Professional
Visual Basic
Project Management

Jake Sturm

Wrox Press Ltd. ®

Professional Visual Basic Project Management

August 1999:   First Edition
December 1999: Reprinted

Published by Wrox Press Ltd
Arden House, 1102 Warwick Road, Acock's Green, Birmingham B27 6BH, UK
Printed in USA
ISBN 1-861002-93-9

Trademark Acknowledgements

Wrox has endeavored to provide trademark information about all the companies and products mentioned in this book by the appropriate use of capitals. However, Wrox cannot guarantee the accuracy of this information.

Credits

Author
Jake Sturm

Editors
Julian Skinner
Tony Davis
Claire Fletcher

Managing Editor
Chris Hindley

Development Editor
John Franklin

Index
Alessandro Ansa

Technical Reviewers
Stephen Danielson
Steven M Fowler
Humberto Lozano Ruiz
Kathleen Peters
Mark Underdown
Chris Vandersluis

Design/Layout
Tom Bartlett
Dave Boyce
Mark Burdett
Will Fallon
Jonathan M Jones
John McNulty

Cover
Chris Morris

About the Author

Jake Sturm has extensive programming experience, throughout all levels of software development. He has been involved in every aspect of Visual Basic application development, from simple executables to complicated Client Server applications and a host of ActiveX controls. Jake has expanded his programming from simply using VB for an entire project, to include the full range of Microsoft BackOffice products such as SQL server, IIS, and MTS. He has also worked extensively with VBA in both Microsoft Office and ASP pages.

Jake has always viewed programming and project management as a creative process, no different from an artist creating a sculpture or painting. Visual Basic, combined with Microsoft's BackOffice products, allows the developer to create a masterpiece.

Presently, Jake is working for Microsoft Corporation as a Consultant. His email address is: jakes@gti.net and his personal web site address is: http://w3.gti.net/jakes. He lives in New Jersey with his wife, Gwen, her two daughters, Jill and Lynzie, his son, Will, and his daughter, Maya.

Jake will be setting up a web site devoted to the Visual Basic language, Enterprise development and the people who use Visual Basic. This site will be up in late October and will have a url of http://www.realworldvb.com.

Dedication:

This book has to be dedicated to my wife, Gwen, my three daughters, Jill, Lynzie and Maya and my son William. This book has consumed most of my time for the last several months. They have all understood the importance of this book and have waited patiently for its completion.

Acknowledgements:

I must begin with my wife, Gwen, who once again has spent long hours editing and reviewing these chapters. She has cleaned up many of my grammatical errors, snapped my run-ons into smaller sentences and kept my writing clear.

The team at Wrox has been an incredible help, working long hours on massaging my text into the final polished work you see before you. Thanks go to the editors Chris Hindley, Julian Skinner, Tony Davis, Claire Fletcher and Dominic Shakeshaft.

I would also like to thank all of the reviewers who have spent their time reading the chapters and making comments. They have worked hard to make this book what it is. I would especially like to thank Kathleen Peters. Her comments have shown an incredible depth of knowledge of project management and the Visual Basic language. Her comments have been to the point, sometimes humorous (definitely something an author needs as they are going through pages of comments) and always accurate. She has added much to this book and deserves special mention.

I also want to thank my readers. May this book give you the knowledge you need to properly manage all of your Visual Basic projects and help you make all of your projects successful.

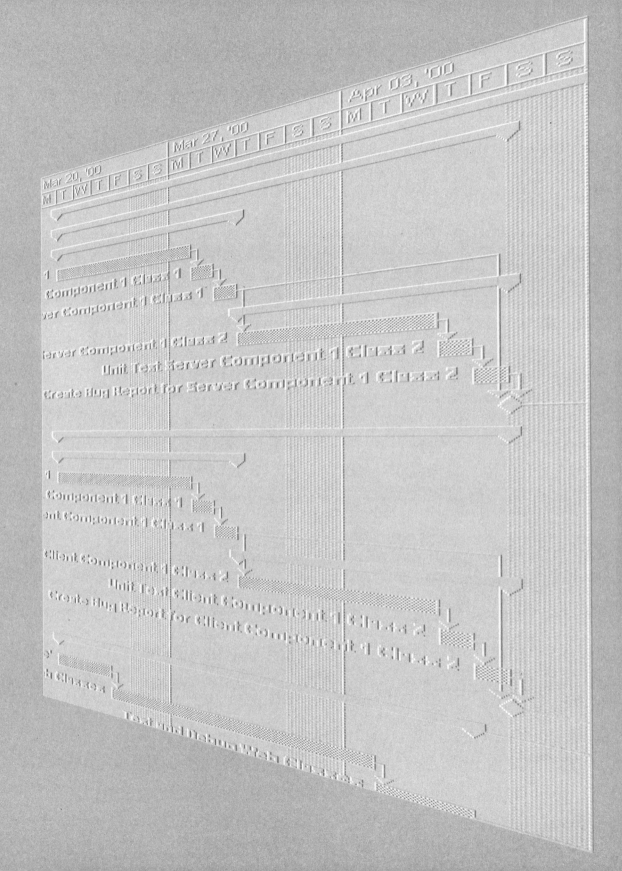

Table of Contents

Chapter 2: Teams 29

Chapter 5: Risk Management   147

Chapter 10: Testing

Chapter 11: Deployment Phase

Chapter 12: Versioning and Sharing Project Files   351

Chapter 13: Creating a Project Schedule   365

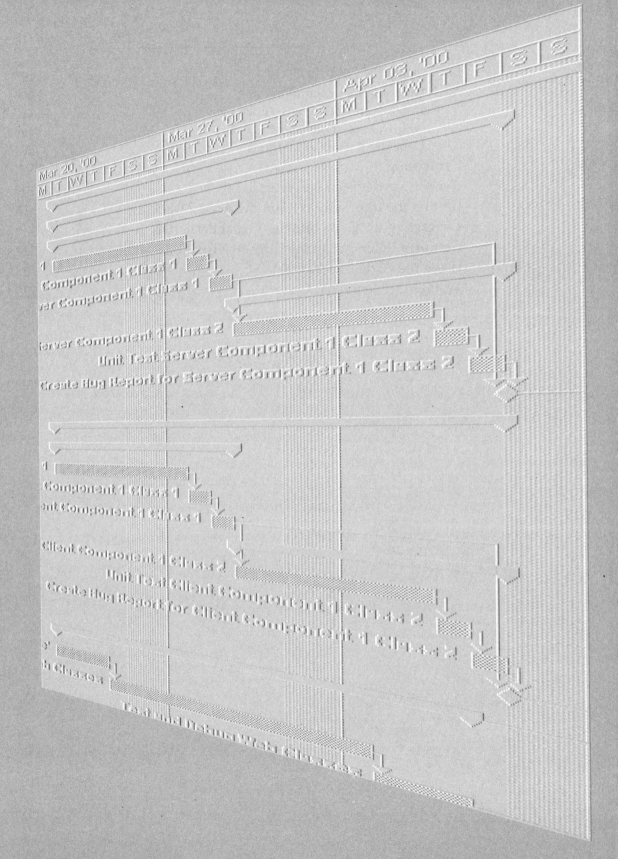

Introduction

Why Do We Need To Know About Project Management?

Modern day software projects are increasingly complex, not only because the functionality of the programming languages has expanded enormously, but also because the Internet has opened up a new way to do business; for corporations to stay afloat, they must have the technology and business processes available to enable them to compete in an online marketplace.

This means that much more is expected of modern applications, making them a serious and complex undertaking. The people working in a project team must have an understanding of what it is they are to do, but they must also understand what everybody else is doing. Project management must be a team effort, with every team member contributing to the success of the project.

This coordination of efforts needs somebody to manage it and make sure that the project is achieving its aims. However, project management is not, and can never be, just about one person arbitrarily taking control of project activities. There should not be one autocratic manager - this is hardly a good grounding for a comfortable team environment!

Tied in with this is the fact that projects are not just about getting the code written and tested (although this is very important!). There are a number of other, non-technical skills that are important within project work, such as communication, leadership and problem solving, amongst others, which are all part of making a project successful.

There are many ways in which a project can be structured; the emphasis on modern-day projects is that they are built so that some parts are reusable and can be utilized in future project undertakings. This is the essence of the object-oriented programming approach; code is written so that it has everything it needs to be able to work - in this way, the code can be moved into other projects without causing a major rewrite.

Who Is This Book For?

This book is aimed primarily at project managers who wish to understand more of the technical issues involved in managing a Visual Basic Software project, and for Visual Basic Developers who would like to progress to managing Visual Basic software projects and would like to understand what is involved at every stage of a project. However, it is important to note that all project team members will benefit from this book - at every phase of the project, each team member's role is described, making the book a comprehensive guide to project management for the whole project team.

For the examples in later chapters and appendices, it is assumed that you have extensive knowledge of Visual Basic. The book as a whole, however, is not aimed specifically at Visual Basic developers (some of you may be pleased to hear!).

What You Need To Use This Book

To try your hand at project schedules, like those found in Chapters 3 and 13, you will need Project 98. If you do not have this, don't worry! You can download a 60-day demo version from the following location:

http://www.microsoft.com/office/98/project/trial/info.htm

For the later chapters of the book, you will need to have Visual Basic 6.0 and also Visual SourceSafe to be able to try the examples found here.

What's Covered In This Book

This book is about effective management of a Visual Basic software project. We learn about the cyclic methodology and how if fits into the four phases of a software project. The book is loosely written in three sections:

> Section 1. Introduction to project management, teams and schedules in Project 98. (Chapters 1, 2 and 3)
> Section 2. The four phases of the cyclic methodology:
> Envisionment (Chapters 4 and 5);
> Design (Chapters 6, 7 and 8);
> Development (Chapter 9);
> Deployment (Chapters 10 and 11)
> Section 3: Source Control (Chapter 12) and Scheduling (Chapter 13).

Throughout the book we will illustrate the development cycle of a DNA project. DNA stands for Windows Distributed interNet Application Architecture and involves programming using Internet techniques, but does not necessarily involve developing Internet applications. Our DNA project will be built on the Northwind company - the end result will be a new order entry application; however, the company wishes to move into electronic commerce, or e-commerce, and also wishes to reuse some of their existing order entry components. You will see many references to this project throughout the book.

Let's look at a more detailed outline of the book.

Chapter 1 serves as an introduction to project management, object-oriented programming and the cyclic methodology. It explains more about why we need project management and tells us why good project management is especially important in object-oriented software projects. This chapter also introduces us to the four phases of the cyclic methodology.

In Chapter 2 we look at teams and team structure. There are a number of different team configurations: we are concerned with the self-directing, goal-oriented team. This chapter also provides a comprehensive list of each team member's role in every phase of the cyclic methodology. Listed also are a number of non-technical skills that are important to team work, as well as information on how to improve these skills.

Chapter 3 is a tutorial on Project 98. Using a Visual Basic developer as the main focus, we create a number of goals, showing how to enter them into Project 98, allocate time and resources to each goal and looking at how each goal is represented on a Gantt chart. This chapter results in a personal schedule, or timetable of events.

The Envisionment phase of the cyclic methodology is the emphasis of Chapter 4. Here, we learn what activities must take place in the initial stages of a project and what goals must be achieved in this phase, as well as discovering the milestones and deliverables for envisionment, and understanding why these must be agreed upon by all team members.

Chapter 5 examines the concept of risk management, showing us how we can identify risks. It provides us with a list of possible risks, saying how they could affect our project and includes a sample risk document. To manage risks, we need to be able to measure them and track them - this chapter shows us how, giving us also a sample risk-tracking document.

In Chapter 6 we look at the Design phase, or, more specifically, the conceptual stage of the design phase. This involves interviewing the users to find out exactly what it is our application must do, and also to find out exactly who our users are! This chapter includes a discussion on Unified Modeling Language (UML) diagrams, work flows and business rules, which are all needed to understand what our system should aim to do.

The emphasis of Chapter 7 is the logical stage of the design phase. Here, we learn about the structure of our application: what components it must be made up of to meet business needs. This stage builds on the information we have gained from the conceptual phase. This chapter also discusses the different frameworks available for our application, along with Microsoft Transaction Server (MTS) and prototyping the user interface.

Chapter 8 concerns the physical stage of the design phase. This is where we actually define how our application is going to be built in Visual Basic. This chapter builds on the groundwork we have carried out in Chapter 6 and Chapter 7 and includes a discussion on mapping out code using activity diagrams. This chapter also covers ActiveX Data Objects (ADO), Remote Data Services (RDS), Distributed Component Object Model (DCOM) and the importance of designing as a team.

In Chapter 9 we move on to the Development phase. This is where we actually begin to code the components we defined in Chapter 8. It suggests guidelines for coding our project and discusses the coding of a business services component and a server component. It also stresses the importance of coding our project so that we can reuse sections with ease in future projects. This chapter also touches upon Active Server Pages (ASP) and Dynamic HyperText Markup Language (DHTML).

Chapter 10 moves swiftly on to testing and debugging our components. It discusses the different ways to test our components; usability, which is testing the user interface, and functional, of which there are a number of different types (two of which are stress and performance testing). This chapter then goes on to discuss debugging Visual Basic MTS components and also logging information.

In Chapter 11 we examine the final phase of the cyclic methodology, the Deployment stage. In this chapter, we will discuss the activities involved in the deployment of a project, such as Beta testing, user training and project documentation. This chapter then goes on to describe the different deployment strategies available to us, before explaining the importance of the final sign off of the project.

Chapter 12 discusses the notion of protecting the integrity of our source code by using Visual SourceSafe to perform version tracking, source control and change management. This chapter discusses why we need different versions of our project, and introduces some scenarios where Visual SourceSafe could be used to protect our source code.

The final chapter provides an example schedule based on the project discussed throughout the book. Chapter 13 covers all four phases of the cyclic methodology and tackles the issue of resource allocation head-on.

Conventions Used

I have used a number of different styles of text and layout in this book to help differentiate between the various types of information. Here are examples of the styles I use along with explanations of what they mean:

Advice, hints or background information comes in this type of font.

Important pieces of information come in boxes like this.

Bulleted lists look like this:

> ➤ **Important words** are in a bold font
> ➤ Words that appear on your monitor in menus or windows, such as in the <u>F</u>ile menu, are presented in a similar font to how they appear on the screen
> ➤ Keys that you press on the keyboard, such as *Enter* or *F5*, are italicized like this

Program code appears in a number of formats. Blocks of code that are to be keyed into Visual Basic or other programs appear in a gray block like this:

```
Private Sub Text1_Change()
    lblTitles.Caption = "Titles published by " & Text1
End Sub
```

Code that appears in the body of the normal text looks like this: Adodc1.Recordset.MoveNext.

Sometimes you'll see code in a mixture of styles, like this:

```
Private Sub Text1_Change()
    lblTitles.Caption = "Titles published by " & Text1
End Sub
```

The code with a white background is code we've already looked at and that we don't wish to examine further.

Source Code

All the code given in this book can be downloaded from the Wrox websites at:

```
http://www.wrox.com
http://www.wrox.co.uk
```

Tell Us What You Think

I've tried to make this book as accurate and enjoyable for you as possible, but what really matters is whether or not *you* find it useful. I would really appreciate your views and comments, so please contact Wrox at:

```
feedback@wrox.com
```

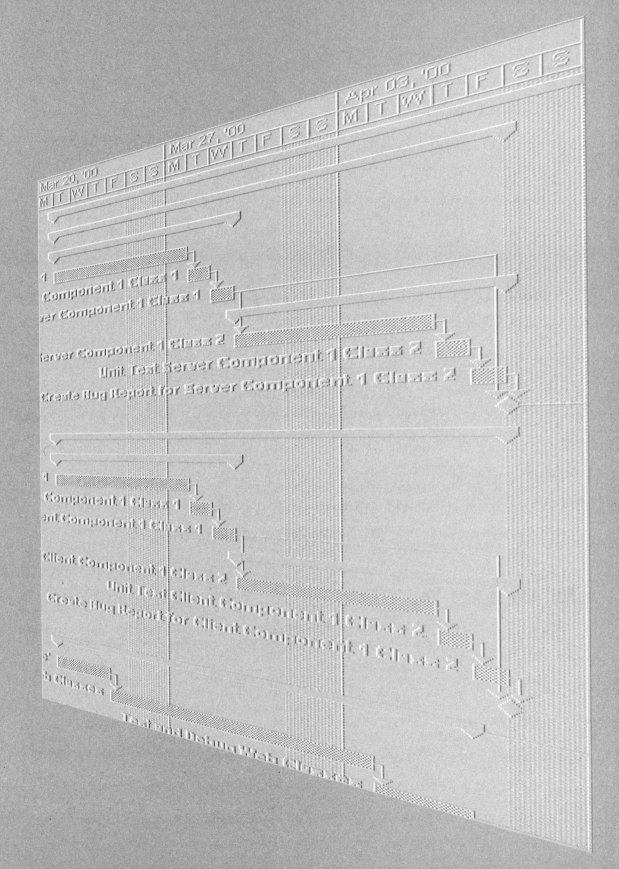

Introduction to Project Management

Complex software projects have always been notoriously difficult to manage successfully. Current projects are required to work across numerous platforms, use multiple databases and operating systems and have to be able to adapt to rapidly changing technology. The complexity of the modern software project has resulted in over half of them either failing completely or not working as planned. There is a desperate need for a structured, clear methodology for building software projects.

Visual Basic has evolved through six versions to become a very powerful programming language. The types of applications we build with Visual Basic have also evolved from monolithic applications, through two-tier applications to DNA applications. As the language has evolved, new features have been added that have made the language more complex. This complexity can make it impossible to build efficient complex enterprise systems using Visual Basic products if you do not properly manage the project. However, in exchange for this added complexity and difficulty, we now can build complete, powerful Visual Basic components within our enterprise systems. These projects can bring the entire enterprise together in a way that could not be imagined just a few years ago. These unifying Visual Basic applications will allow corporations to survive in an ultra-competitive and ever-evolving environment well into the twenty-first century.

An object-oriented programming approach has become the most prominent technique of creating and managing software projects. Over recent years a development model has emerged, encompassed by Unified Modeling Language (UML), which provides a uniform mechanism for the efficient and effective design of object-oriented projects.

Essentially, UML is a set of standard models used to design object-oriented projects (it is not a description of actually how to implement those models). A brief overview of this topic is given in Appendix A. For comprehensive coverage I would refer you to VB6 UML Design and Development, also published by Wrox Press.

The goal of this book is to show how these excellent design principles can be incorporated into a clear methodology which will ensure the efficient and successful undertaking of the project, not just during the design of the object-based Visual Basic application, but right through from initial conception to deployment of the enterprise system.

We have already used terms such as product, project and system on several occasions so it's probably a good idea to set down a few firm definitions so that it is very clear exactly to what we are referring:

> A **project** is defined by a clearly visualized goal e.g. to develop the network and intranet components of a new order entry system for company xyz.

> A **product** is the software delivered to the client or customer, possibly consisting of numerous components, which will satisfy the goals set out in the project.

> A **system** is every component of an enterprise project, including Visual Basic components, infrastructure components such as the physical servers or databases, third party components, etc. It includes everything required to fulfill a certain set of business requirements.

Companies today operate in an ultra-competitive marketplace in the face of rapid advances in technology. In order to prosper, they must constantly review and reassess the technology they have in place and the manner in which they conduct their business. A company may be involved in a continuous process of updating its enterprise systems. This cannot be carried out in a haphazard fashion. The company must be very clear what it wants to achieve and why. Goals must be analyzed closely and prioritized. Each project undertaken in the enterprise development must encompass a clearly defined goal. The project must be carried out with a view to producing a final product that is of the best possible design, embraces all of the required functionality, and is delivered on time.

The best way to achieve this, in my view, is to break each project into well-defined, but often overlapping, phases. These phases, considered together, form a cycle - since they can be repeated endlessly as the enterprise system evolves. Thus we have the **cyclic methodology** that is at the heart of my Visual Basic project management philosophy.

This cyclic methodology shares many features with other methodologies based on repeated stages, such as the Microsoft Solution Framework.

Of course, project management is not just about having a good methodology in place. A methodology is only really as good as the team that implements it. Even relatively simple sounding projects, such as the design of a new order entry system, can be very complex. Such a project may involve:

> A new Visual Basic application which will enable the order entry clerks to enter orders by phone

> A new Internet site that can display products to clients over the Internet, and allow these clients to place orders

> A set of Visual Basic components to move the data from a database to a data warehouse

> A new set of programs to perform analysis on the data

In a sense this illustrates some of the key advantages of projects based around a Visual Basic object-oriented approach:

> The project is easier to break down into component parts, which may be completely different in nature. This is known as modularity.

> Such projects lend themselves very well to a team-based methodology. Small, closely integrated development teams could work on the creation of different product components, either in parallel or sequentially.

In practice this is more difficult than it sounds. Design work on one component almost always impacts the design of others. This is one of the reasons that small, tightly integrated design teams are almost always more desirable than large teams so that the communication between team members during the highly changeable design phase can be fast. Even having said this, it is very clear that without proper management, the project could very quickly spiral out of control. Effective project management is an essential function within every project. It helps to coordinate the work of every team member, not only so that the work gets done and the project is brought to completion, but also so that every team member will know what he or she has to do, why they have to do it and when they have to do it by. Project management is not just performed by the project manager: every member of the team is responsible for the successful management of the project, and so every member of the team should know what good project management entails.

Managing a Visual Basic project can be compared to driving a car. By following a certain set of rules, carefully planning where you are going, keeping an eye out for road signs and road hazards, and responding to them when they arise, your chances of getting to your final destination without having an accident greatly increase. While you can easily find a book on the rules of driving, it is very difficult to find a book explaining all of the rules one must follow for managing a Visual Basic software project. This book is specifically written to provide a methodology for developing Visual Basic products that will be part of a larger enterprise system project. The cyclic methodology I discuss in this book will allow you to see the road signs and road hazards that may "total" your project if you miss them, show you how to respond to them, and how to plan your entire project for maximum success.

While this book is written with the project manager in mind, it is also for all members of a Visual Basic team. In the cyclic methodology, everyone shares responsibility for the project and for making the project succeed. This book will provide the project manager with all of the information they require to oversee the project and the team. The project manager can also share this book with the entire team to provide them with the information they need to know to enable them to be part of a team in which every member works toward the success of the project.

> **Visual Basic project managers often lack technical knowledge. Their ability to lead effectively may be hampered by a lack of credibility within the team if they are not able to understand and discuss critical design issues. They may not understand the impact that the particular technology chosen for the solution has on the manner in which the developers go about their coding. Without this knowledge they may be unable to properly coordinate the efforts of the team and will be less likely to be able to make realistic estimates of schedule and resource requirements etc. This book aims to build a bridge between project managers and developers. It will give project managers a fundamental understanding of some of these issues.**

Before we discuss object-oriented programming, project management and the cyclic methodology, we must first expose and dispel a few myths associated with managing projects.

Project Management Myths

There are several myths surrounding software project management that can often create attitudes that prevent projects from succeeding. The most common ones are discussed in the following sections.

Myth 1: Software Projects are Bound to Fail

It is a widely held belief that software projects are difficult, unpredictable and likely to fail no matter what. It is true that many projects do fail. In the January 1995 issue of Application Development Trends, a survey, based on 835 responses, which represented over 8,000 applications, found the following:

Company Size (in dollars of revenue)	Successful Projects	Projects over budget or schedule, or delivered with incomplete functionality	Projects 100% or more over budget or schedule, or impossible to complete
500 million or greater	9%	62%	30%
200 to 500 million	16%	47%	37%
Less than 200 million	28%	50%	22%

This high rate of failure has been validated in more recent studies. It would seem that the larger the company, the more likely it is that the project will fail. This may be due to the fact that larger companies attempt larger, more complex projects than smaller companies - as size and complexity increase, so does the chance of failure. Nevertheless, the table presents some frightening statistics.

Are software projects doomed from the beginning, or is there a way to improve the chances of your project succeeding? To answer that question, we need to look at the reasons for these projects failing. The top four reasons for failure were as follows:

> ➤ There was a lack of technical sponsorship.
> ➤ The users were not involved in the project.
> ➤ There was inadequate management of the project.
> ➤ There were technical issues.

If you follow the techniques of project management discussed in this book, you will be in a better position to manage and probably reduce the risks posed by of all four of these problems.

The study also found the following reasons for project success:

- ➤ User and sponsorship involvement
- ➤ Clear requirements
- ➤ Clear, well structured and understandable design
- ➤ Realistic management expectations

Finding a way to achieve these essential elements of a successful project will be a central focus of this book. While there may be several ways to manage a project so that it will contain these essential parts, with this book I aim to demonstrate that one of the best ways to achieve them is to build your Visual Basic project using the cyclic methodology.

Myth 2: We Don't Need to Design Visual Basic Projects

This is perhaps one of the most destructive myths to the Visual Basic language. Design can include both what we actually want the product to do, and also how the team decides to develop the product. As the language seems so simple, VB developers are often sent to program with only the smallest amount of design work. The developer will churn out code for weeks on end until the project is about two thirds complete. Unfortunately, without any design work, the code will almost always be illogical in order and extremely difficult to understand: this is what is known as 'spaghetti code'. At this point, the project will have become so complex that it is impossible to debug, clean, or maintain the code and the project starts grinding to a halt.

Adding a single module to the code, and making this module work with the rest of the code, could take weeks. Each step forward is now a slow, and very painful process. The last third of the project may take longer than the first two thirds of the project put together. More often than not, a Visual Basic project will die a painful death at this point. Everyone walks away cursing Visual Basic, when, in reality, all of this could have been prevented if everyone had spent a few days or weeks designing the development of the project thoroughly.

Myth 3: Methodologies Stifle Creativity

It is sometimes suggested that using a well-defined methodology to build a project limits the freedom of the developer. At one point, a methodology was created which tried to break a project into a well-defined set of steps. Each step could be scheduled to take a predetermined amount of time, and a complete code design of each step could be made. The design would specify exactly how every part of the project should be coded. The developers were usually not involved in the design process, and were typically just handed a set of specifications that they must turn into code.

The cyclic methodology detailed in this book allows the developers to design a set of components that will fulfill the goals of the project as specified by the end users and management. The cyclic methodology requires the developers to be creative and use all of their skills to come up with the best possible design for the components within the scope of the project. Designing these components, and basing them on the needs of the end-user and management, is the first goal of the developer: in fact, every member of the team must keep the user, and their needs, in mind at all times, as this methodology is very user-centric. Actually building the components is the second, and most important, goal of the developer. In this way, the developers create their own goals based on the goals of the end users and management.

The final design is detailed enough to say what the code in the components should do, without specifying the exact details on how the code will be written. Thus, the creativity of the developers will once again come into play when they implement the design into actual coded components. We will discuss the importance of creativity of all team members throughout this book.

Programming with Objects

In the real world, 'object' is a word used frequently to describe a lot of things we know, such as an airplane, or a car, or a computer. These objects can also be made up of many other objects: for example, a computer consists of a central processing unit, a monitor, a keyboard, a hard drive, etc. The main point about objects is that they don't need to know anything else in order to work - when you turn a computer on, it knows that there are processes it must go through for you to be able to use it. You just know that you turn it on and then it works.

Every object has characteristics or **properties**. For example, some characteristics of a computer are its dimensions, its weight, its color, etc. In object-oriented terms, the computer object would have properties of size, weight, color, etc. Objects are also able to carry out actions - these are called **methods**. Using our computer object, we can see that one method could be called `SaveFile`, which would allow the computer to save files, whereas another method could be called `ChangeColor`, which would change the color of text on the screen.

Another example would be to use the order entry application. The application can use a `Customer` object. This `Customer` object will have methods that perform services, such as updating a customer's information to the database or deleting the customer. The `Customer` object will also have properties, such as the customer's name, address, phone, fax, etc. These properties can be set to new values or be used to retrieve the current values of these properties.

All objects belong to a **class**. A class is a template for a particular type of object; in real life terms, a class would be, for example, the blueprints for a computer. From the blueprints we could see that they represented a computer - however, it wouldn't be an actual computer. To make a computer we would have to take the blueprints, get some materials and build a computer. In object-oriented terms, we would have to take the class and 'build' an object, or, in other words, make an **instance** of a class. So, when we make an instance of a class, we get an object. If we make multiple instances, we get many objects. One important point to note is that, even though each object is built in exactly the same way from the same class (or same set of blueprints), each object exists in its own right - it is not the same as all the other objects.

Encapsulation and Abstraction

Two important concepts for object-oriented programming are **encapsulation** and **abstraction**. Earlier, I said that we don't need to know how a computer works: we just know that it works. The computer object is hiding its workings from us, because we don't need to know how it works internally: this is encapsulation. This is one reason why we will be developing an object-oriented project: encapsulation means that we can reuse the code we have written, because every object knows what it is supposed to do and doesn't need any other outside information. So, no matter where we use the object, it will always have enough information to work properly.

Abstraction allows us to view things in general terms and not get weighed down with details. If I ask "what is a computer?" you will instantly know what a computer is. I don't have to tell you that a computer is a box with a processor and memory and a monitor and an input device, etc. So, a computer is an abstraction - we know that a computer is a collection of other objects, but we don't need to know every single object, just the fact that they are included in the description of a computer. Abstraction allows us to make sense of our code - if we have somebody in the order entry system who can choose a product, place an order and pay for an order, we don't want to have to go through every item when we want to describe the main object. If we call this person a **customer** and say that it can do these things, it will be easier to explain to everybody, and people will know exactly what you mean without you having to go through every single detail.

Building Components

When we are actually making our Visual Basic project, we will use components. Components are simply sections of precompiled code relating to a specific topic - for example creating a new customer or adding an order. Because a component is precompiled, it does not matter what programming language it was created in. During the course of the project, we will be using components that are already built, such as a text box or a form, and other components that will have to be built from the beginning, such as the customer or order components. When we have to build our own components, we will use one or more Visual Basic classes to make the component. For example, we could build a customer component from two classes arranged in a hierarchy. The bottom class will contain the properties for the component. The middle class will manage the bottom class by retrieving instances of the bottom class and providing methods to create new customers, delete customers, etc. These two classes will be joined together to create a customer component. When the application is running, this component will allow you to retrieve, add or delete customers, and also to get or set information on a customer.

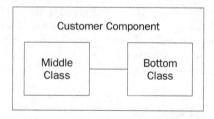

When we build an object, we should consider it as making a contract. This contract says what services (methods) the object will provide, what properties are available for reading (that is, which properties we can get the values of), and what properties are available for writing (that is, which properties we can set). The contract will also state if there are special conditions for reading and writing properties, such as only having write privileges when adding a new object. When making objects, the contract is officially signed when the classes are compiled into a component. Once the contract is signed, we agree not to change any of the existing properties or methods.

Unofficially, the contract is created when the design of the component is created. Once the design is complete, and the methods and properties of the component are determined, other components will be designed and built based on this design.

If you should change any of the methods or properties after the design is complete, you will have to redesign and rebuild all of the components that use the redesigned component. Even worse, if you change the component after it is compiled, you will have to un-register the original component, register the new version, and make all the changes to the dependent components. Both of these scenarios could take days or weeks of work, putting the project behind schedule and budget. This is why we should view the design of our components as a contract. The way to make sure we can honor the object contracts is by carefully designing our components.

Why Do We Need Object-Oriented Programming?

Object-oriented products are a good way to ensure that the company can keep up with evolving technology. Encapsulation means that well-written code can be reused in the future, and the whole idea of using objects and components means that a new component, and therefore new functionality, is easier to add at a later date. This is also known as **extensibility**. This new component can take advantage of advanced technology, but because the original components still expose the same interface (that is, they provide the same methods and properties), they will continue to function with the old technology. This is why we will focus on designing and building object-oriented products when using the cyclic methodology.

It is true that building object-oriented products using the cyclic methodology will require developers who understand how to build object-oriented components, but this is only one requirement for building these products. You do not just have to know how to build object-oriented products to undertake an object-oriented project: the development of an object-oriented product will also require a special team structure, management technique, and design method.

A detailed design methodology is critical for object-oriented products: without detailed design, even the best object-oriented developers will fail to build good products. With the cyclic methodology, design is just one phase in a carefully orchestrated process and, like the others, is a stage that involves everybody within the project team, not just those who will go on to develop the actual code for the component. Every member of the team will contribute to the success of the project, creating a team of peers. This is a critical element in a successful object-oriented project. This book will discuss all of these issues.

The Cyclic Methodology

The cyclic methodology focuses on both the users' goals and their reasons for wanting those goals. The methodology provides a framework that will guide the project from conception through to completion. It splits the project into four distinct linear, often overlapping, phases: envisionment, design, development and deployment. Together, they form one cycle of the project - a cycle can be repeated endlessly as the enterprise system evolves to add new functionality

During the **envisionment phase** the entire system is defined. It is a very thorough assessment of what the company wishes to achieve and why. The goals of the entire system are defined and prioritized. This provides a direction for all of the projects that will need to create the system. The **scope** of each individual project is also carefully defined. The **design phase** defines the components and services that are required to meet the requirements set out in the envisionment phase. During the **development phase** the components are built, unit tested and assembled into a final, compiled application. The **deployment phase** focuses on testing the final complete project and finding and fixing bugs.

We can see the advantages of the cyclic methodology (married with object-oriented programming) when applied to vast enterprise projects, as well as to projects to create a single product (such as new company web site). As was mentioned earlier, enterprise projects may totally redefine the manner in which a company goes about its business and can evolve over many years. The approach I have outlined has several advantages:

> The pace of technological advance is rapid - new versions of software appear with alarming regularity. Rebuilding the corporation in relatively short, well-defined cycles allows the corporation to quickly adapt the business processes to a rapidly changing market.

> In large projects it is likely that by the time the development of the last product component has been completed, several years may have passed since the first of the components was begun. By that time, it is fairly certain that the technology and Visual Basic will have once again evolved and changed. While it is impossible to predict what those changes will be, and what opportunities they may open for this company, developing object-oriented components makes it much easier to add new functionality.

Adding new functionality is never as simple as it seems - there are many areas to consider, such as possible rewriting and probable retesting of the component: all areas which will be explained in more detail later in the book

Bear in mind also that the very nature of certain products (e.g. web sites) requires that they be built in cycles. The first cycle may create the initial site with the basic required functionality. Based on close analysis of how the site is used, the cyclic methodology allows the scope of the product to be continuously refined so that it always uses the most up-to-date and efficient technology.

Each of our four phases will have a set of goals. Each goal should have:

> A purpose (a reason why it is important that this goal is achieved)
> A set of actions that must be performed to achieve the goal
> A set of deliverables when the goal is complete

Each phase of the methodology is associated with a set of **deliverables**. These are the tangible results of the work that has been performed. A deliverable may consist of UML diagrams (you will see more on these later), code modules, risk documents, master schedules, etc. These can be given to all members of the team for review and approval.

The completion of each of the four phases will be a well-defined, measurable point in the project, known as a **milestone**. As each milestone is reached the team must assess whether the customer's requirements are being met and whether the project is on schedule. It is highly recommended that each milestone has one or more associated deliverables. The deliverables will be signed off by the project manager and can be used to determine whether a project is on schedule. When the milestone for a phase has been reached, (which means that the deliverables have been created and completed) you may move onto the next phase. There are no entry requirements for moving into a phase, except that the last phase's milestones must have been completed. Thus, when the final milestone of the first phase is complete you can then move the entire team onto the second phase.

An example of a milestone is as follows: you say that three months from the beginning of the project (or any other pre-determined date) you will have a certain set of documents completed. The documents are the deliverable. At the end of the three months, you either have a completed set of documents signed off by the management, developers and end users, or you do not and the project is behind schedule. When something is either true or false, it is called **binary**. All of your milestones should be based on binaries so that we can determine the progress of the project. These milestones are essential for a software project. Each of the four stages will have milestones marking the end of the stage, as well as several milestones within the stage to monitor progress. Each of these milestones will either have happened by the pre-determined date, or they will not have happened. If they have not happened, the project is behind schedule, and the entire schedule may need to be reassessed.

Once one project cycle completes, the cycle of the next project cycle will begin. When all of the initial development projects are complete, you will then move into the maintenance stage.

When maintenance needs to be performed on the project, another new cycle will be created. Maintenance will usually occur because of some new requirement that did not exist when the project was originally created. For example, an order entry project made four years ago would not have included e-commerce. It is likely, however, that the order-entry application would need to be expanded to also allow orders to be placed by the client over the Internet, in order to remain competitive. This additional Internet component would need to be developed within the four phases. In this way, the cycles never end: the product is always evolving and changing to meet current business requirements.

The Four Phases of the Cyclic Methodology

This section will provide an overview of each of the four stages in the project cycle. The following diagram depicts the four phases arranged into such a cycle.

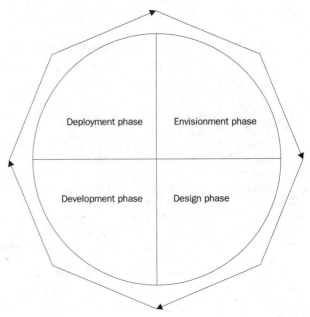

Envisionment Phase

During this first phase, the entire system is defined, and vision and scope statements are created. A **vision statement** states the goals of the entire system and provides a direction for all of the products that are needed to create the system. The **scope** defines the limits of each individual project. Thus, the vision may be to create a revised order entry application (either for use internally or for an external customer) that works on the Internet, an intranet, over the network, is capable of increasing sales by 100%, and able to provide detailed information on sales for management. The scope of the first project might be to create the network and intranet components of the application and increase sales by 40%. Future projects may exist that will fulfill the complete vision statement and additional features can be added at a later date.

Vision and scope statements make sure that the right problem is being solved, which will allows the company to properly plan the rest of the project. Without knowing what the project is supposed to be doing, and why the project is doing this, it is impossible to design or build the project. While this may seem obvious, projects often begin without any clear definition of what they are supposed to be doing, and end up moving haphazardly until either a clear definition is created or the project fails. A project without a clear scope will also suffer from feature creep - features being added throughout the development of the project, rather than being part of a new project. A clear scope freezes the features of the project at the very beginning.

To be able to identify the vision and scope, this phase must go through the following steps:

> Identify and meet with the project's sponsors
> Have a consensus meeting
> Identify the project's goals
> Make an assessment of the resources
> Determine the deliverables of the project
> Assess the benefits of the proposed outline solution

Each of these phases is detailed in a Vision/Scope document.

> **A Vision/Scope document is alternatively referred to as a business case - essentially an analysis and solution document that is drafted when a proposal is made for a product or service.**

The sponsors, who are the people who will provide funding for the project, must be involved from the beginning. It is important to understand their vision and scope of the project, and to make sure that they are committed to the project. Standards for the project must also be defined. If the sponsor is unwilling to get involved or is not interested in the project, there is virtually no possibility the project will succeed. If the sponsor does not feel the project you are building is the correct project for the system being created, it is also likely to fail.

A **consensus meeting** is where all members of the team are brought together to discuss the project. It is essential that these meetings involve the entire team, including the end users. If possible, the sponsors and the stakeholders should also attend. If the sponsors and stakeholders cannot attend, a summary of the meeting should be presented to them to review and approve the results of the meeting.

A consensus meeting should be held at the beginning of the phase to discuss what the vision and scope should be. Goals, resource availability and deliverables are part of this discussion. Another meeting would be held once the vision and scope documents are complete to make sure all team members agree with the contents of the document. If all members of the team agree with the vision and scope documents at the second meeting, this phase is complete.

The primary purpose of the envisionment phase is to reach a vision and scope that all members have agreed upon. The vision will describe what will be in the entire application. The scope will put limitations on the project vision, and define what part of the vision this project will create. There should also be a clear explanation of why the project is being built. The reasons should be focused on the business processes and goals of the corporation.

Milestones and Deliverables

The Vision/Scope Approved milestone is achieved when the team and the customer reach an agreement on what is expected of the project. When this agreement is reached, the project is approved for go-ahead. This milestone is associated with the following deliverables:

Enterprise Architecture Document: Before the project can begin, you must take a look at the current status of the enterprise. This document will detail what the enterprise consists of before the project is undertaken. This will determine if there are the financial, technological, and people resources for the project.

The primary deliverable is the vision and scope document. The vision document should contain the following sections:

The vision statement of the project: The vision should be stated in terms of goals of the project.

The scope statement of the project: The goals that will be accomplished by this project, that is, this cycle. This should define what will be done in this project and what will be delivered at the end of this project.

Team Responsibilities: A list of responsibilities of all the team members should be created during this phase. The list should detail when specific responsibilities need to be completed, (a list of important deadlines) and provide a list of risks to the project that may occur if each team member does not complete their agreed upon responsibilities.

Risk Assessment: A complete list of all risks to the completion of the project should be carefully documented. Examples of some major risks are:

> ➢ Critical resources not being provided
>
> ➢ Little support from high level management
>
> ➢ Unrealistic expectations meaning that the project is too difficult to undertake

The vision and scope document represent a view of what the goals of the project are, why the system is being developed, and how these goals will be reached. These documents must be accepted and signed off by the entire team, including end users and sponsors.

Design Phase

This phase consists of creating a set of documents that define the user requirements, defining the components and services that are required to meet these requirements, and documenting a detailed design of these components. The design phase will make sure that we have properly defined the solution.

We know from our earlier discussion that we must be able to create reusable components, build one part of the system at one time and build another part either in parallel or later. The system must also be able to be upgraded so that it can include future changes that we cannot predict. The way to do this is to build object-oriented projects: We will now discuss the special design considerations of such a project.

Object-Oriented Project Design During the Design Phase

An enterprise Visual Basic project must be designed so that it can help the corporation be competitive in a constantly changing marketplace and help the corporation function as a cohesive unit. This enterprise solution is a combination of software and hardware that works together to run the business processes and also provides the information required to run the corporation.

This enterprise solution will be built from components. If, at some later time, a component of the system is found to be based on an outdated form of technology and needs to be upgraded, this component can be redesigned and replaced without redesigning and rebuilding the entire system. If a new component needs to be added, it needs to be added to the project design, built, and added to the project without affecting the existing components.

Parts of the system that are critical for the corporation can be built in the first project cycles (as defined in the envisionment phase). Less critical components can be added to the system in later cycles. As new business requirements evolve, new components can be designed and added to the system, but always as part of a well-defined cycle with carefully analyzes goals. This type of enterprise solution can adapt to any changes in the market place or technology. As we have said, the best way to build a project with components is to create an object-oriented project.

The Three Stages of the Design Phase

Visual Basic object-oriented enterprise projects can be designed in three stages during the design phase. The three stages are: conceptual, logical, and physical design stages. During the **conceptual design** stage, the needs of the users are analyzed and defined. A detailed description of users' goals is used as a basis for the generation of a detailed solution for the users and the corporation In the **logical design** stage we create a more detailed description of the developers' goals and represents a solution for the overall project team. The users' needs are transformed into a set of services that the project must perform to meet the requirements of the users. The detailed design of the components that will actually perform these services is carried out in the **physical design** stage. This turns the user, development and management goals into a detailed set of design documents for all the system's components, and represents a solution for the developers

This type of design will result in a user-centric approach that means that the project takes advantage of all of the available technology and will be built from components. The most critical components can be built first, and more than one component can be built at any given time (as each component is a separate entity). This will also create a design that takes into consideration the needs of the users, the needs of the developers, and the possibilities and limitations of the technology.

Iterative Design of the Three Stages

The stages of the design phase will build the project using an iterative process. Each iteration will refine the project's design. Initially, in the conceptual phase, the developers will meet with the users and get a rough concept of the project. The developers will then map out their understanding of the project using diagrams, which will be reviewed by the users, who will then add or subtract from the conceptual design. It may take several reviews by the users before the conceptual design fulfills the users' requirements.

Once the conceptual design reaches a point where it seems to meet all of the users' requirements, the design of the project moves into the logical design stage. It is possible that during the physical design stage a user requirement will be discovered that was overlooked in the conceptual design phase. These missed requirements must be added to the conceptual design, refining it even more.

The logical design phase will consist of mapping out all of the services the components must perform. Each service can be traced to one or more business needs. The initial logical design may only include some high level services for the users, such as getting customer or product information. The logical design stage can then be refined by adding the services that will not be visible to the users, such as retrieving data from a customer object. The logical design will also be subject to much refinement.

When the logical design seems complete, the physical design begins. A thorough review of the current technology is made. The technology solutions that will create components that will perform the services efficiently must be chosen. Often, several small test applications will be created to find the best technology for a particular project. Test applications can also determine the most efficient way to use the best technology. An initial concept of the physical design is created and numerous tests will refine and define the physical design. It is likely that there will be missed services that will have to be added to the logical design during the physical design stage.

Milestones and Deliverables

As should be clear from the previous discussion, when the end of design phase milestone has been achieved the user, development and management goals will have been transformed into a detailed set of design documents for all the system's components. Once the design has been approved, it will be frozen and represents a solution for the developers.

The completion of each stage of the design phase represents an interim milestone: a measurable, definable point in the project. When the conceptual design milestone has been reached there will be a clearly defined non-technical description of the product, the functionality it will include and the manner in which the users will interact with the system. The deliverables for the conceptual stage will include a set of documents describing the users' goals for the project, which will most likely be a set of UML **use cases**.

> **Use cases are documents that explain how a particular group of users, called actors, will use the system to perform a particular task. You will see examples of these in chapter six.**

When the logical stage milestone is reached, the deliverables will include a set of documents that identify the components, and the services the components will need to perform, to fulfill the users' goals for the project.

Since it is the goal of the developer to actually build the components, and it is also the developer who will fill in the details of these diagrams, it is important to remember that such diagrams define the developer's goals.

The most common way to document these goals is with UML Sequence diagrams. **Sequence diagrams** show the requests for services between the users and the system and between one component in the system to another component in the system, over time. Sequence diagrams convert the verbal Use Case into a visual diagram. You will see more of these in chapter seven.

In addition to these documents, the following deliverables may also be part of the logical stage:

> ➢ A user interface prototype (how the user will use the system)
> ➢ An evaluation of the user interface prototype
> ➢ A user interface specification
> ➢ Small test applications to test new technology and new solutions
> ➢ An evaluation of the test applications

When the physical design stage milestone is reached we will know exactly what components are required and how the components will be coded, built, and distributed. These components should fulfill the goals of all members of the project. The deliverables of this stage will be a set of documents detailing this information. The usual method of documenting this is by using UML class and activity diagrams:

> ➢ **Activity diagrams** can be used to map out the code steps a component must take to fulfill a request to perform a service. The steps are written in pseudo-code (each step is described in plain English rather than actual code).
> ➢ **Class diagrams** are a set of diagrams that provide a pictorial description of a set of objects with the same attributes, operations and relationships. You will see more on these in Chapter 8.

In addition, another possible deliverable for the physical stage is a document analyzing which components should be built in-house, and which items should come from a third party.

At each stage in the design process the following additional deliverables will be developed and refined:

> ➢ A set of risk documents
> ➢ A detailed schedule for the current stage and the upcoming stage
> ➢ A document showing the distribution of resources and the current responsibilities of all of the team members. It will include the skills required, and assignments in the project

The end of design phase milestone, most importantly, should encompass a fully integrated design that reflects the needs of the users, fulfills essential business requirements of the corporation, and puts reasonable demands on the developers. The design must fit into the existing enterprise solution as well as being able to help create the future enterprise solution. The design must also result in a system that is scalable and extensible

At the end of the design phase all team members should have a clear sense of purpose. There should be a common understanding of what is required of the product, what their responsibilities will be, what resources are required and on what timescale they are expected to complete their work (a realistic project schedule should be in place). Each of these issues will be discussed in detail in the corresponding chapters.

I would like to stress again at this stage that good communication will be the most essential ingredient for success of the project. Communication will have to flow between managers, developers and users. A set of documents that include design specifications and UML documents can form the basis of good communication. Communication also includes learning certain skills. Some important communication skills include: interviewing users, explaining the conceptual design to the users, and getting management involved in the project. All of these skills will be required to be a team member of an object-oriented project. We will discuss team characteristics later in this chapter.

Development Phase

The **development phase** consists of the building and initial testing of the components and the assembly of these components into a final, compiled application. This phase is complete when all new development is complete. This phase will allow you to implement the best possible solution. After this phase is complete, any additions to the product will result in a new project (a new cycle beginning). It is likely that there will be future additions, as the vision statement extends beyond this project, which is limited by the scope statement. In this way, there are many cycles as the product evolves.

This phase will consist of building the components based on the design made in the design phase. Components will be built at the same time or sequentially. After each component is complete, it will be tested by itself (unit testing), and then within part or all of the system (system testing). The testing will be based on a careful plan made by the testers based on standards created by Quality Assurance. Before the components can be built, the design of the system, the schema for any database, and the design of the user interfaces must be frozen. This will prevent feature creep, and also prevent rebuilding entire components. Changes that are made once the coding has started are more expensive than making changes before any components are actually built. It is fairly easy to change a design document. The further along you are in coding a component, the more expensive any changes become. This is why it is essential that all team members sign off the design before coding begins.

Milestones and Deliverables

The development milestone is reached (often referred to as **scope complete** or **first use** milestone) when the team has reached a consensus that the product meets the specifications set out in the Vision/Scope document and the product has been tested in a production environment.

There are many interim milestones and associated deliverables in this phase, including:

> All features are complete
> Testing of individual components complete
> Testing of systems complete
> Internal releases
> Versioned source code complete
> Compiled versions of the code complete

In the development phase developers must put to good use the design documents that reflect the goals of the entire team and must find the most effective and efficient way of building the project within the limitations of the current technology. It will be important that standards created in the conceptual design phase are followed, especially coding and user interface standards. The development phase is where the project is actually coded and built. The bottom line is that the final outcome of this phase must be a project that reflects the best possible solution to improve the business process.

Deployment Phase

When the development stage is finished the project moves into what is termed a "stabilization" phase as the team works toward the release milestone when the product will be shipped and deployed. The deployment phase is where the final testing is completed. The developers fix any problems with the project as they are discovered. Thus, the primary focus of this phase is finding and fixing bugs. Debuggers, and possibly the end-users, will be testing the project, and the developers will be fixing any problems they find with the product. As the release milestone approaches all training aids and help files must be completed and the infrastructure for the new product must be in place.

When the project is complete, stable and there are no longer any problems with it, the project is turned over to the end-users and to the operations and support groups. The completed project is the final deliverable for this phase. It is sometimes called the golden release, essentially being the master copy of the final solution.

Deliverables

There are several deliverables that will occur in this phase. A few of them, not listed in the order they will be completed, are as follows:

> Final release notes
> All project documentation
> Final source code and executables
> Training manuals
> Help Files
> A completed bug database
> Installation plan/instructions

Team Roles for the Cyclic Methodology

When working on a software project, we will find that there are three basic groups involved in the project: **management**, **users** and **developers**. The goals for the project for each group will be different. Management goals will focus on how the project will improve the corporate mission and improve profit: management will want evidence that the project will give a return on investment (ROI). End users are interested in final deliverables, such as the software they will use to do their job, and how they will use this software to make their job easier. End users are mostly interested in seeing how this project will help them to do their day-to-day tasks. Developers are interested in seeing how they will have to build the project

There are six different roles in the software development team, some of which have been touched upon already. People from the developer group will most likely fill the first four roles - development, testing, logistics, and user education. The last two roles, product and component management, will most likely be filled by people in the management group. A definition of the six roles is as follows:

Development: The team members in the development role are responsible for building the components defined in the logical stage of design, as well as creating test applications during the logical stage of design. Members in this role will also make sure that the components are built according to user requirements, make recommendations for technical solutions and coding standards, review testing plans, keep the project within schedule, repair bugs in the components, and integrate the components into a working whole.

Testing: The team members in the testing role will make sure that all of the components function appropriately and that there are no bugs in the code. Other responsibilities include making a test plan that will test each component separately and within the entire system, building test cases, developing automated tests, documenting all bugs, and helping to build a high quality product.

Developing test cases is a very important activity. They specify how a product will be tested in the next phase of the cycle and, critically, ensure that the product complies with the required quality and performance standards.

Logistics: The team members in the logistics role are responsible for integrating the finished product into the enterprise system and the movement of the product into the support and operations groups.

User Education: User Education team members will make sure that the users understand how to use the application, provide training for the user, and work towards making the application easier to understand and use. These team members will be responsible for creating user interface prototypes, setup programs and help files, training aids and all user documentation.

Product Management: The product management team members will create a vision of the project, turn the users' requirements into a coherent set of UML use cases, create the conceptual and logical views, and make sure that the client's requirements are being met. Other responsibilities include making business projections, estimating the cost of the project, and defining key business goals and requirements.

Component management: The team members in this role will be responsible for making the critical decision necessary to create the right project at the right time, ensuring that the project maintains enterprise standards, managing the master schedule, and managing and documenting project changes. They will also work with other team leaders to create the logical and physical views.

Other team members involved in the project are:

Project Manager: In large projects with many teams, the ultimate responsibility for the success of the project may rest with a specifically designated project manager. They would coordinate the efforts of every other team member. For smaller projects this responsibility will rest with a component manager (alternatively referred to as a program manager).

End Users: These are the people who will be using the project's final deliverable (the finished product) on a day-to-day basis.

Sponsor: This will include anyone responsible for the funding of a project. Ideally, this should be one person, but it can include several people.

Stakeholders: These are the managers in charge of the end users.

Reporting Manager: This is the manager who will evaluate the performance of team members and create evaluation reports. However the reporting manager has nothing to do with making project decisions and is not necessarily part of the project team.

Failure to view the end users, sponsors, and stakeholders as members of your team will almost guarantee the failure of your project. Members of all three general groups - management, development, and end users - need to be involved in the project from the beginning to the end and sign off all documentation.

If the project includes building a database, you will also need to add data modeler and database administrator roles. These two team roles will be involved in the design of the database, the structure of the database, finding ways to optimize database components and the design of the data components.

Team Member Involvement in the Four Phases

The involvement of each of the members of these different roles will vary throughout the four phases of the project. The level of involvement of every member during each of the four phases can be summarized as follows:

Role	Envisionment	Design	Development	Deployment
Development	Low	Moderate	Very high	High
Testing	Low	Moderate	Very high	High
Logistics	High	Low	High	Very high
User Education	Low	Low	High	Very high
Product Management	High	Very high	High	High
Component management	Moderate	Very high	Very high	Very high

Table Continued on Following Page

25

Role	Envisionment	Design	Development	Deployment
Project Manager	Very high	Very high	Very high	Very high
End Users	High	Very high	High	Moderate
Sponsor	Low	Low	Low	Low
Stakeholders	Moderate	Moderate	Low	Low

If there are only a few developers for a project, it is possible that one member can play more than one role. Some roles, though, conflict with each other. We will discuss this in more detail in the chapter on teams.

Several small teams, consisting of a component manager, developers, testers, and a person from the user education team, can be used to build these components either at the same time (in parallel) or sequentially. Developers, testers and user education team members should share information with their counterparts in other teams to create a uniform set of components. The number of testers to developers can range from a 1:1 ratio up to a 1:3 ratio, depending on the project. The project manager will determine the best ratio for the project. To better help testers understand the user requirements the testers should join the project from the beginning, if this is possible. The project manager will coordinate the teams and will also put together the vision and scope statement based on the consensus meeting. The component manager is responsible for putting together the documents for the conceptual and logical design views based on documents created by the smaller teams. The project manager will be in charge of the master schedule.

Using small development teams allows for better communication between team members, low management costs, faster implementation of the various components and a higher quality product. Creating the physical design for these components, and building these components, will be the responsibility of the small component groups. Each component group must build their component so that it exposes the methods and properties specified in the logical view. The internal workings of the components, as well as every deliverable of the whole system, should be based on enterprise wide standards of coding and design.

These component teams should be a team of peers. Every member should be equally responsible for the quality of the component, meeting schedules, understanding the client's needs, and contributing to the design and building of the component. The entire team should be focused on fulfilling the users' requirements, identifying risks, keeping the project within budget and time constraints, and making the best component possible. Each team member will have a well-defined role and will submit a schedule for their component, which will become part of the master schedule (you will see more of this in later chapters).

Summary

Visual Basic projects have become more complex as the language has become more powerful and as more complex products are being created with the language. To build efficient Visual Basic projects that meet the needs of the enterprise we need to find an effective methodology to control them. This book will cover the cyclic methodology, which will empower you to build powerful Visual Basic products that will bring the enterprise into the twenty-first century.

The cyclic methodology is based upon the idea of breaking the project into four phases: envisionment, design, development, and deployment. The design phase can be further divided into three small stages: conceptual, logistical, and physical. The members of the team building projects that use the cyclic methodology will all equally share the responsibility for building and creating the project. Everyone on the team has input on the outcome of the final project. By using the cyclic methodology we can build Visual Basic projects that:

- Have a realistic, meaningful vision for the future
- Are centered on the needs of the business
- Are centered on the needs of the end-user
- Are built using binary milestones that are associated with one or more deliverables
- Utilize a team of peers who all contribute to the success of the project
- Fit in with the entire enterprise
- Are built incrementally
- Evolve over time to take advantage of new technology
- Evolve over time to meet new needs in the enterprise

In the next chapter we will discuss the roles of the individual team members. As each team member will share the responsibility of managing their own time and resources, and also need to be able to contribute to the documents and communicate effectively with other team members, all of these topics will also be discussed in the next chapter. The rest of the chapters will cover the four phases of project management and also cover tools for scheduling, risk assessment and bug tracking.

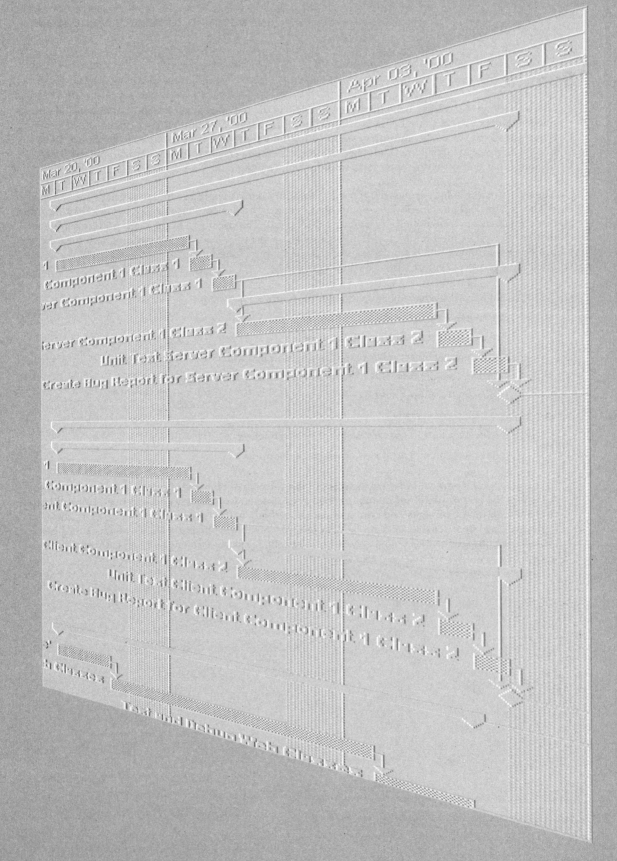

2

Teams

A Visual Basic software team consists of a group of people who work together to fulfill a set of goals that represent the needs of the client and their business. As we will show in this chapter, if you are working on a Visual Basic software team within the cyclic methodology outlined in this book, you will:

> - Be allowed to have input into the project
> - Share in the responsibility for creating and fulfilling the goals of the project
> - Ensure that the schedule is met by giving time estimates for the tasks you are responsible for
> - Have an understanding of the customer's needs and the overall goals of the project

This type of team does not focus on who is in charge. Instead, a set of team roles is created. Each role will have a well-defined set of responsibilities. Instead of having an autocratic project manager who dictates what everyone in the team is doing, we will now give each team member a set of responsibilities that they must accomplish. The project manager has the responsibility of reviewing the recommendations of the team members, putting together a schedule for the complete project, based on the schedules submitted by individual team members, and of producing overall, unified documents, such as the vision/scope and design documents, based on input from all of the team members. The project manager will also manage the resources and make sure all of the critical goals are being accomplished.

When working within this team structure, it is likely that there will still be a reporting manager who will evaluate the performance of team members and create your evaluation reports. However, the reporting manager may not be a member of the software team.

The job of the reporting manager is to make sure that everyone has met their responsibilities for the projects they have been part of. If the reporting manager is part of the project team, he or she can make this evaluation directly; otherwise, the reporting manager will have to speak to the project manager.

If you successfully meet your responsibilities, you can continue in the role you are in, or move up to a role with more responsibilities. If you are not able to meet your responsibilities, then it is likely you will either require more training, coaching, or perhaps even need to be placed in a role with less responsibility. As long as you are willing to put the time in, to learn new skills and improve the ones you have, you should be able to remain in your current position or advance. Ideally, if you are a regular employee, your company should allow a certain number of hours every week in your schedule for training. With the constant changes in Visual Basic, Microsoft Back Office and Enterprise technology, it is essential that all team members be given some time to train in both technical and non-technical skills.

> The reporting manager has nothing to do with making project decisions, and only evaluates whether or not the team members are fulfilling their responsibilities. A reporting manager is part of the organizational chart of the company and has nothing to do with the structure of the software team. Team members can come from many different parts of the company and can belong to completely different groups in the corporate structure.

This chapter will list some important non-technical skills that you will need to be a successful member of this type of team. We will also provide you with suggestions on how to improve these skills.

In this chapter you will learn about the roles within a software team, skills you will need to possess to be a successful member of this team, and how to manage and schedule your time.

The Big Development Team Myth

The philosophy behind this team structure goes against a widely held belief, which I think is one of the biggest myths of project management, and have deliberately ignored. This myth states that only the project manager needs to understand project management. To understand why this is a myth, we must look at the two most common types of management.

The Autocratic Manager

The first type of management involves what I call an 'autocratic manager'. An autocratic manager has complete decision-making power and rules over the systems that he or she manages, dictating tasks to subordinates. A successful autocratic manager must have a complete understanding of the system and the people being managed. Autocratic managers used to be commonly found on assembly lines. Assembly-line autocratic managers usually worked their way up through the ranks. By the time they became managers, they understood every machine and process on the assembly line and knew the entire system intimately.

They were experts on the system they managed. This type of manager would know exactly what to do to speed up or slow down one part of the line, how to improve quality and where costs could be cut. These managers could walk past a machine, hear a squeak in the machine and know if that was normal or abnormal. If it was abnormal, they would get advice from the floor mechanic, and then make a decision on whether a repair was needed. This decision would be based on a full understanding of how taking this machine offline would affect production and whether it was serious enough to do so. These capabilities were based on years of working with the same machines and the same processes.

We can see from this example that since autocratic managers have full decision-making power, they need to be expert in the system they manage. They need to know how to improve the system, how to make it work better, more cheaply and more efficiently. They also need to know when they should ask a question and when something is not serious enough to get advice on. To do this, they need experience based on years of working with the system.

Problems of Autocratic Management in a VB Project

However, when we consider developing software projects using any of Microsoft's products, we immediately see a major problem with the autocratic manager. The system that a Visual Basic project manager manages comprises a set of development technologies, such as Microsoft Transaction Server (MTS) and SQL Server, and the Visual Basic language. I would argue that it is impossible for anyone to be an expert on the entire system. Both the technologies and the Visual Basic language evolve far too rapidly for anyone to become an overall expert. Some people may be experts in certain areas, but I would guess you could count on one hand the number of people who have expert knowledge on everything that is needed for an enterprise project.

While I have worked with SQL Server for four years, the majority of what I knew about administering a SQL server database became redundant with the release of version 7.0. The file systems in this version are completely new, and version 7.0 has added Data Transformation Services. Can anyone claim to be an expert in a technology that is less than a year old?

Two years ago Visual Basic programmers were making two-tier monolithic applications. Over the last two years, Visual Basic developers have started to abandon this method of programming for three-tier object-oriented programming with Windows DNA. While I may have six years experience as a Visual Basic programmer, my experience as an object-oriented Visual Basic programmer only extends back a few years, as these methods did not exist prior to a few years ago.

There are a few basics of development that will never change, such as coding standards and methods of project management. However, most of what is done in a Visual Basic project is less than two years old and a good portion of it is less than a year old. Many developers are working on the cutting edge with technology and techniques that are one to six months old.

In any Microsoft development project, an autocratic manager will usually fail. No single person can possibly have the wide range of expertise and knowledge required to make the appropriate decisions. Even worse, they will often have no idea that they need to get advice from their subordinates. This means that they may not properly manage risks to their projects.

When placed in charge of development teams, autocratic rulers will usually rely on what they know and are familiar with. Unfortunately, this is likely to be outdated technology, and this has resulted in many IT departments developing solutions that do not meet the business needs of the corporation. In the long term, this causes the corporation to become uncompetitive and eventually to fail. As the technology evolves past their expertise, autocratic managers do not know how to identify risks properly in these new situations and often miss important warning signs. Only when a crisis has been reached does the autocratic manager realize there is a problem, and by then it is usually too late. Even when a project can be saved, it usually leads to a development team jumping from one crisis to another. Hours become long, extending into late nights and weekends in order to deal with the latest crisis. Team members burn out and move on.

Some autocratic managers struggle to master every element of development and spend every minute studying, reading and learning. A few of these succeed in mastering the breadth of knowledge for development work, but most of them do not. It is not impossible to be an autocratic project manager, but it is extremely difficult. If you are a project leader and are looking for a better way, this book will show you one.

Self-Directed Work Teams

If the solution does not lie with one autocratic manager, then where does it lie? While one person cannot have the breadth of knowledge required properly to manage, design and oversee an enterprise system, the entire team as a whole will usually have a collective knowledge that will be able to solve any development problem, properly manage the project and all risks to the project, and properly design the project. The management technique used to create a team where everyone contributes to managing the project is called a self-directed work team. Companies that have instituted these self-directed work teams have seen dramatic increases in productivity and performance. When it comes to development, it is the only way to go.

This chapter will describe the fundamental characteristics of a Visual Basic self-directed work team. This chapter, and the entire book, is not written just for the project manager. It is written for the entire team, as everyone on the team must contribute to managing the project, managing their time and managing the risks to the project.

While this idea may seem radical, it is just good common sense. You only need to look at any corporation that teaches a project management discipline to all of the team members to see how successful this method is. I know of one major consulting firm that went from doing no development work to over ten million dollars' worth of development work in a little over one year, and from a staff of four to forty in that time. This company has not had a single project failure and has been successful with numerous large, complex projects. What was the key to their success? Every new employee received extensive training in the methods of project management that the company used, even the new programmers.

A common way of doing this is what is called "training the trainer". In this system, a select group of people is given training, and in turn they train others in the corporation. I know of one Fortune 500 company which trained its project leaders in a project management methodology; they then went on to train the rest of the team.

If you are a project manager, read this book from cover to cover. Learn this way of managing a project, and then pass this book around to your team members (or get them a copy). Every team member should understand his or her responsibilities, how to manage risks, how to manage a schedule and what is expected from them during each phase of the project. Once they have this understanding, they can begin to contribute effectively to a collective knowledge base which the team can use to work together to find solutions with rapidly changing technology.

Team Structure

You, and every member of the team, will be responsible for the success of the project, meeting the client's needs, improving your skills, scheduling your tasks, and meeting your schedule. The tasks you will perform will depend on the role you assume in the team. The roles for the **software team**, as we listed them in Chapter 1, were project, product and component management, development, testing, user education, and logistics. Product management, user education, and logistics will all work with the client.

> *The client can be either external to the corporation or internal to the corporation. There is little difference between these two situations. Therefore, when I refer to client it can mean either an internal or external client.*

Component management, testing and development will have relatively little one-on-one contact with the client and will focus on creating the project components. However, team members in these roles will be involved from the very beginning of the project in meeting the needs of the client. They will have contact with the client during meetings to discuss design and other issues.

The number of people within each role will depend on the number of people available, the size of the project, and the number of end-users and stakeholders. It is best if there is only one stakeholder, so that there is one person who can make final decisions. In this case, one product manager for the project may be sufficient. As we said earlier, a one to one ratio between developers and testers is best. For smaller projects, or when the team is shorthanded, there may be two to three developers per tester. To properly use these testers there must be a good testing plan in place. The number of logisticians and educators depend on the number of end users and what will be required to set up the final project.

When a team is very shorthanded, certain team members can play more than one role. Some roles conflict with each other and so the same person should not be in both roles. An example of this would be the tester and developer (though one developer testing someone else's code will probably not be a problem). Other roles, such as educator and tester, can be performed by the same person. The following lists give some guidelines on which roles are incompatible and which may be held by a single person.

Roles that cannot be filled by the same person:

- Component Management and Product Management
- Component Management and Development
- Project Manager and Development
- Project Manager and Product Management
- Testing and Development
- Product Management and Testing

Roles that can be filled by the same person:

- Product Management and Testing
- Product Management and User Education
- Component Management and Logistics
- Component Management and Project Manager
- Testing and User Education

Roles that have no conflicts but would be difficult for one person to do both:

- Component Management and Testing
- Component Management and User Education
- Product Management and Logistics
- Logistics and Testing

The advantage of creating a team from roles is that you can build a team from a group of people who have a wide range of skills and still have everyone find a role that they can perform well in. As each role has a well-defined set of skills, team members can easily determine what skills they will need to assume any role.

Once the team is assembled, decisions are made on a group consensus. If the members of the development team cannot reach consensus, the component manager will make the final decision; where the disagreement is between teams, rather than within a single team, it will be the project manager who must make the decision. Where consensus between the client and the software team cannot be reached, the stakeholder or the product manager will make the final decision. This means every member needs to understand how to make decisions, and how to participate in group meetings and discussions. Decisions do not always have to be made in formal meetings: a discussion can be started by an email sent to all members of the team. Each person can add to this email their ideas and suggestions, including the previous responses in their reply. The email will become a living document, containing the input of the entire team. Eventually, the discussion will lead to suggestions or solutions and (hopefully) a consensus on which is the best solution. Everyone on the team shares the same responsibility for making the best product within budget and time constraints. Every team member has a right to contribute to the group and to group discussions.

As team members assume responsibility for their tasks and the project, they will begin to identify with the product. They will feel that the quality of the product represents them. This will lead to better work and a more productive work environment.

Large projects will be big enough to have several component teams, consisting of a component manager, developers, testers, logistician(s) and educator(s). The logisticians, testers and educators may belong to more than one team or they may be roles filled by someone who is also in another role. The software team will work in an autonomous manner, coordinated by the project manager. This is possible because the software team will be building components. As long as the component supplies the appropriate public properties and methods, it will fit in with the rest of the project. Thus, each team can build their component separately from the other groups. Of course, best coding methods, techniques, changes in the design of any component, client issues, etc. must flow through the entire team and to all software groups.

A small team of four developers may look as follows:

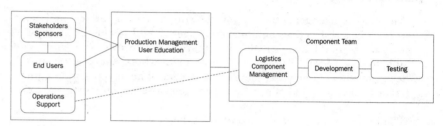

The logistics and component management roles will be filled by one person (who will function as the project manager), as will the product management and user education roles. Operations support is the client's infrastructure support personnel.

In a larger project where there are many people to fill all of the roles, the project team may look as follows:

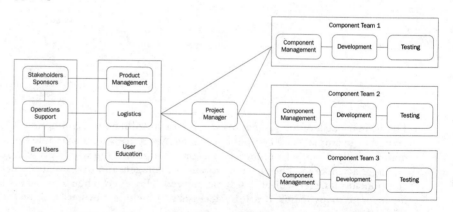

There are no direct lines connecting the component teams to the client groups, as members of the component team will usually communicate to the client through the appropriate liaison. However, if a member of the component team needs to speak directly to the client, this should be possible. If this does happen, the appropriate liaison should be informed of what was discussed. Communication can flow from any member of the team to any other member of the team.

Remember that this is not a hierarchy. This figure shows the flow of communication through the group; it does not indicate that any role is above any other. Again, the testing and development roles are likely to be filled by more than one person.

Visual Basic Software Team Roles

Which role you will fulfill will depend on your skills and your personal career goals. We will look now at each of these roles in more detail; then we will look at the skills needed to work successfully in a team and in each role.

Project Manager

The project manager is the person who coordinates the project and bears overall responsibility for it. It must be stressed that the project manager should *not* be the 'boss' of other team members, and, as we have seen, the team should be self-directed. However, every project does need someone who is able to take a broader view of the project as a whole, and who can coordinate the efforts of other team members (otherwise, there is the danger of developers adding functionality to show off their favorite coding techniques, rather than concentrating on meeting the critical goals of the client.)

The project manager is also likely to be the project team's link to senior management. The project team may look as follows:

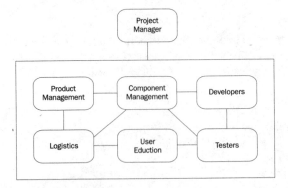

The primary task of the project manager is to coordinate the component managers of each individual team. For example, each component manager will draw up a schedule for the team, and the project manager will compile from these a master schedule for the whole project. In this sense, the project manager acts like a higher-level component manager, and in a small project this role and that of the component manager will probably be merged. However, when a project is large enough to incorporate many teams, it will be necessary to include a project manager who can take an overview of the entire project.

> While the project manager does drive the development process, he or she is not the 'boss'. The project manager will, though, have final authority on disputes within the team.

Envisionment Phase

During this phase, the project manager will take an active part in identifying the more general, top-level goals of the project (the component managers will be more heavily involved in identifying the lower-level, more specific goals). The project manager will also be involved in identifying risks which apply to the entire project (for example, the failure of a piece of key software to work as planned) and managing such risks (in this case, by contacting Customer Support of the software vendors). Another task will be to incorporate the schedules of the individual development teams into a master schedule for the whole project.

Design, Development and Deployment Phases

The chief function of the project manager in these phases will be to manage resources (of time, money and personnel) for the project. Individual component managers will juggle resources within the development teams, but the project manager will have to arrange cover if resources are inadequate within a team. For example, if an unexpected technical issue arises (for example, if changes to the product are required due to feedback from alpha testers), it may be necessary to put together a team of developers at short notice to examine the issue. Since no existing team may have the time to devote to this task, it will be the responsibility of the project manager to assign developers to a new team, created solely for this purpose.

Product Managers

Product managers provide the channel for liaison with the stakeholders and sponsors. Because they are working with the client's management, it is particularly vital that they have a good understanding of the business processes of the client. The product manager works with the rest of the team to make sure that they also understand these business processes. Product managers do not have to be developers; they only need an understanding of the business processes of the client and have the ability to communicate and work with the client. The product managers for a project will work with all of the component teams in the project, usually through the component managers. A **component team** consists of the component manager, developers, educators, testers and logisticians. The educators and logisticians will usually belong to several teams.

Envisionment Phase

During the envisionment phase, the product manager will be responsible for overseeing the analysis of the corporation and the development of the **Enterprise Architecture Document**. This document will contain an overview of the structure of the client's enterprise, including an analysis of the current software systems, a description of the different business processes, and any other factors that may have an impact on the project. This document can be used to develop a vision and scope of the project that suits the current state of the enterprise, instead of creating a solution that is separate from the current system. In our discussion of the envisionment phase, we will give a detailed discussion of how to create the Enterprise Architecture Document.

In the envisionment stage, the product manager primarily works with the stakeholders and the sponsors to help create a project vision and scope that fulfills the critical business goals of the corporation. They will also make sure that the expectations of the stakeholders and sponsors are documented, realistic and understood by the entire team. Product management also creates the Total Cost of Ownership (TCO) and Return On Investment (ROI) estimates with the help of the logisticians, negotiates the contract, and makes any client demonstrations that are required.

The final contribution of the product manager in this stage will be the documentation of the risks of building the product. All team members will contribute to the risk document and be able to review the risk document; each member will also need to be fully acquainted with the potential pitfalls described in the document.

Design Phase

The product manager will be in charge of the conceptual stage of the design phase. The product manager, working with the educators, will determine the different types of end users that will be using the final project defined within the scope document, set up interviews with representatives of these groups, and either perform the interviews or assign another team member to perform them. When the end-user interviews are complete, the product manager will put all of the use cases together in one document, review them for accuracy, and then make arrangements for them to be reviewed by all members of the project (including the end users).

Development Phase

During the development phase, the product manager will help answer any questions the developers may have about the client's requirements. They will also give reports to the stakeholders and the sponsors on the current status of the project. The product manager will be the customer advocate, and help negotiate the removal (or addition) of goals to the scope of the project.

Deployment Phase

In this phase the product manager will find end-users who will perform beta testing (testing of the software before it is officially released). They will do this with the educators. Once the end users for beta testing have been identified, the product manager will coordinate between the testers and the end users doing the beta tests. The product manager will also get the final acceptance of the project from the client.

Component Managers

The component manager's responsibilities will focus on overseeing the development process. A component manager will be in charge of a component team that will include developers, educators, testers and logisticians. The testers, educators and logisticians may belong to more than one team. The project manager will coordinate the component managers within the project.

The component manager will make sure there is open communication within their team, and communicate directly with the product manager. The component manager's responsibilities include: managing the master schedule for the team, keeping the project on time and within budget, and overseeing any design changes. The component manager is the leader of the development process, the facilitator of communication, and the coordinator of the component teams. The product manager must oversee the risks documented by the team and make sure that resources are properly allocated to reduce or eliminate the risks.

Envisionment Phase

During envisionment, the component managers will work closely with the product manager to establish the design goals of the project. The component manager will define what factors and metrics will be used to determine the success of the project, help set up the project infrastructure, and help define the scope of the project. During this time, component management will also set up schedules and determine the software tools that will be used for the project. They will also be responsible for the project's risk management and version control (allowing access to all versions of the code, even after changes have been made and a new version has been created).

Design Phase

The component managers will be responsible for bringing the design phase to the final completed design document milestone, which is at the end of this phase. The component managers will work with the product managers during the conceptual design stage, and will also be responsible for working with the developers to turn use cases into sequence diagrams in the logical stage. They will also oversee the developers creating the final set of documents in the physical stage.

Development Phase

The most important job for the component managers during the development phase is keeping the project on schedule by properly allocating resources. The component managers will keep the schedule for their team, monitor the milestones to make sure they are being reached on schedule and report project status to stakeholders and sponsors. Toward the end of the development phase, the component managers may begin working out the beta testing plan. If there are many teams, each with its own component manager, the project manager will act as a higher-level component manager, who will oversee all of the development teams' component managers.

Deployment Phase

During deployment the component managers will oversee the beta testing program. They will work with the end users that the product manager recommends for beta testing and with the educators and testers.

Developers

Developers take every critical goal of the client and find a programming solution for that goal. They work closely with the component manager to design and build the final business solution. The ideal developer is a person who is creative, is good at problem solving, and is also able to communicate with other members on the team. Developers are the technical experts for the team. Of course, not all developers have these qualities; the component managers and the project manager should encourage developers who do not meet these standards to take courses to improve their technical and non-technical skills. Otherwise, they may have to be assigned to other parts of the team, such as testing, user education or logistics.

Envisionment Phase

In the envisionment phase, developers will help identify possible risks in the development of the project, research existing software components, and determine how feasible the goals of the client are. Risks to the project will be placed into risk documents and recommendations will either be made at a meeting of the whole team or passed on to the project manager.

Design Phase

During the design phase, the developers will work together, coordinated by the component managers, to convert the use cases into sequence diagrams in the logical stage, and convert the sequence diagrams into a final design in the physical stage. The developers will also give estimates as to how long it will take for them to build the components they are responsible for during the physical stage. Developers will also build test applications to make sure that new technologies or new coding methods work correctly and efficiently.

Development Phase

Development will build the project during the development phase. They will do this based on the design documents created in the design phase. Each developer will be responsible for building components or parts of the components. The developers will be coordinated by the component manager, and complete their tasks according to a schedule which they create themselves. If a developer falls behind in their schedule, he or she will need to readjust their schedule. The component manager may then need to readjust the entire team's schedule based on these changes, and this could mean that the schedule for the entire project will have to be amended. Thus, when you are involved in this type of team, it is important that you make accurate time estimates of your work.

Deployment Phase

During the deployment phase, developers will focus on fixing any bugs that are found by testing or beta testers. Development will work with logistics to prepare for the final rollout.

Testing

Testing will make sure that all problems, bugs, and risks to the project are known and documented before the final release of the project. Testers will develop a test plan, implement the test plan, track all bugs, create bug reports, and maintain the bug-tracking database. The test plan must make sure all interfaces and components work properly, and also make sure all of the goals of the project are being met. The bug-tracking database will be used to determine risks to the project and create reports.

> **Quality Assurance (QA) is not testing. Testing is based on a test plan that is specific to the project, whereas QA is concerned with complying with standards and is usually a corporate function. QA may also create documents that illustrate best practices for the corporation and develop standards for the development team.**

Envisionment Phase

Testing will assess the goals with regard to how they can be tested, and what factors are critical for the success of the product, as well as identify any major risks associated with testing. They will also raise any issues connected with the vision or scope which may result in a risk to the project.

Design Phase

During the design phase, the testers will define testing strategies for every goal and create methods and procedures to track problems, bugs and disagreements between members of the team (which includes the client members of the team). We will discuss how to do this in more depth in the testing chapter. Based on the testing strategies, a testing plan and schedule will be created and documented. Testing will also evaluate the overall design, assist in building applications to test new methodologies or technologies, and select appropriate testing software.

Development Phase

During the development phase, testing will make sure that all issues are documented, and known by the entire team. Any bugs that are found by the testers must be documented so that the developers can fix them. The primary focus of testing at this point will be documenting the specifications for testing and designing tests for each goal of the project. The actual tests conducted during the development phase will consist of testing all parts of the components, including private methods and properties, which are used only by the component itself.

If there are enough testers, a one-to-one ratio of testers to developers can be used. In this case, the developer and the tester will work together. The developer will write the code and the tester will test the code as parts of the component are completed. Working with the developer, the tester can create individual test functions for all of the parts of the component the developer is working on. Thus, if the developer is creating a component built out of a two-class hierarchy, when the first class is complete, the tester will create a function to test the class. When the second class is complete, another function can test the second class, and a third function can test both classes together.

Even with the best planning and the most skilled developers, there will often be many small coding mistakes that these tests will uncover. As each mistake is found and documented by the tester, the developer can make the appropriate fixes to the code. Once the component has been completely tested, it will undergo further testing as part of the entire application at the end of the development phase and in the beginning of the deployment phase.

> **It is important to understand that testing of the component does not begin when the component is completely coded and assembled. Testing occurs simultaneously with development - as each part of the component is completed, it is tested. In addition, the design of the components should also be tested, so testing really begins in the design phase.**

When there are not enough testers for a one-to-one ratio, one tester can be used by several developers. Ideally, one should not go beyond a ratio of four developers to one tester, but of course in the real world many teams are too small even for this ratio.

Deployment Phase

The deployment phase will be led by the testers and the logisticians. The testers will be responsible for managing the final testing, the release of the product and making sure that the product meets the goals of the project. The testing will focus on testing the goals of the project and stress-testing (performing tests under stressful conditions, for example by simulating a large number of concurrent users) instead of testing individual components.

For example, during the development phase of an order entry application, the testing may focus on components such as the order component, the customer component, etc. During the deployment phase, the testing will focus on general goals (for example, placing an order), which will include a set of smaller goals, such as being able to begin the order by selecting the customer, selecting a product, or adding a customer, which will itself have a set of smaller goals.

Logistics

The logistician's role is to ensure that there is a smooth rollout and installation of the final project. Logistics will work with the client's operations and support groups, and act as their advocate in the project team. Operations and support will be focused on managing and supporting the final project. Therefore, the logistician will be involved in the addition or removal of any goals that involve the maintainability or supportability of the project. The logistician will help to transfer the project from the control of the developers to the operations and support groups.

Envisionment Phase

The logistician will make a substantial contribution to the assessment of infrastructure for the Enterprise Architecture Document. They will also provide documentation on how manageable and supportable the goals of the project are. They will also work with the product manager to determine the TCO of the project; in this process, those parts of the vision that will not be fulfilled by the end of the project will be included in future maintenance plans.

Design Phase

Logistics will look at the completed design and will document what will be required to maintain and support the project once it is complete. They will also refine the TCO estimates at this point.

Development Phase

During the development phase, the logistician will work as the operations and support advocate. They will bring any issues that operations and support have to the attention of the team and provide reports to operations and support on the status of the project. The logistician will negotiate any issues dealing with the maintenance or support of the project. By the end of this phase, the logistician will make sure that any infrastructure required for the release of the project has been procured.

Deployment Phase

During deployment the logistician will work closely with the testers to get the product through a series of beta tests until a final release candidate is created. The logistician will help to organize the beta sites and deploy the beta versions, and to prepare signoffs from the operations and support groups.

User Education

The educators will work with end users to make sure the final product improves their work performance. Once the project is complete, the educators will help the end users understand how to use the final product in the most efficient way possible. This will reduce the amount of support calls by educating the end users on the appropriate use of the project.

Since the educators will act as an advocate for the end user, they will oversee the building of user interface prototypes, the design of setup programs, and the creation of user documentation and training materials. When making the user interface prototypes, the educator will work closely with the developers and the component manager involved with these developers. They may also work with the product manager to interview the users.

As changes are made to the goals of the project, the educators will make certain that these changes are reflected in the user documentation. They will also make sure that the users are aware of these changes.

Envisionment Phase

The educators will work closely with the product manager to determine the different types of users during the envisionment phase. The educators will also work with the end users to ascertain their general goals, and to make sure that any recommendations from the end users on ways to improve their performance are included in the goals of the project. Towards the end of the envisionment phase, the educators will provide the component manager with an estimate of the cost for training and documentation of the project. Ideally, these estimates should include a range of options so that the product manager, working with the stakeholders and sponsors, can choose an option that fits within the budget and time constraints of the project.

Design Phase

The educators will perform an analysis of the users' needs and create a document based on this analysis. They will work on the design of the user interface with the users and developers. The educators will review the design to determine how usable the project will be, and make recommendations on how to make the final product more efficient for the end users. Towards the end of this phase, the educators will make a more refined estimate of how long it will take to build the end-user documentation and training materials.

Development Phase

During the development phase, the educators will make all of the end-user documentation and training materials, including the online help files. It is important that the design is locked down before this is done, so that nothing has to be redone.

Deployment Phase

In the deployment phase, the educators will be training the users and finishing the user documentation and training materials.

End Users

The end users will contribute ways to improve the efficiency of any business processes that they work with and which are included in the scope of the project. The educators will be the primary members of the software team working with the end user.

Envisionment Phase

During the envisionment phase, the end users will discuss with the educators general goals for making a business process more efficient. They may be involved with the creation of the Enterprise Architecture Document. However, if it is necessary to re-engineer business processes, this will be carried out chiefly by the stakeholders and high-level management.

Design Phase

The end users will allow the educators, product or project manager or developers to interview them to determine the best way to perform their business processes. The end users will also review user-interface prototypes and make recommendations on how to make the interface more efficient. They will make sure that the interface allows them to fulfill all of their goals for this project.

Development Phase

This stage will require beta testing of all the individual components and a review by the users to make sure they meet the goals of the end users.

Deployment Phase

The end users will be involved in beta testing the final releases of the product.

Stakeholders and Sponsors

Stakeholders and sponsors will be responsible for creating the vision and scope of the project. The stakeholder will determine the budget and will have the final say on disagreements that cannot be settled.

Envisionment Phase

Working with the product manager, stakeholders and sponsors will create the vision and scope of the project. They will review the TCO estimates and determine what goals can be included within the project. They will be involved with the creation of the Enterprise Architecture Document. Stakeholders and high-level management may need to become involved in re-engineering business processes.

Design, Development and Deployment Phases

During the design phase, the stakeholders and sponsors will work with the product manager to work out any conflicts over goals. They will also make the final decisions over any conflicts that cannot be resolved.

Team Skills and Abilities

While technical skills are an essential part of being a Visual Basic programmer and the one skill most programmers focus on, it is not the only skill you need to succeed and advance. There is a wide range of skills you need to possess to be a successful member of a software team. We will spend the rest of this chapter going over some of the essential skills you will need to become an effective team member. We will divide each of these skills into three levels: basic, intermediate and advanced.

Read through the skills, and determine what level you are for each of the skills. We indicate for each skill the roles for which it is particularly important. First work toward mastering the basic skills for the roles that you are in, or want to be in, and then work on the intermediate skills. Once you have mastered the intermediate level skills, begin working on the advanced skills.

> While the first level has been termed 'basic', this may include many skills that you are not likely to have learned. It is unlikely that a current college graduate would have most of the basic skills. It is important that your team provides an environment where all team members, new and old alike, can work towards improving themselves and their skills.

While it is important that every team member should strive for as high a level as possible on every skill, it goes without saying that certain skills are more important to certain roles. All team members should try to reach basic level for all skills, but I will indicate which team members really need a higher level for each skill.

Communication

Without a doubt, one of the most essential skills you need to develop is the ability to communicate. You must master both verbal and written communication. You should be able to create well-written documents, as well as speak clearly and concisely to a group. Communication also includes the ability to listen to others.

When working on a project, communication will be the most important skill for making a contribution to the team and becoming part of the collective knowledge base. Communication will impact on your ability to add risks to the risk document, to explain your ideas on design and development and make it possible for you work directly with the client.

The three levels of communication are as follows:

Basic	Intermediate	Advanced
You can get a message across to a listener	You are able to speak or write at the level of the intended audience	You can motivate other people to contribute to the conversation
Your thoughts are organized and you express ideas clearly	You are capable of speaking to small or large audiences, and can answer questions easily	You can give accurate answers to difficult questions
You are comfortable in front of smaller audiences	You are comfortable with communicating with management	You present material in a way that makes the listener or reader interested
You are a good listener	You listen to the viewpoints of others, and are not judgmental if someone's viewpoint is different	You are able to take complex subject matter and present it in a manner that can be understood by the listeners or readers
You are able to express your viewpoint and the viewpoints of others	You help keep the topic of a meeting focused	You make people feel comfortable to speak openly and honestly
You are able to be candid and honest yet still show respect	You do not make assumptions and ask questions when you are not sure	You can effectively and concisely speak and write to senior management

All the roles will require good communication skills. Whether it is speaking to a client, another team member, documenting risks, writing emails or contributing to a meeting, good communication skills will be required.

This skill is perhaps the most important for all team members, and everyone in the team should try to reach as high a level as possible. If every member of the team can reach at least the basic level skills for communication, this will make the entire team more productive as information will flow freely. Those in management roles in particular (the project manager, component managers and product managers) and the user educators should aim to possess communication skills to an intermediate or advanced level.

Good communication involves being able to speak publicly with confidence and to write well, but also, in a less formal context, ensuring that information flows smoothly between team members, so that each member can contribute to the knowledge base of the entire team.

The following suggestions may help you to improve your speaking skills:

> Practise giving a talk to a friend and have the friend make suggestions.
> When asked questions, pause a moment to think about your answer, then begin your answer by paraphrasing the question to give you time to think and make sure you understood the question.
> Show enthusiasm when speaking and do not talk in a monotone.
> Eliminate annoying words such as "um".
> Watch your audience, involve them in your talk, and be aware when they seem bored.
> When giving a presentation, anticipate the questions that may be asked and prepare answers to these questions.
> Make eye contact when speaking or listening to someone.
> Rehearse any presentation you are going to give; if possible, videotape it and review it.
> Use visual aids as an addition to a presentation, but do not let them become the presentation.
> Keep the length of your answers between ten and forty seconds.
> Stay focused on the topic.

Being able to write effectively is also essential when you are part of a team. Whether it is writing an email, adding a risk to the risk documentation or writing design documentation, you must be able to write clearly and effectively. The following are some suggestions on how to improve your writing:

> When you are writing letters or emails, consider what the recipient already knows and concisely provide them with information they do not yet know.
> No matter what you write, whether it is an important report or just a memo, read through it at least once, preferably three times. As you read through it, check the flow of the sentences, the grammar, how clear your sentences are, and whether the document actually means what is intended.
> Write on the level of your readers: do not use technical words when writing to someone who does not have a technical background.

> ➤ Keep a dictionary handy (or have one on your computer or use Internet dictionaries); do not guess at words and do not use words repetitively in a sentence.

> ➤ Organize the information in a way that is easy to read – lists of information can become bulleted lists, structured information can be put into tables, etc.

> ➤ Use spelling and grammar checkers, but do not rely solely on them, as they can be wrong.

> ➤ Paragraphs should deal with one idea and not be too long.

> ➤ Keep a book on grammar close by when you have questions on sentence structure.

> ➤ Identify the mistakes you commonly make in grammar and spelling and watch out for them.

Communication must flow through the team. Following the suggestions below will help to ensure that information is passed through the entire team:

> ➤ Encourage others to share information with you.

> ➤ When in a team meeting make people feel comfortable talking by expressing an interest in their ideas.

> ➤ Document all risks.

> ➤ When creating documents or emails, think who has expressed an interest in this type of information and send them a copy if it is appropriate.

> ➤ Make sure the project, product or component manager has a copy of all correspondence sent to higher management.

> ➤ Return important phone calls promptly.

> ➤ After you meet with someone, write a brief summary of the meeting and send a copy to the person to make sure you properly understood what has been said.

> ➤ When you are assigned a task, add it to your schedule.

> ➤ Respond to important letters, email, etc. quickly.

> ➤ If you become aware of any changes, make sure the entire team also knows about the change.

Making Decisions

Making decisions is another essential skill you must have to work successfully on the team. We generally think of management decisions as the major decisions that cause the project to succeed or fail, such as what the vision and scope should be. However, in reality every person on a team is faced with making decisions that can have a serious impact on the project's success.

For example, when you have a multitude of tasks that need to be performed, such as answering and reading email, meeting the project goals, attending meetings, etc., deciding on how to manage your time will determine whether you meet your goals or fail to meet them. We will discuss time management towards the end of the chapter.

Every member of the team will have to make day-to-day decisions based on their roles. The developer will have to decide the best way to code a module. The tester will have to decide what is the best way to test a module. The educator will have to decide what is the best way to interview and work with the users. The educator, the developer and the tester are not management roles, but they will have to make decisions that can affect the success or failure of the project every day. Every member of the team assumes responsibility for the success or failure of the project. Good decision-making skills are essential for every role and this is something that the entire team should work on.

Below are the three levels for the decision-making skill:

Basic	Intermediate	Advanced
You apply past experiences to current problems

You choose a course of action based on a set of alternative solutions found by doing research and conducting interviews

You make appropriate decisions even when under pressure

You are able to evaluate risky situations and come up with the best solution

You involve other team members in decisions | You come up with a solution to complex, difficult problems based on interviews, research, and past experience

You can help other team members find solutions to their problems

You help others apply their experiences to find solutions to problems

You are able to make far-reaching decisions that not only affect your team, but also beyond your team | You are capable of analyzing a large amount of data and finding and summarizing the important information

You can make decisions that affect the entire enterprise

You will consider the impact a solution has on all levels of the corporation, and all members of the team before implementing them |

This skill is most important for the project manager, who will have the final say on most decisions in the project, and therefore should aim to possess this skill to the advanced level. However, the component managers will also have to make many decisions which affect only their team, and should possess this skill to intermediate-to-advanced level. Imagine one of our developers, who is writing an ASP page which will act as the client-side interface for our order entry application, falls ill. The component manager has to decide whether to cover for the absent developer from within the component team, wait until he returns to work, or ask for cover from outside the component team. To draft in cover may require another developer to be trained in ASP, which could easily take longer than the ill developer's recovery. On the other hand, a lengthy delay could set back the whole project. The project manager and component manager will therefore need to find out if there is a developer who could take over this goal at short notice, without lengthy training in ASP. They will need to consider the impact that removing a developer will have on that developer (who may find it an annoying distraction) and on the team from which he or she is removed. To find the best solution, they will therefore need decision-making skills to the most advanced level.

The first step in making a decision is to gather information and analyze the facts. To get some practice on gathering information, you could try either of the following:

> Research your company's (or your client's) competitors, create a profile on each of them, and see what you can learn from these companies to create improvements and to compete more effectively.

> Research your company's policies and procedures. If there is a policy that everyone complains about because it is not efficient, try to find a better policy than the one currently in place.

There are a number of ways you can improve your decision-making:

> Do not jump to a solution. Take time to gather information and review the facts.

> Take time to get to know the people who are affected by your decisions and find out their opinions.

> Do not just accept the standard solution; ask if it makes sense and if it is the best solution to the problem.

> Determine what time of the day you are best at making decisions, and then schedule that time for making your decisions.

> Write a summary of your research, read through the summary and organize the information. Write out the possible solutions, create experiments to find which solution is best and then go with that solution. Let others look at what you wrote to see if they could add anything.

> Get input from people who are familiar with the subject.

> Recognize when you do not have enough information to make a decision and take the time to gather additional information so you can make a good decision.

> Recognize when you have enough information to make a decision so you do not waste time gathering unneeded information.

> Discuss your ideas with another person. Often, when trying to explain the situation and what your options are, you will get more insight into the situation.

> Create a list of what you need to do to gather the required information to make a decision.

> Focus on the critical decisions. Once the critical decisions are made, then spend time on the less important issues.

> Try to look at the "big picture". Do not get lost in the finer details.

> Before you make a decision, think about how your decision will affect other people involved in the decision.

Proper Planning

With the type of self-directed teams being discussed here, each member will be assigned a task and will have to give an estimate as to how long it will take to complete the task. Therefore, each team member will have to make a plan for the tasks to which they are assigned. Anyone who has not done this before will probably need to get help from someone who has. Once you have made a few plans and estimated the time to complete several tasks, you will start to make better and more accurate plans.

While planning is a skill learned with experience, one can learn a great deal by reviewing previous project schedules. This is one of the reasons that proper documentation is so essential: it provides a library of documents. Estimates usually work best when they start at a fine grain and work upward.

It may be very difficult to estimate the time to build and test a complete server component for an order entry application. Imagine that the server component design is broken down into a design that includes three classes. The class designs are broken down into a design for the methods and properties for the class. Looking at the designs for the methods and properties, each developer should be able to estimate fairly accurately how long it will take for them to code and test each method and property. By summing the times for all of the methods and proprieties you have an estimate for the classes, and summing the times for the classes gives you the components. Good design not only helps you build your project, but also helps you plan it. Make sure you add some extra time for unexpected problems, as these are always going to happen.

The three levels for the planning skill are as follows:

Basic	Intermediate	Advanced
You are capable of planning your own schedule and can stay within that schedule	You are able to see the big picture and put all the pieces of a complex project together	You have a vision level view that takes into account current and future trends
You use your time efficiently and can focus on essential tasks	You perform accurate risk analysis in complex problems	You create enterprise-level plans covering even the most complex problems
You make plans that result in meeting goals within schedule	You are capable of creating effective plans for groups of individuals	You make plans that help the entire team work effectively as a cohesive unit
You properly identify risks and take the appropriate action to handle the risks	You are able to adjust plans according to time and budget constraints	You determine what are the most critical elements and base a plan on these elements
You accurately determine how long it will take to achieve a goal	You are able to identify the tasks required to reach a milestone and reach the milestones in the time assigned.	
	You can adjust the time for your tasks according to the Estimated Time to Finish	

Since all members of the team will need to create their own schedule, everyone will need this skill to at least the basic level. The company should provide software, documentation or training, or a combination of the three, for the members of the team. We will discuss products for drawing up schedules in later chapters. If your company does not provide training, it would be well worth your time to read a few books or even take a course. Several titles are listed at the end of the chapter.

Because the major end product of the project is the code produced by the developers, it is important that this code is completed on time. For this reason, the developers who write the code and the testers who help to ensure that it works as stated should all aim to be on the intermediate level. Even more importantly, the component managers, who create the schedules for the component teams, and the project manager, who draws up the master schedule for the entire project, must be on the intermediate level, and should aim for the advanced level.

Tips for improving your planning skills include the following:

- Once you create a plan, periodically check to make sure the facts you based your plan on still apply. If they do not, revise your plan.
- Break tasks into smaller tasks. Make a detailed plan for the tasks you will complete in the near future and a fluid general plan for the tasks that are in the far future.
- Identify the three to six critical tasks that you must complete to meet your goals and focus on making plans to achieve these.
- Have other people review your plans.
- Periodically review your plans and add more details as you gather more information.
- Set aside some time each day to review your plans.

There's no point in drafting an impeccable schedule if you don't adhere to it. The following guidelines on how to manage your time more efficiently should help you ensure that you don't waste time needlessly:

- Include time in your schedule to do administrative tasks.
- Sort your work by priority and focus on the high priority tasks.
- When making a weekly plan, plan for forty hours.
- For one week write down everything you do in a workday. When the week is done, prioritize your tasks. Non-critical tasks that are taking up a significant portion of your time should be automated, delegated to someone else if possible or a more efficient way of doing these tasks should be found.
- Put some time to examine and adjust your schedule.
- Create folders for your email and try to set up rules with your email program (such as Microsoft Outlook) so that mail will automatically go to the correct folder.
- Create folders for documents, research papers, etc.
- Use a calendar program, such as the one provided with Outlook, to put all your appointments and deadlines in. Set them up so that you get reminders before they are scheduled.
- Read a book on time management or take a course.
- Use a planning tool (such as Microsoft Project 98).
- Begin meetings on time. Do not wait for people who are late unless they are critical to the meeting.
- Keep focused on the topic of the meeting, and ask questions that are only relevant to you after the meeting.
- Try to reduce the amount of paperwork. Automate as many work processes as possible and convert as many paper documents to computer based solutions.
- If you get someone's voice mail, leave a message with what you want from the person. If they get your voice mail, they can leave the answer on your machine. That way you do not have to waste time playing phone tag.

> ➤ When you read a document, letter or email, etc. if a response is necessary, respond immediately, if it needs to be filed, file it; you should strive to look at things only once.

> ➤ Evaluate your tasks in regards to how they will help you accomplish your goals, the goals of the client, and the consequences of not doing the task. Critical tasks are ones that are necessary to accomplish your goals and the goals of the client, and will have serious consequences, such as missing a deadline, if you do not do them.

> ➤ Allocate a time in your schedule for returning phone calls.

> ➤ When responding to paper documents, if possible make a copy of the document and put your answers on the document. When responding to email, include the sender's message in your response, but put your answer at the top of the email, not mixed in with the sender's message.

> ➤ Every morning look at your schedule and create a set of tasks you will complete during the day.

> ➤ Do not keep useless documents.

> ➤ Arrange your office so that things that you use most often are within reach, things used less often are further away.

Solving Problems

Solving problems is an essential skill for a member of a software team. Everyone can learn how to solve problems.

As a member of a Visual Basic development team, you will find yourself constantly find yourself facing problems that need to be solved. The typical questions facing developers include how to code a module or how to ensure the best performance.

Some of the most intense problem solving is trying to figure out why something does not work, especially when it should work. Trying to track down a problem requires a careful process of elimination until you have found the cause of the problem. Sometimes you may find the cause, but there may be no logical explanation. While searching for solutions may be fun, it can be very expensive in terms of time. If a solution cannot be found in a reasonable time, contact Microsoft support. If it is a bug, they will not charge you for the call. For the most part, a support call will cost one or two hours of a developer's time. It is not just money, though. If you turn a problem over to support, while they are searching for a solution your developer can now work on other parts of the project until a solution is found.

Often, the most difficult part of problem solving is not finding the solution, but finding the question. Sometimes you will have to spend hours or even days doing enough research to understand what questions you need to ask. Once you know the questions, it is usually not too difficult to find the answers. With new technologies you usually know the questions only after you have written a few test applications to see how the technology works.

The three levels of problem solving are:

Basic	Intermediate	Advanced
You do not always rely on standard solutions, but instead try to find a better ways of doing tasks You are able to come up with a set of possible solutions and can conduct experiments to find the best one You can solve fairly difficult problems for yourself and other group members You conduct appropriate research and interviews to gather information to solve problems	You are able to identify risks, even those that are not obvious You gather only the required amount of information to solve the problem You find patterns and use them to create solutions You are a leader in making decisions in group meetings You develop creative solutions that solve complex problems that affect their group and other groups You create an environment where other team members are challenged to think creatively and critically	You perform interviews that can pull out all useful information on the problem You are capable of making efficient plans for complex problems that span the enterprise You can see a problem in ways other people can not You can not only find the right answers, but also the right questions

Obviously, the developers will need this skill to a particularly high level, since programming is essentially a problem-solving activity: developers are presented with a problem (such as how to allow a customer to enter an order over the Internet), and must find the best solution to it. They should therefore possess this skill at least to intermediate level. The project and component managers should also possess this skill to intermediate or advanced level, since they must be able to solve administrative and managerial problems. Since the problems faced by the developers, if they are not solved, could cause the entire project to be delayed, these problems are ultimately also issues for the project manager, and may have to be resolved by finding more resources (such as a more experienced developer).

Some things you can do to improve your problem solving skills are:

> Write down the problem, all the information you have gathered on the problem, and then read through everything you have written.
> Play strategy games such as chess or pinochle.
> Discuss the problem with others to help you define the problem.
> Seek advice from people who have had similar problems in the past.
> Work on puzzles or play games in your spare time that require you to solve problems.

Creativity

Creativity is very important for the Visual Basic developer. From finding solutions to design problems to determining the best way to code a module, creativity will help you come up with the answer.

I think that there's an expression, "Get out of the box". This means that you must not get stuck in the box of standard solutions, but instead must look beyond what others have done, and what is usually done, and find a new solution. Whenever you are stepping out of the box, you are being creative. Whenever you tell yourself that this has not been done so I cannot do it, then you not being creative. Sometimes there is no way out of the box, but often there is a way out, it's just that no one is creative enough to find the solution.

Creativity does, though, have to be within the scope of the project and resources. Solutions that create unacceptable risks or break good standards should be avoided. Like everything, the risks of your creative solutions should be investigated and you should determine whether they are within acceptable limits.

The three levels of creativity are as follows:

Basic	Intermediate	Advanced
You help others find new ways of doing a task	You learn new skills to keep up with current technology	You analyze all aspects of a problem and consistently come up with innovative solutions, even for complex problems
You realize when a new method is needed for a task due to a change in technology and find a new way to accomplish the task	You brings good ideas forward	
	You see the "big picture" and can find solutions others missed	You are able to create vision level solutions that solve diverse, and often seemingly unrelated, problems across the enterprise
You find new ways to reach both your goals and team goals	You turn ideas into working solutions	
You are willing to take creative ideas and work them into new ways of doing a task	You help other team members be creative	You motivate the entire team to search for the best way to achieve goals
You question standard practices to see if there is a better way	You are always striving to find the best way of achieving goals	
You contribute good ideas to group meetings		

Creativity is particularly essential for developers, who must devise the best solution for each situation, rather than relying on the standard solution; they should therefore possess this quality to the intermediate-to-advanced level. Testers will also need to think creatively in building functions to test components, and should aim to reach the intermediate level.

Although we may usually think of creativity as an innate quality, which cannot be learned, there are in fact a number of ways you can increase your creative potential:

- Believe in yourself and your ideas. Do not discard an idea until you have explored it and seen that it will not work. Even then, you may find it works for a different problem.

- Learn to walk away from a problem for a while when you get stuck. An answer will often come to you later.

- Create as many options as possible for each problem. If you are not good at this, take a problem, analyze it by yourself, and then talk the problem over with other people and see how they would solve the problem.

- Do not always just ask "Why?" but also sometimes ask "Why not?"

- Evaluate the risks and be willing to choose decisions that have a reasonable risk.

- Put some time aside where it is quiet and you can just think.

- Talk your ideas over with someone that will help you get more insight into a solution.

- The more senses you use to solve a problem, the easier it is to find a solution. Trying to just visualize a solution in your mind is the hardest way to solve a problem. Drawing pictures and writing down information adds vision, talking adds hearing. Doing all of these will help you find better solutions.

- Do not always accept your first ideas; try to see if you come up with other ideas, too. Try seeing the problem from different perspectives.

- Talk to people to see if they have had a similar problem and can share with you how they solved the problem.

- Record all of your ideas, even if you are not going to be using them currently.

- Try to find something that makes you relax and think creatively, such as music.

- Create imaginary problems and try to find solutions to them. Do not be afraid to come up with fantasy-type questions, such as: "What will life be like in one hundred years?"

- Do things that use the creative part of your brain. For example, take a class in drawing even if you cannot draw.

- Try to work in a creative environment. Often, when being creative you can get lost in your work and lose your sense of time. Working where you have constant distractions prevents this. If you are working in cubicles, see if there is any way you can get your company to relocate its "creative" workers, such as developers, into quiet areas, preferably in offices.

Resolving Conflicts

Conflicts can arise in many different ways within a software team. The most common is the conflict caused by the client's desire for as many features as possible versus the constraints of time and budget. Members of the software team must diplomatically work with the client to determine the critical goals of the client and remove the non-critical goals from the project scope.

Within a team there will often be differences in opinions. If you want to hear a heated discussion, put ten Visual Basic programmers in a room and start a conversation on the best coding standards for a Visual Basic project. Creating any standard will result in discussion and compromise.

There will also be differences in personalities, viewpoints, etc. which can create tension between group members. Learning how to resolve these conflicts is an important part of being a member of a team.

Basic	Intermediate	Advanced
You can mediate a disagreement based on the situation and facts and not emotion You stop and think your responses through You express viewpoints to a disagreement that can have a positive outcome on the discussion You are able to withdraw when your viewpoint is not the best, or is wrong You are able to resolve conflicts within your group	You can resolve a conflict without offending anyone You are capable of negotiating conflicts in a fair manner, even in controversial situations You can foresee conflicts and prevent unnecessary conflicts	You can negotiate complex agreements with high level management You can deal with difficult conflicts in a calm, firm and decisive manner You can effectively prevent tense arguments from spiraling out of control

Everyone working in a team will need some ability to resolve conflicts. In our software team, those with particular need for this skill are the product managers, who act as the link between the team and the client, and who will have to resolve any conflict between functionality that the client would like to be provided and what the developers believe is possible with the given resources. The project and component managers will also need this skill to a high level, since they are the ones who must ultimately resolve the issue. Making a decision without first resolving the conflict could fan the flames of any nascent personality clash.

The following tips will be useful for resolving - and even better, avoiding - conflicts:

> If you cannot resolve a conflict, get an impartial third party involved.

> Try to see things from the other person's perspective.

> Think before you speak.

> Clearly explain the areas you agree on and the areas you disagree on. Try to use the areas you agree on as a starting point for resolving the conflict.

> Listen to what the other person's viewpoint is and find out exactly what they want. They may see something that you do not.

> Make it clear to the person you are having a conflict with that you want to find a fair compromise.

> Make your point in a clear, succinct manner. Do not lecture.

> If you feel that you are losing your temper or control, ask for a break to regain your composure.

> Deal with the issues, not personal disagreements that you may have with a particular person.

> Discuss how you handle a conflict situation with others.

> If you feel frustrated, do not be afraid to say that.

> Try to find a reasonable compromise.

A Passion for Building Enterprise Solutions

Being a part of a Visual Basic team requires hard work. Visual Basic is constantly evolving, changing and improving. You must constantly upgrade your skills and learn new programming methods and technologies. To do this, you must constantly read, study and experiment to learn the latest innovations. This requires a passion for building software solutions in the enterprise, as it takes time and dedication.

Perhaps one of the most difficult tasks for a project manager is to nurture a passion for developing solutions in the team. There are many reasons why the team may lack enthusiasm. Team members who are not happy in their job and are dissatisfied will rarely show a passion for anything work-related. The team can be encouraged to give confidential evaluations of the team or team leader to see their perception of how well the team is working. If the same problem is mentioned by a majority of team members, this is a problem that needs to be resolved. One can also have regular discussions on ways to improve the team, or simply have a place to post suggestions.

Another problem is that developers can easily feel isolated and separate. Most development teams get together for short discussions on the project, but then will go off to their cubicles or offices and work alone. Making the project a team effort and bringing the entire team together to find solutions builds team spirit and helps reduce the isolation. The more the team members feel they are part of something and the more they feel that their input is valuable, the more passionate they will become in accomplishing the team goals.

One other possibility is to get your team members to give classes on topics which are important to the team. These classes should not be boring lectures, but should show innovative ways of using Visual Basic or the latest technology, how the technology solves problems, etc. You can even have weekly or monthly contests to see who can come up with the most innovative test project for a particular technology or Visual Basic feature. An award should be given for all entries, and a special award for the best project. This motivates the developers to learn new skills and to take an interest in the technology.

Some of the skills associated with this passion are as follows:

Basic	Intermediate	Advanced
You strive to stay current on the latest technology	You understand new features in Microsoft Back Office products such as SQL Server, MTS, etc.	You can get others excited about current technology
You understand new features in the latest release of Visual Basic	You motivate others to explore new solutions and new technologies	You make major advances in how technology is used
You have a drive to solve problems and find solutions to technical problems	You try to use technology to improve the individual or the enterprise	
You are motivated to try new solutions, new technology, and experiment to find the best technology for each problem		

It is of course particularly important for the developers to feel this passion, and they should strive to reach the intermediate level, but all team members should reach a basic level with this skill. It is particularly important that the project manager and component managers also feel this enthusiasm, since they should be able to instill it into the other team members. Product managers should also emanate a passion for building solutions in their dealings with the client: the client must see that the team is committed to finding the best solution for them.

Visual Basic, combined with Microsoft Back Office, allows one to solve almost any type of enterprise project. Often, the greatest limitation we face is not the Visual Basic language or the Microsoft products, but our own imagination. Microsoft has provided us with a set of products that allows us to define the goals of the client and then find ways to fulfill those goals. Putting together a solution for a client, regardless of your role on the project, should be viewed as an exciting, creative process. If you find working on a Visual Basic software team boring, you should perhaps reassess your role on the team, or try to spend some time working on different aspects of development until you can find a niche that you enjoy.

The following suggestions may help to increase your passion for building enterprise solutions:

> Try to get involved in challenging projects that will require you to make significant contributions.

> Talk to others about the latest features in Visual Basic.

> Work with other team members to learn about new features in Visual Basic, Back Office or other technologies that you work with.

> Become a specialist in developing Visual Basic applications, but also have understanding of the Microsoft Back Office products.

> Try to work with someone who is an expert in the areas you want to learn about.

> Make contacts with people who will be able to give you advice.

> There is no better way to learn than to teach. Present a class on one of the new features in Visual Basic or give a class on programming, such as optimizing Visual Basic middle tier components.

> Attend conferences such as VBITS (the Visual Basic Insiders' Technical Summit) whenever possible.

> Read magazines, such as Visual Basic Professional Journal (VBPJ), to keep up with the latest Visual Basic versions.

> Work as a team to find the best way to build enterprise applications using Visual Basic and Microsoft Back Office.

> Develop plans to incorporate the new Visual Basic features.

Focusing On the Client

The entire project should focus on the client and their business needs. Everyone on the team is working to produce the most efficient product for the client. If a member of the team is simply building components without any thought to how this component will improve the client's business processes, there is something wrong. Through meetings with the client, all members of the team will get to know the client, their needs, and their business processes.

Basic	Intermediate	Advanced
You can work with a client on a one-to-one basis	You act as a liaison between the client and the rest of the group	You are able to represent the entire software team
You can work with a group of clients	You focus on the client's needs and goals	You create long term vision project plans for the client
You work with the entire team to make sure the client gets the best product possible and that the product fully meets the goals of the client	You can create product designs based on the client's needs and goals	You influence the entire team to be client focused
You build long-lasting relationships with the client	You are able to get the client to define their goals in a clear manner	
You follow up with the client		
You respond to the needs of the client and act as their advocate		
You anticipate the needs of the client		

While the product manager, educators, and logisticians are the primary liaisons to the client and should be at the intermediate or advanced level for client focus, all members of the team should be able to discuss issues relating to meeting the client's needs with the client when necessary, and should aim to reach the basic level at least.

The following suggestions should help to ensure that you remain focused on the client and attentive to their needs:

- Make it one of your goals to exceed the client's expectations.
- Explain to the team what the customer's goals are and how this project (or your portion of the project) will help fulfill these goals.
- When reviewing your goals, ask yourself how these meet the client's goals.
- When speaking to a client, listen to what they say.
- Take notes when talking to a client.
- Create a questionnaire for your clients to see how satisfied they are with your work.
- Create a file on your clients.
- Find out what is important to the client.
- Make a list of the goals of the client and then ask the client to review them.
- After each conversation with a client, write a short (a paragraph or so) summary and send it to the client, preferably through email to make sure you understood the client.
- Listen to problems the customer has had with you or your team and work to resolve them.
- Create a team document showing how to handle difficult customers.

Team Spirit

Team spirit helps bind the team together and helps the team achieve its goals because of its members, not in spite of them. Team spirit allows you to look beyond your own personal needs and work toward the goals of the entire team. We have discussed a few possibilities in the section on passion for enterprise solutions. While team spirit is not technically a skill, it is an essential requirement for anyone who has to work in a team.

Other possibilities include activities that you do as a team outside of work, such as a picnic, conference, etc. These can also be done during work hours.

Be careful with out-of-work plans. While some married people might enjoy some time away from the family, the majority of people with families prefer to spend time with them. If possible, include family members in out-of-work activities. I have known some large corporations to have morale-raising events in one central location, flying all their employees into the event from around the world. While it may be fun for some people, others have responsibilities and may find that this event is an inconvenience rather than a morale booster. Make sure you are choosing activities that everyone will enjoy.

Also be sensitive to ethical, cultural and religious customs. Many people have special dietary needs. It may seem like a great idea to order a pizza for a lunchtime meeting but some of the team members may for one reason or another not be able to eat the pizza. Be sensitive to these issues when you plan such activities.

The three levels for team spirit are:

Basic	Intermediate	Advanced
You willingly participate in helping the group achieve its goals	You make sure the goals of the team are being achieved	You bring together diverse teams across the enterprise
You can lead or follow, depending on what is required at the moment	You work towards making members of the team feel they belong and are important	You create successful, productive teams that include all the teams in a software project
You look to help out other group members	You contribute to the creation of the goals of the team	You create teams that work efficiently together and share information
You help bond the group together to achieve the goals of the group	You share credit for successes with other team members	
You help other group members without being asked	You help build the skills and confidence of your team members	
You contribute to the success of the entire group		

Everyone working in a team (and not just a software team) should aim to develop their team spirit skills, and should have most of the basic level qualities. The project and component managers will need to foster these skills in the other team members, so should strive to reach the intermediate or advanced level.

To improve team spirit you can try the following:

> Work with your team members to solve problems and achieve goals.

> Create a team vision.

> Make a list of the strengths of the members of your team and utilize them in these areas.

> Ask your team members which areas they feel they are not strong in and help them improve themselves in these areas.

> Show appreciation to all the people you come in contact with, including those who are not on your team, such as the administrative people.

> Show appreciation for team members who help achieve the team goals.

> Try to make shy members more comfortable and try to help them talk and contribute.

> Listen to your team members.

> Do not judge team members.

> Be open-minded about team members.

> Enjoy your job.

Leadership

While leadership is essential to be in a management role, it is also important for all team members. Knowing how to lead is something that you can learn with experience. As you will be taking responsibility for accomplishing your goals, it is important that you develop some leadership skills. The three levels of leadership are as follows:

Basic	Intermediate	Advanced
You create a clear direction for your group	You lead according to the current situation	You can inspire the entire software team to achieve goals
You motivate the team to accomplish the essential goals	You are able to create a vision for the group	You easily communicate your vision
You enthusiastically work with team members	You involve the entire group in decisions	You can lead in good and bad times
	You successfully get the support of the entire team	You can create new visions

Although not a traditional 'boss', the project manager has ultimate responsibility for the project, so should aim to possess the advanced level for this skill. The other managerial roles, the component and product managers, should also aim for a high (intermediate to advanced) level of leadership.

Ways to improve your leadership skills:

- ➤ Set priorities for yourself and the team.
- ➤ Help create the team's vision.
- ➤ Talk with people who can break complex tasks into smaller, simpler tasks and learn how they do it.
- ➤ Determine the critical goals and focus on them.
- ➤ Stay focused on the client and their needs.
- ➤ Write down your most important convictions. Put them where you can see them and use them to guide you.
- ➤ When in a meeting, mention any risks you may see in the topic being discussed.
- ➤ Think before you speak, and when you speak, talk in a clear, concise manner.
- ➤ Give feedback.
- ➤ Believe that you can make a difference and you will find that you will.
- ➤ If someone who has performed well in the past starts performing poorly, there may be personal problems. Take time to talk to them and find what has caused the change.
- ➤ If someone has always performed poorly, try to find out what areas they are weak in and motivate them to work on those areas.
- ➤ Do not be afraid of superiors; be honest with them when stating your views.
- ➤ Do not be afraid to identify and bring forward risks.
- ➤ Stand by your principles.
- ➤ Accept responsibility for your actions, even your failures.
- ➤ Learn from your mistakes and allow others to learn from theirs.
- ➤ Evaluate the risks involved and then make decisions that have reasonable risks.
- ➤ Do not ask someone to do something you would not do.
- ➤ Give credit to the appropriate people.
- ➤ Encourage your team members to set ambitious goals and acknowledge and reward them when they achieve them.
- ➤ Find out what roles on the team people want to be in and help them gain the skills to be successful in that role.
- ➤ Stand behind your team members.
- ➤ Perform at the best of your ability to set an example for the team.

Accomplishing Goals

Everyone on the software team needs to know how to accomplish goals, as each member is responsible for accomplishing the goals that are assigned to them. The three levels of accomplishing goals are as follows:

Basic	Intermediate	Advanced
You stay focused on goals until they are accomplished	You get other team members to define their assigned tasks in terms of goals to be accomplished	You meet goals even when there are difficult problems or obstacles
You take pride in your work		You take responsibility for the most difficult goals of the group and complete them
You are willing to take on difficult assignments to help the team accomplish its goals	You help other team members to define critical goals and stay focused on accomplishing them	
You take appropriate action when you are diverted from your goals		You perform effective risk analysis and prevent problems from stopping the team from achieving your goals.
You accomplish the assigned task even when it requires extra time and energy to accomplish the task	You help other team members work through difficulties	
	You acknowledge when other team members fulfill their goals within schedule	You are always looking for ways to improve the team
You turn all assigned tasks into personal goals	You create high but realistic standards	
You create realistic schedules based on assigned tasks and goals	You feel your work represents you	
You do not quit when things go wrong or become difficult	You learn how to prioritize your goals	
You are able to help other team members when they need assistance		
You are willing to do routine tasks when they are required		

Since the project depends ultimately on the developers producing working code on schedule, this skill is particularly vital for them, and they should aim for the intermediate to advanced level of this skill. The code will also need to be tested on schedule, so the testers too should try to reach at least the intermediate level. The component managers and the project manager will need to ensure that the goals of the entire team are achieved, so should ideally possess this skill to the advanced level.

Below are some suggestions which might help you to ensure that you accomplish the goals which are assigned to you or which you set for yourself:

> - Do not give up; often one must work hard and keep trying to accomplish a goal.
> - Use the 80/20 rule, which states that you should try to accomplish 80% of your goals in 20% of your time.
> - Reevaluate your goals periodically and adjust your goals as circumstances change.
> - Do not focus on the negative.
> - Do not work the clock; work toward accomplishing tasks.
> - Focus on how to do something; do not focus on why you think it cannot be done.
> - Find the goals that are critical and focus on them.
> - Create rewards for yourself when you accomplish your goals.
> - Accomplish your goals so that you can take on more responsibilities.

System Management

Certain roles in the team, such as product management, require a good knowledge of enterprise systems. The three levels for system management are:

Basic	Intermediate	Advanced
You are able to identify key goals and properly access all risks to the goals	You can manage and design complex processes and systems	You create a vision level design for the enterprise that incorporates both current and future technology
You are able to oversee complex systems and processes	You know what metrics are required to monitor and improve a system	You are able to manage, design and improve enterprise-level systems
You can re-evaluate information on goals to determine risks to goals		

These skills are chiefly important for the product managers and logisticians, who should all aim for intermediate to advanced level for this skill.

These are some ways to improve system management skills:

> - When creating budgets, include only critical items.
> - Understand how systems work within the entire enterprise.
> - Learn any software products that will help you manage the system better.
> - Be familiar with all aspects of the system; past, present and future.
> - Look for ways of improving the system from new technological improvements.
> - Understand how Visual Basic can fit into the enterprise.
> - Do not accept anything that is not up to your standards; find a way to improve poorly working systems.
> - Work with your team and peers to find better solutions.

General Team Skills

Finally, we will put together some general skills necessary to be a successful team member. We could include many more skills in this list, but I've tried to focus on the more important ones. The three levels of these general skills are:

Basic	Intermediate	Advanced
You remain calm and focused during disagreements	You respect all people regardless of their culture, background or opinions	You understand people and can usually predict how they will respond
You build good working relationships with other members of the team	You identify business opportunities and act on them	You do not overreact to problems
You are focused on the goals even when others are being distracted by problems	You can function even during stressful periods	You can stabilize the team during disagreements
You handle stress effectively	You show respect to all others regardless of the situation	You can identify new opportunities and act on them
You are able to keep others focused on the problem when there are disagreements	You do not blame others	You can find solutions even under highly stressful circumstances
You relate to people in a manner that is appropriate for that person	You work towards constructive solutions	You build effective relationships in the enterprise
You treat other people in a courteous manner		
You are honest		
You behave in a professional manner		
You know when and how to respond to a risk		
You respond to changes in technology		

Below are some suggestions on how to improve your general team skills:

> When you make a mistake, admit it.
> Try to learn something from everyone you meet.
> Make realistic schedules and commitments.
> Be honest.
> Be consistent.
> Do not dwell on past mistakes; look towards the future.
> Finish what you start.
> Have a sense of humor.
> Do not get upset when others correct you; look at it as a way to improve yourself.
> Stand up for members of your team.
> Make lists of the things you want to learn.
> Do not bring the job home.
> Say what you think without offending anyone.
> Accept that problems are part of life and learn to adapt your plans when they arise.
> Create personal goals, such as mastering a new feature in Visual Basic, make a plan to achieve that goal, and then accomplish the goal.
> Do not miss deadlines, if possible.
> Allow trust to develop between you and your co-workers, and realize that this may take some time.
> Do not make excuses.

Summary

A Visual Basic team should be comprised of a group of people who are assigned to roles based on their skills and the responsibilities they can assume. The skills for each role should be well-defined, so that team members can develop the necessary skills to succeed in their role and so they can work toward moving into other roles.

Ideally, a company should put time aside for workshops with its employees to train them in non-technical skills. These non-technical skills are as important as the technical ones. Team members should have the skills to manage themselves and also be able to help the team reach its goals.

Skills References

Below is a list of books on topics covered in this chapter. I would recommend that any large company should have a library with both technical and non-technical books that can be borrowed by team members. The following books should be part of any library for a Visual Basic team.

The Art of Communicating by Bert Decker. Crisp Publications, Inc., ISBN 156052409X

You've Got to Be Believed to Be Heard by Bert Decker, James Denney. St. Martin's Press, ISBN 0312099495

People Smarts: Bending the Golden Rule to Give Others What They Want by Tony Alessandra, Michael J. O'Connor. Pfeiffer & Co, ISBN 0883904217

Communicating at Work by Tony Alessandra, Phillip Hunsaker. Fireside, ISBN 0671788558

The Human Touch : Today's Most Unusual Program for Productivity and Profit by William W. Arnold, Jeanne M. Plas. John Wiley & Sons, ISBN 0471572918

Listen to Win: A Manager's Guide to Effective Listening by Curt Bechler, Richard L. Weaver. Master Media, ISBN 1571010025

Basics of Business Writing (Worksmart Series) by Marty Stuckey. AMACOM, ISBN 0814477925

Getting It Done: How to Lead When You're Not in Charge. Harperbusiness, ISBN 0887308422

Discovering Common Ground: How Future Search Conferences Bring People Together to Achieve by Marvin R. Weisbord. Berrett-Koehler Pub, ISBN 1881052087

Breakthrough Innovation, Empowerment, Shared Vision, and Leadership When the Heat's on by Danny Cox, John Hoover. McGraw-Hill, ISBN 0070132674

Leading Self-Directed Work Teams: A Guide to Developing New Team Leadership Skills by Kimball Fisher.

Empowered Teams: Creating Self-Directed Work Groups That Improve Quality, Productivity, and Participation by Richard S. Wellins, William C. Byham. Jossey-Bass Publishers, ISBN 1555425542

Leading the Transition: Management's Role in Creating a Team-Based Culture by Wilbur L. Pike III. AACC Press, ISBN 0527762474

Why Teams Don't Work: What Went Wrong and How to Make It Right by Harvey Robbins, Michael Finley. HighBridge Company, ISBN 1565111923

Why Change Doesn't Work: Why Initiatives Go Wrong and How to Try Again-And Succeed by Harvey Robbins, Michael Finley. Petersons Guides, ISBN 1560799447

Reaching the Peak Performance Zone: How to Motivate Yourself and Others to Excel by Gerald Kushel. AMACOM, ISBN 0814402224

Patterns of High Performance: Discovering the Ways People Work Best by Jerry L. Fletcher. Berrett-Koehler (Short Disc), ISBN 1881052338

Principle-Centered Leadership by Stephen R. Covey. Fireside, ISBN 0671792806

The 2,000 Percent Solution: Free Your Organization from 'Stalled' Thinking to Achieve Exponential Success by Donald Mitchell, Carol Coles, Robert Metz.

Bringing Out the Best in People: How to Apply the Astonishing Power of Positive Reinforcement by Aubrey C. Daniels

If It Ain't Broke, Break It : And Other Unconventional Wisdom for a Changing Business World by Robert J. Kriegel, Louis Patler. Warner Books, ISBN 0446393592

Vision: How Leaders Develop It, Share It, and Sustain It by Joseph V. Quigely. McGraw-Hill, ISBN 0070510849

Building a Shared Vision: A Leader's Guide to Aligning the Organization by C. Patrick Lewis. Productivity Press, ISBN 156327163X

The Confident Decision Maker: How to Make the Right Business and Personal Decisions Every Time. Quill, ISBN 0688142281

Competing for the Future by Gary Hamel, C. K. Prahalad. Harvard Business School Press, ISBN 0875847161

The Profit Zone: How Strategic Business Design Will Lead You to Tomorrow's Profits by Adrian J. Slywotzky, David J. Morrison. Times Books, ISBN 0812929004

Drawing on the Right Side of the Brain: A Course in Enhancing Creativity and Artistic Confidence by Betty Edwards. J P Tarcher, ISBN 0874775132

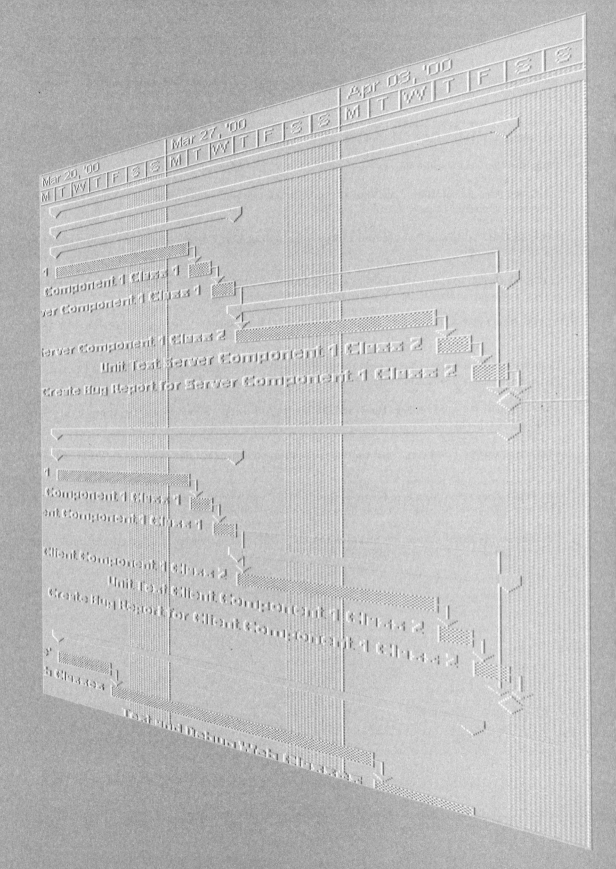

Creating Project Schedules

Now that we have a basic understanding of the cycles of a Visual Basic project, the goals for each cycle and who is responsible for each goal, we can begin to look at making schedules. We will define a **schedule** as a visual document that allows you to see how you will use the time resource towards accomplishing your goals.

A schedule begins with a set of goals that need to be accomplished. Goals can be divided into three priorities: high (critical), medium, and low. Each goal will have one or many milestones that will allow us to measure whether we have accomplished this goal or not. We will have a set of resources, which includes time, money, and human resources, which we can use to accomplish our goals.

Because there will almost always be limitations placed on what we can do with our resources (there is never enough time!), we must balance our schedule so that the high priority goals are met within the limits of our resources. Low priority goals may not get done, and medium priority goals may be done, but not immediately. By using a schedule, we have a visual tool that allows us to adjust the amount of time allotted for our goals until we arrive at a schedule that allows us to complete all of our critical goals, and hopefully most, if not all, of our medium goals. If you can also accomplish your medium priority goals within your normal workday, consider yourself very lucky.

If we are using a scheduling tool, we can extend the definition of a schedule to being a visual document that allows us to see how we are using all of our resources, including time, people, money, and space, towards accomplishing our goals. Using these scheduling tools, you can adjust the usage of all of the available resources until you arrive at a schedule that efficiently uses the resources towards the accomplishment of your goals.

We will use Microsoft Project 98 because it is easy to use and learn, the examples we use with Microsoft Project 98 are useful for any project management software product, and it can be used to demonstrate all of the important concepts of creating a schedule. If you do not have Project 98, you can download a free 60-day trial version at:

http://www.microsoft.com/office/98/project/trial/info.htm

This web site also contains links for Project 98 that can help answer even your most advanced questions about how to use Project 98. I would highly recommend you taking the time to download Project 98 now if you do not already have it.

This chapter is filled with important scheduling skills and will teach you the basics of how to create a project schedule. Two of the visual aids provided by Project 98 are Gantt and Pert charts.

A **Gantt** chart represents each goal as a horizontal bar. The horizontal bar will be placed over a time scale, which is situated at the top of the chart. The length of the horizontal bar shows how long it will take to complete the goal. Using a Gantt chart, one can quickly determine the status of goals over time, the relationship between goals if one exists, and resources associated with the goal.

> In this book, I will be placing goals on the schedule. Normally, most people would call these tasks, instead of goals. Tasks are defined as something that is assigned. In our view of teams, we do not assign work. Goals are created for the team, and each team member assumes the goals that fit with their role and their abilities. The word task just does not fit in with our view of a team. Goals, on the other hand, fit in perfectly with our team view. Project 98 uses the word 'tasks'. Just substitute 'goal' for 'task' when working with Project 98.

A Gantt chart will look something like the following example:

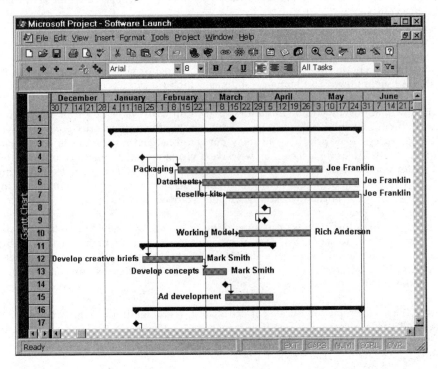

A Pert chart shows the relationships between goals. Goals that are dependent on other goals, for example, one goal requiring another to be completed first or a goal that is a sub-goal of a second, can easily be seen in a Pert chart. Pert charts are useful for visualizing the sequence of goals and they can also show the progress of each goal as time goes on. More information can be found in the Project 98 help files.

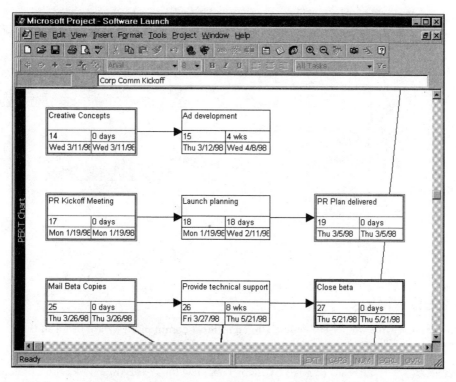

Throughout the rest of the book, we will use a generic Visual Basic DNA project as an example to show you how to manage a project. This project will contain the normal parts of a Visual Basic DNA project: client components, server components and web components. If any of these components are not part of your project, you can remove them from this schedule.

In this chapter, you will start out in the Visual Basic developer role. We will look at your personal schedule for the beginning of a project. We will do this to introduce Project 98, show you some of the basics of this tool and also discuss some special scheduling issues for Visual Basic developers.

Using Project 98 to Schedule Your Goals

Open Project 98. Select View. You will see the following views:

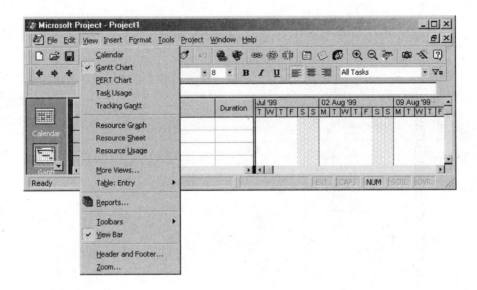

Project 98 Views

Project 98 comes with twenty-six views. The eight most common views are listed in the dropdown menu by default. They are:

Calendar: A view of goals by date. This view looks very much like the calendar in Microsoft Outlook, except that you cannot set the hours for your goals. You can set the range of dates you want to view.

Gantt: Goals are shown as a bar spanning the time it will take to complete the goal.

Pert: A diagram showing all goals and the relationship between goals.

Task Usage: A list of goals showing the resources assigned to each goal.

Tracking Gantt: Used to track the percentage a goal is completed.

Resource Graph: A graph showing resource allocation, cost or work.

Resource Sheet: A place to enter all the resources available to the project.

Resource Usage: A list of resources and the goals associated with the resource.

More Views: Additional ways of viewing the schedule.

We will only discuss the Gantt view in detail because it is one of the most popular views for project management and the best one to manage your schedule and resources.

Project Starting Date

We will begin by creating a schedule for an individual developer. This means creating a new project. Open Project 98, select File and then select New. You will see the Project Information box, as follows:

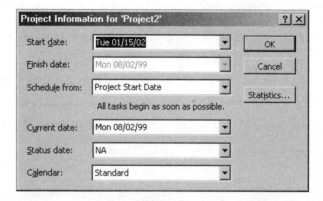

We would like our project to have dates in the future. I have chosen to begin this project on January 15, 2002. We need to tell Project 98 that we are beginning our schedule on this day. The project information can also be seen at any time by selecting Project | Project Information Don't worry about the Finish date: Project 98 will automatically put that in for you.

Gantt View

Now that we have started a new project, we must make sure that we are in Gantt view - do this by selecting View | Gantt Chart or by clicking the Gantt button on the left hand side of the screen.

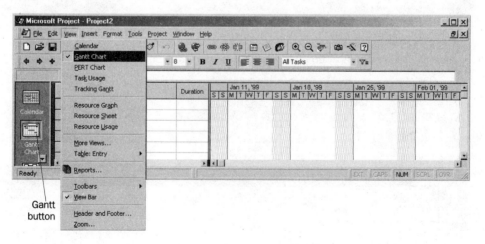

If you don't see these buttons, you can view them by selecting View | View Bar.

On the left side of the screen, you will be able to assign each goal a name, a start and finish date, the duration of the goal, any goals that must be completed before this goal is completed (the Predecessors column), and a list of required resources. This information will be used by Project 98 to create the task bars on the right hand side.

Gantt Chart Timescales

The view on the right hand side will have two timescales, a major timescale and a minor timescale, as shown below.

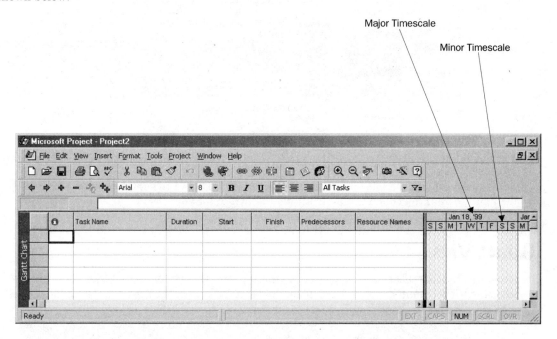

You can change the major and minor timescales by placing the cursor over the timescales and right mouse clicking. Select Zoom to increase or decrease the timescale.

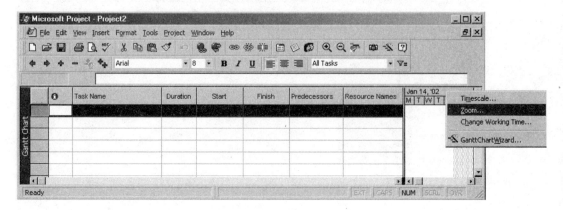

When you select Zoom you will get the following form:

Select the range that you wish to see. You can also select Timescale in the dropdown menu to change both the major and minor times. Selecting Timescale will give you the following form:

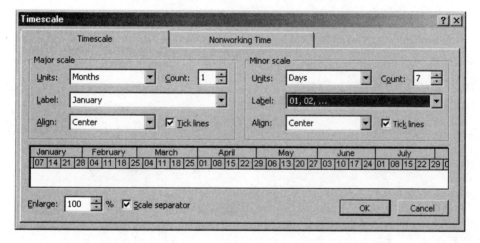

You can now adjust the major and minor time as you wish. Using this feature you can view your project over hours or weeks, or whatever is most appropriate.

When adding goals, you can type the information directly into the left hand side of the screen. Let us begin by making the schedule for our developer during the envisionment phase of our project. During this phase the developer will have minimal input into the project. This is a perfect time for the developer to spend time learning new skills or improving old ones.

When making a Gantt chart, you are showing how the time resource is being used by your goal. You are not making an hourly working schedule. This means that you are not saying that on April 15th from 9 A.M. to 11:00 A.M. I will be working on goal 1 when using a Gantt chart. Instead, a Gantt chart will show that two hours of the time resource have been allocated to working on goal 1 on April 15th without saying which two hours.

Once you have allocated the total time resource for the day to different goals, you can use a standard scheduling program to assign what hours in the day will belong to each goal. Thus, the Gantt chart could allocate one hour to goal 1, four hours to goal 2, and one hour to goal 3 on April 15th. You can then use a calendar program such as the one in Outlook to assign 9 A.M. to 10 A.M. for goal 1, 10 A.M. to 11 A.M. and 12 P.M. to 3 P.M. for goal 2, 3 P.M. to 4 P.M. for goal 3 and 4 P. M. to 5 P.M. for administrative tasks.

Creating the Schedule

Let us begin by typing the following into your schedule:

Task Name	Duration	Start	Finish
Learn VB 6 New Features	0 hrs	Tue 01/15/02	Tue 01/15/02

As soon as you type in the task name, Project 98 will assign it a duration of 1 day. Simply click on the appropriate column and type in 0 hrs as above.

We have said that the duration of this goal is 0 hours - as we break down the goal into sub-goals, and assign durations to them, this main goal will have a duration that is the sum of all the durations of its sub-goals. Don't worry about this for now, it will become clearer later.

Duration Field in a Gantt Chart

Duration can have any of the following values:

m	minute
h	hour
d	day
w	week
em	elapsed minutes
eh	elapsed hours
ed	elapsed days
ew	elapsed week

The elapsed times are used when your goals run through non-working times. Working times are defined in the options. If you wish to change these, go to the menu, select Tools | Options and select the Calendar tab. You will see the following:

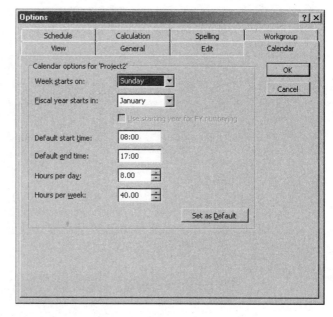

You can set the time for the workday as you need to.

If a goal is to run Friday through Sunday, and you have the default workday as shown above, you can list it as a 3 ed starting on Friday. This means that you were expecting it to run over 3 elapsed days - Friday, Saturday and Sunday. If you used 3 d, Project 98 would see this as meaning 3 work days, and would make the goal run over Friday, Monday and Tuesday of a regular work week.

Entering Goals Into Project 98

Once you have placed your goal into Project 98, your schedule should look as follows:

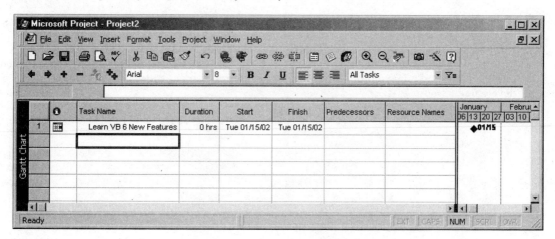

There is another way to enter information into Project 98. Double click on any part of the row you have created. You will now see the following form:

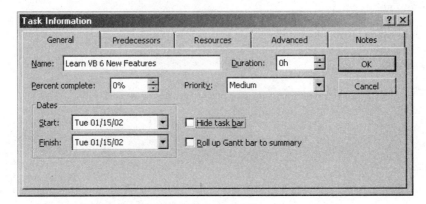

Select the Advanced tab: under Constrain task change the Type to As Soon As Possible:

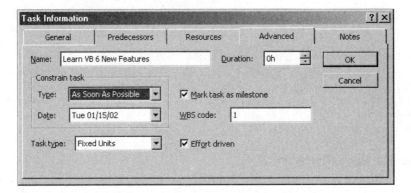

Select the Notes tab and type in the following note:

I will be focusing on learning several of the new features in Visual Basic. The skills I will be focusing on are the new data source classes, web classes and IIS classes. During the envisionment phase I will spend a maximum of five hours on skills and drop to zero hours during the development phase.

This will look as follows:

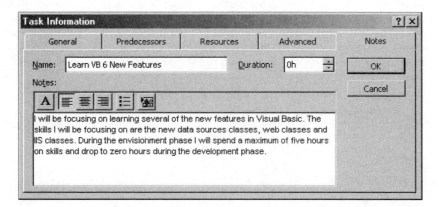

Select **OK**. Notice a note icon has been added to the information column of the left of the goal name.

Some of you may be thinking that it is unrealistic to study at work. I once worked at a large company that did not allow reading of any material at your work desk. I found out about this policy because one of my coworkers spotted me reading a magazine at my cubicle and reported me to my senior manager. I was immediately called into the manager's office. I explained to my manager that I was reading an article in VBPJ and using the code sample in the magazine for the current project I was working on. I was referring to the article as I typed code into my project. I was told that reading any magazine at work was not allowed, and if one of the company's vice presidents had seen me, I would have been fired on the spot. I was advised to go to the cafeteria or step outside if I wanted to do research on my coding during work hours. While this may seem like it came out of a Dilbert cartoon, this really happened to me.

During times when programmers have slack time, such as during the envisionment phase or between projects, team members should be allowed to study. I cannot emphasize this enough. Visual Basic is a constantly evolving language, as is the entire Enterprise technology. There is just too much to learn during off hours. If a company wants highly skilled Visual Basic team members, then they must allow their full time Visual Basic employees to spend some time improving their skills during work time. They should also be willing to invest in training.

I would go as far as setting a quiet office aside and turning it into a study room. The room should be made comfortable and also have one, preferably several, computers set up to work with Visual Basic and Back Office. The computer should have as much source code as possible, the MSDN and tech net loaded onto it, and as many study aids as possible. There should be shelves loaded with good reference materials. A conference room should also be set aside when several developers have downtime so that they can work together on learning a topic. If someone has expertise in a field, they should give a talk on that topic. The company can also pay to have experts in certain areas come in and give classes to the developers.

Learning new Visual Basic 6 skills is a goal that will be scheduled over a one-month period. We would like to see how many hours we can devote to this goal each day. To do this with a Gantt chart we must divide our goal into sub-goals. Each sub-goal can be accomplished within the number of hours you can spend on the overall goal (learning new VB 6 skills in our example) in one day. On Tuesday, January 15 you can put five hours towards learning the new features of Visual Basic 6. This is enough time to learn the basics of Visual Basic 6's new Data provider classes. We will make this a sub-goal for January 15 that will have a duration of five hours.

Goal Name	Duration	Start	Finish
Learn basic skills of VB 6 data source class	5 hrs	Tue 01/15/02	Tue 01/15/02

In our schedule we now have:

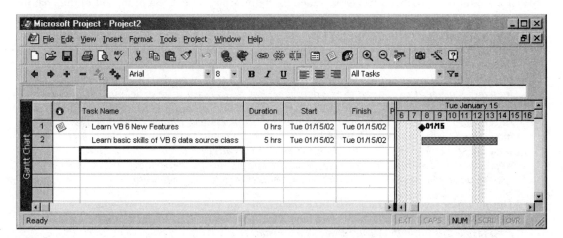

I have changed the major timescale to days and the minor timescale to hours - notice how there is now a bar on the right hand side representing the length of this goal.

Creating Sub-goals

You want to make a sub-goal of the Learn VB 6 New Features goal. We can do this by selecting goal 2 and clicking the arrow pointing to the right on the left hand side of the toolbar:

The left arrow will move a goal up one level:

The plus and minus signs will show or hide the sub-goals:

After clicking the right arrow, you should now have the following:

Notice that there have been a few changes in goal 1. The duration of goal 1 is now 0.63 days. A day is defined as 8 hours; 5 hours is thus 0.63 days. The finish time is now Tue 01/15/02. The main goal can only have a duration that totals the combined durations of its sub-goals. Notice that on the right hand side there is now a black bar indicating that goal 1 is divided up into sub-goals.

Time Estimates and Milestones

In chapter two I said that you should base your daily schedule on accomplishing goals, not on working a certain number of hours. By breaking your larger goals down into daily goals, you can see what you need to accomplish every day. Now, the important question is, "How do we know when we have successfully accomplished the goal?" For the sub-goal, "Learn basic skills of VB data source classes," you might want to say the goal is accomplished when you have completed five hours of studying. Yet, this is not correct. This is working the clock.

The time listed is an estimate of the time we expect this goal to take, not the amount of time we actually must spend to do this goal (though hopefully the two will be nearly the same). We need a milestone here. For example, the book, VB 6 UML, published by Wrox Press, covers data source classes in chapters 12, 13 and 14. Thus, we could create the following milestone for this sub-goal:

> ➤ Read chapters 12, 13 and 14 in the VB 6 UML book and enter the code from these chapters into a test project.

When the chapters are read and the code is written, the goal is complete, regardless of how many hours it takes to reach this point. Hopefully, though, our time estimate of five hours was accurate.

The number of hours assigned to a goal is only an estimate of how long it will take to accomplish the goal. The actual time to complete the goal may be longer or shorter. It is important that you work toward accomplishing goals every day, and have a milestone that tells you when the goal has been reached. When all of your milestones for the day have been reached, you have completed your day's work. If you are new at estimating the time it takes to accomplish a goal, talk to a co-worker who may have more experience. Over time, your estimates should become more accurate and you should be able to properly estimate the goals you can accomplish in a normal workday. Also, actual time spent on working towards a goal can be stored against a goal so that developers and managers can see how accurate time estimates have been and can learn and refine their estimates.

You can enter the milestone in two ways. You can either enter it as a comment or you can create a milestone with Project 98 by entering a goal with a duration of 0, as follows. Enter the following into Project 98:

Goal Name	Duration	Start	Finish
Complete chapters 12-14 in VB6 UML	0	Tue 01/15/02	Tue 01/15/02

Your project should now look as follows:

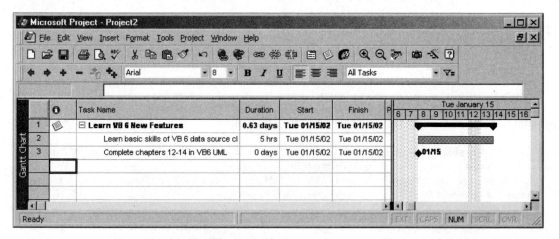

Notice how Project 98 represents a milestone with a diamond.

Let us imagine that on Wednesday, January 16 we will spend the day in meetings so we will not allocate any time to learning VB on this day. On Thursday, January 17 we will spend part of the day reviewing the meeting but will still have two hours to spend working on our VB 6 skills. We will spend this time reviewing MTS. Let us add the following to our schedule:

Goal Name	Duration	Start	Finish
Learn MTS	2h	Thu 01/17/02	Thu 01/17/02
Complete chapter 3 in Wrox MTS MSMQ	0	Thu 01/17/02	Thu 01/17/02

Entering Project Information

Let us now imagine that we are working on a project with the Northwind Company called the Northwind project. We now want to add the Northwind project into our schedule. Under Goal Name in row 6, type in Northwind Project and click the left arrow, as we do not want this to be a sub-goal of Learn VB 6 New Features.

The project should now look as follows:

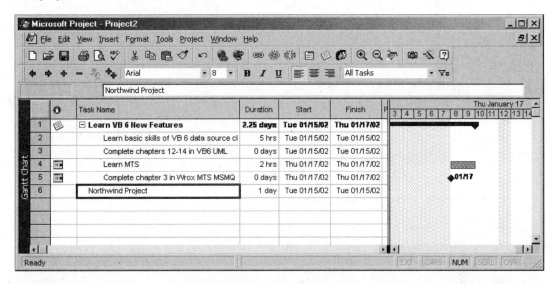

Project 98 automatically gives this a duration of 1 day starting on the first day of the whole project - this will change when we add sub-goals.

Under the Northwind Project on lines 7 and 8 we can add the following sub-goals (don't forget to click the indent arrow):

Goal Name	Duration	Start	Finish
First Envisionment Meeting	7h	Wed 01/16/02	Wed 01/16/02
Review Envisionment Meeting	5h	Thu 01/17/02	Thu 01/17/02

You may have noticed that when you try to enter the date for the First Envisionment Meeting, a wizard pops up, looking like this:

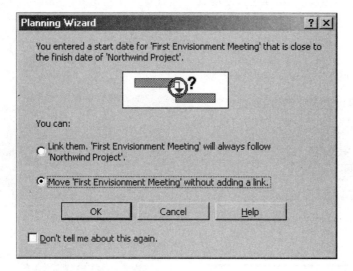

For now, select the second option and press OK.

You should now have the following:

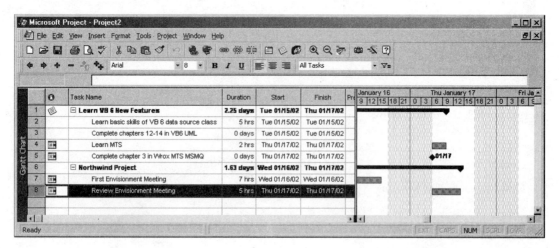

Our scale on the right is too large so we need to change it. Right mouse click on the timescale:

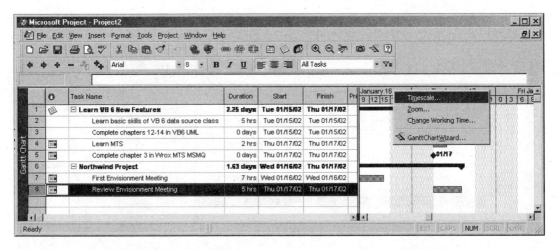

Under Minor scale, change the Count to 8:

We now have the following:

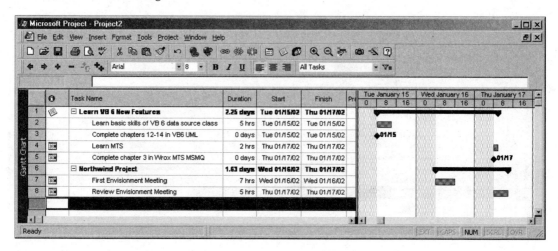

Recurring Goals

Our schedule is beginning to fill out. We would like to allot one hour every day to administrative time, which includes breaks and checking email. We will need to add this in for every day. Microsoft Project 98 allows us to add recurring goals.

Click on the next empty row (number 9) and go to <u>I</u>nsert in the menu. Select <u>R</u>ecurring Task:

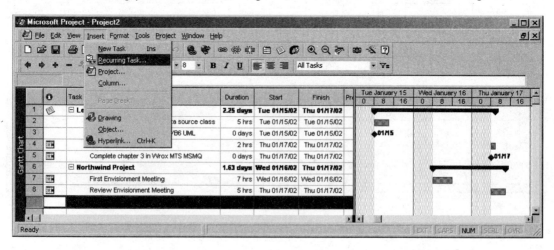

Enter the following information in the Recurring Goal Information form:

Goal Name	Duration	From	To	This occurs	Daily
Administrative	1h	Tue 01/15/02	Wed 01/15/03	Daily	Every Workday

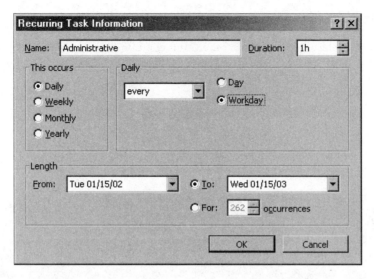

Press OK. Select goal 9 and click on the left arrow to move Administrative up one level. Your schedule should now look as follows:

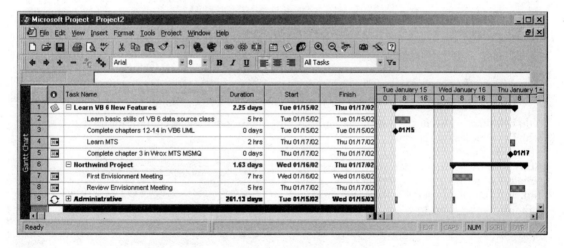

Links

Sometimes one goal is dependent on another goal. Project 98 allows you to set up four types of dependencies:

Finish To Start: One goal must be completed before the next one can start. If we needed to complete the VB6 UML chapters before moving onto MTS, we could add this type of dependency. To make the link, we need to select the first item on the Gantt chart on the right hand side and drag the mouse pointer to the next goal. Select Goal 2 first and drag the mouse to Goal 4. As you do this, you should see the chain link symbol, showing that a link has been made.

The default will be Finish to Start link. Your schedule with the link will look as follows (we have changed the major time scale to week and the minor to day):

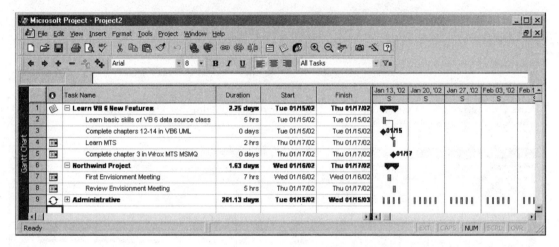

You could have also just typed in the number 2 in the Predecessors column for goal 4. Use whichever is easiest for you.

Start to Start: One goal can start at the same time the other goal starts. Double click on the link and you should see the Task Dependency window. Select Start-to-Start.

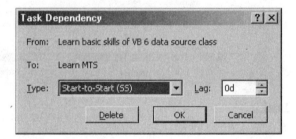

Your link should look as follows:

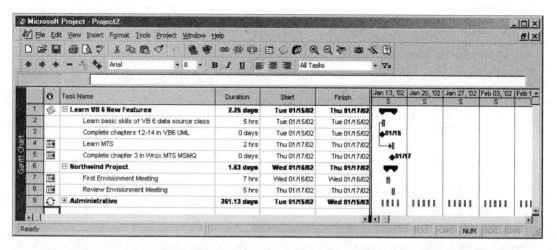

Notice the link has moved from the end of the first goal to the beginning of the first goal. When using start, the link is attached at the beginning of the bar; for finish the link is attached to the end of the bar.

Finish to Finish: This is used when two groups finish at the same time.
Start to Finish: This is used when one group starts when one finishes. For example, you may be upgrading a system. When the new system starts, the old system finishes.

Let us now link together some groups. Insert three new rows into your schedule before goal 9. Make sure that goal 9 is selected, then select Insert | New Task three times:

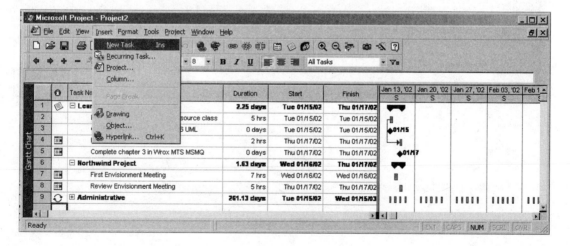

Add the following goals to the Northwind project:

Goal Name	Duration	Start	Finish
Recommendations for Vision/Scope	7h	Tue 01/22/02	Tue 01/22/02
Final Envisionment Meeting	7h	Fri 01/25/02	Fri 01/25/02
First Team Development Meeting	3h	Mon 01/28/02	Mon 01/28/02

Now link all of the Northwind goals together by selecting goals 7 to 11 and clicking the chain link button on the toolbar:

Double click on each link and change it to a Finish to Start link. Your schedule should now look as follows:

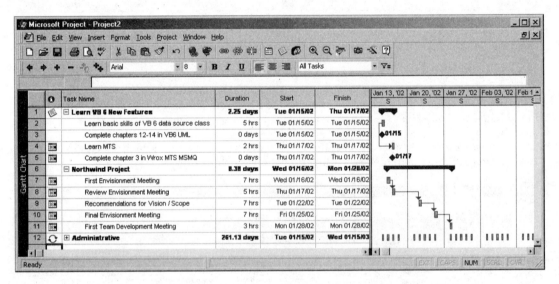

Saving the Schedule

Go to File | Save and name the file DeveloperSchedule.

If you see the following screen just click OK:

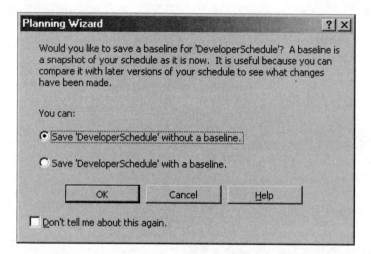

This allows you to save backup copies of your schedule. We do not need to do this, so we select **Save 'DeveloperSchedule' without a baseline.** You can get rid of this by clicking in the box **Don't tell me about this again.** The schedule will then be saved as DeveloperSchedule.mpp

Resources

Up to this point, we have only been working with the time resource. There are many other resources that are available, including people, equipment, rooms, etc. In regards to the schedule we are creating for a developer, some of the resources may be the availability of the study room and the study computer. Let us add these two resources to our schedule.

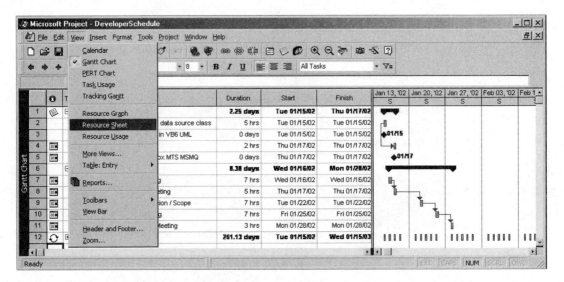

In the resource sheet add Study Room and Study Computer; Project 98 adds the extra information automatically:

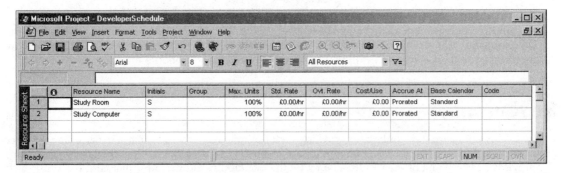

Click <u>V</u>iew and go back to Gantt view. Double click on the Learn basic skills of VB 6 data source class goal to bring up the Task Information window. Select the resources tab, click on the dropdown combo and select Study Room. Since the room can hold four people, you are using 25% (one quarter) of the total resource. Enter 25 for Units. You should see the following:

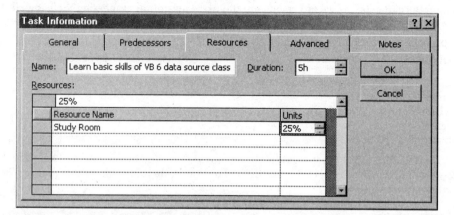

Your schedule will now have the resource added:

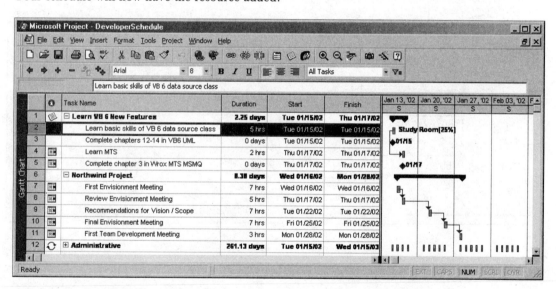

Using this resource information, a master schedule can be put together to make sure that the team is not overusing a resource. In this case, if five team members were trying to use the study room at the same time, the resource would be over utilized and this would show up on the combined master schedule.

Resource Management

What would happen if we did over allocate a resource? Let us deliberately add a conflict to our schedule to see what would happen. We will do this by adding a second envisionment meeting and hold it on the same day as we are reviewing the first envisionment meeting. Select goal 9 and insert a new row (Insert | New Task) and then enter the following into the schedule:

Goal Name	Duration	Start	Finish	Predecessors	Resource name
Second Envisionment Meeting	7h	Thu 01/17/02	Thu 01/17/02	8	

When I was using Project 98, it wouldn't allow me to enter the finish date as Thursday, January 17th 2002, so we must make Project 98 let us do it. To do this, double click on the goal and bring up the task information window.

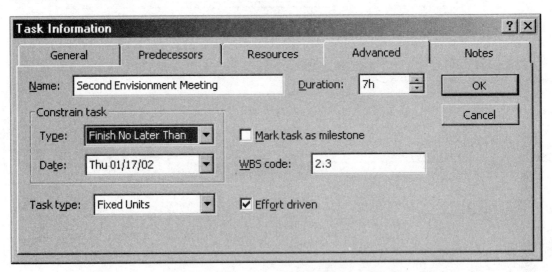

Click on the Advanced tab and make sure that everything looks the same as the above. When you click on OK, you may see this window pop up:

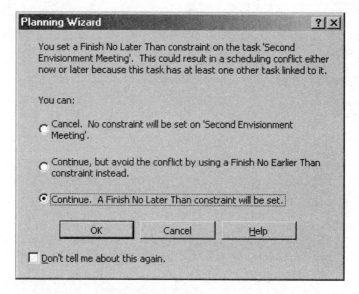

Click on the third option and press OK. This window may then pop up:

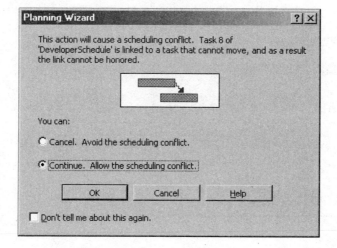

Click on **Continue** and press **OK**. The schedule should then look something like this:

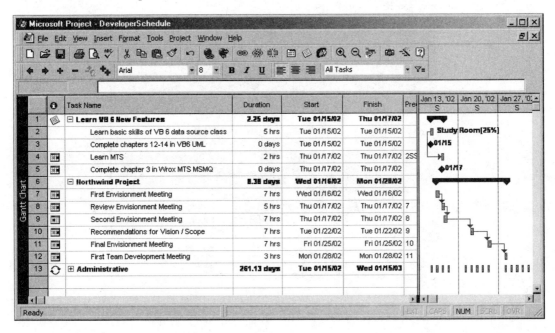

However, we have not yet told Project 98 where we are holding these meetings, so let's add a new resource, the meeting room. Select <u>V</u>iew | Resource <u>S</u>heet and add Meeting Room to the list: it should look something like this:

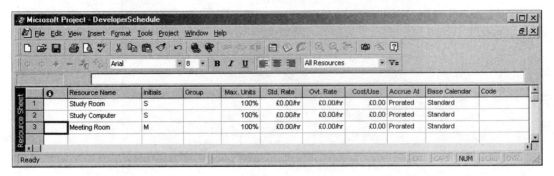

Now we need to tell Project 98 that the First Envisionment Meeting will take place in the meeting room. Click View and go back to Gantt view. Double click on goal 7 to bring up the task information window. We will be using the whole room, so enter the units as 100%. Task information should look as follows:

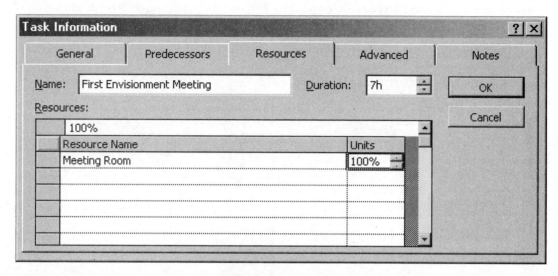

Repeat this for goal 8 and goal 9; the schedule should look like this:

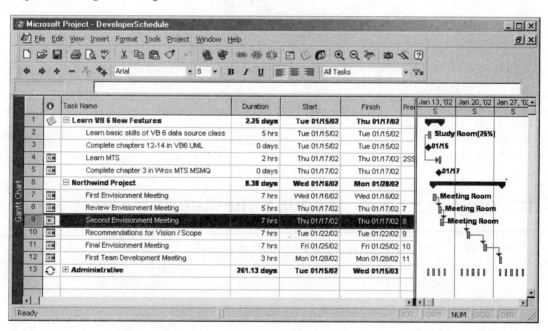

Notice how the resource name appears on the right hand side of each goal in the schedule. As we are fully utilizing the resource, there is no percentage mark beside it.

Now that we have entered this information into our schedule, we would like to look it over and make sure we have used our resources correctly. Go to the menu, select <u>V</u>iew, and then select Resource Graph. Put the cursor over the time scale and right mouse click. Select Timescale from the dropdown menu. Make sure the major scale is in weeks and the minor is in days. Scroll over to January 17 and make sure that you select Meeting Room on the left hand side of the screen. You should see the following:

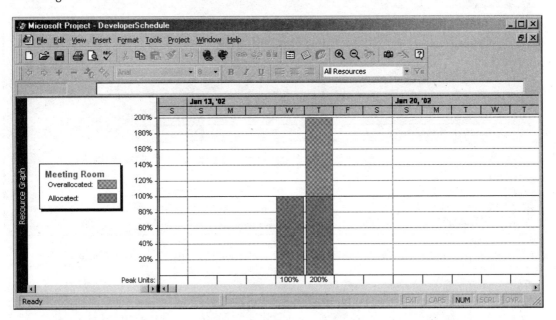

We can see that we have overscheduled our Meeting Room for Thursday, January 17.

Although I had to deliberately insert a conflict of resources into the schedule, you can see that the resource graph tool can be a very powerful aid in helping you manage your project. As you begin to include all of the resources relating to your project, there is an awful lot of room for errors in resource allocation. The resource graph tool can help you keep a check on these, especially when you may not realize that conflicts occur.

Changing the Look of your Schedule

You may have noticed above that the resources are listed on the right hand side of the goals in your schedule. There may be times that you want to change this view, for example, to show the names of the goals next to the bar representing their duration. To do this, you can use the Gantt Chart Wizard.

Right mouse clicking on a link will give us a dropdown list, which includes the Gantt chart wizard:

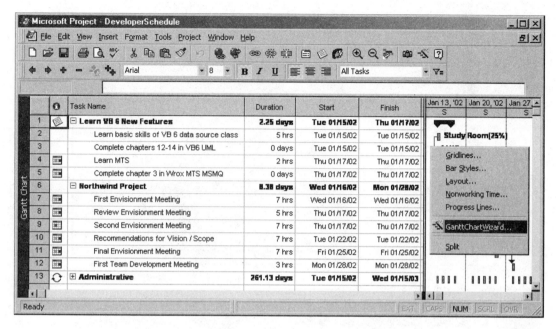

You can also click the Gantt wizard button on the standard Toolbar to open the Gantt wizard:

You must select the rows you want to format. Put the cursor over the numbers on the left column, hold the left mouse button down and select the rows. You should now have:

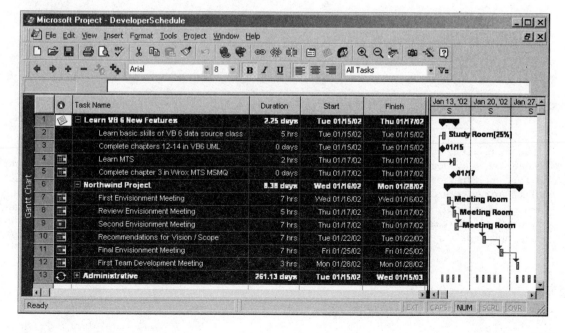

Open the Gantt chart wizard. The first screen of the wizard will look as follows:

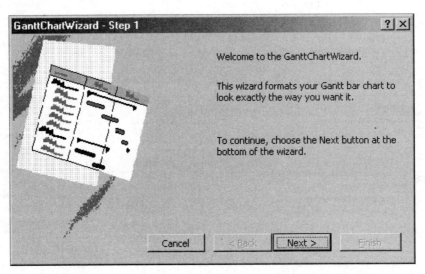

Click next and you will see the following:

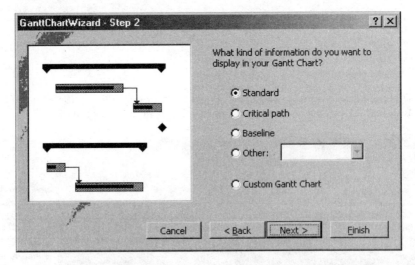

This brings up a very important part of a project, the critical path. At this point, all goals look the same. Yet, some goals are much more important that other goals. **Critical goals** are the ones that must be accomplished for the project to succeed. In our schedule, administrative time and studying Visual Basic are not critical goals. If we do not accomplish these goals, the project should still succeed. It is essential to identify which goals are critical. As this is just a sample project, we will include all goals in the Gantt chart, so leave the Standard button checked. A complete, real schedule might only show the critical goals, in which case we would check the Critical path option button.

Click Next and on the next screen select Custom task information.

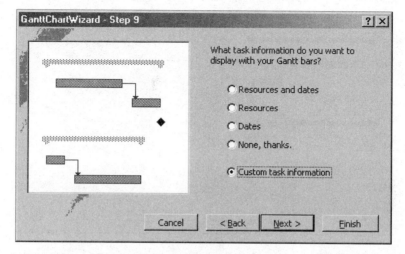

Click Next. On the next screen, select **Name** in the **Left** box. You could add any fields you want, such as the resources, but I am leaving them out to prevent the chart from becoming overcrowded.

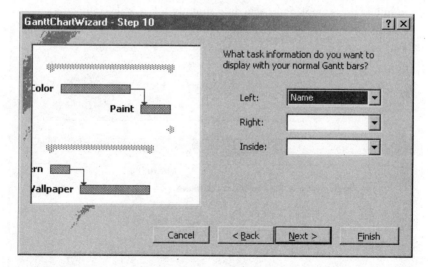

Click Next. Step 11 allows us to add labels to our summary Gantt bars, which are the black bars that represent the goals that have sub-goals. Step 12 gives us the option to include labels for milestones. The next screen in the wizard, Step 13, asks us if we want to include link lines between dependent tasks; leave this option as Yes, please. You should then see the final screen:

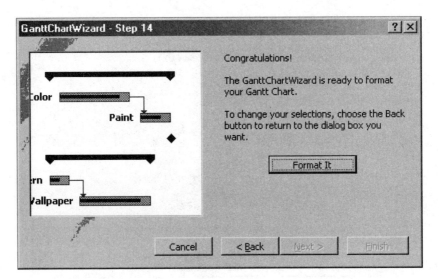

Click the Format It button and your Gantt chart should be transformed: simply press the Exit Wizard button to return to your schedule.

If you chose to follow these steps, your schedule should look like the following:

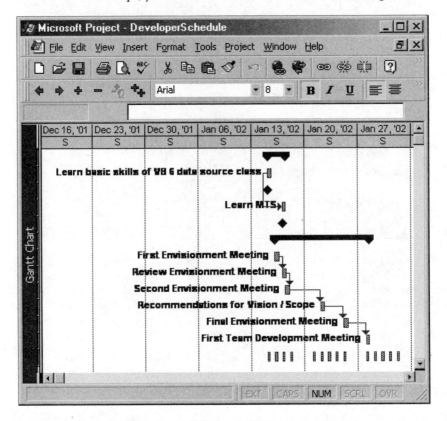

Project 98 Tables

Project 98 uses tables to display the information. Go back to the Gantt view. If you now go to the menu and select <u>V</u>iew, then Ta<u>b</u>le:, you will see the following:

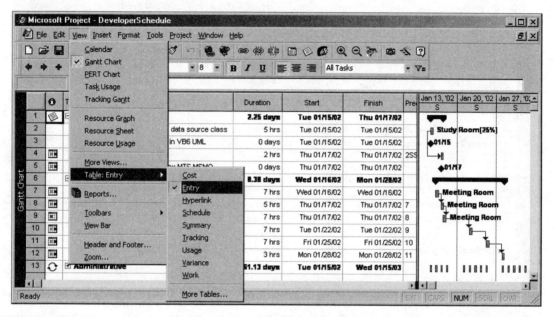

This shows that you are currently viewing the Entry table. This is the table that you use by default to enter information.

Cost Estimates

We can choose other tables to view information. Select Cost from the drop down list. The cost table view should look as follows:

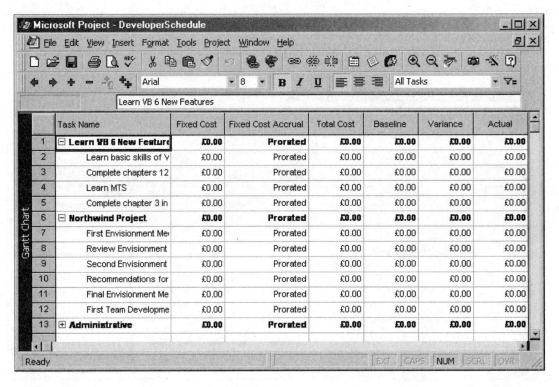

We haven't entered any costs for any of our goals, so our project isn't costing us anything! However, you can see that this can give us an estimate for the cost of each part of the project. The estimate at this stage would be based on our estimates of the time we think the project will take: these are likely to be refined as we go through the project, and so the costs are only as accurate as our estimates allow. Building a software project is not cheap: this is where Visual Basic's wide range of applications and object oriented programming come to the rescue.

By building reusable components that can work in a wide range of environments, from the client exe to the web class to the Office VBA macro, we can reduce the total number of components we need to build. If the components we build in this project will be part of the next project, then we will eliminate a large portion of the cost of the next project.

The cost of the envisionment phase can sometimes be seen as prohibitively high. Visual Basic projects are very complex. The vision/scope document puts this project into a general Enterprise architecture that will allow it to work with existing and future components. The vision/scope will also allow components of this project to be reused in future projects. This in turn will save money. The vision/scope will give the project a clear well defined purpose which will allow the project to have the maximum probability for success.

What happens when you skip this stage? Your project will end up with no well-defined goals or purpose. The project will stumble along and discover its purpose along the way. The design will be in constant flux and the code will be rewritten many times before the Visual Basic team comes close to delivering something acceptable to the user. Let us say that our average VB developer is costing us $75 an hour (a cheap rate in the current market). If we have four developers hacking away and skipping the envisionment phase which results in only four weeks of extra development time, we come up with $75x40x4x4=$48,000. Not too bad, but we must take into account debugging the code. Since the project was not well organized prior to writing the code and many changes have been made in the middle of coding, it is highly unlikely the code will be clean and have well-defined components. This in turn will be a debugging nightmare. Finding a small bug may take days. So, let us add another four weeks of extra debugging time at a cost of another $48,000. We now have reached $96,000.

Am I exaggerating my figures? In my experience, projects that lack an envisionment phase and have a poor design phase will require about one month of extra time for coding and one month of extra time for debugging for approximately every three to six months of the project than a project with an envisionment and design phase. I am not saying this is a hard and fast rule, but this is about average. Besides the extra time and expense, the code of these projects lacking an envisionment phase is almost always not built out of components. They are code islands in which none of the code within them can be reused in future projects. Of course, the argument of cost may be a moot point if the lack of envisionment and design phases results in the complete failure of the project.

While it may seem like a large expense on the front of the project, it is an expense you cannot escape. Either you pay for detailed envisionment and design phases that give you a project that fits in the Enterprise and gives you reusable components or you can pay for a longer development time, unmanageable code and code islands. This is an inescapable truth of managing a Visual Basic project and this must be made clear to all senior managers.

Another point to be made here is that once a thorough vision statement is made for one project, it will be reused in future projects that are fulfilling that vision. Thus, the initial project will incur the most cost and future cycles will only need to define the scope. Therefore, this high cost will only occur during the first cycle.

When you have read through the rest of this book, you will understand the different phases of the cyclic methodology and what they entail. In Chapter 13 you will see an example schedule for the project we build up during this book - here, you will see the complexity of Visual Basic projects and appreciate how a scheduling tool can help you manage your projects. You will also be able to see more on how to make cost estimates for your project and resource allocation.

Creating an Export Table

In this book we will be working on making a Visual Basic project that can present project information on the web. Project 98 allows you to export information from your schedule in HTML format. First though, we must decide how we want to format the information. We do this by building a table. Go to the menu and select View ITable I More Tables.

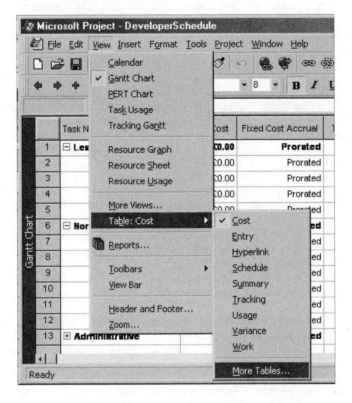

You will now see the following form:

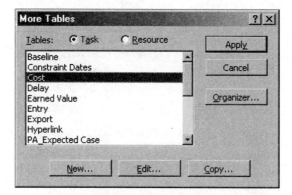

Click the New... button. In the Table Definition form enter the Name as HTML Export. Click on the first row in the Field Name column and the drop down list box of all of the field names will appear. Select Name. In the next rows select Resource Names, Start and Finish. The form should look as follows:

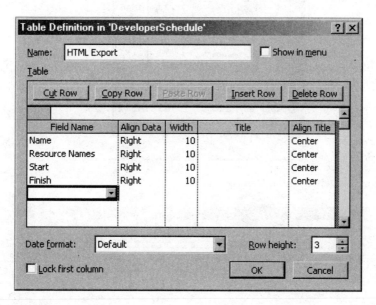

Unclick Lock first column. Change the Row height to 3. Click OK.
Close the More Tables dialog and then go to the menu and click File | Save As HTML:

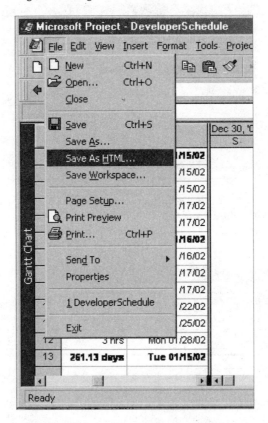

Select a directory and click Save. Call the file DNA.html

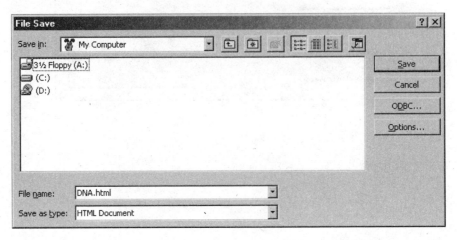

The **Export Format** window will now come up. Click on the <u>N</u>ew Map... button.

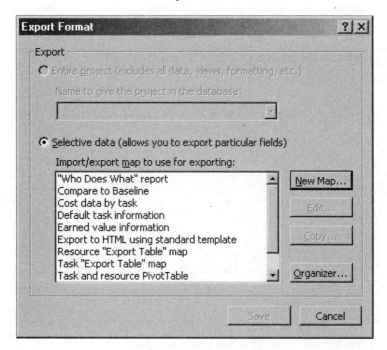

On the Define Import/Export window check the Tasks button. This will make the Task Mapping tab accessible.

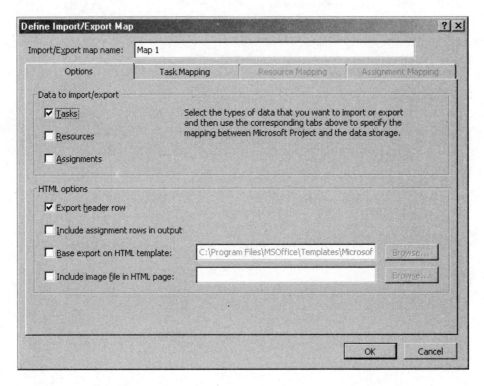

Click Task Mapping and click the Base on Table button.

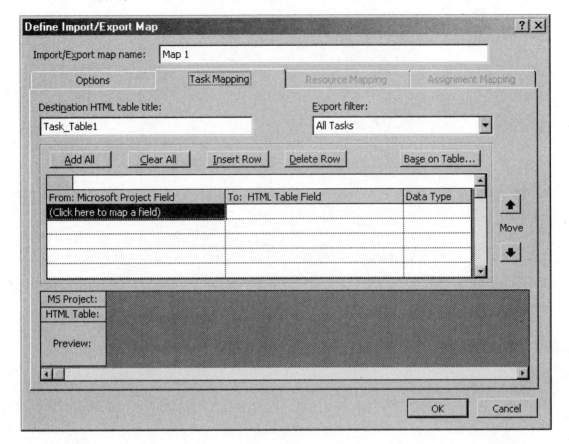

Select HTML Export, which is the table we just created.

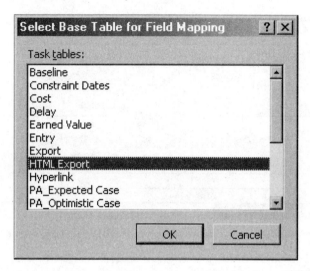

Select OK on the Select Base table form, select OK on the Define Import/Export form and click Save on the Export Format form. The table will now be built. Open the table in your web browser.

Your exported table should look something like the following:

We will use this feature later. If you use this feature, you can build a web application very easily which can be viewed by all team members.

Summary

Making an accurate schedule requires you to balance your resources so that all of your goals get accomplished. Project 98 is an excellent tool that allows you to allocate your resources to your current goals. Project 98 offers a wide range of views of the information that allows you to adjust, refine and improve your schedule so that no resources are over utilized. Project 98 also allows you to export your information into HTML format so that you can build web pages out of your schedule.

There are many more features in Project 98. You can go to the web site we mentioned at the beginning of the chapter to explore some of the additional features. You can create workgroups to share project information and resource information, set the importance of a goal, add additional resources, etc. Explore some of the other views and tables. I really believe this is a product you will find valuable for your Visual Basic projects.

Learn how to accurately estimate the time it takes to accomplish your goals. Keep a record of when you make a mistake so you can learn from it. Keep old schedules as a reference for time estimates. Making an accurate schedule is an essential part of being a team member of a Visual Basic goal-driven team. It is an important skill to learn in order to succeed as a member of the team.

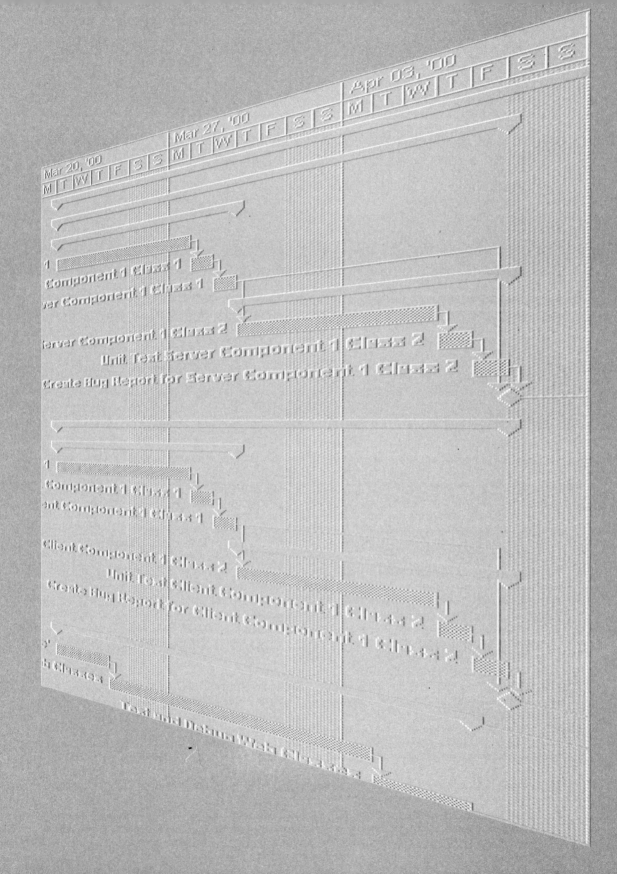

Envisionment Phase

The creation of any new product or system must be driven by the needs of the client organization. The work performed during the envisionment phase is, in broad terms, geared towards obtaining an understanding of these needs. The team must obtain an understanding of exactly what the client requires, what is driving the requirement and, therefore, what problems must be solved and what benefits the client expects to derive from the solution of these problems. In this manner we can move towards a definition of exactly how these requirements may be satisfied.

In this chapter we will:

➢ Demonstrate the assessment of a corporation's current business processes and technological infrastructure, as detailed in an Enterprise Architecture document.

➢ Define the vision for our E-commerce project, in terms of first level goals.

➢ Drill down into these goals to arrive at a level of analysis that will provide a firm basis for product design.

Before we get into a full discussion of envisionment, let's have a summary of the key deliverables from this phase of the cyclic methodology:

➢ Vision/Scope Approved document

➢ Enterprise Architecture Document

➢ Total Cost of Ownership (TCO) and Return on Investment (ROI) estimates

➢ Risk assessment document

➢ Team responsibility definition

Summary of Team Focus

As with every phase in the cyclic methodology, every member of the team will be expected to make a significant contribution, fulfilling various tasks that ensure the completion of each deliverable and, ultimately, attainment of the vision/scope milestone. However, the team focus for this phase revolves largely around the product manager, who will liaise with the client organization and ensure that their needs are being correctly visualized. It is the product manager who will bear ultimate responsibility for the successful achievement of the phase milestone.

The testing members of the development team will be busy reviewing the initial goals of the project and developing general testing scenarios. While the specifics of the components of the project are not defined during this stage, the overall type of the project is known, that is, an E-commerce application or an intranet application, and general methods of testing for different types of applications can be determined at this point.

The component managers and project manager should be working towards building component teams and creating a master schedule for their teams. These schedules will need to be rolled up into one large master schedule(which will look like the schedule we made in the last chapter). By the end of the envisionment phase, the schedule should be revised to give a detailed accurate schedule for the next phase, that is the design phase.

The logistician will be the primary architect of the Enterprise Architecture document, which assesses client infrastructure and business processes. The logistician will deal with infrastructure while the product manager would answer corporate environment issues that would need to be addressed by the high-level client management. The educator would answer any issues in the EAD relating to end users.

Overview of the Envisionment Phase

An entire project will be defined by the vision and scope created in the envisionment phase. The vision will define the goal for the entire system, and the scope will define the goals we will accomplish in the different project cycles that need to be completed in order to create the system. After completion of the first project cycle, future cycles will almost certainly refine or even completely redefine their scope. Every goal that is encompassed by a project cycle has three parts: why, what and how. The Vision/Scope document created in the envisionment phase will define *why* we are trying to achieve the overall goals of the project, and in a general broad manner, what we want the product to do. Until we understand why we are doing something and what we are going to do, it is impossible to determine how we are going to do it.

Thus, the envisionment phase will:

> ➤ determine what problems we are trying to solve.
> ➤ determine what are the important goals of the senior management and end users.
> ➤ create goals for where the corporation wants to be in the future.
> ➤ determine what goals are worth pursuing.
> ➤ explain why the goals are important for the corporation.
> ➤ explain how the goals will change the corporation.

> ➤ show what business processes will be affected by these goals and how these processes will be improved by these goals.

To accomplish all of this during the envisionment phase will require a commitment to the project from the entire team right from the very beginning of this phase. Working together, a consensus can be reached as to what the higher-level goals of the project are. The business processes needed by the enterprise will drive these goals. The available resources and creativity of the team members will shape them.

The conceptual stage of the design phase will redefine these goals from the user's perspective and, in the logical and physical stages, these goals will be turned into an overall design of the Visual Basic product.

The final Vision/Scope document, the main deliverable associated with the Vision/Scope Approved milestone, will represent the goals that were arrived at by the entire team. The fact that the vision will include a measurable result means that not only can we define why the goals *need* to be accomplished; we can verify how successfully they *have* been accomplished.

There are many stages along the way to achieving the Vision/Scope Approved milestone. In this chapter our main focus will be on the Enterprise Architecture document, the consensus meeting and estimation of the Total Cost of Operations (TCO) and Return On Investment(ROI). The chapter will conclude with a listing of each section that should be included in the Vision/Scope document.

The Enterprise Architecture Document (EAD)

While it would be nice if there were one solution that would fit perfectly for every corporation, in the real world such solutions do not exist. We can, and should, build templates that can be the starting point of our Visual Basic applications, but they are only starting points. Every enterprise environment is unique. While there may be similarities between two E-Commerce solutions in two corporations, there will also be major differences that will require differences in their solutions. The existing hardware and software, the corporate environment, the commitment to the project, and a whole range of other factors will influence the final solution. Therefore, before we can begin to discuss where the enterprise needs to go, we need to determine where the enterprise currently is. We will need to look at where the enterprise's corporate infrastructure and business processes currently are. The Enterprise Architecture document will document both of these. The consensus meeting will determine how effective they are.

It is important to remember that, in order to gain a full picture of the organization, business processes as well as technological processes must be assessed in the EAD. It is very important to identify how a business operates now and how the business processes might or should change in future. New computer technology affects the corporation in a fundamental way: it changes the way in which people do their jobs. Looking at the whole picture helps us create a technological solution that helps people do their jobs in the most effective manner possible and supports the goals of the organization.

The corporate infrastructure is the technological foundation of the corporation and provides all of the computing resources for the enterprise. Assessing every single aspect of the business of a huge corporation is a formidable task. It is important that we focus on reviewing the part of the corporate infrastructure that relates directly to our project, whilst giving due consideration to the system of which it forms a part. These resources include hardware, software and people that allow the corporation to perform essential business processes, including the essential functions of the corporation, communications, distribution of information, reporting and achieving the corporate goals.

The Enterprise Architecture Document is a very thorough assessment of the current state of technology in a corporation. It needs to be honest and accurate. There may be some areas in the Enterprise that may be identified as being deficient and needing improvement. You must be professional when making remarks that may be viewed as criticism. For example, you should say, "At this point, there is no effective system to upgrade software and the current software is outdated by at least two years." instead of saying, "Their software is extremely outdated, nearly useless. They do not even have any organized system to get new versions of the software." Remember, everyone on the team, including the client, will see these documents. You also have to be realistic that certain corporations may not be willing to accept the criticism. Yet, most of the time, they will accept your opinion and use your Enterprise Architecture document as a tool to improve their Enterprise Architecture. The investment in the envisionment phase can therefore extend far beyond this project.

As noted earlier, the primary architect of the Enterprise Architecture Document will be the logistician and the product manager with assistance in gathering information and creating the document from the project manager. There will also be sections added at a later time by other members of the team.

In the following sections are the main questions that the EAD seeks to answer.

Evaluation of Technology

> **Current Status of Technology**: This section gives an overview of how current the computer technology is in the enterprise. Is the hardware and software current or outdated? Has the software been updated on a regular basis? Do the system administrators have the authority to release new software? How efficient is their communications system? Do they have email and Internet access? Are they currently using Visual Basic 6? Are they building object-oriented solutions with Visual Basic? Are they building DNA projects with Visual Basic? Are they working with Visual Basic script in Interdev? Are they still building two-tier applications?

> **Flexibility**: How easy or difficult is it for the corporation to change their technology? How flexible are the people involved with the systems that may be changed by this project? How flexible is the entire corporation? Have new technologies been quickly adapted?

> **Technological Importance**: How important is technology to the corporation? Is using new technology a part of the corporation's strategy? Are the members of IT a part of the decision processes for the corporation? Does the person in charge of IT report directly to the CEO? Is technology considered an essential part of accomplishing the corporation's goals? Is technology used to remain competitive and produce the best products?

> **Methodologies**: Is there any form of project planning in existence? Do projects run through a well-defined methodology? (Do projects follow the four phases of the cyclic methodology?) Are the methods used to manage projects successful? Have most of the corporation's products been successful or have they failed? Are they open to new methodologies? Are any Visual Basic frameworks being used? Is UML used to design projects? Are strict coding standards adhered to?

➤ **Component Resources**: Are outside consultants used for building systems? Are pre-packaged solutions commonly used? How much are the internal resources relied on? What role do custom solutions play in the corporation?

➤ **Network:** What is the current bandwidth of the network? What is the total amount of storage space? What types of systems exist: mainframe, UNIX, Microsoft? How much can the network currently handle?

➤ **Client Resources**: What technology exists for the client computers? What systems exist on the client site? Does the client site have Internet and email access?

Evaluation of Value of the Information

➤ **Value of Information to the Corporation**: Does the corporation value information? Are decisions made when new information is presented, or is it ignored? Are decisions more based on time honored traditions or are they based on accurate information? Is there a way to quickly get accurate information, or does information move slowly through a hierarchy?

➤ **Who Uses Information**: Is information only available to senior management, or does everyone have access to the information?

➤ **Access to Information**: How is information accessed? Where does the information come from?

Developer Resources

➤ **Type of Developers**: Are there currently Microsoft developers? Are there Visual Basic Developers? What are the skill sets of the developers?

➤ **Attitude**: What is the attitude toward developing Microsoft solutions?

➤ **Experience**: Has anyone built Visual Basic object-oriented projects? Has anyone built 3-tier applications? Are the team members open to learning new skills? Does anyone have Microsoft certifications in Visual Basic?

➤ **Number**: Are there enough developers for the project? Can additional developers be added to the project?

Geographical

➤ How is the corporation geographically located? Is there one central location? Is the corporation spread across the continent or across the entire world? Are there many small offices, or are there only a few smaller offices? What is the communication between corporate offices in different geographic locations?

Financial Resources

> **Hardware**: What funds have been allocated for upgrade of hardware? Who is responsible for approvals? What has been allocated for hardware upgrades for this project?

> **Training**: What funds are allocated to general training? What funds exist for training for this project? Are there funds to train their developers for this project if it is needed? What training facilities are available? Does training have a priority in the corporation?

> **Continuing Support**: How much money exists for future development?

> **Software**: What funds have been set aside for the development or purchase of new software systems?

> **Overall**: What is the current status of the corporation? Is their budget extremely tight or is there a large financial surplus? How much money can be contributed to development of new technology?

Realistic Expectations

> **General**: How realistic are the expectations of the client? Are there realistic constraints or are the constraints (such as time to complete the project) arbitrary?

The functionality of the project is proportional to the time and financial resources available. If you limit either time or financial resources, functionality must also be limited. Clients often want full functionality completed in a very short amount of time. This time limit is not based on an analysis of the project, but based on when someone would like it done. These projects are bound to fail. If you want full functionality, you need to allow sufficient time for the project as well as substantial financial resources. Time and budget constraints may mean that some of the less important functionality must be left out, or put off until a later date. The purpose of the envisionment phase is to determine what functionality is critical for the system and must be implemented in the first few project cycles and what is not critical and can be left to later cycles. The critical question is: can the highest priority goals be achieved within the financial and time constraints of the project?

The Consensus Meeting-Creating Vision/Scope

A consensus meeting is where a Visual Basic project really begins. This meeting, or series of meetings, will define the goals of the project and define the vision and scope of the project. Consensus meetings for small projects may actually be a series of small meetings or one to three all day meetings for very large projects. To keep things simple, I will divide the consensus meeting into a first and second meeting. The first meeting is with senior management and the second, if possible, is with the entire team. Each of these meetings may actually consist of many meetings depending on the size of the project.

One could give many reasons to invest in a consensus meeting. Certainly getting input from everyone involved will result in more ideas and a better set of goals. Yet, there is something far more important about the consensus meeting. When people are assigned goals that they do not understand the purpose of, nor where the goals come from, they will have little motivation to accomplish the goals. Involving the entire team in the definition and refinement of the project's goals ensures that everyone understands why we are trying to achieve these goals and where these goals come from. The project manager can play a very important role here. Team involvement also means that everyone feels that they had an input into the creation of the goals. The goals therefore belong to every member of the team, and every team member feels they are accomplishing goals they created. This gives a new meaning to achieving the goals and maximizes the possibility that the goals will be successfully accomplished. One word of warning: the more people you involve the more opinions you get and the more difficult it can become to make a final decision. You need to ensure that there is always someone (probably the product manager) who can act as a mediator when differences of opinions arise.

The First Consensus Meeting

In the initial meetings, the product and component managers will meet with the sponsors and stakeholders to determine what their goals for the project are and what business processes will either be improved or created. This is the conceptualization stage. The meetings with the sponsors and stakeholders should not discuss how any of the goals will be achieved, only what the goals are and why they are important. Milestones, which represent the accomplishment of goals, should define measures of success.

The questions that should be answered by the end of this process are:

> What are the needs of the business?
> What are the business processes that fulfill these business needs?
> What business processes might exist in the future to meet the business needs?
> Why are these business processes important to the corporation?
> How can these business processes be improved?
> What are the good and bad aspects of the business processes?
> What are the goals of the senior management?

The sponsor should lead the first meeting and begin with an explanation of the meeting and how it will be run. Once this is done, everyone should introduce themselves and their roles in the project. Some means should be provided to record the meeting in a way that all of the people attending can see summaries of what has been discussed. Either use large white paper or some way to project the notes onto a screen visible to all the participants. The product manager should assist the sponsor in running the meeting, keeping things on track and moving along. Each meeting should not extend much beyond half a day.

The focus of this meeting is defining the project's goals and prioritizing the goals. Prioritizing goals is not as difficult as most people think. We will divide goals into three classifications of priority: high, medium and low. **High priority goals** are the ones that we must do for the project to be successful. If we cannot accomplish our high priority goals, there is no reason for doing the project. **Medium level goals** add value to the project and make the business process more efficient, but they do not have to be in the scope of the first few cycles of the project. **Low priority goals** usually are some unneeded feature someone would like to be added on, and usually are not included in the project. Low priority goals will add little to the efficiency of the business process.

> **It is important to define goals at a high level at this stage, in order to keep the process manageable.**

When we are only comparing two goals it is fairly easily to decide which goal is more important than the other. Yet, what do we do when we have dozens of goals? The easiest way to prioritize a large number of goals is to perform comparisons of two goals at a time. This can be accomplished by building a table whose columns and rows contain the goals. For example, if we have six goals we would have the following:

	Goal 1	Goal 2	Goal 3	Goal 4	Goal 5	Goal 6
Goal 1	–					
Goal 2		–				
Goal 3			–			
Goal 4				–		
Goal 5					–	
Goal 6						–

The dashes (–) represent blocks that are to be ignored. Start at the first column and move down and compare the goal associated with the column with the goals in the row. For example, as we move down the Goal 1 column we will rank Goal 1 against Goals 2 through 6. If Goal 1 has a higher priority than one of the other goals, we place an X in the cell. If it has a lower priority, we do not place a mark in the cell. In the following table, for example, Goal 1 is voted to have a higher priority than Goals 3 and 4 but Goals 2, 5 and 6 are a higher priority than Goal 1:

	Goal 1	Goal 2	Goal 3	Goal 4	Goal 5	Goal 6
Goal 1	–	X			X	X
Goal 2		–				
Goal 3	X		–			
Goal 4	X			–		
Goal 5					–	
Goal 6						–

Notice that since we have rated the priority of Goal 1 against all other goals then, logically, we have also ranked all other goals against Goal 1. Thus, we can fill in these rankings in the Goal 1 row. This process of filling in the chart by comparing two goals at a time is called a **two-goal comparison**. We must perform this comparison for every established goal. Everybody present should be allowed to voice their opinion when prioritizing goals in this manner.

Once we have defined our goals in this manner, we will have our vision. Next, we have to define our scope. To do this, we must begin to make a plan for how we are going to transition from where we are to where we want to be. At this point, we must determine what goals will be accomplished in the first cycle, the second cycle, etc. The goals that will be chosen for the first cycle will be the most critical goals, deliver the most functionality, and fit within the constraints of the project. Once the cycles have been defined, we can focus on the first cycle of the system development.

By the end of the meeting, the project's goals should be defined and prioritized based on a consensus agreement. The results of the meeting must be written up and used to prepare for the next set of consensus meetings.

We will end this section by taking a look at a specific example of the above process. Let's consider our Northwind Company, who wish to establish a new E-commerce site. The company has studied its market and the manner in which it conducts its business and has decided that in order to improve status and profitability it must grab a share of the Internet market. This need has been analyzed and specific goals identified. We join them at the stage where they are choosing the goals to be accomplished in the first project cycle. The goals to be prioritized may be expressed in the following manner.

The product must enable Northwind to:

1. Increase number of orders (and ease and efficiency of ordering process) by transferring a substantial proportion of its order processing from telephone to Internet.

2. Attract new customers

3. Regain customers lost to competition (who have already established this service)

4. Improve customer service (dealing with needs, complaints, problems)

5. Allow customers to link across to other companies in the group

6. Allow customers to see latest research and products due to hit the market in the future

These are all important goals but Northwind is anxious to get the site up and running within a reasonable timescale and it may not be realistic to expect to achieve all of them in the first project cycle. Thus, the goals are prioritized as described above and we end up with the following table:

	1	2	3	4	5	6
1	–		X			
2	X	–	X			
3			–			
4	X	X	X	–		
5	X	X	X	X	–	X
6	X	X	X	X		–

Looking at this chart, we can quickly see that Northwind's top priority is to regain lost customers. This along with Goal 1 may be considered high priority goals. Goals 2 and 4 would probably be assigned as medium priority goals whilst Goals 5 and 6 would almost certainly be classed as low priority goals.

> *It is important to remember that low priority goals are not always unimportant goals. They may be low priority only in the fact that they may be beyond the scope of the first project cycle.*

Thus, using this chart has given Northwind a measurable way of determining what goals are the most important, instead of just a subjective opinion as to what is and is not high priority. Just as important as identifying priority goals is defining measures by which we can determine whether or not the goal has been achieved. This should be accomplished by the end of the first set of consensus meetings with senior management. Thus Northwind's list of prioritized measurable goals for the first project cycle may look as follows:

1. Increase number of orders

   - Capture 25% of market share of the Internet sales of our products within one year of going live.
   - Achieve 50% of market share within two years of going live.
   - Have 50% of orders taken over the Internet within two years.

2. Attract new customers

   - Within one year of going live, 10% of our customers are new customers from the Internet.
   - Within two years of going live, 20% of our customers are new customers from the Internet.

3. Regain customers lost to competition (who have already established this service)

   - Regain 50% of the customers lost over the last two years.
   - Regain 75% of the customers lost over the last year.

4. Improve customer service (dealing with needs, complaints, problems)

   - Have 100% of customer problems resolved within 48 hours of the complaint.
   - Have 90% of customer problems resolved within 24 hours of the complaint.
   - Have 70% of customer problems resolved within 12 hours of the complaint.

The Second Consensus Meeting

As we discussed earlier, we will simply call this the second consensus meeting, though it may actually encompass several meetings. Ideally, these meetings should include the entire development team and the client team members (primarily the end users). This is the analysis stage.

In practice this is sometimes difficult. Some of the current project's development team members may be heavily involved in the latter stages of a different project. It is important that they have access to the reports from these meetings and are allowed to submit their input. There are many ways of doing this, as we will discuss shortly.

These meetings begin with a summary of the first meeting with senior management. The purpose of the second consensus meeting is to take the goals identified by the stakeholders and sponsors to be included within the scope of this cycle, which were defined at a high level, and drill down to the next level of analysis to arrive at a set of second level goals. The stakeholders and sponsors do not need to attend, but their attendance may be of benefit to the meeting. It is possible that upon looking more closely at one of the broader goals of the senior management we may find that it needs to be redefined. We may also find additional broad goals that should be included in the project but were not. If senior management is present, these changes can be made at the meeting and the redefined goals can immediately be broken down into the next level.

If senior management does not attend the later meetings, they should receive a synopsis of the meeting at the end of the day. You could also set up a live hook-up for the senior management who do not attend so that they can watch the meeting as it is happening. If they hear something at some point that they feel they need to comment on, they can join the meeting by electronic media, telephone or by physically joining the meeting. You could even set up a computer in the meeting to receive comments from those watching but not present so the meeting flow is not interrupted by someone suddenly joining in. Today, there is a wide range of technology that allows you to include people who are not physically at the meeting.

Another possibility is to record the meeting and then put the video on the web site. Everyone, including those who did not attend, can review the meeting at their leisure. You can allow a one-day break between meetings to allow everyone time to review the meeting. You can create a web page to submit comments, thoughts and ideas on the meeting.

Use what is appropriate for the situation. If you are designing a large project that will go through many cycles and will reengineer the corporation, then it would make sense for the senior management to be involved in all of the consensus meetings. For example, a corporation that is doing business solely through phone sales decides to build an E-commerce site. They are going to make a major new purchase in hardware and hope to shift most of their business to the E-commerce site. When the E-commerce site becomes functional the current order entry personnel will focus on customer service instead of taking orders. Such a major change in the corporation should have senior management involved in all of the meetings.

On the other hand, we could have a large corporation that is always plagued by personnel shortages that decides to build a special human resources web site. This site will list job openings, information on the corporation, benefits, etc. This HR department is part of a large department that also includes the payroll and benefits departments. The sponsor is the manager of the three departments. While it is important to have this person's commitment to the project and to know what their goals and concerns are, it is unlikely they will have anything to contribute to the second consensus meetings. This is a high level person with limited time resources. It is unlikely that you will be using their time wisely by involving them in these meetings.

If at all possible, the consensus meetings should not be held on site. It is too easy for people to return to their desk at breaks and get caught up in work: people will be returning late, assistants waving at the door, etc. will interrupt others. It is best to get an offsite room - make it a large one so that you can adorn the walls with lots of paper.

The most difficult part of these meetings is defining how deep one should drill and what should be discussed. If you start discussing how something is to be done, then you have strayed out of the envisionment phase and into the design phase. You should be describing the goals in a fairly general way in the envisionment phase. For example, an acceptable goal description for this phase may be: Have a customer enter an order through the Internet using an easy-to-use web page. If the team starts to discuss exactly how this will be done (the customer will navigate to the site, the customer will enter order information etc.) then this would be going too far. At this stage the project manager must get the team back on track. This final level of analysis will be done in the conceptual stage of the design phase.

Let's now take an example of how we might drill down into the high level goals we identified for the Northwind order entry project.

Drilling down into Goals

Following the first consensus meeting with senior management, we can express the established goals in a vision statement, which we now classify as the primary goal. In the initial stages of this drilling down, senior management may have the most input:

> **Primary Goal:**
> Building a customer Internet site that will handle fifty percent of all customer orders, increase orders, regain lost customers, capture new customers, and improve customer service.

The goals expressed in this vision are **first level goals**. I will call the sub-goals of this first level goal the **second level goals**. This is to make it easier to talk about the different sets of goals. I am not limiting the goals defined by management to two levels. It will be necessary to drill down to third or even fourth level goals in order to arrive at the level of analysis that can provide a foundation for the design of the product. I am defining first level goals for the primary goal as defined by management, and second level goals for all of the goals that management creates to support the first level goal.

Thus we may have something like:

1. **First level goal**: Increase orders and improve efficiency.

Second Level Goals:

i) Increase the effectiveness of the role of the customer representatives
> Have the customer service representatives spend 60% of their time taking orders within six months from the start of the E-commerce site.
> Have the customer service representatives spend 40% of their time taking orders within twelve months from the start of the E-commerce site.

ii) Reduce costs of taking orders.
> Have a 30% reduction in the costs of taking orders within six months.

2. First level goal Regain customers that were lost to the Internet market.

Second Level Goals:

Make a better site than our competition.

> ➤ Create a site that is rated easier to navigate than the competitions'.
>
> ➤ Create a site that has more information than the competitions'.

3. First level goal: Make new customers through the internet.

Second Level Goals:

Make it easy for the customer to get information on our products.

> ➤ Have every aspect of product information available immediately for the customer.

4. First level goal: Improve customer service.

Second Level Goals:

i) Be able to respond to each customer's needs.

> ➤ Get higher ratings for meeting customer needs on customer surveys.

ii) Be able to track customer's needs, complaints and problems.

> ➤ Have 100% of customer problems resolved within 48 hours of the complaint.
>
> ➤ Have 90% of customer problems resolved within 24 hours of the complaint.
>
> ➤ Have 70% of customer problems resolved within 12 hours of the complaint.

iii) Improve customer representative's jobs so that they devote more time improving customer service.

> ➤ Get higher ratings for providing customer service on customer surveys.
>
> ➤ See 1 i).

These are broad vision statements. There are no statements in here that describe how these goals will be achieved, only what we want to achieve.

Just where did these vision statements come from? The term vision can be applied to a corporation in many ways. We have been discussing the vision of the project. Each corporation will also have a vision (mission) for the entire corporation. I will call this **corporate vision** to differentiate it from the project vision we have been discussing thus far. In the best corporations, this corporate vision is documented and known to the entire corporation. The corporate vision focuses on the goals of the entire corporation. Examples of corporate visions are:

> ➤ Treat customers and employees with respect.
>
> ➤ Build the best product on the market.
>
> ➤ Offer the best customer services possible.
>
> ➤ Enable the workers to achieve their goals.
>
> ➤ Behave ethically, responsibly and honestly in everything we do.

The vision statement for the project should not be a radical new rethinking of the corporate vision. Instead, the project vision is a subset of the corporate vision. In this case it is clear that the project's second level goals could be considered a subset of the second, third and fourth corporate vision statements listed above.

Notice that not only are the first level goals associated with a way of measuring whether these goals have been achieved, the second level goals are too. Either the corporation has achieved a 30% reduction in the cost of taking orders within six months or they have not. While we have not shown this in our examples, there should also be an explanation as to why a goal is important and what business processes will be improved and/or affected by the achievement of a goal.

Deliverables of the Second Consensus Meeting

Once the second level goals have been defined these meetings will focus on delivering the following:

> An assessment of current business processes as set out in the EAD (notes from the meeting should be added to the EAD)

> A set of third level goals to take forward to the Design phase (to be included in the Vision/Scope Document)

> A definition of the scope for the project cycles (to be included in the Vision/Scope Document)

Business Processes

The meeting(s) should focus on three things: the past, the present and the future. The past and present determine where the corporation currently is. It is important to have an understanding of the corporation's past and present before walking into the consensus meeting. This is why you should create an Enterprise Architecture document prior to the consensus meeting. This document is a tool that can be used to build the corporation's future. When the consensus meeting is finished, the information gathered on the current state of the corporation's technology should be added to the Enterprise Architecture document.

Talking about current business processes also makes it easier for people to think about future business processes they would like to see in the work place. Looking at current business processes, we can see what works very well and what is not working at all.

When beginning the second set of meetings with the entire team, it is a good practice to make it easy to take notes that the entire group can see, just as we did in the first meeting. One possibility is to cover the walls with large sheets of paper and have someone with neat handwriting take notes during the meeting. A piece of paper can be devoted to the current business processes that will be impacted by the project. On top of the sheet should be the name of the business process, and the rest of the sheet should be divided horizontally into three sections labeled **Positive**, **Negative**, **Neutral**. You can then have the group discuss the positive, negative and neutral aspects of the business process. It is quite possible a business process will only have one section filled out. Those processes that have the majority of entries in the Negative should be reworked. The processes that are ranked positive should be used as examples to build new processes and should be maintained if possible.

It is important that everyone is allowed to speak freely during the discussion of the present corporation. No matter how tempting it may be to comment on someone's suggestions, it is important that no comments are made that inhibit people from speaking openly. It is also important that the meeting does not degenerate into a session to air grievances or start running off track.

It is the role of the product manager to be the facilitator, to control the meeting and to make sure everyone stays on track. The product manager keeps the meeting moving, draws everyone in, makes sure all the people are participating and are comfortable enough to be honest. The educator and logistician can assist the product manager.

Once the present has been discussed, the meeting moves into the future. As you start to talk about the future, there should be no constraints, such as budget or time, placed on the initial discussions. In the beginning, the team members can express whatever ideas come to mind to allow a brainstorming session. If a team member feels that, in the past, their job has been made difficult by deficient software, then their input will be valuable in determining exactly the sort of functionality that the new product should embrace. Therefore, it is vital that they are allowed a say as we start to drill down to the third level goals that will provide the foundation for the design of the product.

Third Level Goals

By far, one of the most powerful tools in any brainstorming or consensus type meeting is a simple yellow sticky pad. You can write each goal onto a separate piece of yellow sticky paper and stick it to a page based on its ranking. If another goal is found that outranks this one, you can just stick it further down and place the new goal above the old one. The yellow sticky pages allow you to move goals around until you find the best ranking. You can do this with suggestions for solutions, for mapping out physical layouts of various solutions or just about anything that requires some type of order or ranking. Sometimes the best tools are the simplest. When working with large groups, you can break them into smaller groups and have the group come up with their solutions using sticky paper. When everyone is done, the best solutions can be consolidated onto one page. The final solution will be documented.

You can place on the top of a piece of paper the first and second level goals, as we defined them in the previous section. Each of the second level goals may be expanded down one level further into what I will call third level goals.

> Remember, these goals do not necessarily have to be three levels deep, I am using this term to make it easy to understand the different sets of goals defined at different times. The first level goals are the primary goals of the project, or the vision. The second level goals (defined largely by senior management) support the primary goal. Third level goals are the ones created by the whole team to support the second level goals. It will be necessary to drill down to a sufficient level of detail that the goals can act as a "template" for the design phase. Just how deep we need to drill is an important decision that must be made by the project management.

Again, no constraints. There will be time during the last part of the consensus meeting to sort out what fits within the constraints of the project. When there are no constraints placed on what people can suggest, you will be amazed at how much information flows. Place constraints on what can be suggested and people will often withhold valuable ideas because they are afraid they may not fit within the constraints.

Following is a list of third level goals that may be identified during the second consensus meeting:

> ➤ Document all customer complaints and route the complaint to someone who has the authority to handle the complaint.

> ➤ Make it easier for the customer to submit a complaint.

> ➤ Make it easier for the customer to submit suggestions for improvement.

> ➤ Make it easier for the customer to place an order.

> ➤ Reduce the number of orders the sales people are handling so they can spend more time working with customers.

> ➤ Make customer and product information quickly available to the salesperson.

> ➤ Allow customers to review the billing history.

> ➤ Let customers know about future discounts.

> ➤ Give customers discounts based on the items they buy.

> ➤ Give customers more detailed product information.

These third level goals are the ones that I can come up with immediately. In a real consensus meeting with many people attending, each coming up with a few possible suggestions, this list could be very long. We will need to prioritize the goals, choose the ones we will try to do in the first cycle, and then determine which ones fit into the scope of this particular project.

There is one goal here that illustrates a very valuable point. Looking at the goal "make customer and product information quickly available to the salesperson", we have a goal that seems to have nothing to do with building an Internet site. Normally, this would be part of a regular EXE application that runs on the sales person's workstation, not something that runs over the Internet (though it could work over an intranet). If the goal of the first cycle is to build the first version of the E-Commerce site containing only the critical elements, what does building an EXE for the workstation have to do with this discussion? Everything. Two of our other goals are:

> ➤ Allow customers to review the billing history.

> ➤ Give customers more detailed product information.

If we build a component that retrieves customer information for our Internet site, and another component to retrieve product information for the Internet site, why couldn't these components also be used to build an EXE application for the sales person's workstation? Both the Internet application and the EXE application require identical information, that is customer and product information, so why not use the same components for both applications? If we use the same components, we will substantially reduce the cost of the EXE application. This brings out another major advantage of the consensus meeting (and of object oriented development): we may find that the goals of the current project fulfill the goals of other projects or other cycles.

When we create an Enterprise Architecture Document and review the goals in a consensus meeting, we get to see the big picture: how everything fits together. We can see if goals in one cycle are similar to goals in other cycles. Using this information, we can then see if the components we design to fulfill one set of goals can be used to fulfill another set of goals.

Component reuse reduces the overall costs of development, and will often more than cover the costs of the initial envisionment phase. Without the envisionment phase, these opportunities may be missed, and two or more teams may build components performing the same function at the same time. This duplication is a waste of resources.

At the end of this brainstorming session, the next task is to decide which of the identified goals fit into the vision of the project. Those chosen will then need to be prioritized in order to determine the scope of the first project cycles.

Defining Scope

The first part of this process will determine which of the suggested third level goals will be incorporated into the vision of the project. What suggestions fit within the constraints of the system? Which ideas contribute to the first and second level goals? What are the high, medium and low priority lower level goals? Just as we did previously, making a chart and comparing two goals at a time can rank these goals.

If there are a large number of people participating in the meeting, then it is quite possible that you may have a very large number of high priority third level goals. Even after comparing two goals at a time, you may find that the number of high priority goals far exceeds the limitation of budget and time. There may also be goals that did not rank very high, but may still need to be considered.

You can now start going through the goals that received the highest ratings in the two goal comparisons and start rating them based on the following:

> Will accomplishing this goal be high or low risk?

> What business processes will be affected and/or improved by this goal?

> How critical to the business is the fulfillment of this goal?

> Who will be affected by this goal and why this goal affects them?

> Will this goal reduce the amount of effort required to complete the business process?

> Why is this goal important?

For example, if a critical daily report is currently generated using an Excel spreadsheet by cutting and pasting information from one sheet to the next, a goal may be to create a Visual Basic application that allows the information to be inputted and formatted without cutting and pasting. If we analyze this goal we can see that there is a very low risk here. It will improve the accuracy and the speed to produce the critical report, the person entering the information will be the one affected by having a more efficient way of producing the report, and it will decrease the amount of effort by eliminating a repetitive task (cutting and pasting) and replacing it with an automated process.

Most of the goals will be low to medium risk. We will discuss risk evaluation in detail in the next chapter. For now, realize that risk is both in the process of building the application (not enough resources, time, technology may not yet be available, etc.) and also the risk that the measurable results may not be achieved (such as building an Internet site and getting customers through the site).

Once the third levels goals are chosen, we will have to place the goals into the cycles that we will have to go through to fulfill the vision. These brief summaries of the top ranking goals then can be reviewed by senior management to make a final choice as to what goals form a part of the vision of the project.

The number of cycles there will be depends on the size of the project and what type of project it is. The highest priority goals should be included in the first cycles. In our E-Commerce site we could have the following three scopes: build the base Internet site with minimum order functionality, build the customer suggestion and complaint portions of the web site, and build the product review portion of the web site.

> *In the development phase different teams can build all three of these parts of the project in three different development cycles at the same time. When they are all complete, they can be put together and implemented to become the first version of the E-Commerce site. Additional functionality will be the scope of future cycles.*

In a very large corporation where the project may affect thousands of people, it will be impossible to include everyone in a consensus meeting. In this case, representatives of different groups should attend the meeting. To make sure the final document includes the input of everyone, you can place the summaries of the second consensus meetings on an intranet site. People from the entire corporation can view it and make suggestions. After a period of time, the summary of the second consensus meeting and the comments submitted through the intranet site can be given to senior management to make the final decisions.

Total Cost of Ownership(TCO) and Return on Investment (ROI)

Corporations are becoming more cautious on how they spend their money and sponsors almost always require TCO and ROI estimates. By the end of the envisionment phase, a detailed schedule for the design phase should be created and the goals should be clearly defined. Using this information, we should be able to estimate the total cost of the project.

> **Creating accurate estimates at this stage can be very difficult. We have no solution yet, only goals. We may be able to quantify some of the benefits from the goals but we will only know something about the magnitude of what we want to accomplish once we've done our design and know how the product is going to be built. It is only at this stage that we will be able to put together accurate development estimates. Having said all this, it is unlikely that the sponsor will be willing to proceed to the design phase with just a set of goals. Some estimation of the cost of the project will have to be made.**

In basic terms the TCO is the total cost of investment in an IT asset (such as an operating system). The ROI compares the cost of the investment to the additional profit made by the investment. For example, for an e-commerce site the cost of the investment will be the cost to build the e-commerce project and the TCO (cost of licenses for the operating system, web server and the e-commerce software, the cost for maintaining the site, etc.). Increased sales by having wider access to clients and a decrease in the number of operators required to take orders are all ways the investment can increase profit. If the total cost of the investment is less than the additional profit, it is a good investment.

The Gartner Group does estimates for the cost of computers in a networked environment that can be used to determine some of the hardware costs. There are some software tools that can provide estimates for software, such as Price Systems. Creating a schedule with Microsoft Project 98 will also provide you with a tool to estimate the cost of resources, such as team members. Microsoft provides a spreadsheet tool called "TCO/ROI Desktop Advisor". It can be downloaded from the following site:

http://www.Microsoft.com/office/tco/

It allows you to perform TCO and ROI estimates for desktop applications and operating systems:

The wizard walks you through the data entry process then performs the calculations and produces a report:

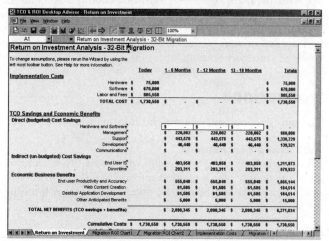

The larger a project is, and the longer it is expected to take, the more difficult it is to estimate the cost of the project. If a project is not broken into cycles but consists of one long development phase extending over several years, it is a much more complex task to estimate costs accurately. If you have any doubt about this, go to your favorite computer dealer and get an estimate for the cost of one specific computer. Check the price of the computer every two months. As new hardware comes out, you can watch the price of the computer drop. Trying to estimate costs two years in advance is very difficult. Even worse, the technology may have completely changed over a single year. New versions of software, or new types of software such as SQL Server 7's data warehouse may make a plan completely obsolete.

By building the project in short cycles, it is unlikely that we will find ourselves using outdated technology or methods in the middle of our project. Our estimates of the cost of the project should remain fairly accurate over a short cycle. The estimate for the next cycle of the project will be the most accurate, the estimate for the entire scope will be less accurate and the estimate for the entire system to be built according to the vision will be the least accurate. Using the cyclic methodology will help us make fairly accurate estimates of the costs of each project of the system.

When making an estimate of the costs of a project, you should make a detailed estimate of the cost of the cycles you are about to design. Future cycles should only have a general estimate, which will be refined when it comes time to actually begin the cycle.

There are also unexpected expenses, such as down times, equipment failures, etc. These should be taken into consideration, included in the risk document, and figured into the total cost of the project.

It sounds like stating the obvious but the safest way of securing a positive ROI is to choose a project where the estimates indicate that there will be a very high ROI. Even in cases where there are unexpected expenses or additional costs, a project with a high ROI estimation will still usually give a significant return. Projects that increase productivity, reduce costs, improve customer service, etc., are all projects that have the potential for a high ROI.

The Vision/Scope Document

We will now list all of the sections that should be included in the Vision/Scope document. Many parts of this document are actually smaller documents included within the larger Vision/Scope document, such as the risk and Enterprise Architecture documents. Each of the sections listed should be included in your Vision/Scope document. You can add or modify the sections according to the needs of your corporation.

Introduction

The introduction contains general information about the document, the project and the team.

Authors and Contributors
This section lists all of the people who wrote the document and which sections they wrote. It also lists all of the people who provided information that was used to build this document. The project manager should put the overall document together but other people will compile many of the additional documents.

Primary Goal
This section will contain the overall goal for the project. In our example above, the overall goal was:

> ➢ Building a customer Internet site that will handle fifty percent of all customer orders, increase orders, regain lost customers, capture new customers, and improve customer service.

Current Enterprise Architecture
This section should include a brief summary of the full Enterprise Architecture document. Issues that are relevant to the project should be listed. Any current problems in the enterprise that will be resolved by the project should also be listed.

Document History

When the first cycle is completed, and the scope of the first project has been implemented, it is time to move to the next cycle with a new scope. This new scope will fulfill another part of the vision of the project.

The initial Vision/Scope document will identify the scope of future cycles in broad terms, which will need to be refined and clearly defined when it is time to begin a new cycle. This in turn will result in the addition of extra information to the Vision/Scope document. It is also possible that the vision may have changed since the last cycle began. New goals may have been established, new technologies may have emerged or Visual Basic may have undergone another revision and offer new opportunities. Any of these will result in an update of the vision statement. These changes should be documented in this section, including a reason for the changes. Copies of the original documents should also be maintained. The Vision/Scope document is a living document that may guide the corporation's development for many years.

Change Control

Change control is necessary for every document in the project. Without this control, anyone could add and remove information in the document. This section needs to identify the following:

- ➢ What types of changes are allowed in the document? Changes can include editorial corrections and updating scope statements or goals.

- ➢ What is required to get approval for changes? For editorial changes, it is likely that these changes can be made easily. Changes of goals may require a meeting with several or all of the team members.

Team Members

This section lists all of the roles for the team and who will be fulfilling the roles. This section should also list responsibilities of each team member and the consequences if they do not fulfill their role. Listing responsibilities and consequences is especially important for the client who may not know what these are.

Purpose of Vision/Scope Document

While the purpose of the document may be well known to the development team, the client team may not know it. This is a living document that will evolve with the corporation. It needs to be written so that future teams, who may not know the methodology used to build this project, can understand the importance of this document. This section should list what is included in the document and also what is not included in the document.

Project Cycles

This section will go through all of the different cycles that will be needed to complete the vision of the document. Each cycle will have a certain scope associated with it, that is a set of goals that will be accomplished in this cycle. Each goal should have a set of milestones associated with them and a set of reasons why these goals need to be accomplished.

First Cycle

Summary

A general discussion of the scope of the current cycle. It will list what is to be included in this cycle, as well as what will not be included in this cycle.

Scope

This subsection will list all first and associated second level goals that will be completed within this cycle. All of the goals that were identified in the consensus meeting will need to be ranked in terms of priority. The highest priority goals will need to be accomplished first. The medium priority goals will be accomplished in later cycles if the resources do not exist to do them during the first cycle. For instance, in our above example we could consider the following goals as our high priority goals and include them in the first cycle:

1. **First level goal**: Increase orders and improve efficiency.

Second Level Goals:

i) Increase the effectiveness of the role of the customer representatives
ii) Reduce costs of taking orders.

2. **First level goal** Regain customers that were lost to the Internet market.

Second Level Goals:

Make a better site than our competition.

3. **First level goal**: Make new customers through the internet.

Second Level Goals:

Make it easy for the customer to get information on our products.

4. **First level goal**: Improve customer service.

Second Level Goals:

i) Be able to respond to each customer's needs.
ii) Be able to track customer's needs, complaints and problems.
iii) Improve customer representative's jobs so that they devote more time improving customer service.

These goals will not only define the initial design of the site, but also what we will need to do to design the web site. Thus, meeting the second level goal "make a better site than the competition", will dictate that during the design phase there will be research of competitor's sites in order to define their strengths and weaknesses along with additional research into very successful E-commerce sites.

The second level goal "track customers' needs, complaints and problems" will also add definition to the site. There will have to be HTML pages devoted to taking customer complaints, and some system to process these complaints. These pages will also help achieve the goal "improve customer service". Of course, there may be many more ways to improve customer service, and this is likely to be a topic that will require a great deal of time in the second consensus meeting.

The first level goal "getting back the customers that were lost to the Internet market" may require several actions. One solution is to get a lost customer list that lists all customers that have not placed orders in the last six months and create a special account for them. A promotion scheme may be devised whereby these customers may have special discount prices for some period of time, probably one or two months. All of the customers on the lost customer list can be sent a letter telling them about the scheme and how to access the corporation's new Internet site with their assigned ID and password. Of course, the site would need to be able to display one set of prices for the special customers and other prices for other customers (that is a promotion component would have to be designed that would function as part of the order entry system). Thus, this goal will also define the features of the site and how it will work.

During the design phase we will take a more in-depth look at how the goals will affect the design of the project.

> **The goals that are defined in the envisionment phase are the starting point for designing the application. Without an envisionment phase, goals are missed, improperly prioritized, or poorly defined. The end result is that the design will not fulfill the primary goals of the corporation, and therefore the project will fail. In the envisionment phase, the goals are defined based on a consensus. Every team member may have important information to contribute and this information will become part of the goals. A design based on these goals has the maximum possibility of meeting the overall goals of the corporation.**

Each goal should be listed separately. For each goal, you should have the following subsections:

Second Level Goals
This section simply states what the goal is, what goals of the corporation will be fulfilled by this goal and the reasons why this goal is important.

Third Level Goals
These will be the additional goals associated with the second level goal identified in the second consensus meeting. As before, we will also list: what goals of the corporation will be fulfilled by this goal, the milestones that will indicate these goals have been accomplished, and the reason(s) why this goal is important. We should also describe whom this goal is important to. Is this goal important to the entire corporation? To the customers? Finally, we should list any resources that may be required to achieve this goal and a list of the people who will need to accomplish the goal.

Putting this all together, the section should look as follows:

First Cycle

Scope

Introduction:
The scope of this cycle is to get the E-Commerce site live with the majority of the essential features. This cycle will not include the building of any of the customer service workstation applications.

Second Level Goal

Be able to respond to customers needs.

Third Level Goals

Allow customers to review the billing history.

Customers want the ability to review their orders and prior billing history online. This feature has been ranked highly as a feature that our customers want in our customer surveys. The customers have also stated concerns about keeping this information secure. Allowing customers to review orders through the Internet will help them determine the status of pending orders without calling the customer service representatives, thereby lessening the number of incoming phone calls. Thus, achieving this goal will achieve the corporate goals of giving the customer the best service possible, improving the quality of work for the workers and decreasing overall expenses. This goal will benefit the sales department.

Give customers more detailed product information.

Customers are interested in a wide range of information on a product. Price, quality, shipping time, options such as color, etc., are all considered important to the customer. With the Internet the customer can compare similar products from many different sources. If it is difficult for a customer to get information on our products, it is likely they will make purchases elsewhere. We not only have to make the best products, but also allow customers to see why our products are best. The customer needs to be able to quickly and easily gather a wide range of information on our products so that they can compare our products to those of our competitors. By allowing customers to gather information, it also ensures that all of the customers know exactly what they are ordering. As a mail order business, we have a large loss of revenue due to customers ordering the wrong product and returning them. By providing the customer with a detailed description of the products, we can reduce the losses due to returns. This goal will improve customer service, allow us to reduce the number of returns and make our service better for the customer. This goal will benefit the shipping and sales departments.

Goal

Allow customers to review the billing history.

Sub Goals

Send the customer an order confirmation via email. Customer representatives and sales managers will accomplish this goal.

Risk Analysis

Documenting potential risks is an essential part of the project. The next chapter will cover risk management and how to create a risk document. The risks identified during the envisionment phase should be listed in a risk document and included with the Vision/Scope document. At least the top ten risks identified by the consensus of the team during the envisionment phase should be included in this section.

Resources

This section will list all of the resources that are available to the project, including financial, time, technological and any other resource that may be needed by the project. A summary of the current resources available and the resources that will become available during the project should be mentioned.

Conflict resolution

It is critical to have some system in place to resolve potential conflicts. What happens when the development team decides that they cannot possibly meet one of the goals of the project due to constraints on finances or time? What if the end users demand that the goal still be met within the projected budget and schedule? Who will resolve this issue? Ideally, there should be one final person to resolve such issues, usually the sponsor. Yet, you do not want to bring every issue to this person, as they usually do not have time. The product manager will be the liaison with the client and can also have the final say. Some system should be put in place to resolve issues first. When every means of resolution fails, then it should be turned over to the person who can make the final decision. This system of conflict resolution should be described in this section.

TCO and ROI Documentation

The completed TCO and ROI documents should be attached. A summary of these initial estimates should be included here. These estimates will be subject to review after the design phase is complete and a note could be included to this effect. As the figures are refined, they can be updated in the Vision/Scope document.

Project Schedule

A copy of the overall schedule should be part of the document. The schedule would look like the template we created in the last chapter, except the schedule for the design phase will be more detailed and complete. The master schedule should be posted on the Internet or secured intranet so everyone can view it.

Definition of Important Terms

As many people of very different backgrounds may read the document, it is important you define all-important terms. This will prevent misunderstandings.

Goals for Later Project Cycles

There will be goals discussed in the consensus meeting that may be medium priority goals that will not be accomplished due to a lack of financial or time resources. While it may not be possible to accomplish these goals at the time the document was created, perhaps at some later time they can be done. Not documenting these goals could result in good suggestions, which may be very useful later on, being lost. Goals that may have been considered medium priority goals may become high priority goals. This process also makes people feel that their suggestions may be included in future cycles. This section should list the medium priority goals and why they were excluded from the scope of all of the cycles.

Business Processes

During the second consensus meeting the major business processes related to the project were discussed and rated. These ratings, and the comments on the strong and weak points of the business processes should be recorded in this section. The weaknesses will show where the project needs to make improvements. The strengths will show how.

The Final Part of the Envisionment Phase

Once the Vision/Scope document is complete, it should be reviewed in one final approval meeting. The entire team should review the final documents, the vision statement and scope statements. Changes should not be made in the approval meeting. Signing off the vision/scope document does not necessarily mean signing off the project. Signing off the vision/scope document means that these documents represents the best solution. Usually, it is after the design phase, when we know exactly what is involved in the project and what the real costs will be in time and money, that a final decision is made to go ahead with the project.

Possible risks, errors or omissions should be found in this final meeting. It is also possible to simply post the information onto an intranet site (or secure Internet site) and allow the team members to review it and submit suggestions. The suggestions can also be put on the web so people can view them and perhaps come up with solutions to potential problems.

Summary

The envisionment phase creates the Vision/Scope document that will guide the entire project. The Enterprise Architecture document, TCO and ROI estimates, and an initial analysis of risks will also be done in this phase of the project. The primary purpose of this meeting is to create the first and second level goals of the senior management and break them down into a set of third level goals. These third level goals form the basis for our product design in the conceptual stage of the design phase. This whole process is geared towards ensuring we have a product designed according to the *needs of the user.*

There are many ways to redesign business processes. One way is to create a radical change in the way a corporation is being run. According to this line of thought, if the corporation is not running successfully now, the business processes are failures and need to be abandoned. Radically new business processes need to be created without any regard to the old ones.

Personally, I feel there are many lessons to be learned from the failures of the current business processes, as well as many lessons to be learned from their successes. I feel that one can still radically reengineer the company based on a careful analysis of the past and current business processes as we did in the Enterprise Architecture Document. This document not only gives an assessment of the current business processes, but also the state of the technology in the enterprise. You cannot realistically restructure the technological infrastructure without understanding what is currently in place.

The reengineering can span across the entire corporation altering workflows, changing job descriptions and roles, organizational structures and virtually the entire company. Everything from the production line in the factory, to the structure of teams, the availability of information and the means of selling products to a customer, can change to meet current market needs. A radical quick reworking of the corporation with a complete disregard to the past is a dangerous undertaking: more than likely it will be too much, too fast and go beyond the corporation's resources.

With a carefully prepared Enterprise Architecture Document, everything will be in black and white in front of you and the entire team. Everyone can review the document in advance of the consensus meetings, look at the available resources, the future needs of the company, and try to find the best ways to improve the corporation's processes.

I highly recommend reading Bill Gate's new book, Business @ The Speed of Thought. You will read about the corporations of the future, and get some insight into where the modern corporation needs to be going. There are many valuable insights into restructuring the corporation in this book. It is definitely worth taking the time to read this book if you intend to be part of reengineering a corporation.

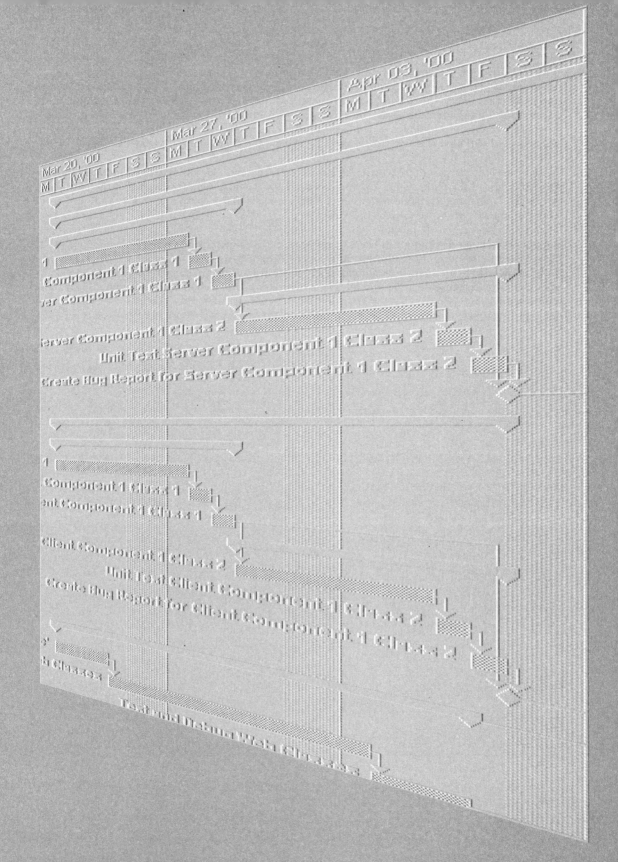

5

Risk Management

Considering the high rate of failure for software projects, we can certainly say that a Visual Basic project has a great deal of risk associated with it. The size and complexity of an enterprise project, and the possible impact the applications could have on the corporation, are two factors that by themselves make the projects risky. By identifying possible risks and properly managing them, we can substantially increase the probability that our project will succeed.

What do we consider to be a risk to our project? A risk is anything that may adversely affect our project. Adversely affecting the project means that something could decrease the functionality of the project or could reduce the probability that our project will succeed. This would include things such as an increase in the cost of the project, an increase in the overall time to complete the project, the inability to complete the project, the project not being able to meet the needs of the client, etc.

Most of the risks to our projects can be managed. Managing risks requires clear guidelines of how risks should be documented and handled. Every member of the team must be able to easily add risks to the risk document. Risk documents, which are documents that list all possible risks to the project, will be described in detail in this chapter. Team members must also feel comfortable with reporting risks. Often it is the team members in the trenches who will be the first to know when something is going wrong, which means that a risk has been realized, and it is usually these people who are most often afraid of reporting bad news. Everyone must be allowed to submit risks without consequences.

One can handle risks proactively by making assessments of possible risks, documenting them, and then creating a plan to deal with them. This plan covers two aspects: the first part is how to reduce the likelihood of a risk happening, and the second is how to deal with the consequences if the risk does happen.

One can also handle risks reactively, waiting for something to happen. Reactive risk handling results in crisis management, jumping from one disaster to another, until finally so much has gone wrong, the project fails. Obviously reactive risk management is not very useful and usually causes the entire team to suffer burnout.

Proper management of risks requires the following:

> - Identification of possible risks
> - Determination of how dangerous the risk is
> - Creation of a plan to minimize the affects of the high probability, high level risks
> - Careful tracking of the risk to make sure that it is under control
> - Adjustment of the plan when the risk is not being properly handled

Identifying risks to the project will be the responsibility of every team member. While every team member may play a role in managing the risks, it will be the component manager who will prioritize risks and determine the probability that the risk will actually occur. The component manager will work with members of the team to find solutions for high probability, high priority risks. Once solutions are found, the product manager will make sure resources are properly allocated to reduce or eliminate the high probability, high priority risks. This will be one of the key roles of the product manager in every part of the project.

Let us begin by looking at how we identify risks.

Identifying Possible Risks

Part of creating an effective Enterprise Architecture document is documenting the possible risks to the project. There are many risks, such as risks related to the corporation, to personal resources, to the attitudes of team members, and to the goals of the project and corporation. All of these risks need to be assessed for every project. While conducting the research for the Enterprise Architecture document, you can research these potential risks and rate their risk level as being high, medium or low.

To perform this assessment a document should be created that lists the standard risks to a project. The senior developers, component and product managers can all come together to create one standard document that lists a general set of risks that need to be ranked for every project.

To give you a place to begin, I have listed some risks to projects that can be included in your general risk document. You can add to this list or modify it to suit the needs of your team.

Risk Assessment Document

These are just some of the standard risks that may affect your project: each comes with a description of how to recognise if it is a high, medium or low risk.

Project Schedule

The risk of a project not being finished by the deadline is dependent on the schedule drawn up for the project. If the project has been assigned an arbitrary schedule, based on the needs of the corporation rather than on those of the project, this risk has a very high probability of being realized. At the other extreme, if we have based the schedule on a detailed review of the project, the vision/scope document and the overall design of the project, we can drastically reduce this risk, and, while we cannot guarantee that the project will be completed on time, we will have a realistic timetable, which we ought to be able to meet. If the schedule has been based on preliminary review of the project, but is determined prior to a detailed analysis of the project, there will be a medium risk: there is a chance that our project will meet the deadline, but unforeseen circumstances could easily cause the deadline to be missed.

Funds

The issue of funding for a project can prove to be a major headache. If funds are extremely limited, this is very likely to cause the project to fail - without funding, there is no way the project can continue. However, if there are sufficient funds available there is less of a risk that the project will fail due to running out of money, and more of a chance that the project can continue as planned and be completed. If there have only been some funds allocated, this is a medium risk: the project can continue, but there is a chance that the project could go over budget.

Resources

A resource is anything that is used within the project to help bring the project to completion - examples are people, money, time, computers, and meeting rooms. The risk to a project of varying availability of resources is also another major consideration. If there are numerous constraints on project resources, the risk is very high that the project will be under threat: if people do not have enough resources to do their job, the project is very likely to fail. Also, if the sponsor is not in control of resources then resource availability will suffer, bringing major flaws to the project. On the other hand, if the sponsor has responsibility for allocating resources, and is committed to the project, there is a low risk: if the resources are made available (for example, if meeting rooms, computers, or money is made available) people will be able to work on the project. A medium risk would be if some resources were limited and some were flexible: the project could continue, but if the limited resources applied to critical tasks, this would be a risk to the completion of the project.

Personnel

The number and type of personnel available to a project can potentially threaten its chance of success. If there aren't enough people available, some may have to undertake conflicting roles (for example, testing and development), or simply have too much work to do in the time available. This is a high risk to the project, because if people are overscheduled, they will not be able to complete their given tasks - for example, the project may not have full functionality as set out in the scope statement: if it doesn't meet expectations, the project could ultimately 'fail'. However, if there are enough people available to fill the different roles sufficiently, this is a low risk: each task will have somebody devoting their full time and attention to it. If there were not enough people, but some people could double up team roles without conflict, this is a medium risk: the tasks will still get done, but there will be less time available to spend on them.

Project Manager

You would be in trouble indeed if you did not have a project manager! Not having a project manager would constitute a high risk, because there would be nobody to coordinate the efforts of the team, see that work was being done and goals were being achieved, and seeing that the project was on time and on schedule. It would be chaos! On the other hand, if there is a project manager with good planning skills, or experience in object-oriented project design, this would pose a low risk - efforts would be coordinated and the project kept on track. A medium risk would present itself if there were a project manager, but they didn't have all the skills needed to manage a project. Some areas of management would be lacking and could cause problems for the project.

Cost Controls (Methods are in place to control costs)

In any large project, there is a danger that costs could spiral out of control. While this risk can be reduced by proper planning and careful allocation of resources, there will always be a danger that unforeseen problems could require additional resources. In order to manage this risk, the project should be subject to tight cost controls. For example, if costs exceed an acceptable level, it may be necessary to abandon non-critical functionality. If no such controls exist, there is a high probability that this risk will be realized. A full set of cost controls combined with a detailed schedule and plan for the allocation of resources will greatly reduce this risk.

Team Member Skills

There is potentially a high risk to the project if team members do not possess the skills needed to be part of a project team. For example, without communication skills, there would be no transfer of information: if things were going wrong, such as sections of code wouldn't compile, but nobody knew about them, this would be dangerous to the success of the project. This risk is low if people have reached competent levels in the skills needed for being a team member: if everybody is aware of what it is they have to do, the project will flow smoothly. If team members have only some of the skills needed, this could pose a medium risk, for example, if some of the skills lacking were needed on critical tasks.

Client Expectations

The client's expectations of the project will have a direct bearing on the success of the project. If the client has unrealistic expectations, such as full functionality in a very limited amount of time, this will pose a high risk to the project: as you will probably not be able to meet these expectations, the client may lose interest in the project and so jeopardize its success. If, however, the client fully understands the nature of the project and what it can offer, this is a low risk. The client knows what the outcome of the project is likely to be and accepts this. A medium risk, in this case, would be if the client still harbored some unrealistic expectations for some parts of the project, but was willing to accept the rest.

Workflows

Workflow is simply a term used to describe the way in which work - information or documents, for example - moves from person to person throughout the company. This movement, however, will adhere to a certain set of rules. If new workflows are created by the project, this is a potential high risk to the success of the project: people may not accept the new ways of working and, in turn, reject the project. If, however, the project fits in with current workflows so that there are no changes to the way people will have to pass on information, or training is implemented so that people know how to perform the new ways of working, this is a low risk. A medium risk would occur if the project introduced only a few new workflows: these may still cause the project to be rejected if opposition is strong enough.

Consensus on the Goals

It is important that all team members agree upon the goals of the project so that everybody can be working towards the same target. Therefore, it is a high risk if management or the end users cannot reach a consensus on the goals: this means that everybody will want the project to achieve different things, which, quite obviously, is not going to make the project a success. If everybody agrees on the goals, and what to expect from the project, this will pose a low risk. If only the critical goals are agreed upon, this will pose a medium risk, as other goals will not have as much impact on the project, and so minor disagreements will not cause a major upset.

Well-Defined Goals

In order to let people know exactly what it is they are supposed to be doing, the goals need to be very well defined. The top-level goals will be broad in design, as by their very nature they encompass the whole project. As you drill down, the goals need to be more detailed so that people can begin working towards specific goals. If these lower level, or third level, goals are not well defined, it could result in poor product design and people will be unsure as to what it is they are to do: this can pose a high risk to the success of the project, as goals will not be able to be achieved. If the goals are well defined, this is a low risk, as people will know what to work towards and what is expected of them. A medium risk would be posed by the fact that, although the goals may have some clear definition, they are hard to accomplish.

Long-Term Results

The corporation needs to be looking towards the future and how it will survive in an ever-changing market place. If the goals are created simply to address a problem the corporation is facing now, this is a high risk: once the project is over, the corporation will still be in the position of having to catch up with the competition, rather than lead it. On the other hand, if the goals are created with the long term future in mind, this is a low risk: goals such as these would look towards utilizing evolving technology and building systems that could easily have new functionality added if and when it was needed. A medium risk would be posed by the fact that the goals were focused only on the short term, but they offered a creative solution to business problems.

Milestones

It is essential that goals have milestones to monitor progress, and also essential that these milestones can be measured. A high risk presents itself when the milestones cannot be measured: there is no way to tell whether the project is on schedule or what stage the project is currently going through. The opposite is also true: if the milestones have binary measurements, these will serve to show exactly where the project is currently and whether it is on schedule. This is a low risk. If the goals have measurements, but they are not binary, this poses a medium risk.

Goals that Meet Corporate Needs

The needs of the corporation will translate into the goals of the project. If the first and second level goals do not match corporate needs, there is a high risk that the project will not reach completion: If the project isn't doing anything for the business, it will not get much support. If the first and second level goals accurately reflect corporate needs there is a low risk of failure, as the project will have the support of upper management. If only the majority of the goals are in line with corporate needs, this is a medium risk: the goals that are not directly related to the needs of the corporation should not adversely affect the success of the project.

Corporate Standards and Vision Statement

Corporate standards lend unity to the team and the vision of the corporation will extend across all projects. If there are no standards, or there isn't a corporate vision, the team may feel as if they are not actually working as one - this could be a high risk to the project, as team members may not feel totally committed to the success of the project. If the standards and vision were well known by every member of the corporation, this would be a low risk to the project, as everybody would feel that they are working together. A medium risk, in this situation, would be if there were standards and a vision, but they weren't widely known throughout the corporation.

Changes in Corporate Vision

The corporate vision is what should drive the corporation in everything it undertakes. If the goals of the project are radically different to the corporate vision, and they could potentially serve to change the corporate vision, this is a high risk: senior management must accept the project in order to support it; if it is going to radically alter the way they think, they are not going to like it! If the goals of the project stick closely to the corporate vision, as they should, this is a low risk. There is a medium risk if the goals of the project make minor changes to the corporate vision: senior management may object to even the slightest change, and so could potentially withdraw their support from the project.

Well-Tested Technology

Well-tested technology means that its functions and methods are widely known and understood. If the project is not based on well-tested technology, and the technology used has not been formally tested, this is a high risk to the success of the project: the 'untested' technology could prove to be unreliable or untrustworthy and the project could fail. If well-tested technology is used, it poses a low risk, as people know and understand how to use it. If untested technology is used, but there are plans to formally test it, this would pose a medium risk: the functionality and methods would be investigated, then understood.

Testing

The project needs to be tested throughout the development phase to ensure that it works as expected without any errors. Developers are not the best people to test their own code. There is a high risk of failure if testing is not carried out until the end of the development phase and it is carried out by the developers. This means that errors will not be found until the last minute, some may be missed because the developers are checking their own code, and any errors found are very expensive and time consuming to correct. If, however, there is a designated tester and testing is performed throughout the development phase, there is a good chance that errors will be found, and corrected, early, presenting a low risk. A medium risk would be posed by the fact that testing is carried out throughout the development phase, but the developers test their own code.

Unit and System Testing

A good testing plan is to test each component on its own - unit testing - and also test it within the whole system - system testing. This is a slightly different risk to the previous testing section. A high risk would present itself if only system testing was carried out: if an error was found, there would be no way to ascertain where the error occurred, as everything would be tested at once. If, however, unit testing had been carried out, this poses a low risk to the project. The components would already have been tested and, if necessary, corrected. System testing would then simply test how the components worked together: if unit testing was carried out properly, there should be few major errors found at this stage: errors here would relate more to the way in which the different components interact with each other than to the functionality and workings of the components themselves. A medium risk would be testing large sections of the project, but not all of it, at once: again, there could be no way to tell where any errors originated.

Stakeholders and Sponsors

The stakeholders and sponsors provide the funding and reason for the project. If they are not committed to the project, or do not see, after defining high level goals, any worth in the project, this is a high risk. In fact, the project would probably never have been undertaken if this were the case! On the other hand, if the stakeholders and sponsors are interested and enthusiastic about the project, and can see how it would benefit them, there is a low risk of failure: they will want the project to succeed. If, however, the stakeholders and sponsors were committed to the project, but didn't fully understand the resource requirements, or didn't fully control the resources available, this would be a medium risk.

Team Members Commitment

It is essential that team members are committed to the project. It is a high risk if they are not, especially with non-self directed work teams where the management imposes a new project, because they may not fully understand why they are working on the project and so will be reluctant to spend time on it. Obviously, the opposite is true: if all team members are committed and there is a consensus on goals, there is a low risk of the project failing, as people will be willing to make the project work. A medium risk would be where some goals were not agreed upon and senior management had to intervene: this may still be seen as solutions being imposed from above.

Roles and Responsibilities

It is important for everybody to know and understand exactly what role they are in and what is expected of them. If the roles and responsibilities are not clearly defined, this could be a high risk to the project: team members may duplicate the work of others, because they don't know that other people are doing the same as them; worse still, no work could be done at all! A low risk ensues when roles and responsibilities are clearly defined: people will know what they are to do, and there is less chance of duplication. If, however, there are roles and responsibilities, but no way of knowing whether people are fulfilling them, this is a medium risk.

User Contribution

It is very important to involve the users and keep their needs in mind throughout the project. If, however, they are not available for interview during the conceptual design phase, they will not be able to make their needs known, and this will be a high risk to the project: how can you keep the users' needs in mind if you don't know what they are? A low risk is presented when the users are available at every stage of the project and are representative of all the users of the system: a medium risk would be when some of the users are available throughout the project, but are not necessarily a representative sample.

User Interest

It is paramount that users are interested in the project to ensure its success. There is a high risk of failure of the project if the users do not see any positive impact of the project on their working life: the project is supposed to focus on the needs of the user; if they don't want it, how can there be a project? If the users can see how the project will improve their working life, and actually want the project, this is a low risk: after all, this is what we are working towards. A medium risk would be if the users could see a potential benefit of the project, but do not fully understand the positive impact it could have on their working life.

Built With Cycles

Building in cycles is a good way to ensure that all functionality is included within a system. There is a high risk of failure if the project is attempted all at once without a design phase - it will more than likely be a monolithic collection of spaghetti code. A low risk situation would be when the project is built in cycles, with each cycle being properly designed. If the project was not built in cycles, but it did have a good design phase, this would pose a medium risk, as there is always a chance that some functionality would have been missed out.

Scope

The scope of a project defines what is to be achieved in one particular cycle. There is a high risk of project failure if there is no project scope: more than likely, the project will try to achieve all the high level goals at once, which, in most cases, cannot be done. A high risk would also be when the scope is unrealistic within the constraints of the project. A low risk would occur when the scope is well defined and realistic in its expectations. If the project has a scope, but it is not clearly defined, feature creep may occur, which would pose a medium risk to the success of the project.

Building Reusable Components

One feature of a modern software project is building components with the aim of being able to reuse them in future projects. There is a high risk that code cannot be reused if the project is not properly designed, or the project is not even built in components at all. The lowest risk occurs when the project is built from components that can be used in future projects: this can save on future development time and investment costs. A medium risk presents itself if the project is built from components, but they do not lend themselves well to being used in future projects.

Change Control

Throughout the life of a project, there is the potential for many things to change - this is not entirely bad, but it must be controlled. A high risk would ensue if there were no guidelines for recording changes to any stage of the project, or if the design was not locked at the start of the development phase: in this way, any part of the project could change without anybody being notified, and nobody would know the correct state of the project. If there are clear guidelines, however, this is a low risk: it is also a low risk if the design has been locked at the start of the development phase - this eliminates feature creep, and everybody knows what he or she is supposed to be developing. A medium risk is when the design may be locked down, but there are unclear guidelines on what to do if a part of the project changes.

Documentation

Documentation is an essential part of any project - it shows exactly how the project progressed and is a reference for future teams. There is a high risk if there is no documentation at all - how will you know what steps you have taken, or what changes have been made, or how the project is progressing if no records are kept? The opposite poses a low risk: if there is detailed documentation for every step of the project, showing how things are changing and progressing (especially the risk document), then it is easier to rectify a mistake if the project should go wrong. There is a medium risk if there is some documentation, but it only covers limited aspects of the project.

Definition of Goals

Goals must be clearly defined. If they are not, this is a high risk, as team members will not know what it is they are working towards. If, however, the goals are detailed and have been drilled down to the correct level for design of the project to commence then this is a low risk. A medium risk would be if the goals were defined, but they were still vague and unachievable: people would have an idea of what they were supposed to achieve, but no detailed way of how to go about it.

Methodologies

Using a methodology is a good way to provide structure to a project. If there isn't a methodology, or any standard way of carrying out the project, there is a high risk that the project will fail: if there are no guidelines, how do you know that what you are doing is correct, or if you are missing out anything important? If, however, a defined methodology is adopted, people will know whether they are doing things in the right order, or in the right way, and this poses a low risk to the project. A medium risk would be if there was a methodology available, but people didn't know how to use it or follow it effectively.

Example Risk Document

In the following, I have selected a few of the most major risks to demonstrate how you could tailor the standard risk document to create a risk document specific to your own project.

Change Control

Rating: Low

Comments: There are very clear guidelines as to how change should be introduced. The design has already been locked down.

Funds

Rating: High

Comments: Funds are extremely limited and it is difficult to see how we will be able to achieve any of the goals set out. In its current state, the project is very likely to go over budget.

Goal Measurement (Milestones)

Rating: Medium

Comments: All goals have milestones that can be measured, but some measurements are not binary. This will need addressing.

User Contribution

Rating: Low

Comments: Every user group is represented and the representatives have attended every meeting. They seem to grasp the underlying concepts of the project and understand and accept what it is we are aiming to do.

This document will give insight into possible risks that may exist within the corporation. Once this document is completed for a particular project, it should be available to the entire team and become part of Vision/Scope document. These risks should be assessed as early as possible, as you may discover that the risks to a project are so great that you may not want to do the project. In addition to the standard risks, there may be risks that are specific to the situation or to the type of the project that should also be added. A review of the Enterprise Architecture document should also reveal risks to the project.

Looking at the master schedule you built with Project 98, you can also find many risks to the project. Are resources (especially personnel) overscheduled? Do you have team members in roles that they are not adequately trained for? Are the cost estimates you arrived at using Project 98 far more than the amount of money allocated to the project? Can you accomplish the items in the critical path in the allotted amount of time? What would happen to the project if one of the key resources left the project (a team member becomes ill or leaves the company)? If there are goals that are dependent on many other goals first becoming accomplished, are all goals in this critical path based on reasonable time estimates, or is likely that some of these goals will take longer than expected and delay all of the dependent tasks? Are there goals that will take a very long time (these tend to have inaccurate time estimates)?

In addition to this risk document, you should also be keeping a separate risk-tracking document with the highest priority critical risks to the project. This second risk document will be discussed below. First, we must determine how critical a risk is.

Creating Risk Metrics

There are many ways to measure the probability of a risk. These are usually subjective measurements, so you should be careful how you view these measurements. For the most part, the measurement of a risk is based on experience with projects. It is useful for junior members of the team to work with the more senior members to learn how to evaluate risk metrics. There are, however, some ways to get a good estimate.

To begin with, you must determine whether the consequences can be tolerated should a particular risk be realized. This will depend on the project. For example, is a possible one million dollar over run in costs in the overall project acceptable? Most people would say no, and in a project that is projected to cost two million dollars this is certainly not acceptable. But, what if you are doing a major Enterprise project that is estimated to cost two hundred million dollars? A one million dollar overrun could be acceptable in this situation.

> We must determine what is and what is not acceptable for each project. These issues should be discussed with the stakeholders and the sponsors at the beginning of the project and documented.

Determining the likelihood that a risk will occur is usually something you can only do by experience and research. At first it may not seem so bad not to include a component manager for a small team of four or five developers. Yet, with experience, you will know that a project will require a constant adjustment in resources. A developer working on critical path goals may get sick and another developer working on another non-critical goal gets assigned to the sick developer's goals. A critical component is taking too long to complete and may throw off the entire schedule, so a developer working on a non-critical goal is reassigned to help with the critical goal. A goal will require additional financial resources to complete so features are removed from another goal. All of these changes must be coordinated, and without someone overseeing the project, these adjustments will not be made. Small issues that could have been easily handled will not be dealt with, and soon the project is running over time and over budget. Through experience, you can know what effect a risk can have on a project. The overall effect of the risk is perhaps one of the most important criteria for determining how critical a risk is.

Another source of information on the effect a risk can have on a project is prior project documents such as status reports, risk documents, etc. This is another reason to document everything. By reviewing previous projects you can see how risks impacted these projects and then make an assessment on how these risks will affect your current project.

Once you have documented and quantified all of the risks, you need to create a plan for each significant risk.

Creating Plans to Eliminate or Reduce Risks

Once we know something is a risk to the project, we must create a plan to either reduce the risk or eliminate it. Some risks are easy to fix. For example, if there is no system of change control then create a system and propose it to the team.

Other risks are far more complicated. If you are building a project that will completely reengineer the corporation, many users may feel resentment toward the project. The end users may not appreciate that the new system will completely change the way they do their job. Many people are afraid of change. It is critical that your end users support your project, so you may find yourself working with management to find a way to help get acceptance for the project. You could build an Intranet site that contains information on the new corporate structure, how old skills and jobs will map to new skills and jobs, etc. The development team's educator can work with the client's education department to conduct training classes. While all of this might seem to have very little to do with building your Visual Basic project, you will quickly see the relevance when users will not work with you.

Each risk will require its own solution. This solution will depend on the corporation, the structure of the corporation and the particular situation. Our initial risk assessment, combined with the Enterprise Architecture document, will tell us what resources we need to make plans to reduce or eliminate the risks to our projects. We will have to make a plan to get access to these resources.

Risks that Cannot be Eliminated or Reduced

Dealing with a risk that cannot be eliminated, and that is almost certainly going to result in the project failing, is perhaps one of the hardest parts of working on a Visual Basic project. What if the stakeholder is not committed to the project? What if there are not enough resources to complete the project? What if the deadlines are impossible? The answer depends on many factors. If you are a contractor you can refuse to take the contract because the risk of failure is too great. If you are a manager, you can recommend the project not be done because of the risks.

It is better to be honest than to take on a project you know cannot succeed. Ideally, the solution is to create a plan to correct the problems and to carry the plan out. Unfortunately, sometimes in the corporate world, creating change simply cannot be done. If you see there is a problem with a project, it is likely that you came to this realization after careful analysis. The rest of the people involved with the project will need to go through the same steps you did to arrive at your conclusions. This may take time and careful explanation. Try to work with the other members of the team and take them through the steps that you took to arrive at the conclusion that the project will not succeed. That is the best way to make someone understand your viewpoint. Sometimes, as you go through the process of explaining, you all get a new insight and find new solutions.

The most difficult position is when you are a developer in a non-self-directed team and are ordered to write Visual Basic code in a manner that is bound to fail. A familiar situation is where the project manager orders a developer to begin writing code without any formal design phase. One of my favorite stories is about the manager who would take the developers to lunch whenever there was a new project. The manager would grab a stack of napkins and start drawing pictures of how the project was supposed to work. After the lunch, the developers would return to their desks with a stack of napkins and start coding. I cannot say if this is a true story, as I heard it second hand, but I would not doubt it. I have seen many projects begun with only that amount of design. This does not only happen to developers. Team leaders will often get orders from much higher to do a project that they know will fail. In the case of the team leader, the responsibility is even worse than for the developer, as accepting this type of project not only means that the team leader must do this, but the entire team as well. I have always viewed it as my responsibility as a leader to protect those I am in charge of, and would try everything in my power to find a way to redefine the project, so it can be completed, or end it.

It is difficult to decide what to do when your manager orders you to do something that is bound to fail. You must evaluate the situation based on your situation. For the most part, it is best to be honest with your manager, explain your concerns and ask if steps can be taken to reduce the risks. Go through the steps that led you to realize this is not the best way of doing things. Your manager does not want the project to fail any more than you do. If you can convince your manager that your way will improve the chances of success of the project, your manager might agree with you. Remember also that your boss is most likely following orders from higher up and the problems may lie with a larger bureaucracy.

Most importantly, when you present your ideas, do not be closed to your manager's viewpoint. Sometimes they have information that you do not. Occasionally, what seems like madness is actually the best solution; it only seems that way to the worker because they do not see the big picture. Before going ahead, do your research and get the best understanding of the situation that you can. Get your facts straight, and when you present your case to your manager, start off by making sure that you both agree on the basic information before getting into the problems and solutions.

It is very easy to be part of the problem. I will admit that there have been times when I have complained about a manager who was leading a project off a cliff. I would make an attempt to steer the project the right way. Sometimes I succeeded and sometimes I did not. In retrospect, I wonder whether I had spent time working on solutions instead of complaining, if I would have succeeded. Now, I focus on finding solutions and not on complaining, and I find that there is almost always a way to reach a mutual consensus that will be acceptable to everyone and will insure the success of the project.

Once we have identified the risks and created a plan, we must monitor them. Let us look at how we can monitor our risks during our projects.

Risk Tracking

Simply defining the risks at the beginning of the project is not enough. You must actually do something about the risks. The best way to do this is to create a tracking document, or use a risk-tracking program.

A risk-tracking document is a living document. Every member of the team should submit a risk document at some interval, usually once a week, to his or her component manager. The component manager will review these risks and make an assessment of the priority of the risks and the probability the risks will occur. High priority, high probability risks must be taken care of immediately. Working with the entire team, the component manager will find ways of reducing or eliminating the risks. If there is a risk caused by a conflict with the client and the development team, the component manager will go to the product manager for help on resolving this issue. If resources are needed, such as a copy of a database for testing and the client is not willing to give this data, the logistician and the product manager will work towards a solution with the component manager. If the problem concerns a bug in one of the primary components of the project, the component manager will work with the developers, testers and even possibly other component managers to find a solution. The component manager manages the resources to find ways of reducing any possible risks to the project.

A typical risk-tracking document could have the following sections:

Name: A unique name used to identify the risk.

Description: This is a detailed description of what the risk is, which parts of the project could be affected by the risk, and the consequences of the risk occurring.

Scenario: The sequence of steps that would need to happen for this risk to affect the project.

Results: What could be the consequences of the scenario occurring.

Probability: The probability that the scenario could actually occur, usually rated high, medium and low.

Resources Affected: What resources will be affected if the scenario occurs? Will there be financial loss? Scheduling delays?

Comments: Additional information on the risk.

Related Risks: Other risks that may be related to this risk.

Plan: The plan to prevent the scenario from happening, or at least to reduce its likelihood of occurring or decreasing the negative consequences to the project, if the scenario occurs.

Risk Metrics: What we will use to determine if the risk is occurring and to determine if the risk has been reduced.

Current Responsibilities: What actions must be taken by team members to reduce the risk and which team members are responsible for these actions.

Trigger: At some point if the risk is not reduced, or the scenario starts and cannot be stopped, we must switch to an alternate plan. This section will explain what must occur for us to switch to the alternate plan.

Alternate Plan: A description of the alternate plan if the first plan is not successful.

Current Risk Assessment: This section should be added to periodically, at the minimum weekly, stating what the assessment of the risk is on that day.

Example Risk Tracking Document

For example, if there was a risk to the project due to a lack of support from the end user, the risk-tracking document may look as follows:

Name: Users not committed.

Description: The users have no interest in the outcome of the project. They see no practical benefits of the system and do not understand the impact it can have on their daily life. This affects all project areas.

Scenario: Vision is defined - users do not agree. Consensus cannot be reached. Negotiations break down and users retract their support from the project.

Results: Without end-user support, the project will no longer be allowed to continue. Work will stop immediately.

Probability: High - the end users see no real benefit to the system and are reluctant to offer their support.

Resources Affected: All resources will be affected - if user support is withdrawn, there is no justification for the project and resources will also be withdrawn. If negotiations continue, this could cause financial loss and scheduling delays.

Comments: We are appointing a new user educator, whom we hope will be able to convince the users that the project will bring many benefits to their working environment.

Related Risks: Sponsors and shareholders might lose interest if we cannot provide a system that is wanted by the users.

Plan: There will be a detailed user education guide to show the users the benefits of the system. This will hopefully allay their fears of change. If the scenario does occur, the plan is to halt work immediately, notify everybody involved and release resources and funds to other projects.

Risk Metrics: We will know if the risk is occurring if the vision and scope cannot be determined or a consensus is continuing to prove difficult to reach. We can see that the risk has been reduced when a consensus is reached and design can begin.

Current Responsibilities: Team members must work to ensure that the end users understand what is happening and the benefits the change can bring to them. This will primarily be the task of the team members occupying the user education role.

Trigger: If the users will not offer their support to the project and a consensus cannot be reached, no matter how much negotiation occurs, we will switch to the alternate plan.

Alternate Plan: If user education cannot describe the benefits to the end users so that they fully understand the benefits the system can bring to them, we must enroll the help of the stakeholders. If the stakeholders see the benefits of the project, the responsibility for the acceptance of the end users must ultimately depend on them. User education will work closely with the stakeholders to make sure they fully understand and accept the benefits the system can bring.

Current Risk Assessment:

May 24, 1999: This risk still has a high probability of occurring. We have begun to educate the users on the importance of the project, but many users still feel resentment because of the attitude that the project could result in layoffs. We have been working with management to create an internal web page showing the future restructuring of the company...(etc.)

May 31, 1999: This risk has dropped to a medium level risk. Our education program has been successful. The users are beginning to see that this project will enhance their jobs and allow some employees to move into other positions, rather than being laid off. We have accomplished this by...(etc.)

Each risk that was labeled high or medium should have a page like this devoted to the risk. Periodically, at the very least every week, the **Current Risk Assessment** section should be updated. Once these updates are done, the document should be reviewed. Periodically, all the team members should review this document to see what risks may impact their portion of the project, which risks have been missed, and which risks may have been improperly assessed.

Summary

One of the most important parts of creating a successful Visual Basic project is the proper management of risks. Assessing the risks at the beginning of the project, developing a plan for medium and high risks, and finally carrying the plan out and monitoring the risk can mean that you can almost guarantee the success of your projects.However, not all risks will be able to be identified at the beginning of the project: risk assessment and risk tracking should carry through the whole of the project to determine whether new risks have presented themselves, or make sure that low risks have not been ignored and allowed to escalate into high risks, almost without notice.

You can use a wide range of resources to find possible risks to the project. You can create a general resource document, as we did above. You can analyze your master schedule in Project 98 for possible resource conflicts. You can create a copy of your master schedule and test 'what if' scenarios and see how they will impact the entire project. You can review documentation from previous projects or speak to senior members of the team. Using all of these techniques, you can assess possible risks to your project and manage them appropriately.

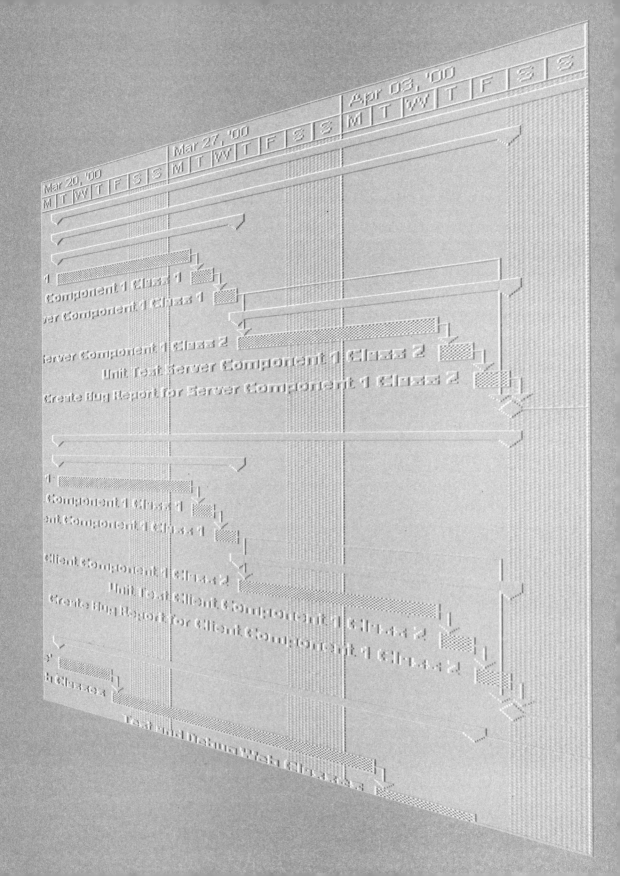

Design Phase: Conceptual Stage

In the conceptual design stage we begin to give some structure to our envisioned solution. We will define how our users will interact with our application and we will step into the roles of the users of our application and find out how they want to accomplish the goals of our application as they are defined in the Vision/Scope Document. In this way, we end up building an application that meets the needs of the customer and of the business, allows the users to accomplish their goals in the way they view as most efficient and makes easy and complicated tasks simple to perform. When the conceptual design milestone has been reached there will be a clearly defined description of the product, the functionality it will include and the manner in which the users will interact with the system

In this chapter we will:

> Create scenarios for third level goals, built upon the needs of the user.

> Discuss roles, workflows, business processes and incorporate this information into our scenarios.

> Create use case documents and diagrams based around our scenarios.

> Identify exactly who the "users" of our application might be.

The key deliverables of this phase are:

> Scenarios for each third level goal identified in the Vision/Scope Document.

> A library of use case documents to take forward into the logical design stage.

Summary of Team Focus

The project and component managers bear responsibility for bringing the whole design phase to the final "Design Approved" milestone. However, during the conceptual design stage the team focus centers very much on the product manager. The ultimate goal of the product manager is to have satisfied clients so they will work very hard during this stage to ensure that the design basis is very much geared towards achieving client goals, as set out in the envisionment phase. The educators will analyze users' needs and create a document based on this analysis. The product manager will work with the educators to determine the different types of end users and set up interviews with representatives of these groups. The product manager or educator will generally perform these interviews, although other team members may help out. The product manager will be responsible for compiling, reviewing and distributing the use case documents.

Overview of the Conceptual Design Stage

In the envisionment phase we began our search for goals. We started with the first level goal of the stakeholders and sponsors and fashioned them into a vision statement (primary goal). We saw how senior management identified first and second level goals, based on the business processes and the needs of the business. We drilled down a level deeper with the client and development team to create the third level goals. The high priority second and third level goals were placed into the Vision/Scope Document and placed into different cycles each with their own scope (this document provides the foundation for the conceptual design stage). The third level goals, though, are still not what we need to design our Visual Basic application. We still have to do some further transformations of the third level goals to arrive at something we can use to design our Visual Basic application. The purpose of the conceptual stage is to make this transformation.

The conceptual stage will allow us to take the third level goals in the Vision/Scope Document and turn them into scenarios.

> *A scenario is an outline of a sequence of events. It provides a step-by-step guide to the procedure that must occur in order to perform an action. A scenario can be used to set out, in clear non-technical language, the exact requirements for a system or component.*

Essentially, we are transforming the third level goals into a set of *requests for services* from the system.

> **We will build a Visual Basic application based on a very detailed set of goals that are defined by scenarios built upon the needs of the user.**

When we eventually build our Visual Basic application in the development phase, we will create methods (functions and subs) that allow a user to make a request to our application to perform some service. Thus, redefining our goals in terms of services will allow us to create methods in our Visual Basic application to fulfill the goals.

Based on these scenarios, we will build the UML use cases, the ultimate deliverable of the conceptual stage. These use cases form the foundation of the design of our Visual Basic application. This type of application is a user-centered application - it will be built to fulfill the goals of the users in the way they feel is best. The users can feel as if the application belongs to them and is a result of their input. This will make the users more productive. In many cases, systems developed in this way make the work more enjoyable and create a better work atmosphere.

> **UML is a highly effective methodology for the successful design of object-oriented projects. It will allow us to design components in an efficient manner, which will make for easier addition, refinement and upgrading in later projects. We are looking to design our application in the best way possible whilst ensuring that user requirements are paramount in our thoughts and that business requirements are effectively managed (for example, ability to adapt to changes in technology and market). It is only natural that UML should be an integral part of the design phase in the cyclic methodology.**

The conceptual stage does not necessarily have to begin at the exact end of the envisionment phase. The conceptual stage is the link between defining the goals of the application and the actual designing of the application. Being a bridge between the two, it usually spans from the envisionment phase into the design phase. Since it is easier to define the beginning of the stage by a milestone, I have defined the beginning of the conceptual stage to be the point where the third level goals start to be transformed into a set of service requests and a set of inputs.

Other methodologies, such as the Microsoft Solution Framework, do not create such a well-defined boundary between envisionment and conceptual design. Much of the information gathering and determination of goals are included as part of the conceptual stage. I feel it is easier to define the envisionment phase and conceptual stage as I have done in this book.

Moving from Third Level Goals to Scenarios

Let's take a look at one of the third level goals we arrived at in the consensus meeting: "Make it easier for the customer to submit a complaint". We recognize that this is still a very general goal - there is no clear way to design a Visual Basic application from this goal. We need to break this goal down into a series of steps that are required to fulfill the goal. These steps will be requests to the system to perform various services or steps that will input information into the system. For example, we can arrive at the following series of steps that a customer could follow to submit a complaint over the Internet:

1. The customer navigates to the complaint page.

2. The customer inputs the type of complaint they want to make into the complaint form and clicks a button to navigate to a page for the complaint they selected.

3. A form specific for the type of complaint will load in the browser.

4. The customer can (optionally) enter their name, address and phone.

5. The customer enters his email address (if logged into site, this is automatically put into the form).

6. The customer selects checkboxes to choose ratings and make the complaint.

7. The customer optionally types information into the form.

8. The customer selects submit.

9. The complaint is routed to the person who handles this type of complaint

10. The complaint is dealt with, and a response is sent to the customer through email.

In these steps we are still not answering how. There is no mention of how the complaint page will be created, how the specific form will be built, how the form gets to the appropriate person, etc. We are only describing what we want the system to do at a finer level of detail. The conceptual stage simply transforms the goals into a series of requests for services from the system or the input of information into the system. This chapter will show how this is achieved using user interviews, surveys and other techniques. The logical design stage will then form the bridge between what we want to do and how we are actually going to do it. The physical design stage will complete the definition of how.

In the conceptual stage, we will view each goal from the perspective of the person who will fulfill the goal (which will be listed in the Vision/Scope document). In our example above, the customer's goal is to easily submit a complaint. We have stepped into their role and found the steps they will want to take to accomplish this goal. Don't forget though, that we will want to create and improve processes for employees as well as customers. A goal, in this regard, might be "improve the efficiency and ease-of-use of the order processing procedure". In the Vision/Scope document we may find that it is the goal of Sales Representatives and Sales Managers to easily process orders. We can step into their role in the same way.

Defining the Different Types of Users

In the previous section we looked at a two examples of the third level goals (which become requests for services) that certain users would want to accomplish. The "customer" is a very broad term and refers to a group of individuals who buy products or services from the corporation. This illustrates an important point: we must build our application to work for entire groups of people and not for individuals.

It would simply be impossible to define a different technique of fulfilling the same goal for every possible user, especially if we have thousands or tens of thousands of users. Therefore, we look at all of the users of the system, place them in groups, and then create a certain type of functionality for the group. The system may have one set of functionality for the "customer" and another set of functionality for an "order entry" group. In other words, we will group people together based on how they interact with the system. For example, anyone entering orders into a database will interact with the system in the same way so we can define an **order entry clerk role**. Sales Representatives and Sales Manager will use this role to enter orders.

In the order processing application we will have many roles besides the **order entry clerk** role. There will be an **inside sales** role for entering new products and updating the inventory along with a **manager** role that will enter employee information and review reports, etc. Since this is an Internet application where the customer can enter orders directly, or directly review product information, there will also be a **customer** role.

It is clear that **roles** define the set of tasks that a group of users need to perform. With this information we can identify the components of the system that the role will need to access. Thus, we can use roles to help us build the security in our system by limiting the services each role is allowed to request. For example, we would not want to allow someone in the **order entry clerk** role to attempt to triple his or her own salary. Only someone in, say, a **manager** role can request the "change an employee's salary" service.

Every role will have certain goals associated with the job, and certain goals that the user in that role is not allowed to perform. Goals the **order entry clerk** role cannot accomplish with the system may be deleting customers, editing employee information and editing product information. Someone who can delete customers cannot be in the **order entry clerk** role.

It is important to remember that the role a person is in has nothing to do with their job title. If a person who is a manager is filling in for a sales representative while they are on a break, and the manager is using the system to accomplish the goals of the **order entry clerk** role, then the manager is in the **order entry clerk** role. The role a person is in is determined only by the goals they are requesting the system to accomplish.

So, we now have roles that will need to accomplish certain goals. The series of steps that are required to accomplish a goal will form our scenario, which is a set of requests for services. How do we know what services each role will request? Are there different routes that may be taken to achieve the same goal? Put another way, these questions mean: How do we know exactly what functionality each group of users needs? In order to find out we need to step into the shoes of a user who will use one of our identified roles. The best way to do that is to talk to them.

Interviewing Users

Basically, once you have identified the roles for your system, you need to interview users who will be in these roles. These interviews will determine what services a person in the role requests from the system, the level of technical expertise a person in this role usually has, their work responsibilities, and their view of the new system you are building.

The best way to learn what a user does is to spend time with the user as they are doing their daily work. Have the user teach you their job. Usually, it will be the educator who will be conducting these interviews, though other team members can help out if need be. The sorts of questions that may be asked are as follows:

> What is their current job description?
> What business processes do they contribute to?
> What systems do they work with, and what requests for services do they request from these systems?
> What services will they be requesting from the new system?
> What business rules are associated with their job?
> What role do they play?
> What information do they need to perform their job?

Of course, you are not going to ask these specific questions. You will need to ask questions based on the user's level of expertise. It is unlikely that a user would understand what you mean by "What services do you request from the system?" On the other hand, they should understand you asking them what tasks they perform and what tasks they ask the computer to do. You will need to talk to the user in terminology they understand.

Following is an example of the sort of interview that might take place with a Northwind Sales Representative, who will use the role of **order entry clerk**:

Interviewer: Valerie, why don't you start by telling me what you're currently doing and how you do it?

Valerie: Basically I'm an Order Entry Clerk - so I enter the new orders. We've got a computer system, which is supposed to make things easier. It's like a database that I can get information from and add things to. Everything I need should be in the database. A customer calls in with an order and I take their details. Then I take their order – which is tells us how many of our products they want.

Interviewer: So could you tell me what customer details you need and why?

Valerie: Well first I need their company name and address so that I can tell whether they're a new or an old customer. We have a list of customers to check from. Each customer has an ID number but I'm not allowed to change that. We have different customers with the same name so that's why we need their address. Also, if we have a new customer call in, I need to set up a new account for them. At this point I also check that the details on our list are correct - maybe the customer's moved.

Interviewer: OK, so what do you do next?

Valerie: Well, then I just take the details of their order, what they want from our catalog and how much. The products are stored in the database too. I confirm these details and the computer works out how much it's all going to cost and then I make sure the customer is happy with the price. Of course, I can't give them a deal or anything, but sometimes they haven't realized how much their order is going to come to. So anyway once the order is taken, I save it to the database and wait for the next one.

Interviewer: Right, so could you tell me how the customer receives his goods?

Valerie: Oh yes, sorry I have to do that too. From another list I select a suitable shipper depending on the company's address and add the cost of shipping to the cost of their goods and then check if the price is OK.

Interviewer: So adding new customers is one of your responsibilities. Could you tell me how you go about setting up an account for a new customer?

Valerie: Yes that is one of my responsibilities. I'm supposed to be adding new customers or changing a customer's details. To check if a customer is new I have to search through our list. If the customer is new I take the customer's company name and address and add it to our list on the database. The computer then generates the customer ID number. Also a customer may call up and say that their address has changed and so one of my responsibilities will be changing the customer's address. I have to get the customer information from the database and modify it. All this can take some time because we have loads of customers. What I would really like is an easier way to check customers – like if I just typed in the company name and it knew if the customer existed or not. Or even if it gave me a list of customers with that name straight away rather than me having to find it myself.

Interviewer: Are there any possible errors that can occur while you are doing this?

Valerie: Yeah, each field can only be a certain length, but the program will allow you to type in as many letters as you want. If you type too much, the program will just chop off the extra letters.

Interviewer: How long can the fields be?

Valerie: Umm, here. I've written it down. The company name can be 40 letters; the contact name, 30 letters; the contact title, 30; the address, 60; city, 15; region, 15; postal code, 10; country, 15; and the phone and fax, 24 digits. I have to remember these.

Interviewer: Do you have any other responsibilities besides taking orders? Can you edit orders or change orders or do things like that?

Valerie: No, I can't change an order. Once I've entered an order, if there's an error in the order, the Sales Manager has to take care of it and she is responsible for modifying the orders.

Interviewer: Can you tell me about the products?

Valerie: No, I don't have anything to do with them, the inside sales person handles that.

Interviewer: Does any one else handle orders?

Valerie: Yeah, sometimes when we are shorthanded or really busy, the Sales Manager will step in and take orders.

Interviewer: Can you think of anything else that you like or dislike about your current system?

Valerie: Well we have loads of products and different products clearly belong to different categories. Sometimes it takes me ages to find the right product because they are all in one long list. I could find each product much more easily if they were split up into the different categories. Another thing that can be frustrating is that if someone else is changing a customer record, I won't be able to modify it until they are done. I understand why this is, but sometimes I can't get a record for an hour or so and you just know that they have gone to lunch leaving the connection open. Also the system can sometimes be very slow.

Interviewer: Thank you for your time.

There is a lot of information here. We found out what Valerie does:

- ➢ Places orders
- ➢ Creates new customers
- ➢ Updates customer information
- ➢ Arranges for orders to be shipped

We found out what she doesn't do: deal with product information; change order information after it has been placed. We found out what she disliked about the current system and what improvements she would like to see. Thus, we can begin to see the sort of things we need to accomplish in order to achieve our "improve the efficiency and ease-of-use of the order processing procedure" goal.

In addition, Valerie confirmed that the business manager would occasionally use the **order entry clerk** role. We even obtained some information about business processes - she couldn't change a customer record while someone else was accessing it (we will discuss business processes again later in the chapter). When we have conducted a series of interview such as these, we will have enough information to start capturing our scenarios.

Creating Scenarios

The four tasks we identified for the **order entry clerk** role (place order, create customer, update customer, arrange to ship order) can be considered sub-goals of our "improve the efficiency and ease-of-use of the order processing procedure" goal. We must look to improve the efficiency of each sub-goal in order to achieve our overall goal. We are now in a position to convert these sub-goals into scenarios:

Order Entry
  Place an Order
- ➢ Customer telephones order or places order via web site
- ➢ If customer is ordering by telephone, request company name
- ➢ Request customer information from system
- ➢ If customer does not exist, **Create Customer**
- ➢ Check customer address, if customer is in system
- ➢ If incorrect, **Update Customer Information**
- ➢ Select product customer wants
- ➢ Enter the number of the product customer wants
- ➢ Calculate total bill
- ➢ Submit order

Create Customer

➤ Enter customer name

➤ Enter customer address

➤ Enter customer telephone number

➤ Enter customer fax number

➤ Enter customer credit card number and expiration date

➤ Verify customer information is correct

➤ Save customer information

Update Customer Information

➤ Retrieve customer information

➤ Replace incorrect information with new information

➤ Save Customer

Ship Order

➤ Shipping gets order

➤ Shipping fills order

➤ Shipping ships order

We have now transformed our original goals into scenarios. By talking to the users, we can find out all the possible scenarios that may occur when trying to accomplish their goals. We have put several scenarios together by using **if** statements in our scenario. This **if** statement means that we could have one scenario where the customer is new and we need to add a new customer, another scenario where we have an existing customer who has moved and requires their information to be updated, and a third scenario where it is an existing customer whose information is correct.

When interviewing users you will want to find out every possible scenario, and then try to put them altogether into one scenario using **if** statements.

In this example we are gathering detailed information on existing processes. If we are going to completely redefine the way a goal is accomplished then matters get more complicated. It is harder trying to invent a scenario for something the user doesn't yet do. You may have to propose something and get comments back before the user will be able to envision the new scenario. Also note that when creating scenarios for the **customer** role you may not be able to have access to real customers and will have to work with a "customer representative" instead (someone from the organization who thinks they know how a **customer** role would work).

Once again, an intranet can provide a resource for recommendations on how to optimize scenarios. Once a set of scenarios is developed based on the Vision/Scope Document and user interviews, you can post them on the company intranet so that everyone can review them. A form to offer suggestions, improvements and additional scenarios should be provided.

Workflows

Now we have defined our scenarios we need to consider **workflows**. Essentially, a workflow is a component part of a business process. A "create new customer" workflow, for example, is part of our "processing an order" business process. Different roles may perform each workflow. It could even be that parts of a business process are not supported by the system – they could be manual activities, be performed by other software tools or even be performed by different organizations.

The workflows in our "processing an order" business process include:

> ➢ Add a Customer if this is a new customer
> ➢ Update customer information if customer information is incorrect
> ➢ Place the order
> ➢ Ship Order

Placing an order, adding a new customer and updating a customer, are all workflows that will be accomplished by someone in the order entry role. Since these workflows are all performed by the same role, we should group them together (perhaps call them the "order entry" goal). In the logical and physical design stages we will see how these three requests will also be grouped in our Visual Basic application. Someone in the **shipping** role will accomplish the final goal, ship order.

It is useful to group scenarios by workflow. We start to see how everything fits together. We start to consider the possibility that an improvement to one process may improve another processes and that we can improve the overall workflow by improving communication between different parts of a workflow.

When we design our application, it will make it easier for a user if a set of scenarios that are usually done together by the same user can all be done at one time. This may have implications for the design of the Graphical User Interface. In this case, we would design our application so that enter orders, add customers and edit customers are all on one form. When a person in the **order entry clerk** role is entering orders, they can accomplish all the goals they normally do in their job by accessing one form. This is much easier than if we had separate forms to accomplish each goal, thus making the user jump from form to form to do their job (see Chapter 7).

Use Cases

We now begin the process of converting our scenarios into a set of use case models that we can take on to the logical design phase. A use case model has numerous sections. We will start by creating a use case Flow of Events. Our scenarios represent every step and every possible flow of events that can occur as a user attempts to achieve a particular goal. The use case Flow of Events encompasses this type of information but there are other important differences:

> *Use cases define the behavior of the system from the standpoint of the user requesting the service.*

We use the generic term **actor** for the user requesting the service. An actor is someone or something that makes a request to the system to perform a set of services. The actor will always be external to the system.

In order to transform our create customer scenario into a use case flow of events, we would make the following alterations:

Create Customer
> **Primary Actor:** Sales Representative
> Actor enters customer name
> Actor enters customer address
> Actor enters customer telephone number
> Actor enters customer fax number
> Actor enter customer credit card number and expiration date
> Actor saves customer information

We have defined a primary actor and we have defined each step from the point of view of the actor. You may also have noticed that we no longer have a "Verify customer information is correct" step. This is not a request to the system or input into the system, it is a manual step, identifying that the information is correct.

> **Requests to the system to perform a service or the inputting of information into the system are the only statements placed into the use case.**

Thus the second point to note is that:

> *Use cases allow the definition of a system's boundaries*

This can be further demonstrated by another example. When we consider the system boundaries, we have to modify our ship order scenario as follows:

Ship Order

> ➢ **Primary Actor:** Shipping Clerk

> ➢ Actor requests new orders

> ➢ If order is shipped, actor marks order as complete

Shipping the order is not something we actually request the system to do. This is done outside of the system.

> *This information will not be lost, though. The services that the system performs internally will be placed into business rules, which we discuss in the next section.*

You may have noticed earlier how I referred to someone or something requesting services. It is quite possible that the actor may not be a person. You may have external computer programs that make requests for services to other programs. If you make a Visual Basic application that validates credit card information that is a separate application, this credit card system may be called by an order entry system. The order entry system would be an actor for the credit card system, as it is external to the credit card validating system and requests it to perform services.

At the moment there is still a lot of information that is missing from our use case - they contain many terms that should be defined. Exactly what is a customer? What defines a product, an order, a bill or a customer address? How do we calculate the total bill? Are we allowed to have a customer with no billing address? We will need to include this information in our list of service requests. Essentially, what are missing are our **business rules**. Business rules define how the business is run. They can be rules governing the definition of business terms, such as "customer" or "billing address". They can be the formulae to calculate a business value such as total bill, or rules that tell us what is allowed, what is not allowed, and what happens when something that is not allowed actually happens.

Business Rules

There are five types of business rules that, generally speaking, place restrictions on the possible outcome of our flow of events.

Requirement Business Rules

This is the most general type of Business Rule. The Requirement can represent any part of the system's operation or any business policy that needs to be taken into consideration when designing the system. Requirements are generally phrased in pure business language, and usually can be broken down into smaller rules.

Example: "Customers are billed on the last day of the month." This rule would be derived from several other rules, such as: "customer's bills include new charges and unpaid balances, calculation of customer's unpaid balance, calculation of unpaid charges, etc."

Definition Business Rules

A Definition defines a **business term** found in a use case. A business term usually refers to a piece of information that's stored (usually in a database) or displayed (such as a calculated value). Business terms usually become classes.

Format: The <business term> has a(n) <attribute>

Example: The customer has a customer billing address where the customer prefers all billing correspondence to be sent. It can be different from the shipping address.
In this example the "customer" is the business term and the "customer billing address" is the attribute.

Factual Business Rules

A Fact relates one business term to another business term. Facts are often relationships, attributes, or generalizations between two business terms.

Format: Every (Each) <business term> <relationship to> <another business term>

Example: "Every ordered item is a product" or "Every customer has a billing address."

Constraint Business Rules

This is a Constraint on the behavior of the system. Any rule that only allows a certain range of values can be considered a constraint. When Constraint Business Rules are applied to terms whose values are inputted by the user, these values are usually checked with an **If** statement. Errors are a result of Constraint Business Rules and code must be written to follow an alternative flow that results from this violation. There should be at least one Constraint Business Rule for every alternative flow of events.

Format: <business term> must <constraint>

Example: "A customer's state must be one of the 50 states" or "The state name must be two letters".

Derivation Business Rules

A Derivation represents any information that is derived from other information in the system. Derivation Business Rules will result in a block of code that performs a task, such as calculating the sales tax. Often Derivations become separate functions or sub-procedures.

Format: <derived item> <rules for derivation>

Example: Net Pay is calculated by subtracting deductions from Gross Pay.

Thus a Requirement business rule that will affect our "Place an Order" flow of events may be: If another user is accessing customer record, system will inform requesting user (remember the information we obtained from Valerie?).

Business rules have a big impact on object-oriented design and on our coding. They can determine what properties an object will have, the correct values for the properties and methods of deriving the information needed by a class.

The Constraint, Fact and Derivation Business Rules are essential elements for converting UML diagrams into a Visual Basic application. It's important to make sure that all of the Fact, Constraint and Derivation Business Rules are implemented in our code.

The easiest way to do this is to put a comment into the code with the name of the Business Rule that the code is based on. We can later do a search on the code for every one of these rules; if we do not find a reference to the Business Rule in our comments, then we know we forgot to implement a rule.

Furthermore:

> ➢ Definition and Fact Business Rules can be used to determine the properties of our objects, and which objects contain other objects, i.e. object hierarchies.

> ➢ Constraint rules will define what users can do, and will form the basis for the type of application errors that may be raised in our code (`IF billing_address is NULL THEN….`).

> ➢ The derivation business rule defines the formulae we will use in our code to derive calculated fields.

We are now ready to look at the full use case model.

The Full Use Case Model

Let's take a look at an actual use case document that describes the process of creating a new customer:

USE CASE: CREATE NEW CUSTOMER

Overview
The main purpose of this use case is to create a new Customer

Primary Actor
Sales Representative

Secondary Actor
None

Starting Point
The use case starts when the actor makes a request to create a new Customer

End Point
The actor's request to create a Customer is either completed or cancelled

Flow of Events
The actor is prompted to enter information that defines the Customer, such as Name, Address, etc. The actor will then enter the information on the Customer.

The actor can choose to save the information or cancel the operation. If the actor decides to save the information the new Customer is created in the system, and the list of Customers is updated.

Alternative Flow of Events
The actor attempts to add a Customer that already exists. The system will notify the user and cancel the create operation. The actor enters an improper value for one of the fields. The system will not allow the update until a proper value for the field is entered.

Measurable Result
A Customer is added to the system

Business Rules
Customer
Customer Fields
Restrict Customer Create

Use Case Extensions
None

There are some new terms here. The only non self-explanatory one is "Use Case Extensions". Occasionally, use cases exist that are a variation of another use case and extend the functionality of the original use case (e.g. create customer and create VIP customer). These extensions are listed here. We also include a Business Rules section. The "Restrict Customer Create" Constraint business rule, for example, has been added to the design of the project to ensure that nobody will be able to create a customer who already exists on the system:

BUSINESS RULE: RESTRICT CUSTOMER CREATE

Overview
This rule is for when a Customer is added to the system

Business Rule Type
Requirement

Business Rule
Each Customer must have a unique CustomerID

Each Customer should only be listed once in the system

Derived Business Rules
None

Business rules are highly contextual to the actual business environment in which the program is being written, but this is a good way to present them clearly and professionally.

We can see that, basically, our final use case documents are a verbal description of what happens when someone using the program we want to design needs to create a new customer. Actors are identified (sales representatives), start and end points are located (in this case, a sales representative asking to create a new customer, and successfully having created a new customer) and a flow of events is drawn up to explain how the system can get from the start point to the end point (information obtained from our scenarios). Further to this, some alternative sequences are identified (perhaps the user decides they don't want to add a customer half way through the process), measurable results are defined, and some business rules are created.

The use case model describes exactly how the goal of the user can be achieved. It provides a comprehensive definition of how a user will interact with the system.

Once a use case is complete, the relevant users should review the document. Once again, the documents can be posted on an intranet or Internet site where all the users can review it and make suggestions. Surveys can also be put on the web site for users to fill out, though it is better to create these after spending some time with some of the users. After everyone has been given time to review the documents, a final set of documents should be physically signed off by members of each group.

It may have seemed like a fairly long road to get here, but we have finally hammered and shaped the original level one and two goals, based on the needs of the business from management, down into a set of user-centered use cases that will form the basis of our Visual Basic project. Before we can move onto the logical design stage, we must talk about how we get information from the user and who the user is.

Who are the Users?

At first, the question "Who are the users?" seems very simple. The initial answer is the people who use the system. Yet, who uses the system becomes a very complex question in our current Enterprise Visual Basic applications. The traditional view of a worker hammering away at a keyboard using a custom built Visual Basic exe application is only one possibility today. With the Internet, we have a new set of users for our applications, the customer.

The customer may be someone we never see and never speak to. If we were building a new Internet site, we could send surveys out to current customers to see what they may want on our new Internet site. Yet, if all of your customers use phone or mail order, it is quite possible that your current customers are not the people who would use the new Internet site and therefore could not give you any useful information.

Even worse, the Internet application creates a whole new group of users who you have no way of contacting prior to building your web site: the potential customer. There is a big difference between the customer, who is someone who is loyal to a corporation and their products, and the potential customer who is trying to decide whether the corporation deserves their business. The Internet application must satisfy the needs of both the loyal and potential customer. Even the loyal customers may have different shopping patterns. Some may like to come and browse through the web pages and take their time selecting goods, others will want to go directly to the product they want, order and leave.

We can begin to see the benefit of creating roles that define the services requested from the system by the user. By creating **a potential customer** role, a **leisure customer** role (for the customer who likes to browse) and a **fast customer** role (for the customer who likes to enter, order and leave) we can define a unique set of use cases for each of these types of customer. Using these use cases, we can then add functionality into our web site for each user. We can even customize the web site so that people in different roles see different web pages and have different options.

One of the most interesting things about building web applications is that we really cannot accurately define the different scenarios a user of the site will use until the site is up and running and people are using it. What we can do is research the best web sites currently in operation, research the potential users of the sites (most likely customers), research successful business patterns, send interviews to potential users, etc. Based on this we can create our first design. Once the site is running, we have users log in and then track what they do. We will see patterns emerging on how users move through the site and place orders (if placing orders is part of the site). Based on these patterns, we can refine the different types of roles that the web application has and what scenarios are associated with these roles. From this we can build and refine our use cases, which in turn will allow us to revise and upgrade the design of our site. This brings up a critical point. When building a web site, you cannot design and build it in one development cycle.

The very nature of web sites requires that they be built in iterative cycles. The first cycle creates the initial site with the basic functionality of the site. Based on how the site is used the roles are refined or new ones created and scenarios are revised or created. These new roles and scenarios will be the basis of the next cycle of development. Once this cycle is complete, the site usage will lead to new refinements of roles and scenarios leading to the next stage. As the market and the Internet itself evolve, so must a good Internet site. The cyclic methodology allows the site to be continuously refined so that it is always the most efficient for the users.

When building a web site, one fundamental question you have to ask is whether to allow users of the site full access without logging in or to require them to log in. By having them fill out a login form and then logging in each time, you can track how users within different categories use your site. Thus, a travel site may be able to compare the difference between how business customers and regular tourists use the site or what pages and what items people in different income brackets order. This information is extremely valuable and can allow you to customize your site for each user type (role). The problem is that many people do not want to give personal information, do not want to waste time logging in, and may simply move on to another site that does not require logins. You can make logging in optional and offer benefits to those who log in, without excluding those users who choose not to log in. You can even use this option to make comparisons between those who log in and those who do not

> **Many sites use cookies to store account and session information that is maintained at the client (system) level. When a customer returns to the site the cookie(s) can relate information about how the customer used the site, which can in turn be used to customize the site for the customer experience. However, some customers are reluctant to store cookies on their computer.**

As we said, some of your users may not be people. As everything starts to become automated, we are now starting to pass information from computer system to computer system. This means that a user of your Visual Basic application may be another computer system. Currently, this may mean that you have to produce output in some standard format, such as EDI (Electronic Data Interchange). With the new emerging XML standard, it is likely that XML will soon become a major part of communications between computer systems.

> *XML is a language similar to HTML. One can make XML files to store data such as a recordset (a set of table from a data source usually held in memory). XML files have tags within the file that identify the structure of the data in the file. As the file is self-defining, it is an excellent choice for sending files across different operating systems and environments. These files also can be easily sent across the Internet and used as a data source for the client.*

Just as you need to determine how a human user of your system will use the system, you will need to do the same for how systems use your computer. These other computer systems will be actors in your use cases, and you can build scenarios based on how they will use your system. You will also need to carefully define how information will be formatted and transferred using business rules.

Your Visual Basic application may need to pass information in disconnected recordsets for a Visual Basic EXE application, in the format of HTML to an ASP page for a web application, and also in the format of XML to transfer information to another system. All of this functionality may be in one component.

> *Disconnected recordsets are copies of information from the database, but once the records have been retrieved into the recordsets, the connection to the database is severed. Later, once the information in the disconnected recorset is updated, it can be reconnected to the database*

For example, if we build an order entry application we could build a product component. For the order entry clerks this product component would be in a Visual Basic EXE application using disconnected ADO recordsets, in the E-Commerce site it would be in an ASP page being controlled by server side Visual Basic script and need to return an HTML page, and finally it could be used in a Visual Basic application that automatically reorders products, when the total items in stock falls below a certain number by sending a message in XML format to the supplier. One product component will be producing information in three formats.

Some of you may be thinking that it is not good design to make one component that performs so many functions. We could just as easily build all of our components so that they only use disconnected ADO recordsets. We can then build another component that takes a disconnected ADO recordset and converts it into either HTML or XML format. In this way, we build all our components to work with disconnected ADO recordsets, and have one component that provides the additional formats when they are needed. This saves us putting the same conversion routines into every component but still allows us to reuse our components in many environments. The best solution depends on the available resources and the requirements of the system.

An application built from the envisionment phase will include the big picture. Between the Enterprise Architecture Documents, the Vision/Scope Document and the use cases, we will have a broad view of how our Visual Basic application will fit into the Enterprise. With this view, we can build reusable components that fit into many projects and diverse situations.

Once the user is identified, we should create a profile of the user and what services they will be requesting our system to perform. The educator and the project manager, assisted by the rest of the team if necessary, should make these profiles. Once the profiles are complete, they should be added to the Enterprise Architecture Document under a new section called User Profiles. The use cases should form their own separate document.

Iterative Cycles

In our schedule template (Chapter 13), we have placed a clear boundary between the different phases of the project and clear boundaries between the stages of the design phase. In reality, though, parts of one cycle or stage may end prior to the cycle or stage being complete, resulting in parts of the next cycle or phase beginning. In this way, there is overlap between the different stages and phases. We have already said that the conceptual stage will usually extend from the envisionment phase to the design phase. It is quite possible that a set of use cases will be completed by the educator and handed over to the developers who will start turning them into the UML sequence diagrams. Building sequence diagrams is part of the logical stage, yet the educator may still have many other use cases they need to complete so the conceptual stage is not actually done. Even when all the use cases are complete and the conceptual stage is complete we may find, while creating a sequence diagram, that something from our use case is missing and have to go back and correct it.

The design of the project is an iterative process. We start with our initial view of the design and then present it to the users who suggest modifications. We make these modifications, show them to the users and again make necessary corrections. We begin to make sequence diagrams, find a few other areas that need to be polished in our use cases and finally, after many iterations, arrive at the correct use cases. While we are doing our sequence diagrams, we will show them to the development team and the users and once again polish them. When the sequence diagrams are complete, we will again go through many iterations until they are complete. We will go through this iterative process with the UML diagrams in the physical stage, too. While our schedule has clear boundaries for the phases, in reality there may be a blurring of the lines between phases and stages.

Summary

In order to design a successful enterprise solution, you must not just look at an individual scenario, you must see the big picture. How does everything fit together? Can one process be improved by improving another process? Does improving communication between different parts of a workflow improve the overall workflow? Be creative, use your imagination. Perhaps one of the best sources of ideas is the brainstorming sessions in the second consensus meeting. Many great ideas will come out of this meeting. The reason I suggested writing down all suggestions, even ones that did not get a high ranking, is that sometimes an idea that seems stupid or just too risky at first, may turn out to be the best solution. The suggestions you gather at the consensus meeting are the creative ideas of the entire team, and more importantly, the people most familiar with the business processes. These are the people who are most likely to come up with the best solutions.

In the conceptual stage we take this a step further. We interview users to find out exactly what goals they need to achieve, how they currently achieve them and exactly how we can improve the ease and efficiency with which they can achieve them. The users are a great source for recommendations on how to improve processes. By reviewing their reasons why a process is poor, we can often see how to improve it. Based on this information we create scenarios and use case models for every third level goal identified in our Vision/Scope Document.

Thus we have a set of use case models based on the goals identified by the client and management (and refined by the whole team) along with detailed information about how exactly the user would interact with the system. By proceeding in this manner, we are well on our way to creating an application that will satisfy both business and user requirements. It is very important that the entire team stops focusing only on building components. Instead, they need to start viewing their coding as the fulfillment of one or more goals of the client. This shift in thinking is critical to producing Visual Basic applications that meet the expectations of the client.

In the next chapter the use cases will be analyzed for a description of the services the system must provide (identified by the verbs in our use case Flow of Events, such as create, update etc.) and in order to start to identify system components (prime candidates are the nouns in our use cases, such as Customer, Order etc.). However, we will see that before we can really identify which components we will need, we need to consider the framework within which they will operate.

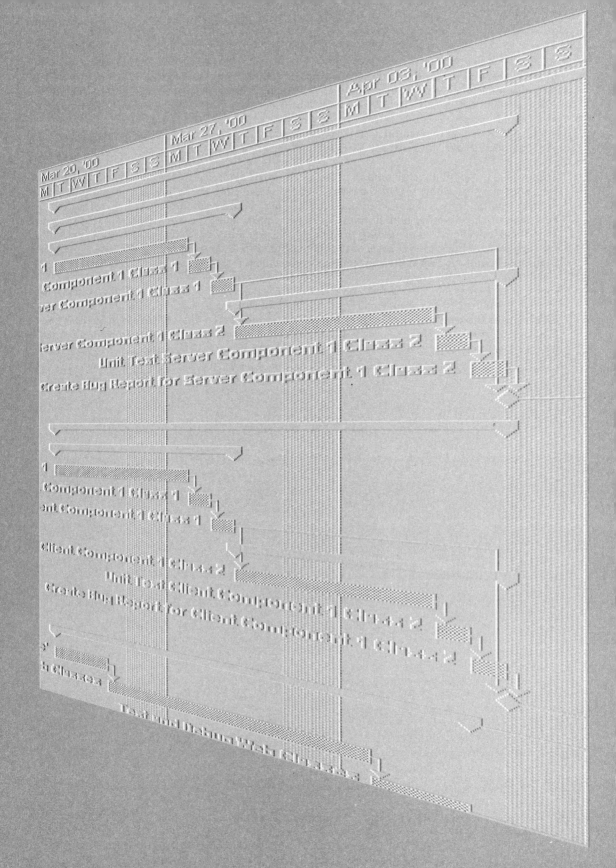

Design Phase: Logical Stage

The logical stage is the point at which the developers really become the focus of the project. Up to here, the focus has been on defining the goals of the client and extracting from those a set of UML use cases. At this point, therefore, we know what the application is going to do, but not how that will be achieved. During this stage, the developers will convert the use cases into a set of sequence diagrams, which define more explicitly the components that the product will contain and the services and properties that these components will require. In order to identify what components we need, it will be necessary to determine the system architecture which will be the most suitable for the product. This stage will also require the user interface to be prototyped and feedback on this prototype to be obtained from the end users.

Therefore, in this chapter we will:

> Refresh and expand on what we've already learned about object-oriented programming
> Examine some of the considerations we need to make in order to choose the framework for our application
> Consider how to convert UML use cases into sequence diagrams
> Take a quick look at prototyping a user-friendly interface for the end user

The logical stage may thus have the following deliverables:

> A set of UML sequence diagrams
> A user interface prototype
> An evaluation of the user interface prototype
> A user interface specification
> Small test applications to test new technology and new solutions
> An evaluation of the test applications

Summary of Team Focus

The most obvious activity during this stage will be the creation of sequence diagrams by the developers. This activity will be coordinated by the project manager and by the component managers, who will be responsible for ensuring that the project remains on schedule. Developers will also be occupied in creating the prototype graphical user interface (GUI).

The testing group will be involved in devising a strategy for testing the components. This will include designing functions to test each component, and every method and property of the components. They will also cooperate with the user educators and the end users in beta testing the GUI prototype. The end users will be interviewed by the educators and invited to give feedback on the prototype.

Overview of the Logical Stage

By the end of the conceptual stage, we have transformed the goals of the client into a set of UML use cases. Each use case will represent a single goal (task) that the user needs the system to accomplish for them. Within these use cases, there will be many services that the user will need the system to perform. It will be the job of our Visual Basic application to perform the services found in these use cases.

During the envisionment phase and conceptual stage, the development team will be working closely with the client to define the goals and services of the system. The logical stage begins when the users and the development team have defined these goals and services and the scope of this current project.

In the logical stage, there is a shift of focus: up to now, the client has been our primary resource for designing the project; from this stage onwards, the members of the software team will take over most of the design work. They will work together to turn the user's goals into objects and to define the interfaces (the methods and properties) for these objects. These interfaces will define the services and attributes of the system's components. The developers will also create a description of the interaction between these components.

Therefore, the logical stage centers on defining the components that will accomplish the business goals of the user. This stage will determine what services these components will perform, what attributes (properties) they will need to perform these services and how they will communicate with each other and with the user. There will be no discussion on how the components will be coded, only what the interfaces will be. Thus, the components designed in the logical phase could be built with any development tool. In the physical stage we will actually begin to look at how our design can be optimized for the development tool we are using, which in our case, is Visual Basic.

The Scope of the Logical Stage

Perhaps one of the most common questions about the cyclic methodology is, "How detailed should I get in each stage?" For the most part, each stage should focus on accomplishing a set of tasks. The conceptual design stage defined the goals of the users. The logical stage will define the interfaces of the components needed to fulfill the user's goals. The physical stage will be used to define the way we will need to code these components.

If we go beyond defining the public properties and methods of our objects in the logical stage, we are probably going too far. If we need to test new methods or techniques and you have to define the private methods and properties in the logical stage, this is fine. Otherwise, in the logical stage it is better just to define the component's interface.

Before the logical stage, we have been viewing the project from the outside. We were not concerned with how the system would fulfill our goals or even what components would exist inside the system. During the logical stage, we take our first peek inside the system. We will not look too deep; we are only going to look at what components are needed to enable our system to accomplish its goals. In the physical stage, we will take a closer look and define how these components will look. Let us a look at an example to get a better idea of what this means.

Imagine we were designing a car with the cyclic methodology. During the envisionment phase and the conceptual stage, we would describe how we want the car to look, the features we want in the car, the way the gauges will look, how the car will drive, etc. Essentially, we would describe every detail about how the car will look and drive by the end of the conceptual stage. In the logical stage, we would lift the hood and start describing the engine and all of the mechanical components.

Every component that we need to make the car perform and function the way we described it in the envisionment phase and conceptual stage will be defined in the logical stage. We will not say how these components will work; only what they must do (what services they must perform) and what characteristics (properties) they will have. Thus, we can say that we will build an engine that will have a certain color, have a certain range of revs per minute, etc. We will need an alternator that will produce a certain voltage, turn at a given rpm, etc. Once we know what components are needed for our car, we can describe how each component will communicate with each other and with the driver.

When we have finished describing the components and how they communicate, we will move on to the physical stage, where we will actually start defining the design of the components. In the physical stage, we would make blueprints of the engine specifying every characteristic of the engine. Finally, in the development phase we would choose the metal, mold it and actually build the engine.

In summary, we will start with the most general goal for the project (the first level goal) in the envisionment phase. We will expand this first level goal into a set of detailed goals that will be used to build the use cases in the conceptual stage. The use cases will be written in the language of application design (that is, we will talk about services and information input and output). In the logical stage, we will expand the use cases into a more detailed design of our application, i.e. a description of the components, the communication between the components, the communication between the components and the user, and the framework for the application, using sequence diagrams. Once we have done this, we will expand our sequence diagrams into a set of pseudo-code instructions in activity diagrams in the physical stage.

Pseudo-code involves summarizing the code you will write in a set of descriptive sentences. For example, the following lines illustrate how we might write pseudo-code instructions for opening a connection to a database:

```
Initialize ADO Connection

Open ADO Connection
```

Each step will become one or more lines of actual Visual Basic code.

The flow of a project from the defining of the general goals to the creating of activity diagrams can be represented as follows:

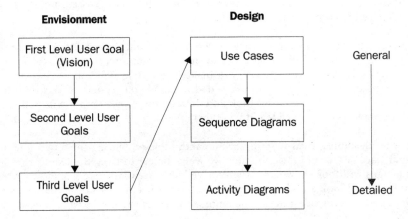

All the way through the envisionment phase, the conceptual stage and the logical stage we are just looking at the system from the outside. In the physical stage we will be looking at the inside of the system. We are doing this because we are designing an object-oriented Visual Basic project. As we will discuss in this chapter, when we are using an object, we are not concerned with how an object does something, only what services it will need to perform and what properties it will have. We will therefore only be concerned with identifying the objects of the system and the properties and services they will have all the way through the logical stage. By the end of the logical stage, we will have a detailed description of the objects we will need to build for our system. These objects can be built from any programming language as long as they can perform the required services. To design an object-oriented Visual Basic application properly, we will need to take a look at some essential properties of objects.

Object Attributes

We met two of the most important attributes shared by objects in Chapter 1: **abstraction** and **encapsulation**. It is worth refreshing and expanding on our definitions of these concepts, since they are vital for a proper understanding of object-oriented programming.

Abstraction

Abstraction is the process of representing a related group of items by a general term that classifies them into one group. For example, the word car is a general classification for something with four wheels, an engine and used to get you from one location to another location. When I say the word car, you immediately know what I am talking about. You do not need a description of what a car is; you immediately know what one is. Abstraction is essentially classification: grouping together things with similar properties (characteristics) and behaviors (things they are capable of doing, such as performing a service) and giving that group a name.

We will want to perform abstraction with the descriptions in the use case. When we look into the use cases, we will find groups that all share the same characteristics and perform the same services. Thus, we could have many customers that share similar characteristics such as having a credit card number, billing address or orders on record. Customers will also have certain behaviors, such as placing orders or changing their address. Thus, I can group all the people with these behaviors (placing orders, changing orders...) and characteristics (a billing address, orders on record, a credit card number...) into one group called customers. Creating abstractions will be the first step in creating objects and this is the first thing we will do in the logical stage.

Abstractions not only help us build our objects, but they also help us view our systems in a simpler manner. By creating these classifications, we will reduce our complicated system into a group of objects. We will find it much easier to talk about abstractions, especially to the client.

Encapsulation

As we have said, we were only interested in what the system is supposed to do (what services it provides) throughout the logical stage. How the system performs these services is something we are not concerned with until we get to the physical design stage. This is encapsulation. Essentially, encapsulation is the process of building components that perform a set of services and have a set of properties. These components will hide how they perform these services.

Encapsulation is one of the fundamental concepts of building objects when working in Windows. Windows 9x and NT all use the Component Object Model (COM). We could write entire books on COM, and indeed, many have been written. Essentially, COM allows components running under Windows to communicate to other components. COM acts as a translator between components. One component will make a request to a second component to perform some service or one component will make a request to set a property on a second component. COM will transfer this request from the first component to the second component, the second component will perform this service or set the appropriate property and COM will carry any messages back to the first component, if necessary.

> *For more information about COM from a Visual Basic perspective, see VB COM: A Visual Basic Programmer's Introduction to COM, ISBN 1-861002-13-0, from Wrox Press.*

The great thing about COM components is that they can be built from any development tool that works with COM. As long as the component exposes its methods (the services it can perform) and properties in a way that COM has access to them, it makes absolutely no difference how they are built. In other words, it does not matter how the object performs its services, only what services it has to offer. Which, of course, is what encapsulation is all about.

Visual Basic components are COM components. Encapsulation and COM allow us to build our Visual Basic components so that they can be used by any other COM component. Our Visual Basic components can also use any other COM component regardless of the development tool which was used to build the component. However, for this all to work, we need to design our Visual Basic components properly. To do this, we need to start with a focus on what the components will do, and not how they will do it. This is exactly what we have done.

Encapsulation offers us other advantages, too. Since we are only concerned with the methods and properties that the object makes available (that is, public properties and methods) we can change the internal workings of our component, keep the external methods and properties the same and not have to change the code in the components which use this component.

For example, imagine we have a Customers component and an Orders component. The Orders component has two public methods, CreateOrder and DeleteOrder and one property, OrderID. The Customers component uses both these methods and also the property. Let us imagine that the Orders component starts off as a COBOL program accessible through COM. Perhaps this is a very old legacy program running on the mainframe that functions as a Windows COM component through the magic of SNA Server (a Microsoft server that allows communication between the Windows world and the mainframe world). Our first cycle is to get the Customers component up and running and to see how it works. Once we have completed this, we now decide it's time to upgrade our old COBOL component, Orders. We rewrite this using Visual C++. Our new C++ component still has CreateOrder, DeleteOrder and OrderID, which all work exactly as they did in the COBOL program. As for the Customers component, we may have to make a few changes in how it references Orders, but any code that calls the methods or properties of Orders can remain unchanged. This is one of the wonderful features of encapsulated objects. Because we don't care how an object performs its services, it makes no difference if it changes how it functions internally as long as the public methods and properties do not change.

This is one of the fundamental concepts of object-oriented programming. The public properties and methods, which we will call the object's **interface**, that you include in the design of your project, must not be altered. You can change the internal, private methods and properties as much as you like, but you had better not change the public ones. If you are building objects with Visual Basic, consider your final object design as an irrevocable contract between you and the developers that will use your object. You will create total havoc to schedules if you initially design your object with a certain set of public properties and methods, give this design to other developers who design other components based on this design, and then later change your design. All the components using your component will have to be redesigned. If the other components are built, they will have to be rebuilt. Doing this will not only make you rather unpopular, but also destroy the integrity of the entire project. This is why it is so important that you take the time to properly design your object right from the start.

If you should need to add functionality to your object after you have designed it, this will not affect any of the objects dependent on your object if you only change internal properties or methods. If you start adding new public properties or methods though, you risk walking into a potential landmine.

Imagine that I have created Version 1 of a Customers component with method CreateCustomer. I release to dozens of developers who use this component in dozens of Visual Basic applications. Later, one of the developers tells me that they really need another function, DeleteCustomer added onto my component. So, I create and release a new version, Customers 2.0, with the CreateCustomer and DeleteCustomer methods. Now, some developers have applications using Version 1 and some using Version 2. What happens if someone installs an application that uses Version 2, which overwrites Version 1? If there are still applications on the machine that use Version 1, there is no problem as the CreateCustomer method is still supported by Version 2. But what happens if we install a Version 2 application, which puts Customers 2.0 on the machine and then someone installs an application on the same computer which installs Customers 1.0? Now there is a problem, as the Version 2 component will be looking for the DeleteCustomer method and it will not be there. Version 2 will probably no longer work.

In an ideal world, this would not be a problem: it is for this very reason that we assign version numbers to components. Setup applications should not install older versions of a component over more recent ones. In reality, however, it is a problem, and it is impossible to guarantee that a newer version won't be overwritten if your component is to be released to other developers and installed by many setup applications.

Thus, you can add public methods and properties to your components without changing the GUID (an identifier that uniquely identifies your component), but you should only do this when you are certain that an earlier version of the component will never overwrite a later version. If you have a Visual Basic server component that only runs on one server, and there is a strict control of what components are placed on that server, it is safe to add public methods and properties, as it is not likely that the older version will be installed. If you are distributing your components over the Internet or over an intranet and you increment your version numbers, you should also try to make sure that the newer version is always installed over the older version. Thus, when you have strict control over the component, it is safe to add public methods or properties. It is a very bad idea to add public methods or properties when you do not have strict control over a component, such as when a component is used by many developers and placed in many setup programs. When you do not have control, it is better to recompile the component with a new name and a new GUID.

We can see that we can adapt our objects to new requirements by adding new private methods or properties or by changing them. Any changes to the internal workings of an object will have no affect on your component. This is all possible because of COM and because encapsulated objects perform services without us caring about how they actually perform these services. As for adding public properties and methods, this can be done when there is strict control over the component. If we do not have strict control, then the component should be renamed and recompiled as a new component.

Encapsulation and abstraction work together. Objects will represent a certain group of things that all share similar properties and methods. Thus, the customers Smith, Jones and Williams will all be objects in an order entry system. They are all customers and a customer is an abstraction. By creating encapsulated objects that contain an interface with public properties and methods, we have found the perfect way to create our abstractions in Visual Basic.

To summarize, encapsulation brings the following benefits:

> It gives users of the object an interface to work with that defines the public property and methods.
> It provides a way of hiding the complexity by creating abstractions.
> It creates an independent, self-contained unit whose internal workings are not important.

Cohesion and Coupling

When working with objects, we can look at how closely the different internal parts of the system are related to each other and we can also look at how closely each object is related to other objects in the system. **Cohesion** is the internal binding of a component, and **coupling** is the external binding of components.

For example, if we consider the computer object we discussed in Chapter 1, we can see that each computer is made up of processors, memory boards, sound cards, etc., that are tightly bound together. There are many different types of internal chips that together create a very tightly bound system. This is a tight form of cohesion. A number of computers can be linked together in an intranet, which forms a much looser coupling. This arrangement - a very tight cohesion associated with a loose coupling - is very common.

Cohesion and coupling do not only refer to our Visual Basic objects. Coupling and cohesion also refer to our methods, the entire application, and essentially any part of the system we are building. Our goal will be to use tight cohesion and loose coupling. Let us look at cohesion and coupling to see why this is the best solution.

Cohesion

There are four types of cohesion that are beneficial to Visual Basic components:

> **Functional Cohesion**. Functional cohesion creates the tightest binding within a component. A component that has functional cohesion only does one thing. If a component performed more than one function, than the component would be doing two separate things, which means the component is not tightly bound. All of your Visual Basic methods, both private and public, should have functional cohesion; that is, they should only do one thing. This makes it very clear what the function does and makes it easy to debug.

> **Sequential Cohesion**. A component that has sequential cohesion will have internal components that must work in a specific order. The internal components will also share internal data. Several internal methods that pass data from method to method through parameters, and work in a specific order, would be considered sequential cohesion. This is common when you create functions or subs in your Visual Basic code that perform some operations on the data. Sequential cohesion makes it easy to follow the flow of the code. Debugging is easier as you can check the parameters which are passed into a method 'by reference'; this means that a variable itself (rather than its value) is passed into the method, so the value of the variable can be changed within the procedure.

> **Temporal Cohesion**. Temporal cohesion means that internal operations are combined so that they can be done at the same time. For example, when you update an order, you will update the `Orders`, `Order Details` and `Products` tables in the database at the same time.

Components with these types of cohesion are tightly bound, perform a clear set of services and are easy to debug and understand.

> **Communicational Cohesion**. In communicational cohesion, the internal operations of the component share the same data but do not communicate with each other. For example, if you create a global connection variable that is used independently by all of your methods, this would be communicational cohesion. You must be careful with global variables, though, as these are not always the best coding technique for Visual Basic. You should be very careful when working with communicational cohesion always to set and retrieve the values of global variables through methods and properties (rather than accessing them directly), even when the variables are only used privately.

All of these types of cohesion result in Visual Basic code that is easy to read and debug. Because components with these types of cohesion are tightly bound, they can easily be tested in isolation from the rest of the project. This means that if an error is found during the testing of an individual component, the error can only be in that component. If each function has a single clear purpose, it should be fairly easy to see what is wrong and find the function in which the error occurred.

On the other hand, there are three other types of cohesion that result in Visual Basic code that is poorly written. These are:

> **Procedural Cohesion**. This is what happens when a series of operations are grouped together because they occur in a specific order. This differs from sequential order in that the operations do not share data. When two routines manipulate different data, they must be performing two completely different functions, so they are very loosely cohesive. There will be no clear logic in the order of the operations and consequently it will be difficult to follow the code. As functions are grouped together without having logical cohesion, it becomes difficult, if not impossible, to test individual functions and components. Often, entire sections of code must be tested at once. If a bug is found, you must search through mountains of code to find it, which could take a very long time.

> **Coincidental Cohesion**: This is simply a worse case of procedural cohesion. In procedural cohesion, there is at least some logic in the order of the procedures, but there is no sharing of data. In coincidental cohesion, there is simply no reason for the order of the code. Code jumps from one module to the next with no obvious pattern or reason. The common term for this is 'spaghetti code'. It is unreadable, un-maintainable and impossible to debug. Visual Basic has evolved to a level where the developers should be professionals. Professional developers should never be writing this type of code. It does not matter how many great features of Visual Basic a developer may know or how deep their knowledge of the language is if they write code that is a tangled, unmanageable mess.

> **Logical Cohesion**: The routines have a logical parameterpassed in that determines what the routine will do. Inside the routine will be a huge `Select Case` (or, even worse, an `If ... ElseIf` statement) that will determine what the routine will do. These routines can stretch to hundreds of lines of codes and become completely unmanageable.

The most common reason for procedural and coincidental cohesion is a total lack of a design phase. During the design phase, and specifically the physical stage, you can see the big picture and organize your components so that there is a logical flow of the internal components. Being given a set of properties and methods that your component is supposed to have, and then just start hacking out code, will result in code that does not have a clear organization. Sometimes a very carefully designed project can end up with spaghetti code because of feature creep. As new features are added in the middle of coding, modules have to be hacked and changed. New modules suddenly need to be stuck in to add this new functionality and all order is soon lost. This is why it is so essential to create a good design and get all team members, especially the stakeholders and sponsors, to sign off on the final design. A clear agreement has to be made that once the design is final, new features will be added in the next cycle. Because there is a documented design, even new team members will be able to work within the existing design and to add features in ways that continue "clean" design in the next cycle.

Coupling

Ideally, we want to be able to test components by themselves first. To do this, each component must be loosely bound to other components. Loose coupling also means that we can remove one component, replace it with another that performs the same services and has the same public properties, and the rest of the project will be unaffected. The connections between components are defined by their interfaces, which gives us maximum flexibility in building components.

Components should have interfaces that are simple to understand. It should be clear what each method and property is. The interface should not be too complicated, and should be kept as small as possible. If the interface begins to get too large, it may be better to break the component into a hierarchy or into smaller components. Nothing should be hidden: everything should be very straightforward. The one exception to this is passing parameters into the initialization event of a class (this occurs when an instance of the object is created). As this cannot be done in Visual Basic, we must initialize our class without passing in any parameters and either have an additional method or use properties to initialize variables that need to be set at the creation of the object. Interfaces should also be as generic as possible to allow the component the maximum amount of flexibility.

Composition and Emergence

Components that are loosely coupled and also have tight cohesion can be thought of as a set of children's building blocks. These blocks will come in many colors and sizes. We can create many different buildings with the same set of blocks. In some cases, we can pull a block out and replace it with another block to create a completely different building. Our components will be like these blocks, usable in many different projects to create applications with different functionality. To add functionality to our applications, we can add methods or properties to our components (but we may never remove them) or remove a component and replace it with a new component that has this new functionality.

The **composition** of a system is the arrangement of the components within the system. A set of components may come together to define a single entity. For example, a set of components may work together to fulfill a particular goal: we can combine Customers, Orders and Products components to allow the user to enter an order, etc.

Associated with composition is the concept of **emergence**. Emergence is the creation of something which is different to the sum of its parts. For example, we can take pasta, tomato sauce, spices, meat, mozzarella and ricotta cheese and put them all together to make baked lasagna. Separately, these ingredients do not make lasagna; it is only when they are all combined that we get lasagna.

Composition and emergence are perhaps two of the most difficult aspects of building a Visual Basic object-oriented application. They require you to look very carefully at all of the components in the system to see how they communicate to each other and what services they will perform. Once we do this, we can build a system from these components, other systems from these components, and different objects from these components. To put all of these pieces together, we will have to place all of the information into some type of model.

Building a system like this is simply too complex to visualize mentally. We can see how components fit together within the entire system more clearly if we create models of the system that allow us to visualize the components. The best tool for doing this is UML. In the conceptual stage, we used UML use cases to create a formal description of each of the users' goals. In the logical stage, we turn these use cases into UML sequence diagrams. Sequence diagrams will show how our objects must communicate to each other, what services they must provide and where in the system they will be located. Just how do we convert UML use cases into sequence diagrams? Once again, there is no black magic. We begin with a careful review of our use cases to define the objects that will be needed by our system. Once we have done this, we will map the communication between our objects using sequence diagrams.

Defining Components from Use Cases

Well, that concludes our refresher of some of the theory behind object-oriented programming. We can now start to think about how we will recognize the components which we need for our application. Finding the components in our use cases that will be performing the basic services for our system is usually not too difficult. When looking at the text in the use cases, we will find that objects will usually be nouns and the things that describe these objects will be properties. We should look for real world objects, such as customer, order, etc. However, some objects will not have any counterparts in the real world; we will discuss these later in the chapter.

The objects that we will define in the logical stage, which will become Visual Basic components in the development phase, should fulfill one or more goals of the user, be loosely coupled and tightly cohesive, encapsulate its functionality, and provide a component that can be easily used by other components. Looking at our use cases, we will usually find that the services our objects will need to perform are verbs. We can either identify the verbs and then ask, "What object will perform this service?" or identify the nouns and ask, "What services (verbs) are associated with this noun?"

To do this, let's take a look at the goal of placing an order. In our initial interview with the user we got what is called a scenario, which is a broad, general description of how something is done. We then removed from this anything which should be placed in a business rule or which was outside the system. By following these steps we created a use case, which describes how the user will interact with the system; that is, it describes exactly how the application will function from the user's perspective.

We will just look at the sequence of events part of the use case, as we have gone into detail about the other sections in the previous chapter. We will underline the nouns that are good candidates for becoming objects in our application and place the verbs that may become services in italics. We will bold anything that can become a separate use case, such as creating a customer:

Order Entry
Place **Order**

>   **Primary Actor:** Sales Representative

>   Actor begins new Order

>   Actor *requests* Customer information from the system

>   Actor will ***Create*** **Customer** if the customer does not exist

> ➤ Actor will *Update* **Customer Information** if the information is incorrect
> ➤ Actor *selects* the <u>Product</u> Customer wants
> ➤ Actor *enters* the quantity of the <u>Product</u> the customer wants
> ➤ (Repeat for each product the customer wishes to order)
> ➤ Actor *submits* the <u>Order</u>

Looking at this use case, we can identify three objects that will be required by our order entry application: `Order`, `Customer` and `Product`. Clearly, we don't want to underline every noun in the use case: objects must provide services (so they must have methods) and have certain attributes (properties). There's no point in making an object out of 'quantity', for example. This doesn't have any attributes, nor does it provide any services. Rather, it is descriptive of the product, so it will become a property of the `Product` object.

We can further see that we have italicized seven verbs, which will give rise to the methods exposed by these components. Three of our verbs - place, create and update - are amongst the goals of the primary actor, the sales representative; these all require a separate use case. 'Place order' is the current use case, and we have to define use cases for 'create customer' and 'update customer'. From this we can see that we will need an `Order` component that has an `Add New` method to allow us to add new orders. Before we can actually use the `Add New` method, though, we will have to perform all the steps listed in the use case. As for the `Customer` component, it will need an `Add New` method to create a customer and an `Edit` method to update a customer. These methods will also require the steps listed in those use cases to be completed.

This leads us to an important observation: the steps listed in the use cases are either a request for information needed to set a property for one of the objects of the use case, the actual setting of the property, or a request for a service from the system. In our example, the `Order` object is the main object of the use case. Note that an object's property can hold another object, so, for example, our `Order` object will have a `Customer` property that will identify who placed the order - this will be one of our `Customer` objects. The following steps will identify the value of that `Customer` property:

> ➤ Actor takes a call from the customer
> ➤ Actor requests customer information
> ➤ If customer does not exist, actor will **Create Customer**
> ➤ Actor checks customer address
> ➤ If incorrect, actor will **Update Customer Information**

An order will also require a list of the products ordered and the following step will determine the value of the `Products` property:

> ➤ Actor selects product customer wants
> ➤ Actor enters the quantity of the product customer wants

In a real system, we would probably have an `Order Details` *object, too, that would hold the list of products. I have left it out to keep the example simple.*

Once we have set all the properties, we can actually submit the order. Notice that only the steps required to get information to set a property of the objects in the use case, actually to set the property or a direct request for a service from the system belong in the use case. If other objects are descended from the main object, as the `Customer` and `Product` objects are derived from the `Order` object, we can include steps to set properties for these objects. However, if setting these properties can be grouped together to form another goal of the user, such as adding a new customer or editing the information on an existing customer, these steps should be moved into a separate use case.

When we reach the point where we are actually trying to identify the objects and the properties and methods of these objects, we might find that we must refine our use cases. A large use case may contain steps that fulfill a goal, such as adding or editing a customer, that need to be separated out into another use case. In our above example, we would probably alter the use case so that it also had an `Order Details` object to hold the product information. Design is an iterative process and often requires many revisions before we reach the best design for our system.

Now that we have identified our objects, we are almost ready to start to define their interfaces - their methods and properties. However, first we must give some consideration to the framework for our application, and think about how to decide where our various components will be located. What we decide will have a significant effect on how we must define our components.

Choosing a Framework

While our choice of programming language may not be a central part of the logical stage, how we are going to distribute the application will have a large impact on our logical stage design. Whether we choose to build an application on a two-tier or three-tier framework will have a major impact on the logical design stage because it directly affects how we will design the component's interfaces.

We have three primary alternatives how to build our systems. These options are the monolithic (single-tiered) model, the two-tier and the three-tier models. Each of these types of applications has its place, but using an inappropriate model could have a serious performance cost to the application. It is vital that everyone in the team understands the implications of choosing a specific architecture, so we will spend some time considering this question.

Single-Tier Applications

One-tier systems run completely from one machine. They tend to be monolithic systems that do not have separate components. If they are monolithic and not built from components, they can only be tested as a single component. Because of the incredible difficulty in testing and maintaining non-modular monolithic system, single-tier systems sometimes have a bad reputation. There are still situations, though, where it makes sense to build this type of application.

An application that runs on a computer and does not need to access data on another machine should use the one-tier model. Examples of such applications are screensaver programs or an appointment scheduler. If you were writing an application that controlled an assembly line that puts caps on bottles and then checks the caps, there would not be enough time to communicate to another computer between each cap. A program that needs response time in milliseconds will probably be one-tier.

Creating one-tier systems is still a large part of what Visual Basic programmers are doing. If you are building these systems, they should be built from components. An excellent example of this is the Microsoft Office suite of products. For the most part, Word, Excel and PowerPoint are one-tier applications.

Two-Tier Applications

However, what if we have a number of order entry clerks, who all need to access the same database from their computers? We will need more than one tier: an order entry application on each clerk's computer (called the 'client') which will retrieve and update data from a database on a server which serves the whole company. Systems with two or more tiers are usually called **client-server** applications. Two-tier systems usually consist of a database server and a client application which retrieves and updates data on the server. This allows a number of people using different client computers to access the same database concurrently.

Data Conflicts and Locking

However, this causes a problem of its own. Suppose we have two users both accessing our products database. If both only want to read the data, there probably won't be a problem. However, if one client wants to change some data and the other wants to read the same data, we will have to step in and do something. Otherwise we may have a situation where one user changes a field a value (say, reducing the stock level of Ipoh Coffee from 20 to 15 when a customer phones in an order) while another is reading the field and sees the original value of 20. Alternatively, one user may change the field value from 20 to 15 and then cancel the change, but another user may view the field and see a value of 15. Finally, two users could access the same field for editing at the same time. One user changes the field value from 20 to 15 and saves it while another (responding to another phoned order) changes it from 20 to 17 and saves it, overwriting the value of 15, instead of further reducing the stock level to 12.

The usual solution to all of these problems is locks. While locks can solve the problem, we will see that they too have some serious problems. If you create a lock that does not now allow a client to look at or change a record when another client is changing a record, all of the problems with client-server go away. Unfortunately, though, locks introduce their own set of problems. Locks can lock more than one record; sometimes they can lock many records. If someone else needs one of these locked records to do their job, they will not be able to do their job until the lock is released. Thus, you will have periods of time where the users are waiting for a record to become unlocked. Sometimes this is not a problem; sometimes this can become a major problem and slow down work performance.

This type of locking, which prevents a record being edited by more than one user at a time, is called **pessimistic locking**. There is another type of locking, called **optimistic locking**, which avoids this problem by locking the record(s) only when the user attempts to update the database. However, as you will appreciate, this has the drawback that two users can still edit the same record concurrently and won't be informed of any conflict until they attempt to update the database. Without going into too much detail, I think you can begin to see that things can get very complicated with client-server and locking records.

Scalability

Another significant problem with two-tier applications is their lack of scalability: we can suffer enormous loss of performance as more and more users are added. Imagine we write an order entry application as a two-tier application. The client application will enter the order and the database will have stored procedures to perform the updating and retrieving of records. The initial two-tier application has about ten users. The company later starts selling over the web, and suddenly the database has to run stored procedures for thousands of clients. Scaling a database is not very easy and we can reach a point where we run out of connections. Thus, a two-tier architecture is not very good for web applications or for large-scale enterprise applications that will need to be scaled.

The solution to this problem is to add an extra tier - we can take any business processing that does not directly produce what the users see on their screens and place it into a middle tier that sits between the client application and the database. The middle tier is then responsible for managing the network traffic and the load on the database. Furthermore, we can decide to have a separate, dedicated machine for our middle tier, which serves our several hundred users. Any updates that need to be made to our business processing can be done quickly and easily - on the middle-tier machine only and not on the many client machines.

However, two-tier is ideal for building small department-size applications. An application that needs to have a central data store used by a few dozen people is perfect for a two-tier application. Most recommendations specify fewer than 100 users, but personally I would consider even 100 users high for a two-tier Visual Basic application. If you are building an application to move graphics into a database that will be used by one user, this is a good candidate for a simple two-tier Visual Basic application.

Three-Tier Applications

In a three-tier model, we separate out the data services, the business services and the client services into separate components. The **data services** are services that deal with direct communication with the database. Data services would include getting all of the customers and returning them to a system object such as a customer object, or getting an updated record from a system object and saving the new information to the database. The **business services** are services that deal with the maintenance of the system's objects. Business services related to a customer object would be retrieving a specific customer, moving to the next customer, adding a customer, etc. The business services are usually in components that encapsulate a business object, such as a customer object or an order object. The **client services** are services that deal with getting information to the user and usually make up the user interface.

In the three-tier framework, we will usually have components for each set of services. The interfaces for these components will be affected by what services these components perform. As we will see below, this three-tier framework will need special server objects for the data services that have no memory of what they did the last time they were called. (This persistence of values between sessions is termed **state**; components that lack this memory are said to be **stateless**.) These server objects will need very special interfaces to work this way. We will describe these in the next chapter.

Physical and Logical Models

Before we move on to discuss some of the considerations we will need to make when we choose the framework for our application, we must first distinguish between two different models for a three-tier application: the logical and the physical.

Physical Three-Tier Model

When people talk about the three-tier model, they almost always mean the physical three-tier model. In this model, we have a client computer, a server middle-tier computer that runs some part of the application, and a database server. Often, the middle tier actually resides on more than one computer. There may also be more than one database server. Because of the possibility for multiple database and middle-tier servers, three-tier is often called n-tier or multi-tier, as there may actually be a number of physical computers. A simple three-tier solution would look as follows:

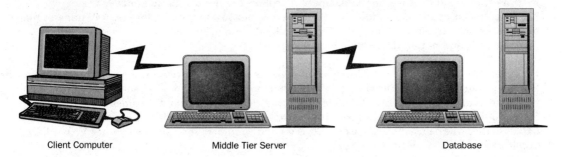

Client Computer   Middle Tier Server   Database

There are many advantages to placing the application onto the third tier. The primary advantage is scalability. If we build our application from components, we can easily divide these components across multiple servers. If we build Component1, which is used by several of our applications to get data from the database, we can place this on its own server. If the server cannot handle the number of requests to use Component1, we can upgrade it, and when the server reaches its maximum capacity, we can add another server and place Component1 on two servers. In this way, we can easily increase the capacity of our system by adding hardware and not by rewriting applications. Applications take one or two years to build and can be very costly. Hardware can be bought for a reasonable price and shipped overnight.

Logical Three-Tier Model

While the physical three-tier framework divides the application across three physical entities (the client computer, the middle tier server and the database server), in the **logical model**, we divide our application into components that perform client services, business services and data services. The actual location of these three services can be anywhere on the three physical tiers.

The data services element of the logical three-tier model is not the database; it is where the components that communicate directly with the data source reside. This could consist of a middle-tier component on a server that retrieves and updates data for the client, or it could be a set of stored procedures in the database. In our application, the data services component will be the server component. The data services can also be a combination of both middle-tier components and stored procedures.

Business services are components that service the client application and usually encapsulate business logic, which validates the data being passed to or from the server. In our application, the business services will be the client components such as the `Order`, `Customer`, `Products` and `Order Details` components. These components can reside on the client computer or on the middle tier. For example, the `Products` component could provide product information to an order entry application on the client. The same business services component could also reside on a web server and retrieve data for a products page to be viewed by potential customers surfing the web. Thus, in the logical three-tier model there is no restriction on where the components will reside, only a placement of the services into three categories according to the functions that the components perform.

Microsoft Transaction Server

One critical part of a three-tier Visual Basic solution is Microsoft Transaction Server (MTS). MTS is essentially a component-based run-time environment that makes it easy to develop and deploy scalable enterprise applications. Its key goals are to relieve the pain of developing the basic infrastructure required for such applications, whilst helping to shield the developer from the many complexities of multi-user development such as concurrent access to resources and distributed transaction processing.

The end result of using MTS is that we can focus on developing middle-tier business objects to solve our business problems, rather than spending 40% of our development time implementing the framework required just to host our objects. Indeed, writing a truly scalable system in Visual Basic is probably not possible without MTS. Even in C++, creating our own scalable infrastructure would be fairly silly, given that somebody else has already done the hard work and is giving it away for free!

MTS is built entirely around COM, and you should think of it as an extension of existing functionality that COM provides. Probably one of the most important features of Windows 2000 is the unification of the COM and MTS programming models (as COM+), bringing context and activity-based concurrency management directly into the COM runtime. The unification means that investment today in MTS won't be wasted with the advent of the next generation of Windows operation systems.

Since the decision whether or not to use MTS will have a major impact on the way we design and code our components, it is worth looking at this topic in some detail.

Transaction Processing

The most powerful feature of MTS is **transaction processing** (hence its name). If you've ever used a relational database, when you read the word transaction your mind probably interprets it to think of database transactions. Whilst this interpretation is correct in many ways, it's important to realize that MTS is designed to deal with transactions for many types of data sources, and not just databases.

What Is a Transaction?

A transaction is best described as one or more actions that are either all performed as a whole or none of them are performed at all. To see why we might want to do this, consider the following scenario.

A customer enters our Northwind e-commerce site and places an order. He enters his name, address, credit card number etc., and the appropriate sum of money is duly removed from his bank account. So far so good, but suppose the system unexpectedly crashes at this point, and all record of the deal is lost. The customer has already paid, and the money been deducted from his account, but we haven't yet updated our database of products to be shipped, so he won't get his goods.

Using MTS, we could place both operations within a transaction. This will ensure that both succeed, or both fail. So, if the system crashes before our database is updated, the transaction will fail and no money will be removed from his account. Similarly, there's no danger that a computer crash will cause the goods to be sent without the customer having to pay.

As in this example, transactions are a vital part of any system which involves the exchange of goods or money, so we really should consider using transactions in any e-commerce site we wish to create.

ACID Properties

A transaction **must** have four properties, which are known from their initials as the **ACID** properties. These four requirements are:

Atomicity

Atomicity dictates that a transaction must execute completely, or not at all. If the process breaks down in the middle, based on atomicity, everything that occurred before the breakdown should be rolled back. So in the example above, our customer wouldn't lose his money.

Consistency

Consistency dictates that the persistent state reflects that which the business rules had intended. In other words, the transaction must not break any rules laid down in the environment by the business rules. That means in our above example, that once the transaction occurred, there should be goods sent to the customer, and money removed from his account. We wouldn't expect goods to be sent to anyone else.

Isolation

Isolation refers to how concurrent transactions are not aware of what each other is doing. The end point of the transaction would be the same no matter what the outcome of the individual transactions. In the above example, imagine if another customer was also purchasing something from our site at the same time. The two transactions would be unaware of each other, but would still successfully result in two orders being dispatched, and a set of funds being removed from both customers' accounts.

Durability

Durability states that when updates have occurred to a resource, only then should the client be notified that a transaction has occurred. If the system failed for any reason after the notification, then the changes would still be reflected once the system was restarted. This allows the user to know that a transaction has been successfully completed even if there is an error later. So relating to the above example, our customer would not think that the money had been transferred when in fact it hadn't.

When Should MTS Be Used?

Besides managing transactions, MTS can be a valuable resource for scaling three-tier Visual Basic applications. If we have Visual Basic middle tier components running on a server, we can run them under MTS. While MTS offers both transaction management and object management, there are times when MTS is not appropriate for our Visual Basic component. Before we discuss the 3-tier solution, let us look at what MTS offers our Visual Basic components and when we should use MTS for our Visual Basic middle tier components.

Visual Basic does a lot of work for us developers. Most of the complicated Windows programming that must be done by C++ developers in their code is already done for us by Visual Basic. Visual Basic allows us to code to our hearts content without ever knowing some of the deeper Windows concepts, such as what a thread is. While we can make working components if we do not understand these things, it is very likely that we will be coding inefficient components without some knowledge of what is going on under the covers. With regards to MTS, the most important Windows concept is that of threading. Let us take a quick look at this.

MTS, Visual Basic and Threading

Imaginethat your application has a small plastic block for every step of code. These blocks are made to snap together. When the blocks are snapped together, they must go in a particular order as specified by the code you write. Each block has only two connectors, which means that as the blocks are snapped together they form a single strand, i.e. a thread. You cannot form a branch in the chain: one block must follow another. These threads made up of programming blocks are used to run your code. One step must always follow another: you cannot place two blocks next to each other on the same thread.

Single-Threading and Multi-Threading

Prior to Windows 95 and Windows NT 3.51, everything in the Windows world ran on a single thread. When a program runs on a single thread, you can only place one block on at a time (run one code step at a time). Since it would be useful to do more than one thing at a time, and a thread is only capable of doing one sequence of steps at one time, later Versions of Windows allowed applications to create more than one thread. Each thread can only do one sequence of events, but you can have many sequences of events running at the same time using more than one thread. This is called **multi-threading** or **free-threading**. Unfortunately, Visual Basic is not one of the programming languages that can create multiple threads (Visual C++ is).

Threading Apartments

Now, threads do not just float around inside your computer's processor. They need to be put somewhere, ideally isolated from other threads. It could be a serious problem if the sequence of steps of one thread was suddenly replaced by a sequence of steps from another thread. To prevent this, threads are placed in apartments. To keep one apartment separated from another apartment, apartments are placed inside a process. This looks as follows:

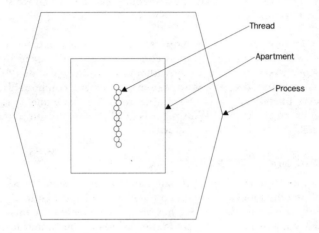

When a client makes a call to a component, COM will create the component in an apartment in a process, and run the code steps on a thread. If we have two clients, Client1 and Client2 and one component called Object1, what happens when Client1 calls Object1 and then Client2 also calls Object1? If Client2 makes a call to Object1 on the same machine as Client1, and Client1 is still using Object1, the second client must wait. Client2 cannot get access into the apartment until Client1 is done:

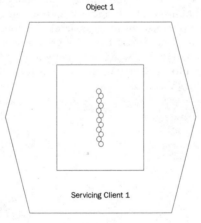

Prior to the current releases of Windows, this is how everything worked. As you can imagine, this does not scale very well. As more and more clients make requests for the component, the queue gets longer and longer. Eventually the computer runs out of memory. In Visual Basic, this is called single-threaded, which is a very poor choice for a name, as all Visual Basic components are single-threaded in the sense that there is only one thread in an apartment. Single-threaded really means that there is a single apartment.

Apartment Threading

The only other option available to Visual Basic programmers is to have COM create multiple apartments within one process, each with a thread in it for each call to a component. Each apartment still has one thread, so this is not multi-threading. This would look as follows:

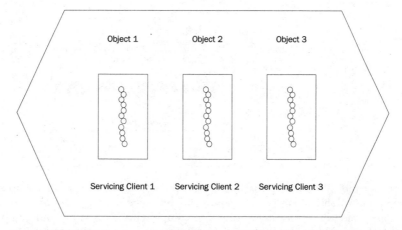

This solution became available in the recent versions of Windows. As you can see, each instance of `Object1` is still not multi-threaded, but now there can be multiple instances of `Object1`. Since there is no waiting for `Object1` to finish servicing `Client1`, all three clients can be serviced at the same time. In Visual Basic and COM, this is called **apartment threading**. If you look at the Properties dialog of a Visual Basic ActiveX DLL, you will see the following options:

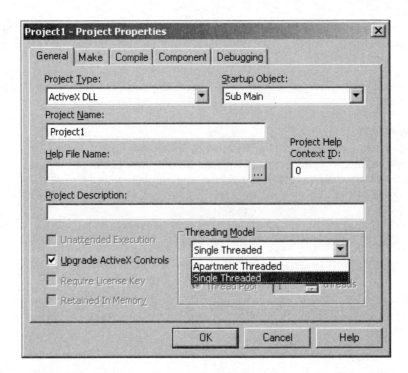

MTS will manage our Visual Basic apartment-threaded components: it will have an apartment waiting for our component when a client is called and will handle the management of creating multiple instances of our Visual Basic apartment-threaded components. This allows our component to be scalable and to be used by multiple clients. If we code our components correctly, we can use this to make our components run faster and scale better. MTS will also create multiple instances of our Visual Basic apartment-threaded components so multiple clients can use the component.

Now that we understand MTS and Visual Basic, let us turn our attention to the 3-tier solution. Perhaps one of the most confusing aspects of the three-tier solution is DNA. Microsoft replaced the term three-tier with n-tier, and now n-tier has now been replaced by DNA. It is important to understand what DNA is if we are going to develop a three-tier application.

Just What is DNA?

In the beginning, DNA was an abbreviation for Distributed interNet Applications, although some documents referred to it as Distributed interNet Architecture. Eventually it mutated to Distributed interNet Application Architecture. Today it stands for Windows Distributed interNet Application Architecture. The name is appropriate, even if the abbreviation is not. DNA is an architecture on which we can build Windows applications.

People are often confused because of the word **Internet**; in fact, DNA does not necessarily involve building internet applications. Actually, it is about building applications using internet programming techniques.

Internet applications can have thousands of users and require components to handle hundreds of simultaneous requests. This means that internet programming techniques must include some methods to make components on the server scalable. One such technique centers around the idea that only the client maintains state between calls to the server, i.e. the client has a memory of what is happening between calls and the server does not. If we maintain state on the server, our server component will need to persist variables for every client currently connected; this could clearly become very costly in terms of resources if we have thousands of users. Performance considerations therefore force us to make our server components stateless. For scalable web applications, information is therefore usually stored on the client in cookies which can be read by the server. Of course, if we are moving information around in cookies, this information should be limited to the smallest size to prevent delays.

From our discussion of MTS, we know that we can build stateless Visual Basic components that run on a server. If we build the components correctly, they will be scalable. Thus, including MTS server components in our application can fulfill the basic requirements of creating an Internet type of application. The best way to use a Visual Basic middle-tier component is to build a three-tier solution.

Another way to make an application scalable is to build the component out of smaller components. We can scale the application by redistributing the components across different servers. Internet-style applications also need the ability to evolve as business requirements and technology change. By building our application with components, we will be able to update or replace individual components over time, without having to rebuild the entire application.

Thus, DNA is about building internet-like applications - applications that can evolve and that have a scalable server component that does not maintain state and a client that does maintain state. DNA could include building an Internet application, an intranet application, or a three-tier solution with a Visual Basic executable on the client.

Defining the Composition of the System

Well, that concludes our diversion into application architecture. It might have seemed a little tough-going, but it is important for all team members to understand the basic issues here. This information will have a major impact on how we design our components. So, now we've got all that under our belt, we can move on to see how to design our object interfaces from the use cases.

Remember that we looked earlier in the chapter at the use case for entering an order and identified three objects: `Product`, `Order` and `Customer`. This use case included the line:

> ➤ Actor will *Create* **Customer** if the customer does not exist

This operation contains a series of steps of its own, and can be expanded into another use case, which will specify exactly what these steps are:

Create Customer

> **Primary Actor:** Order Entry Clerk

> Actor requests to add new customer

> Actor enters customer name

> Actor enters customer address

> Actor enters customer phone number

> Actor enters customer fax number

> Actor enter customer credit card number and expiration date

> Actor saves customer information

We are going to take this use case to create a sequence diagram mapping out the sequence of events that are required to fulfill this goal. Before we even begin, you will notice that we are missing two important objects. Our use case says "Actor enters", which implies that the actor has some way to enter information into the system. In a Visual Basic application, the way for human actors to enter information will be through a user interface. We will therefore, need an additional object to perform services for the user, the User Interface, which will allow information to pass from the user to the system and from the system to the user. All of the client services will be performed by the user interface.

The other object we are missing is the object that will actually perform the updates to the database: our data services object. When building a three-tier project, the middle tier acts as a middleman between the client component and the database. The middle tier will receive requests to retrieve information from or update information to the database from the client component. The client component will gather the information and then send the request to the middle tier. The middle tier will then communicate to the database and perform the request. We therefore need a middle-tier object that will perform these services.

The middle-tier component and the user interface are two objects that are implied in the use case. Remember, the users are more concerned with the goals they want the system to accomplish for them and the services the system must perform than the actual components of the system. The developers must review the use cases, begin to draw out sequence diagrams and find the implied objects.

While we can see that the data services were separated out so that they can be placed into an MTS component for maximum efficiency, scalability and sharing of these services, you may be wondering why we separate out the business services and the client services. The client services will be very specific to the application and will generally not be very reusable. Thus, if I make an order entry application from a Visual Basic executable and remake a similar application for customers to place orders over the Internet, it is unlikely that much of my executable interface code will be reusable for my Internet application. On the other hand, the business objects that I create for my executable, such as the Customers, Orders, Order Details and Products objects, will all be easily reused in my internet application. By creating separate components that perform business services and client services, we have actually separated out the reusable components (the components that perform business services) from those that are probably not reusable (client service components, i.e. user interfaces).

The ability to upgrade the application is another reason we separate the business services and the client services. It is likely that our application will also have to be upgraded at some point to fulfill new business requirements that have resulted from the changes in technology and the market. It is likely that most of these changes will not affect the external methods and properties of the business components, but instead affect the internal rules of these objects. Thus, a change in tax laws may alter the way the order object internally calculates the sales tax, but externally there will still be the same `Save Order` method that will trigger the sales tax calculation. Thus, for the most part, when we have separate business objects we can upgrade our applications by creating internal changes to these objects that will not have any affect on the rest of the system.

When we actually change the way business is done and the interface of the business object must be changed, we can make these changes and plug these business objects into a new interface. The vast majority of the code will be reusable. Usually, only one or two objects will have to change resulting in the change of only a few interfaces. If we needed to make this change in an application where there was no separation of the business and client-service components, we would probably end up rewriting the entire application. Thus, the separation of business and client services allows us to reuse business components and easily upgrade the application.

Because the primary purpose of creating separate components that contain the business logic is for the ability to reuse and upgrade these components, their location in the physical system is usually not that important. Thus, we could place the business logic on the client computer or on a physical server. As these components do not make any direct connections to the database and they will probably maintain state, there is no requirement to place them on a server or to make them MTS components. The factors that will influence the location of the business components will usually be how often they will need to be upgraded (a continually changing component would probably be best on a server since it will only need to be replaced on one machine, rather than on every client), how easy it is to deploy the components to the client and the type of application being built.

The use case has provided us with detailed information on the interaction between the user and the client services object (the user interface). When we look at our use case, we see that it specifies that the actor will request a new `Customer` from the system. The actor will then enter the customer name, address, phone number, fax number and card number and expiration date. Finally, the actor will save customer information. Thus, the use case has given us all of the information for the communication between the user and the client-services component. Each of these operations represents a 'message' sent from the actor to the user interface, and will be represented in the sequence diagram by a line from the user to the interface.

When we reviewed the nouns in our use case, we saw that we needed a `Customers` business services component. We can see from the use case that this component will need to perform two tasks: creating a new customer (`AddNew`) and saving the customer information (`Save`).

The services that will be performed by the data services do not directly come from the use case. The developers will review the services that the business services components will need to perform, and based on these services they will decide what services the data services component will have to perform. In this case, the data services component will save a new customer and indicate whether the save was successful.

Our sequence diagram for creating a customer will thus look as follows:

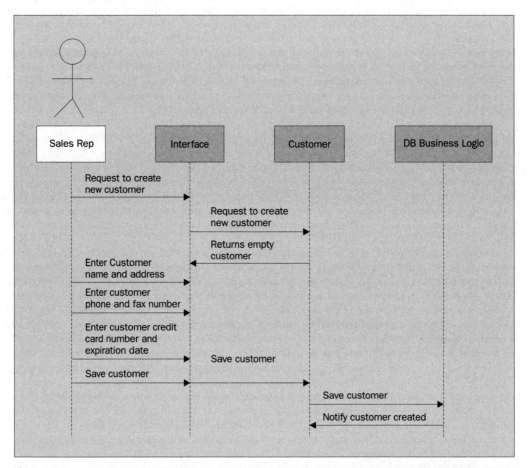

There is really an incredible amount of information in this diagram. We can now see that we will need some additional methods in our customer component. Each arrow represents a request for some object in the system to perform a service. As we said, most of these requests will center on getting information to set properties or will be the actual setting of the properties. Luckily, Visual Basic will allow us to make user interfaces that do not require us to write complicated code to allow the user to enter information into the user information. Most of the requests to the user interface for services will actually be fulfilled simply by creating a text box for the actor to type the information in (or a list or combo box to select the correct information). Other requests, such as 'Request to Create a New Order' will actually require the customer object to have a special object to perform the service (in this case Add New): an object cannot create itself out of nothing, so we need to have an object which has already been created to which we can make the request for a new Customers object. We will see how to do this in the next chapter.

Services performed by the user interface will usually involve adding text boxes or list or combo boxes. The services performed by components will involve setting properties of the object and/or calling methods. Our sequence diagram allows us to see exactly what objects we need, what methods and properties these objects will need, which objects request services from other objects, what information must be supplied to perform the service and what information has to be returned when the service is complete, and what information must be inputted by the user and returned to the user by the system. So there is really a great deal of information in our sequence diagram.

From our 'Add New Customer' diagram, we can see the following:

> The `customers` component will require an `AddNew` method (request to create new customer).

> The `AddNew` method will not require any information passed in (no parameters) but it must return a new `Customers` object (thus it must be a function and have a `Customer` object as its return value).

> The user interface will need a text box or similar control to enter customer name, address, phone and fax numbers, and credit card number and expiration date.

> While it is not explicitly stated, the information placed into the user interface will need to be passed to the customer object before the save occurs. Thus, our `Customers` object will need properties for customer name, address, phone and fax numbers, and credit card number and expiration date.

> The `Customers` object will need to have a method to save a new customer record. This request to save the information will be passed onto the middle-tier component. This `Save` method will take one parameter, a `Customers` object.

> The middle-tier component will need a method actually to save the information to the database. This `Save` method will also take a `Customers` object as a parameter. The database was not listed in this diagram as a separate component, but we could have also included it, as the database is an object of the system. This was not included to keep the diagram simple, but we will show it in a more detailed diagram below.

> The physical location of these components (what tier they will be placed on) could also be placed on the diagram.

When we add the database component to the diagram, we can see that the application is spread across three tiers. The refined sequence diagram looks as follows:

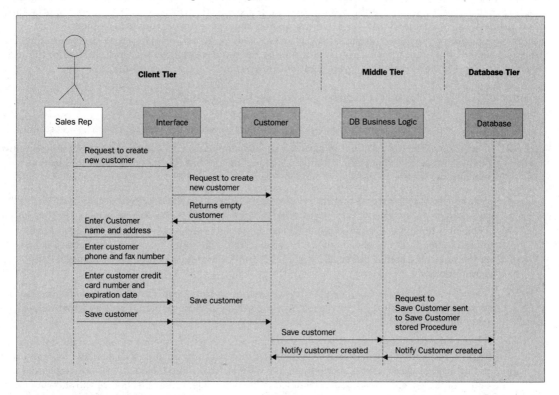

This diagram now tells us that there is a database component. The request to save a customer will be passed from the user interface to the client customer component, to the middle tier component and finally to a stored procedure in the database. We can also see where the components will be placed in our three-tier application. The developer has added numerous components and messages that the user is unaware of, such as the database, middle-tier and user-interface components, and the methods associated with these components. This is the normal process of making a sequence diagram: we begin with the information in the use case and then expand the information to include implied objects and the methods and properties of these implied objects. The sequence diagram may go through many revisions until it reaches its final version. Some of the revisions may force a rethinking of a use case and force it to be redesigned. This is the nature of iterative design.

From these sequence diagrams, we can begin to define our component's public interface. In fact, we have already identified most of the methods and properties we need. As an example, let's look quickly at the interface for the `Customers` component. We have already seen that our `Customers` component will need the following methods:

- ➢ `AddNew`, to create a new customer
- ➢ `Save`, to save the information about a customer
- ➢ `Edit`, to update the customer information

We will also need a way of retrieving a specific instance of our `Customers` object. To do this, we will add methods for moving through the collection of existing customers and retrieving a given `Customers` object:

- ➢   `MoveFirst`, to retrieve the first customer
- ➢   `MovePrevious`, to retrieve the last customer
- ➢   `MoveNext`, to retrieve the next customer
- ➢   `MoveLast`, to retrieve the last customer

The `Customers` object will also need properties that contain information about each of our customers. We can see from the use case and sequence diagram that the information we need to store requires the following properties:

- ➢   `Name`
- ➢   `Address`
- ➢   `Phone`
- ➢   `Fax`
- ➢   `CreditCardNumber`
- ➢   `ExpiryDate`

Sequence diagrams can be built using sophisticated tools such as the UML tools built by Riverton (HOW), Rational (Rational Rose or Visual Modeler) or Visio. You can also hand-draw them on pieces of paper to see the flow of your system, or use graphic programs such as SmartDraw. Use whatever works best for you and the situation you are in. If you are in a meeting with a client and need to show quickly how the components of the system may interact, a sequence diagram quickly hand-drawn can provide an easy way to view the interaction of the different components. If you are preparing documentation for your design document, you should probably use a professional tool.

The advantage of using UML is that there is no longer any guesswork involved. We still have not identified how the methods are going to work - we have not designed a detailed map of what the Visual Basic code will look like in each method, but we will do that in the physical stage. However, we have identified all of our objects and the methods and properties that will belong to these objects. We have also identified where our components will be located, how they will communicate to other objects in the system and how they will communicate to the user.

Before one line of code is actually written we know exactly what the system will do and have a very clear set of documents (the use cases and sequence diagrams) that can be shown to the user. The user can review these documents to make sure that all of the goals that the user needs the system to accomplish can be fulfilled by the system and that the system fulfills these goals in the manner that the user finds most efficient. As the more detailed diagrams may be confusing to the user, it may be best to show them diagrams that only show the interaction between the user and the user services object. When an agreement has been reached on the following items, the developers and users can sign off on the design documents:

> ➤ A list of the objects that will be required to fulfill the services of the system.

> ➤ The public methods and properties of these objects.

> ➤ How the objects will communicate to each other and to the users.

The user will know exactly what the system will do, and the developers will know exactly what they have to build. The testers will know what modules will need to be tested so that they can begin a detailed set of test plans. The educators will know exactly how the system will function so they can begin putting together user documentation and planning training for the new system.

Without use cases and sequence diagrams, there often is nothing more than a list of things the user would like the system to do. From this list, objects are identified and methods and properties for these objects are created. The developer will begin to start coding these objects, putting in the necessary methods and properties. They will then begin to build a user interface based on the developer's concept of what is needed. Once the interface is coded, the developer will begin to write code to pass information into the object. This process may result in the discovery of new methods and properties that the object will need, and these will be added. As the object is coded, the developer will discover that he needs to pass information to the middle-tier component, so methods will be added to the component. This style of coding is much like a man walking into a labyrinth in the dark with a flashlight that only produces a light beam that shines two inches out. In this situation, the person takes a step, examines the next two inches, and depending on what he sees in front of him, makes a decision where his next step will be. It is quite possible that three inches to his right, just outside of the range of the flashlight, is the exit to the labyrinth. But he will not see it unless he is lucky enough to take a turn to the right. He can only make decisions based on what the next immediate step is. He cannot look at the next fifteen steps and see how these fifteen steps may affect his next step.

However, with a detailed set of use cases and sequence diagrams, we can map out the entire system from beginning to end. We can see how changing one component of the system will affect the entire project. In our final sequence diagram, we included a final step that involved saving the customer to the database using a stored procedure. It is also possible that we could use SQL code in our middle-tier component to save the information directly to the database. Which is better? Well, what if we already had a set of stored procedures in our database to save customers? If we did not use stored procedures, we would have to write extra code in our middle-tier component. This could add one day of development time for the component. Adding this functionality into all of the Update methods in the middle-tier component may add several weeks to coding this project. Even if we had the time and financial resources to do this, is there any advantage to be gained by not using the stored procedures? That would allow us to do batch updates with disconnected recordsets in the middle tier and to check for records that failed to update due to inconsistencies. These inconsistent records can then be made consistent by the middle-tier component. Thus, by not using the stored procedures and placing the update functionality in the middle-tier component, we can move to a more flexible three-tier architecture. While this was a fairly simple example, we can investigate completely different scenarios by simply redrawing the sequence diagram.

One thing you must be careful about is not stopping once you find a solution to your problem. Once an initial set of use cases and sequence diagrams have been drawn up, the developers should come together for a brainstorming session. They should review the diagrams and try to find alternative ways of accomplishing the goals of the system. Alternative use cases and sequence diagrams should be created. Once several possible solutions have been arrived at, if this is possible (some systems only have one workable solution), the best solution should be chosen.

> **Often, the best solutions are never found because the people looking for a solution stopped at the first workable solution they came to.**

There is another advantage to using sequence diagrams: they show the details of the services performed by the user, and we can use these to make sure we have a well-designed graphical user interface (GUI). The user interface is the most important part of the system to the user. We can create an application that solves all of the problems of the business, but has a lousy user interface so no one will ever use it. Thus, once the sequence diagrams have been completed, we should go into a detailed design of the user interface. We shall see how this is done in the next section.

Creating a Prototype User Interface

To make our GUI truly user-friendly interface, we must tailor it to the needs of the user and ensure that the processes they follow require as few steps as possible. To illustrate this, let's think about designing a form that the Sales Representative will use to enter an order when a customer phones in. Rather than jumping straight in and designing a GUI, we need first look at the sequence diagram for this task. This will show us exactly what steps the Sales Representative has to carry out, so we can design the GUI to facilitate this goal.

To see how a use case and sequence diagram can help us to prototype a GUI, we will first build the sequence diagram for **Entering an Order**. Since this diagram is going to be used to build a GUI prototype, we will not be interested in the middle and data tier objects. We only want to see how the user interacts with the client side objects, so these are the only ones we will include here.

Building the Order Entry Sequence Diagram

We know that the first thing the actor (in this case the Sales Representative) will have to do is make a request to the retrieve the record for a customer who has just phoned in to place an order. This request will be made to the Customers object via the **Interface** object. There is, as we know the possibility that the customer may not exist in our Customers object or that their details may need amending. This is shown on the diagram as a dotted line from the Customers object back to itself. If this is indeed the case, we know that the flow of events will be somewhat more complicated than shown in this diagram.

As I mentioned earlier, the purpose of this diagram is to help us visualize the communication between our components. We could make a more detailed diagram showing all of these possibilities in full, but for the moment we should just be trying to get an overview of the process of making an order. Editing and creating a customer are not important to our overview of creating an order. For these reasons, we should leave these possibilities out of the diagram.

The Customers component then passes the **CustomerID** onto the Orders object, as this object will need to know which customer this **Orders** belongs to. The Orders object will also need to create an **OrderID**. Once the Customers object has returned the details about a particular customer, the Sales Representative requests the user interface to get products that belong to a certain category. The **Interface** passes this message along to the Products component, which returns the products to the user. Let's take a look and see how our sequence diagram is coming along:

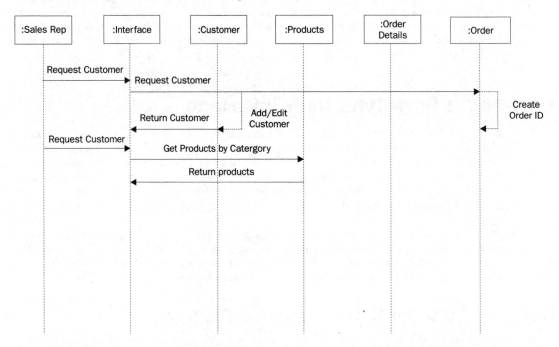

The Sales Representative will then choose a particular product and add it to the **Order Detail** component. The Sales Representative can then select more products from this category or make another request for products from a different one. The Sales Representative will repeat this process until they have completed the Order that the customer desires. A dashed line at the Interface object shows this iterative process.

Once the Sales Representative has finished, they can tell the **Interface** to save the order. This request is passed to the Orders component and the **Order Details** components, which will then add this new record to the disconnected recordset and send the recordset to the middle tier. From here, it is passed to the database so that the database can be updated. As this final part of the operation is outside the realm of our client objects, it will not be shown in our diagram:

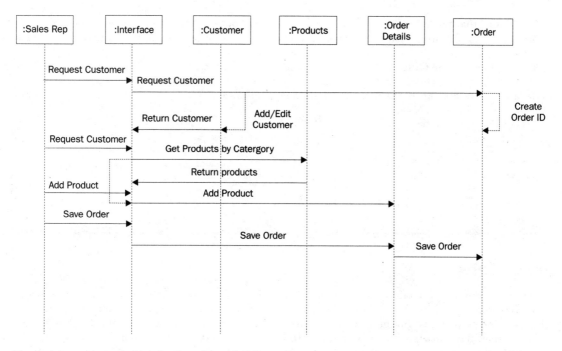

From this we can see that the first thing that happens is a customer will ring in to place an order. Then the Sales Representative will take their name and details. At this point there are three possible things that can be happening:

> The customer already exists and their details are correct.

> The customer is new and the Sales Representative will need to add them to the system.

> The customer's details have changed and the Sales Representative will need to amend them.

Since the customer information is only modified or added while adding an order, it would make sense to add and modify customers on the **Order Entry** form. Now a customer can be added or edited without interrupting the flow of the order by moving in and out of several forms. This part of the GUI could look like this:

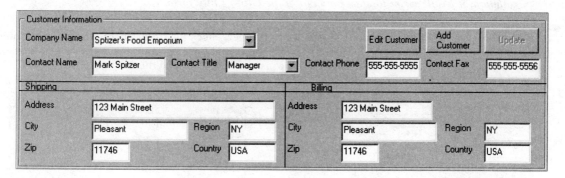

Everything that the Sales Representative needs to carry out this initial part of her task is available to him or her on this form. There is no need to swap between forms to complete this part of the task.

The next part of the Order Entry task is to pick out the products that the customer wants and to add them to the order. This sub-task is quite distinct from taking the customer details and so should occupy a separate part of the form. It could look as follows:

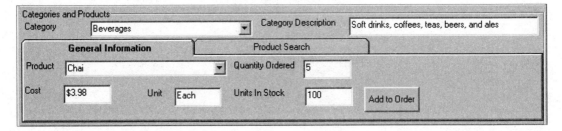

Using Tabs

We have chosen to use tabs in this section. Using tabs on a form can prevent the form from becoming overcrowded and difficult to follow. Here, our user needs to check information about a product, such as cost and availability. So there is a tab to display this general information about the product. Sometimes, particularly when new products have been entered into the system the Sales Representative is not sure to which category the products belong. Therefore we have provided a tab to perform a product search. For most of the time this option will not be used and the tab would not be selected. When it is needed it can be pulled up quickly with a single click of the tab.

The alternative is to open a special product form that allows the user to search for a product. The Sales Representative would then have to close this form when they had finished and return to the Order Entry form. If the user needs to do this a number of times while taking an order, the solution would involve moving back and forth between the forms a lot of times. This doesn't seem very efficient.

> *We could improve the situation by linking the product in the Product Search form to the Order Entry form. Now we can open the Product Search form, find the product we want and choose whether or not to add it to the current order. While this is not a bad solution, it is still easier to click on a tab in the Order Entry form.*

The final part of the Order Entry task is to select a shipper, check the order details with the customer and that they find the total price for the order acceptable and then to cancel the order or go ahead and save it. This information should therefore be grouped together and the final part of the form would probably look as follows:

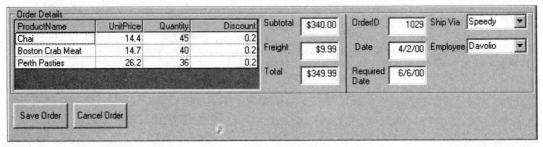

Putting All the Tabs on One Form

Putting all the separate parts together the Order Entry prototype GUI would create one large form as follows:

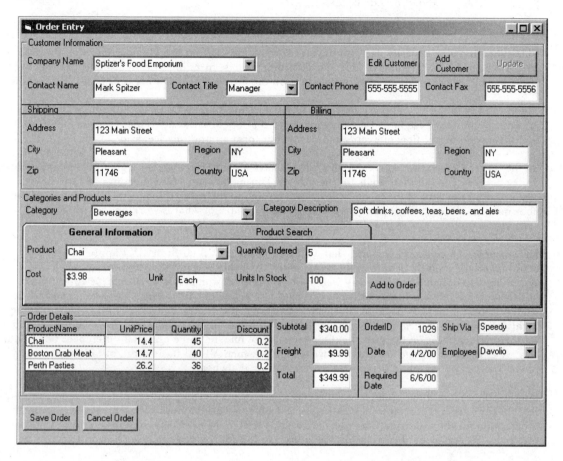

The Sales Representative can spend the entire day using this one form and never have to move away from it.

Most of the information we used to create this GUI came from the use case Create New Order. However, there is at least one aspect of the GUI that follows from the sequence diagram. We have learnt that sequence diagrams place a temporal emphasis on an interaction. They give us the order in which events occur. Bearing that in mind, take another look at the sequence diagram that we created earlier. You can see that the user first selects a customer, then a category and then a product. Once the product is selected, the user enters the required quantity of that product. If you look at the form it is arranged in this order from the top down:

> ➤ First comes the customer information section
>
> ➤ Next, is a product category dropdown listbox
>
> ➤ Next, is a product dropdown listbox
>
> ➤ Finally, the order details and order information

This allows the user to easily perform the task without having to move all over the form. We are not only using our UML diagrams to keep a user within a single form to perform a single task, but we are also using our diagrams to arrange the sections on the form in the order the user is going to use them.

The flexibility of the Visual Basic user interface will allow there to be many different ways to enter information into the system and make requests for services to the system. Ideally, though, we want to find the most efficient flow of events and design our form around this scenario.

By the time we reach the logical design stage we have already put together a great deal of information on the corporation and their goals for the project. During our consensus meetings, we will have reviewed and rated all of the business processes related to the project, listing their good, neutral and poor qualities. From these ratings we should get a good idea of what is working and what is not working.

For example, if a company currently has a custom designed Visual Basic EXE application for entering orders, used by people in the order entry clerk role; we can look at the features of this system to help design an order entry web application for customers. If the forms for entering order information are rated as highly efficient and easy to use (see our last form!), we should consider using similar forms on the web page for the customer to enter the orders. If the order entry system has a highly efficient set of forms for reviewing product information, once again we could use this as a basis for the product pages on the web site. Of course, there may be some essential differences between the way we design a web page and the way we design a regular Visual Basic form, but it is a starting point. There is no reason to be constantly reinventing the wheel.

On the other hand, if the product forms received a very poor rating, and there is a general consensus that these forms are difficult to understand or use, then we need a new way of presenting product information for the web page. The users are a great source for recommendations on how to improve processes. By reviewing their reasons why a process is poor, we can often see how to improve it.

Are Two Forms better than One?

So far, we've been extolling the virtues of a single form where the actor can perform all the duties associated with his particular role. If some of these duties are identical for different actors we need to ask the question "Are two forms for the same activity better than one?"

To address this issue, let's imagine that there is another use case called Review All Customers performed by the Sales Manager actor. Part of this Review All Customers use case is to check if a customer's information is correct. If the information is incorrect, then the Sales Manager has to modify the customer record. If the only place to modify customer information were on the Order Entry form, the Sales Manager would have to perform this task in the Order Entry form, which would make no sense, as this task has nothing to do with Order Entry.

We could make a separate form that is specifically for **Customer Review**. While this may seem redundant, as there are now two places to edit information, there are advantages to doing this. What if the Sales Manager needed to look at a customer's past sales history, balance information, and products purchased as part of the customer review? Now it makes sense to have one individual form to handle customer review.

Most likely the top half of the form will have customer information on it, the bottom half will be a tab control: one tab for sales history, a second for balance information, and a third for products purchased:

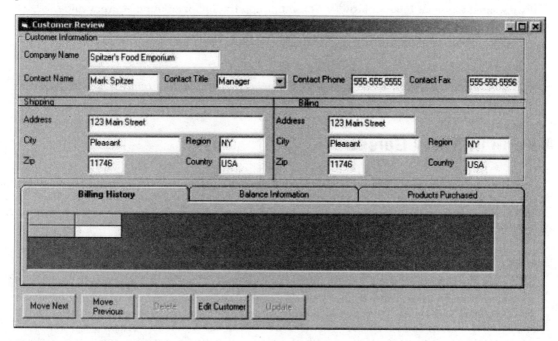

Security

An application that has different actors with different responsibilities will usually have a log in screen and some form of security. If our application employs the **Review All Customers** use case, the application should have security added and only allow a person logged in as a Sales Manager to view the **Customer Review** form. The **Customer Review** form would not be accessible to a Sales Representative.

The Sales Representative has one main role, entering orders. There will only be one form she should have access to, the **Order Entry** form. The Sales Representative would come in at the beginning of the day and log in as a Sales Representative. The application would go directly to the **Order Entry** form, as this is the only form a person in this role can access.

As for our Sales Manager, when he logs in there will either be special forms related to his role, such as the **Customer Review** form, or one form which will provide different functionality for different users, such as the **Order Entry** form.

Internet Applications

There is one other advantage to this single user interface style of programming. Building Internet and intranet applications is becoming more and more common. While we do have the ability to create dynamic web pages that can build new pages on the fly, these only work with certain browsers. Users are usually not too happy when they are constantly waiting for new pages to load. In this case, the usual standard is to minimize the number of pages and try to complete a single task on one page. Internet solutions seem to work best with a single user interface such as the one we have built above.

If we wanted to use an Internet browser to run this application on an intranet, we would not have to make any major changes in the design of my user interface. As this application is being built from the three-tier model, moving the entire project to an intranet solution would be fairly easy.

> *We must build our applications with a focus not only on current needs but also on future needs. The technology is definitely moving toward building Internet and intranet solutions, and our Visual Basic applications should be able to adapt to these changes.* ·

A Form in Many Guises

In our example, the Order Entry form allowed the Sales Representative to add orders, but not to edit or delete them. This same form *could* also provide the ability to edit an order for someone logged in as a Sales Manager. We can create one application, which presents each user with forms that are appropriate for the tasks they need to perform. Each form will provide the actor with everything they need to complete a task in the most efficient manner possible.

This approach does not mean that two different actors may not use the same forms.

In our example, the Sales Representative is allowed to create an order, but not to delete or modify them. The Sales Representative is also allowed to create and modify customers, but not delete them. The Sales Manager, on the other hand, can modify and delete the orders and delete customers. It makes sense that the Sales Manager uses the same form to edit and delete orders as the Sales Representative uses to create them, as both of them will require the same information to perform their task, i.e. order details and customer information.

Even though they are using the same form, the form may present itself differently to the two actors. When a Sales Representative views the Order Entry form, they would only have the ability to add a new order, and edit or add a customer. The buttons to delete or modify an order or delete a customer will be invisible to the Sales Representative. However, when a Sales Manager logs into the system and accesses the same form, they will have the command buttons allowing them to edit and delete orders, and delete customers - as these are tasks this actor can do.

Thus, we have one form that performs several different tasks for two different actors, but this form is designed to perform these tasks in the most efficient manner. This one form will add, delete, and modify both customers and orders.

With this type of form there is always the possibility that it will become quite complex. This is something to take account of when deciding the best way to create the GUI for a particular application.

Although this choice may be guided by the amount of coding that it requires, the main criterion when creating forms should be the user requirements.

Summary

The logical stage is the bridge between defining the goals of the users and defining components, and the services and attributes they will need, to fulfil these goals. In this stage we define the interface for our components, i.e. the public properties and methods of the components.

Our choice of framework will have a major influence on the interfaces that we will choose for our system. We saw that a three-tier architecture is more scalable and makes it easier to upgrade our application; this will result in us dividing the system services into three types: client, business and data. The client services will interact with the user and usually not be reusable. The business services will be easily upgradeable, reusable and allow for a design that can evolve as the needs of the business change. The internet-style techniques of DNA, using stateless server-side components, allow our solution to be scalable. We can further improve scalability by using Microsoft Transaction Server, which provides support for apartment threading, allowing instances of each object to be created on the server, so more than one client can access our server-side objects. MTS has the added advantage of providing support for transactions, which are a prerequisite for any e-commerce application.

The primary tools used in the logical stage are the use cases and sequence diagrams that are built from the use cases. In addition to these, the initial class diagrams can be created with public properties and methods. This stage ends with a set of documents that will allow us to move on to the detailed design of our components.

Finally, this stage also requires the prototype for the user interface to be built, so we also looked at some of the principles behind building a user-friendly GUI, and saw how we should base the design of our GUI on the sequence diagrams we created earlier in this stage.

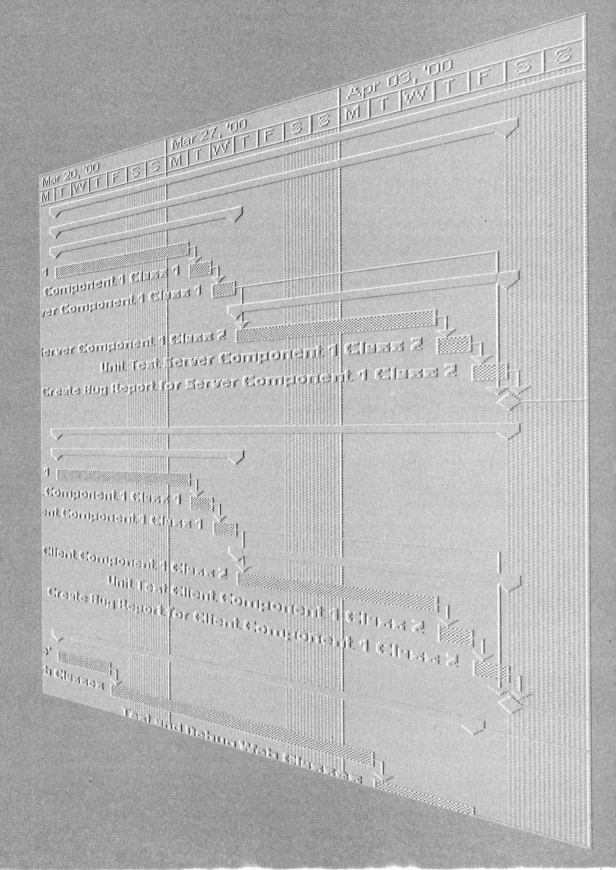

Design Phase: Physical Stage

In the logical stage we explicitly defined the components that the product will contain and the methods and properties that they would require. These definitions were based on the information derived from UML use cases and from the set of framework technologies that would support the product. The logical design was totally independent of programming language. In the physical design stage we will translate this "abstract" design into a concrete physical design for every component in the system and the means by which these components communicate. Essentially, we will define exactly how the system will be implemented.

Thus, in this chapter we will:

> Demonstrate how to allocate services (methods and properties) to components for initial class diagrams.

> Reach a final decision on the framework within which our product will operate.

> Discuss the impact of the technological framework on component design.

> Discuss communication between physically separated components

> Fully specify a component interface.

> Map out the Visual Basic code for selected services.

Thus the primary deliverables for the physical design stage are:

> A library of class diagrams defining the properties and methods of each component. This represents the final interface design of all system components.

> A library of activity diagrams mapping out the Visual Basic code for each component.

The final milestone for this stage represents the completion of the whole design. The team must reach a consensus decision that the final solution embraces the required functionality and will operate at an acceptable performance level. The final approved design will provide a complete functional specification for the development phase.

Summary of Team Focus

The team focus during the physical design phase very much lies with the developers. They, and thus ultimately the component manager, will bear the responsibility for designing components that ensure that the integrity of the logical design is maintained within the physical constraints of the chosen technology. The component managers must carefully co-ordinate the efforts of the developers in their teams. The project manager will coordinate the efforts of each team and liaise with the product manager so that everybody is working towards a common goal. The developers will give estimates as to how long it will take for them to build the components and a development phase schedule will be produced.

As the design phase nears completion the solution will be comprehensively defined so that TCO and ROI can be more accurately estimated. The logistician will be responsible for this.

The product manager will continue to work with the stakeholders and sponsors and will need to ensure that their requirements, as defined by the use cases and sequence diagrams are carried through into the actual physical design.

Testers will play a vital role in this stage. They will develop testing strategies and define criteria by which to measure the product performance. They will create methods and procedures to track problems and bugs. Based on the testing strategies, a testing plan and schedule will be created and documented. Testing will also evaluate the overall design, assist in building applications to test new methodologies or technologies, and select appropriate testing software.

Educators will review the design to determine how usable the project will be, and make recommendations on how to make the final product more efficient for the end users. Towards the end of this phase, the educators will make a more refined estimate of how long it will take to build the end-user documentation and training materials

Overview of the Physical Design Stage

In the previous stages we saw that a component encapsulates certain services, which are accessed through its interface. In the logical design stage we defined these public interfaces. The physical design stage will reveal the internal design of these components.

When it comes to the components we will be creating with Visual Basic, the physical stage is where we map out the code of all of the internal and external properties and methods of these components. This will complete the design of these components.

The physical stage will form a bridge from the interfaces we designed in the logical stage to the actual implementation of the objects with Visual Basic code in the development phase. How you make this mapping will be a topic of this chapter. We will also discuss the most efficient way to build our components and give information on making the decisions that need to be made during this stage.

There will be no coding done in the physical design stage, except to test various techniques or technologies. The physical design stage will be about deciding how the components will be coded, what should be used to code different parts of the system and a choice of technologies.

The physical stage will be based on three steps. The first step is performing research on the best way to implement a component, the second step is evaluating the research material and choosing the best option and the third step is mapping out the solution that has been chosen. This chapter will focus on these three steps. Before we look at these three steps, we must first look at one of the most important concepts of design: designing the product as a team.

Designing as a Team

One of the major advantages of using UML documents to design our components is that they give the development team the ability to design the project as a team. In many organizations, once the initial design of the interfaces is completed, the design is handed off to the developers. The developers will then divide the components amongst themselves and then lock themselves away for a few days or weeks and hammer out mountains of code. The result will be components that will all be coded differently, according to the skill, style and experience of the developer who wrote the individual code module. Testing and debugging will be difficult, as each component will be coded differently. Difficulties will be exacerbated by the lack of clear, coordinated documentation showing how the code was written and how it all fits together.

Using a single set of coding standards is the first step towards solving this problem. One set of standards will allow the testing team members to move from one developer's code module to another developer's code module without having to spend time figuring out how the code was written. Yet, this still does not solve the problem of different skill levels and different styles. Wouldn't it be great if you could take the combined knowledge and talent of the entire team to arrive at the best way to code each module? With UML you can.

It becomes much easier to understand the code if there are design documents, such as activity diagrams, that clearly map it out. Component managers should implement practices that encourage their team to clearly map out the optimum coding solution in such diagrams. How do we arrive at the best solution? Meetings can be arranged whereby the whole team decides the best way to code a particular component. When a consensus as to the best solution is achieved, this can be documented in an activity diagram. Alternatively, individual team members can work out the way to code a module and document their solution in an activity diagram. These diagrams can be circulated to the rest of the team, who can review the coding techniques outlined in the diagrams and comment on alternatives or better methods.

> When the design process becomes a collective activity the solution will represent the collective knowledge and experience of the entire team.

It is important to remember that there will often be significant overlap between each stage of the design phase. The physical stage does not wait for every sequence diagram to be complete before commencing. When code mapping and testing begins, design faults or new ideas may emerge that mean a particular component revisits the logical, or even conceptual, stage. Designing an effective solution requires a significant amount of work and requires planning, creativity and a real commitment to finding the best possible solution. I think it is safe to say that a team of peers working together, rather than a team of individuals working separately, will achieve the best design.

We now need to discuss exactly what is involved in choosing the best solution for your product.

Choosing the Best Solution

The first logical stage in deciding on the best solution for the physical design of your components is to research your options.

Researching the Best Solution

Researching a solution consists of first gathering information from all of the available resources on the issue, and then using that research to create test applications to find the best solution. Finding information is not very difficult with Visual Basic.

One editorial in Visual Basic Programmers Journal commented that one of the major reasons developers chose Microsoft products to build their applications was the wealth of available information. With regard to Visual Basic, this is especially true. A "Visual Basic" search on the Wrox Press site brings up 115 books. The Amazon site lists over 90 books with Visual Basic in the title. Visual Basic has become an extremely complex programming language but, no matter what the topic, there will almost certainly be a book or article on it.

While the MSDN library (Microsoft's library of information on their products - available on their web site and on CD) has received quite a few complaints, it is still an incredibly valuable resource. There are also many additional SDKs (Software Development Kits - special informational files for Microsoft products) that provide additional help. One example is MDAC (Microsoft Data Access Components) that provides information on data access technologies such as ADO, OLE DB, ODBC and ADO MD.

The MSDN allows you to do searches on key words. Unfortunately, the search often brings up dozens of possible titles. Finding the right title might be difficult. Sometimes it is easier to highlight the word in your code that you want help on and click F1 than it is to type the word into the MSDN and search.

In addition to the MSDN and books, we have magazines such as Visual Basic Professional Journal, dozens of web sites such as devx.com and various groups around the world that provide assistance with Visual Basic. If you still can't find the answer, there are still more resources to turn to. Microsoft has the Microsoft Consulting Services for solving the problems of large corporations and the Microsoft Solution Providers for solving the problems of smaller corporations. Of course, if you have a coding problem, there is always Microsoft Support.

When approaching any new project, it is always best to start by searching through the MSDN, `Microsoft.com` and the Visual Basic web sites. While you may not find the specific answer you are looking for, you will often gather code samples and articles that give you enough information to experiment and find the right answer for your problem.

Once information has been gathered from every available resource, you start testing in the environment that your project will run under. You create small prototype testing applications that will test the code to see what its limitations will be. How long will it take to return 1,000 records from a middle tier component running under MTS with 50 simultaneous requests to the component? The answer to such questions depends on the network, the server, the client and a host of other factors. Only through testing can you find the answers for your physical configuration. Based on those answers, you can decide if the solution fits within the constraints of the system. You can test your own coding solutions, third party solutions and your own code that exists from previous projects. Your tests should see how well these solutions meet your project's requirements.

You should carefully document all of your research and your testing. You will use this information to decide what is the best solution for your project. You can also use the results of your tests to determine what are the best methods to code your components

Once you have performed a series of tests and gathered information, you must determine the best solutions for your project. There will be many choices. The first choice is what are we going to use to build each component. Let us look at this issue.

Build, Buy or Reuse?

When deciding how a component should be created you have three choices. The first is to build the component from the ground up. The second is to reuse existing code written by your development team (or another team within your company). The third is to use third party components.

Writing code from the ground up is usually the most costly and difficult. Writing code requires time, training and expertise. Writing your own code also means first performing tests to find the best way to code your component, then performing unit testing of each portion of the component and finally, testing the component as part of the whole system. All of this takes considerable time and money. There is one major advantage to writing your own component: you can customize the component to meet the exact needs of your project.

Using existing components has several advantages. If the component was properly built, it has been documented and tested as an individual component. Therefore, you can save a great deal of time and expense. The usual problem with using existing components is that they usually cannot do exactly what you need them to do. If it is code written with components and you only need to modify a few components, it may be well worth reusing the code.

The greatest danger of code reuse is that the code may not have been properly written. There is an old story about someone using someone else's code, completing a project with it, and then finding out that the code does not work properly. When the person who used the code in the project goes to the person who wrote the code and asks them about the problem, the person who wrote the code says that they had that problem with the code, too. Make sure any code you are reusing or buying has been thoroughly tested and works properly before using it. Also, make sure that you will not spend more time modifying it to your needs than the time that it would take to build it from the ground up.

Using third party components can save a great deal of time. Just be careful to get your components from a reliable source and to use them in the way in the manner in which they were intended. Most third party components are precompiled. This means that you cannot modify them, and that they often have many extra methods and properties that you do not need for your application. This can bloat your application.

Each choice has positive and negative attributes. Which is best will depend on the application and the components you are building. By choosing to build your application with components, you can choose the best solution for each component.

Each choice you make during design has a set of risks. Each choice must be made based on the business requirements of the application, the constraints on resources such as time, number of developers and costs, and what is considered an acceptable risk. One choice Visual Basic programmers seem to hate to make is to use something other than Visual Basic for any part of their Visual Basic application. Sometimes, though, Visual Basic may not be the best choice.

When is Visual Basic not the Right Choice?

There have been endless articles on how to do things with Visual Basic that the language was never meant to do. There are articles and books devoted to using pointers in Visual Basic, changing the functionality of controls and making them do things they never were designed to do, and even how to multi thread Visual Basic components. While we can do these things in Visual Basic, the question really is, *"Should* we do these things in Visual Basic?"

An interesting story revolves around a book that is one of the better books on Visual Basic 5. This book gave a great deal of detailed information on how to do some of the more difficult things in Visual Basic, such as using API functions in Visual Basic. The book also showed how to make Visual Basic do all sorts of things with pointers and other things that the language was never meant to do. This book came with a very useful code library that thousands of people used in their projects.

Everything worked fine until the next release of Visual Basic. The author (and the users of his code) discovered that some of the functions in the code library from the book did not work with the new version of Visual Basic. It turned out that Microsoft plugged a few holes and changed a few things, and some of the tricks the author used to work around Visual Basic no longer worked with Visual Basic 6.

He complained to Microsoft. Microsoft explained that he was doing things that were unsupported and that Microsoft could not be expected to make sure that every unsupported technique people use with Visual Basic is compatible from one version to the next. Microsoft spends a great deal of time and work making sure that supported options work from one version to the next. The author was outraged that Microsoft would not make a minor change in the next release of Visual Basic so that his unsupported techniques would still work. The author published a letter and said that he was disappointed with Visual Basic and would not program with the language anymore.

This situation, which really happened, led me to think about how I programmed in Visual Basic. I had made Visual Basic do some intense things, such as using memory mapping and using pointers to get the parent in class hierarchies.

A pointer is a variable that you can use to store a memory address. The address stored in a pointer usually corresponds to the position in memory where a variable is located, but it can also be the address of a function.

I began to realize that there were other solutions than bending Visual Basic so that it could do things it was not meant to do. I developed a simple set of rules to use when I found that Visual Basic could not do something I needed. They are as follows:

➤ If I need a control to do something that the control cannot do, I will first investigate third party controls. If someone else has already built a control that does what I need, it makes sense to use it instead of forcing a control to work in a way it was not designed to. If you want a control to do something that is reasonable, you can almost be certain that many people needed the same thing. Where there is a need, there is a market, and where there is a market, there usually is a solution. If no control exists that has this functionality, I will try to find another way of doing it. Only when there is no third party alternative, and there is no other solution, will I make a control do something it was not designed to do.

➤ If Visual Basic cannot do a task and C or C++ can, write a C or C++ Dynamic Link Library (DLL). A DLL is a COM-enabled file with a `.dll` extension. Generally, DLLs are made up of a set of classes that that are blueprints for the creation of COM objects. The DLL will be used by Visual Basic to do the task Visual Basic cannot do. Because we have designed COM components, and not a monolithic application, we can choose to make any component from whatever is the best development tool. Thus, I can write 95% of my application using Visual Basic, but the last 5%, which consists of a few components, can be written in C++. I can also write 75% of my code in Visual Basic, 5% in C++ and 20% using third party add-ins. The goal of the physical stage is to choose the best option for each component, not find a way to use Visual Basic for every part of your application no matter what it takes.

➤ Using pointers in Visual Basic makes sense when it comes to using the `AddressOf` function to work with the Windows API functions that require pointers as parameters. This is the one area in which Visual Basic pointer use is supported by Microsoft and a great deal of work has gone into the language to make it compatible with the Windows API functions. Other than accessing a Windows API function, if you are thinking of using pointers in Visual Basic, you probably should be thinking about using a C++ DLL.

In general, any large Visual Basic development team should have at least one C/C++ programmer who can write small DLLs to do the jobs Visual Basic cannot handle. If you are a smaller team and cannot afford a C++ programmer, train one of your Visual Basic programmers to work in both languages. If you cannot get or train a C++ programmer, look into third party solutions.

Using unsupported methods is not wrong - it's just risky and time consuming. When I wrote the memory map program (a program that stores data in an area of memory to be used by components in different processes), I used a code sample from a reliable source. It worked sometimes and other times it did not. We tried everything we could to get it to be stable, but we never made it work properly. Finally, we called Microsoft Support. Microsoft Support helped us even though technically we were doing something we should not have been doing. It turned out that the code sample had a number 2 in one of the pointer formulas that should not have been there, so we were writing in memory somewhere we shouldn't have. It took us about two weeks to straighten it all out. I am certain that a C DLL could have been written in a few days.

For the most part, when you try to make Visual Basic do something it should not be doing, you end up spending a long time making it work. Doing pointers in Visual Basic usually means creating a General Protection Fault (i.e. a fatal error) in the Visual Basic IDE a few dozen times until you get it right. Even worse, unsupported techniques may not work in the next release of Visual Basic. If you need to upgrade your application, you may find yourself rewriting your entire application to work with the new version of Visual Basic if you are using unsupported techniques. Finally, unsupported techniques may work on some platforms, but fail on others.

Some of these techniques allow you to do very powerful things with Visual Basic, but you really need to consider the possible consequences of using these methods in an Enterprise- wide application.

For the parts of your application that you do choose to use Visual Basic for, you should map out how they will be coded in the physical stage.

Resource Estimates

Once the choices have been made, you can give an accurate estimate of what the total cost of the project is going to be. You can also give a good estimate of how long the project will take and the number of people that will be required to build the project.

You can use a tool such as Microsoft Project 98 to map out different solutions to help you find the best project plan. For example, you may be considering how it will affect the overall project if you use three in-house developers or if you hire a consultant for a fourth developer on the team. Will the extra time required to develop with three in house developers be great enough to justify the expense of the consultant? What will the consultant cost? Another question might be, "How much extra time and cost will be added to the project if we use a third party component versus building the component ourselves?" All of these types of questions can be answered by making different schedules and resource plans for each possible situation.

You can make a copy of the Microsoft Project 98 template we created earlier for each solution you want to investigate. Using the templates, you can then map out each solution in terms of time and resources. Doing this can give you a good estimate as to what will be required for each solution. These different solutions can be shown to the client so they can see how each solution affects the available resources.

When the final solution is chosen, it should be documented. The risks associated with this solution should also be documented as well as the resources required for this final solution.

Allocating Services to Components

One of the first tasks of the physical stage is to create class diagrams, which will allocate services to our business services and data services components. The aim is to arrive at a simple static view of the classes that will make up our system. The methods and properties defined in these class diagrams define the component interface. Ultimately, when component design has been completed, the interface defined by these class diagrams become a contract as to the public methods and functions that the classes will provide in their interface. As we stated earlier, this interface should not change.

Designing the Business Services Component

When we analyzed our use cases for the order processing procedure, in the previous chapter, we identified a few of our business services components: Orders, Customers and Products. When we developed our sequence diagram we added two more components: the DB Business Logic object (enabling other objects to communicate with the database) and the Interface object (visual interface of the system). These sequence diagrams mapped out the communication between components and showed the services these components will need to perform. With this information, combined with that in our use cases, we can start to identify the components of the system and their public properties and methods.

Let's have another look at our *Create Customer* sequence diagram:

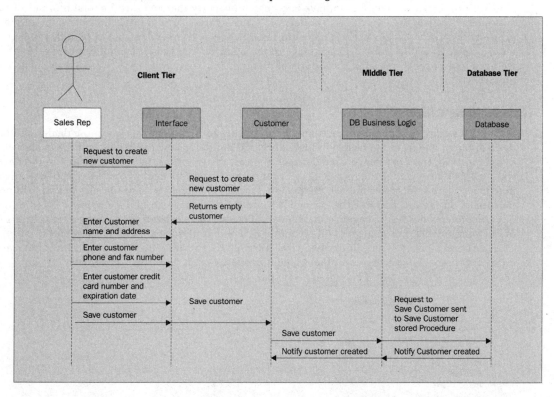

From this diagram we identified two methods for our Customers object: AddNew and Save. Our *Update Customer* sequence diagram must include a request to return an existing customer. Thus we identified the need for methods to navigate through the collection of existing customers to select the appropriate one: Move Previous, Move Next, Move First and Move Last, Get Item, along with an Edit method. In addition we will need a Delete method (we did not discuss the *Delete Customer* use case since this was not a valid goal in the **order entry clerk** role).

We are building the customer component so that it has the ability to return a customer object thus the component must contain all of the properties of a customer - Name, address etc. - that we defined in the previous chapter.

OK, we have identified methods and properties for our Customers component using our sequence diagrams and use cases. We have to stop and think here. The first question we must ask ourselves is: "Does it make sense to put all of these methods and properties into one class, say clsCustomers?" The answer, as I'm sure you knew, is no.

For example, our Customers component needs to perform the service of returning an empty Customers object when requested to create a new customer, that is, it must execute the AddNew method. If the AddNew method were part of our clsCustomers class, we would first have to create the clsCustomers object and then we would need to call the AddNew method in this object to make a new clsCustomers object. We would be asking the customer object to make itself once it already existed!

Another property we might like to have is a Count property that gives us the total number of customer objects in the Customers collection. Once again, it would make little sense to add the property to clsCustomers. Each object in the Customers collection should be independent of any other object. If an object has no knowledge of the other objects then it cannot perform a count. What we need to do here is put all of these sorts of methods into a separate class: we need to create a class hierarchy.

Class Hierarchies

In the real world, objects are made somewhere. If we want a new car, we go to the dealer and have them order us one from the factory. The factory will build our new car for us, and the dealer will deliver it. If we want to change something on the car, then we must take the car back to the dealer, who will then arrange for the repair. If we want to get some information on this type of car, such as how many were sold, we would ask the dealer. The dealer manages all of the services we will need performed on the car. Just like the car needs someone to manage all of the services related to the car, our components need a manager to manage all of the services related to the component. In the case of our components, this manager will be another class that performs these services on the clsCustomers class. Thus, in our two-class hierarchy we would have a managed (bottom) class, clsCustomers, containing all of the relevant properties that describe a customer:

clsCustomers
CustomerID:Text CustomerName:Text ContactName:Text Address:Text City:Text Region:Text PostalCode:Text Country:Text Phone:Text Fax:Text

Normally when we list the properties and methods of a component in a class diagram, a plus sign (+) means the method or property is public, a minus sign (-) means that the property or method is private and a pound sign (#) is used for friend properties (properties that can be seen by everything within the component but cannot be seen outside it). All of our customer properties and methods are public, so in this case we have omitted these signs.

The managing (top) class, `clsCustomersManager`, will contain all of the methods and properties that will be performed on `clsCustomers`:

Managing Class
Count:Integer
AddNew() Edit() Delete() Movefirst() Movelast() MoveNext() MovePrevious() Update()

We can perform this process for all of our components. Our `Products` component, for example, will have different properties but the same methods as the `Customers` component. Thus we will find that `clsProductsManger` may well be identical to `clsCustomersManager`.

> **When designing a Visual Basic class, all of the methods in the class should be services that the object created from the class will perform. If you have a method that performs a service on the object, such as `AddNew`, then it belongs in a separate managing class. Any property that belongs only to the object, such as customer name, should be in the class that belongs to the object. Any property that is shared amongst all of the objects, such as `Count`, belongs in a managing class.**

Not all classes on the bottom of the hierarchy have only properties in their interface. If we wanted to build an animation program with an animated cat, the cat component might look as follows:

clsCat
Color:String Length:Integer · Stripes:Boolean Friendly:Boolean Stray: Boolean Fixed:Boolean
Meow() Walk() WagTail()

Walk, Meow and WagTail are all services that are performed *by* the cat object, not services performed *on* the cat object. Our managed class does not perform any services, so it will not have any public methods.

OK, so we have a two-class hierarchy consisting of a managed class (`clsCustomers`) and a managing class (`clsCustomersManager`). Together, the two classes would make up our `Customers` component. What happens, however, if we have more than one type of customer? Consider the following hypothetical situation. Different users at Northwind may actually need to look at different types of customers. For instance, a Sales Representative may need to view all customers during their working day; but a Sales Analyst at Northwind might need to look at all the customers who have made orders very recently. Or a rather interested Sales Manager somewhere may need to view all customers who are regularly spending over $1000 an order, say. In other words, each different user may need to view a different `Customers` collection. In this situation we would have to deal with three collections of customers. The best way to handle this would be to create a three-level class hierarchy:

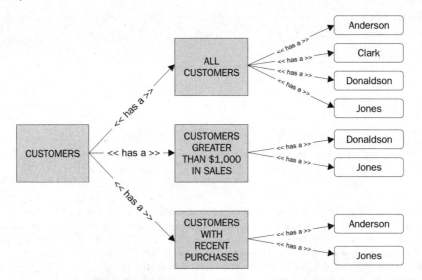

So what's happening in this diagram? Well, if you think back to our two-level class hierarchy, you'll recall that we had a managing class and a managed class. In the diagram above, our managed class is represented by the rightmost collections of actual customer details. And our managing class is in the middle of the diagram, managing those collections of customer details. We've now introduced a third level class (the top class) - which itself manages what was our original managing class.

This is a fairly complex hierarchy. To actually build this component we would need to map out what each class would do and how it would communicate with the other classes. Bearing this in mind, you should not use hierarchies unless you have a need for them. If you find yourself building a hierarchy and the methods and properties all belong to one object, it is likely you should be building a single class. If all of the methods act on one class, and all of the properties belong to that class, then it is unlikely that you need a hierarchy.

A final point to note before we move on is that we can create, for example, a `Products` class hierarchy in a similar manner. If you recall, we noted that the public methods for this class would be the same as for the `Customers` class but the public properties would be different. When public properties are moved in to the bottom class, then `clsProuductsManager` will be virtually identical to `clsCustomersManager`.

We are still not at a stage where we know the exact design of our components. In Chapter 7 we discussed our reasons for choosing a three-tier framework for our project: scalability and upgradability. We now have to choose how to distribute our objects in within this framework.

Distributing the Business Services Objects

In our discussion of the logical three-tier model in Chapter 7, we classified components according to the services they provided:

> ➤ Data services tier - where the components that communicate directly with the data source reside.

> ➤ Business services tier - components that service the client application and usually encapsulate business logic, which validates the data being passed to or from the server (see discussion on Business Rules in Chapter 6).

> ➤ Client service tier - the user interface.

How clear cut is this classification? The main responsibility of our top class (`clsCustomersCollectionManager`) is simply to retrieve a particular `Customers` collection. This functionality could be incorporated into a user control on the user interface. Thus, in effect we are logically spreading our component over two tiers. The next question is: should we physically locate the managing and managed classes on a separate server? With regard to our order processing application executable, the answer is almost certainly "No". Our managing class contains no methods for directly retrieving and manipulating data on a database server, as this is handled by our data services component.

> *The presence of such methods would be a good reason for putting them on a separate server, where they would be most effective in dealing with data manipulation and transactions. The managed class could be placed on the client, where its responsibility would be to maintain state.*

Therefore it makes most sense for the `Customers` component to reside entirely on the client. When the data services component receives a request from `clsCustomersManager` to update a `Customers` object, a disconnected recordset will be passed from the data services server to the client. The managed class objects will contain a disconnected recordset object that will be used to view and update that object's information. We could represent this as follows:

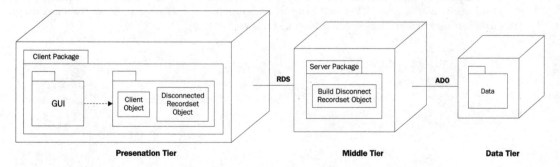

Of course, the "data tier" in our order processing application is simply an `mdb` file that will reside on the data services server. Thus in a physical sense this is two-tier architecture.

We must bear in mind what we are building here is a fairly **fat client**. The client will have numerous components that will communicate with the interface and the data services tier. These client components will not have a connection with the database and, since we don't want them to be constantly communicating with the database to get data, they will store data on the client-side. The client can read the records and return the records to the data services tier to make changes to the database. Yet, having records on the client-side makes this an even fatter client. If this is an order processing application being used by order entry clerks connected to the server through the network, this is a good solution. You want the information to be readily available. As long as you place limits on the amount of information on the client and don't allow huge amounts of data on the client, this will work efficiently.

Yet, this is not a very workable solution for the Internet, which requires a **thin client**. If we wanted a thin, dynamic, interactive Internet client, we could only allow very small sets of data to reside on the client. To resolve this we could place the client-side objects onto a web server. These objects could pass the data to an ASP page, which properly formats the information and passes it back to the client in a standard HTML page.

> *An ASP page is a web page associated with Internet Information Server (IIS), that allows a request to be passed to a server, be processed, and return an HTML page built on the fly.*

In this way, we could create a `Products` object that works in our order-processing project on the client, but resides on the web server in an Internet application, which allows customers to view the products. The Internet application will pass back HTML pages with product information to the client. Therefore, we can use one object to build two applications that have completely different requirements, i.e. a thin and a fat client.

Our Server object has no properties and so it will have no history and no memory of what was requested, i.e. the server does not have any state. The middle-tier objects are simply performing a task. When the task is done they have no memory that they did it.

Designing the Data Services Class

The data services class will contain methods for retrieving and updating recordsets for objects. We will discuss designing a data services class for a 3-tier solution. A data services component in a 3-tier solution will run on a server. We will call this component a server object. A general class diagram for the data services server object would look as follows:

Server Object

+ ValidIDUserPassword (v_sUserID: String, v_sPassword: String)
+ ReturnCustomerRecordset (v_sUserID: String, v_sPassword:
    String,v_sParameter: String): Recordset
+ ReturnEmploeeRecordset (v_sUserID: String, v_sPassword:
    String,v_sParameter: String): Recordset
+ ReturnOrderDetails (v_sUserID: String, v_sPassword:
    String,v_sParameter: String): Recordset
+ ReturnOrdersRecordset (v_sUserID: String, v_sPassword:
    String,v_sParameter: String): Recordset
+ ReturnProductsRecordset (v_sUserID: String, v_sPassword:
    String,v_sParameter: String): Recordset
+ReturnShippersRecordset (v_sUserID: String, v_sPassword:
    String,v_sParameter: String): Recordset
+UpdateCustomerRecordset (v_sUserID: String, v_sPassword:
    String,v_sParameter: String): Recordset
+UpdateEmployeeRecordset (v_sUserID: String, v_sPassword:
    String,v_sParameter: String): Recordset
+UpdateOrderDetailsRecordset (v_sUserID: String, v_sPassword:
    String,v_sParameter: String): Recordset
+UpdateOrdersRecordset (v_sUserID: String, v_sPassword:
    String,v_sParameter: String): Recordset
+UpdateProductsRecordset (v_sUserID: String, v_sPassword:
    String,v_sParameter: String): Recordset
+UpdateShippersRecordset (v_sUserID: String, v_sPassword:
    String,v_sParameter: String): Recordset

As we stated in the last chapter, there are no properties in the data services component because it is stateless - every call the client application makes to the Server object is viewed as a new client. Afterwards, the Server object has no memory of the client and the property values would not persist from one call to the next.

> *This works the same way as an HTML page: using a browser you connect to a server, which returns the page you are requesting. Once the data has been returned to the client, the server and the browser have no knowledge of each other.*

In the case of this component, all of the data resides on a single database and there are only two public methods for each business component: `Return` and `Update`. We could further divide this into separate classes so that we have one class for every business component, but there is no need to do that with only two methods per object. Since all of the components will share the same databases they will have the same internal code for connecting to the database.

What would happen, though, if this data were contained in several databases? Perhaps the employee information is in a completely different database than the rest of the data. In this case, if we were to keep the employee information in the Visual Basic class with the rest of the components, we would need two separate sets of database information. For those of you familiar with the ADO, this means that we will need two connection strings and two connection objects. We would need to place `Select Case` statements in our code to check which database we are connecting to. None of these are good coding techniques. Thus, when it comes to the server component, it may make sense to create separate classes to service different business components if the data comes from different databases. This will make a component that has tight cohesion, as each component will be working from one database.

We've covered a lot of ground in defining the design of our components and their interfaces. However, we are not finished yet. We know that our data services and business services components will reside on different servers but we have not discussed how they will communicate. We have talked about passing data between the two servers in disconnected recordsets, but we have not discussed in any detail the technology that will facilitate this, namely ADO. These framework technologies, along with MTS, will have considerable impact on the way in which we design our components.

ActiveX Data Objects (ADO)

ADO is a set of ActiveX controls (effectively COM objects) that provide programmatic access to Microsoft's latest underlying data access technology - OLE DB. This is a defined set of interfaces that all data sources (relational databases, E-mail, Directory Services, to name but a few) can implement through special drivers, known as providers, and thereby expose their data content in a uniform manner. OLE-DB relies on a low-level Application Programming Interface (API) designed for use with languages such as C++. ADO wraps these interfaces into ActiveX objects that can be used within a far wider range of languages (Visual Basic, Java, VBScript etc.).

The main reasons that we have chosen ADO is so that we can retrieve data from our data source (an `.mdb` file) and pass it in a disconnected recordset from our data services server to our client, where it can be manipulated locally (when the recordset is later reconnected, the server can be updated). ADO allows applications to work in disconnected and stateless environments such as the Internet. Thus ADO is the perfect method of data access in a Windows DNA environment. One of the major benefits we will derive from the use of ADO, is the ability to pool connection objects.

Connection Pooling

The `Connection` object is what connects the consumer to the provider. That is, it's the link between the program and the data. You actually don't need to explicitly create a connection object to do this (you pass a Connection String directly to a `Command` or a `Recordset` object). However, establishing a connection to a data source is a time-consuming event. If you are going to be getting data from the data source more than once it is well worth creating a connection object because, as you will see, the connection won't have to be established each time.

Connection Pooling means that ADO will not actually destroy `Connection` objects unless it really needs to (this is subject to a timeout value - if the connection hasn't been reused within this time, it will be destroyed). So, you open a connection, perform some data access, close the connection and from your point of view, the connection is closed. However, underneath OLEDB keeps the connection in a pool, ready for it to be used again. If you then decide that you need to open the same connection again, you will be given a `Connection` object from the pool of connections, and ADO doesn't actually have to perform all of the expensive data store stuff again. You may not necessarily get your original object back, but may get one that matches the same connection details. In fact, existing objects will be given to anyone who requests them, so this is even better in a multi-user system.

One important point to note about connection pooling is that connections will only be reused if they match the exact connection details. So on multi-user systems, if you specify the same data store, but different user names and passwords, then you will create a new connection, rather than having one reused from the pool. This may seem a disadvantage, but pooling must be done this way to avoid breaking security.

Communication Between Components

The manner in which we distribute our components and how they will be connected will affect the way we code our components, the interfaces we will create and the type of security we will implement (see later). If we were placing all of our components on one computer, then our components would communicate using COM. However, COM objects can communicate directly only if they are running in the same process space. Since we are placing our data and business services components on different machines, we will need to choose some other method of communication. The most common choices for connecting client and server components are Distributed COM (DCOM) and Remote Data Services (RDS).

> With regard to our project, RDS is the perfect choice. For our web application, we can use RDS to make the connection between the server object and the client through a Microsoft Internet Information Server (IIS), using HTTP. RDS also supports DCOM, so for our order processing application this can be our means of communication across a local network.

OK, let's find out how this works.

RDS and DCOM

RDS is a powerful technology that allows us to retrieve recordsets from remote databases and manipulate these databases in client-side script, in a way that minimizes network traffic. Using RDS, an entire set of data can be returned to the client. The client can then filter and manage the recordset without the server.

This is an ideal scenario for our E-commerce site. Let's think again about this application, which allows customers to view the products on a web site. Say a customer is browsing through one range of products and then decides to look at a completely different range. Without RDS, the browser would have to request new data, wait for a response from the server, receive the new data and then reload the page. With RDS, all of the data is on the client so the speed of the web application approaches that of more traditional desktop applications.

The data is held on the client in an ADOR `Recordset` object. This is a smaller, lightweight version of the full ADO `Recordset` object (it doesn't have the explicit `Command` and `Connection` objects). The ADOR `Recordset` object is designed for transmission over the relatively low-bandwidth connections of the Internet and so has a smaller footprint in memory. Our application won't require a constant data connection because the connection is severed without affecting the data. This is because RDS is very closely associated with ADO, which, as we know, provides disconnected recordsets.

How does all this work? Essentially, RDS works by making the connection between the server object and the client through a Microsoft Internet Information Server (IIS) web server. As we discussed earlier, COM objects cannot communicate directly if they are not running in the same process space, therefore there needs to be a mechanism by which they can communicate when they are running in different processes. A full description of how this comes about would include a detailed discussion of the RDS object model. This is beyond the scope of this book.

> For a full description, I would refer you to Professional ADO RDS Programming with ASP, ISBN 1861001649, published by Wrox Press.

However, we must briefly mention the `RDS.DataSpace` object. This object runs on the web client, creates COM objects on an IIS server and returns an object reference from the server to the web client application. These references are called proxies and are a bit like your television remote control. In a similar manner that you can press a button on your remote control to make something happen on your television, a client-side proxy object is the remote control that can be used to make something happen on a server side object across the Internet.

> A *proxy* is an object that provides a pointer to another object in another process. The other object in the other process is known as a *stub*.

RDS will make a proxy of the Server object on the client. The proxy will look exactly like the Server object, that is, it will have the same public properties and methods as the Server object. As far as the client application is concerned, the Proxy object is identical to the Server object. The client will make requests to the Proxy object, and the RDS will pass this request to and from the Server object on the server. This is called marshalling.

Marshaling, through an IIS Web Server, is done using **HyperText Transport Protocol (HTTP)** - the standard Web protocol. The following diagram may help to explain how marshalling works:

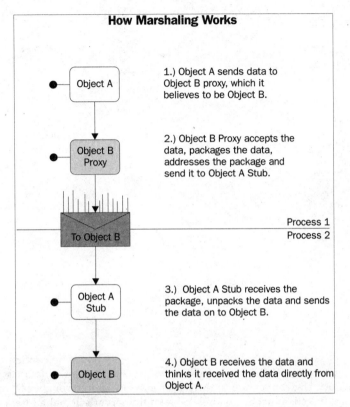

Marshaling is the process that must occur when a proxy communicates with a stub. When they communicate with one another, the message must be packaged for transport across process boundaries. After the message is packaged, it is sent (copied) form the proxy to the stub. When the stub receives the message, it must be unpackaged and sent on to the server object. Marshaling does not include the instantiation or destruction of objects, but is the activity of passing data across process boundaries.

The connection to a Server object using RDS would look as follows:

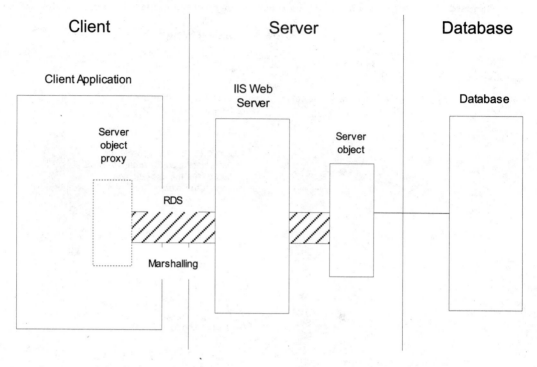

The major advantage of this technique is that the client only has to be configured to have an Internet or an intranet connection. RDS using HTTP allows users to access the database on any client via an Internet connection. The connection to the server may be made through a Domain Server Name (DSN). Therefore, the client needs no knowledge of the server's actual address or, in fact, any information on the server whatsoever. This allows the DSN address to act as a gateway that may actually represent any number of actual Web Servers.

The really great thing about RDS is that as well as supporting HTTP - it also supports DCOM.

> *DCOM is a Microsoft technology that enables COM components to communicate with each other across a network. DCOM extends COM in a transparent fashion, such that any existing COM component can be remotely used without ever changing a single line of code (although it is important to remember that a COM component written without any consideration to DCOM specific issues, probably won't be efficient or scalable). DCOM is language neutral. This means that any language that can produce COM components can have these components run over DCOM. A very good introduction to DCOM can be found in the book VB COM, published by Wrox Press.*

ADO disconnected recordsets are optimized for use with COM/DCOM so DCOM is the perfect means of communication between remote COM components on a local area network, without HTTP. This is a perfect solution for our order processing application!

> DCOM can be difficult to configure when there are thousands of clients (such as for a web application) but is an excellent choice for Intranet or internal applications.

Below is a summary list of components required for an RDS project:

> ➤ **ADO**

> ➤ **Visual Basic ActiveX DLL:** You can actually build your server components as a Visual Basic ActiveX DLL or as a Visual Basic IIS application. The ActiveX DLL will give you a greater degree of control over who can access your data over the Internet than an IIS application. IIS applications, though, give you more flexibility and perform better when there are dozens of forms.

> ➤ **Microsoft Internet Information Server:** This is required for RDS to connect to the server using the HTTP protocol and the Internet. This must be an NT 4.0 Web Server with the Option Pack installed (RDS is installed with the Option Pack by default).

> ➤ **Database:** A database for which there is an OLE DB provider.

> ➤ **Client Machine:** This computer must also be connected to the Internet - usually through an Internet service provider (ISP). To deploy the client application, use the Visual Basic Package and Deployment wizard, which will ensure that both ADO and RDS are installed on the client machine.

Effect of MTS

Finally, before we start creating our activity diagrams we need to consider how the use of MTS will affect the design of our components. Running our components in MTS will add some activities to our diagrams and we at least need to discuss these MTS activities. As we discussed previously, MTS offers two main advantages to our product:

> ➤ It provides scalability by managing object lifetimes.

> ➤ It provides support for transactions.

Object Lifetimes

One of the principal reasons that MTS can easily allow many users to access our objects is that they are only around as long as we need them. When we create an object that is being hosted in MTS, which requires transactional support, the request is intercepted by MTS, which creates an MTS **Context Wrapper** object for our object. Note that our 'real' object is not actually created.

It is only when we actually call a routine on the object that an instance of our object is actually created. This is known as **Just In Time (JIT) activation**. This saves on resources because we don't actually have an instance of the object hanging around until we actually need it. Finally, when the routine ends the 'real' object is destroyed. This is known as **As Soon As Possible (ASAP) deactivation**. The client is completely unaware of any of this happening because it's holding a reference to the Context Wrapper object and not the 'real' object.

Managing Transactions

In order for us to take advantage of many of the features that MTS offers, we need tell MTS when we have finished a transaction and whether it was successful or something went wrong. In order to do this, we need to use the **context object** (also referred to as the `ObjectContext` object). Each of our objects created under MTS has its own context object. This object contains information about the 'real' object's execution environment, such as transactional status and security information.

More importantly, the context object also has two methods:

- ➢   `SetComplete`
- ➢   `SetAbort`

If the transaction was successful then we need call `SetComplete`, and the changes will be committed. If for any reason an error occurred, then we need to call `SetAbort` and all changes will be rolled back.

We only have to call `SetComplete` and `SetAbort` in public routines before we exit. In private methods or properties, we don't have to worry about finishing the transaction because we are not ready to destroy the server object. When the private method or property is done, control will be passed back to the calling routine, which will be responsible for telling MTS to `SetAbort` or `SetComplete`. Remember this rule for making MTS properties and methods:

> **Every public method or property must end the transaction, one way or another, before they finish.**

Think of our public methods as the entry and exit points of our object. When we enter, MTS will create the object; when we leave, we'll be good guests and let our host know we are leaving, by calling `SetComplete` or `SetAbort`.

If we need to call several properties or methods, there should be one method that starts the transaction, calls all of the other private routines, and (if everything is successful) the initial method will close the transaction when it is done.

MTS and Database Transactions

MTS also allows us to perform our database updates under transactions. MTS will do this by using an additional component installed with MTS, or SQL Server, called the **Distributed Transaction Coordinator (DTC)**. All communication to the database will occur through the DTC. Because all updates to the databases go through the DTC, it can control these updates, committing or rolling them back when necessary.

The language that DTC uses to communicate with databases is based on a standard, and most databases conform to this standard.

When a method or property of an object hosted in MTS makes a connection to the database, the DTC will automatically start a database transaction. Yet, to end or cancel the transaction, the component must send a message to the DTC through MTS that the transaction is complete, or has failed.

Non-Transactional Objects

The best part of MTS is that it can manage any object, even one that is not participating in a transaction. MTS does not care if our component does not have any transactions: it will still manage our component so that many clients can access it efficiently. When our non-transactional component tells MTS that is done, MTS will destroy our component at the appropriate time, just like it did with transactional components. The only difference is that MTS will not pass any messages onto the DTC.

The Managing Class Revisited

I've said several times that the choice of technological framework will have a fundamental impact on the way we design our components and thus the resulting component interfaces. Just to prove a point, let's compare the class diagram for the managing class as we defined it from analysis of the sequence diagrams:

Managing Class
Count:Integer
AddNew() Edit() Delete() Movefirst() Movelast() MoveNext() MovePrevious() Update()

with how it looks now that we have taken into consideration the environment in which our components must work(don't forget, the managing class will be common to the Customers, Products, Orders classes etc.):

Middle Class
+BOFAction: ADO BOFActionType +EditMode: ADO EditModeEnum +EOFAction: ADO EOFActionType +Item: ManagedClass +ItemCount: Long #ItemsDataMember: String #ItemsRecordset: ADO Recordset +Password: String +PrimaryKey: String +RecordCount: Long +RecordSetName: String +UserName: String +WhereClause: String
+AddNew() +Cancel() +Delete() +Edit() +Find() +GetProxy() +MoveFirst() +MoveLast() +MoveNext() +MovePrevious() +Refresh() #SetProxyInformation(string,string,string,string) +Update(boolean) -UpdateManagedObjects()

It is clear that we have now gone way beyond our initial interface, comprised exclusively of public properties and methods. We have now defined some friend and private properties and methods. We are not going to get into a full discussion of exactly what every property and method actually does but from our previous discussion of our technological framework, you should have some understanding of where some of them came from. The `GetProxy()` and `SetProxyInformation(…)` methods, for example, relate to our component communication technology, RDS. The `BOFAction` and `EOFAction` properties will describe what should happen if we go beyond the first and last records when navigating through our ADO `Recordset` object. Hopefully, more of this will become clear in the Development phase, when I will show you exactly how class diagrams (and the activity diagrams we will produce shortly) translate into actual Visual Basic code.

One of the goals of this book is to bridge the gap between project management, who may not have extensive coding experience, and developers. Hopefully it will give a much fuller appreciation of the amount of work and consideration that must go in to designing a successful enterprise system and of how technical issues, such as choice of a particular framework technology, can have a fundamental impact on the way in which a component is coded, testing procedure etc.

Mapping Out the Code using Activity Diagrams

We are now (at last!) ready to start mapping out the code for our Visual Basic components. Writing the code out in pseudo code is one solution, yet it can be difficult to read all of the written steps. Activity diagrams are visual and thus make it easier to view the flow of the code.

Before we start I would just like to re-emphasize the importance of creating and documenting UML diagrams at every stage of the design process.

> **Every code module should be traceable back to the original user goal that the module will help fulfill. By creating use cases, sequence diagrams, class diagrams and activity diagrams one can trace back every code module. This allows the developer to easily understand what the purpose of the code is and to optimize the code to fulfill the goals of the user.**

Just as we make code libraries, we can create libraries of UML activity diagrams. These diagrams can be used to show the flow of the code and be used as teaching aids for junior developers or as a starting point for code modules that perform a similar function. As we discussed earlier, activity diagrams can easily be shown to different members of the team for suggestions on ways of improving the coding techniques. It will only take a few seconds to understand the diagram and changes can be made easily and quickly.

Activity diagrams will have a black dot to mark the beginning of the diagram and a black dot with a circle around it to mark the end of the diagram. A lozenge shaped box marks each activity in the diagram. If there are decision points, they are marked by diamonds. First, let us take a look at a relatively simple activity diagram, describing a very important event, that of creating a connection to our data source.

Activity Diagram For Creating an ADO connection

An activity diagram for a method that sets (initializes) the ADO connection for a data services component would look as follows:

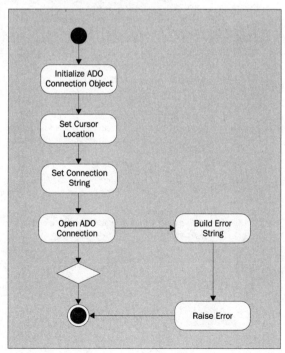

Since this is a fairly straightforward example, we will walk through the code associated with this activity diagram :

```
Private Sub SetADOConnection(v_strDatabasePath As String)

Dim objADOConnection As Object
Dim ADOConnection As ADODB.Connection

' Set the error handler
On Error GoTo SetADOConnectionError

' Initialize the ADO Connection object
Set objADOConnection = CreateObject("ADODB.Connection")

' For disconnected recordsets, set ADO cursor location to client
  With objADOConnection
  .CursorLocation = adUseClient

' Set the ADO connection string
  .ConnectionString = "Provider=Microsoft.Jet.OLEDB.3.51;Persist " & _
  "Security Info=False;Data Source=" & v_strDatabasePath

' Open the connection
  .Open
End With

Exit Sub

'Build the error string
SetADOConnectionError:

Dim lngErrorCounter As Long
Dim strErrors As String

strErrors = Err.Number & ": " & Err.Description

If objADOConnection.Errors.Count > 0 Then

   For lngErrorCounter = 0 To objADOConnection.Errors.Count - 1
      strErrors = strErrors & _
      objADOConnection.Errors(lngErrorCounter).Number & _
      ": " & objADOConnection.Errors(lngErrorCounter).Description & _
         vbCrLf
Next lngErrorCounter

End If

' Rasie the error
Err.Raise 2000 + vbObjectError, "SetADOConnection " & Err.Source, _
   strErrors

End Sub
```

Even for a simple module such as this, it is much easier to understand the flow of the code and what is going on in the code by looking at the activity diagram. This diagram can lead to discussions on the design. To begin with, why do we need a special method to set the ADO connection? From our discussion on the last chapter on ADO connection objects we know that these objects are pooled. We said that we wanted to use them and then throw them back in the pool. This means that we will be opening our connection, using it closing, and then opening it again, etc. Thus, every time we need to connect we will need to open a `Connection` object. Because of connection object pooling, we are not actually opening a connection but taking an existing connection out of the pool.

We can also see there are a few properties that will need to be set on the connection object. One of these is the cursor location. The cursor location can be on the server or on the client. A detailed discussion of these is beyond the level of this book, but they both are used in different situations for different types of data access. The activity diagram makes it clear that we need to set this property, and that we must find the best setting for our particular project.

Retrieve Customer Activity Diagram

How do we take the message *Retrieve a Customer*, which is being sent to the server component, out from the *Modify Customer* sequence diagram and expand this message into an activity diagram? Let's create a new activity diagram called *Retrieve Customer recordset* and find out.

> *There will be variables for a private ADO connection object and a private customer recordset variable in our server component.*

The necessary steps for retrieving a customer recordset are as follows:

> ➤ Initialize the recordset variable
> ➤ Set the properties of the recordset so that it will contain all of the customer records
> ➤ Connect the recordset to the database
> ➤ Retrieve the customer records from the database
> ➤ Disconnect from the database
> ➤ Return the recordset variable filled with customer records to the client

These steps are very high-level. They do not really get into any discussion of the ADO or how the ADO works. They are just a logical series of steps that we need to perform to get information from the database and return it to the client. The next step is to determine exactly how we do each of these steps using ADO.

Following is a table of the steps required to perform the general tasks we listed above using ADO. These are the specific steps our server component must perform to get a customer recordset and pass back a disconnected recordset with the client information in it using ADO. Each step also includes the framework that places this requirement on the system, so you can see where you might have found information on how to perform this step.

Activity	Framework that requires this activity	Requirement
Create ADO connection	ADO Framework	You must make a connection to the database by either creating a `Connection` object prior to retrieving data or passing in a connection string in the open method of the recordset.
	Three-Tier framework	No information can be stored from one call to the next. Therefore a `Connection` object must be created first for every request to get information to the data
If there is an error getting the connection, raise an error and end	ADO Framework	All errors must be handled
If there is no error, initialize the customer recordset object	Three-Tier framework	No information can be stored from one Call to the next; must initialize Recordset for each request
Set customer recordset cursor location to the client	ADO/RDS framework	Updateable disconnected recordsets are required; these recordsets need a cursor location to be on the client
Set customer recordset source equal to the appropriate query string	ADO framework	If a recordset is going to retrieve data from the database, there must be a Query string that specifies what information from which tables will be retrieved (a query string is not required if you accessing a stored procedure).
Set customers recordset connection	ADO framework	To connect a recordset variable to a database you must set the recordset variable's connection property to a valid connection string.
If there is an error getting the connection, raise an error and end	ADO Framework	All errors must be handled

Activity	Framework that requires this activity	Requirement
If there is no error, set the customer recordset `LockType` to the appropriate lock type and set the Recordset's `Connection` object to the `Connection` object.	ADO framework	Must set `LockType` of a recordset before retrieving data from the database (not required for the default optimistic lock)
Open the customer recordset object	ADO framework requirement	Must open a recordset to retrieve the data into the recordset
If there is an error opening the recordset, raise an error	ADO framework requirement	All errors must be handled
If there is no error, return the recordset	Three-Tier framework	Return disconnected recordsets
Close the ADO recordset and set the recordset and `Connection` object to nothing.	ADO framework	Failing to close the `Connection` object leaves it open until it times out. There is a limited number of `Connection` objects, so letting them close by timing out ties up valuable resources.

This table says a great deal about programming in Visual Basic. To make this chart, I had to understand three frameworks (RDS, ADO and Three-Tier). Programming Visual Basic goes beyond knowing just the language syntax. To make Visual Basic projects, we now have to understand the frameworks that our projects are going to work under. We therefore need to do the following:

> Map out the general steps a message requires

> Determine what frameworks you will be using to perform these steps

> Get out your reference books on these frameworks, and find for each framework the specific sub-steps that are required for each general step

255

From this table, we can now draw out our activity diagram. Each activity in the chart above will map to some element of the activity diagram:

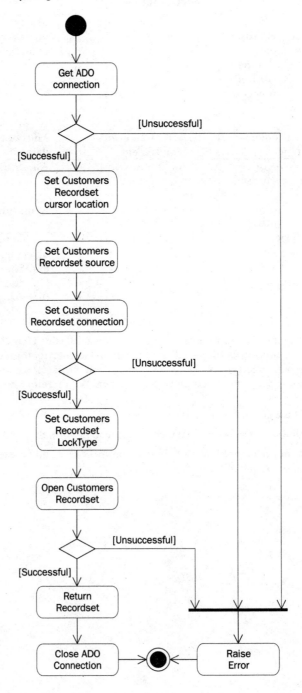

The simultaneous flows that have arisen due to the possibility of errors will come back together at the thick horizontal bar or concurrent join. Of course, as with any activity diagram, the ending point must be shown.

If we were to create a similar diagram for *Retrieve Product*, it would look very similar.

Update Recordset Activity Diagrams

Lastly we will look at some activity diagrams for updating a recordset in the database. If you cast your mind back to Chapter 6 you may recall that our interview with Valerie, the Northwind Sales Representative, highlighted a problem with the old order processing system - if another user was accessing the database table that Valerie wanted to use, she was simply prevented from having access to it until the other user had finished with it. With our ADO disconnected recordsets we have overcome this problem. Each user can work with a recordset on the client machine. The user can then request to update the database. MTS also allows us to perform our database updates under transactions. During this process the system must check for any conflicting records (another user may have been making conflicting changes to the same data), attempt to reconcile any differences then either accept the transaction or rollback the changes. This is not a straightforward process and we will not explore it in all its gory detail. Let's have a look at an activity diagram describing a generic `UpdateRecordset` method:

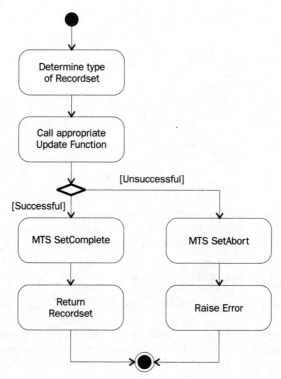

If the transaction was successful we call `SetComplete,` and the changes will be committed. If for any reason an error occurred (such as conflicting records being found) then we need to call `SetAbort` and all changes will be rolled back:

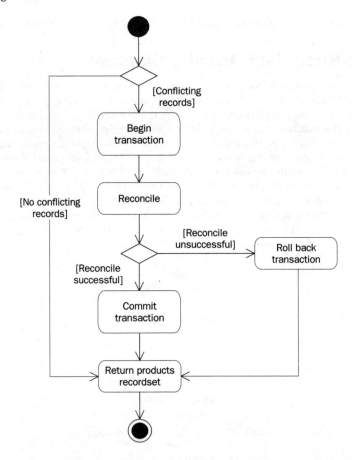

Of course, the Reconcile step is a whole complicated activity diagram on its own. Also the steps that would occur when determining the type of recordset and preparing to send it back would be the focus of yet another activity diagram. As I said, not a simple process.

Benefits of Activity Diagrams

Before we move on let's review the benefits of using activity diagrams.

Listing all of the steps of each of our methods gives a clear, readable way of seeing everything your code must do to perform this task. As such, an activity diagram provides a very useful learning tool. With an activity diagram, a junior developer can go to a more senior developer and ask them "In this diagram, what should I set the cursor property to and how should I raise the error?" Without the diagram, a junior developer may not even know that they are supposed to set the cursor property to a value or that there is any need to build a special error string. Activity diagrams make sure that all of the critical steps are included in the code.

Finding the best solution is usually an iterative process. First you have your initial concept, refine it, test it, then you refine it more and test it more, etc. Activity diagrams will let us go through many refinements of our object's methods before we even write one line of code. Removing something from an activity diagram, means deleting a graphic image. This takes about a second. Changing code means deleting lines of code that may have taken hours to create and adjusting the rest of the code to deal with the deletion. Which one would you rather do?

Effective Testing

We saw in the previous sections that, for example, **Retrieve Recordset** is a task that is required by nearly every client component. Therefore the majority of the tasks the client will be performing will depend on this task functioning correctly. Establishing an ADO connection is a key task performed by the server object. Tasks that are essential to the entire system, such as these two tasks, should always be thoroughly tested during the design phase. If either one of these tasks fails to work, or works inefficiently, the entire project will fail.

With regard to retrieving recordsets from and updating recordsets to the server component, we will need to answer these questions:

> How efficiently will disconnected recordsets work for the Northwind order processing application? How efficiently will they work for the web application?

> Does RDS actually work? If so, how efficiently?

> If RDS works, does it work efficiently enough for this system?

> Can we quantify the benefits to our system derived from MTS?

The testing team should create small test projects to ensure that the chosen technology actually does represent an effective solution for a particular system.

Other Features to be Determined in the Physical Stage

In addition to designing components, there are several other features of your project that need to be determined in the physical stage.

Security

When designing the security for your application, you have many choices. The basic four basic choices are: component- based security, database-based security, MTS security and operating system-based security. You can choose any of these security methods by themselves or you can use a combination of security types.

MTS, database and system security are similar in that they require an administrator to physically add every user into either a group or a role. Because NT system security information is placed in memory on the server, there are limitations on the number of users that can be stored in this type of memory. These three security types were designed prior to the Internet and are not designed to hold information on tens of thousands of users.

MTS security works on top of DCOM security. DCOM security can provide a high grain of security, that is, it can limit access to a complete component such as a DLL. Often, one needs to limit security down to particular parts of a component. For example, you may have an employee component, which has interfaces that can be viewed by anyone within the corporation (such as name and department) and another interface for payroll and personal information that is only available to the human resources and payroll department. With DCOM, we can only create separate security by creating separate components. MTS, though, does allow us to get down to a finer grain of security.

With MTS you can define roles for the users of your components. This will give us a much finer grain of security. Each role can be allowed access to specific interfaces or methods. If you have designed your application with UML and created use cases, you will have defined roles for your users. Based on these roles associated with use cases we can determine the roles for our components, and what these roles are allowed to do. Thus, building applications with UML and using MTS for role-based security go hand in hand. For an excellent discussion of MTS security read Visual Basic 6 MTS Programming by Wrox press.

While DCOM and MTS provide excellent security models for intranet sites and internal distributed applications, they do not provide a practical solution for large-scale web applications. If you are going to need a way of keeping track of thousands of users, your best choice is using a directory service.

A directory service can hold information on each user, including their ID and their password. When developing e-commerce web sites with Site Server, you can use Site Server membership directory to store information. Information can be placed into the membership directory and retrieved from the directory using LDAP (Lightweight Directory Access Protocol). Using the membership directory, we can keep track of thousands of users. Based on the roles we define in our system, we will create different sets of users with different access rights. Ideally, we will be able to tell programmatically what rights a user has, so we can automate adding users to the directory instead of doing it manually. For example, on a web site we could have three levels of membership, each with a different price and different type of access to the site. We can place users into different roles depending on the type of site membership they pay for. This can be done within our code and does not have to be done manually by an administrator. We can see that a directory service will provide the ideal security solution for our large web sites. For more information on Site Servers membership directory read Site Server 3.0 Personalization and Membership from Wrox press.

With Windows 2000, which is to be released sometime in mid 2000, the directory will be part of the operating system. The active directory will allow you to identify both users and resources on the network that can be managed at a single point. At this time there are no books out on the subject, but there certainly will be many of them as we come close to the release of Windows 2000.

Component-based security places the responsibility of validating the user on the components we build. In a data services component that does not maintain state, this type of security requires us to have a userID and password as parameters of every method of the component. In this case, our component would need to have code to actually check to see if the userID and password are valid for each method call. We could then verify the userID and password against a directory.

The userID and password can also be stored in a database or one can simply have regular security on the database and check a user by trying to make a connection to the database. Any of these techniques will work. Since the responsibility of validating users is now taken on by your component, it is important that you code it carefully. This type of security is found in Internet applications and some 3-tier solutions that have a stateless data services component. The Internet applications will usually use a directory. An Intranet application using component security will probably also use either database security or operating system security. If you use Remote Data Services, it is likely you will be using this type of security.

Regardless of the method you choose to use for security, your use cases can help you define roles for your users. In the conceptual stage, we defined a set of roles for our users. These roles can form the basis of our security. Our use cases also tell us what tasks each user is allowed to do.

Error Handling

By the end of the physical stage, you must have documented all of the error statements for your Visual Basic application. The possible errors for your application can be found in the constraint business rules and the alternative flows of the use cases.

Visual Basic allows you to use error numbers ranging from 512 to 32768. You should give each of your components their own range of numbers. If each of your components has 100 possible user-defined errors, this will allow you to make over 300 applications with no conflict of the error numbers. If you set a range of numbers for each component, then you will know exactly which component raised an error when an error occurs in your application. This will make debugging much easier, especially when there are dozens of components that make up the application. For the situations where the same error message may be presented in many different components, you should create a standard for the message, but each component should have their own number assigned to this standard message.

Visual Basic now allows you to use resource files. Resource files are a great place to store error messages. To use a resource file, you will need to add a method into your Visual Basic application to retrieve the string associated with an error. Let us look at how this is done.

In Visual Basic, go to the menu and select Add-Ins|Add-In Manager. The Add-in manager will come up. Double click the VB 6 Resource Editor:

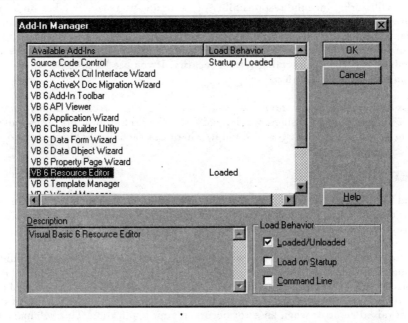

Click OK. Now you can edit resource files in Visual Basic. Go to the menu and select Tools|Resource Editor to open up the resource editor.

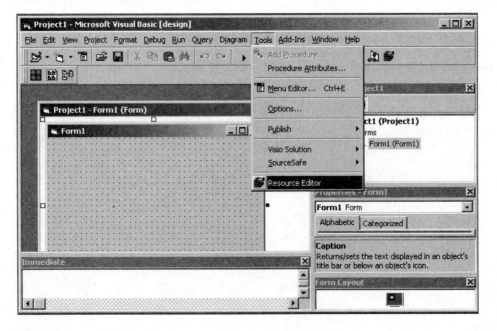

Click on the abc on the toolbar to open the string editor. You can assign each error number to a string that gives a description of the error. It could look as follows:

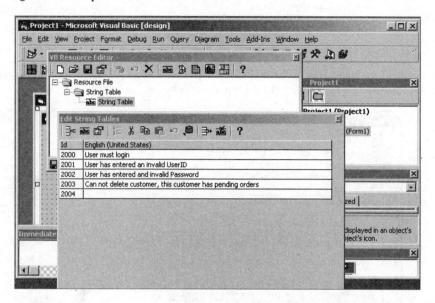

Once you have created your error message strings, you must save them using the VB Resource Editor. The .res file that is created can be shared by all of the components in your project. This .res file should be made during the physical stage.

You can create a function that uses the LoadResString Visual Basic function to retrieve the correct error string:

```
Public Function GetErrorText(ByVal v_lngErrorNumber As Long) as String

    On Error GoTo GetErrorText_Error

    GetErrorText = LoadResString(v_lngErrorNumber)

    Exit Function

GetErrorText_Error:

    If Err.Number <> 0 Then
        GetErrorText = "An unknown error has occurred, the error was not found"
    End If

End Function
```

If the error number is not in the resource file, it will return the default unknown error message. Just to make things a little easier for the Visual Basic programmer, we can make an enumerated type with the error messages. This way the developer does not have to remember all of the error numbers. The enumerated type would look as follows:

```
        Private Enum ErrorCollection
            e_UserMustLogin = 2000
            e_UserEnteredInvalidID = 2001
            e_UserEnteredInvalidPassword = 2002
            e_CanNotDeleteCustomerPendingOrder = 2003
        End Enum
```

These enumerated types should also be made in the physical stage. This type would look as follows to a developer if they hit control-space bar and typed the letter e_ :

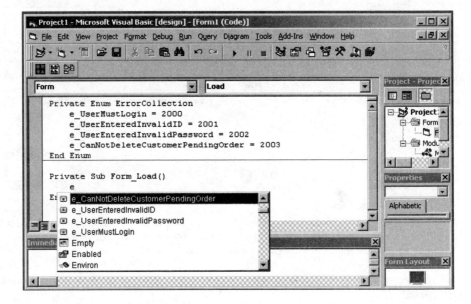

This makes it easy to find the correct error. I do realize this is a bit different than the way most error messages are created. For the most part, developers start coding and as they find they need an error message they add one to the list. This can lead to duplicate numbers and a lack of uniformity in the numbering and content of the error messages.

By defining the errors in the physical stage and designing your technique of coding with activity diagrams before the code is written, developers will know exactly where errors should be placed and which error should be placed there. This is a much cleaner and easier way to code.

One final comment on error messages: try to word your error messages in a way that any user can understand them and understand what has gone wrong. Try to build some intelligence into your applications so that when an error occurs, not only does the user get an error message, but also suggestions on how they may correct the error. Doing this will substantially reduce the number of help desk calls.

Risk Assessment

Once the final design is put together, there will be risks associated with the choices that were made. Each of these risks should be placed in the risk document so that they can be monitored. While risk assessment should be part of every phase of a project, you will have the clearest understanding of the project's risks at the end of the physical stage. A careful review of all of the proposed risks should be done at this time.

Publishing the Final Interface

Once you have completed the design of the interfaces for each component, they should be documented in class diagrams. These diagrams then become a contract as to the public methods and functions that the classes will provide in their interface. As we stated earlier, this interface should not change.

The final interface design of all of your components is one of the final deliverables for the physical stage. When all of your components have been designed and all of the issues, such as security and component distribution have been resolved, the design of the project is complete.

Summary

The physical design stage will first focus on researching the best way to build the components defined in the logical stage. Once the research is completed, you must weigh the options and choose the best solution for each component. Once a solution is chosen, a way to implement that solution must be created and documented.

The physical stage will focus around finding the best possible components for our system. Visual Basic has a wide range of capabilities and can provide us with a wide range of solutions for our enterprise system. When Visual Basic does not provide us with the solutions that we need, we can use other languages or third party components. We can also use third party components when we want to save resources by not reinventing the wheel.

By the end of the physical stage we have mapped out everything we need for our development phase. It is like a play in which the entire script has been written. It is only a matter of the actors acting out their parts. Just as a good actor can bring life to a good script, the skilled developer can take a good design and create a powerful, efficient system.

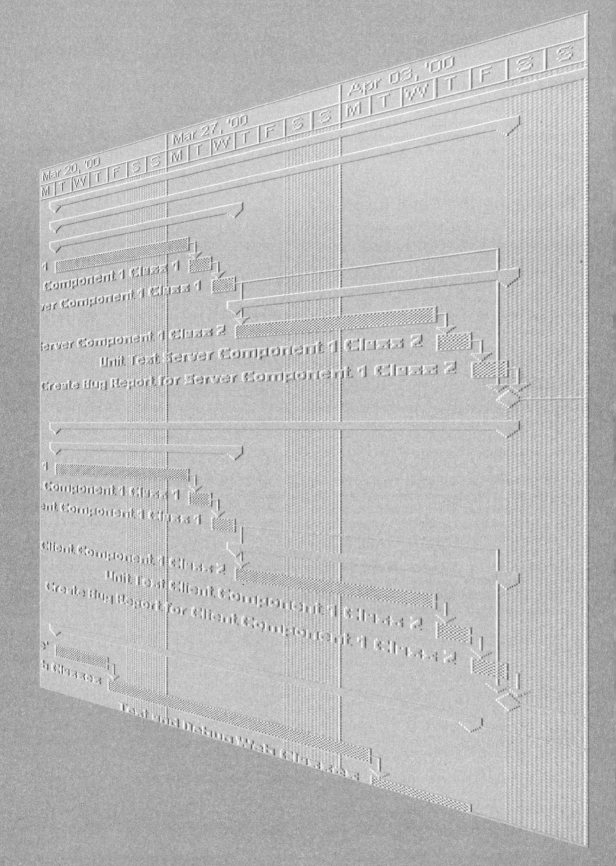

9

Development Phase

The development phase will focus on converting the design created in the physical stage into a working application. This phase begins when the design has been frozen and locked into place. The key players in this phase will be the developers and testers, but the entire team will have work to do in the phase. The two most important activities will be building and testing the solution. This phase is complete when the first release of the project is made.

It is impossible to give a detailed description here of the procedure for creating Visual Basic code from UML activity and class diagrams. However, this can be found in Appendix B. Instead, we will cover some of the issues facing developers in this phase and take an overview of the coding of our DNA application. We will also look at the issue of code reusability, identifying patterns within code and seeing how we can use these to help us write code - even to the extent of automating some code generation.

So, in this chapter we will see:

> How we can identify patterns which will be repeated within our code
> How we can use these patterns to cut development time and costs
> An overview of coding the project
> How we can automate code generation

Since this phase concentrates chiefly on writing code, the deliverables will be:

> Internal code releases
> Versioned source code
> Compiled code
> Updated risk management documents

The final milestone for this phase will be the completion of all the source code, including the testing both of each component individually and of the product as a whole.

Summary of Team Focus

The project manager will be in charge of the master schedule, monitoring risks, generating status reports and handling any changes to the functional specifications. One of the most important jobs of the project manager is adjusting resources so that the critical path tasks get accomplished on time. Thus, if a developer who is working on a critical path task becomes ill and cannot report to work for a week, it is the job of the project manager to make the decision to reassign personnel, if this is the best option. It is important that the critical path tasks are accomplished. Thus, the project manager plays the role of monitoring the project and adjusting resources when necessary to make sure that the project stays on time and on schedule.

The product manager will be responsible for keeping the client informed on the progress of the project, the status of the schedule and costs, and an assessment of the current risks to the project. If there are any issues the client has with the project, the product manager will act as the negotiator between the client and the development team.

The component managers perform the same tasks as the project manager, within each component team. They are responsible for managing the resources within their team and ensuring that the components written by their team are completed on schedule. If personnel need to be reassigned within a component team, that will be the responsibility of the component manager rather than the project manager.

The development team will be driving this phase of the project. They will be building and assembling the components of the system. Development will have numerous deliverables as the code is built in stages from components. These components, whether they are classes, complete business objects built from hierarchies or completed user interfaces, must be thoroughly tested prior to being considered complete.

The testers will be testing the components that the development team is creating. As each component is completed and tested, it will be added to the system and tested within the system. We will discuss the different types of testing in the next chapter.

User education will be busy putting together documentation on the project, based on the design. Because the design has been finalized by this phase, the educators are able write accurate support materials in the knowledge that the system will work as designed. The educators could also be working on creating a web site to support the new product, designing plans to educate the new users or even working with the users on existing portions of the project.

Logistics will be working on procuring the physical components needed for the project and building the required infrastructure for the project. They will work closely with the support groups and bring any issues support may have back to the development team.

Overview of Development Phase

First of all, let's have a quick look at where we are in the project cycle. In the logical stage of the design phase, we identified the components which will be required for our application, and the public methods and properties that each component will need to expose. We also considered some of the possible frameworks for the application. This process continued into the physical stage, where we refined our class diagrams to include friend and private properties and methods which are internal to the component, and cannot be accessed by any other components. This distinction is important because the public methods and properties - the component's public interface - should not be altered once the design has been finalized and signed off by all team members. The internal methods and properties, however, may be altered if this proves necessary.

In the last chapter, we also saw that each component will need to consist of more than one class. For example, as well as a `clsCustomers` class, which will represent an individual customer, we saw that we will need a class to manage the customers: an object from which we will be able to create instances of our customer object. Moreover, if we want to be able to group certain customers together (such as those who spend more than $1,000 dollars a year), we will need yet another object to manage these different collections of customers. We thus saw that we need a three-class system for our business components.

In the development phase, all this design work will be translated into Visual Basic source code. Code will be written to implement all of the methods and properties exposed by our objects, which we identified in the design phase. In other words, it is by this stage absolutely fixed what the application is going to do, but there is still much leeway with regards to how it will perform those services.

The other major activity of this phase is testing. Each routine must be tested as it is written; then each component must be tested as it is completed. Finally, the entire application must be thoroughly tested when all of the code has been written. Bugs will be reported as they are found by the testers, and ranked according to priority. When the code has been completed, the entire product will be beta-tested by end users. This process of testing and debugging overlaps between the development and deployment stage, and will be treated in more detail in the next chapter.

Most of this chapter will focus on the issues facing developers in this phase, but let's first take a quick look at the most important task of the project and component managers: managing risks to the project and ensuring that the project is completed to schedule and on budget.

Risk Management

Risk management is critically important in the development phase. Any risks that go unnoticed can result in the project falling hopelessly behind schedule or over budget. A small problem that could easily be taken care of in its initial stages can quickly snowball into a problem that can destroy an entire project. It is amazing how a project that is properly planned and carefully designed can fall apart very quickly because risks were not properly monitored. A problem that delays a critical task can cause this task to be delayed for weeks. All of the tasks dependent on this critical task must now wait. If some of the dependent tasks are also critical path tasks, then more tasks will wait. One critical task falling behind can cause a chain of events that delay the entire project.

It is the job of the project manager to watch the project and make sure that the risks are being managed properly. It is the job of every single member of the team to document risks and make sure that they are being dealt with. Every week, team members should be submitting a form listing all of the possible risks to their project. Each team member can list risks to the goals they are trying to accomplish. The project manager will then go through these reports from the team members and create a list of risks. Working with team members, a ranking of the risks will be done.

It is likely that a risk will be reduced by the combined efforts of many members of the team, so it is also the team's responsibility to eliminate the risks. The project and component managers should find solutions to risks and divide the responsibility of eliminating the risk amongst the team members.

Another important role of the project manager is change control. If there is any need to make a change to the plan after it is frozen, the component manager will assess the risks. The product manager will bring these risk documents to the client and discuss the consequences of making a change. If the change is put into effect, the project manager will make the necessary changes to the schedule and allocate resources to compensate for this change.

Writing Visual Basic Code

Writing Visual Basic code can be considered an art. A good artist will work hard at developing the best possible solution. The rules of good coding have been discussed throughout this book. Perhaps the most important aspect of team development of a Visual Basic project is having a set of standards. There should be coding standards, standards for documentation, and standards for design. These standards should be understood and followed by the whole team. Coding standards can be made to fit the needs of the team. Coding standards includes all standards related to writing code. This can include naming conventions, error handling, use of `go to` statements, comments, versioning, etc.

> *The basic rule for naming variables is that all variable names should indicate what the variable does, what the variable's type is and what the variable's scope is. It does not matter what specific naming convention you use, as long as it meets this rule.*

It is critical that you create standards for your project, as the code will be passed from the developers to the testers. If the testers must spend days trying to understand each person's code, they will spend little time testing. The code a Visual Basic team writes must be capable of being passed from one Visual Basic developer to another and be understood within a reasonable time. The only way to accomplish this is by using a set of standards, having a detailed design of the project and using deliverables that determine exactly what has and what has not been done in the code. This can all be accomplished by the techniques outlined in this book. Another very useful technique for ensuring that the code is standardized is to use code reiviews.

Code Reviews

Code reviews serve many purposes. One can either review general techniques, such as how to code a module, or review actual code. When reviewing techniques, activity diagrams can be used. A code review can be used for the following:

> ➤ To find ways to make the code more maintainable
>
> ➤ To teach new members the best way to code and what the team's coding standards are
>
> ➤ To help find problems in code that is not working properly
>
> ➤ To help understand the best way to code a difficult section of code

Code reviews should never become personal. While I am promoting standards, I am not saying that each person cannot write code in their own personal style. I am saying that a person's individual style should work within the team's standards. Issues that need to be raised at a code review should be things that affect the performance, readability and maintainability of the code. Issues that revolve around personal preference, that have nothing to do with improving the code or working within the team's standards, should not be included in code reviews.

An impartial moderator should oversee the review and make sure the review does not deteriorate into an attack on the person who wrote the code. The moderator should make sure that comments are constructive and geared towards making the code, and therefore the project, better. If there are mistakes in the code someone writes, the code review should be a learning tool for this person.

In general, the developer or developers who wrote the code should walk through the code and explain the function of the code and how it is supposed to work. The code is then reviewed by the reviewers. In general, one should not try to fix problems during the review, only identify them. If there is time to discuss solutions once all of the problems have been found, then solutions can also be discussed.

All suggestions for change should be logged. It is best to have someone taking notes and keeping a record of all suggestions.

Coding the DNA Visual Basic Project

Now that we have considered some of the ways of managing the process of writing code, we can look at the outline of our Visual Basic DNA project. As we saw, this will be a three-tier application using poolable ADO `Connection` objects, transaction processing with MTS and stateless server components. The application is based on the Northwind database, since this comes supplied with Visual Basic. We won't give all of the code here, although it can be found on our web site, and it is given in 'VB6 UML Design and Development', ISBN 1-861002-51-3.

We made the comment in the last chapter that the client services component is not very reusable. The client services component, which usually consists of the user interface, is very specific to each application. We will therefore not examine this component in great detail; however, some guidelines for creating a user-friendly user interface were given in Chapter 7.

The Business Services Components

The business services components, though, tend to be good candidates for being reusable components. We saw in the last chapter that it is a good strategy to divide our business components into a three-class hierarchy. The middle class will be a managing class, and the bottom class a managed class. The top class manages groups of the objects.

These business services objects are built so that they can provide the attributes of the managed object, such as a customer or order object, by either using a recordset or the properties of the managed object. The properties of the managed class are public. The recordset can only be accessed by binding a control, such as a grid box or text box, to the managed object or to the managing object. This binding is done using Visual Basic's new data source classes (which I call data provider classes, because they provide data).

Bottom Class

The bottom class, which represents objects such as customer, order or employee objects, has a public interface that consists only of properties; these are the attributes of the object that we want to store. For a Customer object, for example, we would find attributes such as Name, Address, City, etc. For this application, we will connect to the Northwind database, so we will add a property for each of the fields of the Customers table in that database. The class diagram looks as follows:

clsCustomers
+Address +City +CompanyName +ContactName +ContactTitle +Country +CustomerID +Fax +Phone +PostalCode +Region +EditMode #ItemsDataMember #ItemsRecordset
#ValidateFields()

Notice that as well as the properties taken from the database, which we use to store the customer information, we have three extra properties - EditMode, ItemsDataMember and ItemsRecordset - and one friend method, ValidateFields.

For each of the properties, we need to write two routines - one for reading the value of the property (Property Get) and one for setting it (Property Let). However, if the property contains an object (rather than, say, a string or a numeric value), Visual Basic requires us to use Property Set instead of Property Let.

Remember that we said that we would allow the attributes of the object to be accessed either through properties or through a recordset? That means we need a property which contains a Recordset object. The ItemsRecordset property holds an ADO recordset which contains this information. This recordset has a field for each of our Customer object's properties, so when we want to read or set one of these properties, we will actually access the appropriate field in this recordset. For example, the routine for getting the value of the Address property looks like this:

```
Public Property Get Address() As String
    On Error Resume Next
    Address = ItemsRecordset.Fields(g_cstrFieldAddress)
    If Err.Number <> 0 Then
        If Err.Number <> 3265 Then
            Err.Raise Err.Number, "AddressGet", Err.Description
        End If
    End If
End Property
```

The variable `g_cstrFieldAddress` is simply a constant (a variable whose value is set when the class is initialized and cannot be changed) which is set to the name of the `Address` field in the database (i.e. `"Address"`). The key line of this routine is therefore equivalent to:

```
Address = ItemsRecordset.Fields("Address")
```

So when the managing class attempts to read the value of the `Address` property, this routine will be executed and the value of the `Address` field in `ItemsRecordset` will be returned. The managing class can thus access the customer's address in two ways: by reading the property directly (that is, by calling `objCustomer.Address`) or by accessing all the customer information by calling `objCustomer.ItemsRecordset`. Similarly, when we wish to set the value of this property, we will set the value of the appropriate field in `ItemsRecordset`:

```
Public Property Let Address(ByVal v_strNewAddress As String)
    On Error GoTo AddressLetError
    If m_blnValidatingFieldChange = True Then
        Exit Property
    End If
    If m_eEditMode = adEditInProgress Or m_eEditMode = adEditAdd Then
        m_blnIgnoreFieldChange = True
        ItemsRecordset.Fields(g_cstrFieldAddress) = v_strNewAddress
    ElseIf m_eEditMode = adEditNone Then
        Err.Raise 1001, "Address Let:", GetErrorText(errChangeFieldNoEdit)
    End If
    Exit Property

AddressLetError:
    Err.Raise Err.Number, "Address Let " & Err.Source, Err.Description
End Property
```

This code is considerably more complex than that for the corresponding `Property Get` because of the need to ensure that we don't allow data conflicts if more than one user is accessing the same record. Firstly, we check whether a change to the property is still being validated; if so, we abandon execution of this routine. Then we check our `EditMode` property; this contains the value of an ADO constant which indicates whether a record is currently being edited, or whether it is being added or deleted. We can use this property to keep track of what operation is being performed, or to check whether a record is being edited by another user. If the record to be changed is being edited or added to the recordset, then we set the field in the recordset in order to set the property; otherwise, we raise an error.

The final property, `ItemsDataMember`, returns a reference to the set of data or 'data member' for the object's attributes, in case the data source is exposing more than one set of data.

The `ValidateFields` method is used to validate a field in our recordset. All of the validation of the fields is done in the properties. However, we can change a field either by using a property or by using the recordset, so we will also need a way to validate the fields when they have been changed using the recordset. `ValidateFields` will be called any time a field changes using the recordset. Since the code to validate a field is already in the properties, the `ValidateFields` method will pass the new field value into the property.

Middle Class

As we noted earlier in the chapter, the middle class of each component will have an identical interface, because the middle class is used not to store data but to manage instances of the bottom class. Each of these objects will therefore require exactly the same functionality. In fact, almost the only difference in the coding of these classes is that we will need a reference to the corresponding bottom class. We will need to declare the reference in the **General Declarations** section of the code. For example, `clsCustomersManager` will need a reference to `clsCustomers`:

```
Private WithEvents m_objManagedObject As clsCustomers
```

And `clsOrdersManager` will need a reference to `clsOrders`:

```
Private WithEvents m_objManagedObject As clsOrders
```

Then, when the class is initialized, we will have to create an instance of the appropriate object:

```
Set m_objManagedObject = New clsCustomers
```

The only other difference occurs when we use the `Item` property to return a specific instance of the class. Since this property returns an instance of the managed object, it will have to be declared As `clsCustomers` or As `clsOrders`, etc.:

```
Public Property Get Item() As clsCustomers
    Set Item = m_objManagedObject
End Property
```

With the exception of these three minor differences, the code will be identical (so long as we give the same name to our managed object).

The class diagram for the middle class looks as follows:

Middle Class
+BOFAction +EditMode +EOFAction +Item +ItemCount #ItemsDataMember #ItemsRecordset +Password +PrimaryKey +RecordCount +RecordSetName +UserName +WhereClause
+AddNew() +Cancel() +Delete() +Edit() +Find() +GetProxy() +MoveFirst() +MoveLast() +MoveNext() +MovePrevious() +Refresh() #SetProxyInformation() +Update() -UpdateManagedObjects()

The methods and properties of this class are used mostly to retrieve a specific object of the bottom class, or to obtain information about the collection as a whole; we have seen most of these, so we will just look at those which we have not yet covered. Also, some of the properties are identical to those of the managed objects, such as `ItemsRecordset`. This property returns the `ItemsRecordset` property for the current managed object:

```
Friend Property Get ItemsRecordset() As ADODB.Recordset
    Set ItemsRecordset = m_objManagedObject.ItemsRecordset
End Sub
```

One consequence of using RDS is that we must create a 'proxy' of the server component in our middle-tier object. That is, we must create an object which looks to our middle-tier object like the server component, but will in fact only be a means for the two objects to communicate with each other. We need two methods to handle this: the `SetProxyInformation` method will set up the information that the proxy needs. Then, the `GetProxy` method will create the proxy object itself:

```
Public Sub GetProxy()
    Set m_objDataSpace = New RDS.DataSpace
    m_objDataSpace.InternetTimeout = 30000
    Set m_objProxy = m_objDataSpace.CreateObject("prjServer.clsServer", "")
End Sub
```

There are two things to notice here: first we must create an instance of the RDS `DataSpace` object. Just as we needed a managing object from which we could create our `clsCustomers` object, so we need an object from which we can create our proxy server object; we can't just wish it out of thin air. The `DataSpace` object fills this function.

The second point to note is that two parameters are passed into the `DataSpace` object's `CreateObject` method (this is the function we use actually to create our proxy server object). The first is the ProgID of the class we want to create: a string which identifies the sort of object of which we want to create an instance. The second indicates the server on which the object itself exists. This can be in any of four formats:

> HTTP (HyperText Transport Protocol, the usual format for transferring information over the Internet). In this case the parameter will be an HTTP address, such as `"http://www.northwind.com"`.

> HTTPS (HTTP over Secure Sockets Layer - a secure form of HTTP). For example: `"https://www.northwind.com"`.

> DCOM (Distributed COM, which works in a similar way to COM, but can operate over a network). The parameter will be the name of the machine on which the server component resides, e.g. `"Northwind1"`.

> In-process, which we use when the client-side and server-side components are on the same machine. In this case, the parameter will be an empty string, as in the example above.

This illustrates the ease with which an RDS connection can be adapted to different circumstances, and shows why RDS is a good choice for reusable components: all we have to do is change this one parameter, and we can adapt a component used by our order entry application running over an intranet via DCOM to run over the Internet via HTTP.

The `UpdateManagedObjects` method is called to update all of the components that are bound to the object. This will happen any time the recordset changes, such as during a `MoveNext` or after an `Edit` or `AddNew` has been saved.

Top Class

We will place the top class into a user control. This allows us to add the control to a form in the client application; we consequently don't need to instantiate a separate component.

The top class will only have two methods, a `Get...` function to retrieve an instance of the corresponding middle class and a `ChangedManagedObjects` method to refresh the bound controls when the recordset changes. There is also one property, based on the primary key of the table. The class diagram for `ctlCustomers`, for example, looks like this:

```
+------------------------------------+
| ctlCustomers                       |
+------------------------------------+
| +CustomerIDEquals                  |
+------------------------------------+
| +GetCustomersCollection()          |
| –ChangedManagedObjects()           |
+------------------------------------+
```

In addition to the object, each component will have a `.bas` module with a `CreateErrorFunc` for error handling and various constants and enumerated types that will be needed for the component.

The Server Component

As we noted in the last chapter, our DNA approach requires us to keep our server component stateless in order to achieve maximum scalability, and this in turn dictates that the component will have only methods: since we are creating an instance of the component only when needed and destroying it afterwards, the values of any properties would not persist from one call to the object to the next.

The following class diagram shows the methods for our `clsServer` class. Because our server component contains only one class, there are no friend methods; all methods which are not public can be accessed only by this class, so will be private:

```
+------------------------------------+
| clsServer                          |
+------------------------------------+
| -CreateInstance()                  |
| +SetComplete()                     |
| +Set Abort()                       |
| -SetADOConnection()                |
| -GetADOConnection()                |
| -CloseADOConnection()              |
| +ValidUserIDPassword()             |
| -GetRecordSet()                    |
| +ReturnCustomersRecordset()        |
| -UpdateCustomersRS()               |
| ...                                |
| +UpdateRecordset()                 |
+------------------------------------+
```

For each of our middle-tier components, we will need two specific methods: a public `Return...Recordset` method and a private `Update...RS` method. The class diagram above shows, as examples of these, `ReturnCustomersRecordset` and `UpdateCustomersRS` methods; we would also need a `ReturnOrdersRecordset` and an `UpdateOrdersRS` method, and so on. The `Return...` methods are public, and can be called directly from our managing class to retrieve a recordset for a specific object from the database. However, the `Update...` methods are private, because we have a generic public `UpdateRecordset` method, which calls the appropriate specific function.

Our decision to use MTS for transaction processing means that we must have some way of telling MTS whether or not the operations within the transaction have succeeded. If all operations succeed, we can 'commit' the transaction: that is, we can tell the database that all the operations within the transaction can actually be performed. We do this through an MTS object known as the ObjectContext object. Every object running under MTS has an associated ObjectContext object, and it provides methods for committing a transaction:

```
Public Sub SetComplete()
    If Not m_objContext Is Nothing Then
        m_objContext.SetComplete
    End If
End Sub
```

Similarly, we need to inform MTS if anything goes wrong and the transaction needs to be aborted or 'rolled back', canceling all the operations within it. Again, we must use the ObjectContext object:

```
Public Sub SetAbort()
    If Not m_objContext Is Nothing Then
        m_objContext.SetAbort
    End If
End Sub
```

The other methods are used mostly for handling our ADO connection to the database: we have separate methods for opening and closing the connection, and for retrieving an existing Connection object. Extracting this functionality into separate methods avoids having to write the same code for each of the Update... and Return... methods. We can just call the method whenever we need to open or close a connection. These methods are all private, because only our server component may have direct access to the database.

Reusing Our Visual Basic Code

We saw in Chapter 8 that for each component you will have decided on one of three possible options: to buy a third party compiled component, to reuse a component, or to build a component from the ground up. If you are choosing a third party component, you will probably only have to test the component to make sure it meets your project's needs, and then add the component into your project. When it comes to code reuse, hopefully you will find that most of the work has been already done.

Building Visual Basic components from the ground up can be a daunting task. Even when the design is created, everything documented, it still takes a long time actually to write and test the code. By reusing code, one can substantially cut costs and time of development.

We can identify two general forms of code reuse. The first form is where we build a component and use the same component in many different applications. An example of this would be building a product component that can be used in an internet application, a Visual Basic EXE application and a Dynamic HTML application. We will see an example of this in the next section.

The second form of reuse is where we identify a pattern, and reuse the same pattern (and coding techniques) to build many different components. We will look at patterns in the next section.

Patterns

We saw in the previous chapters how sequence diagrams can help us to define the public interfaces for our objects and to design a user-friendly GUI. Another great reason for creating sequence diagrams is that they can help us identify patterns.

Patterns are becoming the hottest new idea in OOP. There is good reason for this. A pattern can provide us with a basic blueprint that we can use to design our project.

> **A pattern is a common solution to a common design problem within a project.**

Patterns can allow us to build our components in an assembly line manner. Patterns help a project stay within time deadlines, keep costs down and significantly reduce the amount of coding that needs to be done. Without a pattern telling us how to build our components, we will find ourselves asking questions such as, *"Will we build our customer object for the client as a single class or do we build it as a class hierarchy from one, two or perhaps three classes?"* Having a well-defined pattern, which shows exactly how we should build a component, provides us with the answers to questions like these.

I see patterns being classified as either general or specific.

General Patterns

These apply to a general system and have nothing to do with choices of operating systems, programming languages, or technologies. An example of this type of pattern would be a general pattern for making an Order Entry application. Every order entry application will have certain features regardless of what you use to build it. This type of pattern is useful because it can guide you in a general design of your project. However, in this phase we're more concerned with specific patterns.

Specific Patterns

These can be used to build a particular component of a system, and they are dependent upon the system that we're using. For example, if I were building a three-tier project, I might need to build dozens of client components. It would be really helpful if I could find a pattern to build this type of component. I could then reuse this pattern over and over again, to design and build all of my client components.

UML diagrams will not only provide us with the patterns that exist within our project's components, but also show us how to code these objects. If we are fortunate, there will already be a coding solution for the patterns we find in our UML diagrams. If there isn't already a pattern, we will need to create activity diagrams in order to map out the coding solution.

Unfortunately, you see very little discussion of patterns in the Visual Basic literature, so there are very few patterns for Visual Basic components. Visual Basic has only recently moved toward being object-oriented, and I believe that many developers are still trying to write OO programs using non-OOP techniques. As the Visual Basic community moves more toward using OOP techniques, I think they will also be jumping onto the pattern bandwagon.

Finding Your Own Patterns

Patterns that show how a component will actually perform its required task are not so obvious and are rarely already defined. For example, the three-tier framework dictates that there will be client components with certain properties, but how we actually make this client component have these properties is completely up to us.

There are many resources that can guide us in finding these patterns, but for the most part we will end up designing the patterns for the individual components ourselves. This is especially true because many of the frameworks are so new that there are often very few, if any, patterns created for the framework's components. In addition, since these frameworks are new, they usually have not been thoroughly tested either.

This means that before we use any framework we will have to first create our own patterns and thoroughly test them. While this may sound difficult, it really is not.

These patterns can be found quite easily if we design our components with UML models. The patterns we will use to design our project will be based on object-oriented principles, good coding techniques, and sound project management.

Why Are Patterns So Useful?

Project design really comes from two sides: the inside and the outside. The outside is based on our user requirements, and the inside is based on the programming language, technologies, and server components that we choose.

If we are using the same internal system for all of our projects, then once we've designed and built the internal components for the first time, we can reuse them for all of our projects based on this internal system. By the same reasoning, once we've designed and coded our Enterprise patterns, in order to build future Enterprise projects, we only need to be concerned with the user requirements and building the external part of our project; the patterns will provide everything else.

If we take all of these patterns and put them together, we can build what can be considered our own Visual Basic 6 Enterprise framework. This framework will have a set of rules that must be followed, and will shape how we build the rest of our project, i.e. the external part built from the user requirements (and use cases).

> *Creating entire frameworks to build a particular type of project is perhaps one of the most efficient ways of building projects. Many companies and third-party software vendors are working late hours trying to make frameworks like this for Visual Basic 6 Enterprise projects.*

We can think of this as building prefabricated houses. Every prefabricated house is built from a similar structure, a basic framework that will underlie every house. This doesn't mean that the houses will all look identical. Once we move beyond the basic framework, each house will have certain things added to make it unique: landscaping, color arrangement, bathroom fixtures, carpeting, etc. While the framework of each house is identical, we can place different things within this framework to make completely different houses.

When it comes to our Visual Basic projects, the idea is to make "prefabricated" projects. We make our basic framework and then, based on the users' requirements and the needs of the particular project, we will add the features to make the application unique.

Building the framework is usually the most difficult part of a project. From design to implementation, it can take six months to a year. However, once these frameworks have been established, we don't have to worry about things like making connections to databases. As long as we follow the rules of our Visual Basic Enterprise framework, the framework will handle all of these things. We only need to be concerned with adding features that are required by our project.

Finding Patterns in our Sequence Diagrams

Look at the **Create New Customer** sequence diagram below. Now look at the **Create New Product** sequence in conjunction with **Create New Customer** diagram. It is easy to see that these diagrams are similar. In fact, they are practically identical.

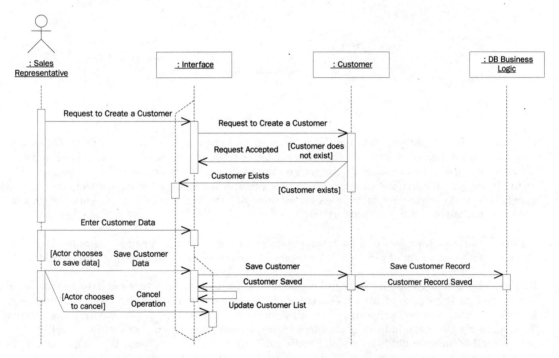

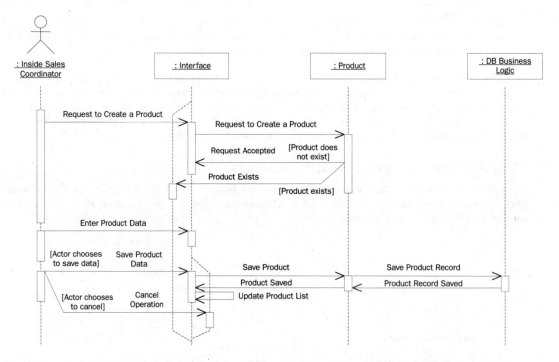

If we were to look at the properties of these customer and product components, they would all seem very different. A sequence diagram, though, only looks at the messages being passed back and forth, which means that it only looks at the **object's public methods**. When we view these three objects' methods, we see that they are all very similar. We can also see that the DB Business Logic component works in an identical manner for all three objects. What does it mean when things have the same methods but different properties?

To answer this question, let's step back for a moment and use *cars* for our next example. Each car is an object with its own set of properties, but every car shares the same underlying functionality.

It might be worth just stopping and thinking about this for a moment. Every car has a unique set of properties that helps us to identify them: color, shape, type of wheels, manufacturer, etc. Yet, even though cars have different properties, they all perform pretty much the same activities: accelerating, braking, turning corners, indicating at junctions, etc. Although every car has a different set of properties that makes it unique, they all function in largely the same manner. We do not have to find a whole new way of making a car each time we want to make a new, unique car. We can use the same technique to build a car whether it is going to be red or metallic silver, four seats or two. Since the way every car works is essentially the same, we only need one way to build an infinite number of unique cars. The way a car is put together (wheels, steering wheel, lights, dashboard...) is a pattern. It is because of this pattern that we can use the same technique to build an infinite number of unique cars (just look down your street).

Components work in the same way. Even though they may have different properties, they can still work in exactly the same way. If we know how to design or build one of these objects, we know how to build all of them. Once I figure out how to build my **Customer** object, I will also know how to build my order and product objects, too. By building similar sequence diagrams from our Modify and Delete use cases, we will find that these tasks are also alike for our Customer, Order and Product objects.

How Can We Take Advantage of Patterns?

Let's take this one step further and try to see how this will affect our Northwind project. If Visual Basic had true inheritance, this certainly would be a place we could use it. We could build one base class that had all of our methods (remember, the methods are the same for all our objects). We could then inherit this class into our **Customer, Order** and **Product** objects. We would then have the same methods within each of our classes but would only have coded these methods once (in the base class). Unfortunately, we don't have inheritance in Visual Basic so let us snap back to the real world and find a way to take advantage of this pattern in Visual Basic.

Interfaces

There's a lot of confusion about Visual Basic interfaces. A Visual Basic interface is a class with methods and properties with no code. Another Visual Basic class can then implement this interface. The class that implements an interface will get all of the methods and properties that are in the interface. These interfaces allow you to have one standard set of methods and properties for a group of similar components.

For example, I could create an `Animal` interface that has a `Move` and a `Sleep` method. I could then implement this interface into a `Rabbit` component. I would then have to write the code to make the `Rabbit` object move or sleep the correct way for a rabbit when these methods are called. I could also make a `Cat` component that implemented the `Animal` interface, and write the appropriate code for that object. If I had an object built from the `Animal` interface, I could call the `Move` method and that object would respond in the way that was appropriate; that is, the rabbit would jump and the cat would walk. This is a form of **polymorphism**.

While this form of polymorphism could be useful in our current example (since we do want all of our components to have the same methods), it will not offer us any advantage in actually coding our components. Remember: an interface has no code within it, the classes that implement the interface must write all of the code for the methods and properties in the interface. We are looking for a solution where we can write code once, and reuse it for all of our components. Interfaces will not provide this type of solution.

While interfaces could apply here, they will greatly complicate the code and offer only a small improvement in our coding solution. It is for this reason we will not discuss them any further.

Object Hierarchies

The other option is to use an object hierarchy to build our objects. The hierarchy would look something like the following:

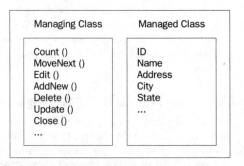

Managing Class	Managed Class
Count ()	ID
MoveNext ()	Name
Edit ()	Address
AddNew ()	City
Delete ()	State
Update ()	...
Close ()	
...	

The hierarchy here is between the Managing Class and the Managed Class.

On the bottom of this hierarchy is a class that could contain the properties of the object (the **Managed Class**). As all of these objects have different properties, this class will be completely different for each of our objects.

Next up in the hierarchy, is a class that will manage the bottom class, which we will call the **Managing Class**. This class will contain all of our client-side methods, such as `Move to the Next Customer`, `Add a New Product`, `Count Customers`, `Update Products`, etc.

When considering this hierarchy, we discover one amazing fact: the Managing Class would be 99% identical for every one of our objects! This is really something - a few hours of work talking to our users, converting this information into use cases and sequence diagrams, has helped us find a pattern within our system. Once we have the middle class coded, we can then build all of the rest of our client side objects by simply making the upper and lower classes - which is a relatively easy task.

The Managing Class performs the same basic tasks for all of these objects.

We can see that our client components will have many methods that will be the same for all the components. Using Visual Basic, we can build one of these client components, such as the Customer component, and use it as a code template to build the other client components – such as the Order component, the Product component, etc. When we look at the sequence diagrams for different components and find patterns like this, we can turn these patterns into code templates. The relationship between patterns and code templates is very similar to the relationship between a component and a class.

Without this ability to identify patterns, we would have been making these components separately… almost certainly we have saved time and development funds by identifying patterns.

> **The time spent using UML has already paid off.**

Exploiting Patterns for Code Reuse

We can use patterns when we find that we are building the same types of components, yet they are different enough to prevent reuse of the code from one component to the next. A `Customer` component and an `Employee` component will have similar functionality but be very different components. Both of these could have a managing class that would allow you to move through either a collection of customers or employees. The methods of the managing class would be identical for the two components. Each component would have methods such as `AddNew`, `Edit`, `Delete`, `MoveNext`, `MoveLast`, etc. in their managing class.

As we have seen, the managed class of an `Employee` and `Customer` component would be very different, as each component would have a different set of properties. In general, we will find that any component that we are building that is based on a managing class and a managed class will have a basic set of functionality that will be identical in every component. Thus, we will find a pattern in all of our components that have a managing class managing a collection of objects belonging to some managed class.

This form of code reuse allows one to build the foundation of your project using code generation. Code generation is where the basic code for a project is generated based on a set of information. The information to generate code can be UML class diagrams or a database. Once I define how to code a particular pattern, I can reuse that code to generate code for any other component built from that pattern. Thus, if I find a way to code my `Customer` component, I can use that method to also build my `Employee`, `Order` and `Order Details` components. While we can do this manually (i.e. cut and paste code and rewrite the code for the new components), we can also write Visual Basic code to generate the required code.

In this way, the basic components of our system can be generated with a Visual Basic code generation project. While this may sound futuristic, it is not. The code for building a simple Visual Basic code generator to create a DNA three-tier project is included in Appendix C. Whenever you find that you are building components from a pattern, you should design and build a code generator. Once the generator is built, the code that is generated can go through rigorous testing. Once the generated code has passed the testing phase, future components should move through testing with a minimum of bugs. Ideally, once the generator creates bug-free code, all future components built from the generator will be bug-free. Realistically, there will always be one or two small things that will need to be adjusted. However, there will be far less time debugging and cleaning the components from a tested code generator than if each component is built from the ground up by developers.

Even if a pattern is found you will still have to write the initial code that will be used to generate future components. Components that are reused in multiple applications will also have to be initially built. You will also have components that cannot be built from either the first or second form of code reuse. In all of these cases, you will have to build your component from the ground up. This will always be an expensive process in terms of time and cost.

If you have followed the rules of good design writing the actual code will be a matter of translating the design into actual code. Providing you have performed thorough testing of your design by creating small testing components, the majority of the hard work has been done. You will need to translate the UML diagrams, in particular the sequence and class diagrams, to code.

Now that we have looked a little at code reuse with patterns, let's see how we can reuse components even in a very different environment. We will take our `Products` component from a fat-client order entry application and reuse it in a thin-client Internet application.

Using an ASP page

It has become common practice to call Visual Basic components from ASP pages. By placing code in the Visual Basic component, many pages can use the same component. If you need several ASP pages to do the same thing, without a Visual Basic component you will have to write the same code in every ASP page. If you need to change something in the code, you will have to go through all of your ASP pages and manually make the changes.

You could include files in your ASP pages for shared code, but this can be complicated. Another problem with ASP pages is that they do not work as efficiently as a Visual Basic component. ASP pages do not have typed variables so everything is a variant. In general, the more complicated the code is, the greater the difference in performance between running the code in a Visual Basic component and running it in ASP pages.

It is also easier to test and debug Visual Basic components. By writing your business logic into a Visual Basic component, you can test the component using standard Visual Basic techniques. When you have worked out all of the bugs in the code, you can integrate it with an ASP page.

Let us now take a look at this example.

Using a Visual Basic Component and an ASP Page

We will use the `Products` component from our DNA application and the VB6 UML book to generate product information for an HTML page. The first question we must ask is, "Is this component appropriate for doing this?" We talked about reusing components so the question is, "Does it make sense to reuse the `Products` component for this application?"

The `Products` component was originally built for a Visual Basic EXE order entry application. The service this component was to perform was to review, update and add product records by either using a recordset bound to a control or by using properties of the object.

In our ASP application, we want a user to be able to submit a request to view all of the products of a particular group. The information will be returned in a standard HTML table. This information is dynamic, so the table must be made for each request.

We could build an ASP page that calls a Visual Basic component, which calls the `Products` component. The Visual Basic component will then use this component to retrieve all of the products for all a particular category.

In this scenario, we would not need the part of our Products component that binds to interface components. We could though use the properties of our products component to get the information. Thus, the products component can be used for our purposes.

Another possibility would be to create a stored procedure. For an application like this, a stored procedure would be the usual choice, though it may not be the best choice. SQL Server 7.0 comes with a web wizard that converts a recordset into an HTML page. With a few modifications, you could use this wizard to build any HTML page you needed from the data. The problem with stored procedures is scalability. What if our web site becomes very popular and we start having hundreds of requests a second? Eventually, our server will reach a point where it will no longer be able to keep up with the requests to build web pages. Scaling databases can be done, but it is difficult.

Let us go back to our original solution, where we had a Visual Basic web component being called from the ASP page that called the products component. Let us place the Visual Basic web component and the products component on the web server. As the demand for the site increases, you can create a web farm; that is, you can use multiple identical web servers to share the load. Each web server will have the Visual Basic web component and the products component on it. This solution will easily scale to be as large as needed. Thus, using a Visual Basic component to build the HTML page makes sense. However, this still does not justify using the Products component.

The Products component calls a server component that then requests the data from the database. Our Visual Basic component could call the database directly and request the data from the database, or it could also directly call the server component for the data. With regards to efficiency, it is possible that calling the Products component, then calling the server component, which retrieves the data, is slightly slower than calling the database directly. The actual difference will depend on the system and the load on the system. There is one advantage, though, to using the Products component.

If, instead of having to create just one set of data, we had to write code to return hundreds of different data sets, writing directly to the database would fill our Visual Basic web component with code to connect and retrieve data from the database. We would need programmers who are experts in ADO and in using stored procedures. We would also be mixing our business services logic with our data services logic. The code could quickly become confusing and hard to maintain and upgrade. If there were a change in the database, it would mean we would have to change our Visual Basic web component. Thus, using the Products component means that the Visual Basic developer creating the component will not have to know anything about ADO and, furthermore, the web component will not be affected by changes to the database. You would have to perform tests comparing performance with and without the Products component to see if the difference in performance is significant. It is very likely that under heavy loads the difference will be very small between using the server component and directly connecting to the database.

Before I would make any decision, I would create small applications (prototypes) for all three methods (using the Products component, calling the server component directly from the web component and connecting directly to the database from the web component). I would then test each of the three solutions under various loads. Based on the performance of each solution, I would make my final choice for the project. Below we will show the code for the solution using the products component. The other two solutions could be written by making minor changes to this application, i.e. by just changing how the data is retrieved.

It is likely that if we were going to use the Products component, we would probably not use our original component. We only need to use the properties; all of the code for binding a recordset is excess code. In a production environment, we would probably reuse all of the code from the products component that is needed for the properties, and remove all of the code related to binding the recordset. Thus, we would reuse the code and not the component. Because I want to show how to use a Visual Basic component from an ASP page and not how to rewrite the Products component, I will only make a few modifications to the Products component so that it will work with this project. We will begin our project with the page that the user will use to make a request for product information.

> The following sections will look quickly at the coding techniques involved in reusing a component in a different environment. If you are not familiar with coding in Visual Basic, you may find it advisable to skip to the section on 'The Future' towards the end of the chapter.

The Client HTML Page

We need a web page with a listbox listing all of the categories. The user selects a category and submits the form. The server will then return a list of all of the products in that category. The HTML page will appear as follows:

The code for this HTML page will look as follows:

```
<HTML>
<HEAD>
<META NAME="GENERATOR" Content="Microsoft Visual Studio 6.0">
<TITLE></TITLE>
</HEAD>

<BODY>
<FORM action=GetProductsByCategory.asp>
<P><STRONG>Select A Category</STRONG>
<P></P>
<P>
<P>
<SELECT id=select1 name=select1 style="HEIGHT: 22px; WIDTH: 150px">
<OPTION Value="0" selected>Beverages Category</OPTION>
<OPTION Value="1" >Condiments Category</OPTION>
<OPTION Value="2" > Confections Category</OPTION>
<OPTION Value="3" >Dairy Products Category</OPTION>
<OPTION Value="4" > Grains/Cereals Category</OPTION>
<OPTION Value="5" > Meat/Poultry Category</OPTION>
<OPTION Value="6" >Produce Category</OPTION>
<OPTION Value="7" >Seafood Category</OPTION>
</SELECT></P>
<P><INPUT id=submit1 name=submit1 type=submit value=Submit></P>
<P></P>
</FORM>
</BODY>
</HTML>
```

When the user selects a category and clicks on the button, a request will be submitted to an ASP page named `GetProductsByCategory.asp` in the same directory as the HTML page we just built. So, our next task is to build this `GetProductsByCategory.asp` page.

Building the ASP Page

The ASP page will take the request and pass it on to a Visual Basic component called `prjRetrieveWebInfo.clsWeb`. This will create an HTML page containing a table with a list of the products in the selected category:

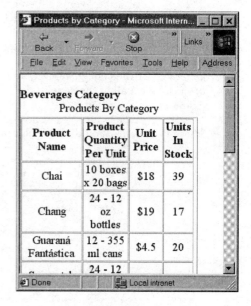

The code for the ASP page looks as follows:

```
<%@ Language=VBScript %>
<%
Dim objGetProducts
Set objGetProducts=CreateObject("prjRetrieveWebInfo.clsWeb")
objGetProducts.GetCategoryInformation "","",Response,Request
%>
<HTML>
<HEAD>
<META NAME="GENERATOR" Content="Microsoft Visual Studio 6.0">
</HEAD>
<BODY>

<P> </P>

</BODY>
</HTML>
```

The ASP code for this page is fairly simple. All this page does is call the Visual Basic component. There is another very interesting thing to notice about this code. The method `GetCategoryInformation` takes four parameters. The first two are the password and user ID, which are empty. The next two are the ASP `Response` and `Request` objects. We are going to pass these into our Visual Basic component so that our Visual Basic component can get all of the request information from the `Request` object. Our Visual Basic component can send information back to the client using the `Response` object. First, though, let us look at the `Products` component and see how we will have to modify it.

Modifying the Products Component

The only change we have to make to the `Products` component is to change the top class from a Visual Basic user control to a Visual Basic class. This change means that we have to change the control's `Initialize` or `ReadProperties` and `Terminate` events to `Class_Initialize` and `Class_Terminate` events. Open a new Visual Basic ActiveX DLL project. Add a reference to the server component from the VB6 UML example or from the code generated by the code generator in Appendix C (if you have not compiled the server DLL, you will have to do that before you can set the reference). Call the project `prjWebProduct`. Add the `clsProduct` and `clsProductManager` classes (these are named `clsProducts` and `clsProductsManager` respectively in the code generated by the code generator, and will need to be renamed) and the `ctlProduct` control into the project. Select all of the code in the `ctlProduct` component, copy it and then remove the control. Add a new class called `clsProducts`. Move the code from the control's `Initialize` or `ReadProperties` and `Terminate` events into the class's `Initalize` and `Terminate` events. These two events should now look as follows:

```
Private Sub Class_Initialize()
    Set ProductCollectionCatalogID = New clsProductManager
    m_lngCategoryIDEquals = m_def_CategoryIDEquals
    ReDim m_acolDataMembersArray(m_def_NumberOfProductCollections)
    ReDim m_blnDataMembersInitialized(m_def_NumberOfProductCollections)
    Set m_acolDataMembersArray(e_ProductsCategoryID) = ProductCollectionCatalogID
    m_blnDataMembersInitialized(e_ProductsCategoryID) = False
End Sub


Private Sub Class_Terminate()
    Set ProductCollectionCatalogID = Nothing
End Sub
```

Compile the new project with a new GUID (that is, with no version compatibility) into a new component.

Building the Visual Basic Component

We will now see how to build the VB component, which will be called from our ASP page. This component will return an HTML page containing a table with the products in the selected category.

Create a new Visual Basic ActiveX DLL project called `prjRetrieveWebInfo`. Add references to the **Microsoft Active Server Pages Object Library** and to the `prjWebProduct` we just created. Make a reference to the MTS library. We will make this an MTS component, though there may not be too much gained by doing this. However, since we are using the `Response` object and `Request` object from the ASP page, and the ASP page is running under MTS, we will choose to run this component under MTS. My computer is using Windows 2000 Beta, so the MTS library is now replaced by **COM+ Services Type Library**.

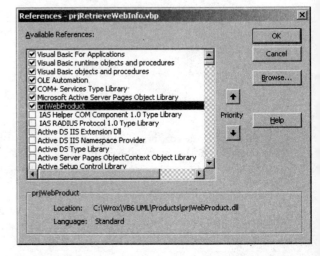

Change the class name to `clsWeb`. Add the following code to the class:

```
Option Explicit
Private m_objContext As ObjectContext
Implements ObjectControl
```

We have implemented the `ObjectControl` interface so that our control can run under MTS. This means we must implement all of the methods of the `ObjectControl`, so we need to add the following code to the `ObjectControl` methods. When our object is instantiated, the `ObjectControl_Activate` event will be fired. We can use this event to get a reference to the `ObjectContext` object:

```
Private Sub ObjectControl_Activate()
    Set m_objContext = GetObjectContext
End Sub
```

When the object is destroyed, the `ObjectControl_Deactivate` event will be raised, and we must destroy the `ObjectContext` object:

```
Private Sub ObjectControl_Deactivate()
    Set m_objContext = Nothing
End Sub
```

Finally, we will also have to implement the `ObjectControl_CanBePooled` function, although this does not actually have any functionality at present. However, we may get an error if we don't implement the entire `ObjectControl` interface:

```
Private Function ObjectControl_CanBePooled() As Boolean
    ObjectControl_CanBePooled = False
End Function
```

We will use a custom function called `CreateInstance` to create our components. If the current component is running under MTS, the `CreateInstance` function will use the MTS `ObjectContext` object's `CreateInstance` function. Otherwise, we will use the `New` keyword:

```
Private Function CreateInstance(ProgID As String) As Object
    On Error GoTo CreateInstanceError

    If Not m_objContext Is Nothing Then
        Set CreateInstance = m_objContext.CreateInstance(ProgID)
    Else
        Select Case ProgID
            Case "prjWebProducts.clsProducts"
                Set CreateInstance = New prjWebProduct.clsProducts
        End Select
    End If

    Exit Function

CreateInstanceError:

    Err.Raise Err.Number, Err.Source & " CreateInstance", Err.Description

End Function
```

We will also create sub routines for `SetComplete` and `SetAbort` to commit or abort the transaction if MTS is running:

```
Public Sub SetComplete()
    If Not m_objContext Is Nothing Then
        m_objContext.SetComplete
    End If
End Sub
```

```
Public Sub SetAbort()
    If Not m_objContext Is Nothing Then
        m_objContext.SetAbort
    End If
End Sub
```

We will create a function called `BuildProductsByCategoryTable`. This function takes the `CategoryID` as a parameter and will return a string with HTML tags to place the product information into a table,

```
Public Function BuildProductsByCategoryTable _
                (ByVal v_vCategoryID As Variant) As Variant
Dim lngCategoryCounter As Long
Dim strHTML As String
Dim strQuery As String
Dim objProduct As prjWebProduct.clsProducts
Dim lngProductCounter As Long
```

This function will use the `Products` object to retrieve the data, so we will create the `Products` component:

```
Set objProduct = CreateInstance("prjWebProducts.clsProducts")
```

We can use the `GetProductCollection` method of this object to build a collection of products with the `ProductID` that was passed into the function:

```
objProduct.GetProductCollection(e_ProductsCategoryID)
```

We will now build an HTML page to place this information into a table using the properties of the product object. We will begin by building the header of the page:

```
strHTML = "<HTML>" & vbCrLf & _
    "<HEAD>" & vbCrLf & _
    "<TITLE>" & "Products by Category" & "</TITLE>" & vbCrLf & vbCrLf & _
    "</HEAD>" & vbCrLf & vbCrLf & _
    "</HEAD>" & vbCrLf & vbCrLf & _
    "<BODY TEXT=" & Chr(34) & "#000000" & Chr(34) & _
    " BGCOLOR=" & Chr(34) & "#FFFFFF" & Chr(34) & " LINK=" & Chr(34) & _
    "#0000FF" & Chr(34) & " VLINK=" & Chr(34) & "#6600CC" & Chr(34) & _
    " ALINK=" & Chr(34) & "#FF0000" & Chr(34) & " TOPMARGIN=" & Chr(34) & _
    "0" & Chr(34) & " LEFTMARGIN=" & Chr(34) & "0" & Chr(34) & ">" & _
    vbCrLf & vbCrLf & vbCrLf & "<BR>" & vbCrLf
```

We have hard coded the category options into the page as there are only a few of them and we did not build a `Category` object in the VB6 UML book (though you can generate one with the code generator in a few seconds). If there were only a few categories then it might save time to create an array of the product names upon initialization to eliminate the need to look up the products every time. This array could then be looped through in the code to get the category names. If a new category were added, only the code for initializing the array would have to be changed. If the categories changed frequently, we would have to get the names dynamically.

```
Select Case v_vCategoryID
    Case 0
        strHTML = strHTML & "<B> Beverages Category </B>" & "<BR>" & vbCrLf
    Case 1
        strHTML = strHTML & "<B> Condiments Category </B>" & "<BR>" & vbCrLf
    Case 2
        strHTML = strHTML & "<B> Confections Category </B>" & "<BR>" & vbCrLf
    Case 3
        strHTML = strHTML & "<B> Dairy Products Category </B>" & "<BR>" & vbCrLf
    Case 4
        strHTML = strHTML & "<B> Grains/Cereals Category </B>" & "<BR>" & vbCrLf
    Case 5
        strHTML = strHTML & "<B> Meat/Poultry Category </B>" & "<BR>" & vbCrLf
    Case 6
        strHTML = strHTML & "<B> Produce Category </B>" & "<BR>" & vbCrLf
    Case 7
        strHTML = strHTML & "<B> Seafood Category </B>" & "<BR>" & vbCrLf
End Select
```

Now we will build the HTML table to put the product information in:

```
strHTML = strHTML & "<TABLE BORDER=1 CELLSPACING=1 CELLPADDING=1 WIDTH=" & _
        Chr(34) & Str(25) & Chr(34) & ">" & vbCrLf & _
        "<CAPTION>" & "Products By Category" & "</CAPTION>" & vbCrLf
```

Next, we put in the headers for the table:

```
strHTML = strHTML & vbCrLf & "<TH>" & _
        "Product Name" & _
        "</TH>"
strHTML = strHTML & vbCrLf & "<TH>" & _
        "Product Quantity Per Unit" & _
        "</TH>"
strHTML = strHTML & vbCrLf & "<TH>" & _
        "Unit Price" & _
        "</TH>"
strHTML = strHTML & vbCrLf & "<TH>" & _
        "Units In Stock" & _
        "</TH>"

strHTML = strHTML & "</TR>" & vbCrLf
```

Then we set the `CategoryID` of the `Product` object and refresh the object:

```
objProduct.CategoryIDEquals = v_vCategoryID + 1
objProduct.GetProductCollection(e_ProductsCategoryID).Refresh
```

We can then use the object to retrieve the information we need:

```
With objProduct.GetProductCollection(e_ProductsCategoryID).Item
    objProduct.GetProductCollection(e_ProductsCategoryID).MoveFirst
    For lngProductCounter = 1 To _
        objProduct.GetProductCollection(e_ProductsCategoryID).RecordCount
```

Now we add the products into the table:

```
        strHTML = strHTML & "<TR>"
        strHTML = strHTML & "<TD align =" & Chr(34) & "center" & Chr(34) & ">"
        strHTML = strHTML & .ProductName & "</TD>"
        strHTML = strHTML & "<TD align =" & Chr(34) & "center" & Chr(34) & ">"
        strHTML = strHTML & .QuantityPerUnit & "</TD>"
        strHTML = strHTML & "<TD align =" & Chr(34) & "center" & Chr(34) & ">"
        strHTML = strHTML & "$" & .UnitPrice & "</TD>"
        strHTML = strHTML & "<TD align =" & Chr(34) & "center" & Chr(34) & ">"
        strHTML = strHTML & .UnitsInStock & "</TD>"
        strHTML = strHTML & "<TD align =" & Chr(34) & "center" & Chr(34) & ">"
```

Move to the next record and loop:

```
        objProduct.GetProductCollection(e_ProductsCategoryID).MoveNext
        strHTML = strHTML & "</TR>" & vbCrLf
    Next
End With
```

End the table and return the HTML string:

```
    strHTML = strHTML & " </TABLE> " & vbCrLf & "<BR>"
    BuildProductsByCategoryTable = strHTML
End Function
```

We will use the `BuildProductsByCategoryTable` function in other functions. For example, we could return all of the products in a function called `GetGeneralProductInformation`. This will be called from the ASP page. We will use an ASP `Response` object as a parameter for this function. This function will loop through all of the products. To keep it simple, I am hardcoding the number of products, but in production code we would use a long constant for the number of categories. We will use the `Write` method of the `Response` object in our Visual Basic web component to return the string:

```
Public Sub GetGeneralProductInformation(ByVal v_vUserID As Variant, _
    ByVal v_vPassword As Variant, ByVal v_oResponse As ASPTypeLibrary.Response)
Dim lngCategoryCounter as Long
For lngCategoryCounter = 0 to 7
    v_oResponse.Write BuildProductTable()
Next
End Sub
```

We can also build another function that reads from the HTML page we initially created, with the combo box with categories. In this case, we will need the ASP `Request` object so we can know which category they selected. The code would look as follows:

```
Public Sub GetCategoryInformation(ByVal v_vUserID As Variant, _
                                  ByVal v_vPassword As Variant, _
                                  ByVal v_oResponse As ASPTypeLibrary.Response, _
                                  ByVal v_oRequest As ASPTypeLibrary.Request)

v_oResponse.Write BuildProductsByCategoryTable(v_oRequest.QueryString("select1"))

End Sub
```

We can create an entire range of pages using Visual Basic. For example, we could create an error page as follows:

```
Private Function BuildLoginErrorPage(ByVal v_sErrorDetails As String) As Variant
Dim strHTML As String

strHTML = "<HTML>" & vbCrLf & _
    "<HEAD>" & vbCrLf & vbCrLf & _
    " <TITLE>Introduction Page</TITLE>" & vbCrLf & vbCrLf & _
    "</HEAD>" & vbCrLf & _
    "<BODY TEXT=" & Chr(34) & "#000000" & Chr(34) & " BGCOLOR=" & Chr(34) & _
    "#FFFFFF" & Chr(34) & "LINK=" & Chr(34) & "#0000FF" & Chr(34) & _
    " VLINK=" & Chr(34) & "#6600CC" & Chr(34) & " ALINK=" & Chr(34) & _
    "#FF0000" & Chr(34) & " TOPMARGIN=" & Chr(34) & "0" & Chr(34) & _
    " LEFTMARGIN=" & Chr(34) & "0" & Chr(34) & ">" & vbCrLf & vbCrLf & vbCrLf & _
    "<!------MAIN INFO---->" & vbCrLf & vbCrLf & _
    "<BR><BR>" & vbCrLf & vbCrLf & _
    "<CENTER>" & vbCrLf & _
    "<FONT FACE=Helvetica, Arial SIZE=+3>" & vbCrLf & _
    "Please try again...login Failed" & vbCrLf & _
    "</FONT>" & vbCrLf & _
    "</CENTER>" & vbCrLf & vbCrLf & _
    "<BR>" & vbCrLf & _
    "<BR>" & vbCrLf & _
    "<BR>" & vbCrLf & vbCrLf & _
    "<CENTER>" & vbCrLf & _
    "<FONT FACE=" & Chr(34) & "Arial, Helvetica" & Chr(34) & " FONT SIZE=" & _
    Chr(34) & "2" & Chr(34) & ">" & Chr(34) & vbCrLf & vbCrLf & _
    v_sErrorDetails & vbCrLf & vbCrLf & _
    "</center>" & vbCrLf & _
    "</FONT>" & vbCrLf & _
    "<FONT FACE=" & Chr(34) & "Arial, Helvetica" & Chr(34) & " FONT SIZE=" & _
    Chr(34) & "1" & Chr(34) & ">" & Chr(34) & vbCrLf & vbCrLf & _
    "All contents ©1999, Northwind, All Rights Reserved." & vbCrLf & _
    "</center>" & vbCrLf & _
    "</FONT>" & "</BODY>" & vbCrLf & "</HTML>" _
    BuildLoginErrorPage = strHTML
End Function
```

There are many different options when it comes to building HTML pages. You could also store the HTML as text in a database and create a component to retrieve and save the HTML pages. There would, however, be extra overhead to connect to the database to get the HTML text. It is only through testing that you could tell if this was a workable solution for your system. If the HTML pages were in the database, hackers could not alter them. You would, though, have to create a staging area where your developers would first place the pages for initial testing. Once the text was correct, they could be moved into the database.

The process of moving pages could be automated. The only pages that could be accessed by a hacker would be the ASP pages that call your Visual Basic components. Even these could be protected by placing the ASP pages in a database and pushing the correct ASP pages out onto the web server periodically. If you needed to make a change to the ASP pages, you would place the new ASP page into the database and when the next push came the new version would go out onto the web server. In this way, no one would have permission to change the ASP pages directly. If someone did find a way to hack into the system and change the ASP pages, the hacked pages would automatically be replaced during the next refresh of the pages. Unfortunately, we must take these things into consideration.

While ASP pages can be replaced without shutting the server down, the same is not true of Visual Basic web classes. Because web classes are DLLs, they will require the web server to be stopped before you can replace them. This is a serious limitation and one of the reasons why ASP is still a better option than web classes.

Let us now turn to a different example where our `products` component can be used.

Using DHTML

Dynamic HTML is a great tool for the intranet. Unfortunately, Netscape Navigator 4.0 and Microsoft Internet Explorer 4.0/5.0 differ considerably in their implementations of DHTML, so DHTML solutions are not useful on the Internet (unless you do not mind creating solutions only for people with current releases of one or the other major browser). On an intranet, you can control what browsers are on the client machines and make sure that everyone has a DHTML-compliant machine.

In this example, we will again use the original `Products` component. We will create the same HTML page with a combo box on it. In addition to the HTML code for the combo box, we will now also have VBScript code in our HTML page. This VBScript code will use the `Products` component to retrieve the products for the category selected and insert a table with those products into the HTML page. This means that we will get the product information directly and rebuild the page without ever going to the web server. This eliminates delay times and makes the web application run just like a Visual Basic EXE application.

Coding the DHTML HTML Page

You can create this page in Microsoft Visual Interdev or any text editor (such as the perennial favorite, Notepad). We will begin by putting the tag in that says we are about to write Visual Basic Script:

```
<HTML>
<SCRIPT LANGUAGE=VBSCRIPT>
```

We will later place a list box onto the page. We will call that list box `lstCategory`. When that list box has been clicked, we will want to place a table with the current products into our HTML page without calling the web server. We will place our code into the `OnPropertyChange` event of the `lstCategory` list box. Add this to your HTML page:

```
Sub lstCategory_OnPropertyChange

Dim strHTML
Dim strQuery
Dim lngProductCounter
Dim e_ProductsCategoryID
e_ProductsCategoryID=1
```

Notice that in VBScript all variables are late-binding variants. With DHTML, you do not create your components with the New keyword. You will create the object in the HTML section of your code. The HTML code later in the page will create an object called objProduct, which is a reference to the product object. We will first initialize the product collection:

```
objProduct.GetProductCollection(e_ProductsCategoryID)
```

We want to place the name of the category selected above our product table. We can access the value of the item selected in the listbox using the expression lstCategory.value.

```
Select Case lstCategory.value
    Case 0
        strHTML = strHTML & "<B> Beverages Category </B>" & "<BR>" & vbCrLf
    Case 1
        strHTML = strHTML & "<B> Condiments Category </B>" & "<BR>" & vbCrLf
    Case 2
        strHTML = strHTML & "<B> Confections Category </B>" & "<BR>" & vbCrLf
    Case 3
        strHTML = strHTML & "<B> Dairy Products Category </B>" & "<BR>" & vbCrLf
    Case 4
        strHTML = strHTML & "<B> Grains/Cereals Category </B>" & "<BR>" & vbCrLf
    Case 5
        strHTML = strHTML & "<B> Meat/Poultry Category </B>" & "<BR>" & vbCrLf
    Case 6
        strHTML = strHTML & "<B> Produce Category </B>" & "<BR>" & vbCrLf
    Case 7
        strHTML = strHTML & "<B> Seafood Category </B>" & "<BR>" & vbCrLf
    End Select
```

We now initialize our table:

```
strHTML = strHTML & "<TABLE BORDER=1 CELLSPACING=1 CELLPADDING=1" & _
        "WIDTH=" & Chr(34) & "25" & Chr(34) & ">" & vbCrLf & _
        "<CAPTION>" & "Products By Category" & "</CAPTION>" & vbCrLf

strHTML = strHTML & vbCrLf & "<TH>" & _
        "Product Name" & _
        "</TH>"
strHTML = strHTML & vbCrLf & "<TH>" & _
        "Product Quantity Per Unit" & _
        "</TH>"
strHTML = strHTML & vbCrLf & "<TH>" & _
        "Unit Price" & _
        "</TH>"
strHTML = strHTML & vbCrLf & "<TH>" & _
        "Units In Stock" & _
        "</TH>"

strHTML = strHTML & "</TR>" & vbCrLf
```

We need to set the `CategoryIDEquals` property of the `Products` component. The `CategoryID` field is one-based, but `lstCategory.value` is zero-based, so we will have to add one first:

```
objProduct.CategoryIDEquals = lstCategory.value + 1
```

Next, we refresh the `Products` component and move through the items. You will notice this is the same code we used in the Visual Basic web component:

```
objProduct.GetProductCollection(e_ProductsCategoryID).Refresh
With objProduct.GetProductCollection(e_ProductsCategoryID).Item
    objProduct.GetProductCollection(e_ProductsCategoryID).MoveFirst
        For lngProductCounter = 1 To _
                objProduct.GetProductCollection(e_ProductsCategoryID).RecordCount
            strHTML = strHTML & "<TR>"
            strHTML = strHTML & "<TD align =" & Chr(34) & "center" & Chr(34) & ">"
            strHTML = strHTML & .ProductName & "</TD>"
            strHTML = strHTML & "<TD align =" & Chr(34) & "center" & Chr(34) & ">"
            strHTML = strHTML & .QuantityPerUnit & "</TD>"
            strHTML = strHTML & "<TD align =" & Chr(34) & "center" & Chr(34) & ">"
            strHTML = strHTML & "$" & .UnitPrice & "</TD>"
            strHTML = strHTML & "<TD align =" & Chr(34) & "center" & Chr(34) & ">"
            strHTML = strHTML & .UnitsInStock & "</TD>"
            strHTML = strHTML & "<TD align =" & Chr(34) & "center" & Chr(34) & ">"
            objProduct.GetProductCollection(e_ProductsCategoryID).MoveNext
            strHTML = strHTML & "</TR>" & vbCrLf
        Next
    End With
strHTML = strHTML & " </TABLE> " & vbCrLf & "<BR>"
```

We will use something that is called a `<DIV>` element. A `<DIV>` element is one of the most important parts of a DHTML application. We can place a `<DIV>` element into our HTML code, and then we can insert text between the element's opening and closing tags. We can also replace text between the `<DIV>` tags. This allows you to add, remove or change sections of your HTML page using script code. In this case, we are inserting `strHTML`, which contains our table in HTML format, into our `<DIV>` element, which we will call `"proddiv"`. The `innerhtml` property contains everything between the opening `<DIV>` tag and the closing `</DIV>` tag, including any other HTML tags. Thus, using the `innerhtml` property, we can insert text between the two tags.

```
document.all.tags("div").Item("proddiv").innerhtml=strHTML
End Sub
```

Finally, we have the closing `</SCRIPT>` tag, and we begin the regular HTML part of our HTML page:

```
</SCRIPT>

<HEAD>
<META NAME="GENERATOR" Content="Microsoft Visual Studio 6.0">
<TITLE></TITLE>
</HEAD>

<BODY>
```

To get a reference to our object, we will use an <OBJECT> element in our HTML page. The object tag has a `classid` attribute, which must be set to the GUID of a public creatable class. Notice that there is the word `clsid` included with the GUID. The `id` attribute gives the object a name that can be referenced in code. CODEBASE gives us the location of the object if it is not on the client machine. You should create a package called a Cab file to distribute your files through the Inter/Intranet. The Visual Basic Package and Deployment wizard can make your Cab files for you (see Chapter 11). In this case, I have created a Cab file called `prjProducts.cab` that is located in the same directory as this HTML file. The string `"1,0,0,0"` is the version number. If there is a copy of `prjProducts` on the client and the version number is higher or equal to this number, the file will not be downloaded. If there is no copy of `prjProducts` on the computer or a copy with a lower version number, the file will be downloaded. We have also set `CategoryIDEquals` to a default of 1.

```
<object classid="clsid:C49C5681-37CC-11D3-A807-009027887C34" id="objProduct"
    CODEBASE="prjProducts.cab#Version=1,0,0,0">
  <param NAME="CategoryIDEquals" = "1">
</object>
```

Next, we build the listbox:

```
<P><STRONG>Select A Category</STRONG>
<P></P>
<P>
<P>
<SELECT id=LstCategory name=1stCategory style="HEIGHT: 22px; WIDTH: 150px">
<OPTION Value="0" selected>Beverages Category</OPTION>
<OPTION Value="1" >Condiments Category</OPTION>
<OPTION Value="2" >Confections Category</OPTION>
<OPTION Value="3" >Dairy Products Category</OPTION>
<OPTION Value="4" >Grains/Cereals Category</OPTION>
<OPTION Value="5" >Meat/Poultry Category</OPTION>
<OPTION Value="6" >Produce Category</OPTION>
<OPTION Value="7" >Seafood Category</OPTION>
</SELECT></P>
<P><INPUT id=ChooseCatagory name=ChooseCatagory Onclick=ChooseCategory type=Button
value=Submit></P>
<P></P>
<INPUT id=text1 name=text1>
```

We will now put our <DIV> tag in. We are placing it below the listbox so we can insert the data directly below the list box.

```
<div ID="proddiv">

</div>
</BODY>
</HTML>
```

There are many possibilities with DHTML. For example, you could bring over information in the form of XML and use that data to create a dynamic application on the client that does not need to communicate to a server. We have only had a glimpse of its potential for use with Visual Basic components.

The Future

Looking at what we have discussed in this book leads us to ask a simple question: "What will be the best way to develop our projects over the next few years?" There will be fundamental principles that will not change in the near future. The basic concept of the logical three-tier model is not likely to change for some time. Building components based on client, business and data services will form the foundation of our object-oriented projects regardless of changes in technology, coding techniques and Visual Basic. Even more importantly, building components based on these three services will shield us from the changes by encapsulating the components of the system.

What we will find changing and becoming more fluid is where we place these components in the physical three-tier model, that is whether these components belong on the client, middle tier server or database server. Technology such as 64 processor NT machines and Windows 2000 with COM + (essentially the next version of MTS) on workstation and server versions will completely rewrite where we place the various components of our system. All assumptions must be assumed false. Never believe what is written or assume that an old technique still applies until you have tested if for yourself and seen that it is really true.

> **You will have to test every assumption.**

Just because you should get maximum efficiency from one solution does not mean you will. The newer technology may have made something else more efficient, or rendered a previously efficient solution useless. The point is, writing testing applications during the development phase will become one of the critical elements in creating an efficient system that fulfills the goals of the client.

This brings out another advantage of using patterns and the second form of code reuse. Imagine that your team develops a set of five workable patterns for a DNA project. For each of the five patterns, you could create a set of testing applications that will test the efficiency of each of the five solutions.

The testing applications could be based on a set of benchmarks that you create, such as the time taken to retrieve or update a recordset or the response time with different numbers of simultaneous users. You can place these testing applications in different arrangements on either the real system or a test system that simulates the production system. You can run the test applications and see how each of the five solutions performs in the real system. Based on these tests, you can determine which solution meets the needs of the system. Using the code generators, you can then generate the framework of your code based on the best solution.

Another vision I have of the future is the inclusion of UML diagrams with code samples. Every developer can relate the story of spending hours stepping through a coding sample trying to figure out what it was doing and how it worked. A simple sequence diagram can explain in a few minutes what could take hours or days to understand by stepping through the code. I would like to see class diagrams and sequence diagrams become a standard for code samples.

Of course, UML diagrams should also become an essential part of every project. Just as it can be very frustrating to step through a code sample, it can be twice as frustrating to spend days trying to understand someone else's code that you must upgrade or debug. A simple sequence diagram could save hours and even days of work when code must pass from one developer to the next. I would hope that the future of Visual Basic development will include the usage of UML and good documentation practices, as outlined in this book.

These are a few of the things I believe will happen over the next few years. We need to reduce the risks of our projects, reduce the amount of time to develop our projects and reduce the costs of our projects. Good project management, proper documentation, a team that manages the project, documentation and managing risks, the usage of UML to perform a thorough design of the system and testing of any assumptions with testing applications will all help our Visual Basic projects meet these requirements. Part of my vision is that through proper project management, Visual Basic projects will begin to reach a 100% success rate.

Summary

In the previous stage of the project, the final decisions were made as to what components will be used. There were many decisions to make in this stage. Do you buy a third party component, reuse existing code or write the code from the ground up? Is using a component the most logical choice or should you use stored procedures? Often, questions can only be answered by creating test applications and finding what solution fits within the parameters of the project. This chapter has shown how these choices can affect your final coding in the development phase.

Visual Basic offers the developer many different ways of doing the same thing. Our Visual Basic order entry application can be built as an EXE with the business and client services on the client machine, as an EXE with the client services on the client and business services on the server (running under MTS or without MTS), or we could make a DHTML application using components. We could also make DHTML applications with XML or a regular Internet application. The choices can make you dizzy. Yet this is what Microsoft Visual Basic is all about: choices. Because we have all of these options, we can choose the best one for our project in the physical design stage.

If you choose to build your components, you have three choices: the first and second form of reuse or building from the ground up. Code reuse in both forms is the best option as it will reduce costs and time. When components are built from the ground up, UML diagrams provide an indispensable tool to allow you to turn the goals of the user into Visual Basic code.

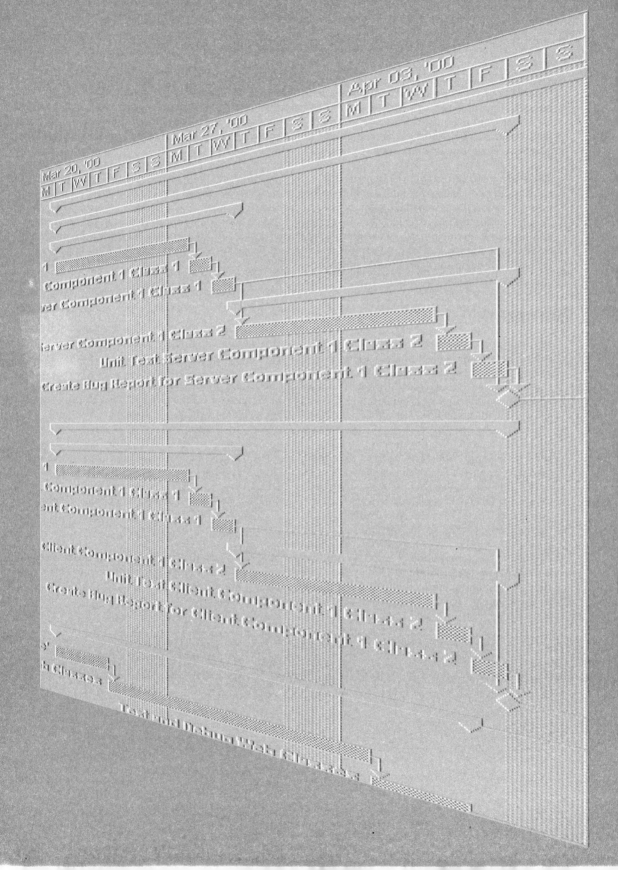

10

Testing

This chapter will provide details of techniques - some general, some specific - for testing and debugging Visual Basic components and products. The testing team can begin to implement some of these techniques as early of the envisionment phase. By carrying out continuous and rigorous testing, with detailed documentation, the team has the best chance of ensuring that the quality of the final product is high and that it meets all requirements.

> The testing that is carried out on the completed product during the "stabilization" stage, leading to product release, is discussed in Chapter 11.

There are two broad categories of testing: **usability testing** and **functional testing**. Usability testing gives the team an idea of how well their solution meets the users' requirements and expectations. Of course, usability testing is performed on the finished product, in order to ensure that it lives up to the expectations of the business and users, but it should be a continuous process starting as early as the envisionment phase. The testing team should create prototype applications to test user interfaces, different methodologies, techniques or technologies and thus arrive at the most effective solution, within the constraints of budget, time and the goals defined in the scope of the project cycle.

Functional testing is the testing of the components of the system, or the system as a whole, to make sure it functions as it is supposed to. Any prototype built for usability testing should first go through functional testing, in order to be sure that the poor performance is not due to a bug in the code. Functional testing will therefore begin in the design phase and extend into the deployment phase (all of the components built in the development phase must undergo functional testing).

We will look at both types of testing in this chapter and also discuss debugging MTS components.

Usability Testing

Usability testing is a very important step in proper design of the project and one of the most often skipped steps of design. I have seen entire projects run for over one year and reach the deployment phase before it is realized that the design that was chosen would not work in the environment in which the application was being deployed. One week of usability testing in the design phase would have found these problems and saved a year of wasted development. Often, there are many possible ways to build a product. The only sure way of finding the one that is best for your project is to build prototypes and usability test each solution.

For the most part, usability testing is divided into two subcategories. The first is testing how usable the user interface is and the second is testing to find the best solution for the business or data services.

User Interface Testing

The user interface needs to be tested for ease of use, to make sure the overall system can accomplish the goals the user needs the system to accomplish and to make sure that the tasks are properly grouped on the forms. User education will be heavily involved in user interface testing. User education may bring user interface prototypes to the end user, and observe them using the prototype with as little interference as possible. User education will take careful notes on any problems the user may have with the interface and any solutions proposed by the user. By a process of improvement and refinement, we can arrive at a GUI that allows the user to harness the product functionality in an easy-to-understand manner.

The developers and testers may also be involved in making the prototypes, and ensuring that they allow the user to perform all necessary services. In order to do this, testers can go through the use cases and make sure every use case can be performed with the user interface prototype. Testers must also make sure that objects on the form and tasks that the forms perform are grouped according to the roles and the tasks performed by people in those roles.

Screenshots of the interfaces can be passed amongst the entire team for suggestions for improvement. Just as we suggested passing around activity diagrams to the entire team to find the best design, we can pass screenshots around to find the best user interface design. You can also post screenshots on an Intranet or build a web application with a user interface prototype and have the entire team (including the users) test the interface.

There are specialized applications that create user interface prototypes or, alternatively, you can just use Visual Basic. The important thing is to remember that a prototype is not the final application and may not be put together in exactly the same way. For this reason, all of the code in the prototype should be discarded and the final product GUI should be built from the ground up *based on the best design found by prototyping.*

Testing of Business and Data Services Components

As we discussed in Chapter 8, when we considered the best way to implement the data and business services components, there will often be a multitude of questions that can only be answered by testing:

> ➤ Should the business services go on the client machine or on the middle-tier server?

> ➤ Should you use MTS on server components?

> ➤ Does an existing component work efficiently enough or does it need to be redesigned for this application?

The testing of business and data services will either be the testing of component solutions or the testing of infrastructure. The component manager should oversee the component solution testing. Testing the infrastructure is the responsibility of the logistician. Our first task is to identify the data and business services that our application will have to perform, and then we can begin searching for the best way for our application to perform these services. For each service, one should document the best way of fulfilling the service. When there are multiple solutions, it is time to do usability testing.

Test Applications

Any development team that is developing more than a few products a year or is developing large enterprise systems, should have a test lab available to test the latest technologies and coding solutions. Ideally, a lab should not only have servers available for testing but also have a repository of information. Each test application should be carefully documented with UML diagrams and text explaining what was tested and what the outcome was. The final conclusions of the tests, such as what was the best way of doing something and why, should be carefully documented. This will provide an invaluable source of information as products evolve in later cycles or new products are designed.

Ideally, the lab should recreate the final production environment as closely as possible. The best situation is to have the same servers and client machines in the lab as in the production environment. The tests should be exhaustive and cover every possible real case scenario.

Test applications can either be structured or unstructured and we will have a brief look at each type.

Unstructured Test Applications

Unstructured test applications are those exploring solutions. These tests answer questions such as, "How do we use the ADO disconnected recordset to handle conflicts?" These tests are performed when trying to find the most efficient way to code a module. It is important to explore different options, coding one way, then a different way until eventually you find the best solution. Along the way you will create a graveyard of unused code modules, variables and methods. The tight cohesion of the components and the loose coupling of the overall project were not there - in a sense you can never truly know where you were going until you arrive. Once you have hit upon the best solution with your test application, you will know how to do it right for the final application design.

Just as we should discard the user interface prototype, we should also discard our unstructured test applications. These test applications are used to find the best solutions and are not intended for use in the final applications. We can use activity diagrams to map out the best coding solutions, and document the best technology, but, ultimately, we should not reuse these test applications.

Structured Test Applications

Structured test applications explore each of several well-defined options that are available for our product. In this case, you would design each of the test applications just as you would design the final application. Again, careful documentation of the results should be kept. It is possible that with this type of test application that you may be able to reuse parts of the test application, but only if you built the test application properly and with reusability in mind.

Creating test applications and exploring options are essential to the success of the project and should be allotted adequate time in the project schedule. You should make a plan for usability testing just as you would for any other part of the project. The weeks you spend finding the best solution, or proving a coding solution, can prevent months of time that could be lost doing the wrong thing.

Functional Testing

Every component that will become part of your system, whether it is a precompiled third party component, a Visual Basic class (or class hierarchy) should be thoroughly tested by itself (unit testing) and within the system. Functional testing begins as soon as components are being built (including components for usability testing). Such testing provides an essential monitor of a project's progress and ensures that, at each step along the way, all of the code modules can be successfully integrated. Functional testing and development occur at the same time, with the testing continuing into the deployment phase.

We should start creating our testing plan in the logical design phase and have it completed by the physical design stage. Complete documentation of the testing plan should be created. Testers should develop testing modules and the development team should develop further modules in the development phase.

Let's consider how we could functionally test our three-level class hierarchy that comprises our `Customer` component in the Northwind project. We could write a sub-routine to test each of the three classes separately, a module to test the middle and bottom classes together and a class to test all three classes together.

To function properly, the bottom class (`clsCustomer`) requires a customer recordset, which is retrieved from the database by the middle class (`clsCustomerManager,`) to be passed in. If we are to test the bottom class separately, our test module will need to retrieve this recordset and then pass it into the bottom class.

Often, when we are testing individual components, we will have to create values for variables that, under normal operating conditions, would be passed into the component.

> *We may only know the exact values for these variables once the design is complete.*

We should test the component with values that are within the boundary conditions of the variable, at boundary conditions of the variable and outside the acceptable range for the variable. For example, our variable might be the index for a 1-based array that has 10 members.

A one based array variable named strArray with ten members will have the following members: strArray(1), strArray(2), strArray(3), strArray(4), strArray(5), strArray(6), strArray(7), strArray(8), strArray(9), strArray(10).

We should pass in variable values:

- At the boundaries: 1 and 10
- Within the boundaries: for example 5
- Outside the boundaries: for example at 0, 11, -2 and 50.

Test performed outside the boundary conditions will ensure that we have proper error handling within our code to handle these errors.

Types of Functional Testing

We have already discussed unit testing, i.e. testing individual components. Below is a list of other types of tests that can be performed on your components:

Coverage Testing: This type of test aims to thoroughly test each major feature of the project. Component coverage testing (white box testing) follows every code path. System or product coverage testing (black box testing) attempts to perform every service without knowing what code is being executed beneath the surface.

Usage Testing: Usage testing is different than coverage testing in that you make each component perform its services. As we said before, you will want to use boundary conditions and values within and out of the range of acceptable values.

Compatibility Tests: These tests make sure that each component is compatible with the other components of the project. As each component is added to other components, compatibility tests must be made to make sure that all of the components work properly together.

Stress Tests: These tests place either the project or components under severe conditions. These are commonly used for the middle tier data services components to see if they can handle the expected loads. They are also commonly used with web components to see if they can handle the expected load of the web server. You can write your own stress tests or, alternatively, there are many programs available that can perform stress testing of your application.

Performance Tests: These tests will see how well a component performs critical tasks. These are commonly used to see if a component will meet the required specifications.

There are other tests, but these are the most important for the Visual Basic development team. Tools such as Radview, which comes with the Interdev Web solutions kit, are essential tools for planning web sites. Testing with automated tools is sometimes useful. Creating your own customized tests may take some time, but if they are carefully planned, they will give you the most accurate testing of your project.

The ultimate goal of all this testing should always be to have no defects in the code. When designing our application with use cases and business rules, we will have a clear set of guidelines as to how our application is supposed to perform. A defect or bug is any system performance that is a deviation from the design of the project. Our use cases should define not only how the system should operate when everything is done correctly, but also how the system handles incorrect input. Any deviation from this is a bug.

Bug Tracking

There are many ways to find bugs. In addition to writing test modules, we can create special programs that test our applications (these are often called test drivers). For example, when writing the code to generate the HTML page for our Northwind project (see Chapter 9), I added a second Visual Basic project. Using this project, I called the function to build product tables. I took the HTML code that was returned and put it into a file with an `.HTM` file extension. I then opened the file with Explorer and viewed the HTML code in the browser. If there were mistakes, I went back and made the corrections. I often test DLLs by adding an EXE Visual Basic project and using this second project to test the first.

No matter how carefully you program there will always be bugs in your code. Using `Option Explicit` at the beginning of all of your code modules makes sure all variables in a project have been properly declared and is a good way of reducing typing errors. Declaring all of your variables and using variants very sparingly will also help the compiler find type errors. In a large project, these two activities can save countless hours of debugging.

Bugs that are trivial to fix, or bugs that are found and fixed during unit testing do not need to be documented or tracked (unless it is an issue that may occur again, such as a bug in Visual Basic, documented knowledge of which could help future development).

However, *all* non-trivial bugs found by the testing team should be carefully documented and tracked. A non-trivial bug is one whose source is not readily identifiable. These bugs are usually found during integration testing versus component testing. This tracking serves as a communication between the testers and the developers. There are several good products on the market to help you track and prioritize bugs. Three of them are PVCS Tracker by Microfocus (InterSolv), Track/TrackWeb by Soffront and Visual Intercept by Elsinore. It is possible to create your own bug tracking documents but, when you have a large project, use of a commercial bug-tracking tool probably represents a better solution.

In general, the following procedure should be followed for every nontrivial bug found by the testing team:

> ➤ Create a Bug Report: A report on the bug should be made. This report should list the steps that are needed to reproduce the bug, what should happen and what does happen, the severity of the bug (see Chapter 11), the priority of the bug, the component the bug is in, and a name assigned to the bug.

➤ Create a Plan to Resolve the Bug: Once the bug has been reported, you should create and document a plan to fix the bug. It is possible that a certain reported bug was known about when the project was designed and was considered minor enough to ignore. These bugs will be labeled as "By Design". There may also be bugs reported that are actually minor enough to ignore and will be labeled "Will Not Fix". Usually "Will Not Fix bugs" are ones that would require a large amount of time and money to repair and will have little effect on the performance of the project. A minor bug that will be fixed when there is time or in the next release will be called "Postponed". Labeling any bug as Will Not Fix, By Design or Postponed should require the signature of the senior members of the team, usually the component manager and the product manager. The stakeholder may also be informed of these decisions if it will have any significant impact on functionality or performance. If the bug has been previously noted, it will be labeled "Duplicate" and closed. If the bug cannot be reproduced, it is labeled "Cannot Reproduce". For the most part, all non-trivial bugs should be taken care of as soon as they are discovered.

➤ Repair the Bug: The developers must find the cause of the bug and repair it.

➤ Retest the components when the bug is fixed: Once the bug has been fixed, the testers need to retest the components to make sure that the repair did not affect another part of the code.

A bug found in a smaller component is usually easy to find. Testing done on assembled components tends be more complicated and usually requires a standardized, careful method of debugging. There is often a lot of work involved in debugging/testing components and it is often not possible to rely on just one method of debugging. Some testing techniques might require test drivers etc. that have to be planned for and built. This should be taken into account when estimating time and other resource requirements for component testing.

Some of the most difficult components to debug are MTS components. For this reason, we are now going to walk through some specific techniques for debugging MTS components. It will illustrate some of these points and act as an illustration of how we debug assembled components in general. Hopefully, for those not experienced with Visual Basic code, Chapter 8 will have given you a firm enough understanding of ADO and MTS to follow through the code and gain some valuable insight into the complexities involved in the debugging process. Of course, it will also give you some valuable code that you can use in your projects.

Debugging Visual Basic MTS Components

There are several techniques for debugging a Visual Basic MTS component. Each of these techniques has their place, and so they all need to be understood by someone working with MTS. As long as you have Service Pack 2 installed, you can debug directly from the Visual Basic IDE. Ideally though, you should have Service pack 3 installed.

> *If service pack 3 is installed, you can go to* Help | About *and you should see* Service Pack 3 *in the About box.*

Let us take a look at an example that shows how this works. We are going to make a request for an ADO recordset from a MTS middle tier component. As we want our MTS component to be stateless, we will make this a disconnected recordset. This example will illustrate perfectly things do not always work in the debugger as they do when the application is compiled.

Begin by creating a new ActiveX DLL project. Add a reference to ADO 2.x. Name the project prjLog. You should have one class, which you should name LogFile. In the properties of the class, set the MTSTransactionMode property to **3-UsesTransaction**. Save the class as Logging and the project as prjLog. We are now ready to start adding code.

We want to see how the context object looks under the debugger, so we will definitively want a reference to the object context.

> *As you may recall from Chapter 8, the context object can be thought of as a wrapper MTS places around our components. The context object allows us to share security and a transaction across several objects.*

We will need to have a private variable that references the ObjectContext object. We will also implement the ObjectControl interface. The ObjectControl interface will give us access to two events associated with the object context: Activate and Deactivate. The ObjectControl will also give us a property, CanBePooled, which we do not really need but will have to implement.

> **We must implement all of the methods and properties of an interface, even the ones we may not need.**

We will need to retrieve an ADO Connection object, so we will also need a private variable for it. Finally we declare a constant that contains the path and filename of our database. Thus we have the following declarations in our LogFile class:

```
Option Explicit

Private m_objADOConnection As ADODB.Connection
Private m_objContext As ObjectContext
Private Const m_cstrDatabasePath As String = "c:\Northwind.mdb"
Implements ObjectControl
```

Don't forget to add a reference to the **Microsoft Transaction Server Type library**. As we discussed earlier, the ObjectControl interface will give us three events. Go to the Object drop down list box in the code window, and select ObjectControl. You should now have the Activate event listed in the Procedure list box. Add the following code to this event:

```
Private Sub ObjectControl_Activate()
    Set m_objContext = GetObjectContext
End Sub
```

With this line of code we are setting a reference to the instance of the ObjectContext object that MTS has automatically created for us. Our ADO Connection object, though, does not exist until we initialize it. If we initialize it as soon as the component is created, there may be some amount of time before that Connection object is actually used. As there are a limited number of connections that can be made to the database, Connection objects are a valuable resource that we want to quickly use, and then destroy. Thus, we do not want to initialise our ADO Connection object until we are ready to use it.

Go to the drop down `Procedure` window and select `CanBePooled` for the `ObjectControl` object. We will need to fill out this code as all parts of the interface must be coded:

```
Private Function ObjectControl_CanBePooled() As Boolean
    ObjectControl_CanBePooled = False
End Function
```

Finally, we want to deactivate our ADO `Connection` object as well as our `ObjectContext` object. We should destroy our ADO connection as soon as we are done using it, but just in case we forget we include a line of code to set the ADO connection to nothing. If it is already set to nothing, then no harm done. Better to be cautious than take a chance that something is overlooked:

```
Private Sub ObjectControl_Deactivate()
    Set m_objADOConnection = Nothing
    Set m_objContext = Nothing
End Sub
```

We will want to see how MTS works with and without an `ObjectContext` object. When there is an `ObjectContext` object, we will want to use its `CreateInstance` method to create our objects. When we use `CreateInstance`, MTS will create the new object within the `ObjectContext` object. Using `CreateInstance` allows security and transactions to be shared over the different objects.

If for some reason something has gone wrong and we do not have an `ObjectContext` object, we would still like our component to function so we can see how an MTS component works without an `ObjectContext` object. Thus, we want the ability to create objects with the `New` keyword. Thus, we will create a function called `CreateInstance` that will allow us to create objects under MTS. Using the `CreateInstance` method when we do have an `ObjectContext` object, and the `New` keyword when we do not have one.

We will need to pass in an identifier for the component we want to build. The ID for a `Recordset` object is `ADODB.Recordset`, and for a `Connection` object it is `ADODB.Connection`. These will be the only two objects we will be creating in our MTS component. Add the following code to your project:

```
Private Function CreateInstance(ProgID As String) As Object
On Error GoTo CreateInstanceError
If Not m_objContext Is Nothing Then
  Set CreateInstance = m_objContext.CreateInstance(ProgID)
Else
  Select Case ProgID
    Case "ADODB.Connection"
        Set CreateInstance = New ADODB.Connection
    Case "ADODB.Recordset"
        Set CreateInstance = New ADODB.Recordset
End Select
End If

Exit Function

CreateInstanceError:

    Err.Raise Err.Number, Err.Source & " CreateInstance", Err.Description
End Function
```

We now want to add three functions to open an ADO connection, close an ADO connection and finally one to set a reference to the ADO connection. Let us begin with the function to set a reference to the ADO connection, which I will call SetADOConnection. Each component - Customers, Orders etc. - will have its own function for calling an ADO connection in the Server component so it makes sense to have one routine which defines and opens the ADO connection, which each function can call (instead of having each function opening connections individually). We will need parameters for the userID and the password in order to make a connection to the database. We will also include an optional parameter for the connection string in case we want to use something other than the default:

```
Private Sub SetADOConnection(ByVal v_strUserID As String, _
    ByVal v_strPassword As String, Optional ByVal _
    v_sConnectionString As String = "Empty")
```

We would like some way of knowing when our variable value has been passed in. The IsMissing function is used to tell if an optional parameter is passed but it only works with variants. As we have made our v_sConnectionString a string, the IsMissing function will not work. Therefore, we have set a default value of Empty for v_sConnectionString so we can know when it actually has a value passed in. We will now put in our error handler:

```
On Error GoTo SetADOConnectionError
```

Next we want to use our CreateInstance function to create our ADO connection:

```
Set m_objADOConnection = CreateInstance("ADODB.Connection")
```

We then set the properties of our Connection object.

```
With m_objADOConnection
    .CursorLocation = adUseServer
    If v_sConnectionString = "Empty" Then
        .ConnectionString = "Provider=Microsoft.Jet.OLEDB.4.0;" & _
            "Persist Security Info=False;Data Source=" & _
            m_cstrDatabasePath
Else
        .ConnectionString = v_sConnectionString
End If
```

Finally, we will open the ADO connection:

```
    .Open
End With

Exit Sub
```

The ADO has its own collection of errors, so we will loop through this error collection to get any errors in this collection:

```
SetADOConnectionError:

    Dim lngErrorCounter As Long
    Dim strErrors As String

    strErrors = Err.Number & ": " & Err.Description

    If m_objADOConnection.Errors.Count > 0 Then

      For lngErrorCounter = 0 To m_objADOConnection.Errors.Count - 1
        strErrors = strErrors & _
        m_objADOConnection.Errors(lngErrorCounter).Number & _
        ": " & m_objADOConnection.Errors(lngErrorCounter).Description & _
        vbCrLf
      Next lngErrorCounter

    End If
    Err.Raise Err.Number, "SetADOConnection", strErrors
End Sub
```

We will create a function to retrieve an ADO connection. We will first make sure the function has been set before we actually return a connection:

```
Private Function GetADOConnection() As ADODB.Connection
    If m_objADOConnection Is Nothing Then
      Err.Raise 2001, "GetADOConnection", _
        "Trying to Get Connection prior to setting it"
    Else
        Set GetADOConnection = m_objADOConnection

    End If
End Function
```

Finally, we will close the connection. As an error would be raised if the connection were not open, we will first check to see if the connection is open:

```
Private Sub CloseADOConnection()
    With GetADOConnection
      If .State = adStateOpen Then
        .Close
    End If

    End With
End Sub
```

Now that we have everything set up to get a connection, we can retrieve a disconnected recordset. Let us create a function called GetRecordset, which will return a Customer recordset from the Northwind database:

```
Public Function GetRecordset() As ADODB.Recordset
```

We will need a string variable to store the connection string, and a recordset variable to build the disconnected recordset:

```
Dim strADOConnection As String
Dim objCustomersRS As ADODB.Recordset
```

Now we will set the connection string:

```
On Error GoTo GetRecordsetError

strADOConnection = "Provider=Microsoft.Jet.OLEDB.4.0;" & _
    "Data Source=C:\Program Files\Microsoft Visual " & _
    "Studio\VB98\Nwind.mdb;Persist Security Info=False"
```

Next we will set the ADO connection, and set all of the properties of the recordset:

```
SetADOConnection "", "", strADOConnection
Set objCustomersRS = New ADODB.Recordset
objCustomersRS.CursorLocation = adUseClient
objCustomersRS.CursorType = adOpenStatic
objCustomersRS.LockType = adLockPessimistic
objCustomersRS.Source = "Customers"
Set objCustomersRS.ActiveConnection = GetADOConnection
```

We will open the `Recordset` object, and disconnect it by setting the `ActiveConnection` to nothing:

```
ObjCustomersRS.Open
Set objCustomersRS.ActiveConnection = Nothing
```

Finally we will return the recordset and create an error handler:

```
Set GetRecordset = objCustomersRS

CloseADOConnection
Exit Function
GetRecordsetError:
    CloseADOConnection
    Err.Raise Err.Number, Err.Source & " GetRecordset", Err.Description
End Function
```

The final part of our middle tier component will be a sub that will change the value of one of the fields of the recordset:

```
Public Sub ChangeRecordset(ByVal v_oCustomerRS As ADODB.Recordset)
    v_oCustomerRS.Fields("ContactTitle") = "NewValue"
End Sub
```

Notice that we intend to pass in the parameter v_oCustomerRS by value (the actual value represented by the variable), as we want to test if the recordset is really going to be passed in by value or by reference.

> If a variable is passed into the middle tier by reference, then any changes to the parameter v_oCustomerRS made here will also change the variable value on the client. If we pass it in by value, any changes made on the middle tier will not affect the values of the recordset on the client.

This completes our middle tier component. Go to **File | Make PrjLog.dll**. Once you do this, go to **Project | prjLog** Properties. From the `Project Properties` form select the `Component` tab, and select binary compatibility (which means that the component will recompile with the same GUID):

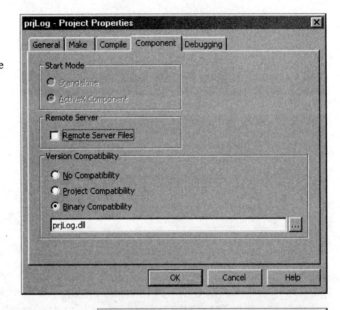

Now we need to build a client component that will test this middle tier component. Go to **File|Add Project**, and add an EXE project. Call this new project `prjTest`, the form `frmTest`. Your project explorer should look as follows:

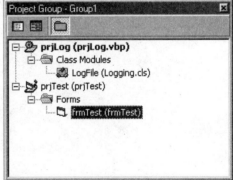

Add a reference to the ADO 2.x library, the Microsoft Transaction Server Type library and to the `prjLog` project. Open up the code window for `frmTest` and put this in the declarations:

```
Option Explicit
Dim WithEvents m_oCustomerRS As ADODB.Recordset
```

We have created a recordset with events so we can use the events associated with the recordset. The event we are interested in is the `WillChangeField` event. If we pass this recordset into the middle tier object by value, and the middle tier changes a field on the recordset, the field event should *not* be raised on the client. If the recordset is passed in by reference, and we try to change a field value in the recordset on the middle tier component, the field change event should be raised. Go to the `Object` drop down of the code window, select `m_oCustomerRS` and type the following code into the `WillChangeField` event, by way of notification if the event is raised:

```
Private Sub m_oCustomerRS_WillChangeField(ByVal cFields As Long, ByVal Fields As
Variant, adStatus As ADODB.EventStatusEnum, ByVal pRecordset As ADODB.Recordset)
    Beep
End Sub
```

Add a command button onto the form and call it **cmdTest**. Add the following code to the click event of the button:

```
Private Sub cmdTest_Click()
    Dim oLog As LogFile
    Dim sReturnValue As String
    Set oLog = New LogFile

    Set m_oCustomerRS = New ADODB.Recordset
    m_oCustomerRS.CursorLocation = adUseClient
    m_oCustomerRS.CursorType = adOpenStatic

    Set m_oCustomerRS = oLog.GetRecordset
    oLog.ChangeRecordset m_oCustomerRS

End Sub
```

Set `prjTest` to be the start up project by placing the cursor over **prjTest** in the project explorer, and select **Set As Start Up**:

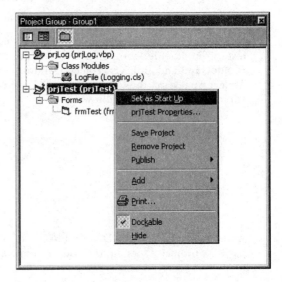

Place a breakpoint in the cmdTest click event:

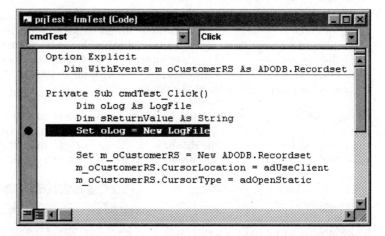

Run the project and click the cmdTest button. When you get to the break point, step through the code using the F8 key on your keyboard. This project runs even though we did not set up the package in MTS. You should notice a few very strange things happen. To begin with, you should not have entered into the ObjectControl event. You will not enter the middle tier component until you reach the Set m_oCustomerRS = oLog.GetRecordset line of code.

Step through the code until you get to the SetADOConnection function. Put the cursor over the m_objConext variable in the If Not m_objContext Is Nothing Then line of code. You should see the following that the variable m_objContext is equal to nothing:

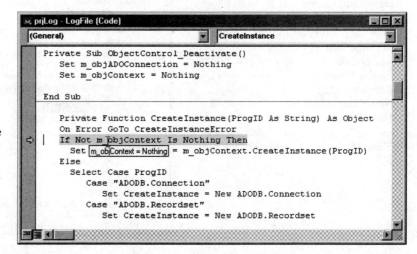

This is why we did not get the ObjectControl events; there is no ObjectContext object. Thus, we have found out something interesting about the Visual Basic debugger: If you do not register the component in MTS, you do not have a reference to the ObjectContext object.

Keep stepping through the code until you reach the point where the client calls the ChangeRecordset sub of the middle tier component. In theory, when we call the ChangeRecordset sub, and the sub changes the value of the field, the FieldChanged event of the recordset on the client should not be raised. Step through the code and you will discover that the FieldChanged event is raised. This means that the parameter has not been passed by value, but actually by reference.

The reason this happens is not important, it has to do with the properties of the ADO recordset. What is important to realize is that very strange things happen in the debug environment that will probably not happen with the final, compiled DLL. In this case, a by value parameter became by reference and we did not get an `ObjectContext` object for our MTS component. If you were not careful, you may think the problem is with your code, and not with the debugger. This in turn could result in hours of wasted testing and rewriting of your code.

This perfectly illustrates the point we made earlier: we need to have several methods of debugging to test our components. The Visual Basic IDE is great for finding errors cause by typos, improper logic (setting the wrong path to the database, not initialising an object, etc.). Yet, it is not our definitive test, as things may behave very differently in the compiled component than in the Visual Basic IDE.

Before we look at some other debugging methods, let us stop for a moment and find out how to improve the situation with our component. The first thing we need to do is add the component to MTS. Open up the Transaction Server Explorer. Drill down until you get to the package explorer. Select **Packages Installed** right-click on the mouse. Select **New|Package** then click the **Create an empty package** button. Call the package **Log**, click **Next** and **Finish**. Expand the new **Log** package, click on **Components**, right mouse click on **Components** and select **New|Component**. Click the **Install New Component** button, and select the `prjLog` DLL you made earlier. Your MTS explorer should look as follows:

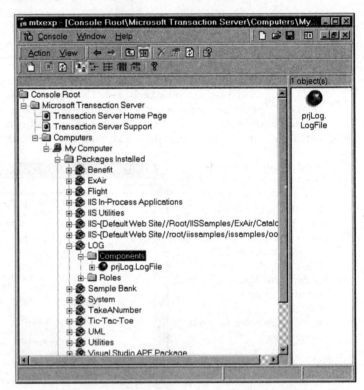

Now run your project again. You will notice that nothing has changed, we are still referencing the ADO recordset by reference and we are still not getting an `ObjectContext` object. What is wrong here? The answer to this question is simple: we are running the client and server components together. When we do this, we will never get an `ObjectContext` object, nor will our by value ADO objects be by value.

To fix this problem, all you have to do is run the two projects in separate instances of Visual Basic. Go to the project explorer; place the cursor over `PrjTest` and right mouse click. Select **Remove Project**:

Now, run the `prjLog` project. You will see the following screenshot:

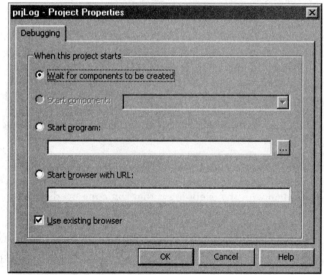

Click **OK**. Open another instance of the Visual Basic IDE, open the `prjTest` project. Put the break point in the `cmdTest` click event again. Run `prjTest`, click the command button and step through the code. This time you will find that your ADO recordset is actually passed in by value (the `FieldChanged` event on the client will not be raised when you change the field). You may not actually enter the `ObjectControl` events, but when you go into the `CreateInstance` function you can check and you will see that `m_objContext` is no longer `Nothing`.

Thus, we have discovered that to properly debug our MTS component using the Visual Basic IDE we need to run our client and server component in two different instances of the Visual Basic IDE, and the component needs to be registered in MTS. Once we do this, we can actually get the behaviour we expect.

You can play around with the code here. You will something very interesting: now that the parameter is behaving properly, that is, it is now being passed by value, Visual Basic still allows you to change the values of the parameter in the sub. These changes, though, are not passed back to the client.

By the way, if you are wondering why we are concerned with using by reference parameters versus using by value parameters, remember that the communication between the client and server is over the network. This means that every change you make to a by reference parameter on the server needs to be passed back to the client. This is not very efficient and limits the scalability of your MTS component. Let us now take a look at some other ways of debugging our component.

Logging Information from an MTS Component

We can now see that even when things work perfectly in the Visual Basic IDE, we still will want to test the final compiled component to make sure that everything works in the compiled component as it does in the IDE. There are other reasons we would not use the Visual Basic IDE. After all of the tests have been completed in the test environment, it is a good practice to run a series of test on the production server. It is unlikely that the production server would have Visual Basic on it, so you will have to use a compiled version of the component. There are basically three ways to test a compiled component: write information to a text file, a database or the NT event log. It is unlikely you would put testing information into the event log, so for testing you would want functions to write to a database or a text file.

If a database is available, such as SQL Server 7, and is legally available (has the proper licensing), it is usually the best option for testing. Test information can be placed into the database. Specialized applications can be written to analyse the data, and these applications can be run from anywhere on the network. This allows everyone from management to development to see the results of the tests. It is possible that something could go wrong, and your component may not be able to write to the database. In this case, you should write to a text file so the information on why this happened is not lost.

Writing to the event log is a good choice for when the final application is rolled out. The event log can keep track of errors, or provide information on how your component is functioning. The major problem with the event log is that someone needs to be looking into the log to find an error. As this may be forgotten, or not done at all, it is advisable to have an additional function that would send an alert to a system administrator. This can be accomplished by creating a function that will e-mail the system administrator, or send a message through the Internet to the system administrator's beeper. Building these components goes beyond the level of this text, but I will show you how to make a function to write to the event log.

We will expand our existing class so that it has the ability to write to a database, a text file and the event log. We will begin by creating a database that will allow us to log information from our MTS component.

The Log Database

We will create two tables. One table, called `ApplicationLog`, will be used for logging general information, and a second table, called `ErrorLog`, will be used for logging errors.

Create a table in a database called `ApplicationLog` with the following fields and data types:

Field Name	Data Type	Size
DateLogged	Date/Time	
Message	Text	100
Level	Integer	5
MethodProperty	Text	15
Class	Text	15
Application	Text	15

Create a second table called `ErrorLog` with the same fields. Call the database `log`.

Let us now code our component, starting with the declarations.

Declarations

We will now add an enumerated type to our declaration for the different types of error levels we may have. The standard levels for the event log are `Informational`, `Warning` and `Error` and we will use these for our enumerated type. We will also make private constants for all of the field names. We will add a constant for the path to the database, for example `C:\log.mdb`:

```
Public Enum e_ErrorLevels
  Informational = 4
  Warning = 2
  Error = 1
End Enum
Private Const m_cstrDatabasePath As String = "C:\log.mdb"
Private m_objADOConnection As ADODB.Connection
Private m_objContext As ObjectContext
Private Const m_cDateField As String = "DateLogged"
Private Const m_cMessageField As String = "Message"
Private Const m_cLevelField As String = "Level"
Private Const m_cMethodPropertyField As String = "MethodProperty"
Private Const m_cClassField As String = "Class"
Private Const m_cApplicationField As String = "Application"
Implements ObjectControl
```

Now, let us add a function called `WriteToDatabase` to log information to the database. We will need to pass in as parameters the name of the application that has requested this log, the name of the class (module, form etc.) that has made the log, the name of the method or property that has made the log, the actual message, and the level of error:

```
Public Function WriteToDatabase(ByVal v_sAppName, ByVal v_sClass, _
             ByVal v_sMethodProperty, ByVal v_sMessage As String, _
             ByVal v_eLevel As e_ErrorLevels) As String
```

We will need a local `Recordset` object to get a reference to the table we need in the logging database and we need to include our usual error handler:

```
Dim recLogRS As ADODB.Recordset
On Error GoTo WriteToDatabaseError
```

We will call `SetADOConnection` and we will not need to pass the path in as we will use the default path:

```
SetADOConnection "", ""
```

Next, we need to set the properties of the ADO recordset:

```
Set recLogRS = New ADODB.Recordset
recLogRS.CursorLocation = adUseServer
recLogRS.CursorType = adOpenDynamic
recLogRS.LockType = adLockPessimistic
```

If the level is informational, we will put in the `ApplicationLog` table. Otherwise, the log is an error and will go into the `ErrorLog` table:

```
If v_eLevel = Informational Then
   recLogRS.Source = "ApplicationLog"
Else
   recLogRS.Source = "ErrorLog"
End If
```

We will set the `ActiveConnection` of the recordset next, and then open it. Once the recordset is open, we can call an `AddNew` method:

```
Set recLogRS.ActiveConnection = GetADOConnection
recLogRS.Open
recLogRS.AddNew
```

Next we will set all of the fields to the values that have been passed in. In a final production version, you would probably want to make sure the parameters have actual values passed in:

```
recLogRS.Fields(m_cApplicationField) = v_sAppName
recLogRS.Fields(m_cClassField) = v_sClass
recLogRS.Fields(m_cDateField) = Now
recLogRS.Fields(m_cLevelField) = v_eLevel
recLogRS.Fields(m_cMessageField) = v_sMessage
recLogRS.Fields(m_cMethodPropertyField) = v_sMethodProperty
```

Finally we update our recordset, exit our function and close the connection:

```
recLogRS.Update
ExitWriteToDatabase:
CloseADOConnection
Exit Function

WriteToDatabaseError:
```

In our error handler, we will set the return value of our function to a string showing the errors. This information can then be written to a text file. You could also write to a text file in the error handler:

```
WriteToDatabase = "Error Description: " & Err.Description & vbCrLf & _
                  "Error Number: " & Err.Number & vbCrLf & _
                  "Error Source: " & Err.Source
```

Finally, we want to clear the error and go to the exit routine:

```
Err.Clear
   GoTo ExitWriteToDatabase

End Function
```

Writing to a Text File

We will create our function to write to a text file with the same parameters as our database function:

```
Public Function WriteToTextFile(ByVal v_sAppName, ByVal v_sClass, _
             ByVal v_sMethodProperty, ByVal v_sMessage As String, _
             ByVal v_eLevel As e_ErrorLevels) As Boolean
```

We will create a text file that has fields of a uniform length so it will be easier to read the text file with an application. To do this, we will create string fields for each of the parameters. We will also need a file number for the log file we are about to open:

```
Dim intFileNumber As Integer
Dim strAppName As String * 15
Dim strClass As String * 15
Dim strMethodProperty As String * 15
Dim strMessage As String * 100
Dim strLevel As String * 5
```

Notice that we have made the fields the same size as they are in the database. We will now set the local strings equal to the parameters that were passed in:

```
strLevel = str(v_eLevel)
strAppName = v_sAppName
strClass = v_sClass
strMethodProperty = v_sMethodProperty
strMessage = v_sMessage
```

We will now use the standard text file methods. We will get a file number using `FreeFile`. If it is `Informational`, we will write to a log file, otherwise we will write to an error file:

```
        intFileNumber = FreeFile
        If v_eLevel = Informational Then
        Open "c:\" & v_sAppName & "Log.txt" For Append As #intFileNumber
        Write #intFileNumber, intFileNumber & Chr(34) & _
                            strAppName & Chr(34) & _
                            strClass & Chr(34) & _
                            strMethodProperty & Chr(34) & _
                            strMessage
    Else
        strLevel = Str(v_eLevel)
        Open "c:\" & v_sAppName & "ErrLog.txt" For Append As _
            #intFileNumber
        Write #intFileNumber, intFileNumber & Chr(34) & _
                            strAppName & Chr(34) & _
                            strClass & Chr(34) & _
                            strMethodProperty & Chr(34) & _
                            strMessage & Chr(34) & _
                            strLevel
    End If
    Close #intFileNumber

    End Function
```

We have not put any error handling in this function, for a final production version you should do this. In this case, it is likely you would raise an error back to the calling application.

Writing to the Event Log

You can write to the event log using the `App` object that comes with Visual Basic. The `App` object has a function called `LogEvent`. You can also set the `App.Title` that will also be written into the event log. Once again, we will use the same parameters:

```
    Public Sub WriteToEventLog(ByVal v_sAppName, ByVal v_sClass, _
        ByVal v_sMethodProperty, ByVal v_sMessage As String, _
        ByVal v_eLevel As e_ErrorLevels)
```

If `App.LogMode` is `vbLogAuto` or `vbLogToNT` then we are logging to the event log in NT. If we are in Windows 95 or 98, we will log to a text file:

```
    If App.LogMode = vbLogAuto Or vbLogToNT Then
        App.Title = v_sAppName
        App.LogEvent v_sMessage & "(" & v_sClass & "/" & v_sAppName & ")", _
            v_eLevel
    Else
        If WriteToDatabase(v_sAppName, v_sClass, v_sMethodProperty, _
            v_sMessage, v_eLevel) <> "" Then
                WriteToTextFile v_sAppName, v_sClass, v_sMethodProperty, _
                    v_sMessage, v_eLevel
        End If
    End If

    End Sub
```

We will now modify some of our previous functions and procedures so that we have a log of any critical errors, such as failing to retrieve an ADO connection.

Modifying the CreateInstance Function

When our MTS component is not able to get the `ObjectContext` object we will write to the event log so we know about it:

```
Private Function CreateInstance(ProgID As String) As Object
   On Error GoTo CreateInstanceError
   If Not m_objContext Is Nothing Then
      Set CreateInstance = m_objContext.CreateInstance(ProgID)
   Else
      WriteToEventLog App.EXEName, "LogFile", "CreateInstance", "Can not get" & _
   "reference to context", Warning
   Select Case ProgID
      Case "ADODB.Connection"
         Set CreateInstance = New ADODB.Connection
      Case "ADODB.Recordset"
         Set CreateInstance = New ADODB.Recordset
   End Select
   End If

   Exit Function

CreateInstanceError:

   Err.Raise Err.Number, Err.Source & " CreateInstance", Err.Description
End Function
```

Modifying the SetADOConnection Procedure

If we have an error getting the `Connection` object, we will want to write this to a text file as it is a critical error. We cannot write to the database if there is something wrong with our connection to the database. If we had the e-mail or beeper function, it is likely we would use it in the error handler of this function.

```
Private Sub SetADOConnection(ByVal v_strUserID As String, _
         ByVal v_strPassword As String, _
         Optional ByVal v_sConnectionString As String = "Empty")

   On Error GoTo SetADOConnectionError

   Set m_objADOConnection = CreateInstance("ADODB.Connection")

   With m_objADOConnection
      .CursorLocation = adUseServer
      If v_sConnectionString = "Empty" Then
         .ConnectionString = "Provider=Microsoft.Jet.OLEDB.4.0;" & _
            Persist Security Info=False;Data Source=" & m_cstrDatabasePath
      Else
         .ConnectionString = v_sConnectionString
      End If
      .Open
   End With
```

Continued on following page.

```
    Exit Sub

SetADOConnectionError:

    Dim lngErrorCounter As Long
    Dim strErrors As String

    strErrors = Err.Number & ": " & Err.Description

    If m_objADOConnection.Errors.Count > 0 Then

      For lngErrorCounter = 0 To m_objADOConnection.Errors.Count - 1
          strErrors = strErrors & _
          m_objADOConnection.Errors(lngErrorCounter).Number & _
          ": " & m_objADOConnection.Errors(lngErrorCounter).Description & _
            vbCrLf
    Next lngErrorCounter

    End If
    WriteToTextFile App.EXEName, "LogFile", "SetADOConnection", _
        "Connection Failed", Informational
    End Sub
```

Now, go to `frmTest` and add another command button called `cmdTest2`. In the click event for
`cmdTest2` add the following code:

```
Private Sub CmdTest2_Click()
    Dim oLog As LogFile
    Dim sReturnValue As String
    Set oLog = New LogFile
    oLog.WriteToEventLog "Test", "FrmMain", "FormLoad", _
      "This is a test", Informational
    oLog.WriteToEventLog "Test", "FrmMain", "FormLoad", _
      "This is a test", Error
    oLog.WriteToEventLog "Test", "FrmMain", "FormLoad", _
      "This is a test", Warning
    oLog.WriteToTextFile "Test", "FrmMain", "FormLoad", _
      "This is a test", Informational
    sReturnValue = oLog.WriteToDatabase("Test", "FrmMain", _
      "FormLoad", "This is a test", Informational)
    If sReturnValue <> "" Then
        oLog.WriteToTextFile "Test", "FrmMain", "FormLoad", _
          sReturnValue, Informational
    End If

End Sub
```

You will notice something rather interesting about this code. Our MTS object is created and held
open until the end of the sub. This means we are holding our server component for a long time, and
also maintaining state across many calls. This will not scale, and is not how we should build our
components. A better way to code this would be as follows:

```
Private Sub CmdTest2_Click()
  Dim oLog As LogFile
  Dim sReturnValue As String
  Set oLog = New LogFile
  oLog.WriteToEventLog "Test", "FrmMain", "FormLoad", _
      "This is a test", Informational
  Set oLog = Nothing
  Set oLog = New LogFile
  oLog.WriteToEventLog "Test", "FrmMain", "FormLoad", _
      "This is a test", Error
  Set oLog = Nothing
  Set oLog = New LogFile
  oLog.WriteToEventLog "Test", "FrmMain", "FormLoad", _
      "This is a test", Warning
  Set oLog = Nothing
  Set oLog = New LogFile
  oLog.WriteToTextFile "Test", "FrmMain", "FormLoad", _
      "This is a test", Informational
  Set oLog = Nothing
  Set oLog = New LogFile

  sReturnValue = oLog.WriteToDatabase("Test", "FrmMain", "FormLoad", _
      "This is a test", Informational)
  If sReturnValue <> "" Then
  oLog.WriteToTextFile "Test", "FrmMain", "FormLoad", _
  sReturnValue, Informational
  End If
  Set oLog = Nothing
End Sub
```

This is still not too readable, though. It would be best to make a log object for each situation: oLogText, oLogDatabase etc. If you are concerned about the work to create the MTS component, MTS will not completely destroy the object when you set it to nothing. It will keep a copy around for the next call, so you are not losing any performance by doing this.

Before you can run this, you will need to remove your component from the MTS package:

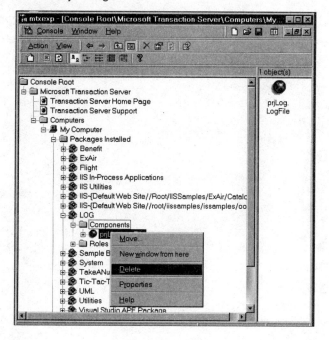

Next recompile the DLL and then add the DLL back into MTS. You will not need to make any changes in `prjTest` as you are adding to the interface and you set binary compatibility (which means that the component will recompile with the same GUID).

As a final comment, you may find that the event log will not work when you debug your component. But, when you compile the component, it will work fine. Once again, things do not always work the same in the debugger as they do in the compiled component.

Conclusion

Testing is an essential part of creating a successful Visual Basic project. Testing begins in the design phase as you build prototypes to find the best way to build your project. Testing continues in the development phase as individual components are tested. In the deployment phase the finished system is beta tested.

There are many different types of testing and many aspects of testing. Smaller problems discovered while testing individual components can usually be fixed quickly without documentation. More complex bugs found during beta testing may require thorough documentation and testing to reveal their causes.

The most essential parts of testing are good coding standards, accurate documentation and a means for excellent communication between team members, including the end users. With these in place, your testing should go smoothly, and it should be easy to find and fix bugs.

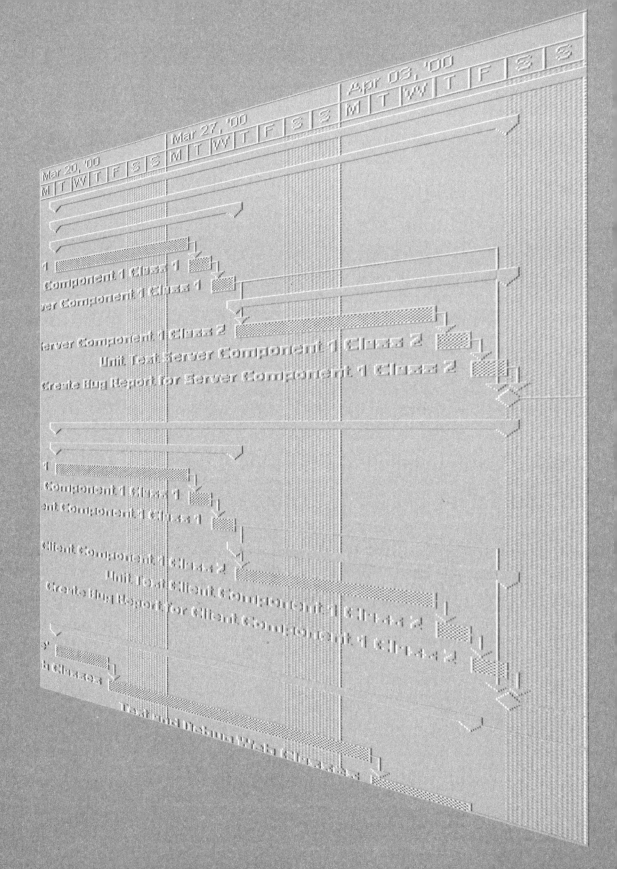

11

Deployment Phase

The deployment phase is where the completed components are deployed. During this phase, the system will be prepared for handover to the end users. Up to this phase, the focus has been on building the components and making sure that the functionality is according to specifications. At this point, the coding and components are complete, but they still need to be prepared for giving to the user. Testing in the final environment, including Beta testing, can occur at this time. The end users must be shown how to use the new application before it goes live. The infrastructure must be in place and the compiled Visual Basic project must be placed on this infrastructure. The documentation for the project must also be completed and given to the users. The final performance of the system must also be determined. The whole team will be heavily involved in the process of deploying the project. The main aim of this phase is to release the system to the users, making sure that all components function accordingly and that users have the backup of good support, should they need it. The end result of this phase is that the system goes live.

In this chapter, we will:

> Examine team member involvement in the deployment phase.
> Investigate the issues of testing in the final environment.
> Look at training the user.
> Examine documentation and support issues.

The deliverables for the deployment phase are:

> Full project documentation
> The release of the system to the users.
> Comprehensive support structure for the users.

Summary of Team Focus

During the deployment phase the product manager assists the educators with setting up beta test sites. The product manager will work closely with the client's senior management, making all of the preparations for final testing and the final installation of the project. Any issues, such as bugs or design flaws, will be passed from the client to the product manager. The product manager will document these bugs or flaws and work with the development team to resolve these issues. The product manager and project manager supervise the whole process of deploying the completed components into the system. Once the system is in place, the product manager and project manager will work with the client to sign off the project.

The component manager continues to manage the schedule, create status reports and oversee debugging of the components. If new risks for the project present themselves, the appropriate team members will report them to the team leaders; the component manager will manage them and balance resources so that the schedule is met and costs stay within budget.

The developers will work closely with testers and the users to identify flaws or bugs in the project, and fix them. Logistics will also be involved, helping to deploy the components, prepare the infrastructure and set up the data stores. Any conflicts between the users and the development team will be handled by the educators. If the educators cannot resolve the issue, the product manager will resolve the issue with the stakeholders. If beta testing is done, logistics will prepare the infrastructure required for the beta test. The educator will find the appropriate testers.

The educators will complete all of the documentation for the user. The documentation will include all help and support files. If a web page is to be used for documenting the application, the educators need to get the page completed and live at this time. The educators will also perform training based on a training plan developed in the design phase.

The entire team, including the client, must work together to deploy the project. Good communication will be essential. The deployment phase is one of the most hectic times of the project. This phase requires constant adjustments to the schedule and a reassignment of resources to deal with serious bugs. If good design is used, as well as many components that have already been thoroughly tested, there should be a minimum of bugs and the adjustments to the schedule should be minimal.

Overview of the Deployment Phase

By the end of the development phase, all code should be written and all components should have been unit and system tested. The focus of this phase shifts from getting the system built to getting the system delivered to the end users. However, the transition from finished code to finished product can be a long and fraught journey.

You have to be very careful during the final deployment phase. As the pace picks up, and the need to fix bugs becomes more urgent, there is a tendency to forget formal procedures and to just start making fixes. There is no better way to destroy Visual Basic code than to perform haphazard fixes. Of course, there are many other issues in the deployment phase, as we shall now see.

Activities in the Deployment Phase

There are a number of things that must be done in this phase: in this section, I will explain the complexity of the different activities within the deployment phase.

Determine the Rollout Schedule

First of all, it must be decided how rollout, or the process of preparing the system for final release, is going to be carried out, and also how long it is going to take. This is a concern for the product and project managers and logistics, in conjunction with the end users and client management. It is important to have some structure for rollout - this means that all goals are coordinated to finish at an appropriate time so that the system is complete and ready for a predetermined date.

It is important also to communicate this schedule to the end users - although they may only be concerned with getting their new system, it must be explained that testing still has to be done and some repairs will have to be made before the system is of a satisfactory level. The system also has to be prepared for deployment, an issue that I will talk more about later.

Beta Testing

Beta testing will involve the testing of the completed system in the production environment by a limited number of people before the final 'usable' version is handed over to the end users. While the key players will be the testers, logisticians and the educators, beta testing will involve the entire team. The educators will meet with the users who will do the beta testing, prepare and train the testers on the new system and help choose appropriate users. The logisticians will be involved in installing the new system. Part of the beta testing may be to see if the software is successfully installed onto the servers and the beta tester's computers. The testers will monitor the end users and, with the educators, document the end users' comments.

One part of beta testing is usability testing. Usability testing is the process of making certain that the system is usable by the end users. Testers and educators should find out what is confusing to the users, and if there are ways of solving these problems without changing the system. If there are problems with how usable the system is that may require a change to the system, these problems will be evaluated and go through change control.

> **Every change should be carefully evaluated. Even the smallest changes can require a large amount of resources.**

Depending on the cost of making the change and the urgency of the change, a decision will be made by the stakeholder, product, project and component managers whether or not to make a usability change. Hopefully, with good user interface prototyping there should not be any usability issues.

Communication is one of the most important parts of a successful beta test. Communication should flow between all team members in this phase. A clear set of tasks for the end users should be developed and be part of the testing plan. Testing may also include automated testing, using testing modules and performing stress tests. Feedback will be essential, and there should be a simple communication system, such as email, intranet or verbal, in place to allow information to flow through the team.

The system is ready for beta testing when it is stable and the testers have tested the entire system. A beta test should have a plan and be documented.

Beta testing allows the whole system to be tested from the viewpoint of a user, rather than a developer. If there are any bugs, or errors, or missing functionality, these can be reported, the system can be refined, and there is a greater likelihood of the system actually representing what the end users expect of it.

Finding bugs during testing should not be difficult if your tests are done properly. Each test should only test one part of your project. In this way, you can find where the problem comes from. This is why we start by testing each component separately. We also test each time we add a component to the system. This helps us limit the places where bugs can be. Unfortunately, when bugs are found in the finished application, it can be difficult to pin down their exact location. If clicking a command button causes an error, did the error come from the command button, the business services component, the data services component or somewhere else? Fortunately, this dilemma can easily be solved by using proper error handling.

Some of the most difficult problems are the ones where something worked perfectly in the testing environment but did not work properly in the production environment. Commonly, these are performance related issues. When the system is actually deployed and used by a multitude of users in different ways, we often find that the system does not perform as expected. The worst situations are where the problems are hard to reproduce. A common example is where some service of the system, such as retrieving data, will normally occur within a second, but occasionally it will take ten or fifteen seconds. Trying to recreate this can be very difficult. Sometimes a component will work flawlessly a certain number of times, but it will fail once in a while. These are all very difficult problems to track down. These are all reasons that Beta testing the components in the production environment is critical.

Every property, function and sub should have error handling. The most important part of your error handling is including the name of the module in the `err.raise` statement. This would look as follows:

```
Err.Raise Err.Number, Err.Source & ''ComponentName.ModuleName'', _
Err.Description
```

If you had a class named clsServer and a module called RetrieveCustomer you would have:

```
Err.Raise Err.Number, Err.Source & ''clsServer.RetrieveCustomer'', _
Err.Description
```

If you place this code in an error handler for every single code module, then when an error is raised the place where the error was initially raised will be in the error string. What will also be in the error message is the name of every code module that the error was passed through. Thus, if frmMain has a command button called cmdGetCustomer that calls a method called GetCustomer in a business component called clsCustomer, and there is an error in GetCustomer, our error source would include the following information:

```
FrmMain.cmdGetCustomer clsCustomer.GetCustomer
```

Thus, we know where the error occurred and what the calling module is. This information can save you hours and hours of searching to find the source of a bug. Placing error handling in every code module does not take much time and it can save you days of frustration.

Ranking Bugs

Bugs can be a serious problem with any application. If an application has already been deployed and is being used by the client, any serious bugs must be taken care of immediately. If the deadline for deploying the application is quickly approaching, it will also be necessary to begin working on the high priority bugs.

Bugs can be ranked two ways. The first way is by how severe the bug is. The second is how reproducible the bug is. Severity can be ranked as follows:

Level 1: System Failure:
A level 1 bug will crash the entire system. A level 1 will require a reboot of the system. For the most part, if you are not playing with pointers in Visual Basic you should rarely see a Level 1 failure. Anything that would cause inconsistent data in the database would also be considered a level 1 failure.

Level 2: Application Failure:
A level 2 is where the application has a major failure. This will result in either a General Protection Fault (GPF) or the application locking up. If a GPF occurs, your application will close unexpectedly and without warning.

Level 3: Incorrect Performance:
A level 3 is where the application does not perform the way it is supposed to, but the application continues functioning normally. A level 3 would be any performance not according to the project's specifications.

Level 4: Cosmetic:
A level 4 is where one or more users do not like the way something looks, but it in no way affects performance.

Level 1 and 2 must be taken care of immediately. They are severe. They can be difficult to debug if the problem does not exist in the test environment and does exist in the production environment as you usually will not have any error messages before the system fails. In this case, you will have to create logs to track the bug. A thorough testing phase should catch any level 1 or 2 bugs, but sometimes components perform differently in the production environment than in the development environment. This is one reason that a beta test should be done before a critical application is installed into an entire corporation. If the application is critical for business, and there is a major bug that prevents the application from running, the corporation can lose a great deal of money.

Even level 3 bugs sometimes can be a serious problem. Imagine building a Visual Basic component that bills credit cards for an E-Commerce site. What happens if this component has a bug such that the component does not actually bill the card; it only appears to bill the card. Thousands of dollars of business may occur and thousands of orders may go out before anyone realizes that the company has been giving out free merchandise. This can happen a lot easier than you would imagine. It might be that testing was done with dummy credit card numbers, as you would not want to really charge your credit card when you are testing. These are real issues and this is why beta testing in the production environment is important.

Some level 3 bugs may not be serious enough to fix in this release. Most level 4 bugs will not be fixed, unless they are very easy to fix. Reproducibility is broken into three categories:

Category 1: Completely Reproducible Simple - The bug can be reproduced every time by following a set of simple steps. Usually, the user would normally perform these steps. It is possible this bug only occurs on one type of computer.

Category 2: Completely Reproducible Complex - This is a bug that can be reproduced, but it takes a very complex set of steps to create the bug. A user will rarely do these steps.

Category 3: Intermittently Reproducible – This is a bug that occurs sometimes, but cannot always be reproduced.

These categories must be combined with the levels to determine the priority of fixing the bug. Category 2 bugs are usually not a high priority, unless they are a level 1 or 2. Category 3 bugs can be very frustrating. I can recall spending days trying to hunt down one of these flaky bugs with Visual Basic 5. It turned out that we had an object hierarchy that we were referencing down to the bottom level in one line, such as:

```
Object1.Object2.Object3. Object4. Object5.Method
```

Using the With statement and breaking up the hierarchy fixed the problem, though I never once saw the error while debugging and only saw it once every twenty or so runs through the application. The working version looked as follows:

```
With Object1.Object2.Object3
    . Object4. Object5.Method
End With
```

If you are using pointers in Visual Basic, it is easy to get these types of intermittent bugs as you will sometimes write to a safe place in memory and other times not.

User Training

The clearer the interface to the application is, the less training the user will require to learn how to use it. The first step in achieving this is a good user prototype and good user interface design. If every form is centered on accomplishing a single task and the controls on the form follow the flow of the task, there should be a minimum of training required. Similarly, if the nature of each form reflects the business process it is supporting, it will be easier for the user to understand what they should do, and in what order. If you have spent time creating user interface prototypes and properly testing them, you will save time and money during training.

However, if your project has introduced a new business process then there are a number of other issues that need addressing. Of course, you will have to tell the users how the new business process is going to work, and how the application follows the new process. There could also be the added difficulty of trying to integrate the new system with the old system - if the new system only covers some functionality, the users will have to know when to use the old system and when to use the new system.

It is very useful to create an internal web site that explains the application and how it functions and answers some of the common questions you would expect to be asked. It can save the help desk people a great deal of work if questions asked to the help desk personnel are posted to a web page with answers. Each question should then only be asked once, which prevents the same question from being asked repeatedly.

User training should use as many different mediums and self-service tools as possible, such as placing information about the application on an Intranet site. The more the user can do on their own, the easier it will be for them to use the application. If the users can teach themselves, it can serve to give them greater confidence in their ability to use the application, and so therefore they will feel more at ease using it.

The educators will work closely with the users on the user education program. If the educators do not have any programming experience, they may need the assistance of the developers to make web pages or help files, which will assist the users in their understanding of the application and how they are supposed to use it.

Prepare Infrastructure

The amount of work the logistician will have to do in preparing the infrastructure depends on what is currently in place in the corporation. There may be large amounts of data in legacy systems that will have to be moved. The Visual Basic programmer may find themselves writing applications to perform these transformations using SQL Server 7's Data Transformation Services. Visual Basic developers may also be called on to create test applications for new systems and to assist in stress testing or performance testing.

Assemble Project Documentation

By the end of the project, there should be a complete set of final documents. These documents will include the Vision / Scope document, the EAD, risk documents, all of the design documents, bug tracking documents, test plans, and test results etc. This collection of documents serves not only a useful tool for future versions of the project, but also a valuable resource for any future project that is similar. These documents show what works and what does not work. The project schedule will show how long each component took to build, which can be used as a basis for an estimate for future projects. The development team and the client should keep a copy of these documents.

When the project is done, the development team should have a review meeting to discuss the project's successes and failures. This information should be included in the developer's documentation and used for future projects. Knowledge is one of the most valuable resources; keeping accurate records allows you to pass knowledge from one project to the next. This is not only important if your project was a failure; future project teams can also learn from the success of this project and incorporate the goal-oriented teams and cyclic methodology into their working life. In this way, good design will become the norm and future projects have a greater chance of success.

Creating Changes in the Code

One of the greatest challenges to the Visual Basic programmer is to keep the design documents up-to-date as changes are made to the code. As changes are made, it is easy for design documents to quickly become out of date. Eventually, there is no accurate documentation for the project. This must be prevented at all costs.

Changes to the code should result in the updating of the design documents and the addition of comments in your code. One easy way to document your code is by adding a comment in the beginning of the module such as the following:

```
'20-06-99-01 Bug Fix: #15-06-99-23.
'Developer: Jake Sturm
```

In the code where changes are made you would add a comment with '20-06-99. You should also have some form of document control, such as SourceSafe, that has the original version of the code prior to the changes. This should be part of the coding standards.

By adding these comments into your code, it becomes easy to see what changes were made, why and by whom. If a change results in additional problems, it will be easy to track down where the changes were made.

Physically Deploying the Application

Once everything has been built and tested, you must actually get the application out onto the desktops. There are many issues involved in this. Do you need to first deploy the server components before you deploy the client components? Do you manually place components on the computers or do you push components onto the computers? What time will you deploy the components, during work hours or after hours? During the development and design phase it will be the job of the logistician to find answers to these questions. Often, it is only through thorough testing and the creation of labs to simulate the production environment that answers to these questions can be found. These answers are not simple, and this is one of the reasons the logistician should be a separate role on your team. To develop a good deployment plan for a large scale deployment could take up to six months.

Deployment Strategies

One thing to consider is how to get your system or application onto the computers of the end users. However, there is not just your application to think about, but also any other files that are needed to make your application work. You cannot be sure that each user computer will have the necessary secondary files needed to make your application work. Some extra files needed to ensure that your application can be used might be:

Any ActiveX controls used in the application. Many computers will already have a copy of the controls; however, if any of them are missing, the application will generate an error. These controls will need to be registered during the setup process when users install them onto their computer.
The Visual Basic Runtime library. For Visual Basic 6.0, the file is `MSVBM60.DLL`.
Any supporting files. If the application is to have its own version of a database, such as Access, you'll need to distribute a copy of it. Don't forget any text files, data files, report files or registry files.
Other Dependency Files. These include DLLs, which are called by the application.
Documentation and Help Files. Many products are available to assist you in creating help files. One of the most popular is RoboHelp.

Of course, some of these files may have to reside in specific directories, and it cannot always be assumed that the user will have read the installation instructions correctly, or that they know how to install a product at all. For this reason, we create a setup program, which will install all included necessary files into the correct subdirectories on the target computer. This is one way of preparing your application for deployment and, luckily, Visual Basic provides us with a Package and Deployment Wizard to help us do just this. Let us look at this facility in more detail.

Visual Basic Deployment Wizard

Visual Basic supplies you with a wizard for almost every task. In this case, it will take your final version of working code and package it so that it can be deployed to the end users. This is useful for every member of the team to know - even if you are not too technically minded, you will still be able to make sure that the application is available to be handed over to the end user.

Open the package and Deployment Wizard from the Visual Basic folder (or the Visual Studio 6.0 Tools folder if you have Visual Studio) from the **Programs** menu. The Package and Deployment Wizard will open and prompt you to select the project you want to deploy. Locate the project file on your computer that you wish to deploy.

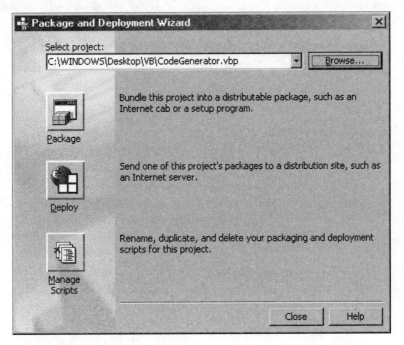

This first screen shows us options for creating, deploying and maintaining application setup files. For now, the only option we are interested in is the Package function, which allows us to create a setup facility, so click on the Package button.

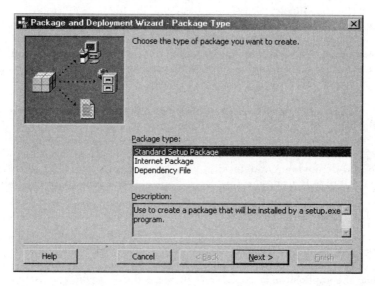

This stage allows us to specify the type of package we wish to create: as you can see, we can say that we want a standard executable package, an Internet package or we can specify it as a dependency file. A dependency file is a file that our application, or components within our application, requires in order to run. It might consist of a DLL, for example, that is used by many clients. If we made revisions to our dependency file, we would want to redistribute it to all users; this utility allows us to do this. We want to create a standard executable file, so select Standard Setup Package and click the Next button.

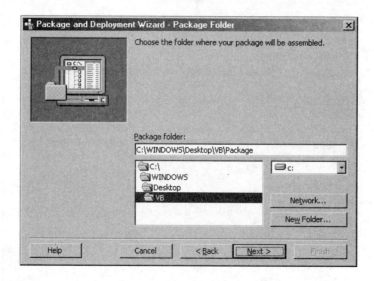

This dialog allows us to specify where we want the setup files to be saved once they have been created. Select where you want them to be saved and then click the Next button

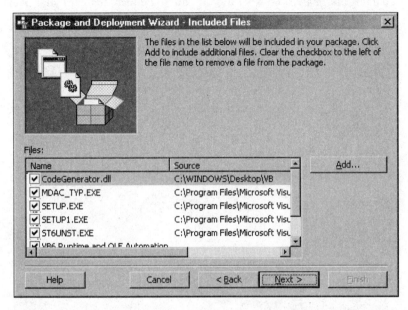

The Included Files dialog shows us what files will be automatically included in the package by Visual Basic. This list is created from the references and components we added to the project. If there are any that we are sure are not needed, we can uncheck the boxes and exclude them from the package. Similarly, if there are any missing, we can make sure they are included by clicking on the Add button and locating the appropriate files.

Dependency Files

A dependency file, which ends in the extension .dep, contains information about what additional files are needed for an application, how these files are to be registered for use and into which specific directories the installed files must be placed on the user's computer. The '.dep' files are what the Package and Deployment Wizard looks for when packaging the application - this file gives the wizard the information it needs to be able to include all of the relevant files in a setup file.

A standard packaged application will have its dependency information stored in a file called Setup.1st, which is separate to the package. An Internet package will store its dependency information in a file ending with the extension '.ini', which is part of the packaged application.

There are two types of file that can contain dependency information:

Component '.dep' files; thesefiles list all of the files that are needed for an individual component to work. If a component you have developed can be used in another project, you would create one of these '.dep' files to tell the next user what information they need and where to find it.

VB6dep.ini file; this file contains the dependency information for the whole environment of Visual Basic and can be found in the '\Wizards\PDWizard' subdirectory of the main Visual Basic directory. This file also contains information on what files are not to be included with your packaged application - this may be because the files need another component to install them.

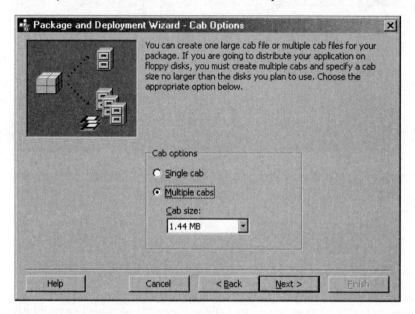

This dialog allows us to specify whether we wish to distribute our application in a single file or in several smaller files. The application will be distributed in Cabinet (Cab) files. These are compressed files, which work similarly to Zip files; each Cab file can contain a number of files which must be extracted before they can be used. In this dialog, we can specify the number of Cab files we want to create and the size of each file. If we plan to distribute this application on floppy disks, then we will want to select the Multiple Cabs option and limit the size of each Cab to 1.44 megabytes. Do this and click on the Next button.

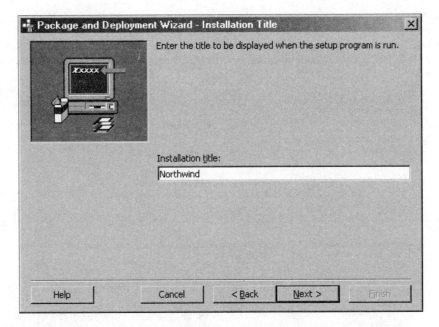

This step asks us what we would like the title of our setup package to be. Click the <u>N</u>ext button.

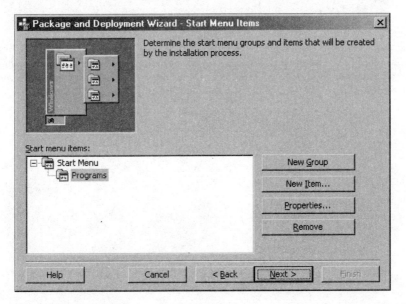

The Start Menu Items dialog allows us to place files in the startup folder, or in the folder that will be created specifically for your application, so that they will be accessible from the Start button. This is a great place to put other executables or help files that are part of your application. Click on the Next button to accept the default values. This takes us to the Install Locations dialog, where we can specify the folders where our individual files will be saved:

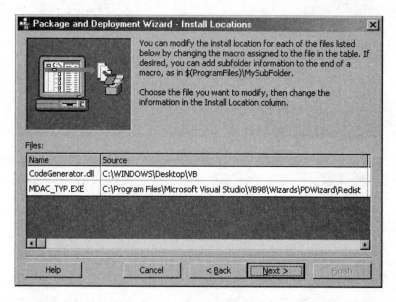

For the most part, Visual Basic knows where the associated files need to be placed, but the Install Locations dialog gives us the option of changing the defaults and placing files in a specific directory. If, for example, we want to place a specific DLL in the application path rather than the Windows Directory, we can change this here. Click on the Next button to accept the defaults.

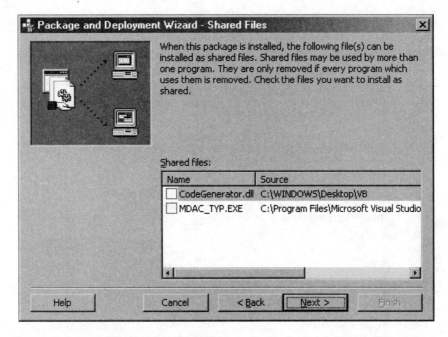

We now have just one final decision to make before the package is created. Visual Basic will identify any applications or DLLs that might be candidates to be shared by other applications. In this case, VB has identified the `CodeGenerator.dll` and the `MDAC_TYP.exe` file. If you want to share the file, click in the box next to the filename. In this case, just click on the **N**ext button, since we don't want any other applications using our program!

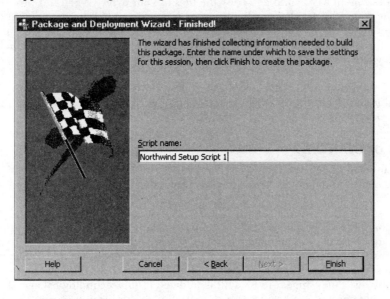

The last dialog is the Finished dialog. Here we can save the script by name so that we can re-use it if we want to make any modifications later. It is quite common to want to modify the setup utility later, so always choose a name that is logical to the project. Finally, click on the Finish button.

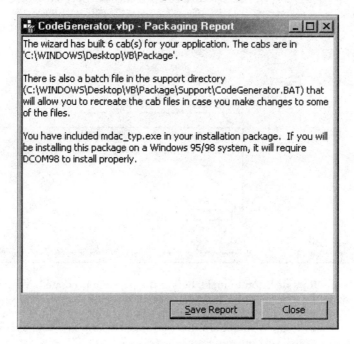

It may take a few minutes to build and copy the files to your drive. When this process has been completed, the dialog shown above will appear, giving us detailed information about the package. This information will change from application to application. Be sure to read the comments closely then click on the Close button. You will be brought back to the original dialog. Click on the Close button unless you want to build another setup utility.

So, now that you have your packaged application, how do you make sure that your end users will be able to install it onto their machines? There are a number of ways that you can do this, as I will now go on to explain.

Floppy Disk or CD-ROM?

The original method of deployment was by floppy disk. In this way, the application could be distributed to many computers by simply making copy after copy and handing over a number of floppy disks.

This method has today been superceded by the CD-ROM. CD-ROMs are easier for the user to utilize - it carries more information than a huge number of floppy disks, and there is no frantic swapping of disks before installation can continue. However, although this may ease the installation technique for some, you must bear in mind that some users will not have a CD-ROM drive on their computer. So, although floppy disks may appear to be a little outdated in this technological age, they are the only way that some of your end users will be able to install your application.

Intranet / Internet Solution

If you have built an Intranet application, then you can use the cab files, perhaps created for you by the Visual Basic Deployment Wizard, to deploy the components. You may, though, want to open the CAB files and verify that the `inf` file in the CAB file has the correct version number. This is usually a good method of deployment, but there can be many factors preventing the successful installation of files over the Intranet. The wrong security settings on the browser can cause endless problems. If the client machines do not all have the same browser settings that cannot be altered by the user, an Intranet cab file download can result in serious problems.

Systems Management Server (SMS) is Microsoft's solution to mass deployment of regular files, such as exes and DLLs, onto thousands of client machines. While it is beyond the level of this book to explain SMS, it is important to make a few comments about this product. In general, if you are using SMS server to deploy to thousands of clients, you need to first assemble a team of one or more people. These people will need to begin by using SMS to determine every type of computer in the company. Once this is done, a lab will need to be set up with client computers that are identical to the client computers that the software will be installed upon. The software should first be installed onto the lab computers. Any problems with the installation should be researched. This entire process can take up to six months. If this is done, SMS server should work very efficiently and successfully install on the client machines.

If you try to push software out onto untested clients do not be surprised if the installation fails. This is not only true with SMS server; this is also true with any method of deployment. I cannot stress enough that you must test everything you do. Getting the software out onto the clients and servers is no trivial matter; it requires a great deal of work to make a successful deployment plan.

The logistician should be working closely with the educators. It would be disastrous to change the client machines if the users have not been trained or prepared for the new system. You must coordinate deployment of the system with the training of the users.

Final Sign Off

When the project is complete, the Beta tests are done and the final application is deployed, the client must sign off the project. By defining the scope of the project in the envisioning phase we can determine exactly what should be delivered in this stage of building the system. Whether it is one part of the system, or the entire system, a well-defined scope will make it clear what should be delivered in the deployment phase. Once these deliverables have been completed and all milestones for the scope have been reached, then the client should sign off the project.

It is important that the project is signed off after completion. The signing off of a project indicates that the client accepts what has been delivered and is happy with the outcome of the project. If the project did not deliver all agreed functionality, meaning that it did not fulfill its scope, it is up to the client whether they accept what work has been done or not. If they are happy that the missing functionality can be delivered in the next project, then they may well sign off the current project and accept the application. More often than not, however, if the project has not fulfilled its scope it will not be accepted by the client, they will not sign off the project, the application is not handed over, and they will definitely not pay up! It is important, therefore, to strive to meet the scope so that the final sign off is merely a formality.

With the final sign off a copy of all documents relevant to the project should be given to the client: these documents will tell the client what their organization was like before the project, what the project aimed to achieve, how it achieved its aims, and also provide any user guides that it is felt necessary to provide. The client will use these documents for future upgrades and maintenance of the system. The development team should also keep a copy of the documents for reference in future projects.

Summary

The deployment phase is the final stage of your project. It is a time of intensive final testing and debugging. All project team members must continue to follow the guidelines of good project management during this stage. Bugs should be documented and changes in code should be made properly and documented in the code. Old versions of the project should be saved.

If the project has been properly designed and built, the final result will fulfill the business needs of the user. Using the cyclic methodology means that we will end up with a user centered application that is built from the best components within the limitations of the project.

Deployment of the application created by the project is not difficult, but there are a number of issues that must be considered, such as including additional necessary files and deciding in which format the application will be sent out. Once the application has been successfully deployed and accepted by the client, all concerned can officially sign off the project.

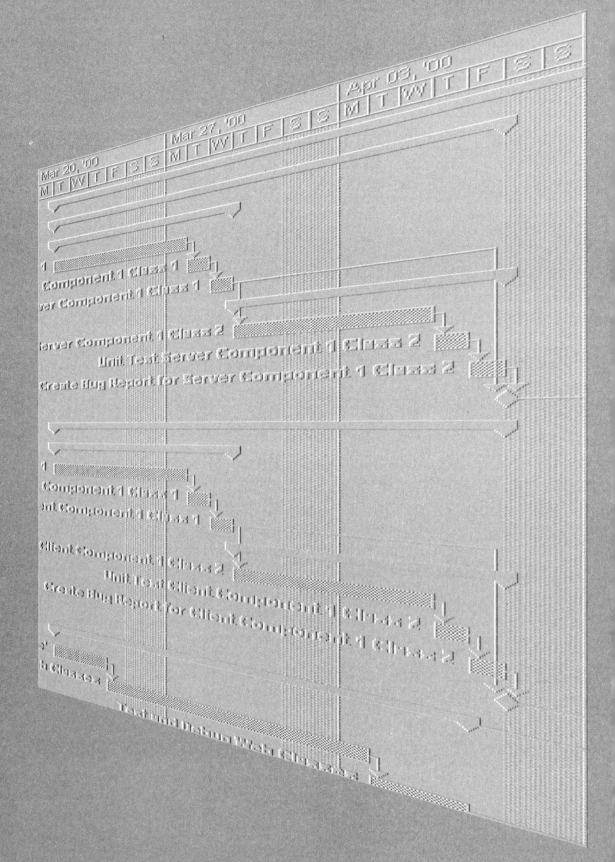

12

Versioning and Sharing Project Files

Nothing can destroy a Visual Basic project faster than creating changes in the source code without properly documenting these changes in the code and in the design documents. Combine these missing updates with a failure to maintain old copies of the source code, and you will quickly find that you have lost all control of your project. Because documentation and code become out of sync, it will be impossible to ensure that our code continues to follow our carefully planned design. And, of course, the best design and plan are useless if not followed.

The process of debugging code must be done scientifically, carefully and with purpose. I cannot tell you how often I have seen developers being told there is a bug in the code, and then watched them start hopping through code sections making random changes. When they have finished hacking, they say, "Try it now and see if it works." More often than not, several other bugs have been introduced. If the original source code is not stored somewhere, there is no going back, as no one can figure out what changes have been made. Changes need to be made in an orderly, organized manner. Using a tool such as Visual SourceSafe allows one to track changes made to the code, and roll back to the previous code. Of course, one should make changes in a careful, organized manner and have a standard for making changes to the code. But it's important to have access to the earlier versions if this doesn't happen.

When a tester identifies a bug, the team will look for a solution to the bug, and this should be found and documented. At this point, a change will have to be made in the code. Prior to making any change, a copy of the original files should be stored. In this chapter, we will look at a tool which can be used to implement change control (the process of ensuring that any changes made to the product are authorized), and to maintain a history of your Visual Basic project files (and other documents, too) so that you can retrieve older versions.

A Look at Visual SourceSafe

Visual SourceSafe is a useful tool supplied with Visual Studio which helps developers share Visual Basic files (called **Source Control**) and maintain different versions of files (**Version Tracking**). Source control is used to try to prevent two copies of the same file being changed at the same time. This can occur when two developers try to change the same file at the same time or when one developer accidentally opens two copies of the same file and tries to edit both of them. While this cannot be entirely prevented (source control will allow any number of developers to open the files as read-only, and these can then be changed and saved under a different file name), using a tool such as Visual SourceSafe (VSS) ensures that there is only one official version. Version tracking enables us to keep a history of the code's development by saving backup copies of the files. These backup copies can be used to recreate the original files exactly as they were at some previous point in time. We can also compare two different versions and see the differences in the two files. This allows us to pull out the precise lines of codes that have been changed.

Visual SourceSafe is a project-oriented version control system. Visual SourceSafe supports any type of Visual Basic project, including web and non-web applications, and it can keep track of changes to both text and binary files so we can use it with all of our project files. We can also use Visual SourceSafe to keep track of the relationships between files. Visual SourceSafe works with groups of files.

In addition, Visual SourceSafe has a report generator, a history tool for showing history of projects or individual files, tools to identify differences between versions of files, a tool for finding strings in text files and a tool for viewing files.

Visual SourceSafe is a tool which allows a team to work cooperatively on code and documents. However, since many readers will not have access to an entire network to explore Visual SourceSafe with, we will create an example on a single machine.

In a real implementation of a change management system, there must be a great deal of planning. It is unlikely the entire team will need access to all files. There must be a decision made on what files and documents each component team will have access to, and what files and documents each member of the team should have access to. The Visual SourceSafe database must be placed where all the team members can have access to it and check out files for editing. There must be enough disk space for the Visual SourceSafe database, and there must be enough room to allow for the expansion of the database as Visual SourceSafe begins to maintain a history of the files. A clear set of rules must be established on when and how files are checked, how they are updated and how they are changed and checked back in. All of these factors take time, planning and research. A good change management system cannot be created without first reviewing these issues.

Adding a Project to Visual SourceSafe

If you have not installed Visual SourceSafe onto a computer and you want to do the examples, install it now; it is supplied with Visual Studio. Once Visual SourceSafe has been installed, you will need to create users who are allowed to use it. To do this, go to the Windows Start menu, select **Microsoft Visual Studio 6/Visual SourceSafe/Visual SourceSafe Administrator 6.0**. You should begin by changing the administrator password: the default password for the administrator is blank. You can also add additional users if you need to. Once you have done this, you can go to the Windows **Start** menu, select **Microsoft Visual Studio 6/Visual SourceSafe/Visual SourceSafe 6.0**. Enter a valid user ID and password. Now open up Visual Basic and create a new project; when you save the project, you will now be asked if you want to add it to Visual SourceSafe. Save the project and add it to SourceSafe.

You will be prompted to log in when you choose to add the project to SourceSafe:

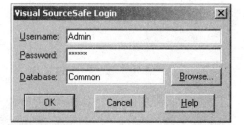

The next screen will require you to select a project to include this in. This is not the name of the Visual Basic project (though it can be the same): it is the name of the Visual SourceSafe project. If you are building an application out of many Visual Basic projects, you may want to group all of the projects into a single VSS project or give each one its own separate Visual SourceSafe project. In this screenshot, I have no VSS projects yet, so I will just save it to `Project1`:

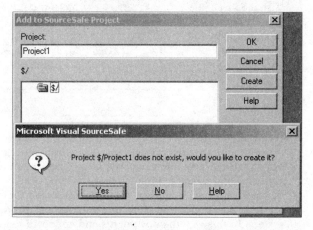

You may be wondering where this file is physically saved. Usually, Microsoft Visual SourceSafe is installed on a server in a development environment. Visual SourceSafe manages all of the documents it stores (these documents can be code, forms, UML diagrams, etc.). Visual SourceSafe will place these files in a special Visual SourceSafe database. The files will also be temporarily placed on one or more of the developer's hard drives as the developers check out the files for editing.

You will next be prompted to choose which files you want to save:

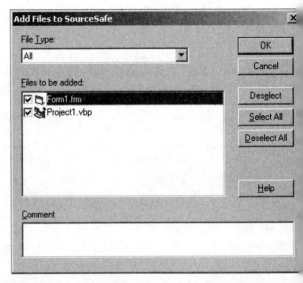

Save all of them. If you close the Visual SourceSafe manager and reopen it, you will see the following:

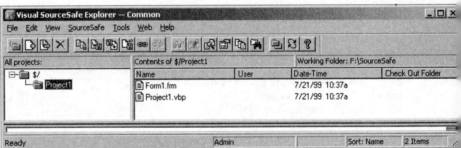

While anyone using Visual SourceSafe can use the manager, most Visual Basic developers will actually never use the Visual SourceSafe Manager or Administrator. These tools will usually be used only by the project manager. In a large corporation with many projects, the change management system would become a library that could be used by many developers. In this case, it is best if a librarian is placed in charge of the database and the change management system. The librarian will establish user rights, locations of databases and procedures and policies for the change management system. In this way the documents and code will belong to the corporation and can be available for reuse, maintenance and future upgrades.

If you return to our Visual Basic project and right mouse click on the program window, you will see the following:

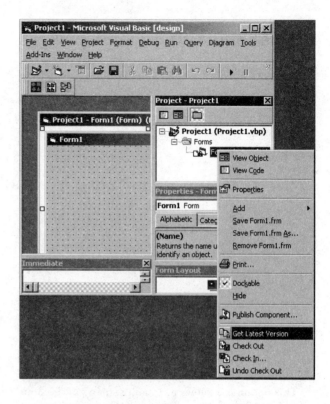

Checking Files Out of Visual SourceSafe

You can see that we now have a few items added to the project menu. Selecting Get Latest Version will retrieve a read-only copy of the latest version of the module, so we cannot make any changes to the file. We will want to do this before we start testing. When we want to edit the module, we must remove or Check Out the file from the Visual Source Safe library. When we check out a module, a copy is written to the local hard drive. If we try to open the module before we have checked it out, we will get an error message and will not be allowed to edit. While one developer has checked it out, no other developer can also check it out for editing. However, other people can still look at the file in read-only mode, or make a copy and add a new file to the database for editing (this is called branching, which will be discussed below). This prevents two people from editing an official version of the same module. Check In saves the new edited code module back into the database and deletes the local copy. This differs from Undo Check Out, which allows us to stop editing without saving any changes.

If a code module is checked out for editing, as we discussed, the last saved version can still be viewed by another developer and even run. The second person cannot, though, change any of the code. This means that while the development team is working on a module, the testing team can be testing completed portions of the module. Thus, Visual SourceSafe allows development and testing to occur together.

Configuring VSS

Many Visual SourceSafe options can be changed. If you go to the Visual SourceSafe menu and select Tools | Options you will see the SourceSafe Option tabs:

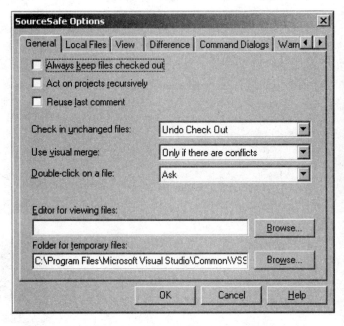

This option tab allows us to adjust many of the SourceSafe configuration settings, such as what action will be taken if an unchanged file is checked in, and what action to take when we double-click on a file in VSS Explorer. It is worth taking some time to look through the tabs and see what options are available.

Merging Files

Using the cyclic methodology will allow us to complete the project in steps. Each step will complete a portion of the project and will have milestones associated with it. Once the milestone is reached, we move onto the next portion of our code. When it comes to writing Visual Basic code, it is best if each step creates and completes a set of functionality of a Visual Basic component. Thus, in our first step we make the Customer component and code the properties of the bottom class. Our milestone will be the writing of the code and the debugging and testing of this code. Once this milestone is reached, we begin work in the next stage, which may include writing the methods for this class. The next stage should not be adding additional functionality to the properties written in the last stage, as this makes it difficult to update changes.

If we are adding methods or properties to a class from one stage to the next, we may run into the situation where a bug is found in an earlier stage while working in a later stage. To fix this, we will have to go back to the code from the earlier stage, fix the bug, and then merge the new version of the earlier phase into the later phase. Visual SourceSafe can do this automatically, but it is recommended to use the Visual Merge tool supplied with VSS. This works a little like Compare Documents in Microsoft Word, and allows us to view each difference between two files:

Ideally, we would want to complete the bottom class in the first phase and then build other classes that used the bottom class in the second phase. This is the best way to build a project and the easiest way to maintain and debug the code.

Versioning Files

The standard project version numbers have used a Dewey decimal notation consisting of numbers separated by periods. The format of a version number appears as *major.minor.revision*, where

> **Major** version numbers identify significant functional changes.
> **Minor** version numbers identify smaller extensions to functionality.
> **Revision** version numbers signify even finer grained changes such as bug fixes.

You can extend this scheme if you need to. Visual SourceSafe's archiving functionality allows you to retrieve any prior version of existing code. This can happen if changes are made to the code that create a serious problem in the functionality of the project. Using the archived versions, you can rollback to the version that did not have the changes.

Versioning with VSS

Visual SourceSafe also allows you to create custom versions of the same application. This could happen if you needed two slightly different versions of a project. In our discussion of reusing the product component for the ASP page, we mentioned that it would be best to create a new application using some of the old code for the product component. In this case, we would want a copy of the original project to become a new project that we could modify according the specifications of the ASP project. Let us look at how Visual SourceSafe allows us to do versioning.

One approach for tracking versions or builds of projects or applications in Visual SourceSafe is to use labels. By placing a label on the parent project of a program, all of the child projects and files will inherit that label. Labels are simply descriptive strings that we can apply to any version of a project. A label is a free-form string which can contain up to 31 characters. The following are all examples of valid labels: `"1.0"`, `"2.01b"`, `"Beta 3"` and `"Approved by Tester1"`. Visual SourceSafe tracks the history of the project, allowing us to label a project when we have reached a certain level of development (for example, version 3.05.234). Later on, we can refer back to the files in the project, as they existed at the time you labeled the project.

We can label a project by going into the SourceSafe Explorer, right mouse clicking on the project and selecting Label:

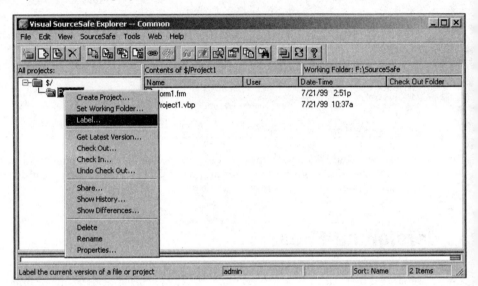

Visual SourceSafe Scenarios

There are two common scenarios with Visual Basic projects. In the first case, we do not expect to change many files. In the second case, we may be changing several files, potentially several times. Visual SourceSafe has two different features to cope with these scenarios. In the first case, we would use Visual SourceSafe's label-promotion feature. In the second case, we would use Share/Pin/Branch.

Label Promotion is the best method to use when your development is done in the same project tree and bug fixes are routinely performed before other changes have been made in the project. A common example is when working on a major release with several milestones, such as Beta 1 and Beta 2. In this instance, we would label the project when we believe we have completed Beta 1, then continue working toward Beta 2. If few fixes are needed for Beta 1, use the label-promotion feature.

Share/Pin/Branch is the best method to use for parallel development on a project over an extended period of time. A common example is when we are working on two releases that share code, both of which have milestones. For example, we have shipped Version 1.0 and now we are working on Version 2.0; however, an interim patch for several bug fixes is needed. This patch will be released as Version 1.1. In this instance, we would work on Version 2.0 and Version 1.1 in different project trees, then merge changes between them as necessary.

The following are three scenarios using the label-promotion feature. For completeness, a fourth scenario using share, pin, and branch is described. These scenarios are presented as a guide.

Scenario #1: Component Development
In this scenario, we are building the project from components. At each release, a component is completed and will not be changed in the next release. Thus, Release 2 does not change Release 1 code; it only adds additional modules to the project.

> ➤ Develop and test the project in the drive toward Release 1.

> ➤ At the point where Release 1 is completely tested, label the project, for example: `"Release 1"`.

> ➤ Begin working on Release 2.

Scenario #2: Changing Files in an Unchanged Previous Release
We will be developing as in Scenario 1, i.e. building separate components in each release. After we have moved to Release 2, we discover there is a major flaw in Release 1 in files that have not been changed while working on Release 2. Release 1 could be in use by the client or the flaw may prevent proper testing of Release 2. Release 1 needs to be fixed and recompiled.

> ➤ Develop and test the project in the drive toward Release 1.

> ➤ At the point where we are ready to go to Release 1, label the project `"Release 1"` (or something similar).

> ➤ Begin working on Release 2.

> ➤ At this point, we realize that the file included in Release 1 has a bug in it that must be fixed. No other files in the project have yet changed.

> ➤ Check out the file, make the changes, then check it back in.

> ➤ Label the project `"Release 1"` again. (You'll be asked to confirm that you want to remove the old label). Projects using version 1 files will not have to be changed. If you want to maintain the original version, rename it Release 1.1 and include the new Release 1.1 files in all of the projects using the Release 1 files.

Scenario #3: Changing Files in an Altered Previous Release
We will be developing as in Scenario 1, i.e. building separate components in each release. After we have moved to Release 2, we discover there is a major flaw in Release 1 in files that have been changed while working on Release 2 (for example: a class may have had additional methods or properties added). Release 1 could be in use by the client, or the flaw may prevent proper testing of Release 2. Release 1 needs to be fixed and recompiled.

> ➤ Develop and test the project in the drive toward Release 1.

> ➤ At the point where we are ready to go to Release 1, give the project an appropriate label, such as `"Release 1"`.

> ➤ Begin working on Release 2.

> ➤ As in Scenario#2, we now realize that the file included in Release 1 has a bug in it that must be fixed. However, this time other files in the project have also been changed and those changes have been checked in.

> Check out the original Release 1 copy of the files that need to changed, make the required changes, and then check the files back in, creating a new version.

> Label the file `"Release 1"` (the same label we gave to the project). This promotes the new version of that file into the project with the label `"Release 1"`.

> Now, if we retrieve the Release 1 project, we will get the project the way it was at the date and time when we labeled it `"Release 1"`, except that we will retrieve the newer version of the file we just labeled individually as `"Release 1"`. This allows us to update specific files in an old version, even after changes have been made to other files.

Scenario #4: Share, Pin and Branch to Create Service Pack Projects to Fix Major Bugs
If the need arises for a bug fix after a project has been labeled and further developed, we can use the following share, pin and branch scenario.

Sharing allows one file or set of files to belong to multiple projects. Unless the file is branched after sharing, each project will have a reference to the shared file: if the file is changed in one project, it will also be changed in the other.

Branching is the process of sharing a file with another project and then separating it into two or more branches. Once a branch has been created, two files (the file in the project and its counterpart in another project) will have a shared history up to a certain point and divergent histories after that time. Branching a file breaks the shared link, making the file in that project independent of all other projects.

Pinning is generally used with shared files, although it is not limited to shared files: we can pin any file. When we pin a shared file, we cannot make any further changes to it. Pinning is like sticking a pin into the file so that a particular version of the file becomes the version that is part of the project. If a pinned version of a file is shared, the projects sharing the file cannot change it. If a file is shared first and then pinned in one project, other projects can still change and update the file.

> In the drive toward Version 1.0, develop and test your project (e.g. `$/Application`).

> When Version 1.0 has been achieved, label the project `"Version 1.0"`.

> Begin changing files in the project in the drive toward Version 2.0 of the project, which will introduce new features.

> If we now realize that an interim Version 1.1 is needed for bug fixes, select the project in SourceSafe Explorer. Then, on the Tools menu, click Show History to display the History Options dialog box:

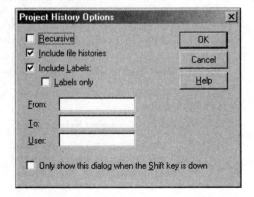

➤ Select the Include Labels box and click on OK to display the History of Project dialog box:

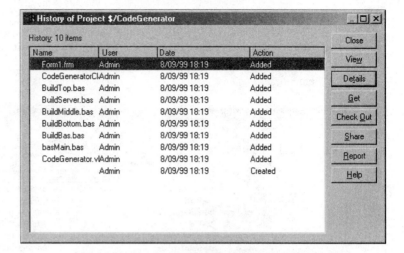

➤ Select the version labeled "Version 1.0" and click Share. The Share from Project dialog box will appear:

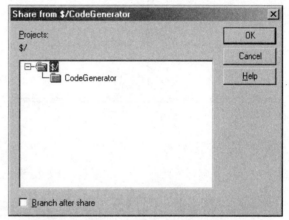

➤ Select the project you want the new project to be part of. This will usually be $/project. We want to fix the bugs in both projects, so ensure that the Branch after Share box is not be checked; otherwise, we will have to make the changes independently to both projects. Now click on OK to display the Share Project dialog box:

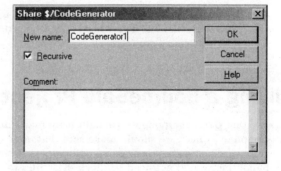

> ➤ Give the project a **New Name** (e.g., $/Application V 1.1). If the project has subprojects, select **Recursive**; this will ensure that all subprojects are also shared. Add any comments in the **Comment** box as needed, then click **OK**. Click **Close** to exit the **History of Project** dialog box.

> ➤ Select the newly created project $/Application V 1.1. All files in this project will now be pinned:

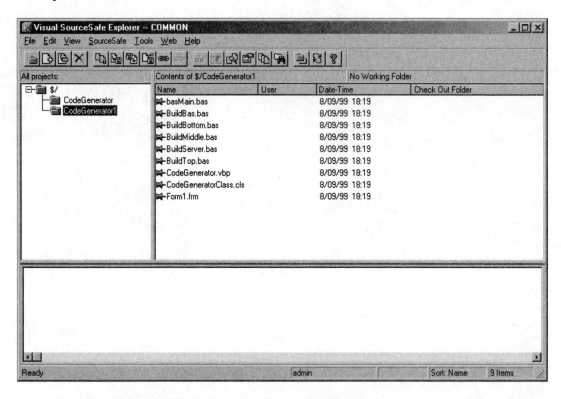

> ➤ Select only those files that need to be changed to address bug fixes, then branch the file(s). Leave pinned any files that do not need to be changed. You can later merge bug fix changes back into your Version 2.0 project.

Building a SourceSafe Project

Most Visual Basic components are built from many different components. Before we start compiling the complete project, we should make sure that none of the files in the entire system are checked out. However, if development is ongoing and the last saved version of a checked out file is acceptable for the build, then we do not need to check these files in. Visual SourceSafe can create a list of all the checked-out files in a project. We can use this recursively to include all subprojects in the current project. Visual SourceSafe will check every file in every relevant project and generate a list including every checked-out file. We thus know immediately whether we can proceed with the build, or who to talk to if we are not able to continue.

File Histories

Visual SourceSafe has the ability to build file history reports. File histories list each version of a file, from the most recent to the oldest, with information such as what happened to the file, who did it, when it was done, and what comment was made.

To tackle this with Visual SourceSafe, we generate a report on the *project itself*. For instance, it might report that a file named COMMON.BAS has just been modified; before that, OPENALL.FRM was changed; before that, FILESUPP.BAS was added to the project, and so on. Visual SourceSafe collates the changes that we would otherwise have to sort through manually, enabling us to view the order of changes over the last week. This can save us a lot of time and help us avoid dead ends.

Maintaining Reusable Code

We will usually find that there are parts of our code that are reusable. In the case of the ASP page Product component and the Visual Basic EXE we saw in Chapter 9, both of them share the non-data provider code. We could have developed this first, shared the project and created two branches at this point. Or, we could have error handling code that is used in all of our applications. Files such as this usually evolve over time because of bug fixes, performance improvements or new features. The benefits of reusing existing code are enormous, but so are the headaches when managing the organizational issues. You have to remember which applications are using each file and propagate every change to all the appropriate places. This is only a minor annoyance when five applications are reusing one file but when twenty applications are mixing and matching fifty different reusable files, the situation can become complicated.

Visual SourceSafe can automate the process completely. Within its database, Visual SourceSafe stores each file only once. Each project that contains a file has a pointer to the location of the file in the database. All versions of the file are available to each project, and a project may "freeze" the version of a file to avoid introducing errors while another development team works on the reused code.

Summary

Visual SourceSafe is a tool that allows a team of developers to share source code. It also provides an easy-to-use versioning system. In this chapter, we outlined some of the more basic features of SourceSafe and discussed how it can be used in managing your Visual Basic project.

We haven't been able to look at all of the features provided by VSS, but this whirlwind tour of this tool has given us the chance to look at some of the issues connected with version tracking and source control. We saw how a tool such as VSS can help us keep track of who is editing which files, and how it can help us maintain a library of previous versions of our code. This means that if we have to fix bugs in an old release, we will still have the appropriate files. We also saw how VSS can help us manage and maintain code modules which are shared by a number of different projects or releases.

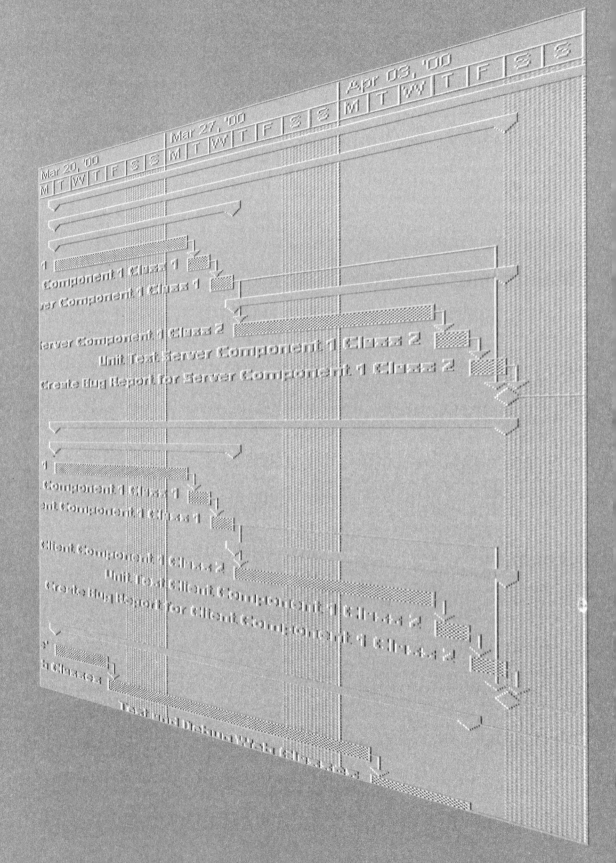

13

Creating a Project Schedule

We are now going to take all of the information we have learned throughout the book about our Visual Basic project and goal oriented Visual Basic teams and create an example schedule for the whole project. Although you can download this schedule from the Wrox Press site, I would recommend you taking the time out to actually input the information into the schedule. This will help you understand the goals of each cycle, and whose responsibility it is to fulfill that goal. We will discuss some ways of improving it at the end of the chapter.

Project Resources

Create a new Project 98 schedule called DNA. You will need to add resources to your project. We will allow for a large development team that incorporates three small teams. Team 1 will focus on server components, Team 2 will work with client side components, and Team 3 will be the web experts. Go to the menu and select View | Resource Sheet.

Resource Name is the label we are going to give to our resource; in this case, our resources are our team members, so their titles will be entered as the resource label. In order for us to make a cost estimate for the project, we must enter the rates of pay for each team member, or the Std. Rate: the total cost of employing each team member will be seen after all the information has been entered into the schedule.

Enter the information from the following table into the resource sheet.

Resource Name	Std. Rate
Component Manager 1	$70.00/h
Developer 1a	$50.00/h
Tester 1a	$45.00/h
Developer 1b	$60.00/h
Tester 1b	$45.00/h
Component Manager 2	$75.00/h
Developer 2a	$50.00/h
Tester 2a	$50.00/h
Developer 2b	$60.00/h
Tester 2b	$45.00/h
Component Manager 3	$70.00/h
Developer 3a	$50.00/h
Developer 3b	$45.00/h
Tester	$40.00/h
Product Management	$75.00/h
Project Manager	$85.00/h
Educator	$40.00/h
Logistics	$40.00/h
End Users	$0.00/h
Client Management	$0.00/h

Your resource list should look as follows:

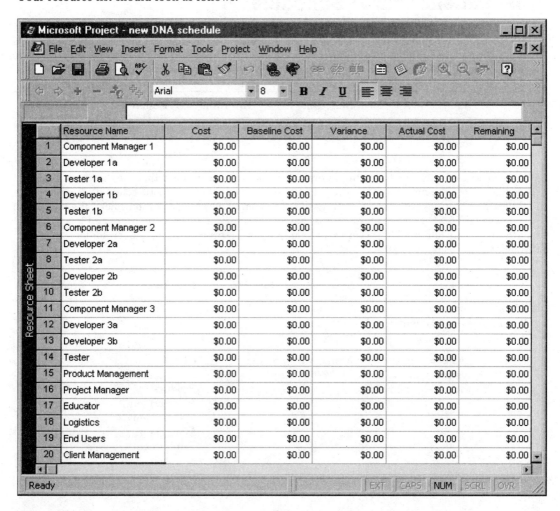

The table is full of zeros because the resources have not yet been assigned to any goals, and so have not yet started costing you any money!

Throughout this chapter, you will see that as you add goals to your schedule, you assign resources to them. In some cases, the resources will have a percentage mark next to them - this is to indicate how much of the resource is being utilized for this particular goal. However, as our resources are all people, we will take the percentage mark to mean the percentage of time each person is spending on the particular goal.

In an ideal world, we would have every member of the project team fully dedicated to only one project at a time; however, this schedule tries to reflect a real life situation, so it must be understood that our team members may sometimes have other, non-project related work to do. Although this may add some length of time to our duration estimates, these responsibilities and prior engagements must be accepted and accommodated.

Envisionment Phase Schedule

Go back to the Gantt view and enter the information below into the schedule. The numbers in parentheses represents how far you should indent the item. Each time the indentation changes, we will list it in the first column in parentheses. A 0 means the item is all the way to the left, a 1 means it is indented once, etc. Make sure that all constraints are set as soon as possible.

		Name	Start Date	Duration	Resources	Predecessors
1	(0)	Notes about this template	Mon 01/17/00	0 days		

When you are entering the following information, please bear in mind that the durations I have given to the goals here are only estimates, based on showing you what a realistic schedule may look like. In real life, the durations will vary according to the size and complexity of the project, the number of people available, what else team members may be working on at the same time, and lots of other factors. This schedule merely serves as an example for the project we have been looking at throughout the book.

		Name	Start Date	Duration	Resources	Predecessors
2		Envisionment	Mon 01/17/00			
3	(1)	Evaluate current systems / meet with client mgmt	Mon 01/17/00	5 days	Client Management, Product Management, Component Manager 1, Component Manager 2, Component Manager 3	
4		Create Enterprise Architecture Document	Fri 01/21/00	0 days		3

	Name	Start Date	Duration	Resources	Predecessors
5	Initial Consensus Meeting	Mon 01/24/00	1 day	Component Manager 1, Developer 1a, Tester 1a, Developer 1b, Tester 1b, Component Manager 2, Developer 2a, Tester 2a, Developer 2b, Tester 2b, Component Manager 3, Developer 3a, Developer 3b, Tester, Product Management, Project Manager, Educator, Logistics, End Users, Client Management	4

In the first part of the envisionment phase, we must evaluate how the client's current Enterprise system works and what their current business processes are. This is essential to give us a good idea of the background of the client. We must then determine how that system will be integrated, or migrated, into the current project.

It is important that every team member attends the initial consensus meeting: everybody should understand the aims of the project and the impact it will have on the client.

It is quite obvious that the Enterprise Architecture Document cannot be created until you have evaluated the current system. Similarly, the initial consensus meeting cannot take place until the current status of the business is known and can be communicated to all.

	Name	Start Date	Duration	Resources	Predecessors
6	Define Vision / Scope				
7 (2)	Determine ROI and TCO	Tue 01/25/00	6 days	Logistics[50%)	5
8	Initial ROI and TCO estimates	Tue 02/01/00	0 days		7

This part of the envisionment phase allows you to make an initial estimate of the Total Cost of Ownership and Return On Investment for the project. At this stage, estimates will be just that - it is only after completing the other phases of the project that these estimates can be refined.

The ROI and TCO cannot be determined until after the initial consensus meeting. Similarly, the milestone cannot be reached until the ROI and TCO have been determined.

	Name	Start Date	Duration	Resources	Predecessors
9	Define Client Requirements	Tue 01/25/00	4 days	Educator	5
10	Define content requirements	Tue 01/25/00	2 days	Component Manager 3	5
11	Define system requirements	Tue 01/25/00	6 days	Logistics[50%]	5
12	Define client / server requirements	Tue 01/25/00	2 days	Component Manager 1, Developer 1a, Developer 1b	5
13	Define specific functionality	Tue 01/25/00	1 day	Component Manager 2, Developer 2a, Developer 2b	5

As you are undertaking the project to deliver some specific functionality to the user, it would be very useful to find out what it is that they require! This cannot take place until after the initial consensus meeting. To define client requirements, you must decide not only what information the users require, but also how they prefer to access that information. From this, you should be able to determine exactly what information each user requires.

Your clients may have strict rules about the configuration of their computers. This may put restrictions on the way that the project can be designed and developed. It is imperative that information such as this is uncovered before any design or development takes place - knowing the restrictions beforehand will save a lot of money and effort in the long run.

To define the specific functionality, you must take the user requirements and translate them into goals for the developers; this will give them more of an idea of what it is they are expected to do when design and development actually take place.

	Name	Start Date	Duration	Resources	Predecessors
14	Define risks and risk management approach	Wed 02/02/00	4 days	Component Manager 1, Developer 1a, Tester 1a, Developer 1b, Tester 1b, Component Manager 2, Developer 2a, Tester 2a, Developer 2b, Tester 2b, Component Manager 3, Developer 3a, Developer 3b, Tester, Product Management, Project Manager, Educator, Logistics, End Users, Client Management	5,7,9,10,11, 12,13

It is important to analyze your concept, the environment you are working in and the potential problems that could arise. These areas of risk should be documented and a plan formulated to mitigate the risk where possible, and manage the risk where necessary. Depending on the degree of risk inherent in the project, you may want to add contingencies to the durations in the project plan. This step would form the basis of the Risk Assessment Document.

This step cannot take place until all the preceding steps have been completed: the risks identified will be specific to what the user wants the system to do. Until the specific functionality and requirements have been defined, the risks cannot be identified.

	Name	Start Date	Duration	Resources	Predecessors
15	Develop project plan	Tue 02/08/00	2 days	Component Manager 1, Developer 1a, Tester 1a, Developer 1b, Tester 1b, Component Manager 2, Developer 2a, Tester 2a, Developer 2b, Tester 2b, Component Manager 3, Developer 3a, Developer 3b, Tester, Product Management, Project Manager, Educator, Logistics, End Users, Client Management	14
16	Develop Testing Plan for project	Thu 02/10/00	4 days	Tester 1a, Tester 1b, Tester 2a, Tester 2b, Tester	15
17	Create Master Schedules	Thu 02/10/00	1 day	Component Manager 1, Component Manager 2, Component Manager 3	15

The project plan should answer the following questions:

> What is the business problem being addressed by this project?
> Who are the users and what are their specific goals?
> Who are the stakeholders and sponsors and what are their specific goals?
> What will the client gain as a result of this project?
> What will be the ROI?

It should also take account of potential risks, so this step cannot take place until the risks and risk approach have been defined.

A testing plan should also be developed to ensure that all code is tested systematically and thoroughly. The master schedule should also be created; this gives an idea as to how long the project will last and can also provide initial cost estimates for the project. These two steps will follow on from the project plan.

	Name	Start Date	Duration	Resources	Predecessors
18 (1)	Final Consensus Meeting	Wed 02/16/00	1 day	Component Manager 1, Developer 1a, Tester 1a, Developer 1b, Tester 1b, Component Manager 2, Developer 2a, Tester 2a, Developer 2b, Tester 2b, Component Manager 3, Developer 3a, Developer 3b, Tester, Product Management, Project Manager, Educator, Logistics, End Users, Client Management	16,17,15
19	Vision / Scope Document Complete	Wed 02/16/00	0 days		18

The final consensus meeting, again attended by every team member, will give the green light for the project. All items should have been agreed upon, and the Vision / Scope document created, becoming the milestone for this phase. The completed Vision / Scope document will be used as a tool to communicate with the development team, whether they are an internal development team or an external vendor. As a result of the briefing you should have committed development resources for the project. Quite obviously, this step cannot take place until all preceding steps are complete.

The Vision / Scope document should include:

> Vision statement
> Scope statement
> Assessment of resources
> Team responsibilities
> Risk Assessment
> ROI / TCO

The schedule for the Envisionment phase will look as follows in Project 98:

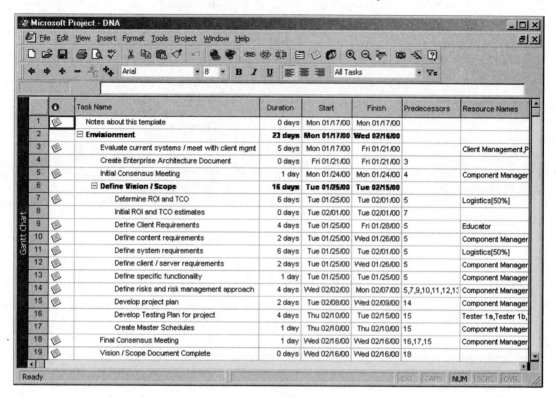

To make the schedule more readable, you can change the color of the goals that are divided into smaller goals. Select an entire row and then go to Format I Font and select a color.

The Gantt chart will look as follows:

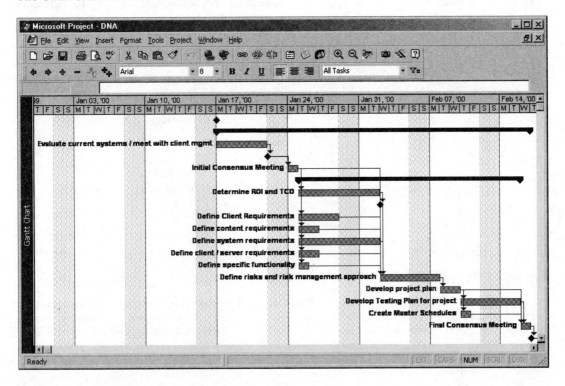

Design Phase Schedule

Add these into the schedule for the design phase:

	Name	Start Date	Duration	Resources	Predecessors
20 (0)	Design	Thu 02/17/00			19
21 (1)	Conceptual	Thu 02/17/00			19
22 (2)	Interview End Users	Thu 02/17/00	2 days	Educator, Product Management, End Users	

	Name	Start Date	Duration	Resources	Predecessors
23	Documentation of User Interviews	Fri 02/18/00	0 days		22
24	Create Use Cases	Mon 02/21/00	2 days	Product Management, Component Manager 1	23
25	Review Use Cases with End Users	Wed 02/23/00	1 day	Educator, Product Management, End Users	24
26	Complete set of Use Cases	Wed 02/23/00	0 days		25

Design cannot begin until the Vision / Scope document is complete.

The conceptual design phase is all about adding structure to the ideas from the envisionment phase. Here, we will find out from the users how they would like the system to work, and how the system can work in the most efficient way to meet business needs. When the conceptual design milestone has been reached - a complete set of finalized Use Cases - there will be a clearly defined description of the product, the functionality it will include and the manner in which the users will interact with the system.

These steps occur in a logical order, each needing to be complete before the next step can begin.

	Name	Start Date	Duration	Resources	Predecessors
27 (1)	Logical	Thu 02/24/00			26
28 (2)	Design User Interface	Thu 02/24/00			
29 (3)	Determine end-user requirements for the forms	Thu 02/24/00			
30 (4)	Create User Interface Prototype	Thu 02/24/00	2 days	Educator	

	Name	Start Date	Duration	Resources	Predecessors
31	Review Prototype with Users	Mon 02/28/00	1 day	Educator, End Users	30
32 (3)	Completed User Interface prototype	Mon 02/28/00	0 days		30,31
33	User Interface designed	Mon 02/28/00	0 days		32
34	For the web component, determine links	Thu 02/24/00	1 day	Developer 3a	
35 (2)	Proof of Concept Testing	Thu 02/24/00	5 days	Component Manager 2 [50%], Developer 2a [50%], Tester 2a	

This stage of the design phase cannot begin until there is a complete set of finalized use cases - otherwise, there would be nothing to build upon!

The logical stage of the design phase is where a prototype of the user interface will be developed; this will allow the developers to ascertain how the users want to interact with the system. Form design will also take place, so that the user's interaction with the system is optimized and both easy and complex tasks are simple to perform.

For the web component, you must figure out conceptually what you want the look and feel of the site / application to be. If the site is large you will want to determine the design and layout of the site. Design should be decided on first and agreed on by all team members. You should also determine conceptually what your 'hot spots' will be and what they will link to.

	Name	Start Date	Duration	Resources	Predecessors
36	Decide how to implement functionality	Tue 02/29/00			32

	Name	Start Date	Duration	Resources	Predecessors
37 (3)	Create Sequence Diagrams	Tue 02/29/00	3 days	Component Manager 1, Developer 1a, Developer 1b, Component Manager 2 [50%], Developer 2a [50%], Developer 2b, Component Manager 3, Developer 3a, Developer 3b, Product Management[33%]	
38	Determine what components are required	Fri 03/03/00	1 day	Component Manager 1, Developer 1a, Developer 1b, Component Manager 2, Developer 2a, Developer 2b, Component Manager 3, Developer 3a, Developer 3b, Product Management[33%]	37

	Name	Start Date	Duration	Resources	Predecessors
39	Determine service for components	Mon 03/06/00	1 day	Component Manager 1, Developer 1a, Developer 1b, Component Manager 2, Developer 2a, Developer 2b, Component Manager 3, Developer 3a, Developer 3b, Product Management[33%]	38
40	Completed Sequence Diagrams	Mon 03/06/00	0 days		38,39

This stage of the design phase is where the developers convert the use cases into sequence diagrams, which indicate which components the project will need, and which properties and services each component will need.

After you have defined the specific functionality in the Conceptual phase, you must decide how to implement it. The decision on how to implement functionality cannot be made until there is a complete user interface prototype - before this, the detailed functionality will not be known. This decision entails whether you will have in-house developers do the work, hire vendor development services, or you will buy a product off-the-shelf to implement the functionality.

For example, functionality important to the users may be the ability to give feedback directly from the website to the content owners. This can be done by implementing a link that sends email to the content owners, or by creating a page that puts the feedback into a database. Creating a hotlink to email needs very little development, but there must be a scheme set up to maintain whom that mail goes to. Creating the direct-feedback page takes more development, but you have greater control over how the feedback is formulated and can be reported on. These types of tradeoffs need to be considered when designing functionality. In this stage you need to perform some cost benefit analysis as to whether it is more beneficial to develop the function in-house, hire vendor development services or buy the product in the form of an off-the-shelf product.

	Name	Start Date	Duration	Resources	Predecessors
41 (1)	Physical	Tue 03/07/00			40
42 (2)	Design Components for the project	Tue 03/07/00			
43 (3)	Create Activity Diagrams	Tue 03/07/00	1 day	Component Manager 1[50%], Developer 1a[50%], Developer 1b[50%], Component Manager 2[50%], Developer 2a[50%], Developer 2b[50%], Developer 3a[50%], Developer 3b[50%], Component Manager 3[50%]	
44	Create Class Diagrams	Tue 03/07/00	1 day	Component Manager 1[50%], Developer 1a[50%], Developer 1b[50%], Component Manager 2[50%], Developer 2a[50%], Developer 2b[50%], Component Manager 3[50%], Developer 3a[50%], Developer 3b[50%]	

	Name	Start Date	Duration	Resources	Predecessors
45	Create Consolidated Design Document	Tue 03/07/00	0 days	Component Manager 1, Developer 1a, Developer 1b, Component Manager 2, Developer 2a, Developer 2b, Component Manager 3, Developer 3a, Developer 3b	43,44

The physical stage of the design phase is where the actual properties and services of each component are defined: this means that there is a concrete design for each component, and also for the way in which the component will interact. The physical design stage of the design phase cannot begin until all sequence diagrams are completed. The logical stage was still very general; the physical stage translates the earlier designs into the programming language of the project, in our case Visual Basic.

In this step of the physical stage, the activity and class diagrams are created - these relate directly to the Visual Basic programming language and will show exactly how each component should work in Visual Basic. The milestone for this step is the completed consolidated design document - it is essential that the design for Visual Basic be agreed upon, as this is what will be developed in the next phase. However, this milestone is dependent on the class and activity diagrams being completed.

	Name	Start Date	Duration	Resources	Predecessors
46 (2)	Design Server Setup	Tue 03/07/00			40
47 (3)	Determine estimated disk space utilization	Tue 03/07/00	1 day	Logistics[33%]	
48	Determine estimated traffic	Tue 03/07/00	1 day	Logistics[33%]	
49	Design access permission	Tue 03/07/00	1 day	Logistics[33%]	
50	Design testing / staging area scheme	Wed 03/08/00	3 days		47,48,49

	Name	Start Date	Duration	Resources	Predecessors
51	Communicate with server operations	Mon 03/13/00	2 days		50
52	Server site live	Tue 03/14/00	0 days		51

There are many things to consider when designing the setup of the server, not least the fact that all sequence diagrams must be complete. First of all, you must determine how much data you will have so that you know how much space it will take up on the server - this is quite important, as vast amounts of data may cause vast increases in total project cost.

You will also want to ensure that, after developing the site, people will be able to view it. You need to determine how much estimated traffic there will be: for example, how many people will visit your site and how often will they visit it? For middle tier components, how many users will try to access the server simultaneously? This will help you figure out what server (hardware and software) configuration you should use.

Security is also an issue when developing a site: who has access to what information on the intranet? Access to information will be based on the roles that were created in the Use Cases.

Since you do not want to make content changes to your application while users are working on it, you need to define how changes will be made and how those changes will be propagated to the server components. You must also communicate all server requirements to the personnel responsible for server operations so that they can prepare and set up the production server. Only after this is complete can server site go live.

	Name	Start Date	Duration	Resources	Predecessors
53 (2)	Develop Server Support Infrastructure	Mon 03/13/00			
54 (3)	Determine network impact	Mon 03/13/00	2 days		50
55	Determine what changes need to be made	Wed 03/15/00	3 days	Logistics	54
56	Communicate with support staff	Mon 03/20/00	1 day	Logistics	55

	Name	Start Date	Duration	Resources	Predecessors
57	Support Requirements Documented	Mon 03/20/00	0 days		56
58 (2)	Completed Design Document	Mon 03/20/00	0 days		45,52,57

Ideally, a lab should be set up to simulate the production network (bandwidth and traffic). Since this is not always feasible, your best guess on impact to the network is important so that different potential solutions to problems can be identified. If your system's speed, reliability or response time will be compromised because of network issues, you must determine what steps need to be taken to address those issues.

Keep your support personnel abreast of any issues you think relevant (network, server or content related) so that they can prepare to staff accordingly. This is important because you want your support staff and intranet site to go live simultaneously. The deliverable for the design phase is a completed design document - dependent on there being a completed consolidated design document, a live server site and full documentation of support requirements - detailing exactly what the system is to include and how this should be developed.

The schedule for the design phase will look as follows:

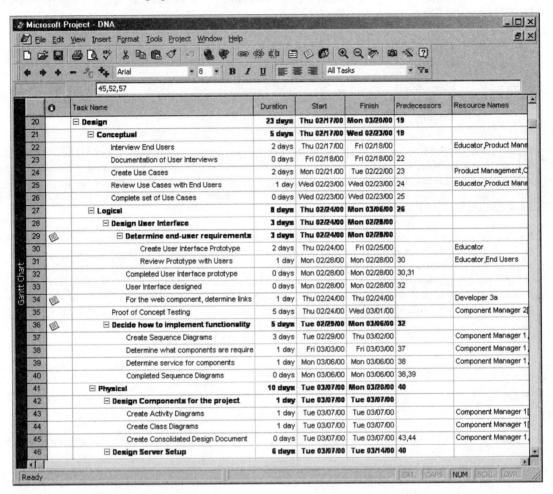

	❶	Task Name	Duration	Start	Finish	Predecessors	Resource Names
20		⊟ Design	23 days	Thu 02/17/00	Mon 03/20/00	19	
21		⊟ Conceptual	5 days	Thu 02/17/00	Wed 02/23/00	19	
22		Interview End Users	2 days	Thu 02/17/00	Fri 02/18/00		Educator,Product Mana
23		Documentation of User Interviews	0 days	Fri 02/18/00	Fri 02/18/00	22	
24		Create Use Cases	2 days	Mon 02/21/00	Tue 02/22/00	23	Product Management,C
25		Review Use Cases with End Users	1 day	Wed 02/23/00	Wed 02/23/00	24	Educator,Product Mana
26		Complete set of Use Cases	0 days	Wed 02/23/00	Wed 02/23/00	25	
27		⊟ Logical	8 days	Thu 02/24/00	Mon 03/06/00	26	
28		⊟ Design User Interface	3 days	Thu 02/24/00	Mon 02/28/00		
29	📝	⊟ Determine end-user requirements	3 days	Thu 02/24/00	Mon 02/28/00		
30		Create User Interface Prototype	2 days	Thu 02/24/00	Fri 02/25/00		Educator
31		Review Prototype with Users	1 day	Mon 02/28/00	Mon 02/28/00	30	Educator,End Users
32		Completed User Interface prototype	0 days	Mon 02/28/00	Mon 02/28/00	30,31	
33		User Interface designed	0 days	Mon 02/28/00	Mon 02/28/00	32	
34	📝	For the web component, determine links	1 day	Thu 02/24/00	Thu 02/24/00		Developer 3a
35		Proof of Concept Testing	5 days	Thu 02/24/00	Wed 03/01/00		Component Manager 2[
36	📝	⊟ Decide how to implement functionality	5 days	Tue 02/29/00	Mon 03/06/00	32	
37		Create Sequence Diagrams	3 days	Tue 02/29/00	Thu 03/02/00		Component Manager 1,
38		Determine what components are require	1 day	Fri 03/03/00	Fri 03/03/00	37	Component Manager 1,
39		Determine service for components	1 day	Mon 03/06/00	Mon 03/06/00	38	Component Manager 1,
40		Completed Sequence Diagrams	0 days	Mon 03/06/00	Mon 03/06/00	38,39	
41		⊟ Physical	10 days	Tue 03/07/00	Mon 03/20/00	40	
42		⊟ Design Components for the project	1 day	Tue 03/07/00	Tue 03/07/00		
43		Create Activity Diagrams	1 day	Tue 03/07/00	Tue 03/07/00		Component Manager 1[
44		Create Class Diagrams	1 day	Tue 03/07/00	Tue 03/07/00		Component Manager 1[
45		Create Consolidated Design Document	0 days	Tue 03/07/00	Tue 03/07/00	43,44	Component Manager 1,
46		⊟ Design Server Setup	6 days	Tue 03/07/00	Tue 03/14/00	40	

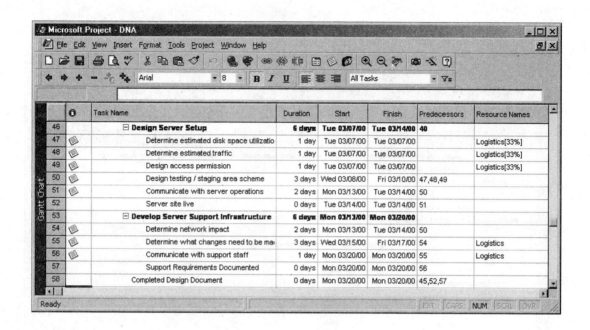

The Gantt chart will look as follows:

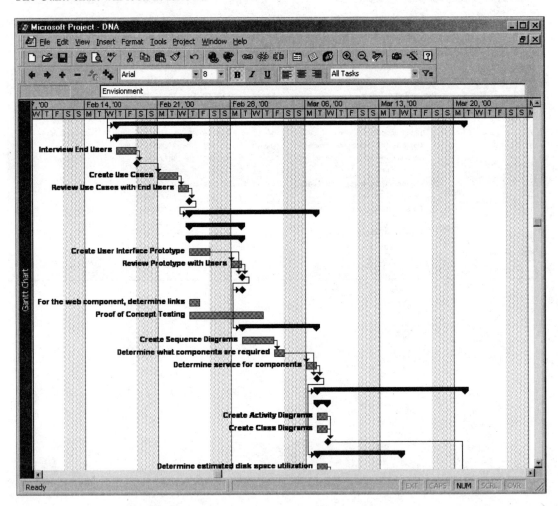

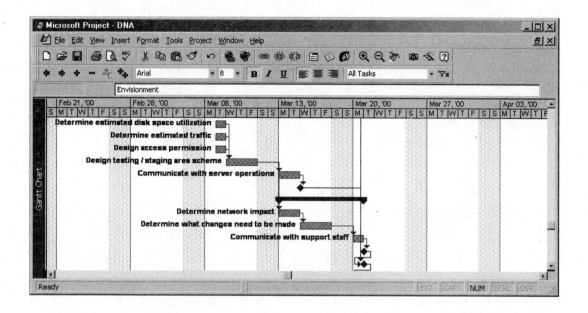

Development Phase Schedule

Add the following information into the schedule for development:

	Name	Start Date	Duration	Resources	Predecessors
59 (0)	Development	Tue 03/21/00			58
60 (1)	Build Server Component 1	Tue 03/21/00			
61 (2)	Create Server Component 1 Class 1	Tue 03/21/00			
62 (3)	Complete Server Component 1 Class 1	Tue 03/21/00	5 days	Component Manager 1, Developer 1a, Tester 1a, Developer 1b, Tester 1b	

	Name	Start Date	Duration	Resources	Predecessors
63	Unit Test Server Component 1 Class 1	Tue 03/28/00	1 day	Component Manager 1, Developer 1a, Tester 1a, Developer 1b, Tester 1b	62
64	Create Bug Report for Server Component 1 Class 1	Wed 03/29/00	1 day	Component Manager 1, Developer 1a, Tester 1a, Developer 1b, Tester 1b	63

Development cannot take place until the final design document is complete - only when the design is locked down is it beneficial to move into development. This means that the project should not suffer from feature creep.

The development phase is where the design from the previous phase is turned into an actual working product. As I said before, three separate development teams will undertake the development of the system. Component 1 is split into two different classes, which was a decision made in the design phase. Here, you can see how the design and testing of Component 1 Class 1 takes place.

	Name	Start Date	Duration	Resources	Predecessors
65 (2)	Create Server Component 1 Class 2	Thu 03/30/00			
66 (3)	Complete Server Component 1 Class 2	Thu 03/30/00	5 days	Component Manager 1, Developer 1a, Tester 1a, Developer 1b, Tester 1b	64
67	Unit Test Server Component 1 Class 2	Thu 04/06/00	1 day	Component Manager 1, Developer 1a, Tester 1a, Developer 1b, Tester 1b	66

	Name	Start Date	Duration	Resources	Predecessors
68	Create Bug Report for Server Component 1 Class 2	Fri 04/07/00	1 day	Component Manager 1, Developer 1a, Tester 1a, Developer 1b, Tester 1b	67
69 (2)	Server Component 1 Completed and Unit Tested	Fri 04/07/00	0 days		64,68

As the same group of people is working on the above two components, it makes sense to schedule the development of Component 1 Class 2 to take place after the completion of Component 1 Class 1. However, it is not enough to simply build the component: it must also be tested to make sure that it functions according to specifications. After unit testing has taken place on the completed component, a bug report must be made, showing any errors that were found, how they were rectified (if a solution was available!) and who was responsible for making the changes. After this has been completed for each individual class of Component 1, the component is complete.

	Name	Start Date	Duration	Resources	Predecessors
70 (1)	Build Client Component 1	Tue 03/21/00			
71 (2)	Create Client Component 1 Class 1	Tue 03/21/00			
72 (3)	Complete Client Component 1 Class 1	Tue 03/21/00	5 days	Component Manager 2, Developer 2a, Developer 2b, Tester 2a, Tester 2b	
73	Unit Test Client Component 1 Class 1	Tue 03/28/00	1 day	Component Manager 2, Developer 2a, Developer 2b, Tester 2a, Tester 2b	72

	Name	Start Date	Duration	Resources	Predecessors
74	Create Bug Report for Client Component 1 Class 1	Wed 03/29/00	1 day	Component Manager 2, Developer 2a, Developer 2b, Tester 2a, Tester 2b	73

The development of this component is able to take place at the same time as the development of the server component, because different team members are involved in the development of each component. Here, we see that it is now Class 1 of the Client Component that is being developed.

	Name	Start Date	Duration	Resources	Predecessors
75 (2)	Create Client Component 1 Class 2	Thu 03/30/00			
76 (3)	Complete Client Component 1 Class 2	Thu 03/30/00	5 days	Component Manager 2, Developer 2a, Developer 2b, Tester 2a, Tester 2b	74
77	Unit Test Client Component 1 Class 2	Thu 04/06/00	1 day	Component Manager 2, Developer 2a, Developer 2b, Tester 2a, Tester 2b	76
78	Create Bug Report for Client Component 1 Class 2	Fri 04/07/00	1 day	Component Manager 2, Developer 2a, Developer 2b, Tester 2a, Tester 2b	77
79 (2)	Client Component 1 Completed and Unit Tested	Fri 04/07/00	0 days		74,78

Again, the component must be unit tested and a bug report created before the milestone for this step of the development phase has been reached.

	Name	Start Date	Duration	Resources	Predecessors
80 (1)	Develop pages and links	Tue 03/21/00			
81 (2)	Create HTML style 'template'	Tue 03/21/00	3 days	Component Manager 3[50%], Developer 3a[50%], Developer 3b[50%], Tester[50%]	
82	Build Visual Basic Web Classes	Fri 03/24/00	7 days	Component Manager 3[50%], Developer 3a[50%], Developer 3b[50%], Tester[50%]	81
83	Test and Debug Web Classes	Tue 04/04/00	3 days	Component Manager 3, Developer 3a, Developer 3b, Tester	82

The third development group is working on this particular step of the project, so this can be scheduled to take place at the same time as the development of Component 1 and Component 2.

This is the stage in which you create the HTML source code. If you do not have developers assigned to this goal, Microsoft FrontPage, Internet Assistant for Word, and other HTML editors can perform this function quickly and easily.

If development is being done in-house, it is useful to have certain standards followed for HTML coding. This makes the code easier to maintain in the long run. Creating a template for your developers will help this effort.

Building the Visual Basic Web Classes can only take place once the template has been created. The size of this goal depends on the amount of content your web site will contain. The more detailed design work done up front, the quicker this goal will be accomplished. Only then can appropriate testing and debugging take place.

	Name	Start Date	Duration	Resources	Predecessors
84 (1)	Develop Functionality	Tue 03/21/00			
85 (2)	Develop any custom functionality	Tue 03/21/00	5 days	Component Manager 3[50%], Developer 3a[50%], Developer 3b[50%], Tester[50%]	
86	Integrate into web site	Fri 04/07/00	4 days	Component Manager 3, Developer 3a, Developer 3b, Tester	83,85
87 (1)	Code Completed	Wed 04/12/00	0 days		69,79,80,84

After you have designed the functionality, you must develop it or buy it, depending on the cost-benefit analysis performed in the design phase. If custom development is the way you want to proceed with getting the functionality you need, you must determine who will be responsible and plug them into this goal.

Once the functionality you need for your web site is complete, either by your own development or by purchasing some third party software, integrate it into the other pages to complete the site. This can only be done when the Visual Basic Web Classes have been tested and debugged and any custom functionality has been developed.

Only after all the components have been developed and tested, and the web pages integrated, can you say that the coding is finished and the code completed milestone has been reached. This is a very important milestone - any delays in reaching this milestone will have a knock-on effect throughout the rest of the project.

	Name	Start Date	Duration	Resources	Predecessors
88	Content Migration / Integration	Tue 03/21/00			

	Name	Start Date	Duration	Resources	Predecessors
89 (2)	Determine what content will be moved / integrated	Tue 03/21/00	3 days	Logistics	
90	Prioritize content conversion	Fri 03/24/00	2 days	Logistics	89
91	Set content conversion standards	Tue 03/28/00	2 days	Logistics	90
92	Implement content migration and conversion	Thu 03/30/00	5 days	Logistics	91
93	Test conversion formats	Thu 04/06/00	5 days	Logistics	92

This step concerns defining what specific content will be converted to HTML to be viewed directly on the site and which content will remain in its native file form and linked to from the intranet. You also need to determine the source and location of each type of content. Each goal follows in a logical order.

It can be beneficial to create a content site map detailing where each content type resides today and where it will reside on the new web server. Prioritize the content migration; that is, determine in what order content will be moved to the web and, if appropriate, what content should be archived. You should also define how you want the content to appear on each page.

Convert necessary content to HTML either manually or by utilizing a set of conversion utilities. The choice is dependent upon the quantity of content requiring conversion.

Once the content has been converted, either manually or with the aid of conversion utilities, an editor should double check the quality of conversion to make sure that standard formats are in place.

	Name	Start Date	Duration	Resources	Predecessors
94 (1)	Testing	Thu 04/13/00			
95 (2)	Page Testing	Thu 04/13/00	1 day	Tester[50%]	87

	Name	Start Date	Duration	Resources	Predecessors
96	Link Testing	Thu 04/13/00	1 day	Tester[50%]	87
97	Usability Testing	Fri 04/14/00	8 days	Tester 1a[50%], Tester 1b[50%], Tester 2a[50%], Tester 2b[50%]	83,86,93,95, 96, 87
98	Stress Testing	Fri 04/14/00	8 days	Tester 1a[50%], Tester 1b[50%], Tester 2a[50%], Tester 2b[50%]	83,86,93,95, 96, 87

Testing is very important; if you do not test your system you could run into insurmountable difficulties when the system goes live, because you won't know what to expect. There are a number of tests you need to perform: first of all, you should test each individual web page. You then need to test the links / connections of all pages of the site, to ensure that users can find the information they want. Quite obviously, testing cannot take place until the code completed milestone has been reached.

Usability testing means that you have the users use the site and conduct testing to see if the site meets the requirements defined in the conceptual phase. Stress testing means that you simulate the load on the system to test the performance of the site according to the predetermined requirements.

The schedule for the development phase should look as follows:

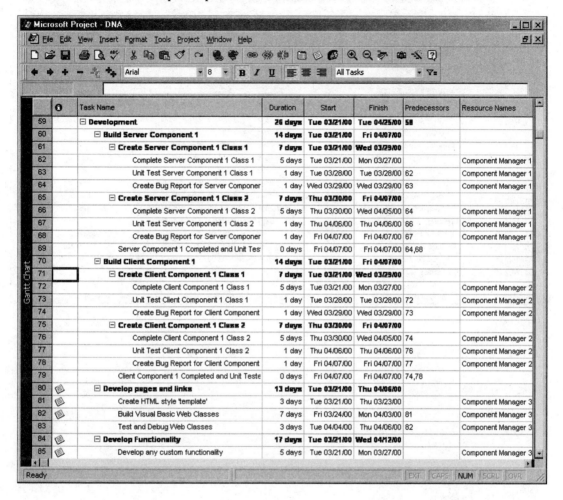

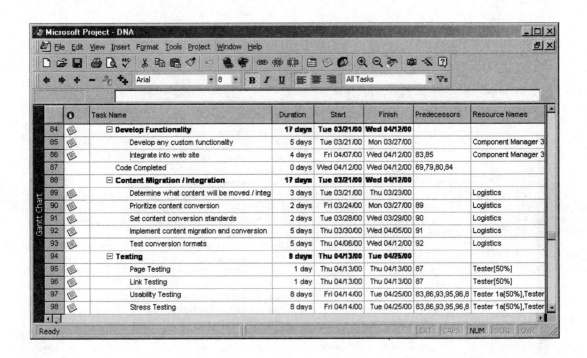

The Gantt chart will look as follows:

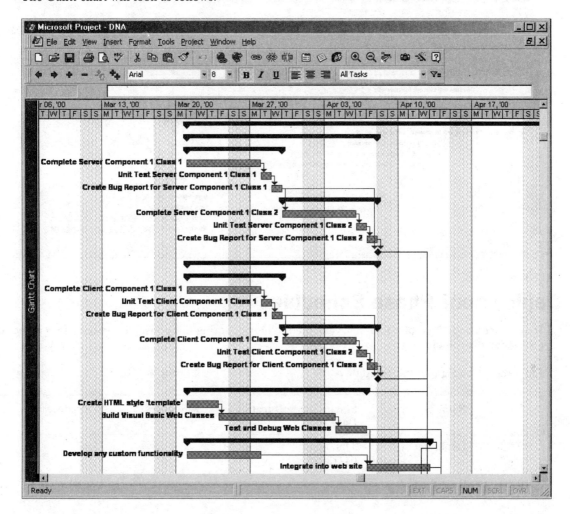

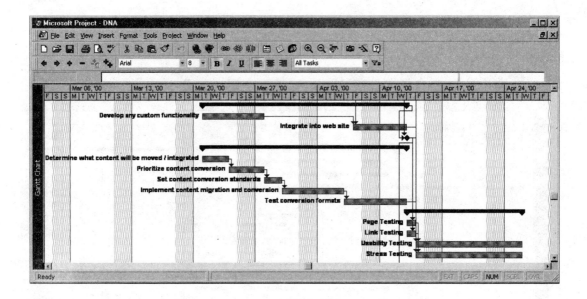

Deployment Phase Schedule

Deployment is the final phase in the cyclic methodology. During this phase, the system is prepared to be handed over to the user.

Enter the following into the schedule:

	Name	Start Date	Duration	Resources	Predecessors
99 (0)	Deployment	Thu 04/13/00			87
100 (1)	Beta Testing	Thu 04/13/00			
101	Roll Out	Thu 04/13/00			100
102 (2)	Move site and server components to production server	Fri 04/14/00	1 day	Logistics[50%]	83,86,93,95,96

	Name	Start Date	Duration	Resources	Predecessors
103	Determine roll out schedule	Thu 04/13/00	3 days	Product Management [33%], Educator[33%], Logistics[50%], End Users [50%], Client Management [50%]	59FS-20days

For the system to be prepared for handover, it is quite obvious that development must have been completed. However, as much of this phase is concerned with planning for the handover, there is no reason why it cannot start while development is still taking place: the design and functionality of the system are known, and the duration of development can be estimated. This is why the deployment and development phases overlap.

It is quite plain to see why there are so many predecessors for goal 102 - obviously, the components cannot be moved to the production server unless they are completed, tested and debugged.

	Name	Start Date	Duration	Resources	Predecessors
104	Communicate roll out plan to users	Tue 04/18/00	10 days	Educator[25%], Logistics, Project Manager [50%]	103
105	Conduct User Training	Tue 04/18/00	10 days	Educator[25%]	103
106	Release internal PR	Tue 04/18/00	10 days	Component Manager 1, Developer 1a, Developer 1b, Component Manager 2, Developer 2a, Developer 2b, Component Manager 3, Developer 3a, Developer 3b	103

	Name	Start Date	Duration	Resources	Predecessors
107	Rollout	Mon 05/08/00	0 days	Product Management, Project Manager, Educator, Logistics, Component Manager 1, Component Manager 2, Component Manager 3	104,105,106, 112

The users will obviously need to know when they are going to get their system, so you must let them know the rollout schedule - this will also help them understand why they cannot have their system yesterday!

It is imperative that the users understand how to use the system before it goes live: not only will this save money in the long run, but it also means that the time taken for the system to become operative and efficient will be shortened.

It is also important to publicize the release of the system internally. Not only can this generate interest in the system, but it might also generate interest in the project team, meaning that (if the project is successful!) their skills are in demand.

The milestone for this step of the deployment phase is the actual handover of the system to the users, otherwise known as rollout. It is clear that this is dependent on all other goals preceding it being completed and all milestones reached.

	Name	Start Date	Duration	Resources	Predecessors
108 (1)	Support	Thu 04/13/00			100
109 (2)	Determine what support resources are needed	Thu 04/13/00	4 days	Educator [33%], End Users [50%], Client Management [50%], Product Management [33%], Project Manager [75%]	57

	Name	Start Date	Duration	Resources	Predecessors
110	Make appropriate staffing changes	Wed 04/19/00	5 days	Educator [25%], End Users, Client Management, Product Management [50%], Project Manager [50%]	109

Although after rollout the project may have officially ended, it is by no means over. It is crucial that the users receive support and guidance in how to use the system, especially if it radically alters business processes or introduces totally new ways of doing things. This step ascertains what support the user will need and makes sure that there are people available to provide it. The level of resources needed relates directly to the documentation of Support Requirements that took place in the physical design stage of the design phase.

	Name	Start Date	Duration	Resources	Predecessors
111	Determine method that users will attain support	Wed 04/26/00	3 days	Educator [33%], End Users, Client Management, Product Management [75%], Project Manager [50%]	110
112	Determine support process	Tue 05/02/00	5 days	Educator, End Users, Client Management, Product Management, Project Manager	111,104,105, 106
113	Support goes live	Mon 05/08/00	0 days		107SS,112

It is important to know how users will seek support: this could be by telephone, by email, over the Internet, or even by post(!). If it is decided that there will be one main way in which users seek support, most of the focus will be given to this; however, the other methods available should not be ignored.

It should also be determined how the process of support takes place - this could include, for example, the description of a hierarchy of support, where increasingly technical queries are passed up the hierarchy to people who are able to deal with them. This process can only be determined after user training has been carried out and the rollout plan communicated to them: before this point, it is unlikely that the users will realize that they may need support with the system.

This phase ends with another milestone - support goes live on the same day as rollout.

The Project 98 schedule for the deployment phase will look as follows:

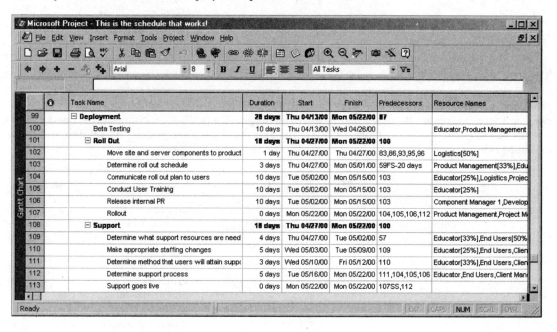

		Task Name	Duration	Start	Finish	Predecessors	Resource Names
99		⊟ **Deployment**	**28 days**	**Thu 04/13/00**	**Mon 05/22/00**	**87**	
100		Beta Testing	10 days	Thu 04/13/00	Wed 04/26/00		Educator,Product Management
101		⊟ **Roll Out**	**18 days**	**Thu 04/27/00**	**Mon 05/22/00**	**100**	
102		Move site and server components to product	1 day	Thu 04/27/00	Thu 04/27/00	83,86,93,95,96	Logistics[50%]
103		Determine roll out schedule	3 days	Thu 04/27/00	Mon 05/01/00	59FS-20 days	Product Management[33%],Edu
104		Communicate roll out plan to users	10 days	Tue 05/02/00	Mon 05/15/00	103	Educator[25%],Logistics,Projec
105		Conduct User Training	10 days	Tue 05/02/00	Mon 05/15/00	103	Educator[25%]
106		Release internal PR	10 days	Tue 05/02/00	Mon 05/15/00	103	Component Manager 1,Develop
107		Rollout	0 days	Mon 05/22/00	Mon 05/22/00	104,105,106,112	Product Management,Project M
108		⊟ **Support**	**18 days**	**Thu 04/27/00**	**Mon 05/22/00**	**100**	
109		Determine what support resources are need	4 days	Thu 04/27/00	Tue 05/02/00	57	Educator[33%],End Users[50%
110		Make appropriate staffing changes	5 days	Wed 05/03/00	Tue 05/09/00	109	Educator[25%],End Users,Clien
111		Determine method that users will attain suppo	3 days	Wed 05/10/00	Fri 05/12/00	110	Educator[33%],End Users,Clien
112		Determine support process	5 days	Tue 05/16/00	Mon 05/22/00	111,104,105,106	Educator,End Users,Client Man
113		Support goes live	0 days	Mon 05/22/00	Mon 05/22/00	107SS,112	

The Gantt chart for deployment should look like the following:

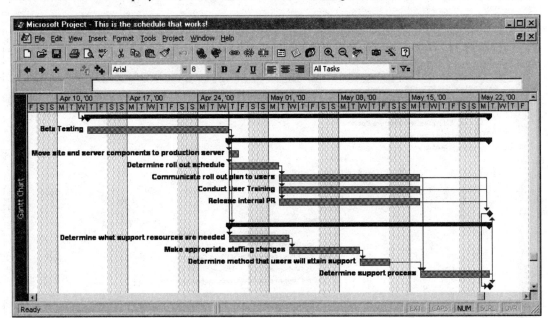

Improvements to the Schedule

As you have entered the goals, resources and durations for each phase, you have seen the schedule expand - you have seen how some goals can be worked on simultaneously and also how some phases can be worked on in parallel. The schedule now represents the timescale for the whole project, looking as follows:

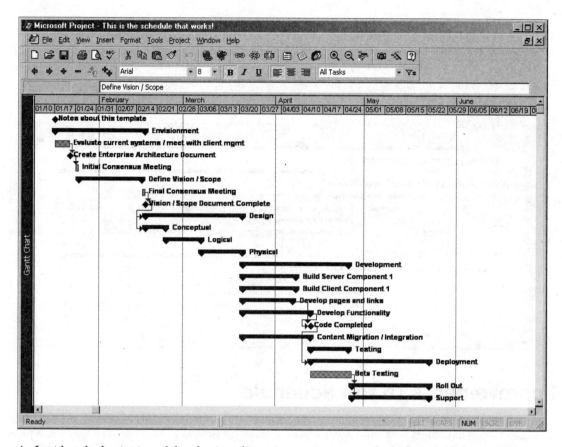

As I said at the beginning of the chapter, there are many ways in which this schedule could be improved. One such area is the fact that some team members aren't always fully dedicated to the project, through no fault of their own. Although this isn't fully under our control, it would be nice to have 100% of resources available to allocate to each goal.

Room for improvement is also available regarding duration estimates. As has already been mentioned, experience is needed when time estimates are being made. As you progress through your project management career, you will become more proficient at estimating the time needed for each goal: therefore, with experience, your schedules will become increasingly more accurate.

Summary

We saw in Chapter 3 how to use Project 98 to make schedules for your projects. This chapter has built on this knowledge to create an entire schedule for a sample project that you can adapt and modify to suit your needs.

This schedule has followed the cyclic methodology detailed in this book. Drawing up an approximate schedule at the beginning of a project will allow us to estimate the resources needed for each phase of the project, and thus the duration and cost of the project. Of course, the schedule will need constant refinement as the project progresses through each phase; as you gain a full appreciation for the complexity of the project, and the effort involved in bringing it to completion, you will be able to make a progressively more accurate assessment of the resources required.

Remember, though, that in real life you will be constrained by a time limit or a set budget - making sure that your project is successful within these constraints is a valuable skill. Hopefully, this skill has been strengthened by the understanding you have gained of the different issues involved in the successful management of a modern-day Visual Basic Enterprise project.

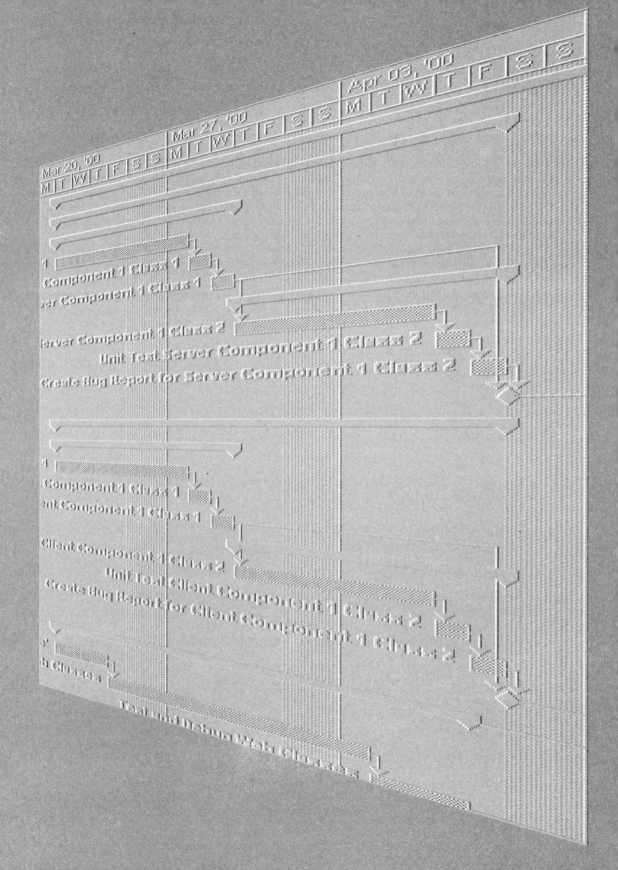

A Brief Overview of UML

For those of you unfamiliar with Unified Modeling Language (UML), this appendix provides a quick tour of some of the terms, concepts and diagrams that are used throughout the book.

What Exactly is a Model?

UML is a set of standard models that we use to design object-oriented programming projects. But what do we mean by a *model*, and what, accordingly, does that mean a *modeling language* is?

A **model** is a description of the problem we are set to solve. It simplifies the reality by capturing a subset of entities and relationships in the problem domain.

> *A problem domain describes not only a particular problem but also the conditions under which the problem occurs. It's therefore a description of a problem and the relevant context of that problem.*

A model shows us what the problem is and how we are going to tackle it. We may use diagrams, text, or any other agreed form of communication to present the model.

Models visualize the system we are about to build.

A **modeling language**, therefore, is a language for describing models. Modeling languages generally use diagrams to represent various entities and their relationships within the model.

UML was created to fulfill these tasks:

> To represent all parts of a project being built with object-oriented techniques
> To establish a way to connect ideas, concepts and general design techniques with the creation of object-oriented code
> To create a model that can be understood by humans and also by computers - so that a computer can generate a major portion of the application automatically

UML accomplishes these tasks by having a series of different models. Each model represents a different view of the project. Some models are built from others, so there is a logical sequence in which the models are built.

The building blocks of the UML are things and relationships:

> **Things** in the UML describe conceptual and physical elements in the application domain
> **Relationships** connect things together

These two elements are brought together in UML **diagrams** to help us visualize things and their relationships in a well-structured format.

UML Diagrams

There are quite a few UML diagrams that we can use when designing our applications, and we can pick and choose those which will be of most use to us. However, there is a basic core set of diagrams that we will almost certainly use. This core set of diagrams includes:

> Use Case Models
> Interaction Diagrams
> Activity Diagrams
> Class Diagrams

We'll now run through these types of diagram at whirlwind pace. You'll notice, as we run through them, that some diagram types have sub-types themselves (such as collaboration and sequence diagrams). This may be your first clue as to the richness and diversity of UML as an analytical design tool.

> Notice that as we progress through this sequence of UML diagrams, we will also be progressing towards an ever more focused and clearly defined idea of the project we are designing and planning to develop. This is one of the fundamental points of the UML approach.

Use Case Models

This is the first step on our journey towards a clear definition of the project we are designing with UML. We go straight to the people who will use the system we're building. The **use case** model translates the user's needs into an easy to understand model. The user may be an individual or an external system and is known as an **actor**. So in a nutshell, the use case model is a representation of how the system, or part of the system, works from the actor's point of view.

Use case models can be built from interviews with the user, and are the first step in converting the user's needs and requirements into a useful model.

> *Use cases are more like a model than a diagram because they describe the system, or parts of the system, with words rather than with pictures.*

Use cases are detailed enough to include all of the information on the project, but simple enough for even the most technically challenged user to understand. Use cases can also be associated with **business rules**, which explain special rules, related to the use case.

Let's take an example. In an order entry application, the use cases could include descriptions of various sub-parts of the system. These sub-parts, that together could make up the whole system, could be such things such as Taking an Order, Creating a New Customer, etc. For the use case Create New Customer, there could be a verbal description of the process of creating a new customer that looked as follows:

USE CASE: CREATE NEW CUSTOMER

Overview
The main purpose of this use case is to create a new Customer

Primary Actor
Sales Representative

Secondary Actor
None

Starting Point
The use case starts when the actor makes a request to create a new Customer

End Point
The actor's request to create a Customer is either completed or cancelled

Flow of Events
The actor is prompted to enter information that defines the Customer, such as Name, Address, etc. The actor will then enter the information on the Customer.

The actor can choose to save the information or cancel the operation. If the actor decides to save the information the new Customer is created in the system, and the list of Customers is updated.

Alternative Flow of Events
The actor attempts to add a Customer that already exists. The system will notify the user and cancel the create operation.

Measurable Result
A Customer is added to the system

Business Rules
Customer
Customer Fields
Restrict Customer Create

Use Case Extensions
None

Without getting too heavily involved right in the details of this use case, what we're seeing here is a verbal description of what happens when a potential user of the program we want to design needs to create a new customer. Possible flows of events are identified to explain how the system can get from the start point to a definite end point. Measurable results are defined, and some business rules are created. One of these business rules is called Restrict Customer Create and might be written as follows:

BUSINESS RULE: RESTRICT CUSTOMER CREATE

Overview
This rule is for when a Customer is added to the system

Business Rule Type
Requirement

Business Rule
Each Customer must have a unique CustomerID

Each Customer should only be listed once in the system

Derived Business Rules
None

Depending on the size of the system we're working one, we may actually need to create quite a few of these use case statements and business rules before we have captured the key aspects of the system we're designing. It's crucial, however, that we draw up these statements from the people who will be using the system, and the people who want to see the system in place. It's the first step in our design process.

Interaction Diagrams

Interaction diagrams are the next step of the UML design process. Interaction diagrams concentrate on showing how objects or things in the system interact with each other to give a dynamic view of the system. There are two basic types of interaction diagram:

> ➤ **sequence** diagrams
> ➤ **collaboration** diagrams

Essentially these both model the same information, except that sequence diagrams emphasize time ordering whereas collaboration diagrams spatial or structural organization.

For the most part, you choose to create either collaboration diagrams or sequence diagrams. For the sake of completeness, this appendix discusses both but we only use sequence diagrams in this book.

Sequence Diagrams

This type of diagram can be used to convert the written use case models that we saw in the previous section into a clearer visual model. This visual model will show how the objects associated with a particular use case communicate with each other and with users over time. Sequence diagrams are very general. For example, they may show that some Object 1 passes a message to some other Object 2, and that Object 2 then performs some operation within itself and finally returns the message back:

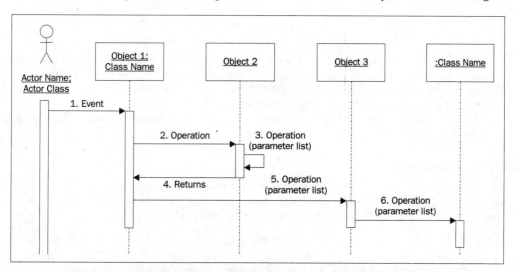

The internal workings of Object 1 that led to the creation of the message, and the internal workings of Object 2 that led to the return message, are not shown in sequence diagrams. (Details of the inner workings of the objects are represented in another type of diagram called an activity diagram - which we'll see in the next phase of the UML design process.)

Sequence diagrams map out every possible sequence of events that can be performed within each use case, including correct and incorrect paths. The correct paths in the sequence diagrams can be used to design the GUI of the project as they show what the user will need to do to interact with the application. Incorrect sequences will later be used to map out errors and how to handle these errors.

Sequence diagrams also show what public methods and properties our components must have. You can compare the sequence diagrams for one or more components and attempt to find patterns that exist that can be used to simplify the coding of the components.

Collaboration Diagrams

Collaboration diagrams are also built from the use cases - but this time the emphasis is on the spatial distribution of the objects involved. This is not to say that there are no temporal elements in collaboration diagrams, since the sequence of events is mapped using numbers:

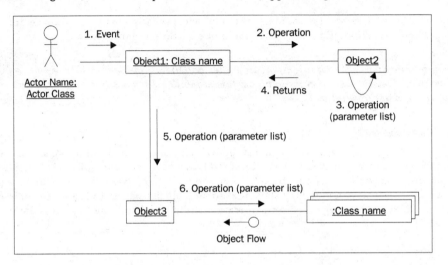

Personally, I often find this type of diagram quite confusing in comparison with the equivalent sequence diagrams. This particular collaboration diagram presents the *same* situation as the sequence diagram we just looked at - Object 1 and Object 2 with exactly the same relationships as before. However, it should be said that there are times when collaboration diagrams can make good sense - especially if we find that we want to emphasize a set of objects themselves rather than any sequence of events between them.

Activity Diagrams

Activity diagrams take the information available from the collaboration and sequence diagrams that we've just looked at, and present that information in a more detailed fashion. The purpose of activity diagrams is now to show the inner workings for a particular object.

> As you may have noticed, we are gradually moving towards more and more detail about our project design as we proceed through the different UML diagrams.

Activity diagrams can map out a method or property showing what that method or property has to do in a step-by-step manner. Activity diagrams will look very similar to mapping out a method or property using pseudo-code. This detailed map can then be used to explore the best method of coding a method or property, check for missing or unnecessary sections, and as a guide to writing the code. Here is a sample activity diagram:

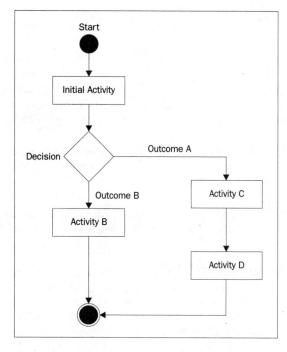

This activity diagram simply specifies what **Activity** is to be initiated at a certain **Decision** point, depending on the outcome of that **Decision**. This is a step-by-step definition of certain situations that pertain to the project we are designing and about to develop in VB, and is a considerable way forward in our journey towards defining a project and preparing it for development and implementation. We're still not finished yet though - the final stage in the overall UML design process is to move on to our class diagrams.

Class Diagrams

Class diagrams ultimately represent the classes that we will build in Visual Basic. They are the most detailed part of the whole UML design definition, inasmuch as they begin to map directly to code objects that we will be writing in Visual Basic. This is where we've been heading all along, and demonstrates how well UML maps our design considerations to the programming language we're using.

A Class diagram is a simple static picture of a class; as such, it will include all of the public and private methods and properties of that class. Class diagrams are, of course, built from use cases, sequence and activity diagrams that we've been developing throughout the UML design process.

Here's a sample class diagram:

Class Name
+ Public Property Name # Friend Property Name – Private Property Name
+ Public Method Name # Friend Method Name – Private Method Name

This sample class diagram is simply a schematic layout of the relevant information that we would need to go away and create the objects we've developed in our UML design process straight into the VB programming environment.

Naturally, for a larger project we would probably need to derive many such class diagrams in order to complete the design of all the objects involved in our system.

Other Diagrams

The diagrams we've looked at so far (use cases-sequence-activity-class diagrams) form the essential parts of UML that we need to build a Visual Basic project, and are the ones we use in this book. There are, however, other models that I will mention now for sake of completeness for the interested reader. These other diagrams include:

> **Statechart Diagrams**: A model of the different possible states of a system's objects

> **Component Diagrams**: A model showing how different objects will be combined to make a component

> **Deployment Diagrams**: A model showing how each component will be placed on various hardware

> **Object Diagrams**: A simplified collaboration diagram.

UML Notation

We have covered the fundamental terms and most important diagrams, but before we move on to demonstrate how to map the UML constructs into VB code (Appendix B) we need to have a look at some more advanced UML notation, including how to depict relationships between classes.

Classes and Objects

As we saw previously, a class is represented in UML like this:

The rectangle representing the class is divided into three compartments, the top one showing the class name, the second showing the attributes and the third showing the methods.

If the class is abstract, then the class name in the first compartment is italicized.

An object looks very similar to a class, except that its name is underlined:

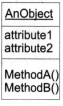

Relationships

Relationships between classes are generally represented in class diagrams by a line or an arrow joining the two classes. UML can represent the following, different sorts of object relationships.

Dependency

If A depends on B, then this is shown by a dashed arrow between A and B, with the arrowhead pointing at B:

Association

An association between A and B is shown by a line joining the two classes:

If there is no arrow on the line, the association is taken to be bi-directional. A unidirectional association is indicated like this:

Aggregation

An aggregation relationship is indicated by placing a white diamond at the end of the association next to the aggregate class. If B aggregates A, then A is a part of B, but their lifetimes are independent:

Composition

Composition, on the other hand, is shown by a black diamond on the end of association next to the composite class. If B is composed of A, then B controls the lifetime of A.

415

Multiplicity

The multiplicity of a relationship is indicated by a number (or *) placed at the end of an association.

The following diagram indicates a one-to-one relationship between A and B:

This next diagram indicates a one-to-many relationship:

A multiplicity can also be a range of values. Some examples are shown in the table below:

1	One and only one
*	Any number from 0 to infinity
0..1	Either 0 or 1
n..m	Any number in the range n to m inclusive
1..*	Any positive integer

Naming an Association

To improve the clarity of a class diagram, the association between two objects may be named:

Inheritance

An inheritance (generalization/specialization) relationship is indicated in the UML by an arrow with a triangular arrowhead pointing towards the generalized class.

If A is a base class, and B and C are classes derived from A, then this would be represented by the following class diagram:

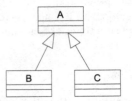

Multiple Inheritance

The next diagram represents the case where class C is derived from classes A and B:

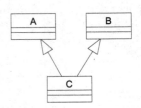

States

States of objects are represented as rectangles with rounded corners. The *transition* between different states is represented as an arrow between states, and a *condition* of that transition occurring may be added between square braces. This condition is called a guard.

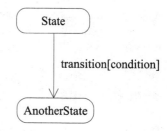

Object Interactions

Interactions between objects are represented by interaction diagrams – both sequence and collaboration diagrams. An example of a collaboration diagram is shown here: Objects are drawn as rectangles and the lines between them indicate links – a link is an instance of an association. The number at the head of the message indicates the order of the messages along the links between the objects.

Sequence diagrams show essentially the same information, but concentrate on the time-ordered communication between objects, rather than their relationships. An example of a sequence diagram is shown here:
The dashed vertical lines represent the lifeline of the object (starting at the top).

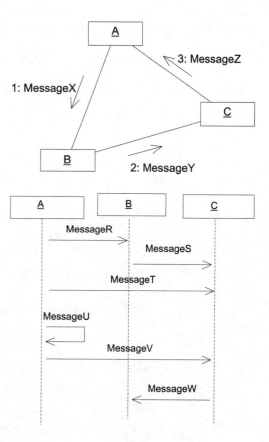

Use Cases

A use case is a description of an interaction between an actor (person or external system) and system under design. In UML it is denoted like this:

Design Patterns

Design patterns are represented in the UML notation by collaborations (shown as dotted elipses) between classes. Each class that is part of the pattern is joined to it by a dotted line labeled with the particular role played by the class:

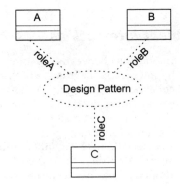

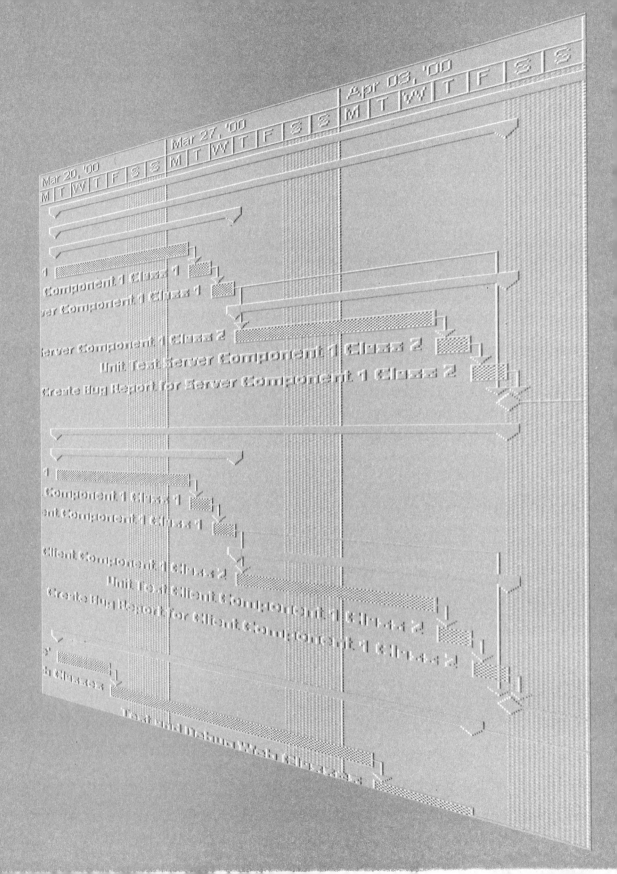

UML to VB Mapping

Purpose of the VB Mapping

UML is a wonderful thing - it allows us to 'see' the design of a system. However the diagrams we take trouble to create are only useful if they directly contribute to our final system. Developers who are new to modeling can understandably wonder whether all the extra effort is worth it. Therefore the point of this mapping is simple: to help the VB developer understand how to map the UML constructs into VB code.

UML Version Covered

The current version of UML as supported by most tools is 1.1.

As of writing, version 1.3 was in draft, although there are no major changes to this version that VB developers need to be aware to.

The current UML documentation can be found on http://www.rational.com/uml/

It is recommended that VB Developers visit this site and review the official documents before trying to understand the mapping in detail.

How the Mapping is Structured

The official UML specification is very detailed and precise but is also very abstract! Most VB developers will find a great deal of the detail unimportant in getting up to speed with mapping the UML.

Therefore, the mapping that follows concentrates on the concrete elements from the UML that have notation and appear on diagrams. These are also the artifacts that the VB Developer will have the most contact with. These include *class*, *attribute*, *operation*, *interface*, etc. Each of these elements will be discussed in turn and references will be made to the more abstract elements in the UML semantics document that they derive from, so that the developer can choose to cross-reference with the official specification.

So to reiterate, the mapping focuses essentially on how the diagrams you draw and communicate with relate to the code you write.

> *Please refer to the Mapping Guide at the beginning of the mapping itself for a breakdown of the sections therein.*

How Well Does the UML Map to VB?

The UML allows you to capture both the static knowledge about your application (packages, classes, associations, etc.) and also the dynamic behavior (operation calls, events, etc.). We will see that most diagrams have a very close mapping to VB but a few are more vague. Class diagrams for instance, are key diagrams to us and it will be quite straightforward to see how these map to VB. The coincidence between 'class' in the UML and 'class' in VB is not a coincidence! These are essentially the same things.

Statechart diagrams, on the other hand, are not so clear. This is because the standard VB language does not come with a 'standard' statechart implementation (often called a 'finite state machine'). This is also partly because of the many different ways we can write them. Nonetheless, some guidelines are provided to help get you started.

UML and Components

It is rather ironic that although the UML is rich and powerful for modeling classes, their relationships and the logical packaging of such things, it is not so good at modeling components, as VB developers know them. This is something that hopefully later revisions of the UML might cover more clearly.

Fortunately for us, we can come up with conventions that developers can follow to help us define components. A further discussion of this can be found in the mapping.

Concrete Or By Convention?

Some mappings from the UML to VB are plain and concrete - there is no debate as to its correctness. Some mappings, on the other hand, are purely by convention because VB simply doesn't support the construct. When convention is used, developers should use their judgment as to whether they follow the convention or invent their own. Remember, though, that the suggestions given are tried and tested.

Upgrade to at Least VB5

If you are currently using a version of VB prior to version 5, I suggest you upgrade immediately! There were some significant features added to VB5 that are key to writing solid components in VB. These include the ability to 'implement' an interface and also the support for 'events' from classes. The features added in VB6 are not so important but there are better storage mapping facilities provided (ADO support).

The mapping assumes that you are using VB5 or later.

Styles Used in the Mapping

Concepts that refer to UML will be stated in *Italics*.

VB Code fragments that are presented in this style:

```
Public m_Car As Car
```

While sections of VB code that are provided as context, but are not directly relevant to the topic under discussion are presented like this:

```
Public m_Car As Car
```

How to Use this Mapping

The mapping is a reference rather than something you would read end-to-end, however it might be worth giving it the 'once over' just to get a feeling for things.

As you become more familiar with the UML, you will soon only need to refer to this Appendix periodically, as the core mappings are very intuitive and easy to remember.

Building Your Diagrams

To help you design your diagrams, it is recommended that you enlist the help of a tool.

There are many choices here from general symbol tools like Visio (UML templates are available for this on the web) to a full-blown repository-based CASE tool that will also ensure your diagrams are in-sync' with each other. Of course never underestimate the power of a whiteboard and marker!

So, without further ado, let's start to look at the VB to UML mapping.

Mapping Guide

These are the sections that are included in this mapping.

1.0 General Extension Mechanisms

1.1 Constraints and Comments

A UML constraint generally maps to a fragment of code in VB that checks the constraint. The location and style of such code depends on the type of constraint. For instance, a UML constraint might suggest that an object be only associated with one object at a time - not two.

In VB, this would translate into validation code inside the procedures of the VB class, such as an `Order` class:

```
'Set the customer related to the order
'Constraints:
'A customer is not already associated

Public Sub SetCustomer(ByVal aCustomer As Customer)

    'we can only be associated with one customer
    'it is an error to set a customer twice
    Debug.Assert m_myCustomer Is Nothing

    Set m_myCustomer = aCustomer
End Sub
```

With this example, an order can only be associated with one customer. It is a constraint that only one customer can be associated at a time. (Assume a separate routine is available to disassociate the customer.)

One useful feature of VB is to make copious use of `Debug.Assert`. This build-in library feature allows us to make assertions in our code that must always be satisfied. If you are running in design mode and an assertion fails, then VB will take you straight to the place where the assertion failed. This is very effective way of catching logic bugs in your code, early.

Sometimes it is not always possible to translate a constraint to code. In these situations, the best you can do is place an appropriate comment into the code to remind yourself and your colleagues that the constraint exists.

1.2 Element Properties

The UML defines *element properties* as values that can be tagged on to arbitrary model elements. In VB, these simply become comments against the related item. A typical property might be the name of the author who created the model. If this property was tagged to a particular diagram, then we would include a author comment inside the definition of each class on the diagram:

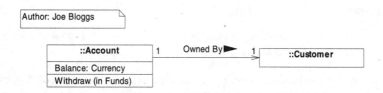

Corresponding Code in `Account.cls`:

```
'Account - defines a single account in the accountancy system
'
'Author: Joe Bloggs

Private m_theBalance As Currency

Public Sub Withdraw(ByVal theFunds As Currency)
'....
End Sub
```

1.3 Stereotypes

Most UML elements come with a set of standard stereotypes. Some CASE Tools also extend the range of stereotypes to match the languages targeted. Here are examples of two class stereotypes:

Stereotypes have a big impact on how we map UML to VB. In some cases, they affect only the properties of the target VB item and sometimes it will completely change the mapping.

When we discuss each UML construct, the standard stereotypes of that item will also be covered.

2.0 Model Management

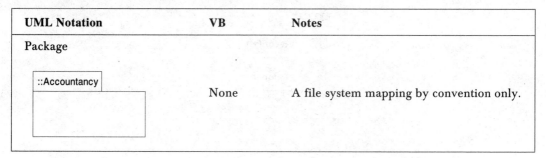

UML Notation	VB	Notes
Package		
::Accountancy	None	A file system mapping by convention only.

2.1 Packages

Packages in the UML are a logical grouping of related items such as *classes*. A *Package* has no direct mapping to VB so conventions are used instead.

A convention typically used is to include the *package* name in the name of contained elements. For instance, an Accountancy Package may contain a class called `Account`. Therefore, the class will have a name in VB of `Accountancy_Account`. This will ensure that classes with similar names in different packages will not collide. This activity is usually called *Name Mangling*.

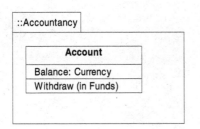
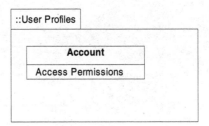

The corresponding class names in VB would look like this:

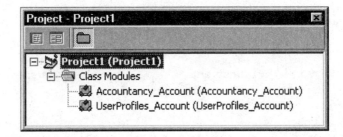

2.1.1 External Libraries as Packages

During modeling, it is also useful to model popular VB libraries as packages. For instance, we can model popular services like RDO as a package:

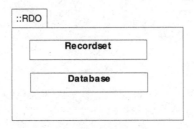

2.1.2 Nested Packages

Packages can be nested. If you choose to map packages to a naming convention, you will need to define 'short' names for the packages so that the class names don't get too long!

2.1.3 Packages and the File System

When deciding how to structure your source code it is a good idea to choose a directory in your file-system that acts as the root for your source code. Each logical package defined can be created as a sub-directory underneath this root. Classes in a particular package are placed in the corresponding directory:

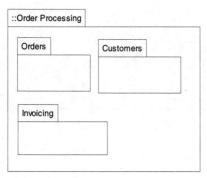

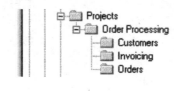

The Nested Packages   The Nested Folder Structure

This technique will not only keep the source code files manageable, but also help partition the work up between developers. For instance, one developer may be working on an Accountancy package, whilst another is working on a User interface package.

2.1.4 Package Stereotypes

The *<<system>> package stereotype* denotes the complete system that is being built in VB. Usually the *<<system>> package* maps to a VB Project group, i.e. the VB project group contains all packages and the elements that define the whole VB application.

A *<<façade>> package* indicates that the *package* is present to provide a façade on to other packages in the system. In VB terms, this could represent a set of related classes that are providing a simple, more high-level interface onto another set of more detailed classes. Again, because *package* is a logical grouping of items, there is no explicit language feature in VB that you can use. It is all defined by convention.

A *<<framework>> package* indicates that the package contains a framework of items. In VB terms, we might design a set of related classes that perform a certain framework service, e.g. generic database access. The *<<framework>>* constraint simply implies that the package would be used as part of a complete system, together with the extra classes that complement the framework and make it complete.

2.1.5 Package Dependencies

A *package* can have *dependencies* to others. A *dependency* of *stereotype* <<*import*>> maps to a reference in a VB project's references list.

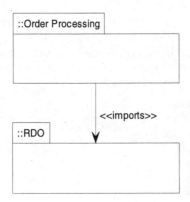

A Package Reference

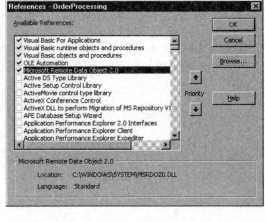

A VB Reference

3.0 Static Structure Diagrams

The static structure diagrams like the Class Diagram are a fundamental tool in the UML toolbox and are used more in practice than any other diagram.

UML Notation	VB	Notes
Association 1 ::Car Transport	Class	Mapping varies. See Association notes.
Attribute - Balance : Currency	Variable	

UML Notation	VB	Notes
Class ::Car	Class, Module or Form	Derived from Classifier
Classifier (no notation)	Class	Abstract class of Class, DataType and Interface
Constraint { ordered }	Assert statement, comment or validation code.	
Interface O———— IPersistent or – «interface» ::IPersistent	Class	A specialization of Classifier. For an ActiveX component, `Instancing = PublicNotCreatable`
Operation `Withdraw()`	Procedure without body	Typically on a VB interface

4.0 Classifiers

4.1 General

A UML *Classifier* is the abstract definition of a *Class, DataType or Interface* in the UML. All of these elements map to a VB Class, Standard Module or Form.

(*Classifiers* are defined in the UML to simply capture the similarities between *Classes, DataTypes* and *Interfaces*. They are abstract however and don't appear directly on diagrams. Consult the UML semantics document for further details about them.)

UML *classes* are the most used of all the *Classifier* types and these map straight to VB Classes or Forms as shown:

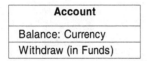

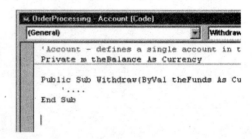

A Class In UML   A Class In Visual Basic

4.1.1 Name

The name of the UML *classifier* becomes the name of the VB item.

4.1.2 Features

All UML *classifiers* have *features*, which are further defined as *attributes* and *operations* and these map to VB Member *Variables* and *Procedures*, respectively. These are discussed later.

4.1.3 Inheritance and Stereotypes

Most VB developers know that VB doesn't support full inheritance. However, VB does support the ability to 'implement' an interface. This is an extremely useful facility that makes regular inheritance 'not so important'.

The first thing we must do is distinguish between two types of inheritance:

> ➢ Inheritance of interface (sub-typing)

> ➢ Inheritance of implementation (class extension or code reuse)

If we consider these two forms of inheritance, it is important to realize that the first form is more important for building components that exhibit good qualities of design like low coupling. (A component with low coupling means that the component has few dependencies on other parts of a system. This means that the component could be used easily in *other* systems without too much work). The details of this are beyond the scope of this book and I suggest you read the 'VB Books On-line' for a background on interfaces and the `Implements` construct.

In UML terminology, a *class* can *realize* many *interfaces*. This directly maps to the meaning of `Implements`, in VB.

4.1.4 Implementation Inheritance

Implementation inheritance or code reuse, as it is often called, is a very useful feature and time saver. However it is not so essential in providing the system your users want. Also code reuse can be achieved by 'aggregating' or 'composing' the object that contains the services (methods) you want to reuse instead.

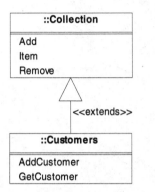

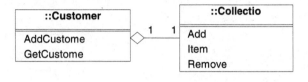

Code reuse via Inheritance   Code reuse via composition (the VB way)

In this situation, any operations you want to reuse, involves writing delegation code to delegate to the reused object. Here is an example 'customers' collection:

```
'this is my hidden implementation of the collection
Private m_myCollection As New Collection

Public Sub AddCustomer(ByVal theCustomer As Customers)
'delegate to my collection
    m_myCollection.Add theCustomer
End Sub

Public Sub RemoveCustomer(ByVal theCustomer As Customers)
'delegate to my collection
    m_myCollection.Remove theCustomer
End Sub
```

Of course this can be very tedious when there are many services involved. This is where CASE tools are useful for doing the 'grunge work'. VB Developers may wish to develop their own VB 'add-in' that performs this task.

So to recap, if you are turning an *<<extends>>* inheritance relationship into containment, do the following:

➤ Add an `Implements` statement for the class being reused.

➤ Add a `Private` variable that holds a reference to the reused object (the aggregation)

➤ Add the set of methods (procedures) that delegate to their counterparts on the aggregated object.

If the stereotype is <<*implements*>> then this maps simply to the VB construct 'implements':

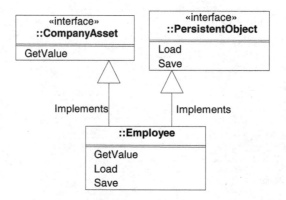

The VB code for the above model could look like this: -

```
'Employee Class

Implements CompanyAsset
Implements PersistentObject

'my implementation of GetValue
Private Property Get CompanyAsset_GetValue() As Variant
    'return asset value of this employee
End Property

'my implementation of load
Private Sub PersistentObject_Load()
    'load employee details from disk
End Sub

Private Sub PersistentObject_Save()
    'save employee details to disk
End Sub
```

4.1.5 Static Members

The UML allows *features* to be either part of each class instance or part of the class itself. This means that the *feature*, whether it is an *attribute* or an *operation* is part of the *class* and not each *instance* of the *class*. These are often called 'static' in VB. VB does not support *features* that are only part of the *class* so, if we wish to model them, we need to define a convention to support them.

One convention we can use is to create a standard (.bas) module for each class that has static members. All static operations and attributes can then be added as members of this module. When naming the module, try to pick a name that relates the module to the VB class. For instance, if we have a class called Account, we may choose to name the module AccountClass.

Account
Balance: Currency
OverdraftRate: double {static}
Withdraw (in Funds)

The Overdraft attribute would be placed in `AccountClass.bas`:

```
'AccountClass - the Account class object
'holds all static features

'the percentage that all overdafts are charged at
'applies to *all* overdrawn accounts
Public OverdraftRate As Double
```

4.1.6 Parameterized Classes (Templates)

VB does not support parameterized classes. This is a tradeoff that VB developers must accept in return for a simpler programming model.

If you include parameterized classes in your design then this is OK but remember that you will have to manually write the specific versions yourself. It may be better to avoid modeling with them to start with.

4.1.7 Class Mapping Advice

If you are using the package to name mapping convention, then the class name will also include the names of its containing packages.

It is good practice to choose a filename for the class that is similar to the class name.

4.2 Interfaces

An *interface*, which is a specialized *Classifier* in the UML maps directly to a class in VB.

This mapping is not explicitly stated and checked in VB - it is only apparent that a VB class is an interface by the way it is used by other classes and the fact that the VB class contains empty procedures.

'IPersistent - responsibilities that must be provided by persistent objects

```
Public Sub Save()
    'abstract operation
End Sub

Public Sub Load()
    'abstract operation
End Sub
```

Interfaces are crucial when building components in VB. To expose an interface from a VB ActiveX Component, the Instancing property of the VB class should be set to PublicNotCreatable.

In all other respects, an *interface* has a similar mapping to a UML *class* in that is also has *features* that can be *operations*, *attributes, associations,* etc.

Note: Developers should not confuse *interface* with user-interface or user-interface class. Refer to the UML documentation for a precise definition of *interface*.

4.3 Attributes

An *attribute* of a UML *classifier* maps to a VB variable.

Account
- Balance: Currency
+ Withdraw (in Funds)

A UML Attribute on Account

```
'Account class
'
Private Balance As Currency
```

A Variable definition in a VB Class

A UML attribute has the following form: -

visibility name : type = { initial-value }

4.3.1 Visibility

The *visibility* of the attribute has a partial mapping to the *access* of the VB attribute as captured in this table:

UML Visibility	UML Notation	VB Access	Notes
Public	+	Public	Same meaning
Protected	#	None	Due to VB not supporting implementation inheritance.
Private	-	Private	Same meaning.

4.3.2 Name

The *name* of the attribute simply maps to the name of the VB variable.

4.3.3 Type

The type specified for the attribute will be the name of either a built-in VB type such as an Integer or a Long, a user-defined type or a VB object type such as a Class or Form.

4.3.4 Initial Value

An attribute in the UML can be given an *initial-value*. In VB, we achieve this by adding initial assignments inside the `Initialize` routine of the class:

Account
- Balance: Currency = 10
+ Withdraw (in Funds)

```
'Account class
'
    Private m_theBalance As Currency

    Private Sub Class_Initialize()
'this generous bank gives you a tenner to
'start!
        m_theBalance = 10
    End Sub
```

An initialized UML Attribute   Variable initialized inside the class initializer

If the attribute is tagged as *{frozen}* then this implies that the attribute is constant. Constant attributes are easily represented in VB as Const variables. For example:

```
Private Const PI As Double = 3.1412
```

Note: VB does not allow classes to declare public constants. This is more of a nuisance rather that a logical restriction. It is recommended that constants that relate to a class be placed in module that is closely related to either the class or the package containing the class. For instance, if you have a package called `Accountancy` that contains the related classes, `Account` and `Ledger`, then you might want to place your constants in a `bas` module that is related to the package called, say, `Accountancy` (`Accountancy.bas`).

4.4 Operations

An *operation* on a UML *class* maps to a VB Procedure.

A UML *operation* has the following form:

visibility name (parameters) : return-type { property string }

4.4.1 Visibility

The *visibility* of the operation has a partial mapping to the access of the VB procedure as captured in this table:

UML Visibility	UML Notation	VB Access	Notes
Public	+	Public	Same meaning
Protected	#	Friend	See notes
Private	-	Private	Same meaning

The actual meaning of public, protected and private really comes down to the language you are using to implement your models in. In C++ for instance, public, protected and private all have quite distinct meanings that are different to VB.

In VB, the visibility options provided in the UML will map to different things in VB. When we are building VB components, we are interested in three levels of access:

➤ Things that are visible only to the inside of a class (Private)

➤ Things that are visible only to the inside of a the component (Friend)

➤ Things that are visible to all other components and classes (Public)

So when using the UML we should choose the mapping as shown in the table.

4.4.2 Name

The *name* of the operation simply maps to the name of the procedure in VB.

4.4.3 Parameters

(see below)

4.4.4 Return Type

The *return-type* specified for the operation will be the name of either a built-in VB type such as an `Integer` or a `Long`, a user-defined type or a VB object type such as a Class or Form.

If a *return type* is present then we map the item to a VB Function, otherwise we map it to a Subroutine:

Account
- Balance: Currency = 10
+ Withdraw (in Funds)
+ IsOverdrawn: Boolean

```
'Account class
    Private m_theBalance As Currency

    Public Sub Withdraw(ByVal theFunds As Currency)
        m_theBalance = m_theBalance - theFunds
    End Sub

    Public Function IsOverdrawn() As Boolean
        IsOverdrawn = (m_theBalance < 0)
    End Function
```

4.4.5 The Operation and Method Distinction

The UML often refers to both *operations* and *methods*, which many VB developers may consider to be the same thing. The UML offers a distinction whereby *operations* define a service, and the *method* is the implementation of that *operation*. In VB terms, the distinction is very subtle as both concepts are implemented with the same language constructs, i.e. as functions or subroutines.

If we really want to make a distinction in VB, then we can say that the empty procedures defined in a VB interface are the *operations* and the *methods* are the actual implementations in each of the VB classes that implement the interface.

4.4.6 Parameters

Each parameter in UML has the following form:

kind name : type = default value

438

Kind

The kind of the operation is either *in*, *out* or *inout*, and indicates how the parameter is passed to the operation's body. VB has an approximate mapping for these:

UML kind	VB	Notes
in	ByVal	
out	ByRef	Not really supported but a compatible mapping
inout	ByRef	

Type

The type specified for the parameter will be the name of either a built-in VB type such as an `Integer` or a `Long`, a user-defined type or a VB object type such as a Class or Form.

Default Value

If a parameter is given a default value then this can be implemented in VB too. For a VB parameter to have a default value, the Optional keyword must be present:

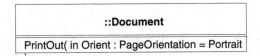

```
Public Sub PrintOut(Optional ByVal Orient As PageOrientation = Portrait)
     'print out
End Sub
```

4.4.7 Polymorphic Operations

If a UML *Operation* is marked as polymorphic (*isPolymorphic = True*), then this signifies that the *operation* can be overridden in subclasses and thus has many implementations. In VB, this property only applies to operations (procedures) defined on a VB interface. (All operations defined on a VB interface are automatically polymorphic because the operation will have many implementations in the classes that implement the interface.)

4.4.8 Stereotypes

A <<get>> or <<set>> operation stereotype is an operation whose role is to provide access to a value on the object. In VB terms, Property procedures are good examples of these types of operations.

4.5 Utilities

A *UML utility class* represents just a cohesive group of global procedures or variables. These are usually mapped to standard (.bas) modules in VB because they don't have multiple instances like a regular class does. Examples of utility classes are the standard procedure libraries that come with VB. It is convenient to show them in this way to make a model easier to understand. These are shown as a stereotype of class:

```
        ┌─────────────────────┐
        │      «utility»       │
        │     ::WINAPI         │
        ├─────────────────────┤
        │  SendMessage        │
        │  PostMessage        │
        │  GetDlgItem         │
        │  CreateWindow       │
        └─────────────────────┘
```

The Windows API as a <<utility>>

4.6 Associations

4.6.1 Multiplicity

The multiplicity of an association determines how we implement the association. If the multiplicity is **1**, then we may choose to implement the association using an object reference. If the multiplicity is a fixed number then we might employ the use of VB arrays. If the multiplicity is unbounded, e.g. **1+** then a collection may be used instead. See the implementation section for examples of this.

4.6.2 Qualifiers

A UML qualifier in is effectively a key for navigating to the object at the other end of an association. For instance, we may initially model that a **Person owns many Cars**. However in later design revisions, we may state that a **Person owns a single Car** when qualified by a particular registration plate. See the following examples for more about this.

4.6.3 N-ary Associations

Most associations involve just two objects - one at each end. However there are occasions when three or more classes are involved in the association. When considering how to map these, look at the example of how we implement link classes. These effectively represent an association of three objects.

4.6.4 Aggregation and Composition

Aggregation and composition are implemented in the same way in VB. This is because unlike some languages such as C++, you cannot physically contain one VB object within another. However VB does allow you to achieve a similar effect by ensuring your composed objects are created at the same time. We achieve this by adding the 'new' keyword to the Private variable that holds the sub-object:

```
'Class Car
'My engine - this will be created when I get created
Dim m_theEngine As New Engine
```

'code for class..

4.6.5 Implementing Associations

Because *associations* are not part of the Visual Basic Language it can be hard for Developers to know how to map them. The follow section provides some techniques and examples for implementing associations in VB.

Let's first look at how we might implement simple associations in VB.

4.6.6 Basic 1-to-1 Unidirectional Associations

The most common way to implement a unidirectional association is to use an object reference embedded in the source class. In the following example, a Person owns a single Car:

Here is the code for a simple unidirectional association (note that the example actually holds a link from Car to Person).

First, let's create a simple definition of the Car (Car.cls):

```
'our private implementation
Private m_Make As String      'make of car

'our hidden link implementation to person
Private m_theOwner As Person

'get the car owner
Public Property Get Owner() As Person
    Set Owner = m_theOwner
End Property

'set the car owner
'note: this makes the owner changeable during
'the car's lifetime
Public Property Set Owner(ByVal theOwner As Person)
    Set m_theOwner = theOwner
End Property

'get the make of the car
Public Property Get Make() As String
    Make = m_Make
End Property

'set the make of the car
Public Property Let Make(ByVal newMake As String)
    m_Make = newMake
End Property
```

Now let's create a simple `Person` class:

```
'private implementation of person
Private m_myName As String

'return person's name
Public Property Get Name() As String
    Name = m_myName
End Property

'set person's name
Public Property Let Name(ByVal newName As String)
    m_myName = newName
End Property
```

To test the association, we will place some code in the main routine of the application:

```
Sub Main()
    'simple 1 to 1 unidirectional association

    '1. create some objects to connect
    Dim aPerson As New Person
    aPerson.Name = "Russell"

    Dim aCar As New Car
    aCar.Make = "Ferrari"

    '2. set the person as the owner of the car
    Set aCar.Owner = aPerson

    '3. print the owner's name via the car
    Debug.Print aCar.Owner.Name + " is driving a " + aCar.Make
End Sub
```

4.6.7 Basic 1-to-Many Unidirectional Associations

If the `Person` gets rich then we might want to model the person owning many cars, as shown:

A basic implementation of this is to embed a collection of `Cars` into `Persons` and then allow client code to add `Cars` to `Person` at will.

Here is some rudimentary code from `Person`:

```
'private implementation of person
Private m_myName As String

Private m_myTransport As New Cars

'return person's name
Public Property Get Name() As String
    Name = m_myName
End Property
```

```
'set person's name
Public Property Let Name(ByVal newName As String)
    m_myName = newName
End Property

Public Property Get Transport() As Cars
    Set Transport = m_myTransport
End Property
```

Note the embedded, hidden `Cars` collection in `Person`. This holds the references to the associated `Car` objects. The code for `Car` follows. (This was generated by the class builder add-in.)

The `Cars` collection code:

```
Option Explicit

'local variable to hold collection
Private mCol As Collection
```

```
Public Function Add(Make As String, Owner As Person, Optional sKey As String) _
                                                                    As Car
    'create a new object
    Dim objNewMember As Car
    Set objNewMember = New Car

    'set the properties passed into the method
    objNewMember.Make = Make
    If IsObject(Owner) Then
        Set objNewMember.Owner = Owner
    Else
        objNewMember.Owner = Owner
    End If
    If Len(sKey) = 0 Then
        mCol.Add objNewMember
    Else
        mCol.Add objNewMember, sKey
    End If

    'return the object created
    Set Add = objNewMember
    Set objNewMember = Nothing

End Function
```

```
Public Property Get Item(vntIndexKey As Variant) As Car
    'used when referencing an element in the collection
    'vntIndexKey contains either the Index or Key to the collection,
    'this is why it is declared as a Variant
    'Syntax: Set foo = x.Item(xyz) or Set foo = x.Item(5)
  Set Item = mCol(vntIndexKey)
End Property
```

```
Public Property Get Count() As Long
    'used when retrieving the number of elements in the
    'collection. Syntax: Debug.Print x.Count
    Count = mCol.Count
End Property
```

```
Public Sub Remove(vntIndexKey As Variant)
    'used when removing an element from the collection
    'vntIndexKey contains either the Index or Key, which is why
    'it is declared as a Variant
    'Syntax: x.Remove(xyz)

    mCol.Remove vntIndexKey
End Sub

Public Property Get NewEnum() As IUnknown
    'this property allows you to enumerate
    'this collection with the For...Each syntax
    Set NewEnum = mCol.[_NewEnum]
End Property

Private Sub Class_Initialize()
    'creates the collection when this class is created
    Set mCol = New Collection
End Sub

Private Sub Class_Terminate()
    'destroys collection when this class is terminated
    Set mCol = Nothing
End Sub
```

To test the collection, we can write some code for the main application routine like this:

```
Sub Main()
    'simple 1 to many unidirectional association

    '1. create some objects to connect
    Dim aPerson As New Person
    aPerson.Name = "Russell"

    Dim aFastCar As New Car
    aFastCar.Make = "Ferrari"

    Dim aSlowCar As New Car
    aSlowCar.Make = "Reliant"

    '2. associate the cars with the person
    aPerson.Transport.Add "Ferrari", aPerson, "R999 ICH"
    aPerson.Transport.Add "Reliant", aPerson, "S111 LOW"

    '3. print the makes of car the person owns
    Debug.Print aPerson.Name + " owns the following car makes: - "
    Dim aCar As Car
    For Each aCar In aPerson.Transport
        Debug.Print "A " + aCar.Make
    Next
End Sub
```

The example code assumes that the collection is not ordered in any way.

Building collection classes can be tedious so it is recommended that developers take a look at the Class Builder add-in, which provides collection-building features.

4.6.8 Implementing Qualifiers

As we elaborate our design model, associations that start off as 1-to-many, often turn out to be 1-to1 when qualified by some index. If we take our Person-to-Car example, we could refine the model to get the following:

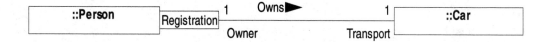

As mentioned in the mapping, a qualifier becomes an index when traversing the association. If we are using property procedures, then the qualifier will become a parameter of that procedure. So, to access a single Car that the Person owns, we must provide a registration number. Clients wishing to access an individual car would supply the registration number of the car of interest:

```
Dim aCar As Car
Set aCar = aPerson.Transport("R999 ICH") 'get a particular car
```

4.6.9 Bi-directional Associations and Referential Integrity

Implementing unidirectional associations with just pointers is just about workable and is quite common. However, in business models, we often need to traverse in both directions. Now we could just implement the above techniques on both ends, i.e. each object has a reference to the other:

First, here is the Car with an Owner link:

```
'our private implementation
Private m_Make As String      'make of car

'our hidden link implementation to person
Private m_theOwner As Person

'get the car owner
Public Property Get Owner() As Person
    Set Owner = m_theOwner
End Property

'set the car owner
'note: this makes the owner changeable during
'the car's lifetime
Public Property Set Owner(ByVal theOwner As Person)
    Set m_theOwner = theOwner
End Property
```

```
'get the make of the car
Public Property Get Make() As String
    Make = m_Make
End Property

'set the make of the car
Public Property Let Make(ByVal newMake As String)
    m_Make = newMake
End Property
```

Here is the code for Person also with a link back to Car:

```
'private implementation of person
Private m_myName As String

'our hidden link implementation to the car
Private m_Transport As Car

'get the person's sole transport
Public Property Get Transport() As Car
    Set Transport = m_Transport
End Property

'set the person's transport
Public Property Set Transport(ByVal someTransport As Car)
    Set m_Transport = someTransport
End Property

'return person's name
Public Property Get Name() As String
    Name = m_myName
End Property

'set person's name
Public Property Let Name(ByVal newName As String)
    m_myName = newName
End Property
```

Here is some simple client code to associate the respective objects:

```
Option Explicit

Sub Main()
    '1 to 1 bidirectional association
    'with *no* referential integrity

    '1. create some objects to connect
    Dim aPerson As New Person
    aPerson.Name = "Russell"

    Dim aCar As New Car
    aCar.Make = "Ferrari"

    '2. set the person as the owner of the car
    Set aCar.Owner = aPerson
```

```
    '3. set the person's means of transport
    Set aPerson.Transport = aCar

    '4. print the car owner's name
    Debug.Print aCar.Owner.Name + " is driving a ";

    '5. print the owner's transport
    Debug.Print aPerson.Transport.Make
End Sub
```

4.6.10 Problems with Simple Associations

Now, it is very difficult to ensure the integrity of these models so far. It would be very easy to accidentally set one end of the association and not the other at run-time. This will ultimately lead to the infamous 'error 91 – object variable or with block not set', when we later try to traverse the association.

If we want to build more robust bi-directional associations, we must build referential integrity into our models. We can do this in a number of ways.

4.6.11 Link Management Routines

These routines are separate routines often placed in standard (.bas) modules and are responsible for attaching both ends of an association at the same time. They are also responsible for disconnecting an association. By performing the connection at the same time, at the same place, we have a better chance of maintaining referential integrity.

So let's revisit our original 1-to-1 bi-directional association between Person and Car but this time, we will add some association link management.

The code for Person and Car is almost the same as before but we have a new module to add which contains the link management:

The code for the PersonOwnsCar_Manager module:

```
'associate a person and car
Public Sub LinkPersonAndCar(ByVal aPerson As Person, ByVal aCar As Car)
    'ensure we are not breaking an existing association
    Debug.Assert aPerson.Transport Is Nothing
    Debug.Assert aCar.Owner Is Nothing

    'link up in both directions
    Set aPerson.Transport = aCar
    Set aCar.Owner = aPerson
End Sub
```

```
'cater for removal of person from model
Public Sub UnlinkPerson(ByVal aPerson As Person)
    'ensure we have a valid person to begin with
    Debug.Assert Not aPerson Is Nothing

    Set aPerson.Transport.Owner = Nothing
    Set aPerson.Transport = Nothing
End Sub
```

```
'cater for removal of car from model
Public Sub UnlinkCar(ByVal aCar As Car)
    'ensure we have a valid car to begin with
    Debug.Assert Not aCar Is Nothing

    Set aCar.Owner.Transport = Nothing
    Set aCar.Owner = Nothing
End Sub
```

We also have one new procedure to add to `Car`:

'Destroy the car from the model

```
Public Sub Destroy()
    'get link manager to sort out the integrity
    PersonOwnsCar_Manager.UnlinkCar Me
End Sub
```

Finally, let's look at some code that tests the association:

```
Option Explicit

Sub Main()
    '1 to 1 bidirectional association
    'with referential integrity

    '1. create some objects to link
    Dim aPerson As New Person
    aPerson.Name = "Russell"

    Dim aCar As New Car
    aCar.Make = "Ferrari"

    '2. Link up the two
    PersonOwnsCar_Manager.LinkPersonAndCar aPerson, aCar

    '3. Test: print the car owner's name
    Debug.Print aCar.Owner.Name + " is driving a ";

    '4. Test: print the owner's transport
    Debug.Print aPerson.Transport.Make

    '5. now write off the car
    '(this will disassociate the person too)
    aCar.Destroy

    '6. check the association no longer exists in both directions
    If aCar.Owner Is Nothing Then
        Debug.Print aPerson.Name + " no longer owns the car."
    End If

    If aPerson.Transport Is Nothing Then
        Debug.Print aPerson.Name + " no longer has transport!"
    End If
End Sub
```

4.6.12 Association Classes and Link Management

If we have a design that incorporates an association class, then we have an alternative home for the link management that Developers may find is more cohesive.

Let's assume that association between `Person` and `Car` is supplemented with a 'Log Book' that records the `Car`'s history:

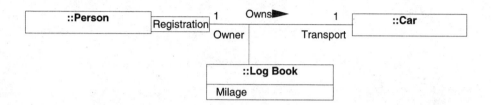

We will now want to ensure that when a `Person` is associated to a `Car`, a `LogBook` is also associated. We will assume that the `LogBook` already exists. If we do this, we can end up with the following implementation.

(Note that some properties in the code have been omitted from the model to make it easier to read. In fact, we can see that the `LogBook` in the code actually has a number of {derived} attributes that get their information from the `Car`.)

Firstly, here is the `LogBook` association class, which also contains the link management code:

```
'LogBook Association Class
'My associations
    Private m_theLoggedCar As Car
    Private m_theOwner As Person

    Private m_myIssueDate As Date

    'to check we have entered an 'initialized state'
    Private m_blnInitialized As Boolean

    'attributes -------------------------------------

    'When was I issued?
    Public Property Get IssueDate() As Date
        IssueDate = m_myIssueDate
    End Property

    'set issue date
    Public Property Let IssueDate(ByVal aDate As Date)
        m_myIssueDate = aDate
    End Property

    'you can only get the milage - you can't set it
    'that would be illegal!
    Public Property Get Milage() As Long
        Debug.Assert m_blnInitialized = True
```

```
        'derived property - get from the car
        Milage = m_theLoggedCar.Milage
End Property

'who owns the car?
Public Property Get RegisteredOwner() As String
    Debug.Assert m_blnInitialized = True

        'derived property - get from the person
        RegisteredOwner = m_theOwner.Name
End Property

'operations --------------------------------
'Register the log book for use
Public Sub Register(ByVal aPerson As Person, ByVal aCar As Car)
        'delegate to link
        Link aPerson, aCar
End Sub

'Unregister the log book from use
Public Sub UnRegister()
        'destroy the asociation
        'just delegate to unlink
        UnLink
End Sub

Private Sub Link(ByVal aPerson As Person, ByVal aCar As Car)
    Debug.Assert Not aPerson Is Nothing
    Debug.Assert Not aCar Is Nothing

        'link up in both directions
    Set aPerson.Transport = aCar
    Set aCar.Owner = aPerson

        'set my links too
    Set m_theLoggedCar = aCar
    Set m_theOwner = aPerson

    m_blnInitialized = True
End Sub

Private Sub UnLink()
        'destroy the asociation

        'deal with person first
    Set m_theOwner.Transport = Nothing      'person looses transport
    Set m_theOwner = Nothing                'log book looses person

        'unlink car now
    Set m_theLoggedCar.Owner = Nothing      'car looses owner
    Set m_theLoggedCar = Nothing            'log book looses car
End Sub
```

Here is the Car source code now (some extra attributes have been added to spice things up):

```
'Car Class
'our private implementation
Private m_Make As String        'make of car
Private m_myRoadMilage As Long  'My Milage
```

```
'our hidden link implementation to person
Private m_theOwner As Person

'attributes --------------------------

'get the car owner
Public Property Get Owner() As Person
    Set Owner = m_theOwner
End Property

'set the car owner
'note: this makes the owner changeable during
'the car's lifetime
Public Property Set Owner(ByVal theOwner As Person)
    Set m_theOwner = theOwner
End Property

'get the make of the car
Public Property Get Make() As String
    Make = m_Make
End Property

'set the make of the car
Public Property Let Make(ByVal newMake As String)
    m_Make = newMake
End Property

'get the car's milage so far
Public Property Get Milage() As Long
    Milage = m_myRoadMilage
End Property

'operations --------------------------
'Bump up the car milage
Public Sub BumpMilageBy(ByVal someMiles As Long)
    m_myRoadMilage = m_myRoadMilage + someMiles
End Sub
```

When we now want to associate `Person` and `Car`, we first create a `LogBook` and then get the `LogBook` to associate all three objects together. In the example client code we first associate the objects and then iterate over the assocation and list the information:

(Code in `App.bas`)

```
Option Explicit

Sub Main()
    '1 to 1 bidirectional association with association class

    '1. create some objects to link
    Dim aPerson As New Person
    aPerson.Name = "Russell"

    Dim aCar As New Car
    aCar.Make = "Ferrari"
    aCar.BumpMilageBy 50
```

```
        Dim aLogBook As New LogBook
        aLogBook.IssueDate = Now

        '2. Link everything up
        aLogBook.Register aPerson, aCar

        '3. Print out the ownership details
        'We can do this solely via the LogBook
        Debug.Print "Car Registration Details:"
        Debug.Print "Registration Date : " + CStr(aLogBook.IssueDate)
        Debug.Print "Owned By : " + aLogBook.RegisteredOwner
        Debug.Print "Milage on Clock : " + CStr(aLogBook.Milage)

        '4. Let's give the car to someone else
        '(I must be mad!)
        'let's take it out for the weekend first!
        aCar.BumpMilageBy 200

        'a new owner gets lucky
        Dim aLuckyPerson As New Person
        aLuckyPerson.Name = "Dave"

        aLogBook.Register aLuckyPerson, aCar

        '5. Print out the new ownership details
        'car should now be registered to Dave:
        Debug.Print "Car Registration Details:"
        Debug.Print "Registration Date : " + CStr(aLogBook.IssueDate)
        Debug.Print "Owned By : " + aLogBook.RegisteredOwner
        Debug.Print "Milage on Clock : " + CStr(aLogBook.Milage)

        '6. finally, write off the car
        'Unregistering the log book is as good as writing off the car
        'so let's do that instead
        aLogBook.UnRegister
End Sub
```

4.6.13 A Final Example: Bi-directional 1-to-Many Association with Link Management and Qualifier

As a final example, here is an implementation of a bi-directional 1-to-many *association* with *association class* and *qualifier,* which is built upon our earlier example. The design model of the implementation looks like this:

The code in `LogBook`, which now deals with multiple `Cars`:

```
'LogBook association class
'
'My associations
Private m_theLoggedCar As Car
Private m_theOwner As Person

Private m_myIssueDate As Date

'to check we have entered an 'initialized state'
Private m_blnInitialized As Boolean
```

```
'attributes  -----------------------------------

'When was I issued?
Public Property Get IssueDate() As Date
    IssueDate = m_myIssueDate
End Property

'set issue date
Public Property Let IssueDate(ByVal aDate As Date)
    m_myIssueDate = aDate
End Property

'you can only get the milage - you can't set it
'that would be illegal!
Public Property Get Milage() As Long
    Debug.Assert m_blnInitialized = True

    'derived property - get from the car
    Milage = m_theLoggedCar.Milage
End Property

'who owns the car?
Public Property Get RegisteredOwner() As String
    Debug.Assert m_blnInitialised = True

    'derived property - get from the person
    RegisteredOwner = m_theOwner.Name
End Property

'operations --------------------------------
'Register the log book for use
Public Sub Register(ByVal aPerson As Person, ByVal aCar As Car)
    'delegate to link
    Link aPerson, aCar
End Sub

'Unregister the log book from use
Public Sub UnRegister()
    'destroy the asociation
    'just delegate to unlink
    UnLink
End Sub

Private Sub Link(ByVal aPerson As Person, ByVal aCar As Car)
    Debug.Assert Not aPerson Is Nothing
    Debug.Assert Not aCar Is Nothing

    'link up in both directions
    Set aPerson.Transport(aCar.Registration) = aCar
    Set aCar.Owner = aPerson
    Set aCar.LogBook = Me

    'set my links too
    Set m_theLoggedCar = aCar
    Set m_theOwner = aPerson

    m_blnInitialised = True
End Sub
```

```
Private Sub UnLink()
    'destroy the asociation

    'deal with owner first
    Set m_theOwner.Transport(m_theLoggedCar.Registration) = Nothing
    'person looses transport
    Set m_theOwner = Nothing                'log book looses person

    'now loose the car
    Set m_theLoggedCar.Owner = Nothing  'car looses owner
    Set m_theLoggedCar.LogBook = Nothing  'car looses log book (me!)
    Set m_theLoggedCar = Nothing            'log book looses car
End Sub
```

Here is the revised `Person` class. Note that the `Transport` property is now qualified with a registration plate:

```
'Person Class with qualified Transport()
'private implementation of person
Private m_myName As String

'our hidden link implementation to the cars
Private m_Transport As Cars

'attributes  -------------------------------

'get the person's transport qualified by registration plate
Public Property Get Transport(ByVal theReg As String) As Car
    Set Transport = m_Transport.Item(theReg)
End Property

'set the person's transport
'note we could have got the registration from the car
'but it makes it easier to understand the client code
'
'If the car passed is nothing then this means we want to drop the
'associated car
Public Property Set Transport(ByVal theReg As String, ByVal someTransport As Car)
    If someTransport Is Nothing Then
        m_Transport.Remove thReg
    Else
        m_Transport.Add someTransport
    End If
End Property

'return person's name
Public Property Get Name() As String
    Name = m_myName
End Property

'set person's name
Public Property Let Name(ByVal newName As String)
    m_myName = newName
End Property
```

```
Public Property Get Cars() As Cars
    Set Cars = m_Transport
End Property

'operations --------------------------------
Private Sub Class_Initialize()
    Set m_Transport = New Cars
End Sub
```

We also have a slightly revised implementation of the `Cars` collection. This is the same as the previous version except that it has been changed to accept an existing object rather than creating it itself. Here is the revised `Add` operation.

```
'add a car
Public Function Add(ByVal aCar As Car) As Car
    mCol.Add aCar, aCar.Registration

    'return the car for convenience
    Set Add = aCar
End Function
```

Finally, here is the client code to test the whole association:

```
Option Explicit

Sub Main()
    '1 to many, bidirectional association with association class

    '1. create some objects to link

    'an owner
    Dim aPerson As New Person
    aPerson.Name = "Russell"

    'the cars
    Dim aFastCar As New Car
    aFastCar.Make = "Ferrari"
    aFastCar.Registration = "R999 ICH"
    aFastCar.BumpMilageBy 50

    Dim anEconomicCar As New Car
    anEconomicCar.Make = "Ford"
    anEconomicCar.Registration = "E123 ECO"
    anEconomicCar.BumpMilageBy 10

    'the log books
    Dim theFerrariLogBook As New LogBook
    theFerrariLogBook.IssueDate = Now

    Dim theFordLogBook As New LogBook
    theFordLogBook.IssueDate = Now

    '2. Link everything up
    theFerrariLogBook.Register aPerson, aFastCar
    theFordLogBook.Register aPerson, anEconomicCar
```

```
     '3. Print out the car details
     'We can do this via the person's cars
     Debug.Print "Car Registration Details for " + aPerson.Name; " : "
     Dim aCar As Car
     For Each aCar In aPerson.Cars
         Debug.Print "Registration Date : " + CStr(aCar.LogBook.IssueDate)
         Debug.Print "Make of Car : " + CStr(aCar.Make)
         Debug.Print "Milage on Clock : " + CStr(aCar.Milage)
     Next
 End Sub
```

Points to note:

➤ `Car` objects can now navigate to their associated `LogBooks`. This was because I wanted to report the issue date of the log book via the car.

➤ This is also a good example of how the UML can help you understand quite a complex code structure. Consider redrawing the model with the extra operations and attributes added and then review the design visually.

➤ I have used the Registration Plate of the `Car` as the qualifier from `Person` to `Car`. This makes sense because the Registration Plate will always identify a single `Car`.

➤ I have chosen in this example to continue to give the `LogBook` class the link management responsibilities. In practice this responsibility will vary depending on your model. The objective is usually to produce a simpler model that other developers can pick up easier later.

4.6.14 Miscellaneous Advice

There are many ways to implement associations. Here are some tips on writing good associations.

Associations Advice: Always Hide Your Implementation

Make sure you always hide the implementation of your association behind a `Property Get` procedure. If you do this, you will benefit in many ways:

➤ It allows you to vary the way you store the reference to the associated object. This hidden reference may change over the lifetime of the system.

➤ It allows you to provide an association that is created "on-demand", to improve performance. For instance, you might have an association to a large collection of objects. By hiding the association behind a property procedure, you could build the collection when the property is first called (which of course may never happen for the object's lifetime).

➤ It allows you to provide a "Derived" association. Because your implementation of the association is hidden, it may never actually take up any fixed storage at all. In other words, you have an algorithm behind the property procedure that calculates the associated object by traversing many other objects.

Associations Advice: Avoid Cyclic Dependencies

Try to avoid cyclic dependencies. Whenever you implement a bi-directional association, you are effectively introducing a cyclic dependency between the two related objects.

For example, given two classes, `Person` and `Car`, `Person` has a reference to `Car`, and `Car` has a reference to `Person`. If you introduce such a cycle, the VB run-times are often unable to clean up the objects, even after you released the objects:

How should you avoid this? There are a number of solutions to this. The first suggestion is to allow cyclic references but make sure you explicitly break the cycles when releasing a model. The technique is to add explicit `Destroy()` routines to classes which are called when the object is ready to be released.

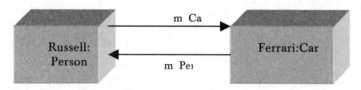

Here is the `Destroy` operation on `Car`:

```
'Car Class
Private m_Engine As Engine
Private m_Alarm As Alarm

'other operations.......

Public Sub Destroy()
    'Destroy all my aggregate objects
    Set m_Engine = Nothing
    Set m_Alarm = Nothing
End Sub
```

Associations Advice: "Keyed" References

Another solution is to avoid cycles to begin with. The technique here is to hold a reference on one object only and an 'object id' on the other (a kind of 'Keyed' pointer, if you like).

So, given the Person-Owns-Car example, we might choose to hold a reference from the `Person` to the `Car`, but on the `Car` we place an ID that uniquely identifies the `Person`. To support this implementation, we will need to introduce a 'registry object' that keeps a track of `Persons` and their associated ID. When the `Car` wants to traverse to its owner, it now consults the registry.

Both techniques have their merits and different performance tradeoffs. It is a judgment call as to which technique is better for a particular situation.

Associations Advice: Use Property Procedures to Provide Read-Only Associations

It is often useful to provide associations that can be traversed but not changed. You can do this by just providing only a property 'Get', without a 'Let' or 'Set'. This will further ensure that your model stays intact for its lifetime.

Associations Advice: Build Type-Safe Collections

As previously mentioned, it is now possible in VB to build fully type-safe collections. Prior to VB5, it was only possible to create collections based on the standard 'Collection' object that comes in the standard VB library. When you build collections of an object, feel free to use `Collection` as your implementation but ensure you wrap up the collection inside your own abstraction. For instance, here's the final version of the type-safe `Cars` collection:

```
'local variable to hold collection
Private mCol As Collection

'add a car
Public Function Add(ByVal aCar As Car) As Car
    mCol.Add aCar, aCar.Registration

    'return the car for convenience
    Set Add = aCar
End Function

Public Property Get Item(vntIndexKey As Variant) As Car
    'used when referencing an element in the collection
    'vntIndexKey contains either the Index or Key to the collection,
    'this is why it is declared as a Variant
    'Syntax: Set foo = x.Item(xyz) or Set foo = x.Item(5)
  Set Item = mCol(vntIndexKey)
End Property

Public Property Get Count() As Long
    'used when retrieving the number of elements in the
    'collection. Syntax: Debug.Print x.Count
    Count = mCol.Count
End Property

Public Sub Remove(vntIndexKey As Variant)
    'used when removing an element from the collection
    'vntIndexKey contains either the Index or Key, which is why
    'it is declared as a Variant
    'Syntax: x.Remove(xyz)

    mCol.Remove vntIndexKey
End Sub

Public Property Get NewEnum() As IUnknown
    'this property allows you to enumerate
    'this collection with the For...Each syntax
    Set NewEnum = mCol.[_NewEnum]
End Property

Private Sub Class_Initialize()
    'creates the collection when this class is created
    Set mCol = New Collection
End Sub

Private Sub Class_Terminate()
    'destroys collection when this class is terminated
    Set mCol = Nothing
End Sub
```

Associations Advice: Use "Debug.Assert" to Firm up the "Contract" of Your Operations

By using `Debug.Assert`, we can ensure that the objects passed are always valid before you try to build the association. By inserting these assertions, we are doing just that - asserting that the client code *must* provide a valid object to create a valid association.

Associations Advice: Consider Using Events to Trigger Link Management

Consider using custom class events to trigger link management routines. For instance, if the `Car` was destroyed, it could fire an event to say 'Hey, I'm a going' without caring who handles it. The `LogBook` could respond by cleaning up the association. The `Car` would never need to explicitly tell the `LogBook`. If the `Car` never needs to know about the `LogBook`, then this is one dependency you could drop, which is also a good thing.

5.0 Use Case Diagrams

UML Notation	VB	Notes
Actor 	None	See below
<name> Use Case	Class	By Convention only. (See below.)

Use case diagrams are basically an analysis tool - they are created to help all parties involved in a development understand *what* is being delivered rather than *how* it is to be built. Therefore it is not usual to map the artifacts from these diagrams to actual source code.

5.1 A Word of Warning

In fact we are actually touching on an area of use cases that is often misunderstood. Often, Developers from a non-object-oriented background will view *use cases* as just a wordy representation of what the system should do in code. As the development cycle moves into the first design phase, the developer then turns the use cases into separate procedures, where the <<*uses*>> relationship between two *use cases* ends up as a procedure call between the two respective procedures. This is wrong and should be avoided!

This is wrong because the *use cases* are there to help the potential users of the system understand what the system will do for them – not how the system should be written.

5.2 Use Cases and Transactions

With the previous comments accepted and understood, there are times when turning *use cases* into code *is* beneficial and as long as we know what we are doing and trying to achieve.

The useful thing about *use cases* is that they clearly define the boundaries of candidate transactions, (where a transaction is defined as a distinct, logical unit of work that our system might perform). 'Create Order' is a good example of a transaction. In other words, the use case 'Create Order' must run to completion or not at all. If we 'half' created an Order, that simply wouldn't do and could leave our system is a nasty state. Therefore it would be useful if we could help ensure that transactions are cleanly defined and applied in our system.

5.3 Use Cases and Controllers

In considering how we might map *use cases* to VB, one useful way is to map them to <<*controller*>> *class stereotypes* that are responsible for 'controlling' the overall use case and also responsible for the transaction as a whole.

(A <<*controller*>> *class stereotype* is a class that is mainly responsible for controlling and coordinating the implementation of a use case but doesn't actually perform any of the use case-specific detail, itself.)

Let's start by looking at a use case model of the example use case:

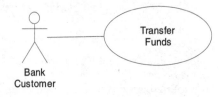

The use case will be performed by the following classes. Note the presence of the use case controller:

This is a high-level model. The two accounts will be the source and target accounts.

As previously stated, the controller is just acting as a coordinator but also knows about the whole transaction. Therefore the lifetime of the controller is synonymous to the lifetime of the transaction and use case. When we discuss collaboration diagrams, we will show how the controller performs the use case.

6.0 Behavioral Diagrams

In contrast to the *static diagram* mapping that is dealing with the static aspects of your design, the *behavioral diagram* mappings deal with how to translate the *dynamic* aspects of your design into VB code.

The UML offers four different diagrams for capturing your design dynamics and these are detailed in two parts: The first part looks at how we map *sequence* and *collaboration diagrams*. They are focused on *object instances* and the *messages* and *events* that travel between them.

In the second part we look at *statechart and activity diagrams*. These are closely tied in with *Collaboration Diagrams* but are focused more on *states* that an item such as an *object* can be in and how external and internal *events* change that *state*.

7.0 Sequence & Collaboration Diagrams

Here is a typical sequence diagram showing some object instances connected by the messages they pass to each other. This is the 'Transfer Funds' use case that was previously discussed:

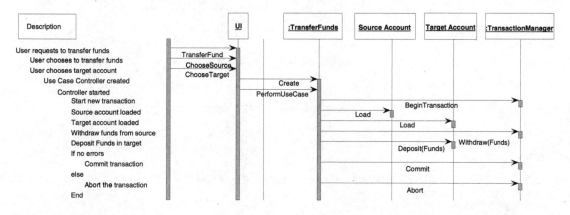

The first thing to note about sequence diagrams (and collaboration diagrams, for that matter) is that they are usually drawn with a context in mind. The first time we use these diagrams is when we are designing how our use cases will be handled. In this case the context is just the system as a whole. Later in the design we will use sequence diagrams to understand how a particular object method behaves. In this case the context is the method.

7.1 Object Instances and Context

This context is important because the object instances we place on the diagram (the columns) are usually named relative to the context. If we are doing the former kind of diagrams, then the objects will usually be given their full names in the system. In the latter case, the object names may relate to local variable names within the method.

Here is an example of a sequence diagram scoped to a method together with the resultant code:

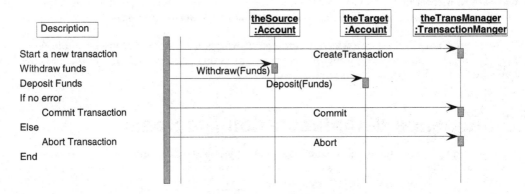

Here is the VB code on the use case controller TransferFunds:

```
Public Sub PerformUseCase(ByVal theSource As Account, ByVal theTarget _
                              As Account, ByVal theFunds As Currency)
    On Error GoTo TransferError:

    Dim theTransManager As New TransactionManager

    'Start a new transaction
    theTransManager.CreateTransaction

    'Withdraw funds
    theSource.WithdrawFunds theFunds

    'Deposit Funds
    theTarget.DepositFunds theFunds

    'commit
    theTransManager.Commit

    Exit Sub

TransferError:
```

```
        'Abort Transaction
        theTransManager.Abort
    End Sub
```

Notice that we have slightly changed the logic so that we can make use of VB's built in error system. This is OK as long as we don't impact the core interaction design.

7.2 Interactions

The horizontal interactions connecting the object instances tell us what operations on the objects need to be called (they also tell us what extra operations we need to add to our static model). The order of these interactions is crucial– this is the main point behind (*message*) *sequence* diagrams. Each horizontal line represents a single message and this represents an actual operation *call*. So we need to map this *call* into an actual VB operation *call*. The next question is 'which VB method makes the call?'

By studying the diagram it is usually easy to see which previous operation is making the call.

7.3 Pseudo-Code

The left-hand side of a sequence diagram usually contains pseudo-code that provides more clues about how the *operations* used on the diagram are actually behaving. This code is usually stated in three basic control constructs: sequence, selection and iteration. The Developer can use these constructs to write the skeleton of the related method's logic. So the mapping here is quite straightforward. Once the Diagram has matured somewhat, the Developer will use the pseudo-code as the basis for the body of the related VB method.

7.4 Collaboration Diagrams

In terms of mapping, collaboration diagrams have a lot in common with sequence diagrams. They differ of course, because they are in network form but we are still mapping the interactions between object instances.

Collaboration diagrams do however allow us to show which associations between two objects are being used to perform the interaction. This will be reflected in the names of the objects being manipulated in the procedure, i.e. if the objects have a 'm_' naming prefix, then it implies that the objects are defined at class scope – not the procedure scope.

8.0 Statechart Diagrams

UML Notation	VB	Notes
state	Depends on implementation	Abstract – see notes
Transition	Depends on implementation	Abstract – see notes

State modeling is one of the more specialized areas of the UML. Although all objects in your system have *state*, many applications such as client-server applications *don't* contain objects with very much *state* so the need to model *state* is less important.

If you *are* using VB in a real-time systems environment, then understanding how to map *statecharts* to VB will be very useful to you.

As was suggested in the introduction, *statecharts* have no straight mapping to VB. The main use behind *statecharts* is to understand clearly how objects with complex state behave. Looking at the source code of a complex object isn't very intuitive. So, once you've created your *statechart* and you are happy with it, what comes next?

8.1 Mapping States and Transitions

Although it is possible to explain where *states* and *transitions* are in a VB program, it can be almost impossible to point them out in code. This is because they are usually implicit in the design of a class and how visible they are depends on how you implement your object's *state*.

8.2 Implementing State

There are generally two ways of implementing *statecharts* in VB (or any other language for that matter). The first way is just to code the object's *state* just like any other. In other words, the member variables of the class *implicitly* define the state of the object. To understand what *state* the object is at any particular time involves inspecting the member's variables. This could be termed an *implicit* implementation of *state*.

Alternatively, if the object in question is going to have a particularly complex *state*, then it is sometimes worthwhile implementing an explicit 'Finite State Machine' inside the object. What we do here is create a machine that is driven from a table loaded with information about what to do for a particular combination of *state* and *event*. It is also possible with this technique to change this data at run-time thus altering the dynamic behavior of the object. (This technique is akin to *data-driven* programming, where the data is partially controlling the program flow.)

8.3 An Example

As always, the best way to understand the difference in implementation is to see some examples.

Let's start by defining a simple statechart for a car's security system. Here is the Car's static class model, showing the objects involved in the state machine activities:

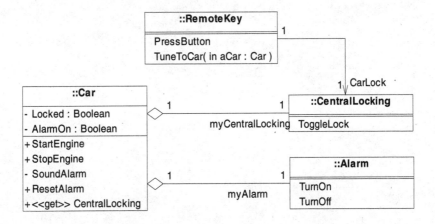

Now, the part we are interested in is the *state* of the Car object as shown:

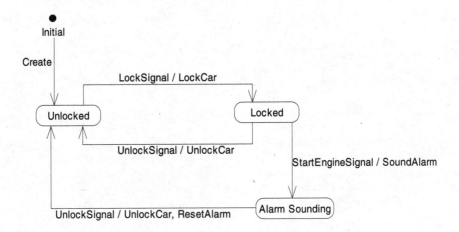

8.4 Implicit Implementation

Let's first take a look at an implicit implementation, where the member variables of the Car define the Car's state:

Firstly, here is the Car implementation:

```
Private m_Locked As Boolean
Private m_AlarmOn As Boolean

Private m_myAlarm As Alarm
Private WithEvents m_myCentralLocking As CentralLocking
'an artifical way to get the car's central locking objects
'this is just to simlate the radio connection between
'the central locking and the remote key
Public Property Get CentralLocking() As CentralLocking
    Set CentralLocking = m_myCentralLocking
End Property
```

```
'initialise self
Private Sub Class_Initialize()
    'create my composite objects
    Set m_myAlarm = New Alarm
    Set m_myCentralLocking = New CentralLocking

    'set initial state
    m_Locked = False    'initially unlocked
    m_AlarmOn = False    'alarm is off
End Sub
```

```
'start the car
'you can't do this unless you're inside!!
Public Sub StartEngine()
    If m_Locked Then
        'uh oh - break in!
        SoundAlarm
    Else
        Debug.Print "Engine started. Brmmmm"
    End If
End Sub
```

```
'here for completeness
Public Sub StopEngine()
    Debug.Print "Engine Stopped"
End Sub
```

```
'I have been locked
Private Sub m_myCentralLocking_Locked()
    m_Locked = True
    Debug.Print "Car locked"
End Sub
```

```
'I have been unlocked
Private Sub m_myCentralLocking_Unlocked()
    m_Locked = False
    If m_AlarmOn Then
        ResetAlarm
    End If
    Debug.Print "Car unlocked, alarm reset"
End Sub
```

```
Private Sub SoundAlarm()
    m_myAlarm.TurnOn
    m_AlarmOn = True
    Debug.Print "alarm sounding..."
End Sub

Private Sub ResetAlarm()
    m_myAlarm.TurnOff
    m_AlarmOn = False
    Debug.Print "alarm cancelled"
End Sub
```

Next, let's look at the code for the `Alarm` (quite simple):

```
'The Car Alarm
Public Sub TurnOn()
    Debug.Print "BEEP! BEEP! BEEP! BEEP! BEEP!"
End Sub
```

```
Public Sub TurnOff()
End Sub
```

Next, we have the code for the `CentralLocking` object:

```
'Central Locking Class
Private m_Locked As Boolean
Public Event Unlocked()
Public Event Locked()
```

```
'this is called by the receiver hardware
'when the driver sends the unlock signal
Public Sub ToggleLock()
    If m_Locked Then
        'locked - now unlock
        Debug.Print "Click"
        m_Locked = False 'set locked state

        RaiseEvent Unlocked
    Else
        'unlocked - now lock
        Debug.Print "Click"
        m_Locked = True 'set unlocked state

        RaiseEvent Locked
    End If
End Sub
```

Finally, we have the code for the `RemoteKey` fob:

```
'Remote Key class
'this is our artificial way of communicating with the
'car. In reality this would be achieved by a radio link
Public CarLock As CentralLocking
```

```
Public Sub TuneToCar(ByVal aCar As Car)
    Set CarLock = aCar.CentralLocking
End Sub
```

```
Public Sub PressButton()
    CarLock.ToggleLock
End Sub
```

Here is some client code to test the state machine:

```
Public Sub Main()
    Dim aCar As New Car
    Dim aKey As New RemoteKey    'to open the car

    '1. (artificially) connect key to car for the demo
    aKey.TuneToCar aCar

    '2. lock car
    aKey.PressButton 'lock

    '3. first use the car legally :)
    aKey.PressButton 'unlock
    aCar.StartEngine
    aCar.StopEngine
    aKey.PressButton 'locked

    '4.someone doesn't have the key....
    aCar.StartEngine 'uh oh!

    '5.owner resets the alarm
    aKey.PressButton 'Unlocked
End Sub
```

Considering the complexity of the statechart (low!) the example is quite easy to follow. If the Car had more states and events (which it could be if we considered the whole Car), then an explicit version might be preferable.

8.5 Explicit Implementation: A Finite State Machine

To contrast the implicit implementation, here is the code for the explicit version where we build an explicit state machine to manage the state of the Car object, starting with the Car class again:

```
'Car Class - external state machine version
Option Explicit

Private m_myAlarm As Alarm
Private WithEvents m_myCentralLocking As CentralLocking
Private m_MyFSM As CarFSM

Private m_CurrentState As CarState

'an artifical way to get the car's central locking objects
'this is just to simlate the radio connection between
'the central locking and the remote key
Public Property Get CentralLocking() As CentralLocking
```

```
        Set CentralLocking = m_myCentralLocking
End Property

'initialise self
Private Sub Class_Initialize()
    'create my composite objects
    Set m_myAlarm = New Alarm
    Set m_myCentralLocking = New CentralLocking
    Set m_MyFSM = New CarFSM
    m_MyFSM.LinkCar Me

    'set initial state
    m_CurrentState = Unlocked
End Sub

'start the car (requested by client)
'remember you can't do this unless you're inside!!
Public Sub StartEngine()
    m_CurrentState = m_MyFSM.ProcessEvent(m_CurrentState, EngineStarted)
End Sub

'here for completeness
Public Sub StopEngine()
    Debug.Print "Engine Stopped"
End Sub

'I have been locked
Private Sub m_myCentralLocking_Locked()
    m_CurrentState = m_MyFSM.ProcessEvent(m_CurrentState, LockSignal)
End Sub

'I have been unlocked
Private Sub m_myCentralLocking_Unlocked()
    m_CurrentState = m_MyFSM.ProcessEvent(m_CurrentState, UnlockSignal)
End Sub

'actions ------------------------------------------------------------

'actually start the engine
Friend Sub InternalStartEngine()
    Debug.Print "Engine started. Brmmmm"
End Sub

Friend Sub LockCar()
    Debug.Print "Car locked"
End Sub

Friend Sub UnlockCar()
    Debug.Print "Car unlocked"
End Sub

Friend Sub SoundAlarm()
    m_myAlarm.TurnOn
    Debug.Print "alarm started"
End Sub

Friend Sub ResetAlarm()
    m_myAlarm.TurnOff
    Debug.Print "alarm reset"
End Sub
```

The `CentralLocking`, `Alarm`, and `RemoteKey` classes are the same but we have now introduced a separate state machine that will drive the `Car` object:

```
'The Car FSM
Option Explicit

Private m_myActionTable(MAX_STATE, MAX_EVENT) As ActionEntry

Private m_theCar As Car
```

```
Public Sub LinkCar(ByVal aCar As Car)
    Debug.Assert Not aCar Is Nothing
    Set m_theCar = aCar
End Sub
```

```
'build up state table
Private Sub Class_Initialize()
    '              (in state, on event) = do actions and then go to [NextState]

    'lock and car is unlocked - just lock car
    m_myActionTable(Unlocked, LockSignal).ActionsToPerform(0) = LockCar
    m_myActionTable(Unlocked, LockSignal).ActionsToPerform(1) = NoAction
    m_myActionTable(Unlocked, LockSignal).NextState = LockedAndIdle

    'unlock and car is already unlock - do nothing
    m_myActionTable(Unlocked, UnlockSignal).ActionsToPerform(0) = NoAction
    m_myActionTable(Unlocked, UnlockSignal).NextState = Unlocked

    m_myActionTable(Unlocked, EngineStarted).ActionsToPerform(0) = _
                                    InternalStartEngine
    m_myActionTable(Unlocked, EngineStarted).ActionsToPerform(1) = NoAction
    m_myActionTable(Unlocked, EngineStarted).NextState = Unlocked

    'lock signal and car's already locked - do nothing
    m_myActionTable(LockedAndIdle, LockSignal).ActionsToPerform(0) = NoAction
    m_myActionTable(LockedAndIdle, LockSignal).NextState = LockedAndIdle

    'unlock signal and car is locked - unlock and reset alarm
    m_myActionTable(LockedAndIdle, UnlockSignal).ActionsToPerform(0) = UnlockCar
    m_myActionTable(LockedAndIdle, UnlockSignal).ActionsToPerform(1) = ResetAlarm
    m_myActionTable(LockedAndIdle, UnlockSignal).ActionsToPerform(2) = NoAction
    m_myActionTable(LockedAndIdle, UnlockSignal).NextState = Unlocked

    'car is locked but engine started!
    m_myActionTable(LockedAndIdle, EngineStarted).ActionsToPerform(0) = SoundAlarm
    m_myActionTable(LockedAndIdle, EngineStarted).ActionsToPerform(1) = NoAction
    m_myActionTable(LockedAndIdle, EngineStarted).NextState = AlarmSounding

    'unlock and alarm is sounding
    m_myActionTable(AlarmSounding, UnlockSignal).ActionsToPerform(0) = UnlockCar
    m_myActionTable(AlarmSounding, UnlockSignal).ActionsToPerform(1) = ResetAlarm
    m_myActionTable(AlarmSounding, UnlockSignal).ActionsToPerform(2) = NoAction
    m_myActionTable(AlarmSounding, UnlockSignal).NextState = Unlocked
End Sub
```

```
Public Function ProcessEvent(ByVal currentState As CarState, ByVal anEvent _
                                    As CarEvent) As CarState
    'first perform all actions for the current state and event combination
    Dim iActionIndex As Integer
    Dim iActionID  As Integer
```

```
        'get first action to perform
        'stop on first "NoAction"
        iActionID = m_myActionTable(currentState _
                            nEvent).ActionsToPerform(iActionIndex)
    Do While NoAction <> iActionID
        'translate action ID into the actual action call
        Select Case iActionID
            Case Is = LockCar
                m_theCar.LockCar
            Case Is = UnlockCar
                m_theCar.UnlockCar
            Case Is = SoundAlarm
                m_theCar.SoundAlarm
            Case Is = ResetAlarm
                m_theCar.ResetAlarm
            Case Is = InternalStartEngine
                m_theCar.InternalStartEngine
        End Select

        'get next action ID
        iActionIndex = iActionIndex + 1
        iActionID = m_myActionTable(currentState, _
            anEvent).ActionsToPerform(iActionIndex)
    Loop

    'move to next state (might be the same)
    ProcessEvent = m_myActionTable(currentState, anEvent).NextState
End Function
```

The state machine data structures are held in a separate module:

```
'data for Car FSM

Public Type ActionEntry
    ActionsToPerform(2) As CarAction      'currently allow max 3 actions per event
processed
    NextState As CarState                 'state to transition to
End Type

'things the car can do in response to state/event combinations
Public Enum CarAction
    NoAction           'used as a placeholder to mark end of actions for an entry
    LockCar
    UnlockCar
    SoundAlarm
    ResetAlarm
    InternalStartEngine
End Enum

'events that a car can receive
'these will be either be sourced from the client or sub components of car
Public Enum CarEvent
    LockSignal
    UnlockSignal
    EngineStarted
    MAX_EVENT
. End Enum
```

```
'states that a car can be in
Public Enum CarState
      none          'intial state
      Unlocked
      LockedAndIdle
      AlarmSounding
      MAX_STATE
End Enum
```

The *state/event/action* information has been stored in a two-dimensional table. To find out what *actions* need to be performed on a given *event*, the state machine just indexes into this table using the current *state* and *event* just received.

Each entry in the table contains a list of *actions* to perform in sequence, terminated by the special *action* "NoAction". Each entry also contains "Next State", which is the *state* that the Car to enter after performing the *actions*.

Note that the finite state machine (FSM) is part of the Car's implementation. The client code has remained the same in both the examples. Clients shouldn't be aware of how you have implemented the state of the object. (This is the power of object encapsulation.)

In the example it was decided that the state machine should be a separate abstraction. By doing this we have made the Car class simpler to understand. However this decision has introduced some compromises. For instance, the actions that Car can perform can no longer be private as the state machine (CarFSM class) needs to call these procedures. These procedures now have 'Friend' access to at least ensure that they are not visible outside of the component - only inside.

9.0 Activity Diagrams

These diagrams have a lot in common with Statechart diagrams in terms of the symbols used and their underlying meaning. However, instead of concentrating on the state of an *object*, they generally focus on the dynamic behavior of individual methods and the flow of *actions* within.

In VB terms, a single activity diagram usually maps to a single VB method. You should use activity diagrams *only* when dealing with *complex operations* that are easier to understand visually than in code.

The interesting items on activity diagrams are *action* and *transitions*. An *action* usually maps to either a single VB statement or a cohesive group of statements. We can see how this relates to our previous example. The procedure *call* to SoundAlarm can be treated as a single *action* in an *activity diagram*. *Transitions* are simply the invisible transition from one VB statement to the next so they don't have any concrete mapping to deal with.

The text associated with an *action*, can also be conveniently mapped to a comment near to the statements, particularly when the statements themselves aren't self-explanatory.

For completeness, here is an example activity diagram. This is the `PerformUseCase` operation on the *<<controller>> class* `TransferFunds` we looked at earlier:

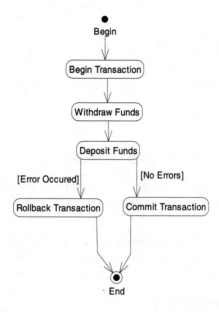

Note that the code mapped from this is identical to that produced from the sequence diagram for the same operation, so we won't repeat it.

10.0 Implementation Diagrams: Component & Deployment Diagrams

UML Notation	VB	Notes
Component	Project	The stereotype of the component determines the type of VB project.
Interface	'PublicNotCreatable' Class	

Table Continued on Following Page

UML Notation	VB	Notes
Node	None	Outside the scope of the language. Relates to a process such as a machine or a process inside that machine that is capable of running a program binary.

10.1 UML Components and Visual Basic

Components are hot stuff at the moment. However, the terminology of *components* can get very confusing at times. A *component* could be defined as any software artifact that is reusable. This could be a *class*, a user control or even a design document.

Still, when developers talk about components, we are usually referring to either *physical components*, i.e. Active X components, DLLs, etc. or *logical components*, i.e. Business Objects, such as Account, Sale, etc., contained and exposed from these *physical components*.

It's important to make a distinction here.

➢ Logical components expose services that applications can use, e.g. Account exposes the service Withdraw Cash.

➢ Physical components, on the other hand, are the *packaging* and *deployment* of these logical *components* and their partitioning is influenced by the technical requirements of the target system.

This is what Component Diagrams help us visualize.

10.2 Logical components

A **logical component** is simply a class in UML terms that expose a number of **interfaces**.

For mapping purposes, it is probably easier to look at an alternative but more familiar representation:

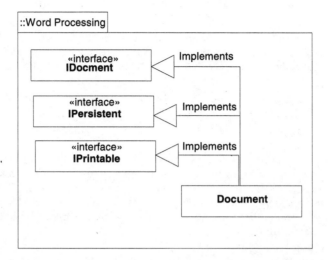

Components also have a private implementation, which typically involves one or more private *classes* that carry out the work for the *component*. The client code using the *component* via *interfaces* is completely unaware of how the services requested are being handled internally. This is the key strength of component development.

Any VB class in a Project that has an instancing property that is *not* private can be treated as a logical component. The classes in the project that have an instancing property of 'Private' are usually there to provide the implementation of the exposed components.

If we consider the Car example introduced in the Statechart mapping, the Car could be exposed as a logical component and the CarFSM would be part of the private implementation.

10.3 Physical Components

A physical *component* in UML is mapped to a VB Project, i.e. the project builds the *component*.

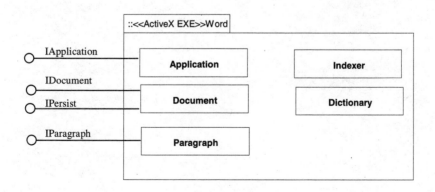

The UML can show a *component* offering many *interfaces* to its prospective users. Here is an example physical component together with exposed logical components and two hidden implementation classes:

However VB Developers should note that it isn't really the UML *component* that is offering *interface* - rather the *classes* within the *component* (project) that are marked as public. This is something that the UML is not clear about. It is likely that the distinction will be clarified in later drafts.

10.4 Stereotypes

The UML comes with a standard set of *stereotypes* for *components*:

An *<<executable>>* stereotype of component simply states that the item represents an executable file, such as 'program.exe', and can be individually deployed onto a node on a network.

A *<<file>>* component stereotype is nothing more than a physical file. However, this notation gives us the opportunity to model files and more importantly, show where files live on a network of *nodes* in the system we are building.

Most CASE tools extend the range of *stereotypes* available for *components* to cover those supported by target programming languages. Visual Basic, for instance, is capable of creating the following *component stereotypes*:

Stereotype	Meaning
<<ActiveX DLL>>	An ActiveX server packaged as a dynamic link library.
<<ActiveX EXE>>	An ActiveX server packaged as an executable program.
<<EXE>>	A regular Win32 executable (without COM).
<<DLL>	A regular Win32 dynamic link library.

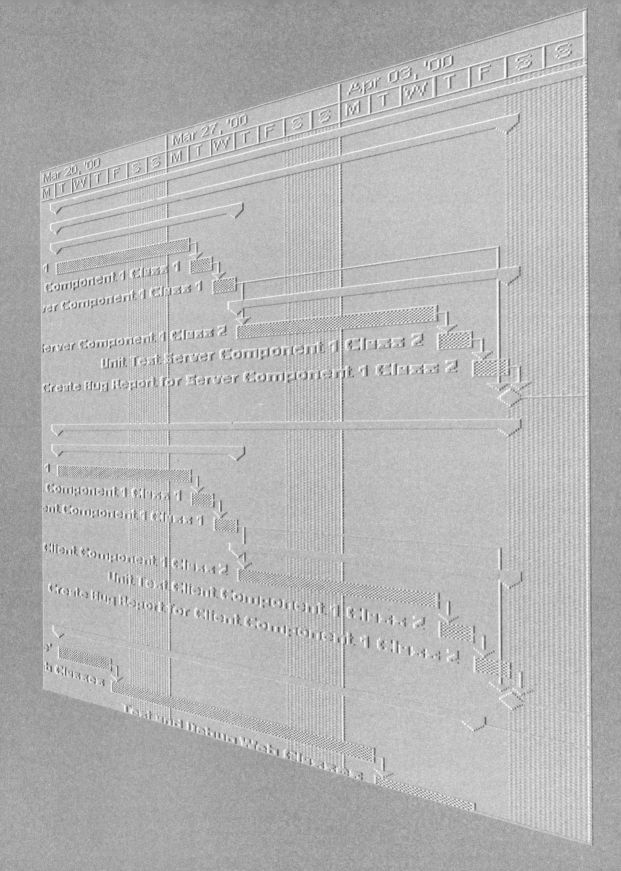

Creating a VB Code Generator Add-In

In this appendix I will show you how to create a Visual Basic application that will read from a database and generate code for a three-tier DNA application which will connect to this database. This code generator can be used to create the basis of any Visual Basic application, including the ones you are currently building. As you have all of the code here, you can customize the code generator for your needs.

When building a Visual Basic code generator application, you will actually have two projects, the application to generate the code and the application that will be generated. The application that is to be generated must be built from patterns so that we can use these patterns to generate the code.

We will covered the basic functioning of the code and provided UML class diagrams for all of the modules that are generated in Chapter 9, and the workings of this code are covered in detail in the VB6 UML book.

I have chosen to use an Access database for generating the code. I made this choice because most Visual Basic programmers are familiar with working with Access databases. We will generate an object for each table in the database. The field names in the tables will become the properties of the objects. The methods will be the standard methods for a recordset.

Instead of using an Access database, we could use the Microsoft Repository as the source of information for the code generator. The Microsoft Repository is a file that allows information, such as certain UML diagrams, to be stored in a universal format. Thus, regardless of the UML tool I am using, I can export my diagrams to the repository in one standard format. Using this standard format, I can read the data out.

If you wanted to use the repository for my code generator instead of the Access database, you would have to write one extra code module that reads the repository and adds tables to an Access database. The table names would be the names of the classes you want to generate and the table fields would be the names of the attributes you want the class to have. Thus, the following project I am providing can easily be expanded to generate code from any source; you just have to convert the information into Access tables.

Before we look at code generator itself, we must first look at the Visual Basic add-in object hierarchy. You might imagine that there would be tons of information on how to this, but actually, there is very little information out there. We will start by building a Visual Basic add-in and then move onto getting information on an Access database.

Building a Visual Basic Add-in

Being able to build your own add-ins is one of the more powerful features of Visual Basic. To make it work, you will need to do a few things. The first thing you must do is add your application into the .ini file that contains a list of Visual Basic add-ins. You may find it hard to imagine that we are still using an .ini file, but we are. If you do not remember what an .ini file is, it is simply a text file that contains information for a particular program. For the most part, it has been replaced by the registry.

The most critical piece of information that we put into the add-in .ini file is the identifier for the add-in. We will be using the standard project name dot class name. Let us begin by creating a function to add the information into the .ini file. Create a new Visual Basic ActiveX DLL project and call it `CodeGenerator`. Call the default class `CodeGeneratorClass`. Add a .bas module to the project and call it `basMain`. We are going to use an API function called `WritePrivateProfileString` to write to the .ini file. If you are not familiar with API functions, they are functions that are provided by Windows. We can use these functions in our Visual Basic application by declaring the function in our Visual Basic application in a .bas module using the `Declare` keyword. Add the following code to `basMain` to declare the windows function `WritePrivateProfileString` in your Visual Basic project:

```
Public Declare Function WritePrivateProfileString _
               Lib "kernel32" _
               Alias "WritePrivateProfileStringA" _
               (ByVal ApplicationName As String, _
               ByVal KeyName As Any, _
               ByVal KeyDefault As Any, _
               ByVal FileName As String) As Long
```

If you are wondering what all of this means, `kernel32` is the DLL where the function resides. The alias, `WritePrivateProfileStringA`, is the real name of the function (there are usually two versions, one for Unicode strings and one for regular strings). `WritePrivateProfileString` is the name we give it and which we will use in our code. `ApplicationName` is the name of the section that you want to add this information to `KeyName` is the information you want to put into the `ApplicationName` section `KeyDefault` is the default value of `ApplicationName`, and `FileName` is the name of the .ini file you want to put the information in. In our case, `ApplicationName` is `Add-Ins32`, the `KeyName` is `CodeGenerator.CodeGeneratorClass`, the `KeyDefault` is 0 and the name of the file is `VBADDIN.INI`. You can probably find `VBADDIN.INI` in your `Windows` directory. My `VBADDIN.INI` has the following entries:

```
[Add-Ins32]
MTxAddIn2.RegRefresh=3
DTCFrameWork.AddIn=0
RVBAddInMenus.Connector=0
RVBAddIn.Connector=0
vbscc=3
VBObjTest.Application.1=0
VisioUMLSolution.VisioUMLSolution=3
```

Of course, we could manually enter the name of our component into the `.ini` file, but it is safer to use the Windows API function.

Fortunately, Visual Basic now comes with a tool that allows us to get the proper declarations for all our Windows API functions. If you go to the Windows **Start/Programs/Microsoft Visual Studio 6/Microsoft Visual Studio 6 Tools/API Text Viewer** you will pull up the API text viewer. If it is the first time you are using it, you will have to load the information first. To do this, in the API Text Viewer Select **File/Load Text File**:

Select `Win32API.txt`. If you select **Declares** from the dropdown list, you will find our API function.

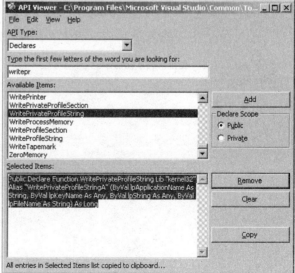

I have changed the names of the parameter in the function declaration. You can do this as long as you have the right number of parameters and each parameter has the correct data type.

API functions can extend the Visual Basic language. For the most part these functions have been wrapped by functions within Visual Basic. Sometimes, though, using an API function is the only way to get the information you require or to do what you need to do.

Next we will add a function that uses our Windows API, called `AddToIni`, to `basMain`:

```
Public Sub AddToINI()
    Dim lngReturn As Long
    lngReturn = WritePrivateProfileString("Add-Ins32", _
    "CodeGenerator.CodeGeneratorClass", "0", "VBADDIN.INI")
    MsgBox "Add-in is now entered in VBADDIN.INI file."
End Sub
```

We will show an easy way to use this sub later. The next step is to get access to the Visual Basic IDE object hierarchy so that we can manipulate objects in the Visual Basic IDE. To do this, we will need access to the extensibility object.

Visual Basic Extensibility Object

For our purposes we will be interested in two parts of the extensibility object. The most important is the `VBIDE` object, which contains everything we need to fully manipulate the Visual Basic IDE. The `VBIDE` main object is the Visual Basic Editor or VBE. The VBE has many objects with many properties and methods. We will only look at a few of the properties and methods. First, let us consider what we want to do. To generate a project we will need to do the following:

> We will make an ActiveX control project for each table in the database. We will therefore need to add a new project to the group for each table.

> As we will discuss in more detail below, each project will consist of two classes, the control and a `.bas` module. Therefore, we will need the ability to add modules to our Visual Basic projects.

> We will need to add references to our project.

> We will need to change the names of the project and the parts of the project.

The VBE object hierarchy looks as follows:

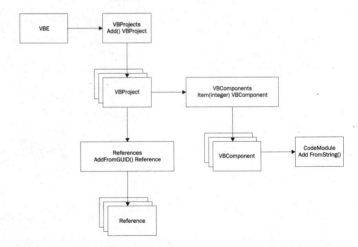

We have included the methods that we will be using with the objects.

You can see that the VBE object is the main managing object of the Visual Basic IDE. The VBProjects object manages VBProject objects, the References object manages Reference objects and the VBComponents object manages VBComponent objects. As you can see, this object hierarchy is built just like the business services components we discussed in Chapter 8, except that this hierarchy is a little more complex and it has more objects and levels. If you look at the managing classes in the Visual Basic object browser, you will see that they consist primarily of methods. The managed classes are primarily properties.

The methods that we will need to use are:

> The Add method of the VBProjects object, which will return a new VBProject object.

> The AddFromGUID method of the References object, which will add a new reference object to the project object based on the GUID of the reference.

> The Item method of the VBComponents object which will return one of the project's components, such as a class or a form.

> The AddFromString method of the CodeModule object that allows you to use a string to add code to a module.

Now let us take a look at the CodeGenerator project that we will use to create this project.

Finishing BasMain

We will need some information from the database so we can know how to write our functions properly. Remember, we are using tables from an Access database as the basis for our components. Therefore, we will need to know the table name so that we can set the name of our component to it. We will also have to know the names of the fields for our properties and we will have to know the data types for each property. We will also need to store information on the queries that will be used to get the information from the database. To help keep track of all of this information, we will add the following enumerated types to the declarations section of the basMain module:

```
Public Type FieldInformation
    FieldName As String
    PropertyName As String
    DataType As String
End Type
```

```
Public Type TableInformation
    TableName As String
    FieldInfo() As FieldInformation
    PrimaryKey As String
End Type
```

It is possible that the field names may have spaces or other characters that will have to be removed if they are going to be used as names of classes, .bas modules or variables in Visual Basic. To do this, we will need a function that strips out these characters. Add this function to basMain:

```
Public Sub CleanFields(ByRef r_uFieldInfo() As FieldInformation, _
                       ByRef r_sFieldNames() As String)
Dim lngFieldCounter As Long
ReDim r_sFieldNames(1 To UBound(r_uFieldInfo))
For lngFieldCounter = 1 To UBound(r_uFieldInfo)
    r_sFieldNames(lngFieldCounter) = r_uFieldInfo(lngFieldCounter).FieldName
    Do While InStr(1, r_sFieldNames(lngFieldCounter), " ") > 0
        If InStr(1, r_sFieldNames(lngFieldCounter), " ") > 0 Then
            Dim lngLocationSpace As Long
            Dim lngLengthString As Long
            Dim strFieldName As String
            strFieldName = r_sFieldNames(lngFieldCounter)
            lngLocationSpace = InStr(1, strFieldName, " ")
            lngLengthString = Len(strFieldName)
            r_sFieldNames(lngFieldCounter) = _
                Left(strFieldName, lngLocationSpace - 1) & _
                Right(strFieldName, lngLengthString - lngLocationSpace)
        End If
    Loop
Next
End Sub
```

This function takes the string array parameter r_sFieldNames() and places names into the array that do not have spaces. The r_uFieldInfo parameter is filled with all of the field names from the table that a business object is currently being built from. The For loop enumerates through all of the fields that are in the r_uFieldInfo variable. Within the For loop we set the current r_sFieldNames() array member equal to the current r_uFieldInfo array member. The Do loop enumerates through the name of the field until all of the spaces have been removed. The Left and Right statements simple divide the string up into two pieces, the section before the space and the section after the space, and then join the two pieces together again.

Writing the Code for the Code Generator

We will use .bas modules to hold the code needed to generate the different modules. For each section, we will build the code modules with a single string. Then, using the Visual Basic IDE, we will add these strings into projects to build our components. Thus, we must take the code from our project and convert it into strings that can be placed into the Visual Basic IDE to generate the code for the project.

Coding the Bas Module

Add a module called BuildBas to your project. This module will be used to build the .bas module associated with each business component. We will begin with a General Declarations section to create enumerated types and constants needed for the project.

In our generated code, the declarations in the .bas module for the customer component will look as follows:

```
Option Explicit

Public Enum CustomerErrors
    errChangeFieldNoEdit = 1001
    errEditPrimaryKey = 1002
    errPrimaryKeyLength = 1003
    errCustomerTitleType = 1004
End Enum

Public Const g_cstrFieldCustomerID As String = "CustomerID"
Public Const g_cstrFieldAddress As String = "Address"
Public Const g_cstrFieldCity As String = "City"
Public Const g_cstrFieldCompanyName As String = "CompanyName"
Public Const g_cstrFieldContactName As String = "ContactName"
Public Const g_cstrFieldContactTitle As String = "ContactTitle"
Public Const g_cstrFieldCountry As String = "Country"
Public Const g_cstrFieldFax As String = "Fax"
Public Const g_cstrFieldPhone As String = "Phone"
Public Const g_cstrFieldPostalCode As String = "PostalCode"
Public Const g_cstrFieldRegion As String = "Region"
Public Const g_cstrFieldProductName As String = "ProductName"

Public Const g_cdmAllCustomers As String = "AllCustomers"
Public Const g_cdmCustomersContactTitleEquals As String = _
    "CustomersContactTitleEquals"
```

For our code generator, we need to find a way to generate these declarations for any component we are generating. Looking at the error-enumerated type, we can see the first three are general errors. We can include these three errors in all of the classes to give the developer a place to add the rest of the errors.

The constants are based on the names of the fields. Thus, if we move through the fields, we can create a template string that will give us all of the public constants. The template for these would look as follows:

```
Public Const g_cstrField & FieldName As String = "FieldName"
```

The last two constants are used for the where clause to create groups. In the case of customer, we can choose all customers or customers whose contact title equals some value. To simplify things, we will only create a where clause from the primary key. If the developer needs additional where clause items, they can add them.

Begin by creating a function called CreateDeclarations. The basis for this code module is the following code:

```
Public Enum CustomerErrors
    errChangeFieldNoEdit = 1001
    errEditPrimaryKey = 1002
    errPrimaryKeyLength = 1003
End Enum

Public Const g_cstrFieldCustomerID As String = "CustomerID"
Public Const g_cdmAllCustomers As String = "AllCustomers"
```

485

Put the following code into the `BuildBas` module:

```
Public Function CreateDeclarations _
                (ByRef v_uFieldInfo() As FieldInformation, _
                ByVal v_sPrimaryKey As String, _
                ByVal v_sTableName As String)
```

The first parameter is a `FieldInformation` object which will have information on the fields in the table that is currently being used to build a business object. The primary key will be used to make where clauses. The table name is needed to make constants.

We will need to declare the following variables:

```
Dim lngFieldCounter As Long
Dim strCode As String
Dim strFieldNames() As String
```

The `strFieldNames` variable will be passed into the `CleanFields` function so it will hold the names of the fields without spaces. The `strCode` variable will be the variable we will use to hold the string with all of the declarations.

Next, send `strFieldNames` and `v_uFieldInfo` into the `CleanFields` function:

```
CleanFields v_uFieldInfo, strFieldNames
```

Now, we can actually start building the code for the module. We want to create an enumerated type with possible errors for this object. We want the enumerated type's name to be based on the table name so we will add that into the name of the enumerated type. First, though, we need to remove any spaces from the name:

```
Dim strTableName As String
strTableName = v_sTableName
Do Until InStr(strTableName, " ") = 0
    Dim lngSpace As Long
    lngSpace = InStr(strTableName, " ")
    strTableName = Left(strTableName, lngSpace - 1) & _
                   Right(strTableName, Len(strTableName) - lngSpace)
Loop
strCode = strCode & "Public Enum " & strTableName & "Errors" & _
          Chr(13) & Chr(10)
```

We will add the three standard errors to our modules:

```
strCode = strCode & " errChangeFieldNoEdit = 1001" & Chr(13) & Chr(10)
strCode = strCode & " errEditPrimaryKey = 1002" & Chr(13) & Chr(10)
strCode = strCode & " errPrimaryKeyLength = 1003" & Chr(13) & Chr(10)
strCode = strCode & "End Enum" & Chr(13) & Chr(10)
```

We want the names of the fields to all be placed into one place. To do this, we will create constants for each field name using the names stored in the `strFieldNames` array. Each constant will begin with `g_cstrField` followed by the name of the field:

```
    For lngFieldCounter = 1 To UBound(v_uFieldInfo)
        strCode = strCode & "Public Const g_cstrField" & _
                strFieldNames(lngFieldCounter) & " As String = " & _
                Chr(34) & v_uFieldInfo(lngFieldCounter).FieldName & _
                Chr(34) & Chr(13) & Chr(10)
    Next
```

Finally, we will make a constant that will be used to make a where clause based on the primary key and set the function to the string we have built.

```
    strCode = strCode & "Public Const g_cdm" & v_sPrimaryKey & _
            " As String = " & Chr(34) & v_sPrimaryKey & "Equals" & _
            Chr(34) & Chr(13) & Chr(10)
    CreateDeclarations = strCode
    End Function
```

The final result of this function for the Northwind database for the `Customers` class would look as follows:

```
Public Enum CustomersErrors
    errChangeFieldNoEdit = 1001
    errEditPrimaryKey = 1002
    errPrimaryKeyLength = 1003
End Enum
Public Const g_cstrFieldAddress As String = "Address"
Public Const g_cstrFieldCity As String = "City"
Public Const g_cstrFieldCompanyName As String = "CompanyName"
Public Const g_cstrFieldContactName As String = "ContactName"
Public Const g_cstrFieldContactTitle As String = "ContactTitle"
Public Const g_cstrFieldCountry As String = "Country"
Public Const g_cstrFieldCustomerID As String = "CustomerID"
Public Const g_cstrFieldFax As String = "Fax"
Public Const g_cstrFieldPhone As String = "Phone"
Public Const g_cstrFieldPostalCode As String = "PostalCode"
Public Const g_cstrFieldRegion As String = "Region"
Public Const g_cdmCustomerID As String = "CustomerIDEquals"
```

When making a code generator, you would start with the coded project. Using this and the UML diagrams as a template, you can find the patterns that you will need to build your code. We will be doing this with the rest of the code from the project in the VB6 UML book. You can compare the generalized code in the generator with the code in the VB6 UML book. Where the code sample used generic terms, we will copy it exactly. Where specific names are used, such as customer or address, we will need to create generic strings and create loops.

Let us now add the function to read errors. Add the following code to `BuildBas`:

```
Public Function CreateErrorFunc()

Dim strCode as String
strCode = "Public Function GetErrorText" & _
    " (ByVal v_lngErrorNumber As Long)" & Chr(13) & Chr(10)
strCode = strCode & " On Error GoTo GetErrorText_Error" & Chr(13) & Chr(10)
strCode = strCode & " GetErrorText = LoadResString(v_lngErrorNumber)" & _
    Chr(13) & Chr(10)
strCode = strCode & " Exit Function" & Chr(13) & Chr(10)
strCode = strCode & "GetErrorText_Error:" & Chr(13) & Chr(10)
strCode = strCode & " If Err.Number <> 0 Then" & Chr(13) & Chr(10)
strCode = strCode & " GetErrorText =" & Chr(34) & _
    "An unknown error has occurred, the error was not found" & _
    Chr(34) & Chr(13) & Chr(10)
strCode = strCode & " End If" & Chr(13) & Chr(10)
strCode = strCode & "End Function" & Chr(13) & Chr(10)
CreateErrorFunc = strCode

End Function
```

Let us now move on to coding the bottom class.

Coding the Bottom Class

For the bottom class we need to take the fields from each Access table and make them into properties in the bottom class. Once again we will need to make the **General Declarations** section. Add a new `.bas` module to the `CodeGenerator` project and call it `BuildBottom` and add the following sections to the `BuildBottom` class:

Bottom Class Declarations

```
Public Function CreateDeclarations() As String
Dim strCode As String
strCode = strCode & " Private m_blnValidatingFieldChange As Boolean" & _
    Chr(13) & Chr(10)
strCode = strCode & " Private m_eEditMode As ADODB.EditModeEnum" & _
    Chr(13) & Chr(10)
strCode = strCode & " Private m_strErrorDetails As String" & Chr(13) & _
    Chr(10)
strCode = strCode & " Private m_blnIgnoreFieldChange As Boolean" & _
    Chr(13) & Chr(10)
strCode = strCode & " Private m_blnInFieldChange As Boolean" & _
    Chr(13) & Chr(10)
strCode = strCode & " Private m_avarAcceptableValuesTitle As Variant" & _
    Chr(13) & Chr(10)
strCode = strCode & " Private m_strManagedObjectDataMember As String" & _
    Chr(13) & Chr(10)
strCode = strCode & " Private WithEvents m_recManagedObjects As " & _
    " ADODB.Recordset" & Chr(13) & Chr(10)
strCode = strCode & " Public Event RefreshDataMember()" & Chr(13) & _
    Chr(10)
strCode =strCode & " Public Event EditInProgress(ByVal v_strEditMode)" & _
    Chr(13) & Chr(10)
CreateDeclarations = strCode
End Function
```

The code that we will generate will have a disconnected `Recordset` object that can be accessed by this class and also by the managing class. This recordset will be passed to controls such as textboxes or gridboxes. The recordset will also be used to retrieve the values of the properties, instead of keeping private variables for all of the properties. The event `RefreshDataMember` will alert the managing class that it needs to refresh the bound controls. `EditInProgress` will alert the managing class that an edit has been started by changing a field value. Let us now add the class `Initialize` event.

Class Initialize

We will have to initialize our objects in the `Class_Initialize` event. Add the function `CreateInitialize` to the `BuildBottom .bas` module to generate the `Class_Intialize` event:

```
Public Function CreateInitialize() As String
Dim strCode As String

strCode = " Private Sub Class_Initialize()" & Chr(13) & Chr(10)
strCode = strCode & " m_blnValidatingFieldChange = False" & Chr(13) & Chr(10)
strCode = strCode & " m_blnIgnoreFieldChange = False" & Chr(13) & Chr(10)
strCode = strCode & " m_blnInFieldChange = False" & Chr(13) & Chr(10) & _
          Chr(13) & Chr(10)
strCode = strCode & " On Error GoTo InitializeError" & Chr(13) & Chr(10)
strCode = strCode & " m_eEditMode = adEditNone" & Chr(13) & Chr(10)
strCode = strCode & " Set m_recManagedObjects = New ADODB.Recordset" & _
          Chr(13) & Chr(10)
strCode = strCode & " Exit Sub" & Chr(13) & Chr(10)
strCode = strCode & "InitializeError:" & Chr(13) & Chr(10)
strCode = strCode & " MsgBox " & Chr(34) & "Error In Class Initialize" & _
          Chr(34) & Chr(13) & Chr(10)
strCode = strCode & "End Sub"
CreateInitialize = strCode
End Function
```

Class Terminate

We will also need to clean up when the class is done. Add the following code to make our `Class_Terminate` event:

```
Public Function CreateTerminate()

Dim strCode As String
strCode = strCode & "Private Sub Class_Terminate()" & Chr(13) & Chr(10)
strCode = strCode & " If Not m_recManagedObjects Is Nothing Then" & Chr(13) & _
          Chr(10)
strCode = strCode & " With ItemsRecordset" & Chr(13) & Chr(10)
strCode = strCode & " If .State = adStateOpen Then" & Chr(13) & Chr(10)
strCode = strCode & " If Not .BOF And Not .EOF Then" & Chr(13) & Chr(10)
strCode = strCode & " If .EditMode <> adEditNone Then" & Chr(13) & Chr(10)
strCode = strCode & " .CancelUpdate" & Chr(13) & Chr(10)
strCode = strCode & " End If" & Chr(13) & Chr(10)
strCode = strCode & " .Close" & Chr(13) & Chr(10)
strCode = strCode & " End If" & Chr(13) & Chr(10)
strCode = strCode & " End If" & Chr(13) & Chr(10)
strCode = strCode & " End With" & Chr(13) & Chr(10)
strCode = strCode & " Set m_recManagedObjects = Nothing" & Chr(13) & Chr(10)
strCode = strCode & " End If" & Chr(13) & Chr(10)
strCode = strCode & "End Sub" & Chr(13) & Chr(10)
CreateTerminate = strCode
End Function
```

Creating the ValidateFields Function

We will need a function to validate the fields if they are changed in the recordset by a bound control. Add this function to `BuildBottom`:

```
Public Function CreateValidateFields(ByRef r_uFieldInfo() As _
                                     FieldInformation) As String
Dim strCode As String
Dim lngFieldsCounter As Long
Dim strFieldNames() As String

CleanFields r_uFieldInfo, strFieldNames


strCode = "Friend Function ValidateFields(ByVal v_vFields As Variant, _" & _
        Chr(13) & Chr(10)
strCode = strCode & " ByVal v_recRecordset As ADODB.Recordset) " & _
        " As Boolean" & Chr(13) & Chr(10)
strCode = strCode & " On Error GoTo ValidateFieldsError" & Chr(13) & _
        Chr(10)
strCode = strCode & " m_blnValidatingFieldChange = True" & Chr(13) & _
        Chr(10)
strCode = strCode & " Select Case LCase(v_vFields(0).Name)" & Chr(13) & _
        Chr(10)
For lngFieldsCounter = 1 To UBound(r_uFieldInfo)
    strCode = strCode & " Case g_cstrField" & _
            strFieldNames(lngFieldsCounter) & Chr(13) & Chr(10)
    strCode = strCode & " " & strFieldNames(lngFieldsCounter) & _
            " = v_recRecordset.Fields(g_cstrField" & _
    strFieldNames(lngFieldsCounter) & ")" & Chr(13) & Chr(10)
Next
strCode = strCode & " Case Else" & Chr(13) & Chr(10)
strCode = strCode & " ValidateFields = False" & Chr(13) & Chr(10)
strCode = strCode & " End Select" & Chr(13) & Chr(10)
strCode = strCode & " m_blnValidatingFieldChange = False" & Chr(13) & _
        Chr(10)
strCode = strCode & " ValidateFields = True" & Chr(13) & Chr(10)
strCode = strCode & " Exit Function" & Chr(13) & Chr(10)
strCode = strCode & "ValidateFieldsError:" & Chr(13) & Chr(10)
strCode = strCode & " ValidateFields = False" & Chr(13) & Chr(10)
strCode = strCode & " m_blnValidatingFieldChange = False" & Chr(13) & _
        Chr(10)
strCode = strCode & " Err.Clear" & Chr(13) & Chr(10)
strCode = strCode & "End Function" & Chr(13) & Chr(10)
CreateValidateFields = strCode
End Function
```

Changed Field Event

We created our recordset variable with events. We want to be able to capture any changes to the recordset using the change field event. When a field has changed, we will want to validate this change if it was made through the recordset. If the change was made through the properties or by the recordset, we want to refresh the controls bound to the bottom and managing objects. We will add the code for this method into our `BuildBottom` module:

```
Public Function CreateChangedField() As String
```

We will begin by coding the event exactly as an ADO recordset would create it:

```
Dim strCode As String
strCode = strCode & "Private Sub " & _
        "m_recManagedObjects_FieldChangeComplete(ByVal cFields As Long," & _
        "ByVal Fields As Variant, ByVal pError As ADODB.Error," & _
        "adStatus As ADODB.EventStatusEnum, " & _
        "ByVal pRecordset As ADODB.Recordset)" & Chr(13) & Chr(10)
```

Next we will set up error handling and check to see if the flag that tells us to not validate field changes has been set:

```
strCode = strCode & " On Error GoTo FieldChangeError" & Chr(13) & Chr(10)
strCode = strCode & " If m_blnIgnoreFieldChange = True Then" & Chr(13) & _
        Chr(10)
```

If the flag is set to true, this change occurred by a property changing the field. In this case, we want to reset it to false, refresh all controls bound to this object and the managing object and exit the function without validating the fields:

```
strCode = strCode & " m_blnIgnoreFieldChange = False" & Chr(13) & _
        Chr(10)
```

When using data provider classes, we must call the `DataMemberChanged` function to refresh the controls bound to this object:

```
strCode = strCode & " DataMemberChanged ItemsDataMember" & Chr(13) & _
        Chr(10)
```

We must now pass a message up to the managing class that it must refresh all of the controls that it is bound to:

```
strCode = strCode & " RaiseEvent RefreshDataMember" & Chr(13) & Chr(10)
strCode = strCode & " Exit Sub" & Chr(13) & Chr(10)
strCode = strCode & " End If" & Chr(13) & Chr(10)
```

If this field change is being called because this routine has made a change to the field value, we will end up in an infinite loop. To check this we check the `m_bInFieldChange` flag. If it is true, this routine has been called by a change in a previous call to this routine and we should exit the function:

```
strCode = strCode & " If m_blnInFieldChange = True Then" & Chr(13) & _
        Chr(10)
strCode = strCode & " m_blnInFieldChange = False" & Chr(13) & Chr(10)
strCode = strCode & " Exit Sub" & Chr(13) & Chr(10)
strCode = strCode & " End If" & Chr(13) & Chr(10)
```

If there are no records to validate or the recordset is not open, there is nothing to check, so we should exit:

```
strCode = strCode & " If m_recManagedObjects.RecordCount = 0 _" & _
    Chr(13) & Chr(10)
strCode = strCode & " Or m_recManagedObjects.State <> adStateOpen Then" & _
    Chr(13) & Chr(10)
strCode = strCode & " Exit Sub" & Chr(13) & Chr(10)
strCode = strCode & " End If" & Chr(13) & Chr(10)
```

If we are in the middle of deleting a record, we do not need to validate a field change:

```
strCode = strCode & " If EditMode = adEditDelete Then" & Chr(13) & Chr(10)
strCode = strCode & " Exit Sub" & Chr(13) & Chr(10)
strCode = strCode & " End If" & Chr(13) & Chr(10)
```

If an edit has been started by changing a field in the recordset, we need to set the EditMode property:

```
strCode = strCode & " If EditMode = adEditNone Then" & Chr(13) & Chr(10)
strCode = strCode & " EditMode = adEditInProgress" & Chr(13) & Chr(10)
strCode = strCode & " RaiseEvent EditInProgress(adEditInProgress)" & _
    Chr(13) & Chr(10)
strCode = strCode & " End If" & Chr(13) & Chr(10)
```

Finally, if we get to this point it means that we are doing an AddNew or Edit and we need to now validate the field. To do this we will pass the fields and the recordset into the ValidateFields function. If this function returns false, the record change is not valid:

```
strCode = strCode & "If ValidateFields(Fields, pRecordset) = False Then" & _
    Chr(13) & Chr(10)
```

If ValidateFields comes back false, this was an invalid change and we must set the value back to the original field value:

```
strCode = strCode & " m_blnInFieldChange = True" & Chr(13) & Chr(10)
strCode = strCode & " m_recManagedObjects.Fields(Fields(0).Name).Value" & _
    " = _ " & Chr(13) & Chr(10)
strCode = strCode & " pRecordset.Fields(Fields(0).Name).UnderlyingValue" & _
    Chr(13) & Chr(10)
strCode = strCode & " m_blnInFieldChange = False" & Chr(13) & Chr(10)
strCode = strCode & " End If" & Chr(13) & Chr(10)
```

As before, we must refresh the bound controls:

```
strCode = strCode & " DataMemberChanged ItemsDataMember" & Chr(13) & _
    Chr(10)
strCode = strCode & " RaiseEvent RefreshDataMember" & Chr(13) & Chr(10)
```

Finally, we write the error trap:

```
strCode = strCode & " Exit Sub" & Chr(13) & Chr(10)
strCode = strCode & "FieldChangeError:" & Chr(13) & Chr(10)
strCode = strCode & " Err.Raise Err.Number, " & Chr(34) & "FieldChange " & _
        Chr(34) & " & Err.Source, Err.Description" & Chr(13) & Chr(10)
strCode = strCode & "End Sub" & Chr(13) & Chr(10)
CreateChangedField = strCode
End Function
```

As you can see, this is no different than coding the real module, except everything is wrapped in quotes and has a `Chr(13) & Chr(10)` at the end to add a carriage return and line feed.

Get and Let Functions

We will now need to add the properties to our bottom class. Add the following function to the `BuildBottom` module:

```
Public Function CreateGetLet(ByRef r_uFieldInfo() As FieldInformation) _
                        As String

Dim strCode As String
Dim lngFieldsCounter As Long
Dim strFieldNames() As String
```

We will need to use the `CleanFields` function again as we want to use names without spaces for our property names:

```
CleanFields r_uFieldInfo, strFieldNames
```

For each member in the fields array, we will need to add a property. To get the total number of items in a one-based array (an array that starts with item 1) we can use `Ubound`. We will show you later how we built our arrays to be one-based instead of zero-based.

```
For lngFieldsCounter = 1 To UBound(r_uFieldInfo)
```

We will now create the `Property Get` using the field name without spaces and the data type parameter of the `r_uFieldInfo` user-defined type:

```
strCode = strCode & "Public Property Get " & _
        strFieldNames(lngFieldsCounter) & "() As " & _
        r_uFieldInfo(lngFieldsCounter).DataType & Chr(13) & Chr(10)
```

We will use the recordset to get the value of the field:

```
strCode = strCode & " On Error Resume Next" & Chr(13) & Chr(10)
strCode = strCode & " " & strFieldNames(lngFieldsCounter) & _
        "= ItemsRecordset.Fields(g_cstrField" & _
        strFieldNames(lngFieldsCounter) & ")" & Chr(13) & Chr(10)
strCode = strCode & " If Err.Number <> 0 Then" & Chr(13) & Chr(10)
```

We will ignore errors caused by a field not being found:

```
strCode = strCode & " If Err.Number <> 3265 Then" & Chr(13) & _
        Chr(10)
strCode = strCode & " Err.Raise Err.Number, " & Chr(34) & _
        strFieldNames(lngFieldsCounter) & "Get" & Chr(34) & _
        ", Err.Description" & Chr(13) & Chr(10)
strCode = strCode & " End If" & Chr(13) & Chr(10)
strCode = strCode & " End If" & Chr(13) & Chr(10)
strCode = strCode & "End Property" & Chr(13) & Chr(10)
```

Our `Let Property` routines will be built in a similar manner:

```
strCode = strCode & "Public Property Let " & _
        strFieldNames(lngFieldsCounter) & "(ByVal v_strNew" & _
        strFieldNames(lngFieldsCounter) & " As " & _
        r_uFieldInfo(lngFieldsCounter).DataType & ")" & Chr(13) & Chr(10)
strCode = strCode & " On Error GoTo " & _
        strFieldNames(lngFieldsCounter) & "LetError" & Chr(13) & Chr(10)
strCode = strCode & " If m_blnValidatingFieldChange = True Then" & _
        Chr(13) & Chr(10)
strCode = strCode & " Exit Property" & Chr(13) & Chr(10)
strCode = strCode & " End If" & Chr(13) & Chr(10)
strCode = strCode & " If m_eEditMode = adEditInProgress " & _
        "Or m_eEditMode = adEditAdd Then" & Chr(13) & Chr(10)
strCode = strCode & " m_blnIgnoreFieldChange = True" & Chr(13) & _
        Chr(10)
strCode = strCode & " ItemsRecordset.Fields(g_cstrField" & _
        strFieldNames(lngFieldsCounter) & ") = v_strNew" & _
        strFieldNames(lngFieldsCounter) & "" & Chr(13) & Chr(10)
strCode = strCode & " ElseIf m_eEditMode = adEditNone Then" & _
        Chr(13) & Chr(10)
strCode = strCode & " Err.Raise 1001," & Chr(34) & _
        strFieldNames(lngFieldsCounter) & " Let:" & Chr(34) & _
        ", GetErrorText(errChangeFieldNoEdit)" & Chr(13) & Chr(10)
strCode = strCode & " End If" & Chr(13) & Chr(10)
strCode = strCode & " Exit Property" & Chr(13) & Chr(10)
strCode = strCode & strFieldNames(lngFieldsCounter) & "LetError:" & _
        Chr(13) & Chr(10)
strCode = strCode & " Err.Raise Err.Number, " & Chr(34) & _
        strFieldNames(lngFieldsCounter) & " Let " & Chr(34) & _
        " & Err.Source, Err.Description" & Chr(13) & Chr(10)
strCode = strCode & "End Property" & Chr(13) & Chr(10)

Next
CreateGetLet = strCode
End Function
```

Miscellaneous Properties

We still have several properties, such as `EditMode`, that need to be created. We will lump these together into one function:

```
Public Function CreateMiscProps(ByVal v_sTableName As String) As String

Dim strCode As String
strCode = "Public Property Get EditMode() As ADODB.EditModeEnum" & _
    Chr(13) & Chr(10)
strCode = strCode & " EditMode = m_eEditMode" & Chr(13) & Chr(10)
strCode = strCode & "End Property" & Chr(13) & Chr(10)
strCode = strCode & "Friend Property Let EditMode" & _
    " (ByVal v_eNewEditMode As ADODB.EditModeEnum)" & Chr(13) & Chr(10)
strCode = strCode & " m_eEditMode = v_eNewEditMode" & Chr(13) & Chr(10)
strCode = strCode & " RaiseEvent EditInProgress(v_eNewEditMode)" & _
    Chr(13) & Chr(10)
strCode = strCode & "End Property" & Chr(13) & Chr(10)
strCode = strCode & "Friend Property Let ItemsDataMember(ByVal v_strNew" & _
    v_sTableName & "DataMember As String)" & Chr(13) & Chr(10)
strCode = strCode & " m_strManagedObjectDataMember = v_strNew" & _
    v_sTableName & "DataMember" & Chr(13) & Chr(10)
strCode = strCode & "End Property" & Chr(13) & Chr(10)
strCode = strCode & "Private Property Get ItemsDataMember() As String" & _
    Chr(13) & Chr(10)
strCode = strCode & " ItemsDataMember = m_strManagedObjectDataMember" & _
    Chr(13) & Chr(10)
strCode = strCode & "End Property" & Chr(13) & Chr(10)
strCode = strCode & "Friend Sub RefreshDataMember()" & Chr(13) & Chr(10)
strCode = strCode & " DataMemberChanged ItemsDataMember" & Chr(13) & _
    Chr(10)
strCode = strCode & "End Sub" & Chr(13) & Chr(10)
strCode = strCode & "Friend Property Get ItemsRecordset() As " & _
    " ADODB.Recordset" & Chr(13) & Chr(10)
strCode = strCode & " Set ItemsRecordset = m_recManagedObjects" & _
    Chr(13) & Chr(10)
strCode = strCode & "End Property" & Chr(13) & Chr(10)
strCode = strCode & "Friend Property Set ItemsRecordset" & _
    " (ByVal v_recNewRecordset As ADODB.Recordset)" & Chr(13) & Chr(10)
strCode = strCode & " Set m_recManagedObjects = v_recNewRecordset" & _
    Chr(13) & Chr(10)
strCode = strCode & "End Property" & Chr(13) & Chr(10)
strCode = strCode & "Private Sub Class_GetDataMember" & _
    " (DataMember As String, Data As Object)" & Chr(13) & Chr(10)
strCode = strCode & " Set Data = m_recManagedObjects" & Chr(13) & Chr(10)
strCode = strCode & "End Sub" & Chr(13) & Chr(10)
CreateMiscProps = strCode
End Function
```

This completes the code to generate the bottom class.

Generating the Middle Class

The middle class will be made up of mostly methods to manage the bottom class. We will begin by adding another `.bas` module to our project and call it `BuildMiddle`.

Creating the Declarations

We will begin with code to create the declarations section of our code. Add a function called `CreateDeclartions`. It will be coded in a similar manner as the previous component. The `r_TableInfo` will be a string array of table names with the spaces removed. We will use `r_TableInfo` to build the following enumerated type:

```
Enum TableName
    e_Categories = 0
    e_Customers = 1
    e_Employees = 2
    e_Order Details = 3
    e_Orders = 4
    e_Products = 5
    e_Shippers = 6
    e_Suppliers = 7
End Enum
```

The `v_sTableName` parameter is the name of the table without spaces of the component it is being built from:

```
Public Function CreateDeclarartions(ByRef r_TableInfo() As String, ByVal _
                              v_sTableName As String) As String
Dim strCode As String
Dim lngTableCounter As Long
Dim strTempTableName As String
```

We will build our enumerated type first:

```
strCode = strCode & "Enum TableName" & Chr(13) & Chr(10)
For lngTableCounter = 1 To UBound(r_TableInfo)
    strTempTableName = r_TableInfo(lngTableCounter)
    strCode = strCode & " e_" & r_TableInfo(lngTableCounter) & _
            "=" & lngTableCounter - 1 & Chr(13) & Chr(10)
Next
strCode = strCode & "End Enum" & Chr(13) & Chr(10)
```

We will now build the `BOFActionType` and `EOFActionType` enumerated types to determine the behaviour at the end of file and beginning of file:

```
strCode = strCode & "Public Enum BOFActionType" & Chr(13) & Chr(10)
strCode = strCode & " adMoveFirst = 0" & Chr(13) & Chr(10)
strCode = strCode & " adStayBOF = 1" & Chr(13) & Chr(10)
strCode = strCode & "End Enum" & Chr(13) & Chr(10)
strCode = strCode & "Public Enum EOFActionType" & Chr(13) & Chr(10)
strCode = strCode & " adMoveLast = 0" & Chr(13) & Chr(10)
strCode = strCode & " adStayEOF = 1" & Chr(13) & Chr(10)
strCode = strCode & " adAddNew = 2" & Chr(13) & Chr(10)
strCode = strCode & "End Enum" & Chr(13) & Chr(10)
```

Finally, we add the constants and variables needed by the managing class:

```
strCode = strCode & "Private m_eRecordsetName As TableName" & Chr(13) & _
    Chr(10)
strCode = strCode & "Private m_strWhereClause As String" & Chr(13) & Chr(10)
strCode = strCode & "Private m_strDataMember As String" & Chr(13) & Chr(10)
strCode = strCode & "Private m_strPrimaryKey As String" & Chr(13) & Chr(10)
strCode = strCode & "Private m_eBOFAction As BOFActionType" & Chr(13) & _
    Chr(10)
strCode = strCode & "Private m_eEOFAction As EOFActionType" & Chr(13) & _
    Chr(10)
strCode = strCode & "Private m_strUserName As String" & Chr(13) & Chr(10)
strCode = strCode & "Private m_strPassword As String" & Chr(13) & Chr(10)
strCode = strCode & "Private m_eEditMode As ADODB.EditModeEnum" & _
    Chr(13) & Chr(10)
strCode = strCode & "Private WithEvents m_objManagedObject As cls" & _
    v_sTableName & Chr(13) & Chr(10)
strCode = strCode & "Public Event ChangeManagedObjects()" & Chr(13) & _
    Chr(10)
strCode = strCode & "Const m_def_BOFAction = BOFActionType.adMoveFirst" & _
    Chr(13) & Chr(10)
strCode = strCode & "Const m_def_EOFAction = EOFActionType.adMoveLast" & _
    Chr(13) & Chr(10)
strCode = strCode & "Const m_def_UserName = " & Chr(34) & Chr(34) & _
    Chr(13) & Chr(10)
strCode = strCode & "Const m_def_Password = " & Chr(34) & Chr(34) & _
    Chr(13) & Chr(10)
strCode = strCode & "Private m_objDataSpace As RDS.DataSpace" & _
    Chr(13) & Chr(10)
strCode = strCode & "Private m_objProxy 'As clsServer" & Chr(13) & Chr(10)
CreateDeclarartions = strCode
End Function
```

Intialize and Terminate Functions

To simplify things, we will start grouping some of the code modules together. The following code will create the `Terminate` and `Initialize` events:

```
Public Function CreateInitTerm(ByVal v_sTableName As String) As String
Dim strCode As String
strCode = strCode & "Private Sub Class_Initialize()" & Chr(13) & Chr(10)
strCode = strCode & " On Error GoTo IntitializeError" & Chr(13) & Chr(10)
strCode = strCode & " Set m_objManagedObject = New cls" & v_sTableName & _
    Chr(13) & Chr(10)
strCode = strCode & " GetProxy" & Chr(13) & Chr(10)
strCode = strCode & " 'Set m_objProxy = New clsServer" & Chr(13) & Chr(10)
strCode = strCode & " m_eBOFAction = m_def_BOFAction" & Chr(13) & Chr(10)
strCode = strCode & " m_eEOFAction = m_def_EOFAction" & Chr(13) & Chr(10)
strCode = strCode & " m_strUserName = m_def_UserName" & Chr(13) & Chr(10)
strCode = strCode & " m_strPassword = m_def_Password" & Chr(13) & Chr(10)
strCode = strCode & " m_eEditMode = adEditNone" & Chr(13) & Chr(10)
strCode = strCode & " Exit Sub" & Chr(13) & Chr(10)
strCode = strCode & "IntitializeError:" & Chr(13) & Chr(10)
strCode = strCode & " MsgBox " & Chr(34) & _
        "Collection Managing Class cannot be initialized" & Chr(34) & _
        Chr(13) & Chr(10)
strCode = strCode & "End Sub" & Chr(13) & Chr(10) & Chr(13) & Chr(10)
strCode = strCode & "Private Sub Class_Terminate()" & Chr(13) & Chr(10)
strCode = strCode & " If Not m_objManagedObject Is Nothing Then" & _
```

Continued...

```
                    Chr(13) & Chr(10)
    strCode = strCode & " Set m_objManagedObject = Nothing" & Chr(13) & _
              Chr(10)
    strCode = strCode & " End If" & Chr(13) & Chr(10)
    strCode = strCode & "End Sub" & Chr(13) & Chr(10)
    CreateInitTerm = strCode
    End Function
```

Non-Data Methods and Properties

We will separate the rest of the properties and methods into those that are related to the recordset, such as MoveNext or BOF, and those that are non-data methods and properties. These properties have no references to property names, so they can all be wrapped exactly as they were in the VB6 UML code, with a few exceptions as noted below. The one thing that we will have to be customizing is the code that is written for the primary key. The primary key is used to determine what record the recordset is on prior to an update and then used to return the recordset to that record. The primary key may be a string or a long. We will use the Boolean, parameter v_bPrimKeyNum, to tell if it is a long primary key (the Boolean is True) or a string (the Boolean is False). Add the following code into the BuildMiddle .bas module:

```
Public Function CreateGeneral(ByVal v_sTableName As String, _
                              ByVal v_bPrimKeyNum As Boolean) As String
Dim strCode As String
strCode = "Private Sub Class_GetDataMember " & _
          "(DataMember As String, Data As Object)" & Chr(13) & Chr(10)
strCode = strCode & " On Error GoTo GetDataMemberError" & Chr(13) & Chr(10)
strCode = strCode & " If ItemsDataMember <> DataMember Then" & _
          Chr(13) & Chr(10)
strCode = strCode & " Exit Sub" & Chr(13) & Chr(10)
strCode = strCode & " End If" & Chr(13) & Chr(10)
strCode = strCode & " Set Data = m_objManagedObject.ItemsRecordset" & _
          Chr(13) & Chr(10)
strCode = strCode & " Exit Sub" & Chr(13) & Chr(10)
strCode = strCode & "GetDataMemberError:" & Chr(13) & Chr(10)
strCode = strCode & " Set Data = Nothing" & Chr(13) & Chr(10)
strCode = strCode & "End Sub" & Chr(13) & Chr(10) & Chr(13) & Chr(10)

strCode = strCode & "Public Sub GetProxy()" & Chr(13) & Chr(10)
strCode = strCode & " Set m_objDataSpace = New RDS.DataSpace" & _
          Chr(13) & Chr(10)
strCode = strCode & " m_objDataSpace.InternetTimeout = 30000" & _
          Chr(13) & Chr(10)
strCode = strCode & " Set m_objProxy = m_objDataSpace.CreateObject _" & _
          Chr(13) & Chr(10)
strCode = strCode & " (" & Chr(34) & "prjServer.clsServer" & _
          Chr(34) & ", " & Chr(34) & Chr(34) & ")" & Chr(13) & Chr(10)
strCode = strCode & "End Sub" & Chr(13) & Chr(10) & Chr(13) & Chr(10)

strCode = strCode & "Friend Function SetProxyInformation " & _
          " (ByVal v_eRecordsetName As TableName, _" & Chr(13) & Chr(10)
strCode = strCode & " ByVal v_strWhereClause As String, " & _
          " ByVal v_strPrimaryKey As String, _" & Chr(13) & Chr(10)
strCode = strCode & " ByVal v_eDataMember As String)" & Chr(13) & _
          Chr(10)
strCode = strCode & " m_eRecordsetName = v_eRecordsetName" & _
          Chr(13) & Chr(10)
strCode = strCode & " m_strWhereClause = v_strWhereClause" & _
```

```
                Chr(13) & Chr(10)
   strCode = strCode & " m_strPrimaryKey = v_strPrimaryKey" & _
                Chr(13) & Chr(10)
   strCode = strCode & " m_strDataMember = v_eDataMember" & _
                Chr(13) & Chr(10)
   strCode = strCode & " m_objManagedObject.ItemsDataMember = " & _
                "v_eDataMember" & Chr(13) & Chr(10)
   strCode = strCode & "End Function" & Chr(13) & Chr(10) & Chr(13) & Chr(10)

   strCode = strCode & "Friend Property Get ItemsDataMember() As String" & _
                Chr(13) & Chr(10)
   strCode = strCode & " ItemsDataMember = m_strDataMember" & _
                Chr(13) & Chr(10)
   strCode = strCode & "End Property" & Chr(13) & Chr(10) & Chr(13) & Chr(10)
   strCode = strCode & "Private Property Get PrimaryKey() As String" & _
                Chr(13) & Chr(10)
   strCode = strCode & " PrimaryKey = m_strPrimaryKey" & Chr(13) & Chr(10)
   strCode = strCode & "End Property" & Chr(13) & Chr(10) & Chr(13) & Chr(10)
   strCode = strCode & "Private Property Get RecordsetName() As TableName" & _
                Chr(13) & Chr(10)
   strCode = strCode & " RecordsetName = m_eRecordsetName" & Chr(13) & Chr(10)
   strCode = strCode & "End Property" & Chr(13) & Chr(10) & Chr(13) & Chr(10)

   strCode = strCode & "Private Property Get WhereClause() As String" & _
                Chr(13) & Chr(10)
   strCode = strCode & " WhereClause = m_strWhereClause" & Chr(13) & Chr(10)
   strCode = strCode & "End Property" & Chr(13) & Chr(10) & Chr(13) & Chr(10)
```

The next property gets the bottom class. As the name of the bottom class will be based on the table name, we will need to use the v_sTableName parameter to build the next line of code:

```
   strCode = strCode & "Public Property Get Item() As cls" & v_sTableName & _
                Chr(13) & Chr(10)
   strCode = strCode & " Set Item = m_objManagedObject" & Chr(13) & Chr(10)
   strCode = strCode & "End Property" & Chr(13) & Chr(10) & Chr(13) & Chr(10)

   strCode = strCode & "Public Property Get ItemCount() As Long" & Chr(13) & _
                Chr(10)
   strCode = strCode & " ItemCount =" & _
                " m_objManagedObject.ItemsRecordset.RecordCount" & Chr(13) & Chr(10)
   strCode = strCode & "End Property" & Chr(13) & Chr(10) & Chr(13) & Chr(10)

   strCode = strCode & "Private Sub UpdateManagedObjects()" & Chr(13) & Chr(10)
   strCode = strCode & " On Error GoTo UpdateManagedObjectsError" & _
                Chr(13) & Chr(10)
   strCode = strCode & " Set m_objManagedObject.ItemsRecordset = _" & _
                Chr(13) & Chr(10)
```

Again, we will need to use the table name in the retrieve methods used with the data services component:

```
strCode = strCode & " m_objProxy.Return" & v_sTableName & _
        "RecordSet(UserName, Password, WhereClause)" & Chr(13) & Chr(10)
strCode = strCode & " DataMemberChanged ItemsDataMember" & Chr(13) & _
        Chr(10)
strCode = strCode & " m_objManagedObject.RefreshDataMember" & Chr(13) & _
        Chr(10)
strCode = strCode & " Exit Sub" & Chr(13) & Chr(10) & Chr(13) & Chr(10)
strCode = strCode & "UpdateManagedObjectsError:" & Chr(13) & Chr(10)
strCode = strCode & " MsgBox Err.Description & Err.Source" & Chr(13) & _
        Chr(10)
strCode = strCode & "End Sub" & Chr(13) & Chr(10) & Chr(13) & Chr(10)

strCode = strCode & "Friend Property Get ItemsRecordset() As " & _
        "ADODB.Recordset" & Chr(13) & Chr(10)
strCode = strCode & " Set ItemsRecordset = " & _
        "m_objManagedObject.ItemsRecordset" & Chr(13) & Chr(10)
strCode = strCode & "End Sub" & Chr(13) & Chr(10) & Chr(13) & Chr(10)

strCode=strCode & "Public Property Get EditMode() As ADODB.EditModeEnum" & _
        Chr(13) & Chr(10)
strCode = strCode & " EditMode = m_eEditMode" & Chr(13) & Chr(10)
strCode = strCode & "End Property" & Chr(13) & Chr(10) & Chr(13) & Chr(10)

strCode = strCode & "Friend Property Let EditMode" & _
        "(ByVal v_eNewEditMode As ADODB.EditModeEnum)" & Chr(13) & Chr(10)
strCode = strCode & " m_eEditMode = v_eNewEditMode" & Chr(13) & Chr(10)
strCode = strCode & " If m_objManagedObject.EditMode <> " & _
        " v_eNewEditMode Then" & Chr(13) & Chr(10)
strCode = strCode & " m_objManagedObject.EditMode = v_eNewEditMode" & _
        Chr(13) & Chr(10)
strCode = strCode & " End If" & Chr(13) & Chr(10)
strCode = strCode & "End Property" & Chr(13) & Chr(10) & Chr(13) & Chr(10)

strCode = strCode & "Public Sub Refresh()" & Chr(13) & Chr(10)
```

We are now starting the code that will require the `v_bPrimKeyNum` Boolean:

```
If v_bPrimKeyNum Then
    strCode = strCode & " Dim strPrimaryKeyValue As Long" & Chr(13) & Chr(10)
Else
    strCode = strCode & " Dim strPrimaryKeyValue As String" & Chr(13) & Chr(10)
End If
strCode = strCode & " If m_objManagedObject.ItemsRecordset.State = " & _
        "adStateOpen Then" & Chr(13) & Chr(10)
strCode = strCode & " If Not m_objManagedObject.ItemsRecordset.BOF " & _
        " And _" & Chr(13) & Chr(10)
strCode = strCode & " Not m_objManagedObject.ItemsRecordset.EOF " & _
        " And _" & Chr(13) & Chr(10)
strCode = strCode & " Not IsNull(m_objManagedObject.ItemsRecordset." & _
        "Fields(PrimaryKey)) Then" & Chr(13) & Chr(10)
strCode = strCode & " strPrimaryKeyValue = _" & Chr(13) & Chr(10)
strCode = strCode & " m_objManagedObject.ItemsRecordset.Fields " & _
        " (PrimaryKey)" & Chr(13) & Chr(10)
strCode = strCode & " End If" & Chr(13) & Chr(10)
strCode = strCode & " End If" & Chr(13) & Chr(10)
strCode = strCode & " UpdateManagedObjects" & Chr(13) & Chr(10)
```

Again, we must check the primary key:

```
If v_bPrimKeyNum Then
    strCode = strCode & " If strPrimaryKeyValue <> 0 Then" & Chr(13) & Chr(10)
    strCode = strCode & " m_objManagedObject.ItemsRecordset.Find " & _
             "PrimaryKey & " & Chr(34) & "=" & Chr(34) & " & _" & _
             Chr(13) & Chr(10) & _
             "strPrimaryKeyValue " & ", , , 1" & Chr(13) & Chr(10)
Else
    strCode = strCode & " If strPrimaryKeyValue <> " & Chr(34) & _
             Chr(34) & " Then" & Chr(13) & Chr(10)
    strCode = strCode & " m_objManagedObject.ItemsRecordset.Find " & _
             " PrimaryKey & " & Chr(34) & "='" & Chr(34) & " & _" & _
             Chr(13) & Chr(10) & "strPrimaryKeyValue & " & Chr(34) & "'" & _
             Chr(34) & ", , , 1" & Chr(13) & Chr(10)
End If
strCode = strCode & " End If" & Chr(13) & Chr(10)
strCode = strCode & "End Sub" & Chr(13) & Chr(10)

strCode = strCode & "Public Sub Update()" & Chr(13) & Chr(10)
```

Another primary key check:

```
If v_bPrimKeyNum Then
    strCode = strCode & " Dim strPrimaryKeyValue As Long" & Chr(13) & Chr(10)
Else
    strCode = strCode & " Dim strPrimaryKeyValue As String" & Chr(13) & Chr(10)
End If

strCode = strCode & " On Error GoTo UpdateError" & Chr(13) & Chr(10)
strCode = strCode & " If m_objManagedObject.ItemsRecordset.State = " & _
         "adStateOpen And _" & Chr(13) & Chr(10)
strCode = strCode & " m_objManagedObject.ItemsRecordset.EditMode " & _
         " <> adEditDelete And (Not IsNull(m_objManagedObject." & _
         "ItemsRecordset.Fields(PrimaryKey))) Then" & Chr(13) & Chr(10)
strCode = strCode & " If " & " m_objManagedObject.ItemsRecordset." & _
         "RecordCount <> 0 Then" & Chr(13) & Chr(10)
strCode = strCode & " strPrimaryKeyValue = _" & Chr(13) & Chr(10)
strCode = strCode & " m_objManagedObject.ItemsRecordset.Fields" & _
         " (PrimaryKey)" & Chr(13) & Chr(10)
strCode = strCode & " End If" & Chr(13) & Chr(10)
strCode = strCode & " End If" & Chr(13) & Chr(10)
strCode = strCode & " If EditMode <> adEditNone Then" & Chr(13) & Chr(10)
strCode = strCode & " Set m_objManagedObject.ItemsRecordset = " & _
         "m_objProxy.UpdateRecordset(UserName, _" & Chr(13) & Chr(10)
strCode = strCode & " Password, m_objManagedObject.ItemsRecordset," & _
         "m_eRecordsetName, _" & Chr(13) & Chr(10)
strCode = strCode & " WhereClause)" & Chr(13) & Chr(10)
strCode = strCode & " EditMode = adEditNone" & Chr(13) & Chr(10)
strCode = strCode & " RaiseEvent ChangeManagedObjects" & Chr(13) & _
         Chr(10)
strCode = strCode & " End If" & Chr(13) & Chr(10)
```

Another primary key check:

```
If v_bPrimKeyNum Then
    strCode = strCode & " If strPrimaryKeyValue <> 0 Then" & Chr(13) & Chr(10)
strCode = strCode & " m_objManagedObject.ItemsRecordset.Find " & _
        " PrimaryKey & " & Chr(34) & "=" & Chr(34) & " & _" & Chr(13) & _
        Chr(10) & "strPrimaryKeyValue " & ", , , 1" & Chr(13) & Chr(10)
Else
    strCode = strCode & " If strPrimaryKeyValue <> " & Chr(34) & _
    Chr(34) & " Then" & Chr(13) & Chr(10)
    strCode = strCode & " m_objManagedObject.ItemsRecordset.Find " & _
    "PrimaryKey & " & Chr(34) & "='" & Chr(34) & " & _" & _
    Chr(13) & Chr(10) & "strPrimaryKeyValue & " & Chr(34) & "'" & _
    "Chr(34) & , , , 1" & Chr(13) & Chr(10)
End If
strCode = strCode & " End If" & Chr(13) & Chr(10)
strCode = strCode & " Exit Sub" & Chr(13) & Chr(10)
strCode = strCode & "UpdateError:" & Chr(13) & Chr(10)
strCode = strCode & " Err.Raise Err.Number, " & Chr(34) & "Update: " & _
        Chr(34) & " & Err.Source, Err.Description" & Chr(13) & Chr(10)
strCode = strCode & "End Sub" & Chr(13) & Chr(10) & Chr(13) & Chr(10)

strCode = strCode & "Public Function Find(ByVal v_strPrimaryKey As " & _
        "String)" & Chr(13) & Chr(10)

If v_bPrimKeyNum Then
    strCode = strCode & " Dim strPrimaryKeyValue As Long" & Chr(13) & Chr(10)
    strCode = strCode & " If v_strPrimaryKey = 0 Then" & Chr(13) & Chr(10)
Else
    strCode = strCode & " Dim strPrimaryKeyValue As String" & Chr(13) & Chr(10)
    strCode = strCode & " If v_strPrimaryKey = " & Chr(34) & Chr(34) & _
    "Then" & Chr(13) & Chr(10)
End If

strCode = strCode & " Exit Function" & Chr(13) & Chr(10)
strCode = strCode & " End If" & Chr(13) & Chr(10)
```

Another primary key check:

```
If v_bPrimKeyNum Then
    strCode = strCode & " If InStr(v_strPrimaryKey, " & Chr(34) & "'" & _
            Chr(34) & ") > 0 Then" & Chr(13) & Chr(10)
    strCode = strCode & " v_strPrimaryKey = " & _
            "Mid(v_strPrimaryKey, 1, InStr(v_strPrimaryKey, " & Chr(34) & _
            "'" & Chr(34) & ") - 1)" & Chr(13) & Chr(10)
    strCode = strCode & " Else" & Chr(13) & Chr(10)
    strCode = strCode & " v_strPrimaryKey = v_strPrimaryKey" & _
            Chr(13) & Chr(10)
    strCode = strCode & " End If" & Chr(13) & Chr(10)
End If
```

Another primary key check:

```
If v_bPrimKeyNum Then
    strCode = strCode & " ItemsRecordset.Find PrimaryKey & " & _
            Chr(34) & "=" & Chr(34) & " & _" & Chr(13) & Chr(10) & _
            "v_strPrimaryKey " & ", , , 1" & Chr(13) & Chr(10)
Else
    strCode = strCode & " ItemsRecordset.Find PrimaryKey & " & Chr(34) & _
            "='" & Chr(34) & " & _" & Chr(13) & Chr(10) & _
            "v_strPrimaryKey & " & Chr(34) & "'" & _
            Chr(34) & ", , , 1" & Chr(13) & Chr(10)
End If

strCode = strCode & " Refresh" & Chr(13) & Chr(10)
strCode = strCode & "End Function" & Chr(13) & Chr(10)
CreateGeneral = strCode
End Function
```

Generate Recordset Methods

```
Public Function CreateDataMethods() As String

Dim strCode As String

strCode = "Public Sub Edit()" & Chr(13) & Chr(10)
strCode = strCode & " If EditMode = adEditNone Then" & Chr(13) & Chr(10)
strCode = strCode & " EditMode = adEditInProgress" & Chr(13) & Chr(10)
strCode = strCode & " End If" & Chr(13) & Chr(10)
strCode = strCode & "End Sub" & Chr(13) & Chr(10) & Chr(13) & Chr(10)

strCode = strCode & "Public Sub Delete()" & Chr(13) & Chr(10)
strCode = strCode & " On Error GoTo DeleteError" & Chr(13) & Chr(10)
strCode = strCode & " If EditMode = adEditNone Then" & Chr(13) & Chr(10)
strCode = strCode & " m_objProxy.UpdateRecordset UserName, " & _
            " Password, _" & Chr(13) & Chr(10)
strCode = strCode & " m_objManagedObject.ItemsRecordset, " & _
            " m_eRecordsetName, WhereClause, True" & Chr(13) & Chr(10)
strCode = strCode & " RaiseEvent ChangeManagedObjects" & Chr(13) & _
            Chr(10)
strCode = strCode & " Else" & Chr(13) & Chr(10)
strCode = strCode & " GetErrorText " & Chr(34) & _
            "CanNotDeleteDuringEdit/AddNew" & Chr(34) & Chr(13) & Chr(10)
strCode = strCode & " End If" & Chr(13) & Chr(10)
strCode = strCode & " Exit Sub" & Chr(13) & Chr(10)
strCode = strCode & "DeleteError:" & Chr(13) & Chr(10)
strCode = strCode & " Err.Raise Err.Number, " & Chr(34) & "Delete " & _
            Chr(34) & "& Err.Source, Err.Description" & Chr(13) & Chr(10)
strCode = strCode & "End Sub" & Chr(13) & Chr(10) & Chr(13) & Chr(10)

strCode = strCode & "Public Sub AddNew()" & Chr(13) & Chr(10)
strCode = strCode & " On Error GoTo AddNewError" & Chr(13) & Chr(10)
strCode = strCode & " If EditMode = adEditNone Then" & Chr(13) & Chr(10)
strCode = strCode & " m_objManagedObject.ItemsRecordset.AddNew" & _
            Chr(13) & Chr(10)
strCode = strCode & " EditMode = adEditAdd" & Chr(13) & Chr(10)
strCode = strCode & " Else" & Chr(13) & Chr(10)
strCode = strCode & " End If" & Chr(13) & Chr(10)
strCode = strCode & " Exit Sub" & Chr(13) & Chr(10)
strCode = strCode & "AddNewError:" & Chr(13) & Chr(10)
strCode = strCode & " Err.Raise Err.Number, " & Chr(34) & "AddNew " & _
            Chr(34) & "& Err.Source, Err.Description" & Chr(13) & Chr(10)
```

```
strCode = strCode & "End Sub" & Chr(13) & Chr(10)

strCode = strCode & "Public Sub Cancel()" & Chr(13) & Chr(10)
strCode = strCode & " If EditMode = adEditAdd Or EditMode = " & _
        "adEditInProgress Then" & Chr(13) & Chr(10)
strCode = strCode & " ItemsRecordset.CancelUpdate" & Chr(13) & Chr(10)
strCode = strCode & " EditMode = adEditNone" & Chr(13) & Chr(10)
strCode = strCode & " End If" & Chr(13) & Chr(10)
strCode = strCode & "End Sub" & Chr(13) & Chr(10)

strCode = strCode & "Public Property Get RecordCount() As Long" & _
        Chr(13) & Chr(10)
strCode = strCode & " RecordCount = m_objManagedObject.ItemsRecordset." & _
        "RecordCount" & Chr(13) & Chr(10)
strCode = strCode & "End Property" & Chr(13) & Chr(10)

strCode = strCode & "Public Sub MoveFirst()" & Chr(13) & Chr(10)
strCode = strCode & " On Error GoTo MoveFirstError" & Chr(13) & Chr(10)
strCode = strCode & " If m_objManagedObject.ItemsRecordset Is Nothing " & _
        "Then" & Chr(13) & Chr(10)
strCode = strCode & " Exit Sub" & Chr(13) & Chr(10)
strCode = strCode & " End If" & Chr(13) & Chr(10)
strCode =strCode & " If m_objManagedObject.ItemsRecordset.RecordCount " & _
        "> 0 Then" & Chr(13) & Chr(10)
strCode = strCode & " m_objManagedObject.ItemsRecordset.MoveFirst" & _
        Chr(13) & Chr(10)
strCode = strCode & " End If" & Chr(13) & Chr(10)
strCode = strCode & " Exit Sub" & Chr(13) & Chr(10)
strCode = strCode & "MoveFirstError:" & Chr(13) & Chr(10)
strCode = strCode & " Err.Raise Err.Number, " & Chr(34) & "Move First " & _
        Chr(34) & "& Err.Source, Err.Description" & Chr(13) & Chr(10)
strCode = strCode & "End Sub" & Chr(13) & Chr(10) & Chr(13) & Chr(10)

strCode = strCode & "Public Sub MoveLast()" & Chr(13) & Chr(10)
strCode = strCode & " On Error GoTo MoveLastError" & Chr(13) & Chr(10)
strCode = strCode & " If m_objManagedObject.ItemsRecordset Is Nothing " & _
        "Then" & Chr(13) & Chr(10)
strCode = strCode & " Exit Sub" & Chr(13) & Chr(10)
strCode = strCode & " End If" & Chr(13) & Chr(10)
strCode = strCode & " If m_objManagedObject.ItemsRecordset.RecordCount " & _
        "> 0 Then" & Chr(13) & Chr(10)
strCode = strCode & " m_objManagedObject.ItemsRecordset.MoveLast" & _
        Chr(13) & Chr(10)
strCode = strCode & " End If" & Chr(13) & Chr(10)
strCode = strCode & " Exit Sub" & Chr(13) & Chr(10)
strCode = strCode & "MoveLastError:" & Chr(13) & Chr(10)
strCode = strCode & " Err.Raise Err.Number, " & Chr(34) & "Move Last " & _
        Chr(34) & "& Err.Source, Err.Description" & Chr(13) & Chr(10)
strCode = strCode & "End Sub" & Chr(13) & Chr(10) & Chr(13) & Chr(10)

strCode = strCode & "Public Sub MoveNext()" & Chr(13) & Chr(10)
strCode = strCode & " On Error GoTo MoveNextError" & Chr(13) & Chr(10)
strCode = strCode & " If m_objManagedObject.ItemsRecordset " & _
        "Is Nothing Then" & Chr(13) & Chr(10)
strCode = strCode & " Exit Sub" & Chr(13) & Chr(10)
strCode = strCode & " End If" & Chr(13) & Chr(10)
strCode = strCode & " If m_objManagedObject.ItemsRecordset.EOF = False " & _
        " Then" & Chr(13) & Chr(10)
strCode = strCode & " m_objManagedObject.ItemsRecordset.MoveNext" & _
        Chr(13) & Chr(10)
strCode = strCode & " End If" & Chr(13) & Chr(10)
strCode = strCode & " If m_objManagedObject.ItemsRecordset.EOF = " & _
```

```vb
                 "True Then" & Chr(13) & Chr(10)
strCode = strCode & " Select Case EOFAction" & Chr(13) & Chr(10)
strCode = strCode & " Case EOFActionType.adAddNew" & Chr(13) & _
          Chr(10)
strCode = strCode & " m_objManagedObject.ItemsRecordset.AddNew" & _
          Chr(13) & Chr(10)
strCode = strCode & " Case EOFActionType.adMoveLast" & Chr(13) & _
          Chr(10)
strCode = strCode & _
              " m_objManagedObject.ItemsRecordset.MoveLast" & Chr(13) & Chr(10)
strCode = strCode & " Case EOFActionType.adStayEOF" & Chr(13) & _
          Chr(10)
strCode = strCode & " Exit Sub" & Chr(13) & Chr(10)
strCode = strCode & " Case Else" & Chr(13) & Chr(10)
strCode = strCode & " Exit Sub" & Chr(13) & Chr(10)
strCode = strCode & " End Select" & Chr(13) & Chr(10)
strCode = strCode & " End If" & Chr(13) & Chr(10)
strCode = strCode & " Exit Sub" & Chr(13) & Chr(10)
strCode = strCode & "MoveNextError:" & Chr(13) & Chr(10)
strCode = strCode & " Err.Raise Err.Number, " & Chr(34) & "Move Next " & _
          Chr(34) & " & Err.Source, Err.Description" & Chr(13) & Chr(10)
strCode = strCode & "End Sub" & Chr(13) & Chr(10)

strCode = strCode & "Public Sub MovePrevious()" & Chr(13) & Chr(10)
strCode = strCode & " On Error GoTo MovePreviousError" & Chr(13) & Chr(10)
strCode = strCode & " If m_objManagedObject.ItemsRecordset Is Nothing " & _
          "Then Exit Sub" & Chr(13) & Chr(10)
strCode = strCode & " If m_objManagedObject.ItemsRecordset.BOF Then" & _
          Chr(13) & Chr(10)
strCode = strCode & " Select Case BOFAction" & Chr(13) & Chr(10)
strCode = strCode & " Case BOFActionType.adMoveFirst" & Chr(13) & Chr(10)
strCode = strCode & " m_objManagedObject.ItemsRecordset.MoveFirst" & _
          Chr(13) & Chr(10)
strCode = strCode & " Case BOFActionType.adStayBOF" & Chr(13) & Chr(10)
strCode = strCode & " Exit Sub" & Chr(13) & Chr(10)
strCode = strCode & " Case Else" & Chr(13) & Chr(10)
strCode = strCode & " Exit Sub" & Chr(13) & Chr(10)
strCode = strCode & " End Select" & Chr(13) & Chr(10)
strCode = strCode & " Else" & Chr(13) & Chr(10)
strCode = strCode & " m_objManagedObject.ItemsRecordset.MovePrevious" & _
          Chr(13) & Chr(10)
strCode = strCode & " End If" & Chr(13) & Chr(10)
strCode = strCode & " Exit Sub" & Chr(13) & Chr(10)
strCode = strCode & "MovePreviousError:" & Chr(13) & Chr(10)
strCode = strCode & " Err.Raise Err.Number, " & Chr(34) & _
          "Move Previous Error" & Chr(34) & "& Err.Source, _" & _
          Chr(13) & Chr(10)
strCode = strCode & " Err.Description" & Chr(13) & Chr(10)
strCode = strCode & "End Sub" & Chr(13) & Chr(10)

strCode = strCode & "Public Property Get UserName() As String" & _
          Chr(13) & Chr(10)
strCode = strCode & " UserName = m_strUserName" & Chr(13) & Chr(10)
strCode = strCode & "End Property" & Chr(13) & Chr(10) & Chr(13) & Chr(10)

strCode = strCode & "Public Property Let UserName" & _
              " (ByVal New_strUserName As String)" & Chr(13) & Chr(10)
strCode = strCode & " m_strUserName = New_strUserName" & Chr(13) & Chr(10)
strCode = strCode & "End Property" & Chr(13) & Chr(10) & Chr(13) & Chr(10)

strCode = strCode & "Public Property Get Password() As String" & _
```

```
                Chr(13) & Chr(10)
    strCode = strCode & " Password = m_strPassword" & Chr(13) & Chr(10)
    strCode = strCode & "End Property" & Chr(13) & Chr(10) & Chr(13) & Chr(10)

    strCode = strCode & "Public Property Let Password " & _
                " (ByVal New_strPassword As String)" & Chr(13) & Chr(10)
    strCode = strCode & " m_strPassword = New_strPassword" & Chr(13) & Chr(10)
    strCode = strCode & "End Property" & Chr(13) & Chr(10)

    strCode = strCode & "Public Property Get BOFAction() As BOFActionType" & _
                Chr(13) & Chr(10)
    strCode = strCode & " BOFAction = m_eBOFAction" & Chr(13) & Chr(10)
    strCode = strCode & "End Property" & Chr(13) & Chr(10)

    strCode = strCode & "Public Property Let BOFAction" & _
                " (ByVal New_BOFAction As BOFActionType)" & Chr(13) & Chr(10)
    strCode = strCode & " m_eBOFAction = New_BOFAction" & Chr(13) & Chr(10)
    strCode = strCode & "End Property" & Chr(13) & Chr(10) & Chr(13) & Chr(10)

    strCode = strCode & "Public Property Get EOFAction() As EOFActionType" & _
                Chr(13) & Chr(10)
    strCode = strCode & " EOFAction = m_eEOFAction" & Chr(13) & Chr(10)
    strCode = strCode & "End Property" & Chr(13) & Chr(10) & Chr(13) & Chr(10)

    strCode = strCode & "Public Property Let EOFAction" & _
                " (ByVal New_EOFAction As EOFActionType)" & Chr(13) & Chr(10)
    strCode = strCode & " m_eEOFAction = New_EOFAction" & Chr(13) & Chr(10)
    strCode = strCode & "End Property" & Chr(13) & Chr(10) & Chr(13) & Chr(10)

    strCode = strCode & "Private Sub m_objManagedObject_EditInProgress" & _
                " (ByVal v_strEditMode As Variant)" & Chr(13) & Chr(10)
    strCode = strCode & " EditMode = v_strEditMode" & Chr(13) & Chr(10)
    strCode = strCode & "End Sub" & Chr(13) & Chr(10)

    strCode = strCode & "Private Sub m_objManagedObject_RefreshDataMember()" & _
                Chr(13) & Chr(10)
    strCode = strCode & " DataMemberChanged ItemsDataMember" & _
                Chr(13) & Chr(10)
    strCode = strCode & "End Sub" & Chr(13) & Chr(10)
    CreateDataMethods = strCode

End Function
```

Generating the Top Class

We will put all of the code for the top class into one function, as there are only a few methods in the top function. Create another .bas module called BuildTop and put the following code into the module:

```
Public Function BuildClass(ByRef r_uTableInfo As TableInformation, _
                        ByVal v_sTableName As String) As String
Dim strCode As String
Dim lngWhereCounter As Long
Dim lngQueryKey As Long
Dim lngQueryCounter As Long
    strCode = strCode & "Public Enum ClientDataMember" & Chr(13) & Chr(10)
    strCode = strCode & "e_" & r_uTableInfo.PrimaryKey & "=" & 1 & Chr(13) & _
                Chr(10)
    strCode = strCode & "End Enum" & Chr(13) & Chr(10)
```

```
strCode = strCode & "Const m_def_" & r_uTableInfo.PrimaryKey & _
          " As String =" & Chr(34) & Chr(34) & Chr(13) & Chr(10)
strCode = strCode & "Private WithEvents m_col" & r_uTableInfo.PrimaryKey & _
          " As cls" & v_sTableName & "Manager" & Chr(13) & Chr(10)

strCode = strCode & "Const m_def_NumberOf" & v_sTableName & _
          Collections =" & 1 & Chr(13) & Chr(10)

strCode = strCode & "Private m_colDataMembersArray() As cls" & _
          v_sTableName & "Manager" & Chr(13) & Chr(10)
strCode = strCode & "Private m_blnDataMembersInitialized() As Boolean" & _
          Chr(13) & Chr(10)
strCode = strCode & "Private m_str" & r_uTableInfo.PrimaryKey & _
          "Equals As String" & Chr(13) & Chr(10)
strCode = strCode & "Private Sub m_col" & r_uTableInfo.PrimaryKey & _
          "_ChangeManagedObjects()" & Chr(13) & Chr(10)
strCode = strCode & " ChangeManagedObjects g_cdm" & _
          r_uTableInfo.PrimaryKey & Chr(13) & Chr(10)
strCode = strCode & "End Sub" & Chr(13) & Chr(10)

strCode = strCode & _
          "Private Sub UserControl_ReadProperties" & _
          "(PropBag As PropertyBag)" & Chr(13) & Chr(10)
strCode = strCode & "If UserControl.Ambient.UserMode = " & _
          "False Then Exit Sub" & Chr(13) & Chr(10)

strCode = strCode & " Set m_col" & r_uTableInfo.PrimaryKey & _
          " = New cls" & v_sTableName & "Manager" & Chr(13) & Chr(10)

strCode = strCode & " m_str" & r_uTableInfo.PrimaryKey & "Equals=" & _
          "m_def_" & r_uTableInfo.PrimaryKey & Chr(13) & Chr(10)

strCode = strCode & " ReDim m_colDataMembersArray(1 To m_def_NumberOf" & _
          v_sTableName & "Collections)" & Chr(13) & Chr(10)
strCode = strCode & "ReDim m_blnDataMembersInitialized" & _
          "(1 To m_def_NumberOf" & v_sTableName & "Collections)" & _
          Chr(13) & Chr(10)
strCode = strCode & " Set m_colDataMembersArray(e_" & r_uTableInfo." & _
          PrimaryKey & ") = m_col" & r_uTableInfo.PrimaryKey & _
          Chr(13) & Chr(10)
strCode = strCode & " m_blnDataMembersInitialized(e_" & _
          r_uTableInfo.PrimaryKey & ") = False" & Chr(13) & Chr(10)
strCode = strCode & "End Sub" & Chr(13) & Chr(10)
strCode = strCode & "Private Sub UserControl_Terminate()" & Chr(13) & _
          Chr(10)
strCode = strCode & " Set m_col" & r_uTableInfo.PrimaryKey & _
          " = Nothing" & Chr(13) & Chr(10)
strCode = strCode & "End Sub" & Chr(13) & Chr(10)

strCode = strCode & "Public Function Get" & v_sTableName & _
          "Collection(ByVal v_eDataMember As ClientDataMember) _" & _
          Chr(13) & Chr(10)
strCode = strCode & " As cls" & v_sTableName & "Manager" & Chr(13) & Chr(10)
strCode = strCode & " If m_blnDataMembersInitialized" & _
          "(v_eDataMember) = False Then" & Chr(13) & Chr(10)
strCode = strCode & " Select Case v_eDataMember" & Chr(13) & Chr(10)
strCode = strCode & " Case e_" & r_uTableInfo.PrimaryKey & _
          Chr(13) & Chr(10)
strCode = strCode & " m_colDataMembersArray(e_" & _
          r_uTableInfo.PrimaryKey & ").SetProxyInformation _" & Chr(13) & _
          Chr(10)
```

```
strCode = strCode & " e_" & v_sTableName & " , " & Chr(34) & _
          Chr(34) & ", g_cstrField" & r_uTableInfo.PrimaryKey & ", g_cdm" & _
          r_uTableInfo.PrimaryKey & Chr(13) & Chr(10)
strCode = strCode & "End Select" & Chr(13) & Chr(10)
strCode = strCode & " m_colDataMembersArray(v_eDataMember).Refresh" & _
          Chr(13) & Chr(10)
strCode = strCode & " m_blnDataMembersInitialized" & _
          "(v_eDataMember) = True" & Chr(13) & Chr(10)
strCode = strCode & " End If" & Chr(13) & Chr(10)
strCode = strCode & " Set Get" & v_sTableName & _
          "Collection = m_colDataMembersArray(v_eDataMember)" & Chr(13) & _
          Chr(10)
strCode = strCode & "End Function" & Chr(13) & Chr(10)

strCode = strCode & "Private Sub ChangeManagedObjects" & _
          " (ByVal v_sDataMember As String)" & Chr(13) & Chr(10)
strCode = strCode & " Dim lng" & v_sTableName & "CollNumber As Long" & _
          Chr(13) & Chr(10)
strCode = strCode & " Dim lngIgnore" & v_sTableName & "Number As Long" & _
          Chr(13) & Chr(10)
strCode = strCode & " Select Case v_sDataMember" & Chr(13) & Chr(10)
strCode = strCode & " Case g_cdm" & r_uTableInfo.PrimaryKey & _
          Chr(13) & Chr(10)
strCode = strCode & " lngIgnore" & v_sTableName & "Number =" & _
          lngWhereCounter & Chr(13) & Chr(10)
strCode = strCode & " End Select" & Chr(13) & Chr(10)
strCode = strCode & " For lng" & v_sTableName & _
          "CollNumber = 1 To m_def_NumberOf" & v_sTableName & _
          "Collections" & Chr(13) & Chr(10)
strCode = strCode & " If lng" & v_sTableName & "CollNumber <> lngIgnore" & _
          v_sTableName & "Number Then" & Chr(13) & Chr(10)
strCode = strCode & " If m_blnDataMembersInitialized(lng" & _
          v_sTableName & "CollNumber) = True Then" & Chr(13) & Chr(10)
strCode = strCode & " m_colDataMembersArray(lng" & _
          v_sTableName & "CollNumber).Refresh" & Chr(13) & Chr(10)
strCode = strCode & " End If" & Chr(13) & Chr(10)
strCode = strCode & " End If" & Chr(13) & Chr(10)
strCode = strCode & " Next" & Chr(13) & Chr(10)
strCode = strCode & "End Sub" & Chr(13) & Chr(10)
strCode = strCode & "Public Property Get " & r_uTableInfo.PrimaryKey & _
          "Equals() As String" & Chr(13) & Chr(10)
strCode = strCode & " " & r_uTableInfo.PrimaryKey & "Equals = m_str" & _
          r_uTableInfo.PrimaryKey & "Equals" & Chr(13) & Chr(10)
strCode = strCode & "End Property" & Chr(13) & Chr(10)

strCode = strCode & "Public Property Let " & r_uTableInfo.PrimaryKey & _
          "Equals(ByVal v_strNew" & r_uTableInfo.PrimaryKey & "Equals" & _
          " As _" & Chr(13) & Chr(10)
strCode = strCode & " String)" & Chr(13) & Chr(10)
strCode = strCode & " m_str" & r_uTableInfo.PrimaryKey & _
          "Equals = v_strNew" & r_uTableInfo.PrimaryKey & "Equals" & _
          Chr(13) & Chr(10)
strCode = strCode & "End Property" & Chr(13) & Chr(10)
BuildClass = strCode
End Function
```

Generating the Data Services Class

The functions to save and retrieve records can also be generated. Add a new .bas module called BuildServer. Add the following code to the module:

```
Public Function CreateServer(ByRef r_TableInfo() As String, _
                             ByRef r_Tables() As TableInformation) As String
Dim strCode As String
Dim lngTableCounter As Long
Dim strTempTableName As String
Dim lngFieldCounter As Long
Dim lngQueryKeyCounter As Long
Dim strTableName As String

strCode = strCode & "Enum TableName" & Chr(13) & Chr(10)
For lngTableCounter = 1 To UBound(r_TableInfo)
    strCode = strCode & " e_" & r_TableInfo(lngTableCounter) & _
            "=" & lngTableCounter - 1 & Chr(13) & Chr(10)
Next
strCode = strCode & "End Enum" & Chr(13) & Chr(10)
For lngTableCounter = 1 To UBound(r_TableInfo)
    Dim strCleanFields() As String
    CleanFields r_Tables(lngTableCounter).FieldInfo, strCleanFields
    Dim strFields As String
    strFields = ""
    For lngFieldCounter = 1 To UBound(r_Tables(lngTableCounter).FieldInfo)
        If lngFieldCounter = 1 Then
            strFields = " [" & r_Tables(lngTableCounter)." & _
            "FieldInfo(lngFieldCounter).FieldName & "]"

        Else
            strFields = strFields & ",[" & r_Tables(lngTableCounter)." & _
            "FieldInfo(lngFieldCounter).FieldName & "]"
        End If
    Next
    strCode = strCode & " Private Const m_cstr" & _
            r_TableInfo(lngTableCounter) & "Query =" & Chr(34) & _
            "Select " & strFields & Chr(34) & " & _" & Chr(13) & Chr(10)
    strCode = strCode & Chr(34) & " From " & _
            r_Tables(lngTableCounter).TableName & Chr(34) & Chr(13) & Chr(10)
    strTableName = r_Tables(lngTableCounter).TableName
    strCode = strCode & " Private Const m_cstr" & _
            r_TableInfo(lngTableCounter) & _
            r_Tables(lngTableCounter).PrimaryKey & " As String = " _
            & Chr(34) & r_Tables(lngTableCounter).PrimaryKey & _
            Chr(34) & Chr(13) & Chr(10)
Next

strCode = strCode & " Private Const m_cstrDatabasePath As String = " & _
         Chr(34) & "C:\Program Files\Microsoft Visual Studio" & _
         "\VB98\NWIND.MDB" & Chr(34) & Chr(13) & Chr(10)
strCode = strCode & " Private m_objADOConnection As ADODB.Connection" & _
         Chr(13) & Chr(10)
strCode = strCode & " Private m_strErrorDetails As String" & Chr(13) & Chr(10)
strCode = strCode & " Private m_strQueryString As String" & Chr(13) & Chr(10)
strCode = strCode & " Private m_objContext As ObjectContext" & Chr(13) & _
         Chr(10)
strCode = strCode & " Implements ObjectControl" & Chr(13) & Chr(10)
strCode = strCode & "Private Sub ObjectControl_Activate()" & Chr(13) & Chr(10)
strCode = strCode & " Set m_objContext = GetObjectContext" & Chr(13) & Chr(10)
```

```
strCode = strCode & "End Sub" & Chr(13) & Chr(10)
strCode = strCode & "Private Function ObjectControl_CanBePooled()" & _
        " As Boolean" & Chr(13) & Chr(10)
strCode = strCode & " ObjectControl_CanBePooled = False" & Chr(13) & Chr(10)
strCode = strCode & "End Function" & Chr(13) & Chr(10)
strCode = strCode & "Private Sub ObjectControl_Deactivate()" & Chr(13) & _
        Chr(10)
strCode = strCode & " Set m_objADOConnection = Nothing" & Chr(13) & Chr(10)
strCode = strCode & " Set m_objContext = Nothing" & Chr(13) & Chr(10)
strCode = strCode & "End Sub" & Chr(13) & Chr(10)
strCode = strCode & "Private Function CreateInstance(ProgID As String)" & _
        " As Object" & Chr(13) & Chr(10)
strCode = strCode & " On Error GoTo CreateInstanceError" & Chr(13) & Chr(10)
strCode = strCode & " If Not m_objContext Is Nothing Then" & Chr(13) & Chr(10)
strCode = strCode & " Set CreateInstance = m_objContext." & _
        CreateInstance(ProgID)" & Chr(13) & Chr(10)
strCode = strCode & " Else" & Chr(13) & Chr(10)
strCode = strCode & " Select Case ProgID" & Chr(13) & Chr(10)
strCode = strCode & " Case " & Chr(34) & "ADODB.Connection" & _
        Chr(34) & Chr(13) & Chr(10)
strCode = strCode & " Set CreateInstance = New ADODB.Connection" & _
        Chr(13) & Chr(10)
strCode = strCode & " Case " & Chr(34) & "ADODB.Recordset" & Chr(34) & _
        Chr(13) & Chr(10)
strCode = strCode & " Set CreateInstance = New ADODB.Recordset" & _
        Chr(13) & Chr(10)
strCode = strCode & " End Select" & Chr(13) & Chr(10)
strCode = strCode & " End If" & Chr(13) & Chr(10)
strCode = strCode & " Exit Function" & Chr(13) & Chr(10)
strCode = strCode & "CreateInstanceError:" & Chr(13) & Chr(10)
strCode = strCode & " Err.Raise Err.Number, Err.Source & " & Chr(34) & _
        "CreateInstance" & Chr(34) & ", Err.Description" & Chr(13) & Chr(10)
strCode = strCode & "End Function" & Chr(13) & Chr(10)
strCode = strCode & "Public Sub SetComplete()" & Chr(13) & Chr(10)
strCode = strCode & " If Not m_objContext Is Nothing Then" & Chr(13) & _
        Chr(10)
strCode = strCode & " m_objContext.SetComplete" & Chr(13) & Chr(10)
strCode = strCode & " End If" & Chr(13) & Chr(10)
strCode = strCode & "End Sub" & Chr(13) & Chr(10)
strCode = strCode & "Public Sub SetAbort()" & Chr(13) & Chr(10)
strCode = strCode & " If Not m_objContext Is Nothing Then" & Chr(13) & _
        Chr(10)
strCode = strCode & " m_objContext.SetAbort" & Chr(13) & Chr(10)
strCode = strCode & " End If" & Chr(13) & Chr(10)
strCode = strCode & "End Sub" & Chr(13) & Chr(10)
strCode = strCode & "Private Sub SetADOConnection(ByVal v_strUserID" & _
        " As String, _" & Chr(13) & Chr(10)
strCode = strCode & " ByVal v_strPassword As String)" & Chr(13) & Chr(10)
strCode = strCode & " On Error GoTo SetADOConnectionError" & Chr(13) & Chr(10)
strCode = strCode & " Set m_objADOConnection = CreateInstance(" & _
        Chr(34) & "ADODB.Connection" & Chr(34) & ")" & Chr(13) & Chr(10)
strCode = strCode & " With m_objADOConnection" & Chr(13) & Chr(10)
strCode = strCode & " .CursorLocation = adUseClient" & Chr(13) & Chr(10)
strCode = strCode & " .ConnectionString = " & Chr(34) & _
        "Provider=Microsoft.Jet.OLEDB.3.51;Persist Security Info=False;" & _
        Chr(34) & " & _ " & Chr(13) & Chr(10)
strCode = strCode & " " & Chr(34) & "Data Source=" & Chr(34) & " & " & _
        "m_cstrDatabasePath" & Chr(13) & Chr(10)
strCode = strCode & " .Open" & Chr(13) & Chr(10)
strCode = strCode & " End With" & Chr(13) & Chr(10)
strCode = strCode & " Exit Sub" & Chr(13) & Chr(10)
```

```vb
strCode = strCode & "SetADOConnectionError:" & Chr(13) & Chr(10)
strCode = strCode & " Dim lngErrorCounter As Long" & Chr(13) & Chr(10)
strCode = strCode & " Dim strErrors As String" & Chr(13) & Chr(10)
strCode = strCode & " strErrors = Err.Number & " & Chr(34) & ": " & _
          Chr(34) & " & Err.Description" & Chr(13) & Chr(10)
strCode = strCode & " If m_objADOConnection.Errors.Count > 0 Then" & _
          Chr(13) & Chr(10)
strCode = strCode & " For lngErrorCounter = 0 To m_objADOConnection." & _
          "Errors.Count - 1" & Chr(13) & Chr(10)
strCode = strCode & " strErrors = strErrors & _" & Chr(13) & Chr(10)
strCode = strCode & " m_objADOConnection.Errors(lngErrorCounter)." & _
          "Number & _" & Chr(13) & Chr(10)
strCode = strCode & " " & Chr(34) & ": " & Chr(34) & " & " & _
          "m_objADOConnection.Errors(lngErrorCounter).Description" & _
          " & vbCrLf" & Chr(13) & Chr(10)
strCode = strCode & " Next lngErrorCounter" & Chr(13) & Chr(10)
strCode = strCode & " End If" & Chr(13) & Chr(10)
strCode = strCode & " Err.Raise 2000 + vbObjectError, " & Chr(34) & _
          "SetADOConnection " & Chr(34) & " & Err.Source, strErrors" & _
          Chr(13) & Chr(10)
strCode = strCode & "End Sub" & Chr(13) & Chr(10)
strCode = strCode & "Private Function GetADOConnection() " & _
          "As ADODB.Connection" & Chr(13) & Chr(10)
strCode = strCode & " If m_objADOConnection Is Nothing Then" & _
          Chr(13) & Chr(10)
strCode = strCode & " Err.Raise 2001, " & Chr(34) & _
          "GetADOConnection" & Chr(34) & ", _" & Chr(13) & Chr(10)
strCode = strCode & " " & Chr(34) & _
          "Trying to Get Connection prior to setting it" & _
          Chr(34) & Chr(13) & Chr(10)
strCode = strCode & " Else" & Chr(13) & Chr(10)
strCode = strCode & " Set GetADOConnection = m_objADOConnection" & _
          Chr(13) & Chr(10)
strCode = strCode & " End If" & Chr(13) & Chr(10)
strCode = strCode & "End Function" & Chr(13) & Chr(10)
strCode = strCode & "Private Sub CloseADOConnection()" & Chr(13) & Chr(10)
strCode = strCode & " With GetADOConnection" & Chr(13) & Chr(10)
strCode = strCode & " If .State = adStateOpen Then" & Chr(13) & Chr(10)
strCode = strCode & " .Close" & Chr(13) & Chr(10)
strCode = strCode & " End If" & Chr(13) & Chr(10)
strCode = strCode & " End With" & Chr(13) & Chr(10)
strCode = strCode & "End Sub" & Chr(13) & Chr(10)
strCode = strCode & "Public Function ValidUserIDPassword" & _
          "(ByVal v_strUserID As String, _" & Chr(13) & Chr(10)
strCode = strCode & " ByVal v_strPassword As String," & _
          " Optional ByRef r_strErrorDetails As String _" & Chr(13) & Chr(10)
strCode = strCode & " = " & Chr(34) & "Empty" & Chr(34) & ") As Boolean" _
          & Chr(13) & Chr(10)
strCode = strCode & " On Error GoTo ValidUserIDPasswordError" & Chr(13) & _
          Chr(10)
strCode = strCode & " SetADOConnection v_strUserID, v_strPassword" & _
          Chr(13) & Chr(10)
strCode = strCode & " ValidUserIDPassword = True" & Chr(13) & Chr(10)
strCode = strCode & " SetComplete" & Chr(13) & Chr(10)
strCode = strCode & " Exit Function" & Chr(13) & Chr(10)
strCode = strCode & "ValidUserIDPasswordError:" & Chr(13) & Chr(10)
strCode = strCode & " If r_strErrorDetails <> " & Chr(34) & "Empty" & _
          Chr(34) & "Then" & Chr(13) & Chr(10)
strCode = strCode & " r_strErrorDetails = " & _
          Chr(34) & "Error Details:" & Chr(34) & " & " & _
          "Err.Description & vbCrLf & _" & Chr(13) & Chr(10)
```

```
strCode = strCode & " " & Chr(34) & "Error Number:" & _
          Chr(34) & " & " & "Err.Number & vbCrLf & " & Chr(34) & _
          "Error Source: " & Chr(34) & " & _" & Chr(13) & Chr(10)
strCode = strCode & " " & Chr(34) & "ValidUserIDPassword " & _
          Chr(34) & " & Err.Source" & Chr(13) & Chr(10)
strCode = strCode & " End If" & Chr(13) & Chr(10)
strCode = strCode & " SetAbort" & Chr(13) & Chr(10)
strCode = strCode & " ValidUserIDPassword = False" & Chr(13) & Chr(10)
strCode = strCode & "End Function" & Chr(13) & Chr(10)
strCode = strCode & "Private Sub GetRecordSet(ByRef r_recRecordset As " & _
          "ADODB.Recordset, _" & Chr(13) & Chr(10)
strCode = strCode & " ByVal v_strSource)" & Chr(13) & Chr(10)
strCode = strCode & " On Error GoTo GetRecordSetError" & Chr(13) & Chr(10)
strCode = strCode & " Set r_recRecordset = New ADODB.Recordset" & _
          Chr(13) & Chr(10)
strCode = strCode & " r_recRecordset.CursorLocation = adUseClient" & _
          Chr(13) & Chr(10)
strCode = strCode & " r_recRecordset.Open _" & Chr(13) & Chr(10)
strCode = strCode & " v_strSource , GetADOConnection, adOpenStatic, " & _
          " adLockOptimistic" & Chr(13) & Chr(10)
strCode = strCode & " Exit Sub" & Chr(13) & Chr(10)
strCode = strCode & "GetRecordSetError:" & Chr(13) & Chr(10)
strCode = strCode & " Err.Raise Err.Number, " & Chr(34) & "ValidUserID" & _
          Chr(34) & " & Err.Source, Err.Description" & Chr(13) & Chr(10)
strCode = strCode & "End Sub" & Chr(13) & Chr(10)
For lngTableCounter = 1 To UBound(r_TableInfo)
    strCode = strCode & "Public Function Return" & _
              r_TableInfo(lngTableCounter) & _
              "RecordSet(ByVal v_strUserID As String, ByVal _" & _
              Chr(13) & Chr(10)
    strCode = strCode & " v_strPassword As String, Optional ByVal " & _
              "v_strParameter As String) As _" & Chr(13) & Chr(10)
    strCode = strCode & " ADODB.Recordset" & Chr(13) & Chr(10)
    strCode = strCode & " Dim rec" & r_TableInfo(lngTableCounter) & _
              " As ADODB.Recordset" & Chr(13) & Chr(10)
    strCode = strCode & " On Error GoTo Return" & _
              r_TableInfo(lngTableCounter) & "RecordSetError" & _
              Chr(13) & Chr(10)
    strCode = strCode & " SetADOConnection v_strUserID, v_strPassword" & _
              Chr(13) & Chr(10)
    strCode = strCode & " GetRecordSet rec" & _
              r_TableInfo(lngTableCounter) & ", m_cstr" & _
              r_TableInfo(lngTableCounter) & "Query & v_strParameter" & _
              Chr(13) & Chr(10)
    strCode = strCode & " Set Return" & r_TableInfo(lngTableCounter) & _
              "RecordSet = rec" & r_TableInfo(lngTableCounter) & _
              Chr(13) & Chr(10)
    strCode = strCode & " Set rec" & r_TableInfo(lngTableCounter) & _
              ".ActiveConnection = Nothing" & Chr(13) & Chr(10)
    strCode = strCode & " SetComplete" & Chr(13) & Chr(10)
    strCode = strCode & " CloseADOConnection" & Chr(13) & Chr(10)
    strCode = strCode & " Set rec" & r_TableInfo(lngTableCounter) & _
              " = Nothing" & Chr(13) & Chr(10)
    strCode = strCode & " Exit Function" & Chr(13) & Chr(10)
    strCode = strCode & "Return" & r_TableInfo(lngTableCounter) & _
              "RecordSetError:" & Chr(13) & Chr(10)
    strCode = strCode & " CloseADOConnection" & Chr(13) & Chr(10)
    strCode = strCode & " SetAbort" & Chr(13) & Chr(10)
    strCode = strCode & " Err.Raise Err.Number, " & Chr(34) & _
              " Return" & r_TableInfo(lngTableCounter) & Chr(34) & " " & _
              " , Err.Source " & " & _" & Chr(13) & Chr(10)
```

```
        strCode = strCode & " m_strErrorDetails" & Chr(13) & Chr(10)
        strCode = strCode & " End Function" & Chr(13) & Chr(10)


        strCode = strCode & "Private Function Update" & _
                r_TableInfo(lngTableCounter) & _
                "RS(ByVal v_recClientRecordSet As _" & Chr(13) & Chr(10)
        strCode = strCode & _
                " ADODB.Recordset, Optional ByVal v_bolDelete " & _
                " As Boolean = False) As ADODB.Recordset" & Chr(13) & Chr(10)
        strCode = strCode & " Dim rec" & r_TableInfo(lngTableCounter) & _
                " As ADODB.Recordset" & Chr(13) & Chr(10)
        strCode = strCode & " Dim lngFieldCounter As Long" & Chr(13) & Chr(10)
        strCode = strCode & " Dim lngRowCounter As Long" & Chr(13) & Chr(10)
        strCode = strCode & " On Error GoTo Update" & _
                r_TableInfo(lngTableCounter) & "RSError" & Chr(13) & Chr(10)
        strCode = strCode & " If v_recClientRecordSet.EditMode = adEditAdd " & _
                "Then" & Chr(13) & Chr(10)
        strCode = strCode & " Set rec" & r_TableInfo(lngTableCounter) & _
                " = CreateInstance(" & Chr(34) & "ADODB.Recordset" & Chr(34) & _
                ")" & Chr(13) & Chr(10)
        strCode = strCode & " With rec" & r_TableInfo(lngTableCounter) & _
                "" & Chr(13) & Chr(10)
        strTableName = r_Tables(lngTableCounter).TableName

        strCode = strCode & " .Source = m_cstr" & _
                "r_TableInfo(lngTableCounter) & "Query & " & Chr(34) & _
                " Where " & Chr(34) & " & m_cstr" & _
                r_TableInfo(lngTableCounter) & _
                r_Tables(lngTableCounter).PrimaryKey & " & " & Chr(34) & _
                " = " & Chr(34) & " & _ " & Chr(13) & Chr(10)
        strCode = strCode & " 0" & Chr(13) & Chr(10)
        strCode = strCode & " .ActiveConnection = GetADOConnection" & _
                Chr(13) & Chr(10)
        strCode = strCode & " .LockType = adLockPessimistic" & Chr(13) & Chr(10)
        strCode = strCode & " .CursorLocation = adUseServer" & Chr(13) & Chr(10)
        strCode = strCode & " .CursorType = adOpenKeyset" & Chr(13) & Chr(10)
        strCode = strCode & " .Open" & Chr(13) & Chr(10)
        strCode = strCode & " .AddNew" & Chr(13) & Chr(10)
        strCode = strCode & " For lngFieldCounter = 0 To v_recClientRecordSet." & _
                "Fields.Count - 1" & Chr(13) & Chr(10)
        strCode = strCode & " If Not " & "IsNull(v_recClientRecordSet.Fields" & _
                "(lngFieldCounter).Value) Then" & Chr(13) & Chr(10)
        strCode = strCode & ".Fields(v_recClientRecordSet.Fields" & _
                "(lngFieldCounter).Name) _" & Chr(13) & Chr(10)
        strCode = strCode & " = v_recClientRecordSet.Fields" & _
                "(lngFieldCounter).Value" & Chr(13) & Chr(10)
        strCode = strCode & " End If" & Chr(13) & Chr(10)
        strCode = strCode & " Next" & Chr(13) & Chr(10)
        strCode = strCode & " .Update" & Chr(13) & Chr(10)
        strCode = strCode & " End With" & Chr(13) & Chr(10)
        strCode = strCode & " Else" & Chr(13) & Chr(10)
        strCode = strCode & " Set rec" & r_TableInfo(lngTableCounter) & _
                " = v_recClientRecordSet" & Chr(13) & Chr(10)
            strCode = strCode & " Set rec" & r_TableInfo(lngTableCounter) & _
                ".ActiveConnection = GetADOConnection" & Chr(13) & Chr(10)
        strCode = strCode & " If v_bolDelete = True Then" & Chr(13) & Chr(10)
        strCode = strCode & " rec" & r_TableInfo(lngTableCounter) & _
                ".Delete" & Chr(13) & Chr(10)
        strCode = strCode & " Else" & Chr(13) & Chr(10)
        strCode = strCode & " On Error Resume Next" & Chr(13) & Chr(10)
        strCode = strCode & " rec" & r_TableInfo(lngTableCounter) & _
```

```
                    ".Filter = adFilterPendingRecords" & Chr(13) & Chr(10)
    strCode = strCode & " rec" & r_TableInfo(lngTableCounter) & _
               ".UpdateBatch" & Chr(13) & Chr(10)
    strCode = strCode & " rec" & r_TableInfo(lngTableCounter) & _
               ".Filter = adFilterConflictingRecords" & Chr(13) & Chr(10)
    strCode = strCode & " If rec" & r_TableInfo(lngTableCounter) & _
               ".RecordCount > 0 Then" & Chr(13) & Chr(10)
    strCode =strCode & " Err.Raise 2002, " & Chr(34) & "Update" & _
               r_TableInfo(lngTableCounter) & "RS" & Chr(34) & "," & Chr(34) & _
               " & Conflicting Errors" & Chr(34) & Chr(13) & Chr(10)
    strCode = strCode & " End If" & Chr(13) & Chr(10)
    strCode = strCode & " rec" & r_TableInfo(lngTableCounter) & _
               ".Filter = adFilterNone" & Chr(13) & Chr(10)
    strCode = strCode & " End If" & Chr(13) & Chr(10)
    strCode = strCode & " End If" & Chr(13) & Chr(10)
    strCode = strCode & " Set Update" & r_TableInfo(lngTableCounter) & _
               "RS = rec" & r_TableInfo(lngTableCounter) & "" & _
               Chr(13) & Chr(10)
    strCode = strCode & " Set rec" & r_TableInfo(lngTableCounter) & _
               " = Nothing" & Chr(13) & Chr(10)
    strCode = strCode & " Exit Function" & Chr(13) & Chr(10)
    strCode = strCode & "Update" & r_TableInfo(lngTableCounter) & _
               "RSError:" & Chr(13) & Chr(10)
    strCode = strCode & " Err.Raise Err.Description, " & Chr(34) & _
               " & Error Update" & r_TableInfo(lngTableCounter) & "RS" & _
               Chr(34) & " & Err.Source, _" & Chr(13) & Chr(10)
    strCode = strCode & " Err.Description" & Chr(13) & Chr(10)
    strCode = strCode & "End Function" & Chr(13) & Chr(10)
Next
strCode = strCode & "Public Function UpdateRecordset" & _
           "(ByVal v_strUserID As String, _" & Chr(13) & Chr(10)
strCode = strCode & " ByVal v_strPassword As String, _" & _
           Chr(13) & Chr(10)
strCode = strCode & " ByVal v_recClientRecordSet As ADODB.Recordset, _" & _
           Chr(13) & Chr(10)
strCode = strCode & " ByVal v_eName As TableName, Optional ByVal " & _
           " v_strWhereClause As String, " & _
           " Optional ByVal v_bolDelete As Boolean = False) " & _
           "As ADODB.Recordset" & Chr(13) & Chr(10)
strCode = strCode & "On Error GoTo UpdateRecordsetError" & Chr(13) & Chr(10)
strCode = strCode & "SetADOConnection v_strUserID, v_strPassword" & _
           Chr(13) & Chr(10)
strCode = strCode & "Select Case v_eName" & Chr(13) & Chr(10)
For lngTableCounter = 1 To UBound(r_TableInfo)
    strCode = strCode & "Case e_" & r_TableInfo(lngTableCounter) & _
               Chr(13) & Chr(10)
    strCode = strCode & "Set UpdateRecordset = Update" & _
               r_TableInfo(lngTableCounter) & _
               "RS(v_recClientRecordSet, v_bolDelete)" & Chr(13) & Chr(10)
Next
strCode = strCode & "End Select" & Chr(13) & Chr(10)
strCode = strCode & "SetComplete" & Chr(13) & Chr(10)
strCode = strCode & "CloseADOConnection" & Chr(13) & Chr(10)
strCode = strCode & "Exit Function" & Chr(13) & Chr(10)
strCode = strCode & "UpdateRecordsetError:" & Chr(13) & Chr(10)
strCode = strCode & "CloseADOConnection" & Chr(13) & Chr(10)
strCode = strCode & "SetAbort" & Chr(13) & Chr(10)
strCode = strCode & "Err.Raise Err.Number, " & Chr(34) & _
           "UpdateRecordset" & Chr(34) & " & Err.Source" & Chr(13) & Chr(10)
strCode = strCode & "End Function" & Chr(13) & Chr(10)
CreateServer = strCode
End Function
```

Getting the Information From the Access Database

Add a form into your Visual Basic project. Call the form `frmMain`. Add the Microsoft ActiveX Data Objects 2.x Library and the Microsoft Visual Basic 6.0 Exensibility Object to your project references:

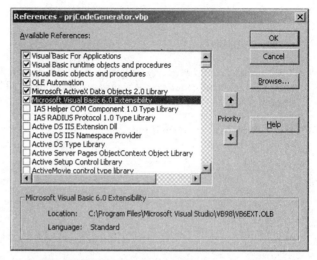

We will need to get the names of the tables and the fields from the Access database. To do this we will use the `OpenSchema` method of the connection object. The `OpenSchema` method will give us access to the structure of the database by returning ADO recordsets with information on the database's schema (structure). Some of the schema information is stored as integers and we will need to convert that to something that is useful. For example, the data types of the fields are stored as numeric values. We will need to convert these numeric values to Visual Basic types. After some digging around I discovered what each of the numbers represented and wrote the following function to convert the numbers to Visual Basic data types:

```
Private Function GetDataType(ByVal v_lngValue As Long) As String

Select Case v_lngValue
   Case 2
      GetDataType = "Integer" '"Short"
   Case 3
      GetDataType = "Long"
   Case 4
      GetDataType = "Single"
   Case 5
      GetDataType = "Double"
   Case 6
      GetDataType = "Currency"
   Case 7
      GetDataType = "Date" '"DateTime"
   Case 11
      GetDataType = "Boolean" '"Bit"
   Case 17
      GetDataType = "Boolean" '"Byte"
   Case 72
      GetDataType = "GUID"
   Case 128
      GetDataType = "Long" '"LongBinary"
   Case 129
      GetDataType = "String" '"Text"
End Select

End Function
```

The types commented out are the actual types listed.

The ADO `OpenSchema` method has the following syntax:

```
Set recordset = connection.OpenSchema (QueryType, [Criteria], [SchemaID])
```

The `Criteria` and `SchemaID` parameters are optional and we will not use them. `QueryType` is the type of schema information we want on the database. The values of `QueryType` are in the MSDN Library. We will only be using three values for `QueryType`. If we choose a `QueryType` `adSchemaTables`, we will get back a recordset filled with information on all of the tables. If you look in MSDN at the values for criteria for `OpenSchema`, you will see some of the field names for the recordset that will be returned. For `adSchemaTables`, the values listed for criteria are:

- TABLE_CATALOG
- TABLE_SCHEMA
- TABLE_NAME
- TABLE_TYPE

We will want to use `TABLE_NAME` to get the names of all of the tables. There are additional fields that are available. If you are curious about them, you can write a small application that loops through all of the fields and writes to a text file the field names and values for the fields.

We will also use `adSchemaColumns` as a `QueryType` to retrieve the information on the columns (fields) of the table. The final `QueryType` we will use is `adSchemaConstraintColumnUsage` to get the names of the primary key fields.

On your form add a textbox named `txtConnection` with a text value of `"C:\Program Files\Microsoft Visual Studio\VB98\Nwind.mdb"`. Add two command buttons to the form called `cmdRetrieveTables` with a caption `"Retrieve Table Info"` and `cmdGenerate` with a caption `"Generate"`. Add a listbox called `lstAvailableTables`. Your form should look as follows:

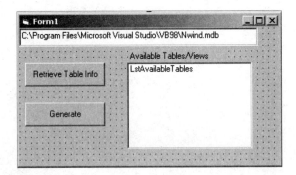

In the declarations section of this form add the following:

```
Private m_oVBInstance As VBIDE.VBE
Private m_uTables() As TableInformation
```

We will use the `m_oVBInstance` variable to get access to the instance of Visual Basic. The IDE `m_uTables` will be used to hold the information on the tables that will be collected when `cmdRetreiveTables` is clicked.

We will add a property to access m_oVBInstance:

```
Friend Property Get VBInstance() As VBIDE.VBE
    Set VBInstance = m_oVBInstance
End Property
```

```
Friend Property Set VBInstance(ByVal v_oNewVBInstance As VBIDE.VBE)
    Set m_oVBInstance = v_oNewVBInstance
End Property
```

Other modules will use VBInstance as we will show later, so it must be a Friend. We cannot include a property for m_uTables as it is an array and we cannot use properties for arrays. We can create a function to retrieve and set array members, but we will not do this to simplify the code. In a real project, you should create such a function.

In the cmdRetrieveTables add the following code:

```
Private Sub cmdRetrieveTables_Click()
Dim objConnection As New ADODB.Connection
Dim objTableInfo As New ADODB.Recordset
Dim objFieldInfo As New ADODB.Recordset
Dim objPrimaryKey As New ADODB.Recordset
Dim lngRecordCounter As Long, lngFieldCounter As Long
Dim lngDisplacement As Long
```

The objTableInfo variable will be used to hold the recordset with the table information returned by OpenSchema. The objFieldInfo variable will hold the field information returned by OpenSchema, and objPrimaryKey will have the detailed field information that will include the primary key information.

If there is no connection string in txtConnection we will exit out, otherwise we will try to open a connection to the database:

```
Screen.MousePointer = vbHourglass
If txtConnection.Text <> "" Then
    On Error Resume Next
    With objConnection
        .Open "Provider=Microsoft.Jet.OLEDB.3.51; " & _
            "Persist Security Info=False;Data Source=" & txtConnection.Text
    If Err.Number <> 0 Then
        MsgBox "The following Error Occurred when trying to connect:" & _
                vbCrLf & "Error Description: " & Err.Description & vbCrLf & _
                "Error Number: " & Err.Number & vbCrLf & _
                "Error Source: " & Err.Source
        Screen.MousePointer = vbDefault
        Exit Sub
    End If
```

If we have successfully opened the database, we will then get a recordset with the table information in it using OpenSchema:

```
Set objTableInfo =.OpenSchema(adSchemaTables)
```

We will now move through the records. Each record contains information on a table in the database. This recordset not only holds information on the regular tables, but also the views and the system tables. We are only interested in the regular tables, so we must skip over the views and system tables. In an Access database, MSYS will be in the name of system tables, so we can eliminate system tables by looking for MSYS in the table name. The recordset returned by OpenSchema will have a field called TABLE_TYPE, which identifies the type of table, i.e. TABLE or VIEW. We can use this to eliminate the views.

```
lngRecordCounter = 1
Do Until objTableInfo.EOF
    If InStr(1, UCase(objTableInfo.Fields("TABLE_NAME")), "MSYS") = 0 _
        And objTableInfo.Fields("TABLE_TYPE") = "TABLE" Then
```

We will want to add each table into the m_uTables array. Since we do not know how many tables there are (the RecordCount of objTableInfo contains the count of regular tables, system tables and views) we must increase the size of the m_uTables array before we add each table. To increase the size of an array, use ReDim. Since we want to keep the information in the array from the previous times through this loop, we use ReDim Preserve, which allows us to increase the size of the array without deleting the current values in the array.

```
ReDim Preserve m_uTables(1 To lngRecordCounter)
```

Now, we can add the table name into m_uTables and into the listbox:

```
m_uTables(lngRecordCounter).TableName = _
    objTableInfo.Fields("Table_Name")
LstAvailableTables.AddItem objTableRecordset.Fields("Table_Name")
```

We will get the primary key next:

```
Set objPrimaryKey = _
    .OpenSchema(adSchemaConstraintColumnUsage)
```

The recordset that is returned contains primary key information on all of the tables, not just the table we want. Therefore, we will have to move through this recordset until we come to the record for the table we are currently working with. Unfortunately, this table holds all of the constraint information on all of the tables. We can have constraints other than the primary key constraint, so we must check to see if this is the primary key constraint, also. If it is the correct table but the wrong constraint, we will ignore it.

```
Do While Not objPrimaryKey.EOF
    If LCase(objPrimaryKey.Fields("TABLE_NAME")) = _
        LCase(objTableInfo.Fields("TABLE_NAME")) Then
        If LCase(objPrimaryKey.Fields("CONSTRAINT_NAME")) = "primarykey" Then
            m_uTables(lngRecordCounter).PrimaryKey = _
                objPrimaryKey.Fields("COLUMN_NAME")
            Exit Do
        End If
    End If
    objPrimaryKey.MoveNext
Loop
```

Next, we will get the field information:

```
Set objFieldInfo =.OpenSchema(adSchemaColumns)
```

Finally, we will loop through the fields and add them to `m_uTables`:

```
objFieldInfo.MoveFirst
lngFieldCounter = 1
Do Until objFieldInfo.EOF
    If objTableInfo.Fields("Table_Name") = _
        objFieldInfo.Fields("Table_Name") Then
```

We will also have to `ReDim` the `FieldInfo` array:

```
ReDim Preserve m_uTables(lngRecordCounter).FieldInfo(1 To lngFieldCounter)
m_uTables(lngRecordCounter).FieldInfo(lngFieldCounter).FieldName = _
    objFieldInfo.Fields("COLUMN_NAME")
m_uTables(lngRecordCounter).FieldInfo(lngFieldCounter).PropertyName = _
    objFieldInfo.Fields("COLUMN_NAME")
```

To get the data type we will use the `GetDataType` function we created:

```
m_uTables(lngRecordCounter).FieldInfo(lngFieldCounter).DataType = _
    GetDataType(objFieldInfo.Fields("DATA_TYPE"))
lngFieldCounter = lngFieldCounter + 1
End If

objFieldInfo.MoveNext
Loop

lngRecordCounter = lngRecordCounter + 1
End If

objTableInfo.MoveNext
Loop

End With

End If

cmdRetrieveTables.Enabled = False
Screen.MousePointer = vbDefault

End Sub
```

Once we have stored all of the schema information that we require into the `m_uTables` array, we can use this to generate our Visual Basic application based on this schema.

Generating the Code into the Visual Basic IDE

Now that we have all of the information we need from the database and we have all of our code that we want to generate wrapped up in functions, we need to start generating the code. Go to the `CmdGenerate_Click` event and add the following code:

```
Private Sub CmdGenerate_Click()
Dim lngTableCounter As Long.
Dim objVBproj As VBProject
Dim objVBClass As vbext_ComponentType
Dim strTempTableName As String
```

We will use the `objVBproj` variable to hold a reference to a Visual Basic project, `objVBClass` will hold a reference to a Visual Basic component, such as a class, control or module, and `strTempTableName` will be used to parse spaces out of the table name. We will loop through all of the tables contained in the `m_uTables` array:

```
For lngTableCounter = 1 To UBound(m_uTables)
```

We will now create a temporary variable with the name of the table. We will remove spaces from the table name.

```
If m_uTables(lngTableCounter).TableName <> "" Then
    strTempTableName = m_uTables(lngTableCounter).TableName
    Do While InStr(1, strTempTableName, " ") > 0
        If InStr(1, strTempTableName, " ") > 0 Then
            strTempTableName = _
                Mid(strTempTableName, 1, InStr(1, strTempTableName, " ") - 1) & _
                    Mid(strTempTableName, InStr(1, strTempTableName, " ") + 1, _
                        Len(strTempTableName))
        End If
    Loop
```

Next, we will use the `Add` method of `VBProjects` to create a new project in the Visual Basic IDE and store a reference to this new project in the `objVBProj` variable:

```
Set objVBproj = VBInstance.VBProjects.Add(vbext_pt_ActiveXControl)
```

We can now start setting the properties of the project:

```
objVBproj.Name = "prj" & strTempTableName
```

We will use the GUIDs to set the proper references. To get these references, I created a Visual Basic EXE project, added the references I needed, saved the project, opened the project in Notepad, and copied the references. We will need references to the ADO 2.x library and remote data services.

```
objVBproj.References.AddFromGUID "{00000200-0000-0010-8000-00AA006D2EA4}", _
    2, 0
objVBproj.References.AddFromGUID "{BD96C556-65A3-11D0-983A-00C04FC29E30}", _
    1, 5
```

Next, we will use the `Add` method of `VBComponents` to add a class module:

```
objVBproj.VBComponents.Add (vbext_ct_ClassModule)
```

This will be the top class so we will name it after the table:

```
objVBproj.VBComponents.Item(1).Name = "ctl" & strTempTableName
```

We will call the `Activate` method to make sure the class is the active code module in the Visual Basic IDE:

```
objVBproj.VBComponents.Item("ctl" & strTempTableName).Activate
```

At this point, we can insert the code into the class code module by using the `AddFromString` method of the `CodeModule` object. We will call the `BuildClass` method of `BuildTop` to get the string containing the code and insert it into the code module:

```
objVBproj.VBComponents.Item("ctl" & strTempTableName)._
    CodeModule.AddFromString _
    BuildTop.BuildClass(m_uTables(lngTableCounter), strTempTableName)
```

Now we will build the bottom class:

```
objVBproj.VBComponents.Item(objVBproj.VBComponents.Count).Name = _
                        "cls" & strTempTableName
objVBproj.VBComponents.Item("cls" & strTempTableName).Activate
```

Because we want the bottom and middle classes to be data providers, we must set the `DataSourceBehavior` to 1. After that, we will use our functions to get the code:

```
objVBproj.VBComponents.Item("cls" & _
    strTempTableName).Properties.Item("DataSourceBehavior").Value = 1
objVBproj.VBComponents.Item("cls" & _
    strTempTableName).CodeModule.AddFromString _
    BuildBottom.CreateDeclarations
objVBproj.VBComponents.Item("cls" & _
    strTempTableName).CodeModule.AddFromString _
    BuildBottom.CreateIntialize
objVBproj.VBComponents.Item("cls" & _
    strTempTableName).CodeModule.AddFromString BuildBottom.CreateTerminate
objVBproj.VBComponents.Item("cls" & _
    strTempTableName).CodeModule.AddFromString _
    BuildBottom.CreateChangedField
objVBproj.VBComponents.Item("cls" & _
    strTempTableName).CodeModule.AddFromString _
    BuildBottom.CreateMiscProps(strTempTableName)
objVBproj.VBComponents.Item("cls" & _
    strTempTableName).CodeModule.AddFromString _
    BuildBottom.CreateValidateFields(m_uTables(lngTableCounter).FieldInfo)
objVBproj.VBComponents.Item("cls" & _
    strTempTableName).CodeModule.AddFromString _
    BuildBottom.CreateGetLet(m_uTables(lngTableCounter).FieldInfo)
```

Next, we will add the middle class:

```
objVBproj.VBComponents.Add (vbext_ct_ClassModule)

objVBproj.VBComponents.Item(objVBproj.VBComponents.Count).Name = _
   "cls" & strTempTableName & "Manager"
objVBproj.VBComponents.Item("cls" & strTempTableName & _
   "Manager").Properties.Item("DataSourceBehavior").Value = 1
objVBproj.VBComponents.Item("cls" & strTempTableName & _
   "Manager").Activate
```

We want to create a string array of the table names without spaces:

```
Dim strTempTable() As String
ReDim strTempTable(1 To UBound(m_uTables))
Dim lngTableCount As Long
For lngTableCount = 1 To UBound(m_uTables)
   strTempTable(lngTableCount) = m_uTables(lngTableCount).TableName
   Do While InStr(1, strTempTable(lngTableCount), " ") > 0
      If InStr(1, strTempTable(lngTableCount), " ") > 0 Then
      Dim lngSpace As Long
      lngSpace = InStr(1, strTempTable(lngTableCount), " ")
      strTempTable(lngTableCount) = _
         Left(strTempTable(lngTableCount), lngSpace - 1) & _
         Right(strTempTable(lngTableCount), _
         Len(strTempTable(lngTableCount)) - lngSpace)
      End If
   Loop
Next
```

We will use AddFromString as before:

```
objVBproj.VBComponents.Item("cls" & strTempTableName & _
   "Manager").CodeModule.AddFromString _
   BuildMiddle.CreateDeclarartions(strTempTable, strTempTableName)
```

We need to find if the primary key field is numeric:

```
Dim bolPrimKeyNum As Boolean
Dim lngFieldCounter As Long
For lngFieldCounter = 1 To UBound(m_uTables(lngTableCounter).FieldInfo)
   If LCase(m_uTables(lngTableCounter).PrimaryKey) = _
      LCase(m_uTables(lngTableCounter).FieldInfo(lngFieldCounter) _
      .FieldName) Then
      If LCase(m_uTables(lngTableCounter) _
         .FieldInfo(lngFieldCounter).DataType) = "string" Then
      bolPrimKeyNum = False
      Else
         bolPrimKeyNum = True
      End If
      Exit For
   End If
Next
```

Again, we will use `AddFromString`:

```
objVBproj.VBComponents.Item("cls" & strTempTableName & _
    "Manager").CodeModule.AddFromString BuildMiddle.CreateDataMethods
objVBproj.VBComponents.Item("cls" & strTempTableName & _
    "Manager").CodeModule.AddFromString _
    BuildMiddle.CreateGeneral(strTempTableName, bolPrimKeyNum)
objVBproj.VBComponents.Item("cls" & strTempTableName & _
    "Manager").CodeModule.AddFromString _
    BuildMiddle.CreateInitTerm(strTempTableName)
objVBproj.VBComponents.Add (vbext_ct_StdModule)
objVBproj.VBComponents.Item(objVBproj.VBComponents.Count).Name = _
    "basMain"
objVBproj.VBComponents.Item("basMain").Activate
objVBproj.VBComponents.Item("basMain").CodeModule.AddFromString _
    BuildBas.CreateDeclarations(m_uTables(lngTableCounter).FieldInfo, _
    m_uTables(lngTableCounter).PrimaryKey, _
    m_uTables(lngTableCounter).TableName)
objVBproj.VBComponents.Item("basMain").CodeModule.AddFromString _
    BuildBas.CreateErrorFunc

End If

Next
```

Finally, we will add our data service class, `clsServer`:

```
Set objVBproj = VBInstance.VBProjects.Add(vbext_pt_ActiveXDll)
objVBproj.Name = "prjServer"
```

We will need references to the ADO 2.0 Library, MTS and remote data services:

```
objVBproj.References.AddFromGUID _
    "{00000200-0000-0010-8000-00AA006D2EA4}", 2, 0
objVBproj.References.AddFromGUID _
    "{BD96C556-65A3-11D0-983A-00C04FC29E30}", 1, 5
objVBproj.References.AddFromGUID _
    "{74C08640-CEDB-11CF-8B49-00AA00B8A790}", 1, 0
objVBproj.VBComponents.Item(objVBproj.VBComponents.Count).Name = _
    "clsServer"
objVBproj.VBComponents.Item("clsServer").Activate
objVBproj.VBComponents.Item("clsServer").CodeModule.AddFromString _
BuildServer.CreateServer(strTempTable, m_uTables)

End Sub
```

While all of our code up to this point is perfectly correct, it will not work. While we have created a reference to the Visual Basic IDE, we have not pointed the reference to the current instance of the Visual Basic IDE that is using our add-in. We still need to get a reference to the Visual Basic IDE that called our Code Generator add-in. Luckily, there are events that are raised that can be used to get this reference.

Getting a Reference to the Current Visual Basic IDE

In the beginning, we named the class associated with this project `CodeGeneratorClass`. We need to put some code into this class. Add the following into the `CodeGeneratorClass`:

```
Option Explicit
Implements IDTExtensibility
```

`IDTExtensibility` will give us the events that we will need to get a reference to the Visual Basic IDE. Remember, when you use an interface you will need to use all of the methods in the interface. If you look in the object drop down of the Visual Basic IDE (the left drop down box) you will see that the `IDTExtensibility` has been added.

We will use `OnConnection` event to get a copy of the Visual Basic IDE. Go to the object drop down of the Visual Basic IDE and select **IDTExtensibility**. `OnConnection` will include a parameter called `VBInst`, which is a copy of the Visual Basic IDE. We will pass this to the `frmMain VBInstance` property:

```
Private Sub IDTExtensibility_OnConnection(ByVal _
  VBInst As Object, ByVal ConnectMode As _
   VBIDE.vbext_ConnectMode, ByVal AddInInst As _
   VBIDE.AddIn, custom() As Variant)
Set frmMain.VBInstance = VBInst
frmMain.Show
End Sub
```

We will now just fill in the rest of the events of the interface with comments:

```
Private Sub IDTExtensibility_OnDisconnection(ByVal _
   RemoveMode As VBIDE.vbext_DisconnectMode, _
   custom() As Variant)
' Comment to prevent procedure from being
' deleted on compilation.

End Sub


Private Sub IDTExtensibility_OnStartupComplete _
   (custom() As Variant)
' Comment to prevent procedure from being
' deleted on compilation.
End Sub

Private Sub IDTExtensibility_OnAddInsUpdate _
   (custom() As Variant)
' Comment to prevent procedure from being
' deleted on compilation.
End Sub
```

Using the Code Generator

Now that we have gone through all of this work, let us use our code generator. Begin by compiling the project into a DLL. Next, without Visual Basic running, open the Immediate Window and type in `AddToIni` and hit return. You should see our message, "Add-in is now entered in VBADDIN.INI file".

Open up another instance of Visual Basic 6 with a new standard exe project. If you want to step through the code in the code generator, place break points in the code generator project and run it.

Go to the menu of the new standard exe project and select **AddIns**. You should see our new code generator project listed:

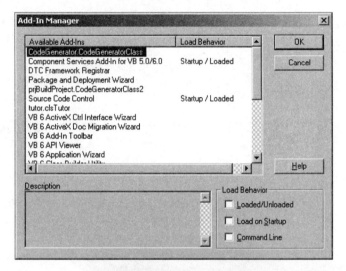

Double-click on **CodeGenerator.CodeGeneratorClass** and select **OK**. This will bring up the form from our add-in:

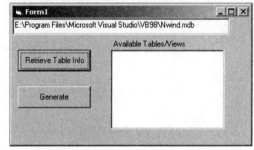

Click **Retrieve Table Info** and then click **Generate**. Set the path to the correct path for your computer. The code generator should now generate the entire project for you.

The generated code for the business services components can form the framework for coding these components. There will be many business rules, such as a customer must have a billing address or a state must be two letters, that will have to be added to this code. We can see that our business components are built from a basic pattern that has specific rules added to them. While we will have to do some refinement to our business services components, the majority of the code can be created from a pattern. This can save a great deal of time in the development phase. Let us now see how to test the generated code.

Testing the Generated Code

You can create as complicated a test as you like. We will offer a very simple one. Go to `Form1` and add a text box and name the text box `txtCategoryName`. Add a command button and call it `cmdMoveNext` with a caption `"Move Next"`. Add a category control onto the form and call it `ctlCategories`. Add the following code to the form:

```
Private Sub cmdMoveNext_Click()
    ctlCategories.GetCategoriesCollection(e_CategoryID).MoveNext
End Sub


Private Sub Form_Load()
    txtCategoryName.DataField = "CategoryName"
    txtCategoryName.DataMember = "CategoryIDEquals"
    Set txtCategoryName.DataSource = _
        ctlCategories.GetCategoriesCollection(e_CategoryID).Item
End Sub
```

Run the generated project. You should see the following:

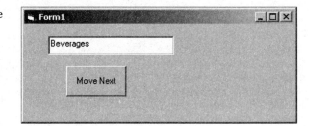

You can now try the project with other Access databases.

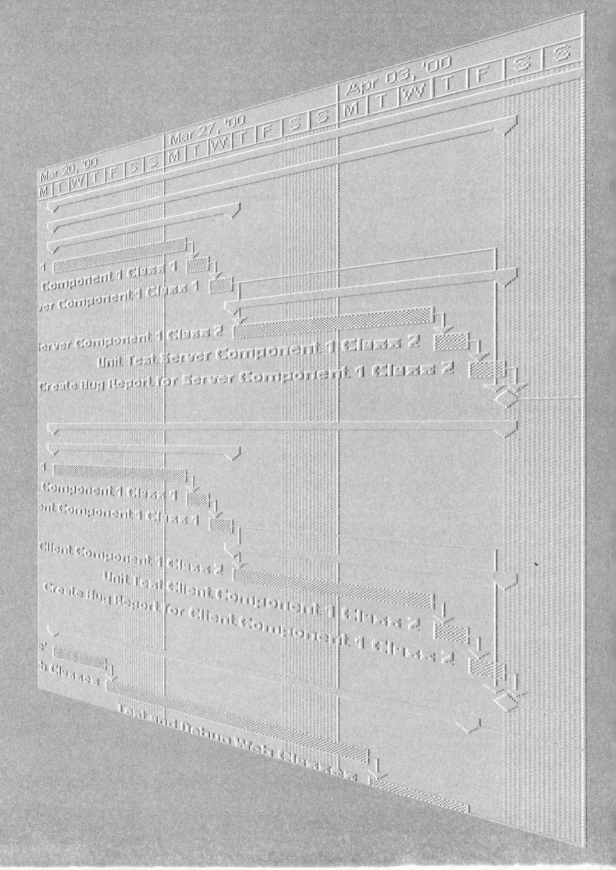

Index

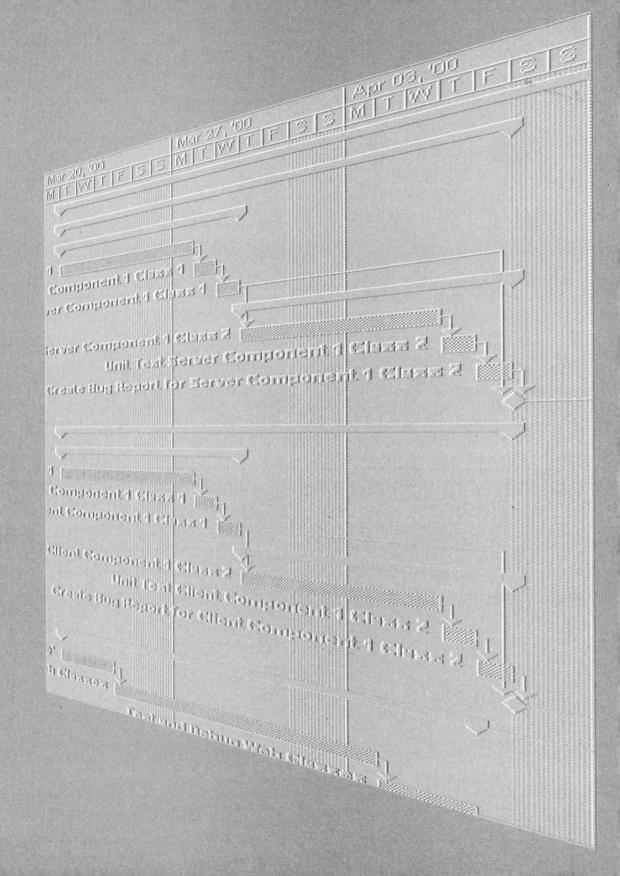